PLAYFAIR CRICKET ANNUAL

59

EDITED BY BILL FRINDALL

All statistics by the Editor unless otherwise stated

PREFACE

This Annual and the 2006 season will be launched with memories of last summer's momentous Ashes campaign still vividly etched. Not since 1953 has a Test series against Australia culminated in the scenes that dominated Kennington Oval on 12 September. Fate decreed that Kevin Pietersen should blast his Ashes-winning 158 on the last day that Test cricket has ever been staged in England. Pertinently, his score equalled that of another South African exile, Basil D'Oliveira, on the same historic ground in another Ashes encounter some 37 years earlier. Whereas 'Dolly's' outstanding innings led to the outlawing of his homeland from the international arena for 22 years, 'KP's resulted in massive celebrations featuring topless buses and a flurry of New Year gongs.

The Ashes series of 2005 has already been hailed as the greatest ever and, having had a box seat from which to record every single nerve-wracking ball, I certainly would not argue with that assessment. Only the 1981 Ashes extravaganza dominated by Ian Botham ranks anywhere near it among those I have been lucky enough to score. Ludicrously crammed into virtually the last eight weeks of the longest-ever English first-class season, it was certainly the most tense, exhilarating, emotional and dramatic of any I have chronicled over the last 40 years. Crucially it caused cricket to dominate the media's sporting coverage and to relegate soccer from the front and back pages of our national press during August and September when kickball would normally hold sway. Significantly bat and ball also held sway in school playgrounds and on recreation sites throughout Britain. The sales of cricket gear have boomed during the winter. Many women with no interest in cricket suddenly became hooked and craved to find the latest score. We must nourish this renewed zest for the game and hope for more dramatic international cricket this summer when Sri Lanka and Pakistan will take the stage with some very talented and exciting players.

The subject of international cricket has dominated the game's statistical discussions this winter because of the ICC's witless decision to award Test match status to a multinational game between the Australians and a World XI in Sydney last October. As I stated on this page last year when this contravention of the ICC's own qualification of Test match status had just been proposed, simple logic dictates that 'international' records should be exactly that – 'contests between nations'. The decision was brought about by sheer greed that demanded Test status to hook deals involving sponsors and television rights. Not only did it totally disregard the long established fabric and traditions of Test match records, it also defied the recommendations of the Association of Cricket Statisticians and Historians. Along with many other statisticians across the globe, I will not be including a game bordering on the farcical in any international records that I compile. It is excluded from this Annual, along with similar multinational contests involving the limited-overs format. For those who wish to add it to their Test match records, a full scorecard appears on page 305. In 2004, the ICC indulged in another piece of gross meddling with their crass decision to regard the toss as the start of a match. This is contrary to Law 16, which clearly states that the umpire's call of play heralds the start. The time has surely come for the MCC, cricket's lawmakers, to assume control of the status of international matches through a committee acting as a House of Lords in these matters. Their first task would be to discard multinational flippancies.

Thankfully Headline have allowed an extra 16 pages to accommodate the host of overseas mercenaries that have flooded county cricket, many under the controversial 'Kolpak' banner. At last the ECB has sought to limit a growing influx that threatens to stifle our own young cricketers by awarding bonuses to counties for fielding England qualified players and allowing overseas players to be replaced only because of international commitments.

BILL FRINDALL
Urchfont, Wiltshire
14 March 2006

ACKNOWLEDGEMENTS
AND THANKS

Headline
Juliana Foster (Editor)
David Mitchell (proofs)
Letterpart
Chris Leggett
Caroline Leggett
Lorraine Byfield
Career Records
Philip Bailey
Robin Abrahams
Debbie Frindall
Christopher Dewing
ECB
Alan Fordham
County Scorer/Statisticians
John Brown (Derbyshire)
Brian Hunt (Durham)
Tony Choat (Essex)
Andrew Hignell (Glamorgan)
Keith Gerrish Gloucestershire)
Vic Isaacs (Hampshire)
Jack Foley (Kent)
Alan West (Lancashire)
Graham York (Leicestershire)
Don Shelley (Middlesex)
Tony Kingston (Northamptonshire)
Gordon Stringfellow (Nottinghamshire)
Gerry Stickley (Somerset)
Mike Charman (Sussex)
Keith Booth (Surrey)
David Wainwright (Warwickshire)
Neil Smith (Worcestershire)
Roy Wilkinson (Yorkshire)

Universities
Ray Markham (Cambridge)
Graeme Fowler (Durham)
Margaret Folwell (Loughborough)
Neil Harris (Oxford)
Tastats
Ric Finlay
David Fitzgerald
Overseas
Rajneesh Gupta (India)
Rajesh Kumar (India)
Andrew Samson (South Africa)
Charlie Wat (Australia)
County Administrations
Gill Hudson (Derbyshire)
Pat Walton (Durham)
Nancy Fuller (Essex)
Caryl Watkin (Glamorgan)
Tom Richardson (Gloucestershire)
Tim Tremlett (Hampshire)
Roz Franklin (Kent)
Diana Lloyd (Lancashire)
James Whittaker (Leicestershire)
Emma Channon (Middlesex)
Lyndsey Hutchings (Northamptonshire)
Mick Newell (Nottinghamshire)
Sally Donoghue (Somerset)
Steve Howes (Surrey)
Francesca Watson (Sussex)
Keith Cook (Warwickshire)
Mark Newton (Worcestershire)
Liz Sutcliffe (Yorkshire)

ENGLAND v SRI LANKA

SERIES RECORDS

1981-82 to 2003-04

HIGHEST INNINGS TOTALS

England	in England	545	Birmingham	2002
	in Sri Lanka	387	Kandy	2000-01
Sri Lanka	in England	591	The Oval	1998
	in Sri Lanka	628-8d	Colombo (SSC)	2003-04

LOWEST INNINGS TOTALS

England	in England	181	The Oval	1998
	in Sri Lanka	148	Colombo (SSC)	2003-04
Sri Lanka	in England	162	Birmingham	2002
	in Sri Lanka	81	Colombo (SSC)	2000-01

HIGHEST MATCH AGGREGATE   1401 for 24 wickets   Lord's   2002
LOWEST MATCH AGGREGATE   645 for 36 wickets   Colombo (SSC)   2000-01

HIGHEST INDIVIDUAL INNINGS

England	in England	174	G.A.Gooch	Lord's	1991
	in Sri Lanka	128	R.A.Smith	Colombo (SSC)	1992-93
Sri Lanka	in England	213	S.T.Jayasuriya	The Oval	1998
	in Sri Lanka	201*	M.S.Atapattu	Galle	2000-01

HIGHEST AGGREGATE OF RUNS IN A SERIES

England	in England	354	(av 88.50)	M.E.Trescothick	2002
	in Sri Lanka	269	(av 67.25)	G.P.Thorpe	2000-01
Sri Lanka	in England	277	(av 55.40)	M.S.Atapattu	2002
	in Sri Lanka	334	(av 83.50)	D.P.M.de S.Jayawardena	2003-04

RECORD WICKET PARTNERSHIPS – ENGLAND

1st	168	M.E.Trescothick (76)/M.P.Vaughan (115)	Lord's	2002
2nd	202	M.E.Trescothick (161)/M.A.Butcher (94)	Birmingham	2002
3rd	167	N.Hussain (109)/G.P.Thorpe (59)	Kandy	2000-01
4th	128	G.A.Hick (107)/M.R.Ramprakash (53)	The Oval	1998
5th	92	M.A.Butcher (113*)/A.J.Stewart (26)	Manchester	2002
6th	87	A.J.Lamb (107)/R.M.Ellison (41)	Lord's	1984
	87	A.J.Stewart (54)/C.White (39)	Kandy	2000-01
	87	A.Flintoff (77)/G.J.Batty (14)	Colombo (SSC)	2003-04
7th	63	A.J.Stewart (113*)/R.C.Russell (17)	Lord's	1991
8th	102	A.J.Stewart (123)/A.F.Giles (45)	Manchester	2002
9th	53	M.R.Ramprakash (42)/D.Gough (15)	The Oval	1998
10th	91	G.P.Thorpe (123)/M.J.Hoggard (17*)	Birmingham	2002

RECORD WICKET PARTNERSHIPS – SRI LANKA

1st	99	R.S.Mahanama (64)/U.C.Hathurusinghe (59)	Colombo (SSC)	1992-93
2nd	92	M.S.Atapattu (201*)/K.C.Sangakkara (58)	Galle	2000-01
3rd	262	T.T.Samaraweera (142)/ D.P.M.de S.Jayawardena (134)	Colombo(SSC)	2003-04
4th	153	D.P.M.de S.Jayawardena (52)/T.M.Dilshan (100)	Kandy	2003-04
5th	150	S.Wettimuny (190)/L.R.D.Mendis (111)	Lord's	1984
6th	138	S.A.R.Silva (102*)/L.R.D.Mendis (94)	Lord's	1984
7th	93	K.C.Sangakkara (95)/H.D.P.K.Dharmasena (54)	Kandy	2000-01
8th	53	H.D.P.K.Dharmasena (54)/W.P.U.C.J.Vaas (36)	Kandy	2000-01

| 9th | 83 | H.P.Tillekeratne (93*)/M.Muralitharan (19) | Colombo (SSC) | 1992-93 |
| 10th | 64 | J.R.Ratnayeke (59*)/G.F.Labrooy (42) | Lord's | 1988 |

BEST INNINGS BOWLING ANALYSIS

England	in England	7-70	P.A.J.DeFreitas	Lord's	1991
	in Sri Lanka	6-33	J.E.Emburey	Colombo (PSS)	1981-82
Sri Lanka	in England	9-65	M.Muralitharan	The Oval	1998
	in Sri Lanka	7-46	M.Muralitharan	Galle	2003-04

BEST MATCH BOWLING ANALYSIS

England	in England	8-115	P.A.J.DeFreitas	Lord's	1991
	in Sri Lanka	8- 95	D.L.Underwood	Colombo (PSS)	1981-82
Sri Lanka	in England	16-220	M.Muralitharan	The Oval	1998
	in Sri Lanka	11- 93	M.Muralitharan	Galle	2003-04

HIGHEST WICKET AGGREGATE IN A SERIES

England	in England	14	(av 32.07)	M.J.Hoggard	2002
	in Sri Lanka	18	(av 29.94)	A.F.Giles	2003-04
Sri Lanka	in England	16	(av 13.75)	M.Muralitharan	1998
	in Sri Lanka	26	(av 12.30)	M.Muralitharan	2003-04

RESULTS SUMMARY

ENGLAND v SRI LANKA – IN ENGLAND

		Series			Lord's			Oval			Birmingham			Manchester		
	Tests	E	SL	D	E	SL	D	E	SL	D	E	SL	D	E	SL	D
1984	1	-	-	1	-	-	1									
1988	1	1	-	-	1	-	-									
1991	1	1	-	-	1	-	-									
1998	1	-	1	-				-	1	-						
2002	3	2	-	1	-	-	1				1	-	-	1	-	-
	7	4	1	2	2	-	2	-	1	-	1	-	-	1	-	-

ENGLAND v SRI LANKA – IN SRI LANKA

		Series			Colombo (PSS)			Colombo (SSC)			Galle			Kandy		
	Tests	E	SL	D	E	SL	D	E	SL	D	E	SL	D	E	SL	D
1981-82	1	1	-	-	1	-	-									
1992-93	1	-	1	-				-	1	-						
2000-01	3	2	1	-				1	-	-	-	1	-	1	-	-
2003-04	3	-	1	2				-	1	-	-	-	1	-	-	1
	8	3	3	2	1	-	-	1	2	-	-	1	1	1	-	1
Totals	15	7	4	4												

ENGLAND v PAKISTAN

SERIES RECORDS
1954 to 2005-06

HIGHEST INNINGS TOTALS

England	in England	558-6d	Nottingham	1954
	in Pakistan	546-8d	Faisalabad	1983-84
Pakistan	in England	708	The Oval	1987
	in Pakistan	636-8d	Lahore	2005-06

LOWEST INNINGS TOTALS

England	in England	130	The Oval	1954
	in Pakistan	130	Lahore	1987-88
Pakistan	in England	87	Lord's	1954
	in Pakistan	158	Karachi	2000-01

HIGHEST MATCH AGGREGATE   1344 for 40 wickets   Manchester   2001
LOWEST MATCH AGGREGATE   509 for 28 wickets   Nottingham   1967

HIGHEST INDIVIDUAL INNINGS

England	in England	278	D.C.S.Compton	Nottingham	1954
	in Pakistan	205	E.R.Dexter	Karachi	1961-62
Pakistan	in England	274	Zaheer Abbas	Birmingham	1971
	in Pakistan	223	Mohd Yousuf Youhana	Lahore	2005-06

HIGHEST AGGREGATE OF RUNS IN A SERIES

England	in England	453	(av 90.60)	D.C.S.Compton	1954
	in Pakistan	449	(av 112.25)	D.I.Gower	1983-84
Pakistan	in England	488	(av 81.33)	Salim Malik	1992
	in Pakistan	431	(av 107.75)	Inzamam-ul-Haq	2005-06

RECORD WICKET PARTNERSHIPS – ENGLAND

1st	198	G.Pullar (165)/R.W.Barber (86)	Dacca	1961-62
2nd	248	M.C.Cowdrey (182)/E.R.Dexter (172)	The Oval	1962
3rd	267	M.P.Vaughan (120)/G.P.Thorpe (138)	Manchester	2001
4th	188	E.R.Dexter (205)/P.H.Parfitt (111)	Karachi	1961-62
5th	192	D.C.S.Compton (278)/T.E.Bailey (36*)	Nottingham	1954
6th	166	G.P.Thorpe (118)/C.White (93)	Lahore	2000-01
7th	167	D.I.Gower (152)/V.J.Marks (83)	Faisalabad	1983-84
8th	99	P.H.Parfitt (119)/D.A.Allen (62)	Leeds	1962
9th	76	T.W.Graveney (153)/F.S.Trueman (29)	Lord's	1962
10th	79	R.W.Taylor (54)/R.G.D.Willis (28*)	Birmingham	1982

RECORD WICKET PARTNERSHIPS – PAKISTAN

1st	173	Mohsin Khan (104)/Shoaib Mohammed (80)	Lahore	1983-84
2nd	291	Zaheer Abbas (274)/Mushtaq Mohammed (100)	Birmingham	1971
3rd	267	Mudassar Nazar (114)/Haroon Rashid (122)	Lahore	1977-78
4th	322	Javed Miandad (153*)/Salim Malik (165)	Birmingham	1992
5th	197	Javed Burki (101)/Nasim-ul-Ghani (101)	Lord's	1962
6th	269	Mohd Yousuf Youhana (223)/Kamran Akmal (154)	Lahore	2005-06
7th	112	Asif Mujtaba (51)/Moin Khan (105)	Leeds	1996
8th	130	Hanif Mohammed (187*)/Asif Iqbal (76)	Lord's	1967
9th	190	Asif Iqbal (146)/Intikhab Alam (51)	The Oval	1967
10th	62	Sarfraz Nawaz (53)/Asif Masood (4*)	Leeds	1974

BEST INNINGS BOWLING ANALYSIS

England	in England	8-34	I.T.Botham	Lord's	1978
	in Pakistan	7-66	P.H.Edmonds	Karachi	1977-78
Pakistan	in England	7-40	Imran Khan	Leeds	1987
	in Pakistan	9-56	Abdul Qadir	Lahore	1987-88

BEST MATCH BOWLING ANALYSIS

England	in England	13- 71	D.L.Underwood	Lord's	1974
	in Pakistan	11- 83	N.G.B.Cook	Karachi	1983-84
Pakistan	in England	12- 99	Fazal Mahmood	The Oval	1954
	in Pakistan	13-101	Abdul Qadir	Lahore	1987-88

HIGHEST AGGREGATE OF WICKETS IN A SERIES

England	in England	22	(av 19.95)	F.S.Trueman	1962
	in Pakistan	17	(av 24.11)	A.F.Giles	2000-01
Pakistan	in England	22	(av 25.31)	Waqar Younis	1992
	in Pakistan	30	(av 14.56)	Abdul Qadir	1987-88

RESULTS SUMMARY
ENGLAND v PAKISTAN – IN ENGLAND

	Tests	Series E	P	D	Lord's E	P	D	Nottingham E	P	D	Manchester E	P	D	The Oval E	P	D	Birmingham E	P	D	Leeds E	P	D
1954	4	1	1	2	–	–	1	1	–	–	–	–	1	–	1	–						
1962	5	4	–	1	1	–	–	–	–	1				1	–	–	1	–	–	1	–	–
1967	3	2	–	1	–	–	1	1	–	–				1	–	–						
1971	3	1	–	2	–	–	1										–	–	1	1	–	–
1974	3	–	–	3	–	–	1							–	–	1				–	–	1
1978	3	2	–	1	1	–	–										1	–	–	–	–	1
1982	3	2	1	–	–	1	–										1	–	–	1	–	–
1987	5	–	1	4	–	–	1				–	–	1	–	–	1	–	–	1	–	1	–
1992	5	1	2	2	–	1	–				–	–	1	–	1	–	–	–	1	1	–	–
1996	3	–	2	1	–	1	–							–	1	–				–	–	1
2001	2	1	1	–	1	–	–				–	1	–									
Total	**39**	**14**	**8**	**17**	**3**	**3**	**5**	**2**	**–**	**1**	**–**	**1**	**3**	**2**	**3**	**2**	**3**	**–**	**3**	**4**	**1**	**3**

ENGLAND v PAKISTAN – IN PAKISTAN

	Tests	Series E	P	D	Lahore E	P	D	Dacca E	P	D	Karachi E	P	D	Hyderabad E	P	D	Faisalabad E	P	D	Multan E	P	D
1961-62	3	1	–	2	1	–	–	–	–	1	–	–	1									
1968-69	3	–	–	3	–	–	1	–	–	1	–	–	1									
1972-73	3	–	–	3	–	–	1				–	–	1	–	–	1						
1977-78	3	–	–	3	–	–	1				–	–	1	–	–	1						
1983-84	3	–	1	2	–	–	1				–	1	–				–	–	1			
1987-88	3	–	1	2	–	1	–				–	–	1				–	–	1			
2000-01	3	1	–	2	–	–	1				1	–	–				–	–	1			
2005-06	3	–	2	1	–	1	–										–	–	1	–	1	–
	24	**2**	**4**	**18**	**1**	**2**	**5**	**–**	**–**	**2**	**1**	**1**	**5**	**–**	**–**	**2**	**–**	**–**	**4**	**–**	**1**	**–**
Totals	**63**	**16**	**12**	**35**																		

TOURING TEAM REGISTERS 2006

Neither Sri Lanka nor Pakistan had selected their 2006 touring teams at the time of going to press. The following players represented these countries in Test matches since 31 August 2005.

SRI LANKA

Full Names	Birthdate	Birthplace	Team	Type	F-C Debut
ATAPATTU, Marvin S.	22.11.70	Kalutara	Sinhalese	RHB/LB	1988-89
BANDARA, C. Malinga	31.12.79	Kalutara	Kalutara Town	RHB/LBG	1996-97
DILSHAN, Tillakaratne M.	14.10.76	Kalutara	Bloomfield	RHB/WK	1993-94
FERNANDO, C.R. Dilhara	19.07.79	Colombo	Sinhalese	RHB/RFM	1997-98
GUNAWARDENA, D. Avishka	26.05.77	Colombo	Nondescripts	LHB/WK	1996-97
HERATH, M. Rangana K.B.	19.03.78	Kurunegala	Moors	LHB/SLA	1996-97
JAYASURIYA, Sanath T.	30.06.69	Matara	Bloomfield	LHB/SLA	1988-89
JAYAWARDENA, D.P. Mahela deS.	27.05.77	Colombo	Sinhalese	RHB/RM	1995-96
MAHAROOF, M. Farveez	07.09.84	Colombo	Bloomfield	RHB/RFM	2001-02
MALINGA, S. Lasith	28.09.83	Galle	Galle	RHB/RMF	2001-02
MUBARAK, Jehan	10.01.81	Washington, USA	Colombo	LHB/OB	1999-00
MURALITHARAN, Muthiah	17.04.72	Kandy	Tamil Union	RHB/OB	1989-90
SAMARAWEERA, Thilan T.	22.09.76	Colombo	Sinhalese	RHB/OB	1995-96
SANGAKKARA, Kumar C.	27.10.77	Colombo	Nondescripts	LHB/WK	1997-98
THARANGA, W. Upul	02.02.85	Balapitiya	Nondescripts	LHB/WK	2000-01
VAAS, W.P.U. Chaminda J.	27.01.74	Mattumagala	Colts	LHB/LFM	1990-91

PAKISTAN

Full Names	Birthdate	Birthplace	Team	Type	F-C Debut
ABDUL RAZZAQ	01.12.79	Lahore	Lahore	RHB/RFM	1996-97
ASIM KAMAL	31.05.76	Karachi	Karachi	LHB	1997-98
DANISH KANERIA	16.12.80	Karachi	Habib Bank	RHB/LB	1998-99
FAISAL IQBAL	30.12.81	Karachi	Karachi	RHB/RM	1998-99
HASAN RAZA	11.03.82	Karachi	Habib Bank	RHB/OB	1996-97
IMRAN FARHAT	20.05.82	Lahore	Lahore	LHB/LB	1998-99
INZAMAM-UL-HAQ	03.03.70	Multan	Multan	RHB/SLA	1985-86
KAMRAN AKMAL	13.01.82	Lahore	Lahore	RHB/WK	1997-98
MOHAMMAD ASIF	20.12.82	Sheikhupura	KRL	LHB/RFM	2000-01
MOHAMMAD SAMI	24.02.81	Karachi	Karachi	RHB/RFM	1999-00
NAVED-UL-HASAN, Rana	28.02.78	Sheikhupura	Sialkot	RHB/RFM	1995-96
SALMAN BUTT	07.10.84	Lahore	Lahore	LHB/OB	2000-01
SHAHID AFRIDI	01.03.80	Khyber Agency	Karachi	RHB/LBG	1995-96
SHOAIB AKHTAR	13.08.75	Rawalpindi	Rawalpindi	RHB/RF	1994-95
SHOAIB MALIK	01.02.82	Sialkot	Sialkot	RHB/OB	1997
YOUNIS KHAN	29.11.77	Mardan, NWFP	Habib Bank	RHB/LB	1998-99
YOUSUF YOUHANA, Mohd	27.08.74	Lahore	Lahore	RHB/OB	1996-97

THE FIRST-CLASS COUNTIES REGISTER, RECORDS AND 2005 AVERAGES

Career statistics are to the end of the 2005 season.
Test Match and LOI career bests have been updated to 26 and 14 February 2005 respectively.

ABBREVIATIONS – General

*	not out/unbroken partnership	l-o	limited-overs
b	born	LOI	Limited-Overs Internationals
BB	Best innings bowling analysis	Tests	Official Test Matches
Cap	Awarded 1st XI County Cap	F-c Tours	Overseas tours involving first-class
f-c	first-class		appearances
HS	Highest Score		

Awards

BHC	Benson and Hedges Cup 'Gold' Award
CGT	Gillette Cup, NatWest/Cheltenham & Gloucester Trophy Match Award
PCA 2005	Professional Cricketer's Association Player of 2005
Wisden 2004	One of *Wisden Cricketers' Almanack's* Five Cricketers of 2004
YC 2005	Cricket Writers' Club Young Cricketer of 2005

ECB Competitions

BHC	Benson & Hedges Cup (1972-2002)
CC	County Championship
CGT	Cheltenham & Gloucester Trophy
NL	National League
NWT	NatWest Trophy (1981-2000)
SL	Sunday League (1969-98)

Education

BHS	Boys' High School
C	College
CFE	College of Further Education
CHE	College of Higher Education
CS	Comprehensive School
GS	Grammar School
HS	High School
I	Institute
IHE	Institute of Higher Education
RGS	Royal Grammar School
S	School
SFC	Sixth Form College
SM	Secondary Modern School
SS	Secondary School
TC	Technical College
T(H)S	Technical (High) School
U	University
UMIST	University of Manchester Institute of Science and Technology
UWIC	University of Wales Institute, Cardiff

Playing Categories

LBG	Bowls right-arm leg-breaks and googlies
LF	Bowls left-arm fast
LFM	Bowls left-arm fast-medium
LHB	Bats left-handed
LM	Bowls left-arm medium pace
LMF	Bowls left-arm medium fast
OB	Bowls right-arm off-breaks
RF	Bowls right-arm fast
RFM	Bowls right-arm fast-medium
RHB	Bats right-handed
RM	Bowls right-arm medium pace
RMF	Bowls right-arm medium-fast
RSM	Bowls right-arm slow-medium
SLA	Bowls left-arm leg-breaks
SLC	Bowls left-arm 'Chinamen'
WK	Wicket-keeper

Teams (see also p 129)

ACT	Australian Capital Territory
ADBP	Agricultural Development Bank of P
B	Bangladesh
CD	Central Districts
EP	Eastern Province
GW	Griqualand West
HK	Hong Kong
K	Kenya
KRL	Khan Research Laboratories
NBP	National Bank of Pakistan
ND	Northern Districts
NSW	New South Wales
NT	Northern Transvaal
(O)FS	(Orange) Free State
PIA	Pakistan International Airlines
Q	Queensland
REDCO	Really Efficient Development Co
SAU	South African Universities
Tas	Tasmania
Vic	Victoria
WA	Western Australia
WAPDA	Water & Power Development Auth.
WP	Western Province

DERBYSHIRE

Formation of Present Club: 4 November 1870
Inaugural First-Class Match: 1871
Colours: Chocolate, Amber and Pale Blue
Badge: Rose and Crown
County Champions: (1) 1936
Gillette/NatWest/C & G Trophy Winners: (1) 1981
Benson and Hedges Cup Winners: (1) 1993
National League (Div 1) Winners: (0); best – 4th (Div 2) 2002
Sunday League Winners: (1) 1990
Twenty20 Cup Winners: (0) best – Quarter-Finalist 2005.
Match Awards: CGT 50; BHC 71

Chief Executive: Tom Sears, County Cricket Ground, Nottingham Road, Derby
DE21 6DA • Tel: 01332 383211 • Fax: 01332 290251 • Email: post@dccc.org.uk • Web:
www.dccc.org.uk

Director of Cricket/1st XI Coach: D.L.Houghton. **Academy Director/2nd XI Coach**:
K.M.Krikken. **Captain**: G.Welch. **Vice-Captain**: **Overseas Players**: M.J.Di Venuto and
Mohammad Yousuf Youhana. **2006 Beneficiary**: K.J.Dean. **Head Groundsman**:
N.Godrich. **Scorer**: J.M.Brown. ‡ New registration. ᴺᴼ Not qualified for England.

ᴺᴼ**ADNAN**, Muhammad **Hassan** SYED (M.A.O. College, Lahore), b Lahore, Pakistan
15 May 1974. 5'10". RHB, OB. Islamabad 1994-95, 2001-02. WAPDA 1997-98 to date (as
an overseas player 2002-03 to date). Gujranwala 1997-98 to 1998-99. Played 49 f-c matches
in Pakistan before his Derbyshire debut in 2003. Cap 2004. 1000 runs (1): 1380 (2004). HS
191 v Somerset (Taunton) 2005. BB 1-4 (CC). LO HS 113* v NZ (Derby) 2004. LO BB
2-13 v Leics (Derby) 2004 (NL). T20 HS 32. T20 BB 1-18.

BORRINGTON, Paul Michael (Repton S; Chellarton S), b Nottingham 24 May 1988. Son
of A.J.Borrington (Derbyshire 1971-80). 5'10". RHB, OB. Debut 2005. HS 28 v Somerset
(Taunton) 2005.

ᴺᴼ**BOTHA, Anthony** Greyvensteyn (Maritzburg C; Maritzburg Technikon), b Pretoria,
South Africa 17 Nov 1976. 6'0". LHB, SLA. Natal/KwaZulu Natal 1995-96 to 1998-99.
EP/Easterns 1999-00 to 2002-03. Derbyshire debut/cap 2004. HS 156* v Yorks (Derby)
2005. BB 8-53 Natal B v Northerns B (Pretoria) 1997-98. CC BB 6-104 v Lancs
(Manchester) 2005. Award: CGT 1. LO HS 60* Easterns v EP (Benoni) 2001-02. LO BB
4-44 v Durham (Chester-le-St) 2005 (CGT). T20 HS 25*. T20 BB 2-16.

DEAN, Kevin James (Leek HS; Leek CFE), b Derby 16 Oct 1975. 6'5". LHB, LMF. Debut
1996. Cap 1998. Benefit 2006. HS 54* v Worcs (Derby) 2002. 50 wkts (2): most – 83
(2002). BB 8-52 v Kent (Canterbury) 2000. 2 hat-tricks (1998, 2000). Award: CGT 1. LO
HS 16* v Glamorgan(Cardiff) 1998 (SL) and 16* v Middx (Derby) 2002 (NL). LO BB 5-32
v Glos (Derby) 1996 (SL). T20 HS 3* T20 BB 2-20.

ᴺᴼ**Di VENUTO, Michael** James (St Virgil's C; Hobart), b Hobart, Australia 12 Dec 1973.
6'0". LHB, RM/LB. Tasmania 1991-92 to date. Sussex 1999; cap 1999. Derbyshire
debut/cap 2000; Appointed captain for 2004 but missed entire season – back surgery. **LOI**
(A): 9 (1996-97 to 1997-98). HS 89 v SA (Johannesburg) 1996-97. F-c Tours: Z 1995-96
(Tas); Sc/Ire 1998 (Aus A). 1000 runs (5): most – 1538 (2002). HS 230 v Northants (Derby)
2002. BB (Tas) 1-0. UK BB (Sx) 1-3. De BB 1-16. Awards: CGT 1; BHC 1. LO HS 173* v
Derbys CB (Derby) 2000 (NWT). LO BB (Tas) 1-10. T20 HS 77*. T20 BB 3-19.

10

FRANCE, Benjaman John (Bromsgrove S; Oxford CFE), b Brunei 14 May 1982. 5'11". LHB, RM. Debut 2004. Suffolk 2003-04. HS 56 v Leics (Derby) 2004 and 56 v Essex (Chelmsford) 2005. BB 1-37 (CC). LO HS 31 v Somerset (Taunton) 2005.

GRAY, Andrew Kenneth Donovan, b Armadale, W Australia 19 May 1974. RHB, OB. British passport. Yorkshire 2001-04. Derbyshire debut 2005. HS 104 Y v Somerset (Taunton) 2003. De HS 77* v Somerset (Derby) 2005. BB 4-128 Y v Surrey (Oval) 2001. De BB 3-56 v Yorks (Leeds) 2005. LO HS 30* Y v Leics (Leicester) 2003 (NL). LO BB 4-34 Y v Kent (Leeds) 2002 (NL). T20 HS 13. T20 BB 3-18.

HUNTER, Ian David (Fyndoune Community C, Sacriston; Durham New C), b Durham City 11 Sep 1979. 6'2". RHB, RMF. Durham 2000-03. Derbyshire debut 2004. HS 65 Du v Northants (Northampton) 2002. De HS 40 v Yorks (Leeds) 2005. BB 5-63 v Du (Chester-le-St) 2005. LO HS 39 Du v Leics (Leicester) 2002 (BHC). LO BB 4-29 Du v Essex (Ilford) 2000 (NL). T20 HS 25*. T20 BB 3-26.

‡**JONES, Philip Steffan** (Stradey CS, Llanelli; Neath TC; Loughborough U; Homerton C, Cambridge), b Llanelli, Carms, Wales 9 Feb 1974. 6'2". RHB, RMF. Cambridge U 1997; blue 1997. Somerset 1997-2003; cap 2001. Northamptonshire 2004-05. Wales MC 1992-96. HS 105 Sm v NZ (Taunton) 1999. CC HS 63 Sm v Northants (Taunton) 2003. Nh 51 v Yorks (Leeds) 2005. 50 wkts (1): 59 (2001). BB 6-67 CU v OU (Lord's) 1997. CC BB 6-110 (match 10-156) Sm v Warwks (Birmingham) 2002. LO HS 27 Sm v Northants (Northampton) 2000 (NL). LO BB 6-56 Nh v Ire (Clontarf) 2004 (CGT). T20 HS 24*. T20 BB 2-24.

LUNGLEY, Tom (St John Houghton SS; SE Derbyshire C), b Derby 25 Jul 1979. 6'1". LHB, RM. Debut 2000. HS 47 v Warwks (Derby) 2001. BB 4-101 v Glamorgan(Swansea) 2003. LO HS 45 v Essex (Chelmsford) 2001 (NL). LO BB 4-28 v Essex (Derby) 2001 (NL). T20 HS 25. T20 BB 4-13.

NEEDHAM, Jake (Nottingham Bluecoat S, Aspley), b Portsmouth, Hants 30 Sep 1986. 6'1". RHB, OB. HS 6 and BB 2-42 v Essex (Derby) 2005 – on debut. LO HS 9* (NL). LO BB 1-35 (NL).

PAGET, Christopher David (Repton S), b Stafford 2 Nov 1987. 6'0". RHB, OB. Debut 2004. No f-c appearances 2005. HS 7 v Yorks (Leeds) 2004. BB 3-63 v WI (Derby) 2004. CC BB – .

‡**PIPE, David James** (Queensbury S, Bradford), b Bradford, Yorks 16 Dec 1977. 5'11". RHB, WK. Worcestershire 1998-2005. HS 104* Wo v Hants (Southampton) 2003. LO HS 56 Worcs CB v Kent CB (Kidderminster) 2000 (NWT). Held 8 catches Wo v Herts (Hertford) 2001 (CGT) to equal l-o record. T20 HS 14.

SHEIKH, Mohammad Avez (Broadway S), b Birmingham 2 Jul 1973. 6'0". LHB, RM. Warwickshire 1997-2003. Derbyshire debut 2004. HS 58* Wa v Northants (Northampton) 2000. De HS 55 v Essex (Derby) 2005. BB 4-9 v Durham (Chester-le-St) 2004. LO HS 50* v Scot (Derby) 2004 (NL). LO BB 4-17 Wa v Yorks (Birmingham) 2001 (NL). T20 HS 20. T20 BB 2-20.

‡NQ**SMITH, Gregory** Marc (St Stithins C), b Johannesburg, S Africa 20 Apr 1983. RHB, RMF. Debut SA Academy 2003-04. Griqualand West 2003-04. HS 56* SA Academy v SL A (Potchefstroom) 2003-04. BB 2-60 GW v Border (E London) 2003-04. LO HS 53 GW v KZNatal (Kimberley) 2003-04. LO BB 1-23.

11

STUBBINGS, Stephen David (Frankston HS, Aus; Swinburne U, Aus), b Huddersfield, Yorks 31 Mar 1978. 6'3". LHB, OB. Debut 1997; cap 2001. 1000 runs (2): most 1126 (2005). HS 151 v Somerset (Taunton) 2005. LO HS 98* v Lancs (Derby) 2002 (NL). T20 HS 8.

‡**TAYLOR, Christopher** Robert (Benton Park HS, Rawdon), b Leeds 21 Feb 1981. 6'4". RHB, RMF. Yorkshire 2001-04. HS 52* Y v Surrey (Leeds) 2002. LO HS 28 Y v Glos (Leeds) 2003 (NL).

‡**WAGG, Graham** Grant (Ashlawn S, Rugby), b Rugby, 28 Apr 1983. 6'0". RHB, LM. Warwickshire 2002-04; contract terminated after ECB imposed a 15-month ban, expiring 1 Jan 2006, for taking cocaine. F-c Tour (Eng A): I 2003-04. HS 74 v Ind A (Birmingham) 2003. BB 4-43 and CC HS 51 Wa v Somerset (Birmingham) 2002 – on debut. LO HS 45 Eng A v Karnataka (Bangalore) 2003-04. LO BB 4-50 v Kent (Birmingham) 2002 (NL). T20 HS 25. T20 BB 3-33.

WALKER, Nicholas Guy Eades (Haileybury Imperial Service C), b Enfield, Middlesex 7 Aug 1984. 6'2". RHB, RFM. Debut 2004. Hertfordshire 2002-04. HS 80 off 57 balls (4 sixes, 11 fours), the record score by a Derbyshire No. 11, adding 103 for 10th wicket with M.A.Sheikh, and BB 5-68, v Somerset (Derby) 2004. LO HS 43 v Scot (Derby) 2004 (NL). LO BB 3-24 v B (Derby) 2005. T20 HS 8. T20 BB – .

WELCH, Graeme (Hetton CS), b Durham City 21 Mar 1972. 5'11½". RHB, RM. Warwickshire 1994-2000; cap 1997. Derbyshire debut/cap 2001. F-c Tour: SA 1994-95 (Wa). HS 115* v Leics (Oakham) 2004. 50 wkts (4); most 65 (1997). BB 6-30 v Durham (Chester-le-St) 2001. Award: BHC 1. LO HS 82 v Sussex (Hove) 2004 (NL). LO BB 6-31 v Middx (Derby) 2002 (NL). T20 HS 20. T20 BB 1-15.

WHITE, Wayne Andrew (John Poet S, Etwall; Nottingham Trent U), b Derby 22 Apr 1985. 6'2". RHB, RMF. Debut 2005. HS 6 v Yorks (Derby) 2005 – on debut. BB 4-77 v Somerset (Taunton) 2005.

‡^{NQ}**YOUSUF** YOUHANA, **Mohammad,** b Lahore, Pakistan 27 Aug 1974. RHB. Debut 1996-97. Bahawalpur 1996-97. Lahore 1996-97 to date. WPDA 1997-98. Peshawar 1998-99. PIA 1999-00, 2001-02. **Tests** (P): 65 (1997-98 to 2005-06, 2 as captain); HS 223 v E (Lahore) 2005-06. **LOI** (P): 206 (1997-98 to 2005-06, 4 as captain); HS 141* v Z (Bulawayo) 2002-03. Tours (P): E 2001; A 1999-00, 2004-05; WI 1999-00; SA 1997-98, 2002-03; NZ 2000-01, 2003-04; I 1998-99, 2004-05; SL 2000-01; Z 1997-98, 2002-03; B 2001-02. HS 223 (*see Tests*). LO HS 141* (*see LOI*). T20 HS 28.

RELEASED/RETIRED

(Having made a first-class County appearance in 2005)

ASTLE, Nathan John, b Christchurch, NZ 15 Sep 1971. RHB, RM. Canterbury 1991-92 to date. Nottinghamshire 1997. Durham 2005. **Tests** (NZ): 73 (1995-96 to 2005); HS 222 v E (Christchurch) 2002-03; BB 3-27 v SL (Wellington) 2004-05. **LOI** (NZ): 206 (1994-95 to 2005-06); HS 145* v USA (Oval) 2004; BB 4-43 v P (Chandigarh) 1996-97). F-c Tours (NZ): E 1999, 2004; A 1997-98, 2001-02, 2004-05; SA 2000-01; WI 1995-96, 2001-02; I 1999-00, 2003-04; P 1996-97; SL 1997-98; Z 1997-98, 2000-01, 2005; B 2004-05. HS 223 NZ v Q (Brisbane) 2001-02. CC HS 100 Nt v Warwks (Nottingham) 1997 and 100 Nt v Essex (Worksop) 1997. Du HS 65 and BB 3-20 v Durham UCCE (Durham) 2005 – on debut. BB 6-22 C v Otago (Christchurch) 1996-97. CC BB 5-46 Nt v Glos (Bristol) 1997. Awards: NWT 2. LO HS 145* (*see LOI*). LO BB 4-14 Canterbury v Otago (Oamaru) 1995-96. T20 HS 75*. T20 BB 3-20.

NQBASSANO, Christopher Warwick Godfrey (Grey S, Port Elizabeth; Launceston Church GS; Tasmania U, Hobart), b East London, South Africa 11 Sep 1975. 6'2". British passport (English mother); son of the late B.S.Bassano (cricket writer, historian and broadcaster). RHB, LB. Derbyshire 2001-05; cap 2002. First from any county to score 100 in each innings on Championship debut – 186* and 106 v Glos (Derby) 2001. Tasmania 2002-03. 1000 runs (1): 1063 (2002). HS 186* (*see above*). Awards: CGT 2. LO HS 126* v Sussex (Arundel) 2003 (NL). T20 HS 43.

NQBRYANT, James Douglas Campbell (Maritzburg C; Port Elizabeth U), b Durban, South Africa 4 Feb 1976. 6'0". RHB. E Province 1996-97 to 2003-04. Somerset 2003. Derbyshire 2005. F-c Tour (SA A): WI 2000-01. HS 234* EP v North West (Potchefstroom) 2002-03. UK HS 109* Sm v LU (Taunton) 2003 – on Sm/UK debut. CC HS 73 Sm v Hants (Taunton) 2003. De HS 61 v Leics (Derby) 2005. BB (EP) 1-22. UK BB – . LO HS 105* EP v WP (Cape Town) 2000-01. T20 HS 53*.

NQFRIEND, Travis John (St George's C, Harare), b Kwekwe, Zimbabwe 7 Jan 1981. Son of I.S.Friend (Rhodesia B 1978-79). 6'2". RHB, RMF. Debut 1999-00 (Zimbabwe Academy). Midlands 2000-01 to date. Derbyshire 2005 (Kolpak registration). Tests (Z): 13 (2001 to 2003-04); HS 81 and BB 5-31 v B (Dhaka) 2001-02. LOI (Z): 51 (2000-01 to 2003-04); HS 91 v K (Kwekwe) 2002-03; BB 4-55 v I (Sharjah) 2000-01. F-c Tours (Z): E 2003; I 2000-01, 2001-02; SL 2001-02; B 2001-02). HS 183 Midlands v Manicaland (Kwekwe) 2003-04. De HS 82 v Durham (Derby) 2005. BB 5-16 Midlands v Matabeleland (Kwekwe) 2003-04. De BB – . LO HS 91 (*see LOI*). LO BB 4-37 Midlands v Mashonaland (Harare) 2002-03. T20 HS 24.

HAVELL, Paul Matthew Roger (Mentone GS, Melbourne; Warden Park S; Haywards Heath C), b Melbourne, Australia 4 Jul 1980. 6'3". LHB, RFM. Sussex 2001 (1 non-CC match). Derbyshire 2003-05. HS 13* v Yorks (Derby) 2004. BB 4-75 v Durham (Chester-le-St) 2004. LO HS 4 and LO BB 3-28 v Scot (Derby) 2004. T20 HS – . T20 BB 2-32.

NQMOSS, Jonathan (Sydney C of E GS; Australian C of PE), b Manly, Sydney, Australia 4 May 1975. 6'1". RHB, RM. Victoria 2000-01 to date. Derbyshire 2004-05; cap 2004. Berkshire 2001. 1000 runs (1): 1021 (2005). HS 172* Vic v WA (Perth) 2003-04. De HS 147* v Durham (Chester-le-St) 2004. BB 4-40 v Lancs (Derby) 2005. LO HS 104 v Worcs (Derby) 2004 (NL). LO BB 5-47 Vic v Q (Melbourne) 2000-01. T20 HS 83. T20 BB 1-16.

SUTTON, L.D. – see LANCASHIRE.

J.R.Chapman, L.J.Goddard, D.R.Hewson and B.J.Spendlove left the staff having not made a first-class appearance in 2005.

DERBYSHIRE 2005

RESULTS SUMMARY

	Place	Won	Lost	Tied	Drew	No Result
County Championship (2nd Division)	9th	1	8		7	
All First-Class Matches		1	8		8	
C & G Trophy	2nd Round					
National League (2nd Division)	5th	9	7	1	—	1
Twenty20 Cup	Quarter-Finalist					

COUNTY CHAMPIONSHIP AVERAGES

BATTING AND FIELDING

Cap		M	I	NO	HS	Runs	Avge	100	50	Ct/St
2000	M.J.Di Venuto	12	24	2	203	1133	51.50	3	5	11
2001	S.D.Stubbings	15	27	1	151	1072	41.23	2	8	8
2004	A.G.Botha	16	27	7	156*	808	40.40	1	2	6
2002	L.D.Sutton	16	28	4	95	816	34.00	—	4	50
2001	G.Welch	16	28	3	112	792	31.68	1	4	9
2004	J.Moss	16	29	—	106	877	30.24	1	7	11
–	A.K.D.Gray	8	13	5	77*	237	29.62	—	1	9
2002	C.W.G.Bassano	8	13	—	87	381	29.30	—	2	4
2004	M.H.Adnan	15	27	—	191	748	27.70	2	2	9
–	T.J.Friend	3	6	—	82	120	20.00	—	1	2
–	J.D.C.Bryant	4	8	1	61	132	18.85	—	1	2
–	M.A.Sheikh	5	8	–	55	137	17.12	–	1	–
–	N.G.E.Walker	9	13	3	79	154	15.40	–	1	3
–	B.J.France	7	13	–	56	189	14.53	–	1	3
–	I.D.Hunter	12	19	5	40	189	13.50	–	–	3
1998	K.J.Dean	3	5	1	12	45	11.25	–	–	–
–	P.M.R.Havell	3	5	4	6*	10	10.00	–	–	–

Also batted: P.M.Borrington (2 matches) 4, 28; T.Lungley (3) 5, 0, 36 (1 ct); J.Needham (1) 1*, 6; W.A.White (2) 2, 6.

BOWLING

	O	M	R	W	Avge	Best	5wI	10wM
G.Welch	527.3	133	1506	58	25.96	5- 63	3	–
M.A.Sheikh	175.5	44	498	13	38.30	4- 67	–	–
J.Moss	315.4	94	906	23	39.39	4- 40	–	–
A.G.Botha	451.4	108	1401	33	42.45	6-104	1	–
I.D.Hunter	356.3	50	1442	33	43.69	5- 63	1	–
A.K.D.Gray	174.4	28	565	12	47.08	3- 56	–	–
N.G.E.Walker	191.5	23	837	16	52.31	4- 69	–	–

Also bowled:

	O	M	R	W	Avge	Best	5wI	10wM
W.A.White	58.5	8	280	5	56.00	4- 77		
T.Lungley	79	12	320	5	64.00	2- 54		
P.M.R.Havell	81.5	9	385	6	64.16	3-106		

M.H.Adnan 13-0-49-0; K.J.Dean 83.5-13-283-3; B.J.France 16-3-70-1; J.Needham 15-4-68-2.

The First-Class Averages (pp 129–145) give the records of Derbyshire players in all first-class matches for the county (Derbyshire's other opponents being Oxford UCCE).

DERBYSHIRE RECORDS

FIRST-CLASS CRICKET

Highest Total	For 707-7d		v	Somerset	Taunton	2005
	V 662		by	Yorkshire	Chesterfield	1898
Lowest Total	For 16		v	Notts	Nottingham	1879
	V 23		by	Hampshire	Burton upon T	1958
Highest Innings	For 274	G.A.Davidson	v	Lancashire	Manchester	1896
	V 343*	P.A.Perrin	for	Essex	Chesterfield	1904

Highest Partnership for each Wicket

1st	322	H.Storer/J.Bowden	v	Essex	Derby	1929
2nd	417	K.J.Barnett/T.A.Tweats	v	Yorkshire	Derby	1997
3rd	316*	A.S.Rollins/K.J.Barnett	v	Leics	Leicester	1997
4th	328	P.Vaulkhard/D.Smith	v	Notts	Nottingham	1946
5th	302*†	J.E.Morris/D.G.Cork	v	Glos	Cheltenham	1993
6th	212	G.M.Lee/T.S.Worthington	v	Essex	Chesterfield	1932
7th	258	M.P.Dowman/D.G.Cork	v	Durham	Derby	2000
8th	198	K.M.Krikken/D.G.Cork	v	Lancashire	Manchester	1996
9th	283	A.Warren/J.Chapman	v	Warwicks	Blackwell	1910
10th	132	A.Hill/M.Jean-Jacques	v	Yorkshire	Sheffield	1986

† 346 runs were added for this wicket in two separate partnerships

Best Bowling	For 10- 40	W.Bestwick	v	Glamorgan	Cardiff	1921
(Innings)	V 10- 45	R.L.Johnson	for	Middlesex	Derby	1994
Best Bowling	For 17-103	W.Mycroft	v	Hampshire	Southampton	1876
(Match)	V 16-101	G.Giffen	for	Australians	Derby	1886

Most Runs – Season	2165	D.B.Carr	(av 48.11)	1959
Most Runs – Career	23854	K.J.Barnett	(av 41.12)	1979-98
Most 100s – Season	8	P.N.Kirsten		1982
Most 100s – Career	53	K.J.Barnett		1979-98
Most Wkts – Season	168	T.B.Mitchell	(av 19.55)	1935
Most Wkts – Career	1670	H.L.Jackson	(av 17.11)	1947-63
Most Career W-K Dismissals	1304	R.W.Taylor	(1157 ct; 147 st)	1961-84
Most Career Catches in the Field	563	D.C.Morgan		1950-69

LIMITED-OVERS CRICKET

Highest Total	CGT	365-3		v	Cornwall	Derby	1986
	NL	304-3		v	Kent	Maidstone	2005
	T20	195-8		v	Yorkshire	Leeds	2005
Lowest Total	CGT	79		v	Surrey	The Oval	1967
	NL	61		v	Hampshire	Portsmouth	1990
	T20	98		v	Lancs	Manchester	2005
Highest Innings	CGT	173*	M.J.Di Venuto	v	Derbys CB	Derby	2000
	NL	141*	C.J.Adams	v	Kent	Chesterfield	1992
	T20	83	J.Moss	v	Yorks	Leeds	2005
Best Bowling	CGT	8-21	M.A.Holding	v	Sussex	Hove	1988
	NL	6- 7	M.Hendrick	v	Notts	Nottingham	1972
	T20	4-13	T.Lungley	v	Notts	Derby	2003

DURHAM

Formation of Present Club: 23 May 1882
Inaugural First-Class Match: 1992
Colours: Navy Blue, Yellow and Maroon
Badge: Coat of Arms of the County of Durham
County Champions: (0) 8th 1999, 8th (Div 1) 2000
Gillette/NatWest/C & G Trophy Winners: (0); best – quarter-finalist 1992, 2001
Benson and Hedges Cup Winners: (0); best – quarter-finalist 1998, 2000, 2001
National League (Div 1) Winners: (0); best – 8th (Div 1) 2002
Sunday League Winners: (0); best – 7th 1993
Twenty20 Cup Winners: (0); best – 4th in Group 2004
Match Awards: CGT 24; BHC 20

Chief Executive: David Harker, County Ground, Riverside, Chester-le-Street, Co Durham DH3 3QR • Tel: 0191 387 1717 • Fax: 0191 387 1616 • Email: marketing@durham-ccc.org.uk • Web: www.durhamccc.co.uk

First XI Coach: M.D.Moxon. **Captain**: M.E.K.Hussey. **Vice-Captain**: P.D.Collingwood. **Overseas Players**: M.E.K.Hussey and M.L.Lewis. **2006 Beneficiary**: N.Killeen. **Head Groundsman**: D.Measor. **Scorer**: B.Hunt. ‡ New registration. ^NQ Not qualified for England.

Durham initially awarded caps immediately their players joined the staff but revised this policy in 1998 and now cap players on merit, past 'awards' having been nullified.

^NQ**BENKENSTEIN, Dale Martin** (Michaelhouse HS), b Salisbury, Rhodesia 9 Jun 1974. Son of M..M.Benkenstein (Rhodesia, Natal B 1970 to 1980); brother of twins B.R. (Natal B 1993-94) and B.N. (Natal B, GW 1994-96). 5'9". RHB, RM. Natal/KZ-Natal 1993-94 to 2003-04. Dolphins 2004-05. MCC 2004. British passport. Durham debut 2005. **LOI** (SA): 23 (1998-99 to 2002-03); HS 69 v WI (Cape Town) 1998-99; BB 3-5 v K (Colombo) 2002-03. F-c Tours (SA A): WI 2000; NZ 1998-99 (SA); SL 1998-99. 1000 (1): 1236 (2005). HS 259 KZ-Natal v Northerns (Durban) 2001-02. Du HS 162* v Derby (Chester-le-St) 2005. BB 4-29 v Northants (Northampton) 2005. LO HS 107* Natal v North West (Fochville) 1997-98. LO BB 4-16 v Surrey (Chester-le-St) 2005. T20 HS 53 T20 BB 3-10.

^NQ**BREESE, Gareth Rohan** (Kingston U of Technology, Jamaica), b Montego Bay, Jamaica 9 Jan 1976. 5'7". RHB, OB. Jamaica 1995-96 to date; captain/overseas player 2003-04 to date. British passport (Welsh father). Durham debut 2004; cap 2005. **Tests** (WI): 1 (2002-03); HS 5 and BB 2-108 v I (Madras) 2002-03. F-c Tours (WI): E 2002 (WI A); I 2002-03. HS 165* v Somerset (Taunton) 2004. BB 7-60 Jamaica v Barbados (Bridgetown) 2000-01. Du BB 5-41 (10-151 match) v Yorks (Scarborough) 2004 – scored 35 and 68 to complete match double. LO HS 52* v Middx (Chester-le-St) 2004. LO BB 3-24 Jamaica v Leeward Is (Spanish Town) 2001-02. T20 HS 24*. T20 BB 4-14.

BRIDGE, Graeme David (Southmoor S, Sunderland), b Sunderland 4 Sep 1980. 5'8". RHB, SLA. Debut 1999. HS 52 v Leics (Chester-le-St) 2001. BB 6-84 v Hants (Chester-le-St) 2001. Awards: CGT 1; BHC 1. LO HS 50* v Leics (Leicester) 2002 (BHC). LO BB 4-20 v Hants (Chester-le-St) 2003 (NL). T20 HS 11. T20 BB 2-16.

COETZER, Kyle James (Aberdeen GS), b Aberdeen, Scotland 14 Apr 1984. RHB, RM. Debut 2004. Scotland 2004. Registered but not contracted. No f-c appearances 2005. HS 133* Scot v Kenya (Abu Dhabi) 2004. Du HS 67 v Glamorgan(Cardiff) 2004. LO HS 30 Durham CB v Glamorgan(Darlington) 2003 (CGT).

COLLINGWOOD, Paul David (Blackfyne CS; Derwentside C), b Shotley Bridge 26 May 1976. 5'11". RHB, RMF. Debut 1996 v Northants (Chester-le-St) taking wicket of D.J.Capel with his first ball before scoring 91 and 16; cap 1998. MBE 2005. **ECB contract 2004.** **Tests:** 5 (2003-04 to 2005-06); HS 96 v P (Lahore) 2005-06. **LOI:** 85 (2001 to 2005-06); HS 112* and BB 6-31 v B (Nottingham) 2005 – first to score a hundred and take six wickets in LOIs. F-c Tours: WI 2003-04; P 2005-06; SL 2003-04. 1000 runs (2); most – 1120 (2005), inc six hundreds (Du record). HS 190 v SL (Chester-le-St) 2002 v190 v Derbys (Derby) 2005. BB 5-52 v Somerset (Stockton) 2005. Awards: BHC 4. LO HS 118* v Notts (Chester-le-St) 2002 (NL). LO BB 6-31 (*see LOI*). T20 HS 46. T20 BB 2-8.

DAVIES, Anthony Mark (Northfield CS, Billingham), b Stockton-on-Tees 4 Oct 1980. 6'3". RHB. RM. Debut 2002; cap 2005. HS 62 v Somerset (Stockton) 2005. 50 wkts (1): 50 (2004). BB 6-32 v Worcs (Chester-le-St) 2005. LO HS 31* v Warwks (Chester-le-St) 2002 (NL). LO BB 4-13 v Sussex (Chester-le-St) 2001 (NL). T20 HS 6. T20 BB 2-14.

‡**GIBSON, Ottis** Delroy (Ellerslie SS), b Sion Hill, Bridgetown, Barbados 16 Mar 1969. 6'2". RHB, RFM. Barbados 1990-91 to 1997-98. 01. Border 1992-93 to 1994-95. Glamorgan 1994-96; cap 1994. Griqualand West 1998-99 to 1999-00. Gauteng 2000-01. Leicestershire 2004-05; cap 2004. Staffordshire 2001. **Tests** (WI): 2 (1995 to 1998-99); HS 37 v SA (Cape Town)1998-99; BB 2-81 v E (Lord's) 1995. **LOI** (WI): 15 (1995 to 1996-97); HS 52 v A (Brisbane) 1995-96; BB 5-40 v SL (Perth) 1995-96. Tours (WI): E 1995; A 1995-96; SA 1997-98 (WI A), 1998-99; SL 1996-97 (WI A). HS 101* WI v Somerset (Taunton) 1995. CC HS 97 Gm v Leics (Swansea) 1996. 50 wkts (2): most – 60 (1994, 2004). BB 7-55 Border v Natal (Durban) 1994-95. CC BB 6-43 (11-141 match) Le v Notts (Leicester) 2004. Award: NWT 1. LO HS 102* Staffs v Northumb (Jesmond) 2001 (CGT). LO BB 5-19 Border v GW (Kimberley) 1992-93. T20 HS 18. T20 BB 2-20.

‡**HARMISON, Ben** William (Ashington HS), b Ashington, Northumb 9 Jan 1986. Younger brother of S.J.Harmison. 6'3". LHB, RMF. Staff 2006 – awaiting f-c debut. LO HS 0. LO BB 1-51.

HARMISON, Stephen James (Ashington HS), b Ashington, Northumb 23 Oct 1978. Elder Brother of B.W. 6'4". RHB, RF. Debut 1996; cap 1999. Northumberland 1996. *Wisden* 2004. MBE 2005. **ECB contracts 2004-05. Tests:** 38 (2002 to 2005-06); HS 42 v SA (Cape Town) 2004-05 – first No. 11 to top-score for England; BB 7-12 (9-73 match) v WI (Kingston) 2003-04. **LOI:** 38 (2002-03 to 2005-06); HS 13* v NZ (Chester-le-St) 2003; BB 5-33 v A (Bristol) 2005; hat-trick v I (Nottingham) 2004. F-c Tours: A 2002-03; SA 1998-99 (Eng A), 2004-05; WI 2003-04; P 2005-06; Z 1998-99 (Eng A); B 2003-04. HS 42 (*see Tests*). Du HS 36 v Kent (Canterbury) 1998. 50 wkts (3); most – 64 (1999). BB 7-12 (*see Tests*). Du BB 6-52 (9-84 match) v Lancs (Manchester) 2005. Hat-trick v Worcs (Chester-le-St) 2005. LO HS 13* (*see LOI*). LO BB 5-33 (*see LOI*). T20 HS – . T20 BB 1-13.

NQ**HUSSEY, Michael** Edward Killeen (Prindiville Catholic C; Curtin U), b Morley, Perth, Australia 27 May 1975. Elder brother of D.J.Hussey (*see NOTTINGHAMSHIRE*). 5'11". LHB, RM. W Australia 1994-95 to date. Northamptonshire 2001-03; cap 2001; captain 2002-03. Gloucestershire 2004; cap 2004. Durham debut/cap/captain 2005. **Tests** (A): 6 (2005-06); HS 137 v WI (Hobart) 2005-06. **LOI:** 29 (2003-04 to 2005-06); HS 88* v NZ (Christchurch) 2005-06; BB 1-31. F-c Tour (Aus A): Sc/Ire 1998. 1000 runs (4); most – 2055 (2001). HS 331* (Northants record) in 651 minutes v Somerset (Taunton) 2003. Also scored 329* Nh v Essex (Northampton) 2001 and 310 Nh v Glos (Bristol) 2002. Du HS 253 v Leics (Leicester) 2005 – on Du debut. BB 3-34 WA v Q (Brisbane) 2004-05. CC BB 1-5. Du BB 1-36. Awards: BHC 3. LO HS 123 Nh v Scot (Northampton) 2003 (NL). LO BB 3-52 WA v Vic (Melbourne) 1999-00 (MM). T20 HS 88. T20 BB – .

KILLEEN, Neil (Greencroft CS; Derwentside C; Teesside U), b Shotley Bridge 17 Oct 1975. 6'2". RHB, RFM. Debut 1995; cap 1999; benefit 2006. HS 48 v Somerset (Chester-le-St) 1995. 50 wkts (1): 58 (1999). BB 7-70 v Hants (Chester-le-St) 2003. Award: BHC 1. LO HS 32 v Middx (Lord's) 1996 (SL). LO BB 6-31 v Derbys (Derby) 2000 (NL). T20 HS 17*. T20 BB 4-7.

LEWIS, Jonathan James Benjamin (King Edward VI S, Chelmsford; Roehampton IHE), b Isleworth, Middx 21 May 1970. 5'9½". RHB, RSM. Essex 1990-96; cap 1994; scored 116* on debut v Surrey (Oval). Durham debut 1997; cap 1998; captain 2000 (*part*) to 2004; benefit 2004. 1000 runs (4); most – 1252 (1997). HS 210* v OU (Oxford) 1997 – on Du debut. CC HS 160* v Derbys (Chester-le-St) 1997. BB 1-73. Award: BHC 1. LO HS 102 v Glos (Cheltenham) 1997 (NL). T20 HS 49*. T20 BB – .

^{NQ}**LEWIS, Mi**chael Llewellyn (Parade C, Bundoora, Vic), b Greensborough, Victoria, Australia 29 Jun 1974. 6'0". RHB, RFM. Victoria 1999-00 to date. Glamorgan 2004. Durham debut 2005. **LOI** (A): 4 (2005-06); HS – ; BB 3-56 v NZ (Wellington) 2005-06. HS 54* Vic v NSW (Sydney) 2001-02. Du/CC HS 20 v Essex (Southend) 2005. BB 6-59 Vic v Q (Melbourne) 2003-04. CC BB 5-80 v Yorks (Chester-le-St) 2005. LO HS 19 Vic v Tas (Melbourne) 2003-04. LO BB 5-48 v Sussex (Chester-le-St) 2005. T20 HS 0. T20 BB 2-18.

LOWE, James Adam (Northallerton C, Yorks), b Bury St Edmunds, Suffolk 4 Nov 1982. 6'2". RHB, WK, occ OB. Debut 2003. HS 80 v Hants (Southampton) 2003 – on debut. LO HS 36 v B (Chester-le-Street) 2005.

MUCHALL, Gordon James (Durham S), b Newcastle upon Tyne, Northumb 2 Nov 1982. 6'1". RHB, RM. Northumberland 1999-2001. Debut 2002; cap 2005. F-c Tours (ECB Acad): SL 2002-03. HS 142* v Yorks (Scarborough) 2004. BB 3-26 v Yorks (Leeds) 2003. LO HS 101* v Yorks (Leeds) 2005 (NL). LO BB 1-15 (NL). T20 HS 64*. T20 BB 1-8.

MUSTARD, Philip (Usworth CS), b Sunderland 8 Oct 1982. 5'11". LHB, WK. Debut 2002. HS 80 v Northants (Northampton) 2005. LO HS 53* v Yorks (Chester-le-St) 2005 (NL). T20 HS 64.

ONIONS, Graham (St Thomas More RCS, Blaydon), b Gateshead 9 Sep 1982. 6'2". RHB, RMF. Debut 2004. HS 20* v Leics (Chester-le-St) 2004. BB 3-110 v Leics (Leicester) 2004. LO HS 5 (Durham CB – CGT). LO BB 3-39 v Derbys (Derby) 2005 (NL). T20 HS 0. T20 BB 2-25.

PLUNKETT, Liam Edward (Nunthorpe SS; Teesside Tertiary C), b Middlesbrough, Yorks 6 Apr 1985. 6'3". RHB, RFM. Debut 2003. **Tests**: 1 (2005-06); HS 9 and BB 2-125 v P (Lahore) 2005-06 – on debut. **LOI**: 5 (2005-06); HS 56 v P (Lahore) 2005-06; BB 3-51v P (Lahore) 2005-06. HS 74* v Somerset (Stockton) 2005. 50 wkts (1): 51 (2005). BB 6-74 v Hants (Chester-le-St) 2004. LO HS 56 (*see LOI*). LO BB 4-28 v Surrey (Chester-le-St) 2005 (NL). T20 HS 8. T20 BB 2-18.

PRATT, Gary Joseph (Willington Parkside CS), b Bishop Auckland 22 Dec 1981. Younger brother of A.Pratt. 6'0". LHB, OB. Debut 2000. 1000 runs (1): 1055 (2003). HS 150 v Northants (Chester-le-St) 2003. LO HS 101* v Somerset (Taunton) 2003 (NL). T20 HS 62*.

SCOTT, Gary Michael (Hetton CS), b Sunderland 21 Jul 1984. 6'0". RHB, OB. Durham 2001 – youngest Durham f-c debutant (17y 19d), 2005. HS 61* v Somerset (Taunton) 2005. BB – . LO HS 100 Durham CB v Herefords (Darlington) 2002 (CGT). LO BB 2-32 Durham CB v Bucks (Beaconsfield) 2001 (CGT). T20 HS 31. T20 BB 3-27.

‡**STONEMAN, Mark** Daniel (Whickham HS), b Newcastle-upon-Tyne, Northumb 26 Jun 1987. Staff 2006 – awaiting f-c debut.

NQ**THORP, Callum** David (Servite C, Tuart Hill, Perth), b Mount Lawley, Perth, Australia 11 Feb 1975. 6'3". British passport (English parents). RHB, RMF. W Australia 2002-03 to 2003-04. Durham debut 2005. HS 26 WA v NSW (Newcastle) 2002-03. Du HS 23 v Derbys (Chester-le-St) 2005. BB 3-10 v Northants (Chester-le-St) 2005. LO HS 52 v B (Chester-le-Street) 2005. LO BB 4-46 WA v Tas (Hobart) 2002-03. T20 HS 12. T20 BB – .

TURNER, Mark Leif (Thornhill CS), b Sunderland 23 Oct 1984. 5'11". RHB, RMF. Debut 2005. HS 18 and BB 1-47 v Essex (Chester-le-St) 2005 – on debut. T20 HS – . T20 BB – .

RELEASED/RETIRED

(Having made a first-class County appearance in 2005)

NQ**MAHER, James** Patrick (St Augustine's C, Cairns), b Innisfail, Queensland, Australia 27 Feb 1974. LHB, RM. Queensland 1993-94 to date. Glamorgan 2001, 2003; cap 2001. Durham 2005. **LOI** (A): 26 (1997-98 to 2003-04); HS 95 v SA (Pretoria) 2001-02. F-c Tour (A): WI 2002-03. 1000 (1+2): most – 1194 (2001-02). HS 217 Gm v Essex (Cardiff) 2001. Du HS 9. BB 3-11 Q v WA (Perth) 1995-96. LO HS 187 Q v WA (Brisbane) 2003-04. LO BB 3-29 Gm v Surrey (Croydon) 2003 (NL). T20 HS 59.

NQ**NOFFKE, Ashley** Allan b Nambour, Queensland, Australia 30 Apr 1977. RHB, RFM. Debut 1998-99 for Australian Academy. Queensland 1999-00 to date. Middlesex 2002-03; cap 2003. Durham 2005. F-c Tours (A): E 2001 (*part*); WI 2003; Z 1998-99 (A Academy). HS 114* Q v S Aus (Brisbane) 2003-04. CC HS 76 M v Worcs (Worcester) 2002. Du HS 65 v Northants (Northampton) 2005. BB 8-24 (12-108 match) M v Derbys (Derby) 2002. Du BB 4-19 v Essex (Chester-le-St) 2005. LO HS 58 M v Sussex (Lord's) 2002 (BHC). LO BB 4-32 Q v Tasmania (Hobart) 2001-02 . T20 HS 7. T20 BB 3-22.

PENG, N. – see GLAMORGAN.

WILLIAMS, Brad Andrew (Frankston HS), b Frankston, Victoria, Australia 20 Nov 1974. 6'0". RHB, RFM. Victoria 1994-95 to1997-98. W Australia 1999-00 to date. Durham 2005. **Tests** (A): 4 (2003-04); HS 10* and BB 4-53 v I (Melbourne) 2003-04. **LOI** (A): 25 (2001-02 to 2004); HS 13*; BB 5-22 v Z (Sydney) 2003-04. HS 41* WA v V (Perth) 1995-96. Du HS 22* v Northants (Chester-le-St) 2005. 50 wkts (0+1): 50 (1999-00). BB 6-74 WA v Vic (Perth) 1999-00. Du BB 3-73 v Derbys (Chester-le-St) 2005. LO HS 23 WA v NSW (Perth) 2002-03. LO BB 5-22 (*see LOI*).

M.Hamilton and A.Pratt left the staff having not made a first-class appearance in 2005.

DURHAM 2005

RESULTS SUMMARY

	Place	Won	Lost	Tied	Drew	No Result
County Championship (2nd Division)	2nd	6	2		8	
All First-Class Matches		6	2		9	
C & G Trophy	1st Round					
National League (2nd Division)	2nd	12	4			2
Twenty20 Cup	5th in North Division					

COUNTY CHAMPIONSHIP AVERAGES

BATTING AND FIELDING

Cap		M	I	NO	HS	Runs	Avge	100	50	Ct/St
2005	M.E.K.Hussey	10	18	4	253	1074	76.71	3	5	19
2005	D.M.Benkenstein	16	23	4	162*	1183	62.26	4	4	12
1998	P.D.Collingwood	13‡	23	3	190	1103	55.15	6	–	15
–	B.A.Williams	3	4	3	22*	51	51.00	–	–	1
–	G.R.Breese	16	22	2	79*	661	33.05	–	7	13
–	N.J.Astle	4	6	–	58	197	32.83	–	2	2
2005	G.J.Muchall	16	27	4	123	754	32.78	1	3	5
–	A.A.Noffke	5	6	2	65	125	31.25	–	1	1
1998	J.J.B.Lewis	9	15	1	52	407	29.07	–	2	6
–	G.M.Scott	7	13	2	61*	307	27.90	–	1	2
–	P.Mustard	16	21	–	80	507	24.14	–	3	38/3
–	L.E.Plunkett	14	19	4	74*	256	17.06	–	1	6
2005	A.M.Davies	11	13	5	62	119	14.87	–	1	2
2001	N.Peng	9	13	–	39	177	13.61	–	–	–
1999	N.Killeen	5	5	1	23	39	9.75	–	–	3
–	M.L.Lewis	5	6	1	20	44	8.80	–	–	2
–	C.D.Thorp	4	5	–	23	44	8.80	–	–	3
–	G.Onions	4	4	2	9*	13	6.50	–	–	1
–	J.P.Maher	2	4	–	9	18	4.50	–	–	3

Also batted: G.D.Bridge (1 match) 6 (2 ct); S.J.Harmison (4 – cap 1999) 0*, 0, 1 (1 ct); J.A.Lowe (1) 26, 14; M.L.Turner (2) 18, 1*.

BOWLING

	O	M	R	W	Avge	Best	5Wi	10wM
S.J.Harmison	131.1	26	392	27	14.51	6-52	2	–
A.M.Davies	263.4	85	731	47	15.55	6-32	2	–
M.L.Lewis	169	27	614	26	23.61	5-80	1	–
A.A.Noffke	140	38	405	15	27.00	4-19	–	–
D.M.Benkenstein	75.4	15	289	10	28.90	4-29	–	–
L.E.Plunkett	423	80	1573	51	30.84	5-43	2	–
P.D.Collingwood	181.3	28	670	21	31.90	5-52	1	–
G.R.Breese	296.1	53	967	27	35.81	5-83	2	–
Also bowled:								
N.Killeen	122.5	37	357	8	44.62	3-40	–	–
B.A.Williams	83.2	12	335	7	47.85	3-73	–	–

N.J.Astle 35-8-80-0; G.D.Bridge 3-1-12-0; M.E.K.Hussey 12-0-59-1; G.J.Muchall 7-0-18-0; G.Onions 67-8-309-4; G.M.Scott 10-1-48-0; C.D.Thorp 69-13-218-3; M.L.Turner 49-5-166-2.

The First-Class Averages (pp 129–145) give the records of Durham players in all first-class matches for the county (Durham's other opponents being Durham UCCE), with the exception of P.D.Collingwood and S.J.Harmison whose full county figures are as above.

‡ Full substitute for N.Peng v Essex at Southend.

DURHAM RECORDS

FIRST-CLASS CRICKET

Highest Total	For 645-6d		v	Middlesex	Lord's	2002
	V 810-4d		by	Warwicks	Birmingham	1994
Lowest Total	For 67		v	Middlesex	Lord's	1996
	V 56		by	Somerset	Chester-le-St[2]	2003
Highest Innings	For 273	M.L.Love	v	Hampshire	Chester-le-St[2]	2003
	V 501*	B.C.Lara	for	Warwicks	Birmingham	1994

Highest Partnership for each Wicket

1st	334*	S.Hutton/M.A.Roseberry	v	Oxford U	Oxford	1996
2nd	258	J.J.B.Lewis/M.L.Love	v	Notts	Chester-le-St[2]	2001
3rd	205	G.Fowler/S.Hutton	v	Yorkshire	Leeds	1993
4th	250	P.D.Collingwood/D.M.Benkenstein	v	Derbys	Derby	2005
5th	197	N.Peng/V.J.Wells	v	Derbys	Derby	2003
6th	193	D.C.Boon/P.D.Collingwood	v	Warwicks	Birmingham	1998
7th	139	M.E.K.Hussey/P.Mustard	v	Lancs	Manchester	2005
8th	134	A.C.Cummins/D.A.Graveney	v	Warwicks	Birmingham	1994
9th	127	D.G.C.Ligertwood/S.J.E.Brown	v	Surrey	Stockton	1996
10th	103	M.M.Betts/D.M.Cox	v	Sussex	Hove	1996

Best Bowling	For 9- 64	M.M.Betts	v	Northants	Northampton	1997
(Innings)	V 9- 36	M.S.Kasprowicz	for	Glamorgan	Cardiff	2003
Best Bowling	For 14-177	A.Walker	v	Essex	Chelmsford	1995
(Match)	V 13-110	M.S.Kasprowicz	for	Glamorgan	Chester-le-St[2]	2003

Most Runs – Season	1536	W.Larkins	(av 37.46)		1992
Most Runs – Career	7449	J.J.B.Lewis	(av 32.04)		1997-2005
Most 100s – Season	6	P.D.Collingwood			2005
Most 100s – Career	14	J.E.Morris			1994-99
	14	P.D.Collingwood			1996-2005
Most Wkts – Season	77	S.J.E.Brown	(av 25.87)		1996
Most Wkts – Career	518	S.J.E.Brown	(av 28.30)		1992-2002
Most Career W-K Dismissals	194	M.P.Speight	(189 ct; 5 st)		1997-2001
Most Career Catches in the Field	116	P.D.Collingwood			2005

LIMITED-OVERS CRICKET

Highest Total	CGT	326-4	v	Herefords	Chester-le-St[2]	1995
	NL	319-3	v	Worcs	Worcester	2004
	T20	180-4	v	Notts	Chester-le-St[2]	2005
Lowest Total	CGT	82	v	Worcs	Chester-le-St[1]	1968
	NL	72	v	Warwicks	Birmingham	2002
	T20	111-8	v	Lancs	Chester-le-St[2]	2005
Highest Innings	CGT	132	M.A.Gough	v	Wales MC	Cardiff	2002
	NL	131*	W.Larkins	v	Hampshire	Portsmouth	1994
	T20	64*	G.J.Muchall	v	Notts	Chester-le-St[2]	2005
Best Bowling	CGT	7-32	S.P.Davis	v	Lancashire	Chester-le-St[1]	1983
	NL	6-31	N.Killeen	v	Derbyshire	Derby	2000
	T20	4- 7	N.Killeen	v	Leics	Leicester	2004

[1] Chester-le-Street CC (Ropery Lane)   [2] Riverside Ground

ESSEX

Formation of Present Club: 14 January 1876
Inaugural First-Class Match: 1894
Colours: Blue, Gold and Red
Badge: Three Seaxes above Scroll bearing 'Essex'
County Champions: (6) 1979, 1983, 1984, 1986, 1991, 1992
Gillette/NatWest/C & G Trophy Winners: (2) 1985, 1997
Benson and Hedges Cup Winners: (2) 1979, 1998
National League (Div 1) Winners: (1) 2005
Sunday League Winners: (3) 1981, 1984, 1985
Twenty20 Cup Winners: (0); best – Quarter-Finalist 2004
Match Awards: CGT 55; BHC 91

Chief Executive: David E.East, County Ground, New Writtle Street, Chelmsford CM2 0PG • Tel: 01245 252420 • Fax: 01245 254030 • Email: administration.essex@ecb.co.uk • Web: www.essexcricket.org.uk

First XI Coach/Captain: R.C.Irani. **Vice-Captain:** D.Gough. **Overseas Players:** A.R.Adams, A.J.Bichel and M.G.Johnson. **2006 Beneficiary:** A.P.Cowan. **Head Groundsman:** S.G.Kerrison. **Scorer:** A.E.Choat. ‡ New registration. NQ Not qualified for England.

NQ**ADAMS, Andre** Ryan (Westlake BHS, Auckland), b Mangere, Auckland, New Zealand 17 Jul 1975. 5'9". RHB, RMF. Auckland 1997-98 to date. Essex debut 2004, scoring 124; cap 2004. Herefordshire 2001. **Tests** (NZ): 1 (2001-02); HS 11 and BB 3-44 v E (Auckland) 2001-02 – on debut. **LOI** (NZ): 38 (2000-01 to 2005-06); HS 45 v P (Rawalpindi) 2001-02; BB 5-22 v I (Queenstown) 2002-03. HS 124 v Leics (Leics) 2004 (91 balls, 7 sixes, 13 fours; 100 off 80 balls) on UK debut. BB 6-25 Auckland v Wellington (Auckland) 2004-05. Ex BB 5-60 v Durham (Southend) 2005. Hat-trick v Somerset (Taunton) 2005. LO HS 90* N Is Selection XI v SL (New Plymouth) 2000-01. LO BB 5-7 Auckland v ND (Auckland) 1999-00. T20 HS 25. T20 BB 2-12.

AHMED, Jahid Sheikh (St Peter's HS, Burnham-on-Crouch; East London U), b Chelmsford 20 Feb 1986. 5'11". RHB, RMF. Debut 2005. HS 14* and BB 1-90 v Worcs (Worcester) 2005 – on debut.

‡NQ**BICHEL, Andrew** John (Laidley HS; Ipswich C, Queensland), b Laidley, Queensland, Australia 27 Aug 1970. RHB, RFM. 5'11". Queensland 1992-93 to date. Worcestershire 2001-02, 2004; cap 2001. Hampshire 2005. **Tests** (A): 19 (1996-97 to 2003-04); HS 71 v WI (Bridgetown) 2002-03; BB 5-60 v WI (Melbourne) 2000-01. **LOI** (A): 67 (1996-97 to 2003-04); HS 64 v NZ (Pt Elizabeth) 2002-03; BB 7-20 v E (Pt Elizabeth) 2002-03. F-c Tours (A): E 1997; SA 1996-97, 2001-02; WI 1998-99, 2002-03; P 2002-03 (in Sharjah); Scot 1998 (Aus A). HS 142 Wo v Northants (Worcester) 2004.. 50 wkts (1+2): most – 66 (2001). BB 9-93 (10-131 match) Wo v Glos (Worcester) 2002. Awards: GGT 1; BHC 3. LO HS 100 Wo v Glam (Cardiff) 2001 (BHC). LO BB 7-20 (*see LOI*). T20 HS 58*. T20 BB 3-36.

BOPARA, Ravinder Singh (Brampton Manor S; Barking Abbey Sports C), b Newham, London 4 May 1985. 5'8". RHB, RMF. Debut 2002; cap 2005. HS 105* and BB 4-93 v Derbys (Chelmsford) 2005. Award: CGT 1. LO HS 96* v Glamorgan(Chelmsford) 2005 (NL). LO BB 2-10 v Hants (Chelmsford) 2004. T20 HS 30. T20 BB 3-18.

CHAMBERS, Maurice Anthony (Homerton TC; Sir George Monoux C), b Port Antonio, Jamaica 14 Sep 1987. 6'3". RHB, RFM. Debut 2005. HS 2* and BB 1-73 v Derbys (Chelmsford) 2005 – on debut.

CHOPRA, Varun (Ilford County HS), b Barking 21 Jun 1987. RHB, LB. Staff 2006 – awaiting f-c debut.

COOK, Alastair Nathan (Bedford S), b Gloucester 25 Dec 1984. 6'3". LHB, OB. Debut 2003; cap 2005. Essex 2nd XI debut 2000 when aged 15y 235d. England U-19 capt 2003-04. YC 2005. 1000 (1): 1466 (2005). HS 195 v Northants (Northampton) 2005. Scored 214 v Australians (Chelmsford) 2005 in 2-day non-f-c match. BB 3-13 v Northants (Chelmsford) 2005. LO HS 94 v Northants (Northampton) 2005 (NL). T20 HS 2.

COWAN, Ashley Preston (Framlingham C), b Hitchin, Herts 7 May 1975. 6'4". RHB, RFM. Debut 1995; cap 1997; benefit 2006. No appearances 2003 (knee surgery). Cambridgeshire 1993. F-c Tour: WI 1997-98. HS 94 v Leics (Leicester) 1998. 50 wkts (1): 52 (1997). BB 6-47 v Glamorgan(Cardiff) 1999. Hat-trick 1996. Award: BHC 1. LO HS 45 v Middx (Chelmsford) 2001 (BHC). LO BB 5-14 v Middx (Southgate) 2001 (NL). T20 HS 14*. T20 BB 2-20.

FLOWER, Andrew (Wainona HS, Harare), b Cape Town, South Africa 28 Apr 1968. 5'10". Elder brother of G.W.Flower (Zimbabwe). LHB, WK, occ RM. Mashonaland 1986-87 to 2002-03. MCC 1996-99. *Wisden* 2001. Essex debut/cap 2002. S Australia 2003-04. British passport after 2003 season. Qualified for England 2005. **Tests** (Z): 63 (1992-93 to 2002-03, 20 as captain); HS 232* v I (Nagpur) 2000-01. **LOI** (Z): 213 (1991-92 to 2002-03, 52 as captain); HS 145 v I (Colombo) 2002-03; scored 115* v SL (New Plymouth) on debut. F-c Tours (Z) (C=captain): E 2000C; SA 1999-00; WI 1999-00C; NZ 1995-96C, 1997-98, 2000-01; I 1992-93, 2000-01, 2001-02; P 1993-94C, 1996-97, 1998-99; SL 1996-97, 1997-98, 2001-02; B 2001-02. 1000 runs (4): 1349 (2005). HS 232* (*see Tests*). Ex HS 201* v Surrey (Oval) 2003. BB (Mashonaland) 1-1. Awards: BHC 2. LO HS 145 (*see LOI*). LO BB (Mashonaland)1-21. T20 HS 83.

NQ**FLOWER, Grant** William (St George's C), b Salisbury, Rhodesia 20 Dec 1970. 5'10". Younger brother of A Flower (*see Essex*). RHB, SLA. Mashonaland 1989-90. Essex debut/cap 2005 (Kolpak registration). **Tests** (Z): 67 (1992-93 to 2003-04); HS 201* v P (Harare) 1994-95 sharing with A.Flower in fourth-wicket partnership of 269, the highest stand between brothers in Test cricket; BB 4-41 (8-104 match) v B (Chittagong) 2001-02. **LOI** (Z): 219 (1992-93 to 2003-04, 1 as captain); HS 142* v B (Bulawayo) 2000-01; BB 4-32 v K (Dhaka) 1998-99. F-c Tours (Z): E 2000; SA 1999-00; WI 1999-00; NZ 1995-96, 1997-98; I 1992-93, 2000-01, 2001-02; P 1993-94, 1996-97, 1998-99; SL 1996-97, 1997-98, 2001-02; B 2001-02. HS 243* Mashonaland v Matabeleland (Harare) 1996-97. Ex HS 115 v Lancs (Manchester) 2005. BB 7-31 Z v Lahore (Lahore) 1998-99. CC BB 4-66 Le v Warwks (Birmingham) 2002. Ex BB 3-112 v Lancs (Manchester) 2005. LO HS 148* Mashonaland v Midlands (Kwekwe) 2002-03. LO BB 4-32 (*see LOI*). T20 HS 4. T20 BB 3-20.

FOSTER, James Savin (Forest S, Snaresbrook; Collingwood C, Durham U), b Whipps Cross 15 Apr 1980. 6'0". RHB, WK. British U 2000. Essex debut 2000; cap 2001. Durham UCCE 2001. British U 2001. **ECB Contract 2002. Tests**: 7 (2001-02 to 2002-03); HS 48 v I (Bangalore) 2001-02. **LOI**: 11 (2001-02); HS 13 v I (Bombay) 2001-02. F-c Tours: A 2002-03; WI 2000-01 (Eng A); NZ 2001-02; I 2001-02. 1000 runs (1): 1037 (2004). HS 212 v Leics (Chelmsford) 2004. LO HS 56* v Sussex (Hove) 2001 (NL). T20 HS 62*.

GOUGH, Darren (Priory CS, Lundwood), b Barnsley, Yorks 18 Sep 1970. 5'11". RHB, RF. Yorkshire 1989-2003; cap 1993; benefit 2004. Essex debut/cap 2004. *Wisden* 1998. **ECB contracts 2000-01-02. Tests**: 58 (1994 to 2003); HS 65 v NZ (Manchester) 1994 – on debut; BB 6-42 v SA (Leeds) 1998; hat-trick v A (Sydney) 1998-99 – first for E v A since 1899. **LOI**: 156 (1994 to 2005); HS 46* v A (Chester-le-St) 2005; BB 5-44 v Z (Sydney) 1994-95 and 5-44 v A (Lord's) 1998. Took wickets with his sixth balls in both Tests and LOI. F-c Tours: A 1994-95, 1998-99; SA 1991-92 (Y), 1992-93 (Y), 1993-94 (Eng A), 1995-96, 1999-00; NZ 1996-97; P 2000-01; SL 2000-01; Z 1996-97. HS 121 Y v Warwks (Leeds) 1996. Ex HS 93 v Yorks (Leeds) 2005. 50 wkts (5): most – 67 (1996). BB 7-28 (10-80 match) Y v Lancs (Leeds) 1995 (not CC). CC BB 7-42 (10-96 match) Y v Somerset (Taunton) 1993. Ex BB 5-57 v Hants (Chelmsford) 2004. 2 hat-tricks (1995, 1998-99); took 4 wkts in 5 balls v Kent (Leeds) 1995. Awards: CGT 2; BHC 1. LO HS 72* Y v Leics (Leicester) 1991 (SL). LO BB 7-27 Y v Ire (Leeds) 1997 (NWT). T20 HS 17. T20 BB 3-16.

IRANI, Ronald Charles (Smithills CS, Bolton), b Leigh, Lancs 26 Oct 1971. 6'3". RHB, RMF. Lancashire 1990-93. Essex debut/cap 1994; captain 2000 to date; benefit 2003. **Tests**: 3 (1996 to 1999); HS 41 v I (Lord's) 1996; BB 1-22. Took wicket of M.Azharuddin with his fifth ball in Test cricket. **LOI**: 31 (1996 to 2002-03); HS 53 and BB 5-26 v I (Oval) 2002. F-c Tours: NZ 1996-97, 1999-00 (Eng A); P 1995-96 (Eng A); Z 1996-97; B 1999-00 (Eng A). 1000 runs (6); most – 1202 (2005). HS 207* v Northants (Ilford) 2002. 50 wkts (1): 51 (1999). BB 6-71 v Notts (Nottingham) 2002. Awards: CGT 5; BHC 5. LO HS 158* v Glamorgan(Chelmsford) 2004 (NL). LO BB 5-26 (*see LOI*). T20 HS 64*.

JEFFERSON, William Ingleby (Beeston Hall S, Norfolk; Oundle S; St Hild & St Bede C, Durham U), b Derby 25 Oct 1979. Son of R.I.Jefferson (Cambridge U and Surrey 1961-66); grandson of J.Jefferson (Army 1919, Comb Services 1922). 6'10½". RHB, RMF. British U 2000-01. Essex debut 2000; cap 2002. Durham UCCE 2001-02. Scored 50 and 65 in first two LO innings. 1000 runs (1): 1555 (2004). HS 222 v Hants (Southampton) 2004. BB 1-16 (CC). Awards: CGT 2. LO HS 132 v Essex CB (Chelmsford) 2003 (CGT). BB 2-9 v Worcs (Worcester) 2005 (NL). T20 HS 19.

‡NO**JOHNSON, Mitchell** Guy, b Townsville, Queensland, Australia 2 Nov 1981. LHB, LFM. Queensland 2001-02 to date. **LOI** (A): 1 (2005-06); HS – v NZ (Christchurch) 2005-06. HS 51* .Q v S Aus (Brisbane) 2005-06. BB 5-43 Q v S Aus (Adelaide) 2005-06. LO HS 27 Q v Vic (Ballarat) 2004-05. LO BB 4-37 Q v Tas (Brisbane) 2003-04.

MIDDLEBROOK, James Daniel (Pudsey Crawshaw S), b Leeds, Yorks 13 May 1977. 6'1". RHB, OB. Yorkshire 1998-2001. Essex debut 2002; cap 2003. HS 115 v Somerset (Taunton) 2004. 50 wkts (1): 56 (2003). BB 6-82 (10-170 match) Y v Hants (Southampton) 2000 – including 4 wickets in 5 balls. Ex BB 6-123 v Kent (Chelmsford) 2003. Hat-trick 2003. LO HS 47 v Worcs (Worcester) 2004 (CGT). LO BB 4-33 v Hants (Southend) 2002 (NL). T20 HS 29. T20 BB 3-25.

NAPIER, Graham Richard (The Gilberd S, Colchester), b Colchester 6 Jan 1980. 5'9½". RHB, RM. Debut 1997; cap 2003. F-c Tour (Eng A): I 2003-04. HS 106* v Notts (Nottingham) 2004. BB 5-56 v Derbys (Derby) 2004. Award: CGT 1. LO HS 79 Essex CB v Lancs CB (Chelmsford) 2000 (NWT). LO BB 6-29 v Worcs (Chelmsford) 2001 (NL). T20 HS 38. T20 BB 3-13.

PALLADINO, Antonio Paul (Cardinal Pole SS; Anglia Polytechnic U), b London Hospital 29 Jun 1983. 6'0". RHB, RMF. Cambridge UCCE 2003. Essex debut 2003. HS 41 v Notts (Nottingham) 2004. BB 6-41 v Kent (Canterbury) 2003. LO HS 16 Essex CB v Essex (Chelmsford) 2003. LO BB 3-32 v Glamorgan(Chelmsford) 2003 (NL). T20 HS – . T20 BB 2-3.

PETTINI, Mark Lewis (Comberton Village C; Hills Road SFC, Cambridge; Cardiff U), b Brighton, Sussex 7 Aug 1983. RHB, RM. 5'10". Debut 2001. British U (captain) 2004. HS 78 v Warwks (Chelmsford) 2003. LO 92* v Warwks (Birmingham) 2003 (CGT). T20 HS 60.

PHILLIPS, Timothy James (Felsted S; St Hild & St Bede C, Durham U), b Cambridge 13 Mar 1981. 6'1". LHB, SLA. Essex debut 1999. No appearances 2003-04. Durham UCCE 2001-02. HS 89 v Worcs (Worcester) 2005. BB 4-42 v SL A (Chelmsford) 1999 – on debut. CC BB 4-102 v Middx (Southgate) 2002. LO HS 24* v Lancs (Manchester) 2005 (CGT). LO BB 3-31 v Hants (Southampton) 2005 (NL).

NO**Ten DOESCHATE, Ryan** Neil (Fairbairn C; Cape Town U), b Port Elizabeth, South Africa 30 Jun 1980. 5'10½". RHB, RMF. Debut 2003. EU passport – Dutch ancestry. Holland 2005. HS 98 v Worcs (Worcester) 2005. BB 3-29 v CU (Cambridge) 2004. CC BB 2-52 v Durham (Chester-le-St) 2004. LO HS 89* v Lancs (Chelmsford) 2005 (NL). LO BB 4-18 Holland v Papua New Guinea (Belfast) 2005 T20 HS 42*. T20 BB 2-27.

TUDOR, Alex Jeremy (St Mark's S, Hammersmith; City of Westminster C), b West Brompton, London 23 Oct 1977. 6'5". RHB, RF. Surrey 1995-2004; cap 1999. Essex debut 2005. YC 1999. **Tests**: 10 (1998-99 to 2002-03); HS 99* v NZ (Birmingham) 1999 – record score by an England 'night-watchman'; BB 5-44 v A (Nottingham) 2001. **LOI**: 3 (2002); HS 6; BB 2-30 v I (Oval) 2002. F-c Tours: A 1998-99, 2002-03; SA 1999-00; WI 2000-01 (Eng A). HS 116 Sy v Essex (Oval) 2001. Ex HS 57 v Somerset (Taunton) 2005. BB 7-48 Sy v Lancs (Oval) 2000. Ex BB 2-30 v Yorks (Chelmsford) 2005. LO HS 56 Sy v Lancs (Croydon) 2004 (NL). LO BB 4-26 Sy v Hants (Oval) 2000 (NL).

WESTFIELD, Mervyn Simon (Barking C), b Romford 5 May 1988. 6'0". RHB, RFM. Debut 2005. HS 0 and BB 1-90 v Durham (Chester-le-St) 2005 – on debut.

RELEASED/RETIRED

(Having made a first-class County appearance in 2005)

BISHOP, Justin Edward (Bury St Edmunds County Upper S; John Snow C, Durham U), b Bury St Edmunds, Suffolk 4 Jan 1982. 6'0". LHB, LMF. Essex 1999-2005. Durham UCCE 2002-04. British U 2003. HS 66 DU v Northants (Northampton) 2004. Ex HS 23* v Worcs (Southend) 2002.BB 5-148 v Leics (Chelmsford) 2001. LO HS 16* v Hants (Colchester) 2000 (NL). LO BB 3-33 v Worcs (Worcester) 2001 (NL).

[NQ]**DANISH PARABHA SHANKER KANERIA** (St Patrick's HS; Government Islamia C), b Karachi, Pakistan 16 Dec 1980. 6'1". Cousin of Anil Dalpat (Pakistan) and second Hindu to represent Pakistan. RHB, LB. Karachi 1998-99. PNSC 1998-99. Habib Bank 1999-00 to date. Essex 2004-05; cap 2004. **Tests** (P): 34 (2000-01 to 2005-06); HS 15 v A (Sharjah) 2002-03; BB 7-77 v B (Dhaka) 2001-02. Test debut was his fourth f-c match. **LOI** (P): 15 (2001-02 to 2005-06); HS 3*; BB 3-31 v NZ (Dambulla) 2003. F-c Tours (P): A 2004-05; WI 2004-05; NZ 2003-04; I 2004-05; SL 2001 (Pak A); K 2000 (Pak A). 50 wkts (1+1); most 63 (2004). HS 47 Karachi Blues v Karachi Whites (Karachi) 2004-05. Ex HS 22 v Northants (Chelmsford) 2005. BB 7-39 Karachi Whites v Gujranwala (Karachi) 2000-01. Ex BB 7-65 (13-186 match) v Yorks (Chelmsford) 2004. LO HS 15 PCB Whites v PCB Reds (Lahore) 2002-03. LO BB 5-24 Habib Bank v Lahore Blues (Lahore) 2001-02. T20 HS 5. T20 BB 4-31.

[NQ]**NEL, Andre** (Dr E.G.Jansen S, Boksburg), b Germiston, South Africa 15 Jul 1977. 6'4". RHB, RFM. Easterns 1996-97 to date. Northamptonshire 2003. Essex 2005 (one match). **Tests** (SA): 18 (2001-02 to 2005-06); HS 14 v A (Melbourne) 2005-06; BB 6-32 (10-88 match) v WI (Bridgetown) 2004-05. **LOI** (SA): 43 (2000-01 to 2005-06); HS 4*; BB 4-39 v P (Rawalpindi) 2003-04. F-c Tours (SA): A 2002-03 (SA A – part), 2005-06; WI 2000-01, 2004-05; NZ 2003-04; P 2003-04; Z 2001-02. HS 44 Easterns v FS (Benoni) 2000-01. CC HS 42 Nh v Glamorgan (Cardiff) 2003. Ex HS – and BB 2-12 v Somerset (Colchester) 2005 – on debut. BB 6-25 Easterns v Gauteng (Jo'burg) 2001-02. CC BB 5-47 Nh v Glos (Gloucester) 2003. LO HS 21* Easterns v Boland (Benoni) 2003-04. LO BB 6-27 Easterns v GW (Benoni) 2000-01. T20 HS 12. T20 BB 2-19.

[NQ]**STEYN, Dale** Willem (Hans Merensky HS, Phalaborwa), b Phalaborwa, N Province, South Africa 27 Jun 1983. RHB, RF. Northerns 2003-04. Titans 2005-05. Essex 2005. **Tests** (SA): 3 (2004-05); HS 8 (twice); BB 2-26 v E (Durban) 2004-05. **LOI** (SA): 2 (2005-06); HS – ; BB 1-58. HS 82 v Durham (Chester-le-St) 2005. BB 5-30 Titans v Warriors (East London) 2004-05. Ex BB 3-69 v Leics (Chelcmsford) 2005 – on debut. LO HS 3. LO BB 3-34 v Glamorgan (Chelmsford) 2005. T20 HS 0. T20 BB 2-10.

THORNICROFT , N.D. – *see YORKSHIRE*

A.J.Clarke and A.P.Grayson left the staff having not made a first-class appearance in 2005.

ESSEX 2005

RESULTS SUMMARY

	Place	Won	Lost	Tied	Drew	No Result
County Championship (2nd Division)	5th	5	4		7	
All First-Class Matches		6	4		7	
C & G Trophy	2nd Round					
National League (1st Division)	1st	13	1			2
Twenty20 Cup	5th in South Division					

COUNTY CHAMPIONSHIP AVERAGES

BATTING AND FIELDING

Cap		M	I	NO	HS	Runs	Avge	100	50	Ct/St
2002	A.Flower	15	24	5	188	1239	65.21	5	4	11
1994	R.C.Irani	15	21	2	103	1133	59.63	1	9	5
2005	A.N.Cook	16	28	2	195	1249	48.03	4	5	12
2004	Danish Kaneria	7	6	5	22	47	47.00	–	–	2
2002	W.I.Jefferson	14	24	2	149	842	38.27	2	3	10
2001	J.S.Foster	16	23	4	107*	696	36.63	1	4	33/6
2005	R.S.Bopara	16	27	4	105*	792	34.43	1	4	7
2004	A.R.Adams	12	12	1	103	373	33.90	1	–	14
2004	D.Gough	9	9	1	93	260	32.50	–	2	1
2003	J.D.Middlebrook	15	21	3	71	548	30.44	–	3	9
2005	G.W.Flower	11	17	–	115	382	22.47	1	3	5
2003	G.R.Napier	8	7	–	55	153	21.85	–	2	2
–	D.W.Steyn	6	7	2	82	94	18.80	–	1	2
–	A.P.Palladino	5	7	4	17	40	13.33	–	–	1

Also batted: J.S.Ahmed (1 match) 14*; M.A.Chambers (1) 2*; A.P.Cowan (1 – cap 1997) 0, 27 (1 ct); T.J.Phillips (2) 0, 2*, 89; R.N.ten Doeschate (1) 98; N.D.Thornicroft (1) 0, 4*; A.J.Tudor (2) 57 (2 ct); M.S.Westfield (1) 0, 0. A.Nel (1) (1 ct) did not bat.

BOWLING

	O	M	R	W	Avge	Best	5wI	10wM
D.Gough	271.5	67	781	25	31.24	5- 85	1	–
Danish Kaneria	394.4	86	1069	32	33.40	6- 74	3	1
A.R.Adams	391.3	111	1218	36	33.83	5- 60	1	–
R.S.Bopara	202.2	26	871	20	43.55	4- 93	–	–
G.R.Napier	166.2	32	634	14	45.28	3- 25	–	–
J.D.Middlebrook	439.4	85	1348	26	51.84	4- 60	–	–
D.W.Steyn	199.2	38	838	14	59.85	3- 69	–	–
Also bowled:								
A.J.Tudor	40	9	118	5	23.60	2- 30	–	–
G.W.Flower	110.3	25	339	9	37.66	3-112	–	–
T.J.Phillips	61	7	242	6	40.33	3- 24	–	–
A.P.Palladino	75.2	16	271	6	45.16	3- 24	–	–

J.S.Ahmed 27-4-141-1; M.A.Chambers 16-1-84-1; A.N.Cook 13-1-54-3; A.P.Cowan 25-6-99-1; W.I.Jefferson 20-6-60-1; A.Nel 23-3-88-4; N.D.Thornicroft 22-6-70-1; M.S.Westfield 18-0-90-1.

The First-Class Averages (pp 129–145) give the records of Essex players in all first-class matches for the county (Essex's other opponents being Cambridge UCCE), with the exception of A.N.Cook, A.Flower, and A.P.Palladino whose full county figures are as above, with the exception of M.L.Pettini whose only first-class appearance was for the MCC.

ESSEX RECORDS

FIRST-CLASS CRICKET

Highest Total	For 761-6d		v	Leics	Chelmsford	1990
	V 803-4d		by	Kent	Brentwood	1934
Lowest Total	For 30		v	Yorkshire	Leyton	1901
	V 14		by	Surrey	Chelmsford	1983
Highest Innings	For 343*	P.A.Perrin	v	Derbyshire	Chesterfield	1904
	V 332	W.H.Ashdown	for	Kent	Brentwood	1934

Highest Partnership for each Wicket

1st	316	G.A.Gooch/P.J.Prichard	v	Kent	Chelmsford	1994
2nd	403	G.A.Gooch/P.J.Prichard	v	Leics	Chelmsford	1990
3rd	347*	M.E.Waugh/N.Hussain	v	Lancashire	Ilford	1992
4th	314	Salim Malik/N.Hussain	v	Surrey	The Oval	1991
5th	316	N.Hussain/M.A.Garnham	v	Leics	Leicester	1991
6th	206	J.W.H.T.Douglas/J.O'Connor	v	Glos	Cheltenham	1923
	206	B.R.Knight/R.A.G.Luckin	v	Middlesex	Brentwood	1962
7th	261	J.W.H.T.Douglas/J.Freeman	v	Lancashire	Leyton	1914
8th	263	D.R.Wilcox/R.M.Taylor	v	Warwicks	Southend	1946
9th	251	J.W.H.T.Douglas/S.N.Hare	v	Derbyshire	Leyton	1921
10th	218	F.H.Vigar/T.P.B.Smith	v	Derbyshire	Chesterfield	1947

Best Bowling	For 10- 32	H.Pickett	v	Leics	Leyton	1895
(Innings)	V 10- 40	E.G.Dennett	for	Glos	Bristol	1906
Best Bowling	For 17-119	W.Mead	v	Hampshire	Southampton	1895
(Match)	V 17- 56	C.W.L.Parker	for	Glos	Gloucester	1925

Most Runs – Season	2559	G.A.Gooch	(av 67.34)		1984
Most Runs – Career	30701	G.A.Gooch	(av 51.77)		1973-97
Most 100s – Season	9	J.O'Connor			1929, 1934
	9	D.J.Insole			1955
Most 100s – Career	94	G.A.Gooch			1973-97
Most Wkts – Season	172	T.P.B.Smith	(av 27.13)		1947
Most Wkts – Career	1610	T.P.B.Smith	(av 26.68)		1929-51
Most Career W-K Dismissals	1231	B.Taylor	(1040 ct; 191 st)		1949-73
Most Career Catches in the Field	519	K.W.R.Fletcher			1962-88

LIMITED-OVERS CRICKET

Highest Total	CGT	386-5		v	Wiltshire	Chelmsford	1988
	NL	316-4		v	Glamorgan	Chelmsford	2004
	T20	175-5		v	Middlesex	Chelmsford	2003
Lowest Total	CGT	57		v	Lancashire	Lord's	1996
	NL	69		v	Derbyshire	Chesterfield	1974
	T20	109		v	Sussex	Hove	2005
Highest Innings	CGT	144	G.A.Gooch	v	Hampshire	Chelmsford	1990
	NL	176	G.A.Gooch	v	Glamorgan	Southend	1983
	T20	83	A.Flower	v	Middlesex	Chelmsford	2003
Best Bowling	CGT	5- 8	J.K.Lever	v	Middlesex	Westcliff	1972
		5- 8	G.A.Gooch	v	Cheshire	Chester	1995
	NL	8-26	K.D.Boyce	v	Lancashire	Manchester	1971
	T20	4-20	S.A.Brant	v	Kent	Maidstone	2004

GLAMORGAN

Formation of Present Club: 6 July 1888
Inaugural First-Class Match: 1921
Colours: Blue and Gold
Badge: Gold Daffodil
County Champions: (3) 1948, 1969, 1997
Gillette/NatWest/C & G Trophy Winners: (0); best –
finalist 1977
Benson and Hedges Cup Winners: (0); best – finalist 2000
National League (Div 1) Winners: (2) 2002, 2004
Sunday League Winners: (1) 1993
Twenty20 Cup Winners: (0); best – Semi-Finalist 2004
Match Awards: CGT 45; BHC 56

Chief Executive: M.J.Fatkin, Sophia Gardens, Cardiff, CF1 9XR • Tel: 029 2040 9380 •
Fax: 029 2040 9390 • email: info@glamorgancricket.co.uk • Web:
www.glamorgancricket.com

First XI Coach: J.Derrick. **Captain**: R.D.B.Croft. **Vice-Captain**: No appointment.
Overseas Players: M.T.G.Elliott and M.S.Kasprowicz. **2006 Beneficiary**: S.D.Thomas.
Head Groundsman: L.A.Smith. **Scorer**: Dr Andrew K.Hignell. ‡ New registration.
NQ Not qualified for England.

CHERRY, Daniel David (Tonbridge S; U of Wales, Swansea), b Newport, Gwent 7 Feb 1980. 5'9". LHB, RM. Debut 1998. No f-c appearances 2000-01. HS 226 v Middx (Southgate) 2005. LO HS 42 v Middx (Lord's) 2005 (NL). T20 HS 43*. T20 BB 2-6.

COSKER, Dean Andrew (Millfield S), b Weymouth, Dorset 7 Jan 1978. 5'11". RHB, SLA. Debut 1996; cap 2000. F-c Tours (A): SA 1998-99, SL 1997-98; Z 1998-99, K 1997-98. HS 52 v Glos (Bristol) 2005. BB 6-140 v Lancs (Colwyn Bay) 1998. LO HS 27* v Somerset (Taunton) 1999 (NL). LO BB 5-54 v Essex (Chelmsford) 2003 (NL). T20 HS 10*. T20 BB 2-24.

CROFT, Robert Damien Bale (St John Lloyd Catholic CS, Llanelli; Neath Tertiary C; W GlamorganIHE), b Morriston 25 May 1970. 5'10½". RHB, OB. Debut 1989; cap 1992; benefit 2000; captain 2003 (*part*) to date. Tests: 21 (1996 to 2001); HS 37* v SA (Manchester) 1998; BB 5-95 v NZ (Christchurch) 1996-97. **LOI**: 50 (1996 to 2001); HS 32 v SL (Perth) 1998-99; BB 3-51 v SA (Oval) 1998. F-c Tours: A 1998-99; SA 1993-94 (Eng A), 1995-96 (Gm); WI 1991-92 (Eng A), 1997-98; NZ 1996-97; SL 2000-01, 2002-03; Z 1990-91 (Gm), 1994-95 (Gm), 1996-97. HS 143 v Somerset (Taunton) 1995. 50 wkts (7); most – 76 (1996). BB 8-66 (14-169 match) v Warwks (Swansea) 1992. Awards: CGT 2; BHC 2. LO HS 143 v Lincs (Lincoln) 2004 (CGT). LO BB 6-20 v Worcs (Cardiff) 1994 (SL). T20 HS 62*. T20 BB 3-32.

DAVIES, Andrew Philip (Dwr-y-Felin CS; Christ C, Brecon), b Neath 7 Nov 1976. 5'11". LHB, RMF. Debut 1995. Wales (MC). No appearances 2000. HS 41* v Notts (Nottingham) 2005. BB 5-79 v Worcs (Cardiff) 2002. LO HS 24 v Sussex (Hove) 2001 (NL). LO BB 5-19 v Lincs (Sleaford) 2002 (CGT). T20 HS 11. T20 BB 3-17.

NQELLIOTT, Matthew Thomas Gray (Kyabram Secondary C; La Trobe U), b Chelsea, Victoria, Australia 28 Sep 1971. 6'3". LHB, LM/SLC. Victoria 1992-93 to date. Glamorgan 2000, 2004; cap 2000. Yorkshire 2002. *Wisden* 1997. Tests (A): 21 (1996-97 to 2004); HS 199 v E (Leeds) 1997. **LOI** (A): 1 (1997); HS 1 v E (Lord's) 1997. F-c Tours (A): E 1995 (Young A), 1997; SA 1996-97; WI 1998-99. 1000 runs (3+5); most – 1429 (2003-04). HS 203 v Tasmania (Melbourne) 1995-96. UK HS 199 (*see Tests*). Gm HS 177 v Sussex (Colwyn Bay) 2000. BB 3-68 V v Q (Melbourne) 2004-05. Awards: CGT 3. LO HS 156 v Dorset (Bournemouth) 2000 (NWT). T20 HS 52*.

GRANT, Richard Neil (Cefn Saeson CS; Neath Port Talbot C), b Neath 5 Jun 1984. 5'10". RHB, RM. Debut 2005. HS 33 v Notts (Nottingham) 2005. LO HS 29 v Lancs (Colwyn Bay) 2005 (NL). LO BB 1-18 (NL). T20 HS 36. T20 BB 4-38.

HARRISON, Adam James (W Monmouth CS), b Newport, Gwent 30 Oct 1985. RHB, RMF. Younger brother of D.S.Harrison; son of S.C.Harrison (Glamorgan 1971-77). MCC 2004. Glamorgan debut 2005. HS 34* and BB 2-65 MCC v Sussex (Lord's) 2004. Gm HS 0 and BB 1-54 v Sussex (Swansea) 2005 – on debut. T20 HS 1*. T20 BB 2-12.

HARRISON, David Stuart (W Monmouth CS; Usk C, Pontypool), b Newport, Gwent 30 Jul 1981. Elder brother of A.J.Harrison; son of S.C.Harrison (Glamorgan 1971-77). 6'4". RHB, RM. Glamorgan debut 1999. HS 88 v Essex (Chelmsford) 2004. 50 wkts (1): 57 (2004). BB 5-48 v Somerset (Swansea) 2004. LO HS 37* and LO BB 5-26 v Yorks (Leeds) 2002 (NL). T20 HS 4. T20 BB 2-17.

HEMP, David Lloyd (Olchfa CS; Millfield S; W Glamorgan C; Birmingham U), b Hamilton, Bermuda 8 Nov 1970. UK resident since 1976. 6'0". LHB, RM. Glamorgan 1991-96; cap 1994. Warwickshire 1997-2001; cap 1997. Wales (MC) 1992-94. F-c Tours: SA 1995-96 (Gm); I 1994-95 (Eng A); Z 1994-95 (Gm). 1000 runs (5); most – 1452 (1994). HS 186* Wa v Worcs (Birmingham) 2001. Gm HS 157* v Kent (Canterbury) 2005. BB 3-23 v SA A (Cardiff) 1996. CC BB 2-29 Wa v Glos (Birmingham) 2000. Awards: CGT 4; BHC 2. LO HS 121 v Comb U (Cardiff) 1995 (BHC). LO BB 4-32 Wa v Minor C (Lakenham) 1998 (BHC). T20 HS 74.

JONES, Simon Philip (Coedcae CS; Millfield S), b Swansea 25 Dec 1978. Son of I.J.Jones (Glamorgan and England 1960-68). 6'3½". LHB, RF. Debut 1998; cap 2002. Unavailable 2003 (knee reconstruction). MBE 2005. **ECB contracts 2004-05. Tests:** 18 (2002 to 2005); HS 44 v I (Lord's) 2002 – on debut; BB 6-53 v A (Manchester) 2005. **LOI:** 8 (2004-05 to 2005); HS 1; BB 2-43 v Z (Bulawayo) 2004-05 – on debut. F-c Tours: A 2002-03 (part); SA 2004-05; WI 2003-04; I 2003-04 (Eng A – part). HS 46 v Yorks (Scarborough) 2001. BB 6-45 v Derbys (Cardiff) 2002. LO HS 12* v Notts (Nottingham) 1999 (NL). LO BB 3-19 v Lancs (Manchester) 2005 (NL).

NQ**KASPROWICZ, Michael** Scott (Brisbane State HS), b South Brisbane, Australia 10 Feb 1972. 6'4". RHB, RFM. Queensland 1989-90 to date. Essex 1994; cap 1994. Leicestershire 1999; cap 1999. Glamorgan 2002-04; cap 2002. **Tests** (A): 35 (1996-97 to 2005); HS 25 v I (Calcutta) 1997-98; BB 7-36 v E (Oval) 1997. **LOI** (A): 43 (1995-96 to 2005); HS 28* v E (Lord's) 1997; BB 5-45 v SL (Colombo) 2003-04. F-c Tours (A): E 1995 (Young A), 1997, 2005; NZ 2004-05; I 1997-98, 2000-01; 2004-05; P 1998-99; SL 2003-04. HS 92 Australians v India A (Nagpur) 2000-01. Gm HS 78 v Glos (Cardiff) 2003. 50 wkts (4+3); most: 77 (2003). BB 9-36 (11-77 match) v Durham (Cardiff) 2003. Also 9-45 (13-110 match) v Durham (Chester-le-St) 2003. Hat-trick (Queensland 1998-99). LO HS 40 Le v Warwks (Leicester) 1999 (BHC). LO BB 5-45 (see LOI). T20 HS 31. T20 BB 4-29.

O'SHEA, Michael Peter, b Cardiff 24 Oct 1986. RHB, OB. England U-15, U-16, U-19. Debut 2005. HS 24 v Kent (Canterbury) 2005. LO HS 0.

‡**PENG GILLENDER, Nicky** (Newcastle upon Tyne RGS), b Newcastle upon Tyne, Northumb 18 Sep 1982. 6'2". RHB, OB. Durham 2000-05; cap 2001. HS 158 Du v Durham UCCE (Chester-le-St) 2003. CC HS 133 Du v Glamorgan(Cardiff) 2003. Scored 90 Du v Surrey (Chester-le-St) on debut. BB – Award: CGT 1. LO HS 121 Du v Worcs (Worcester) 2001 (NL). T20 HS 49.

POWELL, Michael John (Crickhowell SS; Pontypool CFE), b Abergavenny, Gwent 3 Feb 1977. 6'1". RHB, RSM. Debut 1997 scoring 200* v OU (Oxford); cap 2000. 1000 runs (4): most – 1234 (2003). HS 200* (*see above*). CC HS 198 v Durham (Chester-le-St) 2003. BB 2-39 v OU (Oxford) 1999. CC BB – . LO HS 91* v Leics (Cardiff) 2003 (NL). LO BB 1-26 (CGT). T20 HS 68*.

‡**SHINGLER, Aaron** Craig (Pontardulais CS; Gorseinon TC), b Aldershot, Hants 7 Aug 1987. RHB, RFM. Glamorgan2nd XI debut aged 16yr 271d. Staff 2006 – awaiting f-c debut.

THOMAS, Stuart Darren (Graig CS, Llanelli; Neath Tertiary C), b Morriston 25 Jan 1975. 6'0". LHB, RFM. Debut v Derbys (Chesterfield) 1992, taking 5-80 when aged 17yr 217d; cap 1997; benefit 2006. F-c Tours (Eng A): SA 1995-96 (Gm), 1998-99; NZ 1999-00; Z 1994-95 (Gm), 1998-99. HS 138 v Essex (Chelmsford) 2001. 50 wkts (5); most – 71 (1998). BB 8-50 Eng A v Zim A (Harare) 1998-99 – record Eng A analysis. CC BB 7-33 (10-83 match) v Durham (Cardiff) 2002. Award: BHC 1. LO HS 71* v Surrey (Oval) 2002 (CGT). LO BB 7-16 v Surrey (Swansea) 1998 (SL). T20 HS 43*. T20 BB 3-32.

WALLACE, Mark Alexander (Crickhowell HS), b Abergavenny, Gwent 19 Nov 1981. 5'9". LHB, WK. Debut 1999; cap 2003. F-c Tour (ECB Acad): SL 2002-03. HS 121 v Durham (Chester-le-St) 2003. LO HS 48 v Suffolk (Bury St Edmunds) 2005 (CGT). T 20 HS 32*.

WATERS, Huw Thomas (Monmouth S), b Cardiff 26 Sep 1986. 6'2". RHB, RMF. Debut 2005. HS 34 v Kent (Canterbury) 2005. BB 4-75 v Notts (Nottingham) 2005 – on debut. LO HS 8.

WATKINS, Ryan Edward (Pontllanfraith CS; Cross Keys TC), b Abergavenny, Gwent 9 Jun 1983. 6'0". LHB, RM. Wales MC. Debut 2005. HS 41 v Hants (Cardiff) 2005. BB 2-14 v Sussex (Hove) 2005. LO HS 26 and BB 2-33 v Glos (Bristol) 2005 (NL). LO BB – T20 HS 6*. T20 BB 2-8.

WHARF, Alexander George (Buttershaw Upper S; Thomas Danby C), b Bradford, Yorks 4 Jun 1975. 6'5". RHB, RMF. Yorkshire 1994-97. Nottinghamshire 1998-99. Glamorgan debut 2000, scoring 100* v OU (Oxford); cap 2000. **LOI**: 13 (2004 to 2004-05): HS 9; BB 4-24 v Z (Harare 2004-05). HS 113 v Notts (Cardiff) 2005. 50 wkts (1): 52 (2003). BB 6-59 v Glos (Bristol) 2005. LO HS 72 v Lancs (Manchester) 2004 (NL). LO BB 6-5 v Kent (Cardiff) 2004 (NL). T20 HS 16. T20 BB 3-23.

‡**WRIGHT, Ben** James, b Preston, Lancs 5 Dec 1987. RHB, RM. Joined staff 2005 – awaiting f-c debut.

RELEASED/RETIRED

(Having made a first-class County appearance in 2005)

NQ**GANGULY, Sourav** Chandidas (St Xavier's Collegiate S), b Calcutta, India 8 Jul 1972. Brother of Snehasish C. Ganguly (Bengal 1986-87 to 1996-97). 5'11". LHB, RM. Bengal 1989-90 to date. Lancashire 2000. Glamorgan 2005. **Tests** (I): 88 (1996 to 2005-06, 49 as captain); HS 173 v SL (Bombay) 1997-98; BB 3-28 v A (Calcutta) 1997-98. **LOI** (I): 278 (1991-92 to 2005), 146 as captain); HS 183 v SL (Taunton) 1999; BB 5-16 v P (Toronto) 1997-98. F-c Tours (I) (C=captain): E 1996, 2002C; A 1991-92, 1999-00, 2003-04C; SA 1996-97, 2001-02C; WI 1996-97, 2001-02C; NZ 1998-99, 2002-03C; P 2003-04C, 2005-06; SL 1997-98, 1998-99, 2001C; Z 1998-99; Z 2001C, 2005-06C; B 2000-01C, 2004-05C. HS 200* Bengal v Tripura (Calcutta) 1993-94 and 200* Bengal v Bihar (Calcutta) 1994-95. CC HS 142 Gm v Kent (Cardiff) 2005. BB 6-46 Bengal v Orissa (Calcutta) 2000-01. CC BB 3-68 Gm v Notts (Nottingham) 2005. Awards: NWT 2; BHC 1. LO HS 183 (*see LOI*). LO BB 5-16 (*see LOI*). T20 HS 36. T20 BB 3-27.

HUGHES, Jonathan (Coed-y-Land CS, Pontypridd), b Pontypridd 30 Jun 1981. 5'10". RHB, RM. Glamorgan 2001-05. MCC YC. HS 134* (and 100*) v Middx (Southgate) 2005. LO HS 51 v Derbys (Cardiff) 2003 (CGT). T20 HS 7.

MAYNARD, Matthew Peter (David Hughes S, Anglesey), b Oldham, Lancs 21 Mar 1966. 5'10½". RHB, RM. Glamorgan 1985-2005; cap 1987; captain 1996-2000; benefit 1996; testimonial 2005. Scored 102 out of 117 in 87 min, reaching 100 with 3 sixes off successive balls, v Yorks (Swansea) on debut. *Wisden* 1997. N Districts 1990-91 to 1991-92. Otago 1996-97 to 1997-98. YC 1988. **Tests**: 4 (1988 to 1993-94); HS 35 v WI (Kingston) 1993-94. **LOI**: 14 (1993-94 to 2000); HS 41 v P (Manchester) 1996. F-c Tours: SA 1989-90 (Eng XI), 1995-96 (Gm – captain); WI 1993-94; Z 1994-95 (Gm). 1000 runs (13); most – 1803 (1991). HS 243 v Hants (Southampton) 1991. BB 3-21 v OU (Oxford) 1987. CC BB 1-3. Awards: CGT 5; BHC 9. LO HS 151* v Durham (Darlington) 1991 (NWT) and 151* v Middx (Lord's) 1996 (BHC). LO BB 1-13 (NL). T20 HS 72.

THOMAS, Ian James (Bedwas CS; Bassaleg CS; UWIC), b Newport, Gwent 9 May 1979. 5'11". LHB, OB. Glamorgan 1998-2005. Wales MC. HS 82 v Essex (Southend) 2000 – on CC debut. BB 1-26 (CC). LO HS 93 v Durham CB (Darlington) 2003 (CGT). LO BB 1-24 (NL). Retired to become a Performance Lifestyle Advisor. T20 HS 116*. T20 BB 1-5.

G.P.Rees and A.D.Shaw left the staff having not made a first-class appearance in 2005.

COUNTY BENEFITS AWARDED FOR 2006

Derbyshire	K.J.Dean
Durham	N.Killeen
Essex	A.P.Cowan
Glamorgan	S.D.Thomas
Gloucestershire	M.G.N.Windows
Hampshire	T.C.Middleton (Testimonial)
Kent	D.P.Fulton
Lancashire	A.Flintoff
Leicestershire	D.L.Maddy
Middlesex	–
Northamptonshire	–
Nottinghamshire	–
Somerset	R.L.Johnson
Surrey	M.P.Bicknell (Testimonial)
Sussex	R.J.Kirtley
Warwickshire	A.F.Giles
Worcestershire	G.A.Hick (Testimonial)
Yorkshire	–

GLAMORGAN 2005

RESULTS SUMMARY

	Place	Won	Lost	Tied	Drew	No Result
County Championship (1st Division)	9th	1	14		1	
All First-Class Matches		1	14		2	
C & G Trophy	2nd Round					
National League (1st Division)	4th	6	6			4
Twenty20 Cup	6th in Mid/West/Wales Division					

COUNTY CHAMPIONSHIP AVERAGES

BATTING AND FIELDING

Cap		M	I	NO	HS	Runs	Avge	100	50	Ct/St
–	S.C.Ganguly	5	9	2	142	438	62.57	1	3	2
2000	M.T.G.Elliott	7	14	–	162	746	53.28	2	5	6
1994	D.L.Hemp	16	32	1	171*	1369	44.16	3	8	9
2000	M.J.Powell	15	30	2	96	927	33.10	–	6	9
–	D.D.Cherry	13	26	–	226	834	32.07	2	1	1
1992	R.D.B.Croft	16	29	2	90	703	26.03	–	3	5
2003	M.A.Wallace	16	29	2	96	695	25.74	–	5	31/4
–	J.Hughes	12	24	2	134*	498	22.63	2	–	10
2000	D.A.Cosker	11	19	6	52	293	22.53	–	1	5
–	A.P.Davies	6	11	4	41*	157	22.42	–	–	3
1997	S.D.Thomas	7	14	–	63	274	19.57	–	1	–
2000	A.G.Wharf	11	20	–	113	353	17.65	1	–	9
–	R.N.Grant	4	7	1	33	103	17.16	–	–	1
–	I.J.Thomas	4	8	–	40	129	16.12	–	–	2
–	R.E.Watkins	4	8	–	41	118	14.75	–	–	–
–	D.S.Harrison	16	29	2	75*	318	11.77	–	1	8
–	M.P.O'Shea	2	4	–	24	42	10.50	–	–	1
2002	S.P.Jones	3	6	4	12*	19	9.50	–	–	2
–	H.T.Waters	6	12	7	34	40	8.00	–	–	–

Also batted (1 match each): A.J.Harrison 0; M.P.Maynard (cap 1987) 20, 0 (1 ct).

BOWLING

	O	M	R	W	Avge	Best	5wI	10wM
H.T.Waters	100	15	332	11	30.18	4- 75	–	–
S.P.Jones	93.4	19	322	10	32.20	3- 62	–	–
A.G.Wharf	292.2	40	1209	28	43.17	6- 59	2	1
R.D.B.Croft	577.4	77	2134	43	49.62	5- 57	2	1
D.A.Cosker	395.4	60	1405	28	50.17	4- 57	–	–
D.S.Harrison	387.3	64	1547	27	57.29	5-117	1	–
A.P.Davies	163	28	647	11	58.81	3-121	–	–
Also bowled:								
S.D.Thomas	122.3	9	611	9	67.88	3- 63	–	–

D.D.Cherry 3-1-9-0; M.T.G.Elliott 5-0-20-0; S.C.Ganguly 38-4-148-3; R.N.Grant 3-0-18-0;
A.J.Harrison 15-2-54-1; R.E.Watkins 37-5-125-3.

The First-Class Averages (pp 129–145) give the records of Glamorgan players in all
first-class matches for the county (Glamorgan's other opponents being Bangladesh A), with
the exception of D.S.Harrison and S.P.Jones whose full county figures are as above, and:
 M.J.Powell 16-31-2-111-1038-35.79-1-6-9ct. Did not bowl.

GLAMORGAN RECORDS

FIRST-CLASS CRICKET

Highest Total	For 718-3d		v	Sussex	Colwyn Bay	2000
	V 712		by	Northants	Northampton	1998
Lowest Total	For 22		v	Lancashire	Liverpool	1924
	V 33		by	Leics	Ebbw Vale	1965
Highest Innings	For 309*	S.P.James	v	Sussex	Colwyn Bay	2000
	V 322*	M.B.Loye	for	Northants	Northampton	1998

Highest Partnership for each Wicket

1st	374	M.T.G.Elliott/S.P.James	v	Sussex	Colwyn Bay	2000
2nd	252	M.P.Maynard/D.L.Hemp	v	Northants	Cardiff	2002
3rd	313	D.E.Davies/W.E.Jones	v	Essex	Brentwood	1948
4th	425*	A.Dale/I.V.A.Richards	v	Middlesex	Cardiff	1993
5th	264	M.Robinson/S.W.Montgomery	v	Hampshire	Bournemouth	1949
6th	230	W.E.Jones/B.L.Muncer	v	Worcs	Worcester	1953
7th	211	P.A.Cottey/O.D.Gibson	v	Leics	Swansea	1996
8th	202	D.Davies/J.J.Hills	v	Sussex	Eastbourne	1928
9th	203*	J.J.Hills/J.C.Clay	v	Worcs	Swansea	1929
10th	143	T.Davies/S.A.B.Daniels	v	Glos	Swansea	1982

Best Bowling	For 10- 51	J.Mercer	v	Worcs	Worcester	1936
(Innings)	V 10- 18	G.Geary	for	Leics	Pontypridd	1929
Best Bowling	For 17-212	J.C.Clay	v	Worcs	Swansea	1937
(Match)	V 16- 96	G.Geary	for	Leics	Pontypridd	1929

Most Runs – Season	2276	H.Morris	(av 55.51)		1990
Most Runs – Career	34056	A.Jones	(av 33.03)		1957-83
Most 100s – Season	10	H.Morris			1990
Most 100s – Career	54	M.P.Maynard			1985-2005
Most Wkts – Season	176	J.C.Clay	(av 17.34)		1937
Most Wkts – Career	2174	D.J.Shepherd	(av 20.95)		1950-72
Most Career W-K Dismissals	933	E.W.Jones	(840 ct; 93 st)		1961-83
Most Career Catches in the Field	656	P.M.Walker			1956-72

LIMITED-OVERS CRICKET

Highest Total	CGT	429		v	Surrey	The Oval	2002
	NL	305-6		v	Worcs	Cardiff	2001
	T20	194-2		v	Somerset	Taunton	2004
Lowest Total	CGT	76		v	Northants	Northampton	1968
	NL	42		v	Derbyshire	Swansea	1979
	T20	113		v	Warwicks	Birmingham	2003
Highest Innings	CGT	162*	I.V.A.Richards	v	Oxfordshire	Swansea	1993
	NL	155*	J.H.Kallis	v	Surrey	Pontypridd	1999
	T20	116*	I.J.Thomas	v	Somerset	Taunton	2004
Best Bowling	CGT	5-13	R.J.Shastri	v	Scotland	Edinburgh	1988
	NL	7-16	S.D.Thomas	v	Surrey	Swansea	1998
	T20	4-38	R.N.Grant	v	Worcs	Worcester	2005

GLOUCESTERSHIRE

Formation of Present Club: 1871
Inaugural First-Class Match: 1870
Colours: Blue, Gold, Brown, Silver, Green and Red
Badge: Coat of Arms of the City and County of Bristol
County Champions (since 1890): (0); best – 2nd 1930, 1931, 1947, 1959, 1969, 1986
Gillette/NatWest/C & G Trophy Winners: (5) 1973, 1999, 2000, 2003, 2004
Benson and Hedges Cup Winners: (3) 1977, 1999, 2000
National League (Div 1) Winners: (1) 2000
Sunday League Winners: (0); best – 2nd 1988
Twenty20 Cup Winners: (0); best – Semi-Finalist 2003
Match Awards: CGT 65; BHC 72

Chief Executive: Tom E.M.Richardson, County Ground, Nevil Road, Bristol BS7 9EJ • Tel: 0117 910 8000 • Fax: 0117 924 1193 • Email: info@glosccc.co.uk • Web: www.glosccc.co.uk

First XI Coach: M.W.Alleyne. **Captain**: J.Lewis. **Vice-Captain**: No appointment.
Overseas Players: S.E.Bond and H.J.H.Marshall. **2006 Beneficiary**: M.G.N.Windows.
Head Groundsman: S.P.Williams. **Scorer**: K.T.Gerrish. ‡ New registration. NQ Not qualified for England.

Gloucestershire revised their capping policy in 2004 and now award players with their County Caps when they make their first-class debut.

ADSHEAD, Stephen John (Bridley Moor HS, Redditch), b Worcester 29 Jan 1980. 5'9". RHB, WK. Herefordshire 1999. Leicestershire 2000 (one non-CC match). Worcestershire 2003 (2 matches). Gloucestershire debut/cap 2004. HS 148* v Surrey (Oval) 2005. Gs HS 61 v Worcs (Worcester) 2004. LO HS 77* Shropshire v Northumb (Oswestry) 2003 (CGT). T20 HS 81.

ALI, Kadeer (Handsworth GS), b Moseley, Birmingham 7 Mar 1983. 6'1". Brother of M.M.Ali (*see WARWICKSHIRE*), cousin of Kabir Ali (*see WORCESTERSHIRE*). RHB, LB. Worcestershire 2000-04. Gloucestershire debut/cap 2005. F-c Tour (Eng A): I 2003-04. HS 99 Wo v Yorks (Worcester) 2003. Gs HS 66 v Surrey (Oval) 2005. BB 1-4 (CC). LO HS 66 Worcs CB v Sussex CB (Kidderminster) 2002 (CGT). LO BB 1-4 (Wo – GT). T20 HS 53.

AVERIS, James Maxwell Michael (Cathedral S, Bristol; Portsmouth U; St Cross C, Oxford), b Bristol 28 May 1974. 5'11". RHB, RMF. Oxford U 1997; blue 1997; rugby blue 1996-97. Gloucestershire debut 1997; cap 2001. HS 48* v Surrey (Oval) 2004. BB 6-32 v Northants (Bristol) 2004. Award: BHC 1. LO HS 23* v Lancs (Manchester) 2000 (NL). LO BB 6-23 v Bucks (Ascott Park) 2003 (CGT). T20 HS 4. T20 BB 3-7.

BALL, Martyn Charles John (King Edmund SS; Bath CFE), b Bristol 26 Apr 1970. 5'8". RHB, OB. Debut 1988; cap 1996; benefit 2002. F-c Tours: I 2001-02; SL 1992-93 (Gs). HS 75 v Somerset (Taunton) 2003. BB 8-46 (14-169 match) v Somerset (Taunton) 1993. Award: CGT 1. LO HS 51 v SL A (Cheltenham) 1999. LO BB 5-33 v Yorks (Leeds) 2003 (NL). T20 HS 21. T20 BB 3-24.

34

‡^{NQ}**BOND, Shane** Edward (Papanui HS; Lincoln U), b Christchurch, NZ 7 Jun 1975. 6'2". RHB, RF. Canterbury 1996-97 to date. Warwickshire 2002. **Tests** (NZ): 12 (2001-02 to 2005); HS 41* v Z (Harare) 2005; BB 6-51 v Z (Bulawayo) 2005. **LOI** (NZ): 40 (2001-02 to 2005-06); HS 31* v I (Auckland) 2002-03; BB 6-19 v I (Bulawayo) 2005. F-c Tours (NZ): A 2001-02; WI 2001-02; SL 2002-03; Z 2005. HS 100 Canterbury v ND (Christchurch) 2004-05. BB 5-37 Canterbury v ND (Gisborne) 2001-02. CC HS 29* and BB 5-64 Wa v Somerset (Taunton) 2002. LO HS 40 Canterbury v Wellington (Christchurch) 2002-03. LO BB 6-19 (*see LOI*). T20 HS 8*. T20 BB 2-15.

FISHER, Ian Douglas (Beckfoot GS, Bingley; Thomas Danby C, Leeds), b Bradford, Yorks 31 Mar 1976. 5'10½". LHB, SLA. Yorkshire 1995-96 (Y in Zim) to 2001. Gloucestershire debut 2002; cap 2004. F-c Tour: Z 1995-96 (Y). HS 103* v Essex (Gloucester) 2002. BB 5-30 (10-123 match) v Durham (Bristol) 2003. LO HS 23 and BB 3-18 v Northants (Northampton) 2004 (NL). T20 HS 8. T20 BB 4-22.

GIDMAN, Alex Peter Richard (Wycliffe C), b High Wycombe, Bucks 22 Jun 1981. 6'3". RHB, RM. Debut 2002; cap 2004. MCCYC. Appointed captain of Eng A tour to India 2003-04 but withdrawn because of hand injury. 1000 (1): 1012 (2005). HS 142 v Surrey (Bristol) 2005. BB 4-47 v Glamorgan (Cardiff) 2005. LO HS 73 v Warwks (Birmingham) 2003 (NL). LO BB 3-26 v Warwks (Gloucester) 2003 (NL). T20 HS 61. T20 BB 1-25.

GREENIDGE, Carl Gary (Lodge S and St Michael S, Barbados; Heathcote S, Chingford; W Hatch HS; City of Westminster C), b Basingstoke, Hants 20 Apr 1978. Son of C.Gordon Greenidge (Hampshire, Barbados and West Indies 1970-92). 5'10". RHB, RMF. MCC YC. Surrey 1999-2000. Northamptonshire 2002-04. Gloucestershire debut/cap 2005. HS 46 Nh v Derbys (Derby) 2002. Gs HS 25 v Kent (Maidstone) 2005. 50 wkts (1): 53 (2002). BB 6-40 Nh v Durham (Chester-le-St) 2002. Gs BB 2-78 v Warwks (Gloucester) 2005. LO HS 20 Nh v Sussex (Northampton) 2002 (NL). LO BB 3-22 Nh v Derbys (Northampton) 2002 (NL). T20 HS 5*. T20 BB 3-15.

HARDINGES, Mark Andrew (Malvern C; Bath U), b Gloucester 5 Feb 1978. 6'1". RHB, RMF. Debut 1999; cap 2004. British U 2000. HS 172 v OU (Oxford) 2002. CC HS 68 v Warwks (Bristol) 2004. BB 5-51 v Kent (Maidstone) 2005. Award: CGT 1. LO HS 111 v Lancs (Manchester) 2005 (NL). LO BB 4-19 v Salop (Shrewsbury) 2002 (CGT). T20 HS 40. T20 BB 3-18.

HODNETT, Grant Phillip (Durban Preparatory HS; Nortwood HS), b Johannesburg, S Africa 17 Aug 1982. 6'4". RHB, LB. Debut/cap 2005. HS 49 v Warwks (Birmingham) 2005 – on debut.

KIRBY, Steven Paul (Elton HS; Bury C), b Ainsworth, nr Bolton, Lancs 4 Oct 1977. 6'3½". RHB, RF. Leicestershire staff 1998 – no f-c appearances. Yorkshire 2001-04, debut as sub for M.J.Hoggard (England duty) taking 7-50; cap 2003. Gloucestershire debut/cap 2005. F-c Tour (Eng A): I 2003-04 (*part*). HS 57 Y v Hants (Leeds) 2002. Gs HS 15* v Middx (Lord's) 2005. 50 wkts (1): 67 (2003). BB 8-80 (13-154 match) Y v Somerset (Taunton) 2003. Gs BB 4-20 v OU (Oxford) 2005 – on debut. LO HS 15 Y v Leics (Leicester) 2003 (NL). LO BB 3-27 Y v Worcs (Scarborough) 2003 (NL). T20 HS 1*. T20 BB 2-15.

LEWIS, Jonathan (Churchfields S. Swindon; Swindon C), b Aylesbury, Bucks 26 Aug 1975. 6'2". RHB, RMF. Debut 1995; cap 1998. Northamptonshire staff 1994. **LOI**: 3 (2005); HS 7*; BB 3-32 v B (Oval) 2005 – on debut. F-c Tour: WI 2000-01 (Eng A). HS 62 v Worcs (Cheltenham) 1999. 50 wkts (5); most – 74 (2003). BB 8-95 v Z (Gloucester) 2000. CC BB 7-56 (10-92 match) v Notts (Bristol) 1999. Hat-trick 2000. Awards: CGT 1; BHC 2. LO HS 40 and LO BB 5-19 v Hants (Southampton) 2005 (NL). LO BB 5-23 v Lancs (Cheltenham) 2004 (NL). T20 HS 34. T20 BB 4-24.

‡**NQMARSHALL, Hamish** John Hamilton (Mahurangi C, Warkworth; King C, Auckland), b Warkworth, NZ 15 Feb 1979. twin brother of J.A.H.Marshall (ND and NZ). 5'9". RHB, RM. N Districts 1998-99 to date. Gloucestershire 2005. **Tests** (NZ): 95 (2000-01 to 2005); HS 160 v SL (Napier) 2004-05. **LOI** (NZ): 50 (2003-04 to 2005-06); HS 101* v P (Faisalabad) 2003-04. F-c Tours (NZ): SA 2000-01; Z 2005; B 2004-05. HS 160 (*see Tests*). BB 1-12. LO HS 111 NZ v Essex (Chelmsford) 2004 LO BB 1-14. T20 HS T20 BB.

RUDGE, William Douglas (Clifton C), b Southmead, Bristol 15 Jul 1983. 6'4". RHB, RM. Debut/cap 2005. HS 15 v Surrey (Oval) 2005. BB 3-46 v Bangladesh A (Bristol) 2005 – on debut. CC BB 3-75 v Middx (Bristol) 2005. LO HS (Gs CB) 3 (CGT).

SNELL, Stephen David (Sandown HS), b Winchester, Hampshire 27 Feb 1983.6'0". RHB, WK. Debut/ cap2005. HS 83* v Bangladesh A (Bristol) 2005 – on debut. CC HS 13 v Warwks (Birmingham) 2005. LO HS 17 v Glamorgan (Cardiff) 2005 (NL).

SPEARMAN, Craig Murray, b Auckland, New Zealand 4 Jul 1972. RHB. Auckland 1993-94 to 1995-96. Central Districts 1996-97 to date. Gloucestershire debut/cap 2002. Qualified for England 2005. **Tests** (NZ): 19 (1995-96 to 2000-01); HS 112 v Z (Auckland) 1995-96. **LOI** (NZ): 51 (1995-96 to 2000-01); HS 86 v Z (Harare) 2000-01. F-c Tours (NZ): SA 2000-01; WI 1995-96; I 1999-00; P 1996-97; SL 1997-98; Z 1997-98, 2000-01. 1000 runs (2): 1462 (2004). HS 341 v Middx (Gloucester) 2004 – record Gloucestershire score. BB 1-37 CD v Wellington (New Plymouth) 1999-00. Awards: CGT 3; BHC 1. LO HS 153 v Warwks (Gloucester) 2003 (NL). T20 HS 88.

TAYLOR, Christopher Glyn (Colston's Collegiate S), b Southmead, Bristol 27 Sep 1976. 5'7". RHB, OB. Debut 2000, scoring 104 v Middx – first to score a hundred at Lord's in a Championship match on his first-class debut. Cap 2001. Captain 2004-05(part). 1000 runs (1): 1077) 2004. HS 196 v Notts (Nottingham) 2001. BB 3-126 v Northants (Cheltenham) 2000. Award: BHC 1. LO HS 93 v Warwks (Bristol) 2002 (BHC). LO BB 2-5 v Northants (Northampton) 2004 (NL). T20 HS 36.

WESTON, William Philip Christopher (Durham S), b Durham City 16 Jun 1973. Son of M.P.Weston (Durham; England RFU); brother of R.M.S.Weston (*see MIDDLESEX*). 6'3". LHB, LM. Worcestershire 1991-2002; cap 1995. Gloucestershire debut 2003; cap 2004. F-c Tours (Wo): Z 1993-94, 1996-97. 1000 runs (4); most – 1389 (1996). HS 205 Wo v Northants (Northampton) 1997. Gs HS 179 v Somerset (Taunton) 2003. BB 2-39 Wo v P (Worcester) 1992. CC BB – . Gs BB 1-8 (CC). Awards: CGT 2. LO HS 134 Wo v Derbys (Derby) 2001 (NL). LO BB (Wo) 1-2 (SL). T20 HS 73*.

WINDOWS, Matthew Guy Newman (Clifton C; Durham U), b Bristol 5 Apr 1973. Son of A.R.Windows (Glos and CU 1960-68). 5'7". RHB, LM. Debut 1992; cap 1998; benefit 2006. Combined U 1995. F-c Tours (Eng A): SA 1998-99; Z 1998-99. 1000 runs (3); most – 1173 (1998). HS 184 v Warwks (Cheltenham) 1996. BB (Comb U) 1-6. Gs BB – . Awards: CGT 1; BHC 2. LO HS 117 v Northants (Cheltenham) 2001 (NL). T20 HS 27.

RELEASED/RETIRED

(Having made a first-class County appearance in 2005)

ALLEYNE, Mark Wayne (Harrison C, Barbados; Cardinal Pole S, London E9; Haringey Cricket C), b Tottenham, London 23 May 1968. 5'10". RHB, RM. Gloucestershire 1986-2005; cap 1990; captain 1997-2003; club/limited-overs captain/1st XI coach 2004; benefit 1999. Wisden 2000. MBE 2004. **LOI:** 10 (1998-99 to 2000-01); HS 53 v SA (E London) 1999-00; BB 3-27 v SL (Sydney) 1998-99. F-c Tours (Eng A) (C=captain): WI 2000-01C; NZ 1999-00C; SL 1986-87 (Gs), 1992-93 (Gs); B 1999-00C. 1000 runs (6); most – 1189 (1998). HS 256 v Northants (Northampton) 1990. 50 wkts (1): 54 (1996). BB 6-49 v Middx (Lord's) 2000. Awards: CGT 3; BHC 3. LO HS 134* v Leics (Bristol) 1992 (SL). LO BB 5-27 v Comb U (Bristol) 1988 (BHC). T20 HS 35. T20 BB 2-23.

NQBANDARA, Charitha Malinga, b Kalutara, Sri Lanka 31 Dec 1979. RHB, LBG. Galle. Kalutara Town, Nondescripts. Gloucestershire 2005; cap 2005. **Tests** (SL): 4 (197-98 to 2005-06); HS 28* and BB 3-84 v I (Ahmedabad) 2005-06. **LOI** (SL): 11 (2005-06); HS 12 v NZ (Wellington) 2005-06; BB 4-31 v sa (Hobart) 2005-06. F-c Tour (SL): I 2005-06. HS 79 Sri Lanka A v Pakistan A (Dambulla) 2004-05. Gs HS 70 v Middx (Bristol) 2005. BB 8-49 Sri Lanka v England A (Colombo) 2004-05. Gs BB 5-45 v Bangladesh A (Bristol) 2005. CC BB 5-71 v Middx (Bristol) 2005. LO HS 46* Galle v Colombo (Colombo) 2004-05. LO BB 5-22 Nondescripts v Sebastianites (Colombo) 1999-00. T20 HS 8. T20 BB 1-29.

NQCHANDANA, Umagiliya Durage Upul, b Galle, Sri Lanka 5 Jul 1972. 5'8". RHB, LB. Tamil Union 1991-92 to date. Gloucestershire 2005; cap 2005. **Tests** (SL): 16 (1998-99 to 2004-05); HS 92 v Z (Galle) 2001-02; BB 6-179 v P (Dhaka) 1998-99 – on debut. **LOI** (SL): 146 (1993-94 to 2005-06); HS 89 v WI (Bridgetown) 2003; BB 5-61 v SA (Colombo) 2004. F-c Tours (SL): E 1998, 2002; A 2004; SA 1997-98; 2000-01; NZ 2004-05; I 2001-02 (Colombo Dist); P 1999-00; B 1998-99. HS 194 SL A v K (Matara) 2001-02. Gs HS 49* v Notts (Bristol) 2005. BB 7-80 Tamil U v Bloomfield (Colombo) 1998-99. Gs BB 5-117 v Glamorgan(Cardiff) 2005. LO HS 108 SL A v K (Moratuwa) 2001-02. LO BB 5-22 Tamil U v Chilaw Marians (Colombo) 2001-02. T20 HS 11. T20 BB 3-18.

HANCOCK, Timothy Harold Coulter (St Edward's S, Oxford; Henley C), b Reading, Berks 20 Apr 1972. 5'10". RHB, RM. Gloucestershire 1991-2005; cap 1998; benefit 2005. Oxfordshire 1990. F-c Tour: SL 1992-93 (Gs). 1000 runs (1): 1227 (1998). HS 220* v Notts (Nottingham) 1998. BB 3-5 v Essex (Colchester) 1998. Awards: CGT 4. LO HS 135 v Bucks (Ascott Park) 2003 (C&G). LO BB 6-58 v Scot (Bristol) 1997 (NWT). T20 HS 56.

PEARSON, James Alexander, b Bristol 11 Sep 1983. LHB. Gloucestershire 2002-05 (no appearances 2003-04); cap 2004. HS 68 v Notts (Bristol) 2005. LO HS 7 and BB 1-29 Glos CB v Herefords (Brockhampton) 2001.

NQSARWAN, Ramnaresh Ronnie (North Gromuel S), b Wakenaam Island, Essequibo, Guyana 23 Jun 1980. 5'7½". RHB, LB. Guyana 1995-96 to date (youngest to play f-c cricket in WI, previously R.E.Marshall). Gloucestershire 2005; cap 2005. **Tests** (WI): 58 (1999-00 to 2005-06); HS 261* v E (Kingston) 2004; BB 4-37 v B (St Lucia) 2004. **LOI** (WI): 88 (2000 to 2005-06); HS 104* v E (Bridgetown) 2003-04; BB 3-31 v NZ (Lord's) 2004. F-c Tours (WI): E 2000, 2004; A 2000-01, 2005-06; SA 2003-04; SL 2001-02; Z 2001, 2003-04; B 2002-03. HS 261* (see Tests). Gs HS 117 v Sussex (Hove) 2005. BB 6-62 Guyana v Leeward Is (Antigua) 2000-01. Gs BB 2-38 v Glamorgan (Bristol) 2005. LO HS 118* v Lancs (Manchester) 2005 (NL). LO BB 5-10 Guyana v Bermuda (Hampton Court) 1998-99.

SILLENCE, R. J. – see WORCESTERSHIRE.

GLOUCESTERSHIRE 2005

RESULTS SUMMARY

	Place	Won	Lost	Tied	Drew	No Result
County Championship (1st Division)	8th	1	10		5	
All First-Class Matches		2	10		6	
C & G Trophy	2nd Round					
National League (1st Division)	7th	6	9			1
Twenty20 Cup	4th in Mid/West/Wales Division					

COUNTY CHAMPIONSHIP AVERAGES
BATTING AND FIELDING

Cap		M	I	NO	HS	Runs	Avge	100	50	Ct/St
2004	A.P.R.Gidman	14	26	1	142	857	34.28	2	4	12
2005	R.R.Sarwan	7	14	–	117	442	31.57	1	2	9
2001	C.G.Taylor	8	15	–	176	457	30.46	1	1	5
2004	S.J.Adshead	16	30	3	148*	817	30.25	1	4	33/6
2002	C.M.Spearman	13	25	–	73	696	27.84	–	3	12
2005	Kadeer Ali	11	21	2	66	449	23.63	–	4	7
2004	W.P.C.Weston	11	20	–	66	465	23.25	–	3	4
1998	J.Lewis	10	18	6	55	277	23.08	–	1	5
1998	M.G.N.Windows	11	22	1	65*	479	22.80	–	2	2
2004	J.A.Pearson	4	8	–	68	182	22.75	–	2	–
2004	I.D.Fisher	8	15	2	43	274	21.07	–	–	7
2005	U.D.U.Chandana	6	10	2	49*	136	17.00	–	–	4
1998	T.H.C.Hancock	4	7	1	41*	96	16.00	–	–	9
2004	M.A.Hardinges	12	24	1	58*	363	15.78	–	1	9
2005	C.G.Greenidge	3	6	2	25	61	15.25	–	–	–
2005	C.M.Bandara	7	13	–	70	190	14.61	–	1	6
2001	J.M.M.Averis	8	14	1	29*	148	11.38	–	–	2
2005	S.P.Kirby	12	21	11	15*	105	10.50	–	–	–
2005	W.D.Rudge	4	7	1	15	35	5.83	–	–	1
1996	M.C.J.Ball	3	6	–	7	10	1.66	–	–	5

Also batted (1 match each): M.W.Alleyne (cap 1990) 16, 51; G.P.Hodnett (cap 2005) 49, 10 (1 ct); R.J.Sillence (cap 2004) 12, 0; S.D.Snell (cap 2005) 13, 3 (2 ct).

BOWLING

	O	M	R	W	Avge	Best	5wI	10wM
C.M.Bandara	314.1	57	981	39	25.15	5- 71	1	–
J.Lewis	368.3	94	1111	40	27.77	5- 57	2	–
S.P.Kirby	326.5	67	1124	40	28.10	4- 53	–	–
M.A.Hardinges	243.1	47	878	28	31.35	5- 51	1	–
A.P.R.Gidman	112.1	9	475	12	39.58	4- 47	–	–
U.D.U.Chandana	239.1	38	740	16	46.25	5-117	1	–
I.D.Fisher	234.4	42	791	15	52.73	4- 89	–	–
J.M.M.Averis	198	36	788	14	56.28	3- 54	–	–
Also bowled:								
C.G.Greenidge	61.5	13	224	5	44.80	2- 78	–	–
W.D.Rudge	93.1	17	436	9	48.44	3- 75	–	–
M.C.J.Ball	149	38	400	6	66.66	3- 99	–	–

Kadeer Ali 24-4-69-2; M.W.Alleyne 24-3-84-1; T.H.C.Hancock 5-2-14-1; R.R.Sarwan 32-5-99-2; R.J.Sillence 30-3-144-2; C.G.Taylor 13-1-43-1.

The First-Class Averages (pp 129–145) give the records of Gloucestershire players in all first-class matches for the county (Gloucestershire's other opponents being Bangladesh A and Oxford UCCE), with the exception of:
J.Lewis 11-19-6-55-324-24.92-0-1-5ct. 397.3-98-1237-43-28.76-5/57-2-0.

GLOUCESTERSHIRE RECORDS

FIRST-CLASS CRICKET

Highest Total	For 695-9d		v	Middlesex	Gloucester	2004
	V 774-7d		by	Australians	Bristol	1948
Lowest Total	For 17		v	Australians	Cheltenham	1896
	V 12		by	Northants	Gloucester	1907
Highest Innings	For 341	C.M.Spearman	v	Middlesex	Gloucester	2004
	V 310*	M.E.K.Hussey	for	Northants	Bristol	2002

Highest Partnership for each Wicket

1st	395	D.M.Young/R.B.Nicholls	v	Oxford U	Oxford	1962
2nd	256	C.T.M.Pugh/T.W.Graveney	v	Derbyshire	Chesterfield	1960
3rd	336	W.R.Hammond/B.H.Lyon	v	Leics	Leicester	1933
4th	321	W.R.Hammond/W.L.Neale	v	Leics	Gloucester	1937
5th	261	W.G.Grace/W.O.Moberley	v	Yorkshire	Cheltenham	1876
6th	320	G.L.Jessop/J.H.Board	v	Sussex	Hove	1903
7th	248	W.G.Grace/E.L.Thomas	v	Sussex	Hove	1896
8th	239	W.R.Hammond/A.E.Wilson	v	Lancashire	Bristol	1938
9th	193	W.G.Grace/S.A.P.Kitcat	v	Sussex	Bristol	1896
10th	131	W.R.Gouldsworthy/J.G.Bessant	v	Somerset	Bristol	1923

Best Bowling	For 10-40	E.G.Dennett	v	Essex	Bristol	1906
(Innings)	V 10-66	A.A.Mailey	for	Australians	Cheltenham	1921
	10-66	K.Smales	for	Notts	Stroud	1956
Best Bowling	For 17-56	C.W.L.Parker	v	Essex	Gloucester	1925
(Match)	V 15-87	A.J.Conway	for	Worcs	Moreton-in-M	1914

Most Runs – Season	2860	W.R.Hammond	(av 69.75)	1933
Most Runs – Career	33664	W.R.Hammond	(av 57.05)	1920-51
Most 100s – Season	13	W.R.Hammond		1938
Most 100s – Career	113	W.R.Hammond		1920-51
Most Wkts – Season	222	T.W.J.Goddard	(av 16.80)	1937
	222	T.W.J.Goddard	(av 16.37)	1947
Most Wkts – Career	3170	C.W.L.Parker	(av 19.43)	1903-35
Most Career W-K Dismissals	1054	R.C.Russell	(950 ct; 104 st)	1981-2004
Most Career Catches in the Field	718	C.A.Milton		1948-74

LIMITED-OVERS CRICKET

Highest Total	CGT	401-7	v	Bucks	Wing	2003
	NL	344-6	v	Northants	Cheltenham	2001
	T20	221-7	v	Glamorgan	Bristol	2003
Lowest Total	CGT	82	v	Notts	Bristol	1987
	NL	49	v	Middlesex	Bristol	1978
	T20	128	v	Glamorgan	Cardiff	2005
Highest Innings	CGT	177	A.J.Wright	v	Scotland	Bristol	1997
	NL	153	C.M.Spearman	v	Warwicks	Gloucester	2003
	T20	100*	I.J.Harvey	v	Warwicks	Birmingham	2003
Best Bowling	CGT	6-21	C.A.Walsh	v	Kent	Bristol	1990
		6-21	C.A.Walsh	v	Cheshire	Bristol	1992
	NL	6-52	J.N.Shepherd	v	Kent	Bristol	1983
	T20	4-22	I.D.Fisher	v	Somerset	Bristol	2004

HAMPSHIRE

Formation of Present Club: 12 August 1863
Inaugural First-Class Match: 1864
Colours: Blue, Gold and White
Badge: Tudor Rose and Crown
County Champions: (2) 1961, 1973
Gillette/NatWest/C & G Trophy Winners: (2) 1991, 2005
Benson and Hedges Cup Winners: (2) 1988, 1992
National League (Div 1) Winners: (0); best – 3rd 2004
Sunday League Winners: (3) 1975, 1978, 1986
Twenty20 Cup Winners: (0) – best Quarter-Finalist 2004
Match Awards: CGT 67; BHC 67

Chief Executive: Nick S.Pike, The Rose Bowl, Botley Road, West End, Southampton
SO30 3XH • Tel: 023 8047 2002 • Fax: 023 8047 2122 • Email:
enquiries@rosebowlplc.com • Webs: www.hampshire.cricinfo.com •
www.rosebowlplc.com

First XI Manager/Coach: V.P.Terry. **2nd XI Coach/Academy Director**: T.C.Middleton.
Captain: S.K.Warne. **Vice-Captain**: S.D.Udal. **Overseas Players**: D.J.Thornely and
S.K.Warne. **2006 Beneficiary**: T.C.Middleton (Testimonial). **Head Groundsman**: N.Gray.
Scorer: A.E.Weld. ‡ New registration. ^{NQ} Not qualified for England.

ADAMS, James Henry Kenneth (Sherborne S; University C, London; Loughborough U), b
Winchester 23 Sep 1980. 6'2". LHB, LM. British U 2002-03. Hampshire debut 2002.
Loughborough UCCE 2003-4 – scoring 107 v Somerset (Taunton) on debut. Dorset 1998.
HS 107 (*above*). H HS 75 v Glamorgan(Cardiff) 2004. BB 2-16 v Durham (Chester-le-St)
2004. LO HS 40 v Glamorgan(Southampton) 2004 (NL). BB – T20 HS 17*.

BENHAM, Christopher Charles (Yately CS; Loughborough U), b Frimley, Surrey 24 Mar
1983. 6'1". RHB, RM/OB. Loughborough UCCE 2004. Hampshire debut 2004. HS 74 v
Derbys (Derby) 2004 – on county debut. LO HS 0 (Hants CB) (CGT).

BROWN, Michael James (Queen Elizabeth GS, Blackburn; Collingwood C, Durham U), b
Burnley, Lancs 9 Feb 1980. 6'0". RHB, OB. Middlesex 1999-2003. Durham UCCE
2001-02. British U 2001-02. Hampshire debut 2004. HS 109* v Glamorgan(Southampton)
2004. LO HS 35 v Lancs (Southampton) 2004 (NL). T20 HS 14.

BRUCE, James Thomas Anthony (Eton C; St Hild & St Bede C, Durham U), b
Hammersmith, London 17 Dec 1979. 6'1". RHB, RMF. Durham UCCE 2001-02. Hampshire
debut 2003. Cumberland 2001. HS 21* v Glamorgan (Southampton) 2003. BB 3-42 v
Glamorgan (Southampton) 2003 and 3-42 v Glos Cheltenham) 2005. LO HS 10* v Notts
(Southampton) 2005 (NL). LO BB 3-45 v Sussex (Hove) 2003 (NL). T20 HS 12. T20 BB
3-20.

BURROWS, Thomas George (Reading GS; Southampton Solent U), b Wokingham,
Berkshire 5 May 1985. 5'8". RHB, WK. Berkshire 2001 to 2003. Debut 2005. HS 42 v Kent
(Canterbury) 2005 – on debut. LO HS 1 (Berks).

‡CARBERRY, Michael Alexander (St John Rigby Catholic C), b Croydon, Surrey 29 Sep
1980. 6'0". LHB, OB. Surrey 2001-02. Kent 2003-05. HS 153* Sy v CU (Cambridge) 2002.
K HS 137 v CU (Cambridge) 2003 – on Kent debut inc 109* before lunch 1st day. CC HS
112 K v Worcs (Canterbury) 2004. BB (K) 1-45. LO HS 79 K v Worcs (Canterbury) 2003
(NL). LO BB (K) 1-21 (NL). T20 HS 59*.

CRAWLEY, John Paul (Manchester GS; Trinity C, Cambridge), b Maldon, Essex 21 Sep 1971. Brother of M.A.Crawley (Oxford U, Lancs and Notts 1987-94) and P.M. (Cambridge U 1992). 6'1". RHB, RM, occ WK. Lancashire 1990-2001; cap 1994; captain 1999-2001. Cambridge U 1991-93; blue 1991-92-93; captain 1992-93. Hampshire debut/cap 2002. YC 1994. **Tests**: 37 (1994 to 2002-03); HS 156* v SL (Oval) 1998. **LOI**: 13 (1994-95 to 1998-99); HS 73 v Z (Harare) 1996-97. F-c Tours: A 1994-95, 1998-99, 2002-03; SA 1993-94 (Eng A), 1995-96; WI 1995-96 (La), 1997-98, 2000-01 (Eng A); NZ 1996-97; Z 1996-97. 1000 runs (9); most – 1851 (1998). HS 311* v Notts (Southampton) 2005. BB 1-7. Awards: BHC 2. LO HS 114 La v Notts (Manchester) 1995 (BHC). T20 HS 23.

NQERVINE, Sean Michael (Lomagundi C, Chinhoyi), b Harare, Zimbabwe 6 Dec 1982. Son of R.M.Ervine and nephew of B.B.Ervine (both Rhodesia 1977-78). Irish passport. 6'2". LHB, RM. Zimbabwe Academy 2000-01. Mashonalands 2001-02 to date. Hampshire debut/cap 2005 (Kolpak registration). **Tests** (Z): 5 (2003 to 2003-04); HS 86 v B (Harare) 2002-04; BB 4-146 v A (Perth) 2003-04. **LOI** (Z): 42 (2001-02 to 2003-04); HS 100 v I (Adelaide) 2003-04; BB 3-29 v P (Sharjah) 2002-02. F-c Tours: E 2003; A 2003-04. HS 126 Midlands v Manicaland (Mutare) 2002-03. H HS 75 v Glamorgan (Cardiff) 2005. BB 6-82 Midlands v Mashonaland (Kwekwe) 2002-03. H BB 5-60 v Glamorgan (Cardiff) 2005. Awards: CGT 2. LO HS 104 v Warwks (Lord's) 2005 (CGT). LO BB 5-50 v Glamorgan (Cardiff) 2005 (CGT). T20 HS 46. T20 BB 2-13.

‡GRIFFITHS, David Andrew, b Newport, IOW 10 Sep 1985. LHB, RFM. Joined staff 2005 – awaiting f-c debut.

NQLAMB, Gregory Arthur (Lomagundi C, Chinhoyi; Guildford C, Surrey), b Harare, Zimbabwe 4 Mar 1980. 5'11". RHB, RM/OB. CFX Academy 1998-99 to 1999-00. Mashonaland 2000-01. Hampshire debut 2004. F-c Tour (Zim A): SL 1999-00. HS 100* CFX Academy v Manicaland (Mutare) 1999-00. H HS 94 v Derbys (Derby) 2004 – on UN debut. BB 7-73 CFX Academy v Midlands (Kwekwe) 1999-00. H BB 2-30 v Middx (Southgate) 2005.. LO HS 100* v Northants (Southampton) 2005 (NL). LO B3-24 v Middx (Southampton) 2005 (NL). T20 HS 67. T20 BB 4-28.

LATOUF, Kevin John (Millfield S; Barton Peveril C), b Pretoria, South Africa 7 Sep 1985. 5'10". RHB, RM. Staff 2004 – awaiting first-class debut. LO HS 25 v Surrey (Oval) 2005 (CGT) on 1st XI debut.

LOGAN, Richard James (Wolverhampton GS), b Stone, Staffs 28 Jan 1980. 6'1". RHB, RMF. Northamptonshire 1999-2000. Nottinghamshire 2001-04. Hampshire debut 2005. HS 37* Nt v Hants (Nottingham) 2001. H HS 28 v Glos (Southampton) 2005 – on debut. BB 6-93 Nt v Derbys (Nottingham) 2001. H BB 3-59 v Kent (Canterbury) 2005. Award: CGT 1. LO HS 28* v Northants (Northampton) 2005 (NL). LO BB 5-24 Nt v Suffolk (Mildenhall) 2001 (CGT). T20 HS 11*. T20 BB 5-26.

NQMcLEAN, Jonathan ('Jono') James (St Stithian's S; Cape Town U), b Johannesburg, South Africa 11 Jul 1980. 6'0". RHB, RM. W Province 2001-02 to 2002-03. SA Acad 2003-04. Hampshire debut 2005. British passport. HS 68 v Glos (Cheltenham) 2005 – on debut. LO HS 36 v Notts (Southampton) 2005 (NL).

MASCARENHAS, Adrian Dimitri (Trinity C, Perth, Australia), b Hammersmith, London 30 Oct 1977. 6'2". Resident in Australia 1979-96. RHB, RMF. Debut 1996, taking 6-88 v Glamorgan (Southampton); took 16 wickets in first two CC matches; cap 1998. Dorset 1996. HS 104 v Worcs (Southampton) 2001 and 104 v Durham (Chester-le-St) 2004. 50 wkts (1): 56 (2004). BB 6-25 v Derbys (Southampton) 2004. Awards: CGT 3. LO HS 79 v Worcs (Southampton) 1999 (NL) and 79 v Kent (Canterbury) 2004 (NL). LO BB 5-27 v Glos (Southampton) 2002 (NL). T20 HS 52. T20 BB 5-14.

PIETERSEN, Kevin Peter (Maritzburg C; Natal U), b Pietermaritzburg, South Africa 27 Jun 1980. British passport (English mother) – qualified for England Oct 2004. 6'4". RHB, OB. MBE 2005. Natal/KwaZulu-Natal 1997-98 to 1999-00. Nottinghamshire 2001-04; cap 2002. Hampshire debut/cap 2005. **Tests**: 8 (2005 to 2005-06); HS 158 v A (Oval) 2005. **LOI**: 23 (2004-05 to 2005-06); HS 116 v SA (Pretoria) 2004-05; scored 454 runs (av 151.33) in 7-match series, including fastest England 100 off 69 balls (E London), v SA 2004-05. F-c Tours: I 2003-04 (Eng A), 2005-06. 1000 runs (3): most – 1546 (2003). HS 254* Nt v Middx (Nottingham) 2002. H HS 126 v Glamorgan (Southampton) 2005. BB 4-31 Nt v DU (Nottingham) 2003. CC BB 3-72 Nt v Hants (Nottingham) 2004. Award: CGT 1. LO HS 147 Nt v Somerset (Taunton) 2002 (NL). LO BB 3-14 Nt v Middx (Lord's 2004 (NL). T20 HS 67. T20 BB 2-9.

NQPOTHAS, Nic (King Edward VII S; Rand Afrikaans U), b Johannesburg 18 Nov 1973. ECB qualified – EU (Greek) passport. 6'3". RHB, WK. Transvaal 1993-94 to 2000-01. Hampshire debut 2002; cap 2003. **LOI** (SA): 3 (2000-01); HS 24 v P (Singapore) 2000 – on debut. F-c Tours (SA): E 1996 (SA A); WI 2000-01 (SA A); SL 1998-99. HS 165 Gauteng v KZ-Natal (Johannesburg) 1998-99. H HS 146* v Worcs (Worcester) 2003. Award: CGT 1. LO HS 114* v Glamorgan (Cardiff) 2005 (CGT). T20 HS 59.

TAYLOR, Billy Victor (Bitterne Park S, Southampton), b Southampton, Hants 11 Jan 1977. Brother of J.L.Taylor (Wiltshire 1998 to date). 6'3". LHB, RMF. Sussex 1999-2003. Hampshire debut 2004. Wiltshire 1996-98. HS 40 v Essex (Southampton) 2004. BB 6-45 v Glos (Southampton) 2005. Awards: CGT 1; BHC 1. LO HS 21* Sx v Notts (Cleethorpes) 1999 (NL). LO BB 5-28 Sx v Middx (Lord's) 2002 (BHC). T20 HS 12*. T20 BB 1-14.

‡NQTHORNELY, Dominic** John, b Albury, NSW, Australia 1 Oct 1978. RHB, RM. NSW 2003-04 to date. Surrey 2005. 1000 (0+1): 1065 (2004-05). HS 261* NSW v WA (Sydney) 2004-05. UK HS 81 and BB 2-40 Sy v Middx (Lord's) 2005 – on UK debut. BB 3-52 NSW v Vic (Melbourne) 2003-04. LO HS 78 NSW v Tas (Hobart) 2003-04. LO BB 3-32 NSW v S Aus (Sydney) 2002-03. T20 HS 67*. T20 BB 3-22.

TOMLINSON, James Andrew (Harrow Way S, Andover; Cardiff U), b Winchester 12 Jun 1982. 6'1". LHB, LFM. Wiltshire 2001. British U 2002-03. Hampshire debut 2002. No f-c appearances 2005. HS 23 v I (Southampton) 2002. CC HS 12* v Derbys (Derby) 2004. BB 6-63 v Derbys (Derby) 2003. LO HS 6 (NL). LO BB 2-15 v Sussex (Southampton) 2002 (NL).

TREMLETT, Christopher Timothy (Thornden S, Chandler's Ford; Taunton's C, Southampton), b Southampton 2 Sep 1981. Son of T.M.Tremlett (Hampshire 1976-91); grandson of M.F.Tremlett (Somerset, CD and England 1947-60). 6'7". RHB, RMF. Debut v NZ A (Portsmouth) 2000 taking wicket of M.H.Richardson with his first ball. Cap 2004. **LOI**: 3 (2005); HS 8; BB 4-32 v B (Nottingham) 2005 – on debut (hat-trick ball hit stump without dislodging bails). F-c Tour (ECB Acad): SL 2002-03. HS 64 v Glos (Southampton) 2005. BB 6-44 v Sussex (Hove) 2005. Hat-trick v Notts (Nottingham) 2005. LO HS 38* v Cheshire (Alderley Edge) 2004 (CGT). LO BB 4-25 v Essex (Southend) 2002 (NL). T20 HS 13. T20 BB 3-20.

UDAL, Shaun David (Cove CS), b Cove, Farnborough 18 Mar 1969. Grandson of G.F.U.Udal (Middx 1932 and Leics 1946); great-great-grandson of J.S.Udal (MCC 1871-75). 6'2". RHB, OB. Debut 1989; cap 1992; benefit 2002. **Tests**: 3 (2005-06); HS 33* and BB 1-31 v P (Faisalabad) 2005-06. **LOI**: 11 (1994 to 1995, 2005-06); HS 11* v Z (Brisbane) 1994-95; BB 2-37 v A (Sydney) 1994-95. F-c Tours: A 1994-95; I 2005-06; P 1995-96 (Eng A). HS 117* v Warwks (Southampton) 1997. 50 wkts (7); most – 74 (1993). BB 8-50 v Sussex (Southampton) 1992. Awards: CGT 1; BHC 2. LO HS 78 v Surrey (Guildford) 1997 (SL). LO BB 5-43 v Surrey (Oval) 1998 (SL). T20 HS 37. T20 BB 2-6.

[NQ]**WARNE, Shane** Keith (Hampton HS; Mentone GS), b Upper Ferntree Gully, Melbourne, Australia 13 Sep 1969. 6'0". RHB, LBG. Victoria 1990-91 to date; captain 1997-98 to 1998-99. Hampshire 2000, 2004-05; cap 2000; captain 2004 to date. *Wisden* 1993 (also one of *Five Cricketers of the Century*). **Tests** (A): 134 (1991-92 to 2005-06; HS 99 v NZ (Perth) 2001-02; BB 8-71 v E (Brisbane) 1994-95; hat-trick v E (Melbourne) 1994-95. **LOI** (A): 193 (1992-93 to 2002-03, 11 as captain); HS 55 v SA (Pt Elizabeth) 1993-94; BB 5-33 v WI (Sydney) 1996-97. F-c Tours (A): E 1993, 1997, 2001, 2005; SA 1993-94, 1996-97, 2001-02; WI 1994-95, 1998-99; NZ 1992-93, 1999-00; I 1997-98, 2000-01, 2004-05; P 1994-95, 2002-03 (in SL/Sharjah); SL 1992-93, 1999-00, 2003-04; Z 1991-92 (Aus B), 1999-00. HS 107* v Kent (Canterbury) 2005 – maiden 100 in his 321st innings. 50 wkts (5+1); most – 87 (2005). BB 8-71 (*see Tests*). H BB 6-34 v Kent (Canterbury) 2000. Award: BHC 1. LO HS 55 (*see LOI*). LO BB 5-33 (*see LOI*). T20 HS 12. T20 BB 1-29.

RELEASED/RETIRED

(Having made a first-class County appearance in 2005)

[NQ]**BICHEL, A.J.** -*see ESSEX.*

[NQ]**KATICH, Simon** Mathew (Trinity C, WA; U of WA), b Middle Swan, Midland, W Australia 21 Aug 1975. 6'0". LHB. SLC. W Australia 1996-97 to 2001-02. NSW 2002-03. Durham 2000; cap 2000. Yorkshire 2002 (one match). Hampshire 2003-05; cap 2003. **Tests** (A): 22 (2001 to 2005-06); HS 125 v I (Sydney) 2003-04; BB 6-65 v Z (Sydney) 2003-04. **LOI** (A): 30 (2000-01 to 2005-06); 107* v SL (Brisbane) 2005-06. F-c Tours (A): E 2001, 2005; I 2004-05; SL 1999-00, 2003-04. 1000 runs (2+3): most – 1632 (1998-99). HS 228* WA v S Aus (Perth) 2000-01. UK HS 168* A v MCC (Arundel) 2001. CC HS 143* v Yorks (Scarborough) 2003. BB 7-130 NSW v Vic (Melbourne) 2002-03. UK BB 4-21 H v Northants (Southampton) 2003. LO HS 136* NSW v Vic (Bowral) 2003-04. LO BB 3-21 Aus A v SA (Adelaide) 2001-02. T20 HS 59*.

KENWAY, Derek Anthony (St George's S, Southampton; Barton Peveril C, Eastleigh), b Fareham 12 Jun 1978. 5'11". RHB, RM, occ WK. Hampshire 1997-2005; cap 2001. 1000 runs (1): 1055 (1999). HS 166 v Notts (Southampton) 2001. BB 1-5. Award: CGT 1. LO HS 120* v Z (Southampton) 2003. LO BB 1-16 (CGT). T20 HS 40.

[NQ]**McMILLAN, Craig** Douglas (Shirley BHS), b Christchurch, NZ 13 Sep 1976. 5'11". RHB, RM. Canterbury 1994-95 to date. Hampshire 2005. **Tests** (NZ): 55 (1997-98 to 2004-05); HS 142 v Z (Wellington) 2001-02; BB 3-48 v P (Lahore) 2001-02. **LOI** (NZ): 174 (1996-97 to 2005-06, 8 as captain); HS 105 v P (Rawalpindi) 2001-02; BB 3-20 v P (Dunedin) 2000-01. F-c Tours (NZ): E 1999, 2004; A 1997-98, 2001-02, 2004-05; SA 2000-01; WI 2000-01; I 1999-00, 2003-04; P 2001-02; SL 1997-98; Z 2000-01. HS 168* New Zealanders v Indian Board President's XI (Jodhpur) 1999-00. H HS 52 and BB 2-49 v Notts (Nottingham) 2005 – on debut. BB 6-71 Central Conference v Pakistan A (Blenheim) 1998-99. LO HS 125 Canterbury v ND (Hamilton) 1998-99. LO BB 5-38 Canterbury v ND (Whangarei) 1996-97. T20 HS 65*. T20 BB 2-21.

[NQ]**WATSON, Shane** Robert (Ipswich GS), b Ipswich, Queensland, Australia 17 Jun 1981. 6'0". RHB, RFM. Tasmania 2000-01 to date. Hampshire 2004-05; cap 2005. **Tests** (A): 2 (2004-05 to 2005-06); HS 31 v P (Sydney) 2004-05 – on debut; BB 1-25. **LOI** (A): 37 (2001-02 to 2005); HS 77* v K (Nairobi) 2002; BB 3-27 v SL (Perth) 2002-03. F-c Tour (Aus): SA 2001-02 scoring 100* in only innings. HS 203* v Warwks (Southampton) 2005. Scored 112* v Somerset (Southampton) 2004 on UK debut. BB 6-32 Tas v Q (Hobart) 2001-02. H BB 2-33 v Kent (Southampton) 2005. Award: CGT 1. LO HS 132 v Surrey (Oval) 2005 (CGT). LO BB 3-27 (*see LOI*). T20 HS 97*. T20 BB 1-35.

A.D.Mullally and L.R.Prittipaul left the staff without making a first-class appearance in 2005.

HAMPSHIRE 2005

RESULTS SUMMARY

	Place	Won	Lost	Tied	Drew	No Result
County Championship (1st Division)	2nd	9	3		4	
All First-Class Matches		9	3		4	
C & G Trophy	Winners					
National League (1st Division)	9th	5	10			1
Twenty20 Cup	4th in South Division					

COUNTY CHAMPIONSHIP AVERAGES

BATTING AND FIELDING

Cap		M	I	NO	HS	Runs	Avge	100	50	Ct/St
2005	S.R.Watson	5	8	1	203*	540	77.14	1	3	10
2003	N.Pothas	15	24	5	139	973	51.21	3	5	48/3
2003	S.M.Katich	7	13	1	128	597	49.75	1	4	7
1998	A.D.Mascarenhas	11	18	7	103*	540	49.09	2	1	5
2002	J.P.Crawley	16	29	2	311*	1246	46.14	3	4	14/1
2005	K.P.Pietersen	6	11	–	126	424	38.54	2	1	4
2000	S.K.Warne	11	18	3	107*	493	32.86	2	1	13
2005	S.M.Ervine	16	28	1	75	821	30.40	–	7	8
–	J.J.McLean	6	9	1	68	242	30.25	–	3	4
2004	C.T.Tremlett	11‡	5	–	64	219	24.33	–	1	3
–	C.D.McMillan	4	8	1	52	169	24.14	–	1	–
–	J.H.K.Adams	8	13	–	71	310	23.84	–	3	8
–	M.J.Brown	13	25	1	54	560	23.33	–	3	13
1992	S.D.Udal	11	14	4	47*	196	19.60	–	–	7
–	G.A.Lamb	9	15	–	75	250	16.66	–	2	13
–	C.C.Benham	5	10	–	41	117	11.70	–	–	5
–	R.J.Logan	6	9	2	28	61	8.71	–	–	–
–	B.V.Taylor	8	14	6	24	66	8.25	–	–	–

Also batted: A.J.Bichel (4 matches) 138, 87, 2 (1 ct); J.T.A.Bruce (4) 0, 0*, 2 (3 ct); T.G.Burrows (1) 42, 13 (5 ct); D.A.Kenway (1 – cap 2001) 0, 20 (3 ct).

BOWLING

	O	M	R	W	Avge	Best	5wI	10wM
S.D.Udal	274.3	54	832	44	18.90	6- 44	3	–
J.T.A.Bruce	91	13	324	14	23.14	3- 42	–	–
A.D.Mascarenhas	273.4	65	801	34	23.55	5- 55	2	–
S.K.Warne	397.4	61	1161	47	24.70	6- 88	1	–
C.T.Tremlett	334	57	1232	46	26.78	6- 44	2	–
B.V.Taylor	187.4	34	587	19	30.89	6- 45	1	–
S.M.Ervine	374.1	79	1360	42	32.38	5- 60	3	–
Also bowled:								
S.R.Watson	112	22	372	9	41.33	2- 33	–	–
R.J.Logan	128.4	15	572	7	81.71	3- 59	–	–

J.H.K.Adams 6-1-26-0; J.P.Crawley 2.5-0-7-1; S.M.Katich 25-4-86-4; G.A.Lamb 36.4-5-145-3; C.D.McMillan 41-7-150-3; K.P.Pietersen 2-1-7-0.

Hampshire played no fixtures outside the County Championship in 2005. The First-Class Averages (pp 129–145) give the records of Hampshire players in all first-class matches for the county, with the exception of S.M.Katich, K.P.Pietersen and S.K.Warne whose full county figures are as above.

‡ Full substitute for J.T.A.Bruce v Gloucestershire at Cheltenham and for B.V.Taylor v Sussex at Southampton.

HAMPSHIRE RECORDS

FIRST-CLASS CRICKET

Highest Total	For 714-5d		v	Notts	Southampton	2005
	V 742		by	Surrey	The Oval	1909
Lowest Total	For 15		v	Warwicks	Birmingham	1922
	V 23		by	Yorkshire	Middlesbrough	1965
Highest Innings	For 316	R.H.Moore	v	Warwicks	Bournemouth	1937
	V 303*	G.A.Hick	for	Worcs	Southampton	1997

Highest Partnership for each Wicket

1st	347	V.P.Terry/C.L.Smith	v	Warwicks	Birmingham	1987
2nd	321	G.Brown/E.I.M.Barrett	v	Glos	Southampton	1920
3rd	344	C.P.Mead/G.Brown	v	Yorkshire	Portsmouth	1927
4th	263	R.E.Marshall/D.A.Livingstone	v	Middlesex	Lord's	1970
5th	235	G.Hill/D.F.Walker	v	Sussex	Portsmouth	1937
6th	411	R.M.Poore/E.G.Wynyard	v	Somerset	Taunton	1899
7th	325	G.Brown/C.H.Abercrombie	v	Essex	Leyton	1913
8th	257	N.Pothas/A.J.Bichel	v	Glos	Cheltenham	2005
9th	230	D.A.Livingstone/A.T.Castell	v	Surrey	Southampton	1962
10th	192	H.A.W.Bowell/W.H.Livsey	v	Worcs	Bournemouth	1921

Best Bowling	For 9- 25	R.M.H.Cottam	v	Lancashire	Manchester	1965
(Innings)	V 10- 46	W.Hickton	for	Lancashire	Manchester	1870
Best Bowling	For 16- 88	J.A.Newman	v	Somerset	Weston-s-Mare	1927
(Match)	V 17-119	W.Mead	for	Essex	Southampton	1895

Most Runs – Season	2854	C.P.Mead	(av 79.27)	1928
Most Runs – Career	48892	C.P.Mead	(av 48.84)	1905-36
Most 100s – Season	12	C.P.Mead		1928
Most 100s – Career	138	C.P.Mead		1905-36
Most Wkts – Season	190	A.S.Kennedy	(av 15.61)	1922
Most Wkts – Career	2669	D.Shackleton	(av 18.23)	1948-69
Most Career W-K Dismissals	700	R.J.Parks	(630 ct/70 st)	1980-92
Most Career Catches in the Field	629	C.P.Mead		1905-36

LIMITED-OVERS CRICKET

Highest Total	CGT	371-4		v	Glamorgan	Southampton	1975
	NL	353-8		v	Middlesex	Lord's	2005
	T20	192-7		v	Middlesex	Southampton	2005
Lowest Total	CGT	98		v	Lancashire	Manchester	1975
	NL	43		v	Essex	Basingstoke	1972
	T20	95		v	Essex	Chelmsford	2004
Highest Innings	CGT	177	C.G.Greenidge	v	Glamorgan	Southampton	1975
	NL	172	C.G.Greenidge	v	Surrey	Southampton	1987
	T20	97*	S.R.Watson	v	Kent	Southampton	2004
Best Bowling	CGT	7-30	P.J.Sainsbury	v	Norfolk	Southampton	1965
	NL	6-20	T.E.Jesty	v	Glamorgan	Cardiff	1975
	T20	5-14	A.D.Mascarenhas	v	Sussex	Hove	2004

KENT

Formation of Present Club: 1 March 1859
Substantial Reorganisation: 6 December 1870
Inaugural First-Class Match: 1864
Colours: Maroon and White
Badge: White Horse on a Red Ground
County Champions: (6) 1906, 1909, 1910, 1913, 1970, 1978
Joint Champions: (1) 1977
Gillette/NatWest/C & G Trophy Winners: (2) 1967, 1974
Benson and Hedges Cup Winners: (3) 1973, 1976, 1978
National League (Div 1) Winners: (1) 2001
Sunday League Winners: (4) 1972, 1973, 1976, 1995
Twenty20 Cup Winners: (0); best – 3rd in Group 2003
Match Awards: CGT 56; BHC 96

Chief Executive: Paul E.Millman, St Lawrence Ground, Canterbury, CT1 3NZ • Tel: 01227 456886 • Fax: 01227 762168 • Email: kent@ecb.co.uk • Web: www.kentccc.com

First XI Coach: G.Ford. **Captain**: R.W.T.Key. **Vice-Captain**: M.M.Patel. **Overseas Players**: A.J.Hall and J.M.Kemp. **2006 Beneficiary**: D.P.Fulton. **Head Groundsman**: M.G.Grantham. **Scorer**: J.C.Foley. ‡ New registration. NQ Not qualified for England.

COOK, Simon James (Matthew Arnold S), b Oxford 15 Jan 1977. 6'4". RHB, RM. Middlesex 1999-2004; cap 2003. Kent debut 2005. HS 93* M v Notts (Lord's) 2001. K HS 38 v Notts (Nottingham) 2005. BB 8-63 v Northants (Northampton) 2002. K BB 5-54 v Notts (Nottingham) 2005. LO HS 67* M v Durham (Lord's) 2003 (NL). LO BB 6-37 M v Leics (Leicester) 2004 (NL). T20 HS 20. T20 BB 3-14.

CUSDEN, Simon Mark James (Simon Langton GS, Canterbury), b Canterbury 21 Feb 1985. 6'5". RHB, RFM. Debut 2004. HS 12* v Sussex (Canterbury) 2004. BB 4-68 v Northants (Canterbury) 2004. LO HS 3 (NL). LO BB 1-29 (NL).

DENLY, Joseph Liam (Chaucer TC), b Canterbury 16 Mar 1986. 6'0". RHB, LB. Debut 2004. HS 10 v Glos (Canterbury) 2005. LO HS 49 v Yorks (Leeds) 2005 (NL). T20 HS 4.

DENNINGTON, Matthew John (Northwood BS; UNISA), b Durban, South Africa 16 Oct 1982. 6'1". RHB, RFM. Debut 2004. HS 55 v Hants (Canterbury) 2005. BB 3-23 v Bangladesh A (Canterbury) 2005. CC BB 3-48 v Sussex (Canterbury) 2004. LO HS 26* v Glos (Cheltenham) 2004 (NL). LO BB 3-53 v Glamorgan(Canterbury) 2004 (NL). T20 HS 12. T20 BB 4-28.

DEXTER, Neil John (Northwood HS; Varsity C; U of South Africa), b Johannesburg, S Africa 21 Aug 1984. 6'0". RHB, RM. Debut 2005. HS 79* and BB 1-42 v Notts (Canterbury) 2005. LO HS 5 (NL). LO BB 2-33 v Leics (Leicester) 2005 (NL).

DIXEY, Paul Garrod (King's S, Canterbury), b Canterbury 2 Nov 1987. 5'8". RHB, WK. Debut 2005. Awaiting CC debut. HS 24 v Bangladesh A (Canterbury) 2005 – on debut.

FERLEY, Robert Steven (King Edward VII HS; Sutton Valence S; Grey C, Durham U), b Norwich, Norfolk 4 Feb 1982. 5'8". RHB, SLA. Durham UCCE 2001-03. British U 2001-03. Kent debut 2003. Norfolk 2001. HS 78* DU v Durham (Chester-le-St) 2003. K HS 29 v Surrey (Canterbury) 2004. BB 4-76 v Surrey (Oval) 2003. LO HS 42 v Lancs (Manchester) 2004 (NL). LO BB 3-36 v Scotland (Canterbury) 2005 (NL). T20 HS 16*. T20 BB 1-9.

FULTON, David Paul (The Judd S; Kent U), b Lewisham 15 Nov 1971. 6'2". RHB, SLA, occ WK. Debut 1992; cap 1998; captain 2002 –05; benefit 2006. PCA 2001. 1000 runs (3): most – 1892 (2001). HS 208* v Somerset (Canterbury) 2001. Scored 9 hundreds in 2001, including 208*, 104* and 197 in successive innings. BB 1-37 (not CC). LO HS 82 v Yorks (Leeds) 2001 (NL). T20 HS 15.

NQ**HALL, Andrew** James (Alberton HS), b Alberton, Johannesburg, South Africa 31 Jul 1975. 6'0". RHB, RFM. Transvaal/Gauteng 1995-96 to 2001-02. Easterns 2001-02 to 2003-04. Lions 2004-05. Durham CB 1999. Suffolk 2002. Worcestershire 2003-04. Kent debut/cap2005. **Tests** (SA): 15 (2001-02 to 2004-05); HS 163 v I (Kanpur) 2004-05; BB 3-1 v SL (Johannesburg) 2002-03. **LOI** (SA): 66 (1998-99 to 2005-06); HS 81 v SL (Galle) 2000-01; BB 4-23 v NZ (Pretoria) 2005-06. F-c Tours (SA): E 2003; WI 2004-05; I 2004-05. HS 163 (*see Tests*). UK HS 133 K v Glam (Canterbury) 2005. BB 6-77 (11-99 match) Easterns v WP (Port Elizabeth) 2002-03. CC BB 4-32 K v Glamorgan (Canterbury) 2005. Award: CGT 1. LO HS 129* Gauteng v Border (E London) 1999-00. LO BB 4-26 Wo v Leics (Oakham) 2004 (NL). T20 HS 59. T20 BB 2-17.

JONES, Geraint Owen (Harristown State HS, Toowoomba and MacGregor State HS, Brisbane, Australia), b Kundiawa, Papua New Guinea 14 Jul 1976. RHB, WK. Debut 2001; cap 2003. MBE 2005. **ECB Contracts 2004-05**. **Tests**: 23 (2003-04 to 2005-06); HS 100 v NZ (Leeds) 2004. **LOI**: 38 (2004 to 2005-06); HS 80 v Z (Bulawayo) 2004-05. F-c Tours: SA 2004-05; WI 2003-04; I 2005-06; SL 2003-04. HS 108* v Essex (Chelmsford) 2003. Award: CGT 1. LO HS 80 (*see LOI*). T20 HS 22.

JONES, Kevin John Francis (Sittingbourne Community C), b Gillingham 9 Sep 1986. 5'11". RHB, RM. Debut 2005. Awaiting CC debut. HS 14 v Bangladesh A (Canterbury) 2005 – on debut. T20 HS T20 BB

JOSEPH, Robert ('Robbie') Hartman (Sutton Vallence S; St Mary's C, Twickenham), b Antigua 20 Jan 1982. Resided in England since 1997. RHB, RF. First-Class Counties XI 2000. Kent debut 2004. HS 26 and CC BB 3-47 v Middx (Canterbury) 2004. BB 5-19 v Bangladesh A (Canterbury) 2005. LO HS 15 v (Canterbury) 2005 (NL). LO BB 2-21 v Warwks (Canterbury) 2005 (NL).

NQ**KEMP, Justin** Miles (Queens C; Port Elizabeth U), b Queenstown, South Africa 2 Oct 1977. Son of J.W.Kemp (Border 1975-76 to 1976-77); grandson of J.M.Kemp (Border 1947-48). RHB, RFM. E Province 1996-97 to date. Worcestershire 2003. Kent debut 2005. **Tests** (SA): 4 (2000-01 to 2005-06); HS 55 v A (Perth) 2005-06; BB 3-33 v SL (Pretoria) 2000-01 on debut. **LOI** (SA): 46 (2000-01 to 2005-06); HS 80 v E (E London) 2004-05; BB 3-20 v I (Durban) 2001-02. F-c Tours (SA): A 2005-06; WI 2000 (SA A), 2000-01; Z 1998-99 (SA Acad). HS 188 EP v North West (Port Elizabeth) 2000-01. CC HS 124 K v Surrey (Oval) 2005. BB 6-56 EP v Border (Port Elizabeth) 2000-01. CC BB 5-48 Wo v Glam (Cardiff) 2003 – on Worcs debut. K BB 3-53 v Middx (Lord's) 2005. LO HS 107* Northerns v GW (Centurion) 2003-04. LO BB 6-20 EP v FS (Port Elizabeth) 2000-01. T20 HS 85*. T20 BB 3-19.

KEY, Robert William Trevor (Colfe's S), b East Dulwich, London 12 May 1979. 6'1". RHB, RM/OB. Debut 1998; cap 2001, captain 2006. *Wisden* 2004. **Tests**: 15 (2002 to 2004-05); HS 221 v WI (Lord's) 2004. **LOI**: 5 (2003); HS 19 v WI (Lord's) 2004. F-c Tours: A 2002-03; SA 1998-99 (Eng A), 2004-05; SL 2002-03 (ECB Acad); Z 1998-99 (Eng A). 1000 runs (4): most – 1896 (2004). HS 221 (*see Tests*). K HS 199 v Surrey (Oval) 2004. LO HS 114 v Notts (Nottingham) 2002 (NL). T20 HS 66*. T20 BB

^{NQ}**KHAN, Amjad** (Skolenpa Duevej, Denmark), b Copenhagen, Denmark 14 Oct 1980. 6'0". RHB, RFM. Debut 2001. Denmark 1998-2000. HS 78 v Middx (Lord's) 2003. 50 wkts (2); most – 63 (2002). BB 6-52 v Yorks (Canterbury) 2002. LO HS 65* Denmark v Ire (Harare) 1999-00. LO BB 4-26 v Leics (Leicester) 2003 (NL). T20 HS 15. T20 BB 3-24.

^{NQ}**O'BRIEN, Niall** John (Marian C, Dublin), b Dublin, Ireland 8 Nov 1981. 5'6". LHB, WK. Irish passport. Debut 2004. HS 176 Ireland v UAE (Windhoek) 2005. K HS 69 v Warwks (Birmingham) 2004. LO HS 43 v Surrey (Canterbury) 2005 (NL). T20 HS 12.

PATEL, Minal Mahesh (Dartford GS; Erith TC), b Bombay, India 7 Jul 1970. 5'9". RHB, SLA. Debut 1989; cap 1994; benefit 2004. No appearances 2003 (back injury). **Tests**: 2 (1996); HS 27 and BB 1-101 v I (Nottingham) 1996. F-c Tour: I 1994-95 (Eng A). HS 87 v Glamorgan (Cardiff) 2005. 50 wkts (4); most – 90 (1994). BB 8-96 v Lancs (Canterbury) 1994. LO HS 27* v Somerset (Canterbury) 2001 (CGT). LO BB 3-22 v Essex (Canterbury) 1999 (NL).

SAGGERS, Martin John (Springwood HS, King's Lynn; Huddersfield U), b King's Lynn, Norfolk 23 May 1972. 6'2". RHB, RMF. Durham 1996-98. Norfolk 1995-96. Kent debut 1999; cap 2001. **Tests**: 3 (2003-04 to 2004); HS 1 and BB 2-29 v B (Chittagong) 2003-04 on debut. F-c Tours: SL 2003-04; B 2003-04. HS 64 v Worcs (Canterbury) 2004. 50 wkts (4); most – 83 (2002). BB 7-79 v Durham (Chester-le-St) 2000. Awards: CGT 1; BHC 1. LO HS 34* Minor C v Leics (Jesmond) 1996 (BHC). LO BB 5-22 v Glos (Canterbury) 2001 (NL). T20 HS 5. T20 BB 2-14.

STEVENS, Darren Ian (Hinckley C), b Leicester 30 Apr 1976. 5'11". RHB, RM. Leicestershire 1997-2004; cap 2002. Kent debut/cap 2005. F-c Tours (ECB Acad): SL 2002-03. 1000 (1): 1277 (2005). HS 208 v Glamorgan (Canterbury) 2005. BB 3-19 v Glos (Maidstone) 2005. Award: CGT 1. LO HS 133 Le v Northumb (Jesmond) 2000 (NWT). LO BB 5-32 v Scotland (Edinburgh) 2005 (NL). T20 HS 39. T20 BB 1-13.

STIFF, David Alexander (Batley GS; Wakefield C), b Dewsbury, Yorks 20 Oct 1984. RHB, RFM. England U-19 to Australia 2002-03. Debut 2004. HS 18 and CC BB 2-58 v Lancs (Tunbridge W) 2004. BB 3-88 v NZ (Canterbury) 2004. LO HS – and BB 1-27 Yorks CB v Glos CB (Bristol) 2001 (CGT).

TREDWELL, James Cullum (Southlands Community CS, New Romney), b Ashford 27 Feb 1982. 6'0". LHB, OB. Debut 2001. F-c Tour (Eng A): I 2003-04 (capt). HS 61 v Yorks (Leeds) 2002. BB 5-101 Eng A v E Zone (Amritsar) 2003-04. CC BB 4-48 v Sussex (Hove) 2003. LO HS 71 Kent CB v Bucks (Maidstone) 2001 (CGT). LO BB 4-16 v Scotland (Canterbury) 2005 (NL). T20 HS 34. T20 BB 2-16.

NQVAN JAARSVELD, Martin (Warmbaths S; Pretoria U), b Klerksdorp, South Africa 18 Jun 1974. 6'2". RHB, OB. N Transvaal/Northerns 1994-95 to 2003-04. Titans 2004-05. Northamptonshire 2004. Kent debut/cap 2005 (Kolpak registration) scoring 118 and 111 v Warwicks (Canterbury) – second player after C.W.G.Bassano (Derbyshire) to score two hundreds on a county debut. **Tests** (SA): 9 (2002-03 to 2004-05); HS 73 v WI (Johannesburg) 2003-04. **LOI** (SA): 11(2002-03 to 2004); HS 45 v E (Birmingham) 2003; BB 1-0. Took wickets with his first and third balls in LOI. F-c Tours (SA): NZ 2003-04; I 2004-05; SL 1998-99 (SA A), 2004; Z 1998-99 (SA Acad). 1000 runs (1+1); most – 1268 (2001-02). HS 262* v Glamorgan (Cardiff) 2005. BB 2-30 SA A v SL A (Potchefstroom) 2003-04. Award: CGT 1. LO HS 123 NT v EP (Pretoria) 1996-97. LO BB 1-0 (*see LOI*). T20 HS 61*. T20 BB 2-19.

WALKER, Matthew Jonathan (King's S, Rochester), b Gravesend 2 Jan 1974. Grandson of Jack Walker (Kent 1949). 5'8". LHB, RM. Debut 1992-93 (Z tour); UK Debut 1994; cap 2000. F-c Tour: Z 1992-93 (K). 1000 runs (2); most 1266 (2004). BB 2-21 v Middx (Canterbury) 2004. Awards: BHC 3. LO HS 117 v Warwks (Canterbury) 1997 (BHC). LO BB 4-24 v Yorks (Leeds) 2001 (NL). T20 HS 48*.

RELEASED/RETIRED

(Having made a first-class County appearance in 2005)

CARBERRY, M.A. – *see HAMPSHIRE.*

SHERIYAR, Alamgir (George Dixon S; Joseph Chamberlain SFC; Oxford Poly), b Birmingham 15 Nov 1973. 6'1". RHB, LFM. Leicestershire 1994-95. Worcestershire 1996-2002, 2005 (*on temporary loan*); cap 1997. Kent 2003-04. F-c Tours (Eng A): NZ 1999-00; B 1999-00. HS 21 Wo v Notts (Nottingham) 1997 and 21 Wo v Pak A (Worcester) 1997. K HS 18* v Essex (Chelmsford) 2003. 50 wkts (4); most – 92 (1999). BB 7-130 (10-172 match) Wo v Hants (Southampton) 1999. K BB 5-65 v Sussex (Hove) 2003. Hat-tricks (2): 1994 (Le), 1999 (Wo). LO HS 19 Wo v Derbys (Chesterfield) 1996 (SL). LO BB 4-18 Wo v Yorks (Leeds) 1997 (SL). T20 HS 9*. T20 BB 1-18.

SCORING OF EXTRAS 2006

The variable penalties involved in scoring no-balls and wides in our international and county cricket remain unchanged from last season:

COMPETITION	NO-BALL PENALTY	WIDE PENALTY
Test Matches Limited-Overs Internationals }	1 + other runs scored	1 + other runs scored
County Championship Second XI Championship }	2 + other runs scored	1 + other runs scored
Tourist Matches (First-Class) Tourist Matches (Limited-Overs) }	1 + other runs scored	1 + other runs scored
C & G Trophy Totesport National League Twenty20 Cup }	2 + other runs scored + for a foot fault a free hit next ball	1 + other runs scored

KENT 2005

RESULTS SUMMARY

	Place	Won	Lost	Tied	Drew	No Result
County Championship (1st Division)	**5th**	6	3		7	
All First-Class Matches		7	3		7	
C & G Trophy	Quarter-Finalist					
National League (2nd Division)	8th	6	10			2
Twenty20 Cup	6th in South Division					

COUNTY CHAMPIONSHIP AVERAGES
BATTING AND FIELDING

Cap		M	I	NO	HS	Runs	Avge	100	50	Ct/St
2001	R.W.T.Key	15	27	1	189	1556	59.84	4	8	8
–	J.M.Kemp	8	12	2	124	527	52.70	2	2	8
2005	D.I.Stevens	16	27	1	208	1277	49.11	4	6	13
2005	M.van Jaarsveld	16	28	1	262*	1198	44.37	4	4	18
–	N.J.Dexter	2	4	1	79*	121	40.33	–	1	1
2000	M.J.Walker	16	28	3	173	993	39.72	3	4	8
2005	A.J.Hall	11	16	2	133	538	38.42	1	2	9
1998	D.P.Fulton	16	29	1	110	833	29.75	1	5	16
1994	M.M.Patel	16	21	4	87	487	28.64	–	4	3
–	M.J.Dennington	3	6	1	55	136	27.20	–	2	1
–	N.J.O'Brien	13	20	4	64	429	26.81	–	3	46/5
2001	M.J.Saggers	8	12	5	45	172	24.57	–	–	4
–	A.Khan	14	17	9	58*	170	21.25	–	1	2
2003	G.O.Jones	3	6	1	36*	101	20.20	–	–	13/1
–	S.J.Cook	14	18	2	38	193	12.06	–	–	3

Also batted: S.M.J.Cusden (1 match) 6*; J.L.Denly (1) 4, 10; R.H.Joseph (1) 0, 0* (1 ct); J.C.Tredwell (2) 27, 0, 15.

BOWLING

	O	M	R	W	Avge	Best	5wI	10wM
A.J.Hall	347.5	71	1028	40	25.70	4-32	–	–
M.M.Patel	598.4	132	1626	59	27.55	6-53	3	–
A.Khan	415.2	80	1555	55	28.27	6-73	1	–
S.J.Cook	397.1	103	1247	41	30.41	5-44	2	–
J.M.Kemp	109.5	14	359	11	32.63	3-53	–	–
D.I.Stevens	199.4	28	655	17	38.52	3-19	–	–
M.J.Saggers	232.3	47	782	13	60.15	2-64	–	–

Also bowled: S.M.J.Cusden 28-1-107-3; M.J.Dennington 52-13-160-4; N.J.Dexter 29-2-150-2; D.P.Fulton 2-0-5-0; R.H.Joseph 24.5-4-102-3; R.W.T.Key 1-0-5-0; J.C.Tredwell 35-7-142-3; M.van Jaarsveld 35-11-82-3; M.J.Walker 35-1-164-4.

The First-Class Averages (pp 129–145) give the records of Kent players in all first-class matches for the county (Kent's other opponents being the Bangladesh A), with the exception of G.O.Jones whose full county figures are as above, and A.Sheriyar whose only first-class appearances were made whilst on loan to Worcestershire.

KENT RECORDS

FIRST-CLASS CRICKET

Highest Total	For	803-4d		v	Essex	Brentwood	1934
	V	676		by	Australians	Canterbury	1921
Lowest Total	For	18		v	Sussex	Gravesend	1867
	V	16		by	Warwicks	Tonbridge	1913
Highest Innings	For	332	W.H.Ashdown	v	Essex	Brentwood	1934
	V	344	W.G.Grace	for	MCC	Canterbury	1876

Highest Partnership for each Wicket

1st	300	N.R.Taylor/M.R.Benson	v	Derbyshire	Canterbury	1991
2nd	366	S.G.Hinks/N.R.Taylor	v	Middlesex	Canterbury	1990
3rd	323	R.W.T.Key/M.van Jaarsveld	v	Surrey	Tunbridge W	2005
4th	368	P.A.de Silva/G.R.Cowdrey	v	Derbyshire	Maidstone	1995
5th	277	F.E.Woolley/L.E.G.Ames	v	New Zealand	Canterbury	1931
6th	315	P.A.de Silva/M.A.Ealham	v	Notts	Nottingham	1995
7th	248	A.P.Day/E.Humphreys	v	Somerset	Taunton	1908
8th	159	M.van Jaarsveld/M.M.Patel	v	Glamorgan	Cardiff	2005
9th	171	M.A.Ealham/P.A.Strang	v	Notts	Nottingham	1997
10th	235	F.E.Woolley/A.Fielder	v	Worcs	Stourbridge	1909

Best Bowling	For	10- 30	C.Blythe	v	Northants	Northampton	1907
(Innings)	V	10- 48	C.H.G.Bland	for	Sussex	Tonbridge	1899
Best Bowling	For	17- 48	C.Blythe	v	Northants	Northampton	1907
(Match)	V	17-106	T.W.J.Goddard	for	Glos	Bristol	1939

Most Runs – Season	2894	F.E.Woolley	(av 59.06)	1928
Most Runs – Career	47868	F.E.Woolley	(av 41.77)	1906-38
Most 100s – Season	10	F.E.Woolley		1928
	10	F.E.Woolley		1934
Most 100s – Career	122	F.E.Woolley		1906-38
Most Wkts – Season	262	A.P.Freeman	(av 14.74)	1933
Most Wkts – Career	3340	A.P.Freeman	(av 17.64)	1914-36
Most Career W-K Dismissals	1253	F.H.Huish	(901 ct/352 st)	1895-1914
Most Career Catches in the Field	773	F.E.Woolley		1906-38

LIMITED-OVERS CRICKET

Highest Total	CGT	384-6		v	Berkshire	Finchampstead	1994
	NL	327-6		v	Leics	Canterbury	1993
	T20	182-9		v	Surrey	The Oval	2004
Lowest Total	CGT	60		v	Somerset	Taunton	1979
	NL	83		v	Middlesex	Lord's	1984
	T20	113-9		v	Hampshire	Southampton	2004
Highest Innings	CGT	136*	C.L.Hooper	v	Berkshire	Finchampstead	1994
	NL	146	A.Symonds	v	Lancs	Tunbridge Wells	2004
	T20	112	A.Symonds	v	Middlesex	Maidstone	2004
Best Bowling	CGT	8-31	D.L.Underwood	v	Scotland	Edinburgh	1987
	NL	6- 9	R.A.Woolmer	v	Derbyshire	Chesterfield	1979
	T20	4-28	M.J.Dennington	v	Essex	Chelmsford	2003

LANCASHIRE

Formation of Present Club: 12 January 1864
Inaugural First-Class Match: 1865
Colours: Red, Green and Blue
Badge: Red Rose
County Champions (since 1890): (7) 1897, 1904, 1926, 1927, 1928, 1930, 1934
Joint Champions: (1) 1950
Gillette/NatWest/C & G Trophy Winners: (7) 1970, 1971, 1972, 1975, 1990, 1996, 1998
Benson and Hedges Cup Winners: (4) 1984, 1990, 1995, 1996
National League (Div 1) Winners: (1) 1999.
Sunday League Winners: (4) 1969, 1970, 1989, 1998
Twenty20 Cup Winners: (0); best – Finalist 2005
Match Awards: CGT 81; BHC 86

Chief Executive: Jim Cumbes, Old Trafford, Manchester M16 0PX • Tel: 0161 282 4000 • Fax: 0161 282 4100 • Email: enquiries@lccc.co.uk • Web: www.lccc.co.uk

Cricket Manager/First XI Coach: M.Watkinson. **Captain**: M.J.Chilton. **Vice-Captain**: S.G.Law. **Overseas Player**: B.J.Hodge. **2006 Beneficiary**: A.Flintoff. **Head Groundsman**: P.Marron. **Scorer**: A.West. ‡ New registration. NQ Not qualified for England.

ANDERSON, James Michael (St Theodore RC HS and SFC, Burnley), b Burnley 30 Jul 1982. 6'2". LHB, RFM. Debut 2002. Cap 2003. YC 2003. **ECB contracts 2004-05. Tests**: 12 (2003 to 2004-05); HS 21* v SA (Lord's) 2003; BB 5-73 v Z (Lord's) 2003 on debut. **LOI**: 44 (2002-03 to 2005-06); HS 11 v NZ (Chester-le-St) 2004; BB 4-25 v Holland (E London) 2002-03. Hat-trick v P (Oval) 2003 – 1st for Eng in 373 LOI. F-c Tours: SA 2004-05; WI 2003-04; SL 2003-04. HS 37* v Durham (Manchester) 2005. 50 wkts (2); most – 60 (2005). BB 6-23 v Hants (Southampton) 2002. Hat-trick (Lancs) 2003. LO HS 13* v Notts (Manchester) 2005. LO BB 4-25 (*see LOI*). T20 HS 16. T20 BB 2-25.

‡BROWN, Karl Robert (Hesketh Fletcher HS, Atherton), b Bolton 17 May 1988. 5'10". RHB, RMF. Staff 2006 – awaiting f-c debut.

CHAPPLE, Glen (West Craven HS; Nelson & Colne C), b Skipton, Yorks 23 Jan 1974. 6'1". RHB, RFM. Debut 1992; cap 1994; benefit 2004. F-c Tours (Eng A): A 1996-97; WI 1995-96 (La); I 1994-95. HS 155 v Somerset (Manchester) 2001. Scored 100 off 27 balls in contrived circumstances v Glamorgan(Manchester) 1993. 50 wkts (4); most – 55 (1994). BB 6-30 v Somerset (Blackpool) 2002. Awards: CGT 1; BHC 2. LO HS 81* v Derbys (Manchester) 2002 (CGT). LO BB 6-18 v Essex (Lord's) 1996 (NWT). T20 HS 55*. T20 BB 2-13.

CHILTON, Mark James (Manchester GS; Durham U), b Sheffield, Yorks 2 Oct 1976. 6'3". RHB, RM. Debut 1997. Cap 2002. Captain 2005-. British U 1998. 1000 runs (1): 1154 (2003). HS 130 v Yorks (Manchester) 2005. BB 1-1. CC BB 1-10. Awards: CGT 2; BHC 4. LO HS 115 v Surrey (Croydon) 2004 (NL). LO BB 5-26 v Brit U v Sussex (Cambridge) 1997 (BHC). T20 HS 23*.

CORK, Dominic Gerald (St Joseph's C, Stoke-on-Trent; Newcastle CFE), b Newcastle-under-Lyme, Staffs 7 Aug 1971. 6'2". RHB, RFM. Derbyshire 1990-2003; cap 1993; captain 1998-2003; benefit 2001. Lancashire debut/cap 2004. *Wisden* 1995. PCA 1995. Staffordshire 1989-90. **ECB contract** 2001. **Tests**: 37 (1995 to 2002); HS 59 v NZ (Auckland) 1996-97; BB 7-43 v WI (Lord's) 1995 – on debut (record England analysis by Test match debutant); hat-trick v WI (Manchester) 1995 – the first in Test history to occur in the opening over of a day's play. **LOI**: 32 (1992 to 2002-03); HS 31* v NZ (Napier) 1996-97; BB 3-27 v WI (Lord's) 1995. F-c Tours: A 1992-93 (Eng A), 1998-99; SA 1993-94 (Eng A), 1995-96; WI 1991-92 (Eng A); NZ 1996-97; I 1994-95 (Eng A); P 2000-01 (*part*). HS 200* De v Durham (Derby) 2000. HS 149 v Surrey (Croydon) 2004. 50 wkts (7); most – 90 (1995). BB 9-43 (13-93 match) De v Northants (Derby) 1995. Took 8-53 before lunch on his 20th birthday for De v Essex (Derby) 1991. 2 hat-tricks: 1994 and 1995 (*see Tests*). La BB 7-120 v Middx (Lord's) 2004. Awards: CGT 4; BHC 4. LO HS 93 De v Derbys CB (Derby) 2000 (NWT). LO BB 6-21 De v Glamorgan(Chesterfield) 1997 (SL). T20 HS 28. T20 BB 3-9.

CROFT, Steven John (Highfield HS, Blackpool; Myerscough C), b Blackpool 11 Oct 1984. 5'10". RHB, RMF. Debut 2005. HS 6 v OU (Oxford) 2005 – awaiting CC debut. LO HS 7 and LO BB 1-27 La CB v Oxon (Bodicote) 2002 (CGT).

NQ**CROOK, Andrew** Richard, b Modbury, S Australia 14 Oct 1980. 6'1". Elder brother of S.P.Crook (see NORTHAMPTONSHIRE). RHB, OB. British passport. S Australia 1999-00 (one match). Lancashire debut 2004. HS 88 v OU (Oxford) 2005. BB 3-71 and CC HS 43 v Essex (Manchester) 2005. Award: CGT 1. LO HS 162* v Bucks (Wormsley) 2005 (Lancs CGT record). LO BB 3-32 v Hants (Manchester) 2005. T20 HS 15. T20 BB 2-25.

CROSS, Gareth David (Moorside S; Eccles C), b Bury 20 Jun 1984. 5'9". RHB, WK. Debut 2005. HS 22 v Leics (Manchester) 2005. LO HS 21 La CB v Scot (Aberdeen) 2002 (CGT).

FLINTOFF, Andrew (Ribbleton Hall HS), b Preston 6 Dec 1977. 6'4". RHB, RFM. Debut 1995; cap 1998; benefit 2006. YC 1998. *Wisden* 2003. PCA 2004, 2005. MBE 2005. BBC Sports Personality of 2005. **ECB contracts 2000-02-03-04-05. Tests**: 55 (1998 to 2005-06); HS 167 v WI (Birmingham) 2004; BB 5-58 v WI (Bridgetown) 2003-04. **LOI**: 95 (1998-99 to 200506); HS 123 v WI (Lord's) 2004; BB 4-14 v B (Chittagong) 2003-04. F-c Tours (Eng): A 2002-03 (*part*), SA 1998-99 (Eng A), 1999-00, 2004-05; WI 2003-04; NZ 2001-02; I 2001-02; P 2005-06SL 1997-98 (Eng A), 2003-04; Z 1998-99 (Eng A); K 1997-98 (Eng A). HS 167 (*see Tests*). BB 5-24 v Hants (Southampton) 1999. Awards: CGT 3; BHC 1. LO HS 143 (off 66 balls) v Essex (Chelmsford) 1999 (NL). LO BB 4-11 v Yorks (Leeds) 2002 (BHC). T20 HS 85. T20 BB 2-15.

NQ**HODGE, Bradley** John (St Bede's C, Mentone; Deakin U), b Sandringham, Victoria, Australia 29 Dec 1974. 5'8". RHB, OB. Victoria 1993-94 to date. Australia A debut 1999-2000. Durham 2002. Leicestershire 2003-04; cap 2003; captain 2004 (*part*). Lancashire debut 2005. **Tests** (A): 5 (2005-06); HS 203* v SA (Perth) 2005-06. **LOI** (A): 5 (2005-06) HS 59 v NZ (Christchurch) 2005. F-c Tours (A): I 2004-05; Z 1998-99 (A Academy). 1000 runs (2+2); most 1548 (2004). HS 302* (Leics record) v Notts (Nottingham) 2003. La HS 110* v Somerset (Taunton) 2005. BB 4-17 Aus A v WI (Hobart) 2000-01. UK BB 3-35 Le v LU (Leicester) 2003. CC BB 2-18 Le v Yorks (Leicester) 2004. La BB 1-14. Award: CGT 1. LO HS 164 Aus A v SA A (Perth) 2002-03. LO BB 5-28 Aus A v SA A (Canberra) 2002-03. T20 HS 97. T20 BB 4-17.

HOGG, Kyle William (Saddleworth HS), b Birmingham 2 Jul 1983. Son of W.Hogg (Lancashire and Warwickshire 1976-83; grandson of S.Ramadhin (Trinidad, Lancashire and West Indies 1949-50 to 1965). 6'4". LHB, RFM. Debut 2001. F-c Tour (ECB Acad): SL 2002-03. HS 53 v Notts (Nottingham) 2003. BB 5-48 v Leics (Manchester) 2002 – on CC debut. LO HS 41* v Glamorgan (Manchester) 2005 (NL). LO BB 4-20 v Hants (Southampton) 2002 (NL). T20 HS 7. T20 BB 1-16.

HORTON, Paul James (St Margaret's HS, Liverpool), b Sydney, Australia 20 Sep 1982. 5'10". RHB, RM. UK resident since 1997. Debut 2003. HS 99 v Essex (Manchester) 2005. LO HS 42 v Warwks (Birmingham) 2004 (NL). T20 HS 11.

KEEDY, Gary (Garforth CS), b Wakefield, Yorks 27 Nov 1974. 6'0". LHB, SLA. Yorkshire 1994 (one match). Lancashire debut 1995; cap 2000. F-c Tour: WI 1995-96 (La). HS 57 v Yorks (Leeds) 2002. 50 wkts (2): most – 72 (2004). BB 7-95 (14-227 match) v Glos (Manchester) 2004. LO HS 10* v Essex (Manchester) 2002 (NL). LO BB 5-30 v Sussex (Manchester) 2000 (NL). T20 HS 0. T20 BB 3-25.

LAW, Stuart Grant (Craigslea State HS), b Herston, Brisbane, Australia 18 Oct 1968. 6'1". RHB, RM/LB. Queensland 1988-89 to 2003-04; captain 1994-95 to 1996-97, 1999-00 to 2001-02. Essex 1996-2001; cap 1996. Lancashire debut/cap 2002. *Wisden* 1997. PCA 1999. British Citizenship after 2004 season. **Tests** (A): 1 (1995-96); HS 54* v SL (Perth) 1995-96. **LOI** (A): 54 (1994-95 to 1998-99); HS 110 v Z (Hobart) 1994-95; BB 2-22 v P (Sydney) 1996-97. F-c Tours: E 1995 (Young A); Z 1991-92 (Aus B). 1000 runs (7+2); most – 1833 (1999). HS 263 Ex v Somerset (Chelmsford) 1999. La HS 236* v Warwks (Manchester) 2003. BB 5-39 Q v Tasmania (Brisbane) 1995-96. CC BB 3-27 Ex v Worcs (Chelmsford) 1997. La BB 1-24. Awards: CGT 5; BHC 1. LO HS 163 Young A v Surrey (Oval) 1995. LO BB 5-26 Q v SL (Cairns) 1995-96. T20 HS 101.

LOYE, Malachy Bernhard (Moulton S), b Northampton 27 Sep 1972. 6'2". RHB, OB. Northamptonshire 1991-2002; cap 1994. PCA 1998. Lancashire debut 2003 – scoring 126 v Surrey (Oval) and 113 v Notts (Manchester) in his first two innings; cap 2003. F-c Tours (Eng A): SA 1993-94, 1998-99; Z 1994-95 (Nh), 1998-99. 1000 runs (5); most – 1198 (1998, 2005). HS 322* Nh v Glamorgan(Northampton) 1998 – record Northants score until 2001. La HS 200 v Durham (Chester-le-St) 2005. BB 1-8. Awards: CGT 2; BHC 1. LO HS 124* Nh v Northants CB (Northampton) 2001 (CGT). T20 HS 100.

MAHMOOD, Sajid Iqbal (North C, Bolton), b Bolton 21 Dec 1981. 6'4". RHB, RF. Debut 2002. **LOI**: 1 (2004); HS 1 and BB – v NZ (Bristol) 2004. F-c Tour (Eng A): I 2003-04. HS 94 v Sussex (Manchester) 2004. BB 5-37 v DU (Durham) 2003. CC BB 4-59 v Surrey (Manchester) 2004. LO HS 29 v Staffs (Stone) 2004 (CGT). LO BB 4-39 v Glamorgan-(Manchester) 2004 (NL). T20 HS 21. T20 BB 1-20.

MARSHALL, Simon James (Birkenhead S; Pembroke C, Cambridge), b Arrowe Park, Wirral, Cheshire 20 Sep 1982. 6'3". RHB, LB. Cambridge U 2002-04; blue 2002-03-04. British U 2004. Lancashire debut 2005. Cheshire 2001-03. Hockey blue. HS 126* CU v OU (Cambridge) 2003. La HS 35* v OU (Oxford) 2005. CC HS 26* v Worcs (Manchester) 2005. BB 6-128 CU v Essex (Cambridge) 2002. La BB 2-23 v OU (Oxford) 2005 – on La debut. CC BB 1-8. LO HS 8.

NEWBY, Oliver James (Ribblesdale HS; Muerscough C), b Blackburn 26 Aug 1984. 6'5". RHB, RMF. Debut 2003. Nottinghamshire 2005 (whilst on loan). HS 38* Nt v Kent (Nottingham) 2005 – on Notts debut. La HS 0* and BB 2-32 v Northants (Liverpool) 2004 on CC debut. LO HS 7* (NL). LO BB 2-37 v Glos (Manchester) 2004 (NL). T20 HS – . T20 BB 1-20.

SMITH, Thomas Christopher (Parkland HS, Chorley; Runshaw C, Leyland) B Liverpool 26 Dec 1985. 6'3". LHB, RMF. Debut 2005. Awaiting CC debut. HS 0 and BB 1-24 v OU (Oxford) 2005. LO HS 8 (NL).

SUTCLIFFE, Iain John (Leeds GS; Queen's C, Oxford), b Leeds, Yorks 20 Dec 1974. 6'2". LHB, occ LB. Oxford U 1994-96; blue 1995-96; boxing blue 1993-94. Leicestershire 1995-2002; cap 1997. Lancashire debut/cap 2003. F-c Tour (Le): SA 1996-97. 1000 runs (3): most – 1088 (2002). HS 203 Le v Glamorgan(Cardiff) 2001. La HS 153 v Yorks (Leeds) 2005. BB 2-21 OU v CU (Lord's) 1996. CC BB (Le) 1-7. La BB 1-11. Awards: CGT 1; BHC 1. LO HS 105* Le v Notts (Nottingham) 1998 (BHC). T20 HS 4.

‡**SUTTON, Luke** David (Millfield S; Durham U), b Keynsham, Somerset 4 Oct 1976. 5'11". RHB, WK. Somerset 1997-98. Derbyshire 2000-05; cap 2002; captain 2004-05. HS 140* (carried bat) De v Sussex (Derby) 2001. LO HS 83 De v Lancs (Derby) 2003 (NL). T20 HS 61*. T20 BB

YATES, Gary (Manchester GS), b Ashton-under-Lyne 20 Sep 1967. 6'0". RHB, OB. Lancashire 1990-2002; cap 1994; benefit 2005. Lancashire 2nd XI captain 2002-04. Appointed Assistant Coach 2005. HS 134* v Northants (Manchester) 1993. BB 6-64 v Kent (Manchester) 1999. LO HS 38 v Essex (Chelmsford) 1996 (SL). LO BB 4-34 v Warwks (Birmingham) 1994 (SL). Now Assistant Coach, he has made no f-c appearances since 2002.

RELEASED/RETIRED

(Having made a first-class County appearance in 2005)

NQ**CROOK, S.P.** – see NORTHAMPTONSHIRE.

HEGG, Warren Kevin (Unsworth HS, Bury; Stand C, Whitefield), b Whitefield 23 Feb 1968. 5'8". RHB, WK. Lancashire1986-2005; cap 1989; benefit 1999; captain 2002-04. **Tests**: 2 (1998-99); HS 15 v A (Sydney) 1998-99. F-c Tours: A 1996-97 (Eng A), 1998-99; WI 1986-87 (La), 1995-96 (La); NZ 2001-02; SL 1990-91 (Eng A); Z 1988-89 (La). HS 134 v Leics (Manchester) 1996. Held 11 catches (equalling world f-c match record) v Derbys (Chesterfield) 1989. Award: BHC 1. LO HS 81 v Yorks (Manchester) 1996 (BHC). T20 HS 45.

NQ**KARTIK, Murali,** b Madras, India 11 Sep 1976. LHB, SLA. Railways 1996-97 to date. Lancashire 2005. **Tests** (I): 8 (1999-00 to 2004-05); HS 43 v B (Dhaka) 2000-01; BB 4-44 v A (Bombay) 2004-05. **LOI** (I): 31 (1999-00 to 2005-06); HS 32* v A (Perth) 2003-04; BB 3-36 v A (Jodhpur) 2002-03. F-c Tours (I): A 2003-04; B 2001-02. HS 79 Railways v Baroda (Baroda) 2000-01. La HS 7. BB 9-70 Rest of India v Bombay (Bombay) 2000-01. La BB 5-75 (10-168 match) v Essex (Chelmsford) 2005. LO HS 37* Central Zone v South Zone (Poona) 2004-05. LO BB 4-13 Railways v Rajasthan (Jaipur) 1996-97.

NQ**MURALITHARAN, Muthiah** (St Anthony's C, Kandy), b Kandy, Sri Lanka 17 Apr 1972. 5'5". RHB, OB. Central Province 1989-90 to date. Tamil Union 1991-92 to date. Lancashire 1999 (taking 7-44 and 7-73 v Warwks at Southport on debut), 2001, 2005; cap 1999. Kent 2003; cap 2003. *Wisden* 1999. **Tests**: 91 (1992-93 to 2004); HS 67 v I (Kandy) 2001-02; BB 9-51 (13-115 match) v Z (Kandy) 2001-02. **LOI** (SL): 263 (1993-94 to 2005-06); HS 27 v A (Sydney) 2005-06; BB 7-30 v I (Sharjah) 2000-01. F-c Tours (SL): E 1991, 1998, 2002; A 1995-96; SA 1992-93 (SL U-24), 1994-95, 1997-98, 2000-01, 2002-03; WI 1996-97, 2003; NZ 1994-95, 1996-97; I 1993-94, 1997-98; P 1995-96, 1999-00, 2001-02; Z 1994-95, 1999-00, 2003-04. HS 67 (*see Tests*). 50 wkts (2+3); most – 97 (2001-02). Took 66 wkts in 7 CC matches 1999. BB 9-51 (13-115 match) (*see Tests*). La HS 24* v Derby (Derby) 2005. La BB 7-39 (11-61 match) v Derbys (Derby) 1999. Award: BHC 1. LO HS 19 (*see LOI*). LO BB 7-30 (*see LOI*). T20 HS 9. T20 BB 4-19. T20 HS 9. T20 BB 4-19.

NQNORTH, Marcus James (Kent Street Sr HS), b Pakenham, Melbourne, Australia 28 Jul 1979. 6'1". LHB, OB. W Australia 1998-99 to date. Durham 2004. Lancashire 2005. Tour (A Academy): Z 1998-99. 1000 runs (0+1): 1074 (2003-04). HS 219 Du v Glam (Cardiff) 2004. La HS 60 v Worcs (Manchester) 2005. BB 4-16 Du v Durham UCCE (Chester-le-St) 2004 – on DU debut. CC BB 2-45 Du v Yorks (Chester-le-St) 2004. La BB 1-16. LO HS 134* WA v Q (Perth) 2004-05. LO BB 4-26 Durham CB v Bucks (Beaconsfield) 2001 (CGT). T20 HS 21.

NQSYMONDS, Andrew (All Saints Anglican School, Mudgeeraba, Queensland), b Birmingham 9 Jun 1975. 6'1½". RHB, RMF/OB. Emigrated to Australia when 18 months old. Queensland 1994-95 to date. Gloucestershire 1995-96; cap 1996. Kent 1999, 2001, 2004; cap 1999. Lancashire 2005; cap 2005. YC 1995. Surrendered England qualification by appearing for Australia A v WI 1996-97. **Tests** (A): 7 (2003-04 to 2005-06); HS 72 and BB 3-50 v SA (Melbourne) 2005-06. **LOI** (A): 138 (1998-99 to 2005-06); HS 156 v NZ (Wellington) 2005-06; BB 5-18 v B (Manchester) 2005. F-c Tours (A): Sc 1998 (Aus A); NZ 1994-95 (Aus Academy); SL 2003-04. 1000 runs (2); most – 1438 (1995). HS 254* Gs v Glam (Abergavenny) 1995 (including record 16 sixes); hit record 20 sixes in match. La HS 146 v Yorks (Manchester) 2005. BB 6-105 K v Sussex (Tunbridge Wells) 2002. La BB 3-80 v Northants (Northampton) 2005. Awards: CGT 3; BHC 2. LO HS 146 K v Lancs (Tunbridge W) 2004 (NL). LO BB 6-14 Australia A v India A (Los Angeles) 1999. T20 HS 112. T20 BB 2-14.

T.M.Rees left the staff without making a first-class appearance in 2005.

COUNTY CAPS AWARDED IN 2005

Derbyshire	–
Durham	D.M.Benkenstein, A.M.Davies, M.E.K.Hussey, G.J.Muchall
Essex	R.S.Bopara, A.N.Cook, G.W.Flower
Glamorgan	–
Gloucestershire	Kadeer Ali, C.M.Bandara, U.D.U.Chandana, C.G.Greenidge, G.P.Hodnett, S.P.Kirby, W.D.Rudge, R.R.Sarwan, S.D.Snell
Hampshire	S.M.Ervine, K.P.Pietersen, S.R.Watson
Kent	A.J.Hall, D.I.Stevens, M van Jaarsveld
Lancashire	A.Symonds
Leicestershire	H.D.Ackerman
Middlesex	A.Richardson, E.T.Smith
Northamptonshire	U.Afzaal, B.J.Phillips
Nottinghamshire	S.P.Fleming
Somerset	C.K.Langeveldt, G.C.Smith, M.J.Wood
Surrey	R.Clarke, S.A.Newman
Sussex	Naved-ul-Hasan, M.H.Yardy
Warwickshire	N.M.Carter, H.H.Streak, I.J.L.Trott
Worcestershire	S.M.Davies, Z.de Bruyn, C.H.Gayle, D.K.H.Mitchell, Shoaib Akhtar, W.P.U.C.J.Vaas, S.A.Wedge
Yorkshire	P.A.Jaques

Gloucestershire award caps on first-class debut. Worcestershire award club colours on Championship debut.

LANCASHIRE'S FIRST-CLASS AVERAGES 2005

BATTING

Name	M	I	NO	Runs	HS	Avge	100	50	Ct	St
A.R.Crook	2	2	0	131	88	65.50	–	1	4	–
A.Symonds	7	10	0	623	146	62.30	3	1	4	–
M.B.Loye	16	25	1	1198	200	49.91	4	3	11	–
I.J.Sutcliffe	15	25	3	1046	153	47.54	2	7	15	–
S.G.Law	15	24	2	858	143	39.00	3	2	18	–
P.J.Horton	6	9	0	350	99	38.88	–	2	2	1
A.Flintoff	4	6	1	184	83	36.80	–	2	4	–
M.J.Chilton	17	28	3	895	130	35.80	3	2	10	–
S.P.Crook	2	2	0	71	66	35.50	–	1	–	–
S.J.Marshall	4	6	3	104	35*	34.66	–	–	1	–
W.K.Hegg	15	21	6	502	77*	33.46	–	3	41	5
B.J.Hodge	7	11	1	331	110*	33.10	1	1	6	–
D.G.Cork	14	19	2	540	102*	31.76	1	5	12	–
M.J.North	3	4	0	101	60	25.25	–	1	2	–
G.Chapple	14	20	1	422	82	22.21	–	3	5	–
S.I.Mahmood	7	10	0	177	57	17.70	–	1	–	–
G.Keedy	9	10	7	47	34	15.66	–	–	1	–
M.Muralitharan	6	8	2	78	24*	13.00	–	–	3	–
G.D.Cross	2	3	0	38	22	12.66	–	–	9	2
J.M.Anderson	16	19	5	145	37*	10.35	–	–	8	–
S.J.Croft	1	1	0	6	6	6.00	–	–	–	–
K.W.Hogg	2	4	0	18	9	4.50	–	–	2	–
M.Kartik	2	3	0	11	7	3.66	–	–	1	–
T.C.P.Smith	1	1	0	0	0	0.00	–	–	1	–

BOWLING

Name	O	M	R	W	Avge	Best	5w	10w	SR
M.J.Chilton	5	1	9	1	9.00	1-9	–	–	30.00
M.Muralitharan	233.2	69	540	36	15.00	6-50	4	–	38.88
M.Kartik	90	21	260	16	16.25	5-75	2	1	33.75
G.Chapple	383.1	98	1010	47	21.48	5-22	2	–	48.91
G.Keedy	265.3	67	753	33	22.81	6-33	2	1	48.27
D.G.Cork	395.3	98	1118	43	26.00	4-27	–	–	55.18
J.M.Anderson	512.4	99	1813	60	30.21	5-79	1	–	51.26
A.Symonds	177	37	484	16	30.25	3-80	–	–	66.37
S.I.Mahmood	128.2	22	450	14	32.14	3-21	–	–	55.00
A.R.Crook	35	7	132	4	33.00	3-71	–	–	52.50
B.J.Hodge	17	3	35	1	35.00	1-14	–	–	102.00
K.W.Hogg	34.2	9	113	3	37.66	2-40	–	–	68.66
S.J.Marshall	94.3	15	266	7	38.00	2-23	–	–	81.00
T.C.P.Smith	20	8	46	1	46.00	1-24	–	–	120.00
A.Flintoff	20	6	59	1	59.00	1-11	–	–	120.00
M.J.North	56	10	176	2	88.00	1-16	–	–	168.00
S.J.Croft	11	1	49	0	–	–	–	–	–
S.P.Crook	29	6	80	0	–	–	–	–	–

* Not out

	8		TITUS SALT (USA) (F8) M D Hammond 4 9 8	R Lee
SS	9	P5-50U	WESTERN BLUEBIRD (F13) (C) K Milligan 7 10 12	M J McAlister (7)
	10	000-5	NIGHT PEARL (FR) (32) B Storey 4 10 5	B Harding
	11	0522P	STAFF NURSE (IRE) (12) N Wilson 5 10 5	K Renwick

BETTING: 3-1 Possible Gale, 9-2 Obay, 6-1 Staff Nurse, 7-1 Ball Games, 8-1 Seafire Lad, Always Flying, Free Will, 10-1 others.

3.05 YOUNGS CHARTERED SURVEYORS HANDICAP CHASE (CLASS F) £4,500 added 5YO PLUS (3m 1f)

	1	065514	INNISFREE (IRE) (21) J G Carr(IRE) 7 11 12	R Johnson
	2	2B3PP-	ALFY RICH (233) (C) M Todhunter 9 11 12	A Dobbin
	3	1U0F02	ASTON (USA) (7) D R C Guest 5 11 10	W Kennedy (5)
	4	205-14	TA TA FOR NOW (9) (C) Mrs S Bradburne 8 11 7	M Bradburne
	5	052105	SWALLOW MAGIC (IRE) (31) T Murphy 7 11 3	K Mercer (3)
	6	P33342	TEE-JAY (IRE) (31) (BF) M D Hammond 9 10 11	G Lee
	7	-06156	TOAD HALL (31) N Normile 11 10 8	D Flavin (5)
	8	-31126	STARBUCK (98) (BF) A Crow 11 10 7	D McGann (5)
	9	0060P0	NORTHERN ECHO (31) (C) K S Thomas 8 10 2	G Thomas (7)
	10	PU0-P4	MIDDLEWAY (125) (CD) Miss K Milligan 9 10 0	M J McAlister (7)

BETTING: 4-1 Tee-Jay, 5-1 Ta Ta For Now, 6-1 Innisfree, Aston, Swallow Magic, Starbuck, 8-1 Toad Hall, 10-1 others.

3.40 TARMAC NORTHERN MARES' ONLY NOVICES' HURDLE (CLASS E) £4,700 added 4YO PLUS (2m 4f 110yds)

	1	32R-11	OSTFANNI (IRE) (F19) (D) M Todhunter 5 11 10	G Lee
	2	U21325	REEM TWO (31) D McCain 4 11 2	S J Craine (5)
	3		ENTRE AMIS (69) M Moore 5 10 10	F Keniry
	4		SOLWAY CLOUD B Storey 5 10 10	M J McAlister (7)
	5	0/000	TERIMONS DAUGHTER (111) E W Tuer 6 10 10	N Mulholland
	6	0-2U	CADEAUX ROUGE (IRE) (99) D W Thompson 4 10 9	K Mercer (3)
	7	F404	OSCAR'S LADY (IRE) (34) G A Swinbank 4 10 9	J Crowley

BETTING: 4-6 Ostfanni, 9-2 Reem Two, 8-1 Oscar's Lady, 10-1 Cadeaux Rouge, 12-1 Entre Amis, 20-1 Solway Cloud, 25-1 Terimons Daughter.

4.15 SIS NOVICES' HURDLE (CLASS E) £4,700 added 4YO PLUS (2m 110yds)

	1	236-1	CRATHORNE (IRE) (F59) M Todhunter 5 11 5	A Dobbin
	2	1	HIGH COUNTRY (IRE) (31) M D Hammond 5 11 5	G Lee
	3	25/0-2	ACES FOUR (IRE) (21) M McKeown 6 10 12	R Johnson
	4	3-P04	BEAVER (AUS) (15) R C Guest 6 10 12	H Oliver
	5	6/	LONER (F423) W Coltherd 7 10 12	D O'Meara
	6	0350-0	MR TWINS (ARG) (32) M Barnes 4 10 12	Ben Orde-Powlett (7)
	7	6-	ONTARIO SUNSET (160) M Moore 4 10 12	D C Costello (7)
	8	00-33	PEARSON GLEN (IRE) (128) J Moffatt 6 10 12	J Crowley
	9	000224	SKIDDAW JONES (8) M Barnes 5 10 12	P Whelan (3)
	10	4-	TIMBUKTU (209) B Storey 4 10 12	B Harding

BETTING: 9-4 Crathorne, 7-2 High Country, 5-1 Skiddaw Jones, 7-1 Aces Four, 8-1 Beaver, Pearson Glen, 16-1 Timbuktu, 20-1 others.

4.50 ALAN MERRIGAN HANDICAP CHASE (CLASS F) £4,500 added 5YO PLUS (2m 110yds)

	1	3F2F/0	LOY'S LAD (IRE) (92) (CD) Miss V Scott 9 11 12	
	2	6352-5	BOB'S BUSTER (117) (CD) R Johnson 9 11 7	K Johnson
	3	031330	RISKY WAY (8) (CD) W Coltherd 9 11 4	G Lee
	4	40300-	MOSS BAWN (239) B Storey 9 11 3	A Dobbin
	5	6-F543	LASCAR DE FERBET (FR) (23) (BF) R Ford 6 11 2	J M Maguire
	6	0F4515	LOULOU NIVERNAIS (FR) (8) (D) M Todhunter 6 11 1	A Dempsey
	7	260004	HE'S HOT RIGHT NOW (NZ) (23) (D) R C Guest 6 10 11	H Oliver
	8	-PP004	PARTNERS CHOICE (IRE) (31) (C) GAMFarrell 8 10 0	James Davies
	9	P-P05P	RATTY'S BAND (23) (D) Mrs L Normile 11 10 0	
	10	4P/6P5	DOTTIE DIGGER (IRE) (9) (D) Miss L Russell 6 10 0	P Buchanan (3)

BETTING: 7-2 Lascar de Ferbet, 4-1 Loulou Nivernais, 11-2 Bob's Buster, 7-1 Risky Way, Partners Choice, 8-1 others.

	16	345203	SAPPHIRE (S
	16	000	DISTANT SHO
	17	00	MANNELLO (
	18	0003	MACS ALL IN

BETTING: 2-1 Outlook, 11

4.00 INTERCASIN (CLASS 5) £

	1		DANISH BLU
	2	3	DIDN'T WE (IF
	3	00	GIFT AID (28
	4	535326	LOUA (11) C
	5		PICADOR S H
	6	03	PRINCE TAMI
	7		PROTESTER
	8		TARANIS SIN
	9	0	AMYGDALA
	10	32	BALIK PEARL
	11	644	DISCOTHEQU
	12		KENTAVR'S

BETTING: 5-2 Didn't We,

4.35 H.B.L.B. HA (7f)

	1	221	OVERLORD
	2	430222	FANTAISISTE
	3	610205	BIRD OVER (
	4	205031	RESPLENDE
	5	460015	DANEHILL DA
	6	010600	AASTRAL MA
	7	6510D3	PAMIR (IRE)
	8	000050	LOUPHOLE
	9	006050	MISS MEGG
	10	411	DIG DEEP (IR
	11	2401	HAYYANI (IR
	12	4-0622	TOP MARK (
	13	-21600	LANGSTON
	14	301004	PIPPA'S DAN

BETTING: 9-2 Dig Deep,

5.05 BOSCH MA added 3YO

	1	00	COEUR D'AL
	2	3-3360	HILLS SPITF
	3	00	MOSTAKBEL
	4	5350-	NATION STA
	5	00-0	LITTLE GANN
	6		BEAUCHAM
	7	06	LOW FOLD F
	8	0-	PATAU (427)
	9		TIPES (39) C
	10		WAR FEATH
	11	56-0	ALWAYS MIN
	12	35	AVICIA (24)
	13	0	GAMBLING S
	14	05	PERFUMERY

BETTING: 7-4 Hills Spitfire

5.40 MOORCRO HANDICAP

	1	304302	SCOTT (13)
	2	31410-	SALUT SAINT
	3	552102	DISTANT CO
			SERRANE

LANCASHIRE 2005

RESULTS SUMMARY

	Place	Won	Lost	Tied	Drew	No Result
County Championship (2nd Division)	1st	7	3		6	
All First-Class Matches		8	3		6	
C & G Trophy	Semi-Finalist					
National League (1st Division)	6th	6	9			1
Twenty20 Cup	Finalist					

COUNTY CHAMPIONSHIP AVERAGES
BATTING AND FIELDING

Cap		M	I	NO	HS	Runs	Avge	100	50	Ct/St
2005	A.Symonds	7	10	–	146	623	62.30	3	1	4
2003	M.B.Loye	16	25	1	200	1198	49.91	4	3	11
2003	I.J.Sutcliffe	14	23	2	153	1007	47.95	2	7	15
2002	S.G.Law	15	24	2	143	858	39.00	3	2	18
1998	A.Flintoff	4	6	1	83	184	36.80	–	2	4
2002	M.J.Chilton	16	26	2	130	847	35.29	3	2	10
1989	W.K.Hegg	15	21	6	77*	502	33.46	–	3	41/5
–	P.J.Horton	5	8	–	99	266	33.25	–	1	1/1
–	B.J.Hodge	7	11	1	110*	331	33.10	1	1	6
2004	D.G.Cork	14	19	2	102*	540	31.76	1	5	12
–	M.J.North	3	4	–	60	101	25.25	–	1	2
–	S.J.Marshall	3	5	2	26*	69	23.00	–	–	–
1994	G.Chapple	14	20	1	82	422	22.21	–	3	5
2000	G.Keedy	8	9	7	34	44	22.00	–	–	1
–	S.I.Mahmood	6	9	–	57	139	15.44	–	1	–
1999	M.Muralitharan	6	8	2	24*	78	13.00	–	–	3
2003	J.M.Anderson	16	19	5	37*	145	10.35	–	–	8
–	K.W.Hogg	2	4	–	9	18	4.50	–	–	2

Also batted: A.R.Crook (1 match) 43; S.P.Crook (1) 5; G.D.Cross (1) 14, 22 (5 ct, 1 st); M.Kartik (2) 0, 7, 4 (1 ct).

BOWLING

	O	M	R	W	Avge	Best	5wI	10wM
M.Muralitharan	233.2	69	540	36	15.00	6-50	4	–
M.Kartik	90	21	260	16	16.25	5-75	2	1
G.Chapple	383.1	98	1010	47	21.48	5-22	2	–
D.G.Cork	395.3	98	1118	43	26.00	4-27	–	–
G.Keedy	222	53	674	23	29.30	6-60	1	–
J.M.Anderson	512.4	99	1813	60	30.21	5-79	1	–
A.Symonds	177	37	484	16	30.25	3-80	–	–
S.I.Mahmood	94.3	13	351	11	31.90	3-21	–	–

Also bowled: M.J.Chilton 5-1-9-1; A.R.Crook 10-2-71-3; S.P.Crook 9-2-28-0; A.Flintoff 20-6-59-1; B.J.Hodge 17-3-35-1; K.W.Hogg 34.2-9-113-3; S.J.Marshall 68.3-9-215-4; M.J.North 56-10-176-2.

The First-Class Averages (pp 129–145) give the records of Lancashire players in all first-class matches for the county (their other opponents being Oxford UCCE), with the exception of A.Flintoff and B.J.Hodge whose full county figures are as above, O.J.Newby whose only first-class appearances were made whilst on loan to Nottinghamshire, and:
  S.P.Crook 2-2-0-66-71-35.50-0-1-0ct. 29-6-80-0.
  S.I.Mahmood 7-10-0-57-177-17.70-0-1-0ct. 128.2-22-450-14-32.14-3/21.

LANCASHIRE RECORDS

FIRST-CLASS CRICKET

Highest Total	For 863		v	Surrey	The Oval	1990
	V 707-9d		by	Surrey	The Oval	1990
Lowest Total	For 25		v	Derbyshire	Manchester	1871
	V 22		by	Glamorgan	Liverpool	1924
Highest Innings	For 424	A.C.MacLaren	v	Somerset	Taunton	1895
	V 315*	T.W.Hayward	for	Surrey	The Oval	1898

Highest Partnership for each Wicket

1st	368	A.C.MacLaren/R.H.Spooner	v	Glos	Liverpool	1903
2nd	371	F.B.Watson/G.E.Tyldesley	v	Surrey	Manchester	1928
3rd	364	M.A.Atherton/N.H.Fairbrother	v	Surrey	The Oval	1990
4th	358	S.P.Titchard/G.D.Lloyd	v	Essex	Chelmsford	1996
5th	360	S.G.Law/C.L.Hooper	v	Warwicks	Birmingham	2003
6th	278	J.Iddon/H.R.W.Butterworth	v	Sussex	Manchester	1932
7th	248	G.D.Lloyd/I.D.Austin	v	Yorkshire	Leeds	1997
8th	158	J.Lyon/R.M.Ratcliffe	v	Warwicks	Manchester	1979
9th	142	L.O.S.Poidevin/A.Kermode	v	Sussex	Eastbourne	1907
10th	173	J.Briggs/R.Pilling	v	Surrey	Liverpool	1885

Best Bowling	For 10-46	W.Hickton	v	Hampshire	Manchester	1870
(Innings)	V 10-40	G.O.B.Allen	for	Middlesex	Lord's	1929
Best Bowling	For 17-91	H.Dean	v	Yorkshire	Liverpool	1913
(Match)	V 16-65	G.Giffen	for	Australians	Manchester	1886

Most Runs – Season	2633	J.T.Tyldesley	(av 56.02)	1901
Most Runs – Career	34222	G.E.Tyldesley	(av 45.20)	1909-36
Most 100s – Season	11	C.Hallows		1928
Most 100s – Career	90	G.E.Tyldesley		1909-36
Most Wkts – Season	198	E.A.McDonald	(av 18.55)	1925
Most Wkts – Career	1816	J.B.Statham	(av 15.12)	1950-68
Most Career W-K Dismissals	925†	G.Duckworth	(635 ct/290 st)	1923-38
Most Career Catches in the Field	556	K.J.Grieves		1949-64

† *W.K.Hegg (1987-2005) has retired with the second-highest aggregate of 919 dismissals (825 ct; 94 st)*

LIMITED-OVERS CRICKET

Highest Total	CGT	381-3		v	Herts	Radlett	1999
	NL	310-7		v	Somerset	Taunton	2003
	T20	217-4		v	Surrey	The Oval	2005
Lowest Total	CGT	59		v	Worcs	Worcester	1963
	NL	68		v	Yorkshire	Leeds	2000
		68		v	Surrey	The Oval	2002
	T20	91		v	Derbyshire	Manchester	2003
Highest Innings	CGT	162*	A.R.Crook	v	Bucks	Wormsley	2005
	NL	143	A.Flintoff	v	Essex	Chelmsford	1999
	T20	101	S.G.Law	v	Yorkshire	Manchester	2005
Best Bowling	CGT	6-18	G.Chapple	v	Essex	Lord's	1996
	NL	6-25	G.Chapple	v	Yorkshire	Leeds	1998
	T20	4-17	B.J.Hodge	v	Derbyshire	Manchester	2005

LEICESTERSHIRE

Formation of Present Club: 25 March 1879
Inaugural First-Class Match: 1894
Colours: Dark Green and Scarlet
Badge: Gold Running Fox on Green Ground
County Champions: (3) 1975, 1996, 1998
Gillette/NatWest/C & G Trophy Winners: (0); best –
finalist 1992, 2001
Benson and Hedges Cup Winners: (3) 1972, 1975, 1985
National League (Div 1) Winners: (0); best – 2nd 2001
Sunday League Champions: (2) 1974, 1977
Twenty20 Cup Winners: (1) 2004
Match Awards: CGT 49; BHC 79

Operations Manager: Angus J.Mackay, County Ground, Grace Road, Leicester LE2
8AD • Tel: 0871 282 1879 • Fax: 0871 282 1873 • Email:
enquiries@leicestershireccc.co.uk • Web: www.leicestershireccc.co.uk

Director of Cricket: T.Boon. **Head Coach/Academy Director**: P.Whitticase. **Captain**:
J.N.Snape. **Vice-Captain**: D.L.Maddy. **Overseas Players**: Mohammad Asif and
D.Mongia. **2006 Beneficiary**: D.L.Maddy. **HeadGroundsman**: A.Whiteman. **Scorer**:
G.A.York. ‡ New registration. NQ Not qualified for England.

ALLENBY, James (Christ Church GS, Perth), b Perth, W Australia 12 Sep 19182. RHB,
RM. Durham CB 2003. Leicestershire 2005 (no f-c appearances). LO HS 7* (NL). T20 HS
17.

BROAD, Stuart Christopher John (Oakham S), b Nottingham 24 Jun 1986. 6'6". LHB,
RMF. Son of B.C.Broad (Glos, Notts, OFS and England 1979-94). Debut 2005. HS 31 and
BB 4-64 v Worcs (Worcester) 2005. LO HS – . LO BB 2-35 v Kent (Manchester) 2005
(NL).

CUMMINS, Ryan Anthony Gilbert (Wallington CGS; Loughborough U), b Sutton, Surrey
14 Apr 1984. 6'4". RHB, RM. Loughborough UCCE 2003-05. Leicestershire debut 2005.
HS 26 LU v Sussex (Hove) 2005. Le HS 4*. BB 3-32 v Lancs (Leicester) 2005.

HABIB, Aftab (Millfield S; Taunton S), b Reading, Berks 7 Feb 1972. Cousin of Zahid
Sadiq (Surrey and Derbys 1988-90). 5'11". RHB, RM. Middlesex 1992 (one match).
Leicestershire 1995-2001, 2005; cap 1998. Essex 2002-04; cap 2002. **Tests**: 2 (1999); HS 19
v NZ (Lord's) 1999. F-c Tours (Eng A): WI 2000-01 (*part*); NZ 1999-00; B 1999-00. 1000
runs (2); most – 1055 (1999). HS 215 v Worcs (Leicester) 1996. BB 1-10. Award: BHC 1.
LO HS 111 v Durham (Chester-le-St) 1997 (BHC). LO BB 2-5 v Ire (Dublin) 1999. T20 HS
16*.

NQ**HENDERSON, Claude** William (Worcester HS), b Worcester, South Africa 14 Jun
1972. Elder brother of J.M.Henderson (Boland, North West and Transvaal 1994-95 to date).
6'1½". RHB, SLA. Boland 1990-91 to 1997-98. W Province 1998-99 to 2003-04. Leicestershire debut/cap 2004 (first Kolpak registration). **Tests** (SA): 7 (2001-02 to 2002-03); HS
30 and BB 4-116 v A (Adelaide) 2001-02. **LOI** (SA): 4 (2001-02); HS – ; BB 4-17 v Z
(HarareaRAhhhhh) 2001-02. F-c Tours (SA): A 2001-02; SL 1998-99 (SA A); Z 2001-02.
HS 71 WP v KZ-Natal (Cape Town) 2003-04. Le HS 63 v Glamorgan (Leicester 2004) – on
UK debut. BB 7-57 Boland v EP (Paarl) 1994-95. Le HS 7-74 v Durham (Leicester) 2004.
LO HS 32 Worcs CB v Kent CB (Kidderminster) 2000. LO BB 6-29 Boland v Easterns
(Paarl) 1997-98. T20 HS 9*. T20 BB 3-26.

LIDDLE, Christopher John (Nunthorpe CS), b Middlesbrough, Yorks 1 Feb 1984. 6'5". RHB, LFM. Debut 2005 – awaiting CC debut. HS – .

MADDY, Darren Lee (Wreake Valley C), b Leicester 23 May 1974. 5'9". RHB, RM/OB. Debut 1994; cap 1996; benefit 2006. **Tests**: 3 (1999 to 1999-00); HS 24 v SA (Durban) 1999-00. **LOI**: 8 (1998 to 1999-00); HS 53 v Z (Harare) 1999-00. F-c Tours (Eng A): SA 1996-97 (Le), 1998-99, 1999-00 (Eng); SL 1997-98; Z 1998-99; K 1997-98. 1000 runs (4); most – 1187 (2002). HS 229* v LU (Leicester) 2003. CC HS 162 v Durham (Darlington) 1998. BB 5-37 v Hants (Southampton) 2002. Awards: CGT 1; BHC 8 (inc 5 in 1998). LO HS 151 v Minor C (Leicester) 1998 (BHC). LO BB 4-16 v Somerset (Taunton) 2000 (NL). T20 HS 111. T20 BB 2-18.

MASTERS, David Daniel (Fort Luton HS; Mid Kent CHE), b Chatham, Kent 22 Apr 1978. Son of K.D.Masters (Kent 1981-85, Surrey 1986). 6'4". RHB, RMF. Kent 2000-02. Leicestershire debut 2003. HS 119 v Sussex (Hove) 2003. BB 6-27 K v Durham (Tunbridge Wells) 2000. Le BB 6-74 v Durham (Chester-le-St) 2005. LO HS 27 v Kent (Canterbury) 2003 (NL). LO BB 5-20 K v Durham (Maidstone) 2002 (NL). LO BB 2-16 v Warwks (Birmingham) 2005 (CGT). T20 HS 7. T20 BB 3-7.

MAUNDERS, John Kenneth (Ashford HS; Spelthorne C), b Ashford, Middx 4 Apr 1981. 5'10". LHB, RM. Middlesex 1999 (one non-CC match); 2nd XI debut aged 16y 19d. Leicestershire debut 2003. HS 171 v Surrey (Leicester) 2003. BB 4-28 v Lancs (Manchester) 2005. LO HS 49 M v Glamorgan(Cardiff) 2001 (NL). T20 HS 10.

NQ**MONGIA, Dinesh**, b Chandigarh, India 17 Apr 1977. LHB, SLA. Punjab 1995-96 to date. Lancashire 2004. Leicestershire debut 2005. **LOI** (I): 49 (2000-01 to 2004-05); HS 159* v Z (Gauhati) 2001-02; BB 3-31 v Z (Mohali) 2001-02. F-c Tours (I): E 2002; WI 2001-02; SL 2001. 1000 runs (0+1): 1041 (2000-01). HS 308* Punjab v Jammu & Kashmir (Jullundur) 2000-01. Le HS 164 v Durham (Chester-le-St) 2005. BB 4-34 Punjab v Kerala (Palghat) 2003-04. CC BB 2-8 v Worcs (Leicester) 2005. LO HS 159* (*see LOI*). LO BB 4-12 v Somerset (Oakham) 2005 (NL). T20 HS 50. T20 BB 3-19.

‡NQ**MOHAMMAD ASIF**, b Sheikhupura, Pakistan 20 Dec 1982. LHB, RFM. Debut 2000-01. Khan Research Labs. Lahore. Sheikhupura. **Tests**: 3 (2004-05 to 2005-06); HS 12* v A (Sydney) 2004-05 – on debut; BB 4-78 (7-126 match) v I (Karachi) 2005-06. **LOI** (P): 4 (2005-06); HS 2; BB 3-30 v I (Peshawar) 2005-06. Tour (P): A 2004-05. HS 42 KRL v Allied Bank (Karachi) 2002-03. BB 7-35 Sialkot v Multan (Multan) 2004-05. LO HS 12* Pakistan A v Sri Lanka A (Colombo) 2004-05. LO BB 4-30 KRL v Rawalpindi (Rawalpindi) 2001-02. T20 HS 12. T20 BB 5-11.

NEW, Thomas James (Quarrydale S), b Sutton in Ashfield, Notts 18 Jan 1985. 5'10". LHB, WK. Debut 2004 HS 89 v Derbys (Leicester) 2005. LO HS 47 v Yorks (Leicester) 2005 (NL).

NIXON, Paul Andrew (Ullswater HS, Penrith), b Carlisle, Cumberland 21 Oct 1970. 6'0". LHB, WK. Leicestershire 1989-99, 2003; cap 2000. Kent 2000-02; cap 2000. Cumberland 1987. MCC YC. F-c Tours: SA 1996-97 (Le); I 1994-95 (Eng A); P 2000-01; SL 2000-01 (*no f-c*). 1000 runs (1): 1046 (1994). HS 134* K v Hants (Canterbury) 2000. Le HS 131 v Hants (Leicester) 1994. BB – Awards: CGT 1; BHC 3. LO HS 101 v SL A (Galle) 1998-99. LO BB – T20 HS 43.

ROBINSON, Darren David John (Tabor HS; Braintree; Chelmsford CFE), b Braintree, Essex 2 Mar 1973. 5'10½". RHB, RMF. Essex 1993-2003; cap 1997. Leicestershire debut 2004. 1000 runs (3): most – 1474 (2002). HS 200 Ex v NZ (Chelmsford) 1999. CC HS 175 Ex v Glos (Gloucester) 2002. Le HS 154 v Yorks (Leicester 2004). BB 1-7 (Ex). Awards: BHC 2. LO HS 137* Ex v Sussex (Hove) 1998 (BHC). LO BB (Ex)1-7 (SL). T20 HS 7*.

SADLER, John Leonard (St Thomas A'Beckett S, Sandal), b Dewsbury, Yorks 19 Nov 1981. 5'11". LHB, LB. Yorkshire 2nd XI 2000-02. Leicestershire debut 2003. HS 145 v Surrey (Leicester) 2003 and 145 v Sussex (Hove) 2003. BB 1-22 (not CC). LO HS 88 v Yorks (Leeds) 2004 (NL). T20 HS 73. T20 BB

SNAPE, Jeremy Nicholas (Denstone C; Durham U), b Stoke-on-Trent, Staffs 27 Apr 1973. 5'8½". RHB, OB. Northamptonshire 1992-97. Combined U 1994. Gloucestershire 1999-2002; cap 1999. Leicestershire debut 2003. **LOI**: 10 (2001-02 to 2002-03); HS 38 v I (Madras) 2001-02; BB 3-43 v Z (Bulawayo) 2001-02. F-c Tour: Z 1994-95 (Nh). HS 131 Gs v Sussex (Cheltenham) 2001. Le HS 66 v Notts (Leicester) 2004. BB 5-65 Nh v Durham (Northampton) 1995. Le BB 3-108 v Surrey (Leicester) 2003. Awards: BHC 3. LO HS 104* Gs v Notts (Nottingham) 2001 (NL). LO BB 5-32 Nh v Leics (Northampton) 1997 (BHC). T20 HS 39*. T20 BB 3-14.

RELEASED/RETIRED

(Registered players who made a first-class appearance in 2005)

NQ**ACKERMAN, Hylton** Deon ('HD') (Rondebosch BHS), b Cape Town, South Africa 14 Feb 1973. 5'11". Son of H.M.Ackerman (Border, NE Transvaal, Natal, Northants, W Province 1963-81). RHB, RM. W Province 1993-94 to 2002-03. Gauteng 2003-04. Lions 2004-05. Leicestershire debut/captain/cap 2005 (Kolpak registration). **Tests** (SA): 4 (1997-98): HS 57 v P (Durban) 1997-98 – on debut. F-c Tours (SA): E 1996 (SA A); A 1995-96 (WP); SL 1995-96 (SA U-24), 1998-99; Z 2001-02, 1000 runs (1+1); most – 1373 (1997-98). HS 202* WP v Northerns (Pretoria) 1997-98. Le HS 125 v Derbys (Leicester) 2005. LO HS 114* v Sussex (Hove) 2005 (NL). T20 HS 80*.

BRIGNULL, David Stephen (Lancaster BSS; Wyggeston & Queen Elizabeth I SFC), b Forest Gate, London 27 Nov 1981. 6'4". RHB, RMF. Leicestershire 2003-05. HS 46 v Middx (Leicester) 2003. BB 3-36 v Durham UCCE (Leicester) 2005. CC BB 2-30 v Kent (Canterbury) 2003 – on debut. LO HS (Leics CB) 9* (NWT). LO BB 3-40 v Worcs (Oakham) 2003 (NL).

DeFREITAS, Phillip Anthony Jason (Willesden HS, London), b Scotts Head, Dominica 18 Feb 1966. 6'0". RHB, RFM. UK resident since 1976. Leicestershire 1985-88, 2000-05; cap 1986; captain 2003-04 (*part*); benefit 2004. Lancashire 1989-93; cap 1989. Boland 1993-94 and 1995-96. Derbyshire 1994-99; cap 1994; captain 1997 (*part*). *Wisden* 1991. MCC YC. **Tests**: 44 (1986-87 to 1995-96); HS 88 v A (Adelaide) 1994-95; BB 7-70 v SL (Lord's) 1991. **LOI**: 103 (1986-87 to 1997); HS 67 v SL (Faisalabad) 1995-96; BB 4-35 v A (Adelaide) 1986-87. F-c Tours: A 1986-87, 1990-91, 1994-95; WI 1989-90; NZ 1987-88, 1991-92; P 1987-88; I 1992-93; Z 1988-89 (La). HS 123* v Lancs (Leicester) 2000. 50 wkts (14); most – 94 (1986). Took his 1000th f-c wicket 1999. BB 7-21 La v Middx (Lord's) 1989. Le BB 7-44 (13-86 match) v Essex (Southend) 1986. Hat-trick 1994. Awards: CGT 6; BHC 4. LO HS 90 v Glos (Bristol) 2003 (NL). LO BB 5-13 La v Cumb (Kendal) 1989 (NWT). T20 HS 18. T20 BB 3-39.

GIBSON, O.D. – *see DURHAM*.

NQ**KREJZA, Jason** John, b Newtown, Sydney, Australia 14 Jan 1983. RHB, OB. New South Wales 2004-05 to date. Leicestershire 2005 (one match). HS 63 NSW v Vic (Melbourne) 2004-05. Le HS 38 v A (Leicester) 2005. BB 2-11 NSW v Vic (Melbourne) 2004-05. LO HS 19 NSW vTas (Newcastle) 2004-05. LO BB 3-45 NSW v Tas (Newcastle) 2004-05.

NQ**ROGERS, C.J.H.** – *see NORTHAMPTONSHIRE*

NQ**WILLOUGHBY, C.M.** – *see SOMERSET*

C.E.Dagnall and N.J.Ferraby left the staff without making a first-class appearance in 2005.

LEICESTERSHIRE 2005

RESULTS SUMMARY

	Place	Won	Lost	Tied	Drew	No Result
County Championship (2nd Division)	7th	3	6		7	
All First-Class Matches		3	6		9	
C & G Trophy	2nd Round					
National League (2nd Division)	4th	10	7			1
Twenty20 Cup	Semi-Finalist					

COUNTY CHAMPIONSHIP AVERAGES
BATTING AND FIELDING

Cap		M	I	NO	HS	Runs	Avge	100	50	Ct/St
–	C.J.L.Rogers	2	4	–	93	176	44.00	–	1	4
–	D.D.J.Robinson	15	25	1	139	1027	42.79	4	3	12
2005	H.D.Ackerman	16	27	2	125	1027	41.08	2	7	9
–	D.Mongia	10	16	–	164	627	39.18	1	4	5
–	T.J.New	5	8	–	89	306	38.25	–	2	4
1994	P.A.Nixon	16	27	7	85	708	35.40	–	6	40/4
1998	A.Habib	12	20	2	153*	623	34.61	1	2	8
–	J.L.Sadler	4	7	1	56*	180	30.00	–	2	4
–	J.K.Maunders	14	23	–	148	607	26.39	1	2	6
–	J.N.Snape	2	4	–	31	101	25.25	–	–	–
2004	C.W.Henderson	14	20	3	55	396	23.29	–	2	6
1996	D.L.Maddy	14	24	–	53	536	22.33	–	1	14
–	D.D.Masters	11	14	6	36	172	21.50	–	–	4
2004	O.D.Gibson	14	23	4	91	349	18.36	–	2	2
–	S.C.J.Broad	8	10	2	31	96	12.00	–	–	1
1986	P.A.J.DeFreitas	4	7	–	20	62	8.85	–	–	–
–	C.M.Willoughby	13	16	4	16*	68	5.66	–	–	2

Also batted: R.A.G.Cummins (2 matches) 4*, 1*, 1 (1 ct).

BOWLING

	O	M	R	W	Avge	Best	5wI	10wM
D.D.Masters	264.2	80	739	31	23.83	6-74	1	–
S.C.J.Broad	177.1	31	714	27	26.44	4-64	–	–
J.K.Maunders	84	15	295	11	26.81	4-28	–	–
P.A.J.DeFreitas	111	21	406	12	33.83	4-76	–	–
O.D.Gibson	480.3	83	1605	44	36.47	6-56	1	–
C.M.Willoughby	412.5	96	1308	33	39.63	4-92	–	–
D.L.Maddy	181	36	568	13	43.69	4-65	–	–
C.W.Henderson	494.2	107	1356	29	46.75	5-63	1	–
Also bowled:								
R.A.G.Cummins	42	9	136	8	17.00	3-32		
D.Mongia	76.2	14	209	5	41.80	2- 8		

D.D.J.Robinson 2-0-3-0; C.J.L.Rogers 3-0-9-0; J.N.Snape 11-1-39-1.

The First-Class Averages (pp 129–145) give the records of Leicestershire players in all first-class matches for the county (their other opponents being the Australians and Durham UCCE), with the exception of R.A.G.Cummins whose full county figures are as above.

LEICESTERSHIRE RECORDS

FIRST-CLASS CRICKET

Highest Total	For 701-4d		v	Worcs	Worcester	1906
	V 761-6d		by	Essex	Chelmsford	1990
Lowest Total	For 25		v	Kent	Leicester	1912
	V 24		by	Glamorgan	Leicester	1971
	24		by	Oxford U	Oxford	1985
Highest Innings	For 302*	B.J.Hodge	v	Notts	Nottingham	2003
	V 341	G.H.Hirst	for	Yorkshire	Leicester	1905

Highest Partnership for each Wicket

1st	390	B.Dudleston/J.F.Steele	v	Derbyshire	Leicester	1979
2nd	289*	J.C.Balderstone/D.I.Gower	v	Essex	Leicester	1981
3rd	436*	D.L.Maddy/B.J.Hodge	v	L'boro UCCE	Leicester	2003
4th	290*	P.Willey/T.J.Boon	v	Warwicks	Leicester	1984
5th	322	B.F.Smith/P.V.Simmons	v	Notts	Worksop	1998
6th	284	P.V.Simmons/P.A.Nixon	v	Durham	Chester-le-St	1996
7th	219*	J.D.R.Benson/P.Whitticase	v	Hampshire	Bournemouth	1991
8th	172	P.A.Nixon/D.J.Millns	v	Lancashire	Manchester	1996
9th	160	W.W.Odell/R.T.Crawford	v	Worcs	Leicester	1902
10th	228	R.Illingworth/K.Higgs	v	Northants	Leicester	1977

Best Bowling	For 10- 18	G.Geary	v	Glamorgan	Pontypridd	1929
(Innings)	V 10- 32	H.Pickett	for	Essex	Leyton	1895
Best Bowling	For 16- 96	G.Geary	v	Glamorgan	Pontypridd	1929
(Match)	V 16-102	C.Blythe	for	Kent	Leicester	1909

Most Runs – Season	2446	L.G.Berry	(av 52.04)	1937
Most Runs – Career	30143	L.G.Berry	(av 30.32)	1924-51
Most 100s – Season	7	L.G.Berry		1937
	7	W.Watson		1959
	7	B.F.Davison		1982
Most 100s – Career	45	L.G.Berry		1924-51
Most Wkts – Season	170	J.E.Walsh	(av 18.96)	1948
Most Wkts – Career	2130	W.E.Astill	(av 23.19)	1906-39
Most Career W-K Dismissals	903	R.W.Tolchard	(794 ct/109 st)	1965-83
Most Career Catches in the Field	427	M.R.Hallam		1950-70

LIMITED-OVERS CRICKET

Highest Total	CGT	406-5		v	Berkshire	Leicester	1996
	NL	344-4		v	Durham	Chester-le-St	1996
	T20	221-3		v	Yorkshire	Leeds	2004
Lowest Total	CGT	56		v	Northants	Leicester	1964
	NL	36		v	Sussex	Leicester	1973
	T20	137		v	Derbyshire	Derby	2005
Highest Innings	CGT	201	V.J.Wells	v	Berkshire	Leicester	1996
	NL	154*	B.J.Hodge	v	Sussex	Horsham	2004
	T20	111	D.L.Maddy	v	Yorkshire	Leeds	2004
Best Bowling	CGT	6-16	C.M.Willoughby	v	Somerset	Leicester	2005
	NL	6-17	K.Higgs	v	Glamorgan	Leicester	1973
	T20	4-22	C.E.Dagnall	v	Notts	Leicester	2004

MIDDLESEX

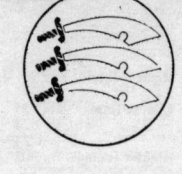

Formation of Present Club: 2 February 1864
Inaugural First-Class Match: 1864
Colours: Blue
Badge: Three Seaxes
County Champions (since 1890): (10) 1903, 1920, 1921, 1947, 1976, 1980, 1982, 1985, 1990, 1993
Joint Champions: (2) 1949, 1977
Gillette/NatWest/C & G Trophy Winners: (4) 1977, 1980, 1984, 1988
Benson and Hedges Cup Winners: (2) 1983, 1986
National League (Div 1) Winners: (0); best – 1st (Div 2) 2004
Sunday League Winners: (1) 1992
Twenty20 Cup Winners: (0); best – Quarter-Finalist 2005
Match Awards: CGT 63; BHC 62

Secretary: Vincent J.Codrington, Lord's Cricket Ground, London NW8 8QN •
Tel: 020 7289 1300 • Fax: 020 7289 5831 • Email: enquiries@ middlesexccc.com • Web:
www.middlesexccc.com

Head Coach: J.E.Emburey. **Assistant Coach**: J.C.Pooley. **Captain**: B.L.Hutton.
Vice-Captain: no appointment. **Overseas Player**: S.B.Styris. **2006 Beneficiary**: none.
Head Groundsman: M.Hunt. **Scorer**: D.K.Shelley. ‡ New registration. NQ Not qualified
for England.

‡NQALI, Syed Mohammad Bukhari (Punjab C of Commerce), b Bahawalpur, Pakistan
8 Nov 1973. 6'0". Nephew of Taslim Arif (Pakistan 1979-80 to 1980-81). British passport.
RHB, LFM. Lahore 1993-94. Railways 1993-94. Islamabad 1994-95. United Bank 1994-95.
Rawalpindi 1995-96 to 1998-99. ADBP 1995-96 to 1998-99. Bahawalpur 1998-99. 55 f-c
matches in Pakistan before his UK debut in 2002. Derbyshire 2002-04. HS 92 Bahawalpur v
Lahore (Rahim Yar Khan) 1998-99. CC HS 53 De v Durham (Derby) 2002 – on debut. 50
wkts (0+1): 56 (1993-94). BB 6-37 Railways v National Bank (Faisalabad) 1993-94. CC BB
4-75 De v Glam (Cardiff) 2004. LO HS 19 De v Lancs (Manchester) 2002 (CGT). LO BB
4-34 Railways v United Bank (Karachi) 1993-94. T 20 HS – . T20 BB 3-24.

BETTS, Melvyn Morris (Fyndoune CS, Sacriston), b Sacriston, Co Durham 26 Mar 1975.
5'10". RHB, RFM. Durham 1993-2000; cap 1998. Warwickshire 2001-03; cap 2001.
Middlesex debut 2004. F-c Tour (Eng A): Z 1998-99. HS 73 Wa v Lancs (Birmingham)
2003. M HS 36* v Sussex (Hove) 2005. BB 9-64 (Durham record; 13-143 match) v
Northants (Northampton) 1997. M BB 5-89 v Worcs (Worcester) 2004. Award: BHC 1. LO
HS 21 Du v Hants (Chester-le-St) 1997 (SL). LO BB 4-15 v Wales MC (Lamphey) 2004
(CGT). T20 HS 13*. T20 BB 2-51.

COMPTON, Nicholas Richard Denis (Harrow S), b Durban, South Africa 26 Jun 1983.
6'1". Grandson of D.C.S.Compton (Middlesex, England, Holkar, Europeans, Commonwealth and Cavaliers 1936-64); great-nephew of L.H.Compton (Middlesex 1938-56). RHB,
OB. Middlesex staff 2002. Debut 2004. Hs 56* v CU (Cambridge) 2005. CC HS 40 v Worcs
(Worcester) 2004 – on CC debut. LO HS 86* v Lancs (Shenley) 2002 (NL). T20 HS 17.

DALRYMPLE, James William Murray (Radley C; St Peter's C, Oxford), b Nairobi, Kenya
21 Jan 1981. 5'11". RHB, OB. Oxford UCCE 2001-02; captain 2002; blue 2001-02. British
U 2002-03. Middlesex debut 2001; cap 2004. HS 244 v Surrey (Oval) 2004. BB 5-49 OU v
CU (Cambridge) 2003. M BB 4-53 v Hants (Southgate) 2005. Awards: CGT 2. LO HS 107
v Glamorgan(Lord's) 2004 (CGT). LO BB 4-14 v Essex (Southgate) 2001 (NL). T20 HS 39.
T20 BB 2-26.

FINN, Steven Thomas (Parmiter's S, Garston), b Watford, Herts 4 Apr 1989. 6'5½". RHB,
RMF. Debut 2005. Awaiting CC debut. HS – and BB 1-16 v CU (Cambridge) 2005.

GODLEMAN, Billy Ashley (Islington Green S), b Islington, London 11 Feb 1989. 6'3". LHB, LB. Debut 2005. Awaiting CC debut. HS 69* v CU (Cambridge) 2005.

HUTTON, Benjamin Leonard (Radley C; Durham U), b Johannesburg, South Africa 29 Jan 1977. Elder son of R.A.Hutton (Yorkshire, Transvaal & England 1962 to 1975-76); grandson of Sir Leonard (Yorkshire and England 1934-60); elder brother of O.R.Hutton (OU 2004). 6'2". LHB, RMF. British U 1998-99. Middlesex debut 1999; cap 2003; captain 2005-. 1000 runs (2); most – 1129 (2004). HS 152 v Kent (Lord's) 2005. BB 4-37 v SL (Shenley) 2002. CC BB 3-14 v Northants (Lord's) 2004. LO HS 77 v Durham (Chester-le-St) 2001 (NL). LO BB 5-45 v Derbys (Southgate) 2001 (NL). T20 HS 27*. T20 BB 2-21.

JONES, Craig Michael Parry, b Tamworth, NSW, Australia 13 Apr 1978. RHB, RMF. Debut 2005. Awaiting CC debut. HS – and BB 2-26 v CU (Cambridge) 2005. LO HS 0*. LO BB 1-47.

JOYCE, Edmund Christopher (Presentation C, Bray, Co Wicklow; Trinity C, Dublin), b Dublin, Ireland 22 Sep 1978. 5'11". LHB, RM. Ireland 1997 to date. Middlesex debut 1999; cap 2002. Qualifies for England during 2005. 1000 runs (4); most 1668 (2005). HS 192 v Notts (Lord's) 2005. BB 2-34 v CU (Cambridge) 2004. CC BB 1-4. Award: CGT 1. LO HS 115* Ireland v UAE (Belfast) 2005. LO BB 2-10 v Notts (Nottingham) 2003 (NL). T20 HS 31.

KEEGAN, Chad Blake (Durban HS), b Sandton, near Johannesburg, South Africa 30 Jul 1979. 6'1". RHB, RF. Debut 2001; cap 2003. MCC YC. Qualified for England March 2005. HS 44 v Surrey (Oval) 2004. 50 wkts (1): 63 (2003). BB 6-114 v Leics (Southgate) 2003.LO HS 50 v Notts (Lord's) 2003 (NL). LO BB 6-33 v Notts (Nottingham) 2005 (NL). T20 HS 42. T20 BB 3-34.

‡**NQLOUW, Johann** (Fraserburg HS; Port Elizabeth U), b Cape Town, South Africa 12 Apr 1979. 6'2". RHB, RFM. Griqualand West 2000-01 to 2002-03. E Province 2003-04. Dolphins 2004-05. Northamptonshire 2004-05 (Kolpak registration). HS 124 EP v Boland (Pt Elizabeth) 2003-04. CC HS 64 Nh v Somerset (Taunton) 2005. 50 wkts (1): 60 (2004). BB 6-51 Nh v Essex (Northampton) 2005. LO HS 72 GW v Northerns (Kimberley) 2000-01. LO BB 5-27 Nh v Warwks (Northampton) 2004 (NL). T20 HS 17. T20 BB 3-25.

NQ**MORGAN, Eoin** Joseph Gerard, b Dublin, Ireland 10 Sep 1986. LHB, RM. British passport. Ireland 2004-05. Middlesex summer contract 2004. Ireland U-19 in 2003-04 youth world cup. Awaiting County debut. HS 151 Ireland v UAE (Windhoek) 2005 LO HS (Ire) 93 v Ireland v Bermuda (Belfast) 2005

‡**NAMBIAR**, Aneil Padman ('**Johnny**'), b Trivandrum, India 2 Mar 1984. RHB, RM. Awaiting f-c debut. LO HS (Oxon) 0 (CGT).

NASH, David Charles (Sunbury Manor S; Malvern C), b Chertsey, Surrey 19 Jan 1978. 5'8". RHB, occ LB, WK. Debut 1997; cap 2000. F-c Tour: SL 1997-98 (Eng A). HS 114 v Somerset (Lord's) 1998. BB 1-8. LO HS 67 v Sussex (Lord's) 2002 (BHC).

PEPLOE, Christopher Thomas (Twyford C of E HS; Surrey U, Roehampton), b Hammersmith, London 26 Apr 1981. 6'4". LHB, SLA. MCC YC. Debut 2003. HS 42 v Sussex. (Lord's) 2005. BB 4-65 v Sussex (Hove) 2004. LO HS 14* v Hants (Southampton) 2005 (NL). LO BB 4-38 v Glamorgan (Cardiff) 2005 (NL). T20 HS 3* T20 BB 3-35.

POYNTER, Andrew David, b Hammersmith, London 25 Apr 1987. RHB, OB. Debut 2005. Awaiting CC debut. HS 1.

‡**RANKIN, William** Boyd, b Londonderry, Co Derry, N Ireland 5 Jul 1984. RHB, RMF. Brother of R.J.Rankin (Ireland U-19). Summer contract 2004-05. Ireland U-19 in 2003-04 youth world cup. Awaiting f-c debut.

RICHARDSON, Alan (Alleyne's HS; Stafford CFE; Durham U), b Newcastle-under-Lyme, Staffs 6 May 1975. 6'2". RHB, RMF. Derbyshire 1995 (one match). Warwickshire 1999-2004, cap 2002. Middlesex debut/cap 2005, taking 7-113 v Notts (Lord's) on debut. Staffordshire 1996-98. HS 91 Wa v Hants (Birmingham) 2002 – adding 214 for 10th wicket with N.V.Knight. M HS 25 v Notts (Nottingham) 2005. 50 wkts (1): 57 (2005). BB 8-46 Wa v Sussex (Birmingham) 2002. M BB 7-113 (*see above*). LO HS 21* v Lancs (Lord's) 2005 (NL). LO BB 5-35 Wa v Staffs (Stone) 2002 (CGT). T20 HS 6*. T20 BB 3-13.

SAVILL, Thomas Edward (Bilborough C; Homerton C, Cambridge), b Sheffield, Yorks 16 May 1983. 6'6". RHB, RFM. Cambridge UCCE 2002-03. Nottinghamshire 2002 – no CC appearance. Middlesex summer contract 2003-05 – no 1st XI appearances. HS 59 CU v CU (Cambridge) 2005. BB 3-86 CU v Essex (Cambridge) 2003. LO HS 35* Notts CB v Oxon (Oxford) 2001 (CGT). LO BB 1-45 (Notts CB – CGT).

SCOTT, Ben James Matthew (Whitton S, Richmond; Richmond C), b Isleworth, Middx 4 Aug 1981. 5'8". RHB, WK. Surrey 2003. Middlesex debut 2004. HS 101* v Northants (Lord's) 2004. LO HS 50* v Essex (Southend) 2005 (NL). T20 HS 17*.

SHAH, Owais Alam (Isleworth & Syon S), b Karachi, Pakistan 22 Oct 1978. 6'0". RHB, OB. Debut 1996; cap 2000; captain 2004 (*part*). YC 2001. **LOI**: 15 (2001 to 2002-03); HS 62 v P (Lord's) 2001. F-c Tours (Eng A): A 1996-97; SL 1997-98. 1000 runs (5); most 1728 (2005). HS 203 v Derbys (Southgate) 2001. BB 3-33 v Glos (Bristol) 1999. Award: BHC 1. LO HS 134 v Sussex (Arundel) 1999 (NL). LO BB 2-2 v Glamorgan(Cardiff) 1998 (BHC). T20 HS 79.

‡SILVERWOOD, Christopher Eric Wilfred (Garforth CS), b Pontefract, Yorks 5 Mar 1975. 6'1". RHB, RFM. Yorkshire 1993-2005; cap 1996; benefit 2004. YC 1996. **Tests**: 6 (1996-97 to 2002-03); HS 10 v A (Perth) 2002-03; BB 5-91 v SA (Cape Town) 1999-00. **LOI**: 7 (1996-97 to 2001-02); HS 12 v NZ (Auckland) 1996-97; BB 3-43 v Z (Bulawayo) 2001-02. F-c Tours: A 2002-03 (*part*); SA 1999-00 (*part*); WI 1997-98, 2000-01 (Eng A); NZ 1996-97; Z 1996-97 (Y), 1996-97. HS 80 Y v Durham (Chester-le-St) 2005. 50 wkts (2); most – 59 (1999). BB 7-93 (12-148 match) Y v Kent (Leeds) 1997. Awards: CGT 2; BHC 2. LO HS 61 Y v Northants (Northampton) 2002 (CGT). LO BB 5-28 Y v Scot (Leeds) 1996 (BHC). T20 HS 13*. T20 BB 2-22.

SMITH, Edward Thomas (Tonbridge S; Peterhouse, Cambridge), b Pembury, Kent 19 Jul 1977. 6'2". RHB, RM. Cambridge U 1996-98, scoring 101 v Glamorgan(Cambridge) on debut; blue 1996-97 (*injured 1998*). Kent 1996-2004; cap 2001. Middlesex debut/cap 2005. British U 1998. **Tests**: 3 (2003); HS 64 v SA (Nottingham) 2003 on debut. F-c Tour (Eng A): I 2003-04. 1000 runs (6): most – 1534 (2003). Scored 135, 0, 149, 113, 203 and 108 in successive f-c innings 2003. HS 213 K v Warwks (Canterbury) 2003. M HS 145 v Glamorgan (Southgate) 2005. LO HS 122 K v Glamorgan(Maidstone) 2003 (NL). T20 HS 85.

STRAUSS, Andrew John (Radley C; Durham U), b Johannesburg, South Africa 2 Mar 1977. 5'11". LHB, LM. Debut 1998; cap 2001; captain 2002 (*part*) to 2004 (*part*). Oxfordshire 1996. *Wisden* 2004. MBE 2005. **ECB contracts 2004-05**. **Tests**: 21 (2004 to 2005-06); HS 147 v SA (Johannesburg) 2004-05. Scored 112 & 83 (run out) v NZ (Lord's) on debut and 126 & 94* v SA (Pt Elizabeth) 2004-05 on his debut overseas. **LOI**: 44 (2003-04 to 2005-06); HS 152 v B (Nottingham) 2005. F-c Tours: A 2004-05; P 2005-06. 1000 runs (3); most – 1529 (2002). HS 176 v Durham (Lord's) 2001. BB 1-27. Award: CGT 1. LO HS 152 (*see LOI*). T20 HS 60.

NQSTYRIS, Scott Bernard (Hamilton BHS), b Brisbane, Australia 10 Jul 1975. 5'10". RHB, RM. N Districts 1994-95 to date. Middlesex debut 2005. **Tests** (NZ): 21 (2002 to 2005); HS 170 v SA (Auckland) 2003-04; BB 3-28 v I (Wellington) 2002-03. **LOI** (NZ): 110 (1999-00 to 2005-06); HS 141 v SL (Bloemfontein) 2002-03; BB 6-25 v WI (Pt-of-Spain) 2002. F-c Tours (NZ): E 2004; A 2004-05; WI 2001-02; I 2003-04; SL 2002-03; Z 2005; B 2004-05. HS 212* ND v Otago (Hamilton) 2001-02. UK HS 108 NZ v E (Nottingham) 2004. M HS 100* v Surrey (Oval) 2005. BB 6-32 ND v Otago (Gisborne) 1999-00. M BB 6-73 (10-118 match) v Hants (Southampton) 2005. LO HS 141 (*see LOI*). LO BB 6-25 (*see LOI*). T20 HS 73*. T20 BB 2-20.

WEEKES, Paul Nicholas (Homerton House SS, Hackney), b Hackney, London 8 Jul 1969. 5'10". LHB, OB. Debut 1990; cap 1993; benefit 2002. F-c Tour: I 1994-95 (Eng A). MCC YC. 1000 runs (2); most – 1218 (1996). HS 171* v Somerset (Uxbridge) 1996. BB 8-39 v Glamorgan (Lord's) 1996. Awards: CGT 3; BHC 4. LO HS 143* v Cornwall (St Austell) 1995 (NWT). LO BB 4-17 v Kent (Lord's) 2001 (BHC). T20 HS 56. T20 BB 2-20.

WHELAN, Christopher David, b Liverpool, Lancs 8 May 1986. RHB, RMF. Debut 2005. HS 9* and CC BB 2-54 v Hants (Southampton) 2005. BB 2-34 v CU (Cambridge) 2005. LO HS 6 (NL).

WRIGHT, Christopher Julian Clement (Eggars S, Alton; Anglia Polytechnic U), b Chipping Norton, Oxon 14 Jul 1985. 6'3". RHB, RFM. CU 2004. Middlesex debut 2004. HS 76 CU v Essex (Cambridge) 2005. M HS 13 v Surrey (Lord's) 2005. BB 2-36 CU v Middx (Cambridge) 2005. LO HS 0 (NL). LO BB 1-34 (NL). T20 HS 1*. T20 BB 2-24.

RELEASED/RETIRED

(Having made a first-class County appearance in 2005)

[NQ]**CLARK, Stuart** Rupert, b Sutherland, Sydney, Australia 28 Sep 1975. 6'5½". RHB, RFM. NSW 1997-98 to date. Middlesex 2004. **LOI** (A): 10 (2005-06); HS 15 v SA (Brisbane) 2005-06; BB 4-55 v NZ (Christchurch) 2005-06. HS 35 NSW v WA (Newcastle) 2002-03. M HS 34 v Northants (Northampton) 2004 – on UK debut. BB 6-84 NSW v Tas (Hobart) 2002-03. M BB 5-61 v Warwks (Lord's) 2005. LO HS 26* v Sussex (Hove) 2004 (NL). LO BB 4-26 NSW v Tas (Sydney) 1997-98. T20 HS – . T20 BB 1-35.

[NQ] **GOLWALKAR, Yogesh** Ashok (educated in Indore), b Indore, India 13 Feb 1980. 5'7". LHB, LB. Madhya Pradesh 2000-01 to date. Middlesex 2005. HS 41* Madhya Pradesh v Orissa (Gwalior) 2000-01. BB 8-127 Madhya Pradesh v Railways (Indore) 2004-05. M HS 3 and BB 3-41 v Kent (Lord's) 2005. LO HS 6*. LO BB 3-34 Madhya Pradesh v Vidarbha (Delhi) 2000-01.

[NQ]**HAYWARD**, Mornantau (*'Nantie'*) (Daniel Pienaar THS), b Uitenhage, South Africa 6 Mar 1977. RHB, RF. E Province 1995-96 to2003-04. Warriors 2004-05. Worcestershire 2003. Middlesex 2004-05. **Tests** (SA): 16 (1999-00 to 2004); HS 14 v A (Melbourne) 2001-02; BB 5-56 v P (Durban) 2002-03. **LOI** (SA): 21 (1998 to 2001-02); HS 4; BB 4-31 v I (Sharjah) 1999-00. F-c Tours (SA): A 2001-02; I 1999-00; SL 2000-01, 2004. HS 55* EP v Boland (Pt Elizabeth) 1997-98. CC HS 28 Wo v Durham (Stockton) 2003. M HS 12* v Notts (Lord's) 2004. 50 wkts (1): 67 (2003). BB 6-31 (12-94 match) EP v Easterns (Pt Elizabeth) 1999-00. CC BB 5-46 Wo v Somerset (Worcester) 2003. M BB 4-41 v Surrey (Lord's) 2004. LO HS 19* EP v WP (Cape Town) 1996-97. LO BB 5-37 EP v KZ-Natal (Durban) 1998-99. T20 HS 3. T20 BB 3-21.

[NQ]**HUTCHISON, Paul** Michael (Crawshaw HS, Pudsey), b Leeds, Yorks 9 Jun 1977. 6'3". LHB, LFM. Yorkshire 1995-96 (Y in Zim) to 2001; cap 1998. Sussex 2002-03. Middlesex 2004-05. F-c Tours (Eng A): SL 1997-98; Z 1995-96 (Y); K 1997-98. HS 30 Y v Essex (Scarborough) 1998. M HS 26* v Warwks (Birmingham) 2005. 50 wkts (1): 59 (1998). BB 7-31 Y v Sussex (Hove) 1998. M BB 3-50 v Surrey (Oval) 2004. Award: CGT 1. LO HS 20 Sx v Northants (Northampton) 2003 (NL). LO BB 4-29 Sx v Scot (Edinburgh) 2003 (NL). T20 HS 0*. T20 BB 2-22.

[NQ] **PATHAN, Irfan** Khan, b Baroda, India 27 Oct 1984. LHB, LMF. Baroda 2002-01 to date. Middlesex 2005. **Tests** (I): 21 (2003-04 to 2005-06); HS 93 v SL (Delhi) 2005-06; BB 7-59 (12-126 match) v Z (Harare) 2005-06. **LOI** (I): 51 (1999-00 to 2005-06); HS 83 v SL (Nagpur) 2005-06; BB 5-27 v Z (Harare) 2005. F-c Tours (I): A 2003-04; P 2003-04, 2005-06; Z 2005-06; B 2004-05. HS 93 (*see Tests*). M HS 68 v Surrey (Lord's) 2005. BB 7-59 (*see Tests*). M BB 4-81 v Sussex (Hove) 2005 – on UK debut. LO HS 83 (*see LOI*). LO BB 5-27 (*see LOI*). T20 HS 21*. T20 BB 4-27.

TREGO, P.D. – *see SOMERSET.*

MIDDLESEX 2005

RESULTS SUMMARY

		Place	Won	Lost	Tied	Drew	No Result
County Championship (1st Division)		6th	4	5		7	
All First-Class Matches			4	6		7	
C & G Trophy		2nd Round					
National League (1st Division)		2nd	10	5			1
Twenty20 Cup		Quarter-Finalist					

COUNTY CHAMPIONSHIP AVERAGES

BATTING AND FIELDING

Cap		M	I	NO	HS	Runs	Avge	100	50	Ct/St
2000	O.A.Shah	16	30	4	173*	1650	63.46	7	7	22
–	I.K.Pathan	3	4	2	68	126	63.00	–	1	1
2002	E.C.Joyce	16	29	2	192	1668	61.77	3	13	15
1993	P.N.Weekes	16	26	7	128*	842	44.31	1	5	7
2005	E.T.Smith	16	30	–	145	1228	40.93	2	7	12
2004	J.W.M.Dalrymple	12	22	2	108	701	35.05	1	6	3
2003	B.L.Hutton	16	30	2	152	899	32.10	1	4	23
–	S.B.Styris	9	17	1	100*	484	30.25	1	3	4
–	P.D.Trego	7	10	1	72	234	26.00	–	2	2
–	B.J.M.Scott	15	22	4	64*	399	22.16	–	3	37/5
–	C.T.Peploe	6	9	2	42	143	20.42	–	–	2
–	M.M.Betts	9	10	2	36*	136	17.00	–	–	1
2001	A.J.Strauss	4	8	–	37	118	14.75	–	–	3
2005	A.Richardson	13	16	5	25	137	12.45	–	–	2
–	S.R.Clark	4	7	3	17*	47	11.75	–	–	1
–	M.Hayward	4	5	3	12*	20	10.00	–	–	1

Also batted: Y.A.Golwalkar (2 matches) 3, 2; P.M.Hutchison (2) 0, 26*, 2 (2 ct); C.B.Keegan (2) 28, 17, 3; D.C.Nash (1 – cap 2000) 12, 0; C.D.Whelan (1) 1, 9*; C.J.C.Wright (2) 13, 0 (1 ct).

BOWLING

	O	M	R	W	Avge	Best	5wI	10wM
S.B.Styris	230.5	44	730	31	23.54	6- 73	2	1
A.Richardson	471.4	109	1438	57	25.22	7-113	3	–
S.R.Clark	120.4	22	412	15	27.46	5- 61	1	–
P.D.Trego	131	21	576	16	36.00	6- 59	1	–
M.M.Betts	229.1	45	838	22	38.09	4- 58	–	–
J.W.M.Dalrymple	215.4	19	820	18	45.55	4- 53	–	–
C.T.Peploe	216	45	749	15	49.93	3- 77	–	–
P.N.Weekes	237.5	33	765	14	54.64	3- 83	–	–
Also bowled:								
Y.A.Golwalkar	104.4	25	329	7	47.00	3- 41	–	–
M.Hayward	94	9	380	8	47.50	2- 23	–	–
P.M.Hutchison	53.4	3	255	5	51.00	2- 43	–	–
I.K.Pathan	89	13	324	5	64.80	4- 81	–	–

B.L.Hutton 86-10-363-0; E.C.Joyce 32.3-1-204-3; C.B.Keegan 70-18-233-1; O.A.Shah 40-3-171-2; C.D.Whelan 22-4-112-3; C.J.C.Wright 38-3-159-0.

The First-Class Averages (pp 129–145) give the records of Middlesex players in all first-class matches for the county (their other opponents being Cambridge UCCE), with the exception of O.A.Shah, A.J.Strauss and C.J.C.Wright whose full county figures are as above, and T.E.Savill whose only first-class appearances were for Cambridge UCCE.

MIDDLESEX RECORDS

FIRST-CLASS CRICKET

Highest Total	For 642-3d		v	Hampshire	Southampton	1923
	V 734-5d		by	Lancashire	Manchester	2003
Lowest Total	For 20		v	MCC	Lord's	1864
	V 31		by	Glos	Bristol	1924
Highest Innings	For 331*	J.D.B.Robertson	v	Worcs	Worcester	1949
	V 341	C.M.Spearman	for	Glos	Gloucester	2004

Highest Partnership for each Wicket

1st	372	M.W.Gatting/J.L.Langer	v	Essex	Southgate	1998
2nd	380	F.A.Tarrant/J.W.Hearne	v	Lancashire	Lord's	1914
3rd	424*	W.J.Edrich/D.C.S.Compton	v	Somerset	Lord's	1948
4th	325	J.W.Hearne/E.H.Hendren	v	Hampshire	Lord's	1919
5th	338	R.S.Lucas/T.C.O'Brien	v	Sussex	Hove	1895
6th	270	J.D.Carr/P.N.Weekes	v	Glos	Lord's	1994
7th	271*	E.H.Hendren/F.T.Mann	v	Notts	Nottingham	1925
8th	182*	M.H.C.Doll/H.R.Murrell	v	Notts	Lord's	1913
9th	160*	E.H.Hendren/T.J.Durston	v	Essex	Leyton	1927
10th	230	R.W.Nicholls/W.Roche	v	Kent	Lord's	1899

Best Bowling	For 10- 40	G.O.B.Allen	v	Lancashire	Lord's	1929
(Innings)	V 9- 38	R.C.R-Glasgow†	for	Somerset	Lord's	1924
Best Bowling	For 16-114	G.Burton	v	Yorkshire	Sheffield	1888
(Match)	16-114	J.T.Hearne	v	Lancashire	Manchester	1898
	V 16-109	C.W.L.Parker	for	Glos	Cheltenham	1930

Most Runs – Season	2669	E.H.Hendren	(av 83.41)	1923
Most Runs – Career	40302	E.H.Hendren	(av 48.81)	1907-37
Most 100s – Season	13	D.C.S.Compton		1947
Most 100s – Career	119	E.H.Hendren		1907-37
Most Wkts – Season	158	F.J.Titmus	(av 14.63)	1955
Most Wkts – Career	2361	F.J.Titmus	(av 21.27)	1949-82
Most Career W-K Dismissals	1223	J.T.Murray	(1024 ct/199 st)	1952-75
Most Career Catches in the Field	561	E.H.Hendren		1907-37

LIMITED-OVERS CRICKET

Highest Total	CGT	304-7		v	Surrey	The Oval	1995
		304-8		v	Cornwall	St Austell	1995
	NL	337-5		v	Somerset	Southgate	2003
	T20	210-6		v	Hampshire	Southampton	2005
Lowest Total	CGT	41		v	Essex	Westcliff	1972
	NL	23		v	Yorkshire	Leeds	1974
	T20	136		v	Sussex	Hove	2003
Highest Innings	CGT	158	G.D.Barlow	v	Lancashire	Lord's	1984
	NL	147*	M.R.Ramprakash	v	Worcs	Lord's	1990
	T20	85	E.T.Smith	v	Kent	Beckenham	2005
Best Bowling	CGT	6-15	W.W.Daniel	v	Sussex	Hove	1980
	NL	6- 6	R.W.Hooker	v	Surrey	Lord's	1969
	T20	4-27	I.K.Pathan	v	Essex	Southgate	2005

† R.C.Robertson-Glasgow

69

NORTHAMPTONSHIRE

Formation of Present Club: 31 July 1878
Inaugural First-Class Match: 1905
Colours: Maroon
Badge: Tudor Rose
County Champions: (0); best – 2nd 1912, 1957, 1965, 1976
Gillette/NatWest/C & G Trophy Winners: (2) 1976, 1992
Benson and Hedges Cup Winners: (1) 1980
National League (Div 1) Winners: (0); best – 3rd 2000, 2005
Sunday League Winners: (0); best – 3rd 1991
Twenty20 Cup Winners: (0); best – Quarter-Finalist 2005
Match Awards: CGT 58; BHC 62

Chief Executive: Mark J.Tagg County Ground, Wantage Road, Northampton, NN1 4TJ ∙ Tel: 01604 514455 ∙ Fax: 01604 514488 ∙ Email: post@nccc.co.uk ∙ Web: www.nccc.co.uk

Director of Cricket/First XI Coach: K.P.Wessels. **Captain**: D.J.G.Sales. **Vice-Captain**: none. **Overseas Players**: M.J.Nicholson and C.J.L.Rogers. **2006 Beneficiary**: none. **Head Groundsman**: P.Marshall. **Scorer**: A.C.Kingston. ‡ New registration. NQ Not qualified for England.

AFZAAL, Usman (Manvers Pierrepont CS; S Notts C), b Rawalpindi, Pakistan 9 Jun 1977. 6'0". LHB, SLA. Debut 1995; cap 2000. Northamptonshire debut 2004; cap 2005. **Tests**: 3 (2001); HS 54 v A (Oval) 2001; BB 1-49. F-c Tours: SA 1996-97 (Nt); WI 2000-01 (Eng A); NZ 2001-02. 1000 runs (5): most – 1365 (2004). HS 168* v Essex (Northampton) 2005. BB 4-101 v Glos (Nottingham) 1998. Nh BB 3-65 v Kent (Northampton) 2004. Award: CGT 1. LO HS 122* v Middx (Northampton) 2005 (NL). LO BB 3-4 v Cambs (Northampton) 2004 (CGT). T20 HS 46.

BAKER, Thomas Michael (Whitcliffe Mount S; Huddersfield C), b Dewsbury, Yorks 6 Jul 1981. 6'4". RHB, RM. Debut 2005. HS 0 and BB 1-55 v Leics (Leicester) 2005. LO HS 63 Northants CB v Yorks CB (Northampton) 2002. LO BB 2-13 Yorks v Derbys (Leeds) 2001.

BROWN, Jason Fred (St Margaret Ward HS & SFC), b Newcastle-under-Lyme, Staffs 10 Oct 1974. 6'0". RHB, OB. Debut 1996; cap 2000. Staffordshire 1994-95. F-c Tours: WI 2000-01 (*part*) (Eng A); SL 2000-01 (*no f-c*). HS 38 v Hants (Northampton) 2003. 50 wkts (3): most – 66 (2003). BB 7-69 v Durham (Chester-le-St) 2003. Award: CGT 1. LO HS 16 v Lancs (Manchester) 2002 (NL). LO BB 5-19 v Cambs (Northampton) 2004 (CGT). T20 HS – . T20 BB 5-27.

COVERDALE, Paul Stephen (Wellingborough S; Loughborough U), b Harrogate, Yorks 24 Jul 1983. Son of S.P.Coverdale (Yorkshire, Cambridge U and Northamptonshire 1973-80, 1987; Northants Secretary-Manager/**Chief Executive** 1985-2004). 5'10". RHB, RM. Emerging player contract – awaiting f-c debut. LO HS 19 Northants CB v Leics CB (Barwell) 2001. LO BB 1-21 (CGT).

‡**NQCROOK, Steven** Paul (Rostrevor C; Magill U), b Modbury, S Australia 28 May 1983. Younger brother of A.R.Crook (see LANCASHIRE). 5'11". RHB, RFM. British passport. S Australia U-17, U-19. Lancashire 2003-05. Northamptonshire debut 2005 (whilst on loan from Lancashire). HS 97 v Notts (Northampton) 2005. BB 3-54 v Durham (Chester-le-St) 2005. LO HS 21 La v Warwks (Birmingham) 2004 (NL). LO BB 2-47 La v Notts (Nottingham) 2005. T20 HS 27.

70

FRIEDLANDER, Matthew James (Hilton C; Anglia Polytechnic U), b Durban, S Africa 1 Aug 1979. 6'0". RHB, RFM. Boland 2001-04. Cambridge UCCE 2005. British U 2005. Northamptonshire 2005. Awaiting CC debut. HS 81 CU v Essex (Cambridge) 2005. Nh HS 7. BB 3-67 v Bangladesh A (Northampton) 2005.

‡^{NQ}**KLUSENER, Lance** (Durban HS), b Durban, South Africa 4 Sep 1971. 5'10". LHB, RM/OB. Natal/KwaZulu-Natal 1993-94 to date. Nottinghamshire 2002. *Wisden* 1999. Kolpak Registration. **Tests** (SA): 49 (1996-97 to 2004); HS 174 v E (Pt Elizabeth) 1999-00; BB 8-64 v I (Calcutta) 1996-97 – on debut. **LOI** (SA): 171 (1995-96 to 2004); HS 103* v NZ (Auckland) 1998-99; BB 6-49 v SL (Lahore) 1997-98. F-c Tours (SA): E 1998; A 1997-98, 2001-02; WI 2000-01; NZ 1998-99; I 1996-97, 1999-00; P 1997-98; SL 1998-99, 2000-01, 2004; Z 1999-00, 2001-02. HS 174 (*see Tests*). CC HS 68* M v Glos (Gloucester) 2004. BB 8-34 Natal v WP (Durban) 1995-96. CC BB 4-89 v Lancs (Lord's) 2004 – on Middx debut. Award: BHC 1. LO HS 142* SA v Northants (Northampton) 1998. LO BB 6-49 (*see LOI*). T20 HS 63*. T20 BB 2-13.

‡^{NQ}**NICHOLSON, Matthew** James (Knox GS; Edith Cowan U, Perth), b St Leonards, Sydney, Australia 2 Oct 1974. 6'6". RHB, RFM. W Australia.1996-97 to 2002-03. NSW 2003-04 to date. Missed entire 1997-98 season (salmonella poisoning, glandular fever, Ross River fever, chronic fatigue syndrome). Registered as an overseas player by Sussex for 2005 but was unable to take up his contract because of injury. **Tests** (A): 1 (1998-99); HS 9 and BB 3-56 v E (Melbourne) 1998-99. Tour (A): Z 1999-00. HS 101* WA v S Africans (Perth) 2001-02. BB 7-77 WA v Eng XI (Perth) 1998-99. LO HS 25 NSW v Q (Sydney 2003-04. LO BB 3-34 NSW v S Aus (Sydney) 2003-04. T20 HS 2*. T20 BB 2-18.

PANESAR, Mudhsuden Singh '*Monty*' (Stopsley HS; Bedford Modern S; Loughborough U), b Luton, Beds 25 Apr 1982. 6'0". LHB, SLA. Bedfordshire 1998-99. Debut 2001. Loughborough U 2004. F-c Tour (ECB Acad): SL 2002-03. HS 39* v Worcs (Northampton) 2005. BB 7-181 v Essex (Chelmsford) 2005. 50 wkts (1): 51 (2005). LO HS 16* v Essex (Colchester) 2002 (NL). LO BB 5-20 ECB Acad v SL Acad XI (Colombo) 2002-03.

‡**PETERS, Stephen** David (Coopers Coborn & Co S), b Harold Wood, Essex 10 Dec 1978. 5'11". RHB, occ LB. Essex 1996-2001, scoring 110 and 12* v CU (Cambridge) on debut. Worcestershire 2002-05. 1000 runs (1): 1177 (2003). HS 165 Wo v Somerset (Bath) 2003. BB (Ex) 1-19 (not CC). Award: CGT 1. LO HS 82 Wo v Leics (Oakham) 2003 (NL). T20 HS 26*.

PHILLIPS, Ben James (Langley Park S and SFC, Beckenham), b Lewisham, London 30 Sep 1974. 6'6". RHB, RFM. Kent 1996-99. Northamptonshire debut 2002; cap 2005. HS 100* K v Lancs (Manchester) 1997. Nh HS 90 v Warwks (Birmingham) 2004. BB 5-47 K v Sussex (Horsham) 1997. Nh BB 5-106 v Glos (Bristol) 2004. Award: CGT 1. LO HS 44* v Kent (Canterbury) 2004 (NL). LO BB 4-25 K v Northants (Canterbury) 2000 (NL). T20 HS 41*. T20 BB 4-18.

‡**PHYTHIAN, Mark** John (Durham U), b Peterborough 26 Apr 1985. RHB, WK. Durham UCCE 2005. Awaiting Northamptonshire debut. HS (DU) 0.

^{NQ}PIETERSEN, Charl (Northern Cape HS, Kimberley), b Kimberley, South Africa 6 Jan 1983. 5'8". LHB, LMF. Griqualand West 2001-02 to 2003-04. Northamptonshire debut 2005 (Kolpak registration). HS 45 GW v N West (Kimberley) 2003-04. Nh HS 1. BB 6-43 GW v Boland (Kimberley) 2002-03. Nh BB 3-74 v B (Northampton) 2005. CC BB 1-31. Award: CGT 1. LO HS 14* GW v KZ-Natal (Kimberley) 2003-04. LO BB 7-10 v Denmark (Brondby) 2005 (Nh CGT record) .

‡^{NQ}ROGERS, Christopher John Llewellyn (Wesley C, Perth; Curtin U, Perth), b St George, Sydney, Australia 31 Aug 1977. Son of W.J.Rogers (NSW 1968-69 to 1969-70). 5'10". LHB, LBG. W Australia 1998-99 to date. Shropshire 2003. Derbyshire 2004. Leicestershire 2005. HS 209 Le v A (Leicester) 2005 – on Le debut. CC HS 156 De v Durham (Derby) 2004. LO HS 117* WA v Q (Perth) 2003-04. T20 HS 35.

SALES, David John Grimwood (Caterham S; Cumnor House S), b Carshalton, Surrey 3 Dec 1977. 6'0". RHB, RM. Debut 1996 v Worcs (Kidderminster) scoring 0 and 210* – record Championship score on f-c debut; youngest (18yr 237d) to score 200 in a Championship match; cap 1999; captain 2004-. Wellington 2001-02. F-c Tours (Eng A): NZ 1999-00; SL 1997-98; K 1997-98; B 1999-00. Sustained severe knee injury prior to start of England A tour of WI 2000-01 – no f-c appearances 2001. 1000 runs (3); most – 1291 (1999). HS 303* v Essex (Northampton) 1999 – youngest Englishman (21y 240d) to score a f-c 300. BB 4-25 v SL A (Northampton) 1999. CC BB 2-7 v Yorks (Scarborough) 1999. Award: BHC 1. LO HS 133* v Notts (Northampton) 2003 (NL). T20 HS 78*. T20 BB 1-10.

SHAFAYAT, Bilal Mustapha (Greenwood Dale; Nottingham Bluecoat SFC), b Nottingham 10 Jul 1984. 5'7". RHB, RMF. Nottinghamshire 2001-2004. Northamptonshire debut 2005. Captained Eng U-19 tour of Australia 2002-03. F-c Tour (Eng A): I 2003-04. 1000 (1); 1058 (2005). HS 161 v Derbys (Derby) 2005. BB (Nt) 1-22 (not CC). LO HS 97* v Glos (Stowe) 2005 (NL). LO BB 4-33 v Worcs (Worcester) 2005 (NL). T20 HS 40. T20 BB 2-13.

^{NQ}WESSELS, Matthewus Hendrik ('Riki') (Woodridge C, Pt Elizabeth; Northants U), b Nambour, Queensland, Australia 12 Nov 1985. Left Australia when 2 months old. Son of K.C.Wessels (OFS, Sussex, WP, NT, Q, EP, Australia and South Africa 1973-74 to 1999-00). 5'11". RHB, WK. MCC 2004. Northamptonshire debut 2005 (Kolpak registration). HS 107 v Durham (Chester-le-St) 2005. LO HS 80 v Glamorgan (Northampton) 2005 (NL). T20 HS 49*.

WHITE, Andrew Rowland (Regent House GS; Ulster U), b Newtownards, Co Down, N Ireland 3 Jul 1980. 6'0". RHB, OB. Ireland 2004, scoring 152* on debut (*see HS*). Northamptonshire debut 2004. HS 152* Ire v Holland (Deventer) 2004 – on f-c debut. Nh HS 30* v Bangladesh A (Northampton) 2005. CC HS 22 v Middx (Lord's) 2004 – on Northants debut. BB 3-24 Ireland v Kenya (Windhoek) 2005. CC BB 2-19 v Warwks (Northampton) 2004. Award: CGT 1. LO HS 45 Ireland v Uganda (Comber) 2005. LO BB 3-17. Ireland v Denmark (Bangor) 2005.

WHITE, Robert Allan (Stowe S; Durham U; Loughborough U), b Chelmsford, Essex 15 Oct 1979. 5'11". RHB, LB. Debut 2000. Loughborough UCCE 2003. British U 2003. HS 277 and BB 2-30 v Glos (Northampton) 2002 – highest maiden f-c hundred in UK; included 107 before lunch on first day. LO HS 101 v Glamorgan(Northampton) 2004 (NL). LO BB 2-18 v Sussex (Northampton) 2002 (NL). T20 HS 28.

‡**WIGLEY, David** Harry (St Mary's RCS, Menstom, Ilkley; Loughborough U), b Bradford, Yorks 26 Oct 1981. 6'4". RHB, RFM. Yorkshire 2002 (one match). Loughborough UCCE 2003-04. British U 2004. Worcestershire 2003, 2005. HS 23* LU v Somerset (Taunton) 2004. CC HS 15 Y v Surrey (Guildford) 2002 – on debut – and 15 v Yorks (Worcester) 2003 – on Worcs debut. BB 4-68 v Derbys (Derby) 2005. LO HS 2 (NL). LO BB 4-37 v Leics (Worcester) 2004 (NL). T20 HS 1. T20 BB 1-8.

WOLSTENHOLME, John Paul (Northampton S; University C, Northampton), b Northampton 7 May 1982. 6'10". RHB, RFM. Debut 2005. Awaiting CC debut. HS – . LO HS 10 Northants CB v Northumb (Northampton) 2000.

RELEASED/RETIRED

(Having made a first-class County appearance in 2005)

NQ**BROPHY, G.L.** – *see YORKSHIRE.*

HUGGINS, Thomas Benjamin (Kimbolton S; De Montfort U), b Peterborough 8 Mar 1983. 6'3". RHB, OB. Northamptonshire 2003-05. Cambridgeshire 2001. HS 82* v Middx (Lord's) 2004. LO HS 16 v Kent (Canterbury) 2004 (NL). T20 HS 19.

JONES, P. S. – *see DERBYSHIRE.*

KING, Richard Eric (Bedford Modern S; Loughborough U), b Hitchin, Herts 3 Jan 1984. 6'0". RHB, LMF. Loughborough UCCE 2003. Northamptonshire 2005 (one match – v Bangladesh A). HS 17 LU v Somerset (Taunton) 2003 – on debut. Nh HS – . BB 1-32 (Nh). LO HS 2 (Northants CB). LO BB 2-39 Northants CB v Yorks CB (Northampton) 2002 (CGT).

NQ**LOUW, J.** – *see MIDDLESEX.*

NQ**LOVE, Martin** Lloyd (Toowoomba GS; Queensland U), b Mundubbera, Queensland, Australia 30 Mar 1974. 6'1". RHB, OB. Queensland 1992-93 to date. Durham 2001-03; cap 2001. Northamptonshire 2004-05. **Tests** (A): 5 (2002-03 to 2003); HS 100* v B (Cairns) 2003. F-c Tours (A): E 1995 (Young A); WI 2003. 1000 (2+3): most – 1364 (2001). HS 300* Q v Vic (Melbourne) 2003-04. CC HS 273 (Durham record) v Hants (Chester-le-St) 2003 . Nh HS 177 v Derbys (Northampton) 2005. BB (Q) 1-5. LO HS 127* Q v NSW (Brisbane) 2001-02. T20 HS 53.

ROBERTS, Timothy William (Bishop's Stopford S, Kettering; Durham U), b Kettering 4 Mar 1978. Younger brother of A.R.Roberts (Northants 1987-98). 5'7". RHB, OB. British U 1999. Bedfordshire 2000. Lancashire debut 2001. Northamptonshire 2003-05. HS 89 v Lancs (Northampton) 2004. BB 1-10 (not CC). LO HS 131 v Notts (Nottingham) 2003 (NL). T20 HS 43.

NQ**WRIGHT, Damien** Geoffrey (Terrigal HS, NSW), b Casino, NSW, Australia 25 Jul 1975. 6'1". RHB, RFM. Tasmania 1997-98 to date. Scotland 2001 (CGT). Northamptonshire 2003, 2005. Withdrew from 2004 overseas player contract with Derbyshire because of a knee injury. F-c Tours (Aus A): SA 2002-03. HS 111 Tas v Vic (Hobart) 2004-05. Nh HS 85 v Worcs (Worcester) 2005. 50 wkts (1): 53 (2005). BB 8-60 v Yorks (Leeds) 2005. LO HS 55 Scot v Middx CB (Southgate) 2001 (CGT). LO BB 5-37 v Notts (Northampton) 2005 (NL). T20 HS 38*. T20 BB 3-17.

C.M.Goode and C.J.Wade left the staff without making a f-c appearance in 2005.

NORTHAMPTONSHIRE 2005

RESULTS SUMMARY

	Place	Won	Lost	Tied	Drew	No Result
County Championship (2nd Division)	4th	5	3		8	
All First-Class Matches		5	3		9	
C & G Trophy	Quarter-Finalist					
National League (1st Division)	3rd	7	7			2
Twenty20 Cup	Quarter-Finalist					

COUNTY CHAMPIONSHIP AVERAGES

BATTING AND FIELDING

Cap		M	I	NO	HS	Runs	Avge	100	50	Ct/St
–	S.P.Crook	3	4	2	97	217	108.50	–	2	–
–	M.L.Love	15	25	1	177	1345	56.04	4	6	36
1999	D.J.G.Sales	16	27	2	190	1171	46.84	3	6	20
2005	U.Afzaal	16	27	2	168*	1140	45.60	5	1	8
–	B.M.Shafayat	16	27	–	161	982	36.37	2	5	21
2005	B.J.Phillips	13	20	6	58	447	31.92	–	2	2
–	M.H.Wessels	13	22	3	107	593	31.21	3	2	23/4
–	R.A.White	14	23	2	95	630	30.00	–	2	10
–	D.G.Wright	16	25	2	85	609	26.47	–	4	6
–	T.W.Roberts	2	4	–	53	98	24.50	–	1	–
–	J.Louw	15	20	3	64	277	16.29	–	2	2
–	P.S.Jones	6	6	–	51	78	13.00	–	1	–
–	M.S.Panesar	8	11	4	39*	75	10.71	–	–	2
2000	J.F.Brown	15	16	7	22	47	5.22	–	–	1

Also batted: T.M.Baker (1 match) 0 (1 ct); G.L.Brophy (3) 52*, 0, 0 (6 ct); C.Pietersen (3) 1, 0, 0 (2 ct); A.R.White (1) 0, 6.

BOWLING

	O	M	R	W	Avge	Best	5wI	10wM
M.S.Panesar	389.1	95	991	46	21.54	7-181	4	1
D.G.Wright	480	139	1398	53	26.37	8- 60	2	–
J.F.Brown	629.4	184	1551	55	28.20	6-112	6	2
J.Louw	415.5	94	1424	44	32.36	6- 51	2	–
B.J.Phillips	254	73	728	21	34.66	3- 42	–	–

Also bowled:

P.S.Jones	144	34	474	9	52.66	4- 74	

U.Afzaal 23-5-94-1; T.M.Baker 13-2-55-1; S.P.Crook 54.3-8-206-4; C.Pietersen 32-1-130-1; B.M.Shafayat 20.5-2-61-0; R.A.White 11-3-27-0.

The First-Class Averages (pp 129–145) give the records of Northamptonshire players in all first-class matches for the county (Northamptonshire's other opponents being Bangladesh), with the exception of S.P.Crook and M.S.Panesar whose full county figures are as above, M.J.Phythian whose only first-class appearances were made for Durham UCCE, and:

M.J.Friedlander 1-1-0-7-7-7.00-0-0-1ct. 14-1-67-3-22.33-3/67.

NORTHAMPTONSHIRE RECORDS

FIRST-CLASS CRICKET

Highest Total	For 781-7d		v	Notts	Northampton 1995
	V 673-8d		by	Yorkshire	Leeds 2003
Lowest Total	For 12		v	Glos	Gloucester 1907
	V 33		by	Lancashire	Northampton 1977
Highest Innings	For 331*	M.E.K.Hussey	v	Somerset	Taunton 2003
	V 333	K.S.Duleepsinhji	for	Sussex	Hove 1930

Highest Partnership for each Wicket

1st	375	R.A.White/M.J.Powell	v	Glos	Northampton 2002
2nd	344	G.Cook/R.J.Boyd-Moss	v	Lancashire	Northampton 1986
3rd	393	A.Fordham/A.J.Lamb	v	Yorkshire	Leeds 1990
4th	370	R.T.Virgin/P.Willey	v	Somerset	Northampton 1976
5th	401	M.B.Loye/D.Ripley	v	Glamorgan	Northampton 1998
6th	376	R.Subba Row/A.Lightfoot	v	Surrey	The Oval 1958
7th	293	D.J.G.Sales/D.Ripley	v	Essex	Northampton 1999
8th	164	D.Ripley/N.G.B.Cook	v	Lancashire	Manchester 1987
9th	156	R.Subba Row/S.Starkie	v	Lancashire	Northampton 1955
10th	148	B.W.Bellamy/J.V.Murdin	v	Glamorgan	Northampton 1925

Best Bowling	For 10-127	V.W.C.Jupp	v	Kent	Tunbridge W 1932
(Innings)	V 10- 30	C.Blythe	for	Kent	Northampton 1907
Best Bowling	For 15- 31	G.E.Tribe	v	Yorkshire	Northampton 1958
(Match)	V 17- 48	C.Blythe	for	Kent	Northampton 1907

Most Runs – Season	2198	D.Brookes	(av 51.11)	1952
Most Runs – Career	28980	D.Brookes	(av 36.13)	1934-59
Most 100s – Season	8	R.A.Haywood		1921
Most 100s – Career	67	D.Brookes		1934-59
Most Wkts – Season	175	G.E.Tribe	(av 18.70)	1955
Most Wkts – Career	1102	E.W.Clark	(av 21.26)	1922-47
Most Career W-K Dismissals	810	K.V.Andrew	(653 ct/157 st)	1953-66
Most Career Catches in the Field	469	D.S.Steele		1963-84

LIMITED-OVERS CRICKET

Highest Total	CGT	360-2		v	Staffs	Northampton 1990
	NL	319-7		v	Scotland	Northampton 2003
	T20	224-5		v	Glos	Milton Keynes 2005
Lowest Total	CGT	62		v	Leics	Leicester 1974
	NL	41		v	Middlesex	Northampton 1972
	T20	128-5		v	Glos	Bristol 2003
Highest Innings	CGT	145	R.J.Bailey	v	Staffs	Stone 1991
	NL	172*	W.Larkins	v	Warwicks	Luton 1983
	T20	88	M.E.K.Hussey	v	Somerset	Northampton 2003
Best Bowling	CGT	7-10	C.Pietersen	v	Denmark	Brondby 2005
	NL	7-39	A.Hodgson	v	Somerset	Northampton 1976
	T20	5-27	J.F.Brown	v	Somerset	Northampton 2003

NOTTINGHAMSHIRE

Formation of Present Club: March/April 1841
Substantial Reorganisation: 11 December 1866
Inaugural First-Class Match: 1864
Colours: Green and Gold
Badge: **Badge** of City of Nottingham
County Champions (since 1890): (5) 1907, 1929, 1981, 1987, 2005
Gillette/NatWest/C & G Trophy Winners: (1) 1987
Benson and Hedges Cup Winners: (1) 1989
National League (Div 1) Winners: (0); best – 5th 2001, 2005
Sunday League Winners: (1) 1991
Twenty20 Cup Winners: (0); best – 6th in Group 2003, 2004, 2005
Match Awards: CGT 47; BHC 76

Chief Executive: Derek Brewer, Trent Bridge, Nottingham NG2 6AG • Tel: 0115 982 3000 • Fax: 0115 945 5730 • Email: administration@nottsccc.co.uk • Webs: www.nottsccc.co.uk • www.trentbridge.co.uk

First XI Coach: M.Newell. **Captain**: S.P.Fleming. **Vice-Captain**: tba. **Overseas Players**: C.L.Cairns, S.P.Fleming and D.J.Hussey. **2006 Beneficiary**: none. **Head Groundsman**: S.Birks. **Scorer**: G.Stringfellow. ‡ New registration. NQ Not qualified for England.

ALLEYNE, David (Enfield GS; Hertford Regional C; City & Islington C), b York 17 Apr 1976. 5'11". RHB, WK. Middlesex 2001-02. Nottinghamshire debut 2004. HS 49* M v Derbys (Derby) 2002. Nt HS 43* v OU (Oxford) 2004 on Nt debut. LO HS 58 M v Notts (Nottingham) 2000 (NL). T20 HS 24*.

BICKNELL, Darren John (Robert Haining County SS; Guildford TC), b Guildford, Surrey 24 Jun 1967. Elder brother of M.P.Bicknell (*see SURREY*). 6'4". LHB, SLA. Surrey 1987-99; cap 1990; benefit 1999. Nottinghamshire debut/cap 2000. F-c Tours (Eng A): WI 1991-92; P 1990-91; SL 1990-91; Z 1989-90. 1000 runs (9); most – 1888 (1991). HS 235* Sy v Notts (Nottingham) 1994. Nt HS 180* v Warwks (Birmingham) 2000 – sharing unbroken 1st wkt stand of 406 with G.E.Welton. BB 3-7 Sy v Sussex (Guildford) 1996. Nt BB 3-33 v Essex (Nottingham) 2004. Awards: CGT 1; BHC 6. LO HS 135* Sy v Yorks (Oval) 1989 (NWT). LO BB (Sy) 1-11 (SL). T20 HS 10.

NQ**CAIRNS, Christopher** Lance (Christchurch BHS), b Picton, New Zealand 13 Jun 1970. Son of B.L.Cairns (CD, Otago, ND and NZ 1971-86). 6'2". RHB, RFM. Nottinghamshire 1988-89, 1992-93 and 1995-96; cap 1993; limited-overs captain 2003. N Districts 1988-89. Canterbury 1990-91 to date (*occasionally*). *Wisden* 1999. **Tests** (NZ): 62 (1989-90 to 2004); HS 158 v SA (Auckland) 2003-04; BB 7-27 v WI (Hamilton) 1999-00. **LOI** (NZ): 214 (1990-91 to 2005-06, 7 as captain); HS 115 v I (Christchurch) 1998-99; BB 5-42 v A (Napier) 1997-98. F-c Tours (NZ): E 1999, 2004; A 1989-90, 1993-94, 1997-98, 2001-02; WI 1995-96 (part); I 1995-96, 1999-00; P 1996-97; SL 1997-98; Z 1997-98, 2000-01. 1000 runs (1): 1171 (1995). HS 158 (*see Tests*). Nt HS 115 v Middx (Lord's) 1995. 50 wkts (3); most – 56 (1992). BB 8-47 (15-83 match) v Sussex (Arundel) 1995. Awards: CGT 2; BHC 1. LO HS 143 Canterbury v Auckland (Christchurch) 1994-95. LO BB 6-12 NZ v FICA World XI (Hamilton) 2004-05. T20 HS T20 BB

76

CLOUGH, Gareth David (Pudsey Grangefield S), b Leeds, Yorks 23 May 1978. 6'0". RHB, RM. Yorkshire 1998. Nottinghamshire debut 2001. No f-c appearances 2004. HS 55 v Ind A (Nottingham) 2003. CC HS 33 Y v Glamorgan(Cardiff) 1998 – on debut. BB 3-69 v Glos (Nottingham) 2001. LO HS 42* v Durham (Nottingham) 2003 (NL). LO BB 4-32 v Sussex (Horsham) 2003 (NL). T20 HS 30*. T20 BB 2-18.

EALHAM, Mark Alan (Stour Valley SS, Chartham), b Willesborough, Ashford, Kent 27 Aug 1969. Son of A.G.E.Ealham (Kent 1966-82). 5'9". RHB, RMF. Kent 1989-2003; cap 1992; benefit 2003. Nottinghamshire debut/cap 2004. **Tests**: 8 (1996 to 1998); HS 53* v A (Birmingham) 1997; BB 4-21 v I (Nottingham) 1996. **LOI**: 64 (1996 to 2001); HS 45 v WI (Bridgetown) 1997-98; BB 5-15 v Z (Kimberley) 1999-00 – Eng record. F-c Tours: A 1996-97 (Eng A); SA 1999-00 (part); SL 1997-98; Z 1992-93 (K); K 1997-98. 1000 runs (1): 1055 (1997). HS 153* K v Northants (Canterbury) 2001. Nt HS 139 v Leics (Leicester) 2004. BB 8-36 (10-74 match) K v Warwks (Birmingham) 1996. 50 wkts (1): 56 (2005). Nt BB 5-31 v Glos (Nottingham) 2005. Awards: CGT 3; BHC 6. LO HS 112 K v Derbys (Maidstone) 1995 (off 44 balls – SL record). LO BB 6-53 K v Hants (Basingstoke) 1993 (SL). T20 HS 91. T20 BB 2-22.

NQFLEMING, Stephen Paul (Cashmere HS, Canterbury; Christchurch C of Ed), b Christchurch, New Zealand 1 Apr 1973. 6'3". LHB, RSM. Canterbury 1991-92 to 1999-00. Wellington 2000-01 to date. Middlesex 2001; cap 2001. Yorkshire 2003. Nottinghamshire debut/captain/cap 2005. **Tests** (NZ): 96 (1993-94 to 2004-05, 72 as captain); HS 274* v SL (Colombo) 2002-03. **LOI** (NZ): 246 (1993-94 to 2005-06, 184 as captain); HS 134* v SA (Johannesburg) 2002-03; BB 1-8. F-c Tours (NZ) (C=captain): E 1994, 1999C, 2004C; A 1997-98C, 2001-02C, 2004-05C; SA 1993-94 (Cant), 1994-95, 2000-01C; WI 1995-96; I 1995-96, 1999-00C, 2003-04C; P 1996-97; SL 1997-98C, 2002-03C; Z 1997-98C, 2000-01C, 2005. 1000 (1): 1091 (2001). HS 274* (see Tests). UK HS 238 v Surrey (Oval) 2005. LO HS 139* Y v Warwks (Leeds) 2003 (NL). LO BB (NZ) 1-3. T20 HS 58.

FOOTITT, Mark Harold Alan (West Notts C), b Nottingham 25 Nov 1985. RHB, LFM. Debut 2005. HS 19* v Hants (Southampton) 2005. BB 4-45 v Glamorgan (Nottingham) 2005 – on debut. LO HS (Nt CB) – .

FRANKS, Paul John (Southwell Minster CS), b Mansfield 3 Feb 1979. 6'2". LHB, RMF. Debut 1996; cap 1999. Canterbury 2002-03. YC 2000. **LOI**: 1 (2000); HS 4 v WI (Nottingham) 2000. F-c Tours (Eng A): SA 1998-99; WI 2000-01; NZ 1999-00; B 1999-00. HS 123* v Leics (Leicester) 2003. 50 wkts (2); most – 63 (1999). BB 7-56 v Middx (Lord's) 2000. Hat-trick 1997. Awards: CGT 2. LO HS 84* v Lincs (Lincoln) 2003 (CGT). LO BB 6-27 v Durham (Chester-le-St) 2000 (NL). T20 HS 29*. T20 BB 2-31.

GALLIAN, Jason Edward Riche (Pittwater House S, Sydney; Keble C, Oxford), b Manly, Sydney, Australia 25 Jun 1971. Qualified for England 1994. 6'0". RHB, RM. Lancashire 1990-97, taking wicket of D.A.Hagan (OU) with his first ball; cap 1994. Oxford U 1992-93; blue 1992-93; captain 1993. Nottinghamshire debut/cap 1998; captain 1998 (part) to 2004; benefit 2005. Captained Australia YC v England YC 1989-90, scoring 158* in 1st 'Test'. **Tests**: 3 (1995 to 1995-96); HS 28 v SA (Pt Elizabeth) 1995-96. F-c Tours: A 1996-97 (Eng A); I 1995-96 (La); SA 1995-96 (part); I 1994-95 (Eng A); P 1995-96 (Eng A). 1000 runs (6); most – 1220 (2005). HS 312 La v Derbys (Manchester) 1996 (record score at Old Trafford). Nt HS 199 v Sussex (Nottingham) 2005. BB 6-115 La v Surrey (Southport) 1996. Nt BB 2-28 v Warwks (Nottingham) 1999. Awards: CGT 2; BHC 2. LO HS 134 La v Notts (Manchester) 1995 (BHC). LO BB 5-15 La v Minor C (Leek) 1995 (BHC). T20 HS 62.

HARRIS, Andrew James (Hadfield CS; Glossopdale Community C), b Ashton-under-Lyne, Lancs 26 Jun 1973. 6'1". RHB, RM. Derbyshire 1994-99; cap 1996. Nottinghamshire debut/cap 2000. F-c Tour: A 1996-97 (Eng A). HS 41* v Northants (Northampton) 2002. Dismissed 'Timed Out' v DU (Nottingham) 2003 – third instance in f-c cricket. 50 wkts (2); most – 72 (1996). BB 7-54 (11-122 match) v Northants (Nottingham) 2002. Award: CGT 1. LO HS 16* v Kent (Tunbridge Wells) 2002 (NL). LO BB 5-35 v Hants (Nottingham) 2000 (NL). T20 HS 0*. T20 BB 2-30.

NQ**HUSSEY, David** John, b Morley, Perth, Australia 15 Jul 1977. Younger brother of M.E.K.Hussey (*see DURHAM*). RHB, OB. Victoria 2002-03 to date. Nottinghamshire debut (and cap) 2004 scoring 107* v Oxford UCCE (Oxford) – UK debut. 1000 runs (2); most – 1315 (2004). HS 232* v Warwks (Nottingham) 2005 Scored 170, 116 and 140 in successive innings 2004. BB 4-105 v Hants (Nottingham) 2005. LO HS 128 Australia A v WI (Hobart) 2004-05. LO BB 3-48 Sussex CB v Glos (Horsham) 2001 (CGT). T20 HS 50.

McMAHON, Paul Joseph (Trinity RC CS, Nottingham; Wadham C, Oxford), b Wigan, Lancs 12 Mar 1983. 6'2". RHB, OB. Debut 2002. Oxford UCCE 2003-04-05; captain 2004-05; blue 2003-04-05. British U 2004. HS 99 OU v CU (Oxford) 2004. Nt HS 30 v Middlesex (Lord's) 2003. BB 5-30 OU v CU (Cambridge) 2005. Nt BB 4-59 v Essex (Chelmsford) 2003. LO HS 0 (NL). T20 HS – . T20 BB 1-22.

NOON, Wayne Michael (Caistor S), b Grimsby, Lincs 5 Feb 1971. 5'9". RHB, WK. Northamptonshire 1989-93. Nottinghamshire debut 1994; cap 1995; benefit 2003. Canterbury 1994-95. Worcs 2nd XI debut when aged 15yr 199d. F-c Tours: SA 1991-92 (Nh), 1996-97 (Nt). No f-c appearances 2004-05. HS 83 v Northants (Northampton) 1997. LO HS 46 v Warwks (Birmingham) 1998 (BHC).

PATEL, Samit Rohit (Worksop C), b Leicester 30 Nov 1984. 5'8". RHB, SLA. Debut 2002. Notts 2nd XI debut 1999 when aged 14yr 274d. No f-c appearances 2004. HS 55 v Lancs (Nottingham) 2003 – on CC debut. BB 3-73 v Kent (Nottingham) 2005. LO HS 82 v Middx (Southgate) 2005 (NL). LO BB 2-14 v Yorks (Leeds) 2002 (NL). T20 HS 32. T20 BB 2-22.

READ, Christopher Mark Wells (Torquay GS; Bath U), b Paignton, Devon 10 Aug 1978. 5'8". RHB, WK. Gloucestershire (L-O) 1997. Nottinghamshire debut 1998; cap 1999. Devon 1995-97. **Tests**: 11 (1999 to 2003-04); HS 38* v B (Chittagong) 2003-04. **LOI**: 28 (1999-00 to 2003-04); HS 30* v SA (Manchester) 2003. F-c Tours: SA 1998-99 (Eng A), 1999-00; WI 2000-01 (Eng A); SL 1997-98 (Eng A), 2002-03 (ECB Acad), 2003-04; Z 1998-99 (Eng A); B 2003-04; K 1997-98 (Eng A). HS 160 v Warwks (Nottingham) 1999. Award: CGT 1. LO HS 119* v Northants (Northampton) 2003 (NL). T20 HS 44*.

SHRECK, Charles Edward (Truro S), b Truro, Cornwall 6 Jan 1978. 6'7". RHB, RFM. Cornwall 1997-2002. Nottinghamshire debut 2003. No appearances 2005 (injured). Award: CGT 1. HS 19 v Essex (Chelmsford) 2003. BB 6-46 v Durham (Chester-le-St) 2004. LO HS 9 Cornwall v Cumb (Netherfield) 1999 (CGT). LO BB 5-19 Cornwall v Worcs (Truro) 2002 (CGT). Took 5-35 v Worcs (Nottingham) 2002 (NL) – on 1st XI debut. T20 HS 1*. T20 BB 1-25.

SIDEBOTTOM, Ryan Jay (King James's GS, Almondbury), b Huddersfield, Yorks 15 Jan 1978. Son of A.Sidebottom (Yorks, OFS and England 1973-91). 6'3". LHB, LFM. Yorkshire 1997-2003; cap 2000. Nottinghamshire debut/cap 2004. **Tests**: 1 (2001); HS 4 v P (Lord's) 2001; **LOI**: 2 (2001-02); HS 2*; BB 1-42 (twice). F-c Tour (Eng A): WI 2000-01. HS 54 Y v Glamorgan (Cardiff) 1998. Nt HS 31 and Nt BB 5-61 v Kent (Nottingham) 2005. 50 wkts (1): 50 (2005). BB 7-97 Y v Derbys (Leeds) 2003. LO HS 32 v Middx (Nottingham) 2005 (NL). LO BB 6-40 Y v Glamorgan(Cardiff) 1998 (SL). T20 HS 10. T20 BB 3-20.

SINGH, Anurag (King Edward's, Birmingham; Gonville & Caius C, Cambridge), b Kanpur, India 9 Sep 1975. 5'11½". RHB, OB. Warwickshire 1995-2000. Cambridge U 1996-98; blue 1996-97-98; captain 1997-98. British U 1998 (captain). Worcestershire 2001-03. Nottinghamshire debut 2004. 1000 runs (2); most – 1167 (2002). HS 187 Wo v Glos (Bristol) 2002. Nt HS 131 v LU (Nottingham) 2005. Awards: CGT 1; BHC 1. LO HS 123 Brit U v Somerset (Taunton) 1996 (BHC).

NOSMITH, Gregory James (Pretoria BHS; Pretoria Technikon), b Pretoria, South Africa 30 Oct 1971. ECB qualified – British passport. 6'4". RHB, LFM. N Transvaal/Northerns 1993-94 to 2001-02. Nottinghamshire debut/cap 2001. F-c Tour (SA A): E 1996. HS 68 NT v WP (Pretoria) 1995-96. Nt HS 44* v Sussex (Nottingham) 2001. 50 wkts (3): most – 51 (2003, 2005). BB 8-53 (11-74 match) v Essex (Nottingham) 2002. Awards: BHC 2. LO HS 17* v Durham (Chester-le-St) 2004 (NL). LO BB 5-11 NT v GW (Kimberley) 1995-96. T20 HS 11*. T20 BB 1-17.

SMITH, Will Rew (Bedford S; Collingwood C, Durham), b Luton, Beds 28 Sep 1982. 5'9". RHB, OB. Debut 2002. Durham UCCE 2003–04-05; captain 2004-05. British U 2004-05. Notts 2nd XI debut 1999 when aged 16y 309d. HS 156 DU v Somerset (Taunton) 2005, sharing opening partnership of 304 with A.J.Maiden. Nt HS 38* v WI A (Nottingham) 2002 – on debut. CC HS 13 v Hants (Southampton) 2005. BB 3-34 DU v Leics (Leicester) 2005. Nt BB 1-21 (not CC). LO HS 36 v Worcs (Nottingham) 2005 (NL). T20 HS 55.

SWANN, Graeme Peter (Sponne SS, Towcester), b Northampton 24 Mar 1979. Son of R.Swann (Northumberland 1969-72; Bedfordshire 1988-95); younger brother of A.J.Swann (*see LANCASHIRE*). 6'0". RHB, OB. Northamptonshire 1998-04; cap 1999. Nottinghamshire debut 2005. Bedfordshire 1996. **LOI**: 1 (1999-00); dnb v SA (Bloemfontein) 1999-00. F-c Tours (Eng A): SA 1998-99, 1999-00 (Eng); WI 2000-01 (*part*); Z 1998-99. HS 183 Nh v Glos (Bristol) 2002 – including 114 before lunch on third day. Nt HS 63 v LU (Nottingham) 2005. 50 wkts (1): 57 (1999). BB 7-33 Nh v Derbys (Northampton) 2003. Nt BB 6-57 v Warwks (Birmingham) 2005. LO HS 83 Nh v Leics (Northampton) 2001 (NL). LO BB 5-35 Nh v Durham (Chester-le-St) 1999 (NL). T20 HS 62. T20 BB 3-22.

WARREN, Russell John (Kingsthorpe Upper S), b Northampton 10 Sep 1971. 6'1". RHB, OB. Northamptonshire 1992-2002; cap 1995. Nottinghamshire debut 2003. Cap 2004. 1000 runs (1): 1303 (2001). HS 201* Nh v Glamorgan(Northampton) 1996. Award: CGT 1. Nt HS 134 v Leics (Nottingham) 2004. LO HS 100* Nh v Ire (Northampton) 1994 (NWT). T20 HS 26.

RELEASED/RETIRED

(Having made a first-class County appearance in 2005)

NEWBY, O.J. – see LANCASHIRE.

NOYOUNIS KHAN, Mohammad, b Mardan, North-West Frontier Province, Pakistan 29 Nov 1977. RHB, RM/LB. Peshawar 1998-99. Habib Bank 1999-00 to date. Nottinghamshire 2005. **Tests** (P): 42 (1999-00 to 2005-06, 2 as captain); HS 267 v I (Bangalore) 2004-05; BB 1-24. **LOI** (P): 126 (1999-00 to 2005-05, 2 as captain); HS 144 v Hong Kong (Colombo) 2004; BB 1-24. F-c Tours (P): E 2001; A 2004-05; SA 2002-03; WI 1999-00, 2004-05; NZ 2000-01; I 2004-05; SL 2000-01, 2002-03; Z 2002-03; B 2001-02. 1000 (0+1): 1315 (1999-00). HS 267 (*see Tests*). Nt HS 53 v Glamorgan (Cardiff) 2005. BB 3-24 Habib Bank v Faisalabad (Faisalabad) 1999-00). Nt BB 2-21 v Warwks (Nottingham) 2005. Nt LO: 144(*see LOI*). LO BB 3-5 v Glos (Cheltenham) 2005 (NL). T20 HS 35.

R.Hodgkinson left the staff without having made a first-class appearance in 2005.

NOTTINGHAMSHIRE 2005

RESULTS SUMMARY

	Place	Won	Lost	Tied	Drew	No Result
County Championship (1st Division)	1st	9	3		4	
All First-Class Matches		9	3		5	
C & G Trophy	2nd Round					
National League (1st Division)	5th	6	7			3
Twenty20 Cup	6th in North Division					

COUNTY CHAMPIONSHIP AVERAGES

BATTING AND FIELDING

Cap		M	I	NO	HS	Runs	Avge	100	50	Ct/St
1999	P.J.Franks	4	5	3	104*	189	94.50	1	–	–
2004	D.J.Hussey	15	20	2	232*	1231	68.38	3	7	29
2005	S.P.Fleming	11	16	1	238·	908	60.53	4	2	14
1998	J.E.R.Gallian	16	26	4	199	1163	52.86	3	4	14
2000	D.J.Bicknell	16	26	3	123	1131	49.17	2	9	2
1999	C.M.W.Read	15	20	4	103*	715	44.68	1	7	58/2
2004	M.A.Ealham	15	19	3	72	484	30.25	–	3	5
2004	R.J.Warren	8	12	1	60*	330	30.00	–	3	6
–	Younis Khan	5	7	1	53	131	21.83	–	1	4
–	A.Singh	6	9	–	57	170	18.88	–	1	2
–	G.P.Swann	14	16	2	53	259	18.50	–	1	5
2001	G.J.Smith	14	15	3	26	135	11.25	–	–	4
2000	A.J.Harris	11	11	4	35	75	10.71	–	–	4
2004	R.J.Sidebottom	14	14	3	31	107	9.72	–	–	5
–	W.R.Smith	3	5	1	13	34	8.50	–	–	1
–	S.R.Patel	3	4	–	12	27	6.75	–	–	–

Also batted: D.Alleyne (1 match) 6, 40 (5 ct); G.D.Clough (1) 14*, 0; M.H.A.Footitt (2) 16, 0, 19* (1 ct); O.J.Newby (2) 11, 38*, 0.

BOWLING

	O	M	R	W	Avge	Best	5wI	10wM
M.A.Ealham	390.5	90	1165	56	20.80	5- 31	1	–
R.J.Sidebottom	415.3	122	1096	48	22.83	5- 61	1	–
A.J.Harris	303.5	48	1214	47	25.82	6- 76	3	–
G.J.Smith	374.5	86	1295	46	28.15	4- 28	–	–
G.P.Swann	364.2	77	1140	30	38.00	6- 57	1	–
Also bowled:								
S.R.Patel	77.1	17	218	6	36.33	3- 73	–	–
M.H.A.Footitt	43.3	6	260	6	43.33	4- 45	–	–
O.J.Newby	47	10	223	5	44.60	2- 78	–	–
P.J.Franks	87	13	360	8	45.00	2- 37	–	–
D.J.Hussey	56	8	254	5	50.80	4-105	–	–

D.J.Bicknell 5.3-0-46-0; G.D.Clough 24-2-84-1; J.E.R.Gallian 30-4-180-0; W.R.Smith 9.3-0-70-0; Younis Khan 37.1-1-151-4.

The First-Class Averages (pp 129–145) give the records of Nottinghamshire players in all first-class matches for the county (Nottinghamshire's other opponents being Loughborough UCCE), with the exception of W.R.Smith whose full county figures are as above, P.J.McMahon whose only first-class appearances were for Oxford UCCE and:
G.P.Swann 15-17-2-63-322-21.46-0-2-5ct. 367.2-79-1141-30-38.03-6/57-1-0.

NOTTINGHAMSHIRE RECORDS

FIRST-CLASS CRICKET

Highest Total	For	739-7d		v	Leics	Nottingham	1903
	V	781-7d		by	Northants	Northampton	1995
Lowest Total	For	13		v	Yorkshire	Nottingham	1901
	V	16		by	Derbyshire	Nottingham	1879
		16		by	Surrey	The Oval	1880
Highest Innings	For	312*	W.W.Keeton	v	Middlesex	The Oval	1939
	V	345	C.G.Macartney	for	Australians	Nottingham	1921

Highest Partnership for each Wicket

1st	406*	D.J.Bicknell/G.E.Welton	v	Warwicks	Birmingham	2000
2nd	398	A.Shrewsbury/W.Gunn	v	Sussex	Nottingham	1890
3rd	369	W.Gunn/J.R.Gunn	v	Leics	Nottingham	1903
4th	361	A.O.Jones/J.R.Gunn	v	Essex	Leyton	1905
5th	266	A.Shrewsbury/W.Gunn	v	Sussex	Hove	1884
6th	372*	K.P.Pietersen/J.E.Morris	v	Derbyshire	Derby	2001
7th	301	C.C.Lewis/B.N.French	v	Durham	Chester-le-St	1993
8th	220	G.F.H.Heane/R.Winrow	v	Somerset	Nottingham	1935
9th	170	J.C.Adams/K.P.Evans	v	Somerset	Taunton	1994
10th	152	E.B.Alletson/W.Riley	v	Sussex	Hove	1911
	152	U.Afzaal/A.J.Harris	v	Worcs	Nottingham	2000

Best Bowling	For	10-66	K.Smales	v	Glos	Stroud	1956
(Innings)	V	10-10	H.Verity	for	Yorkshire	Leeds	1932
Best Bowling	For	17-89	F.C.Matthews	v	Northants	Nottingham	1923
(Match)	V	17-89	W.G.Grace	for	Glos	Cheltenham	1877

Most Runs – Season	2620	W.W.Whysall	(av 53.46)		1929
Most Runs – Career	31592	G.Gunn	(av 35.69)		1902-32
Most 100s – Season	9	W.W.Whysall			1928
	9	M.J.Harris			1971
	9	B.C.Broad			1990
Most 100s – Career	65	J.Hardstaff jr			1930-55
Most Wkts – Season	181	B.Dooland	(av 14.96)		1954
Most Wkts – Career	1653	T.G.Wass	(av 20.34)		1896-1920
Most Career W-K Dismissals	957	T.W.Oates	(733 ct/224 st)		1897-1925
Most Career Catches in the Field	466	A.O.Jones			1892-1914

LIMITED-OVERS CRICKET

Highest Total	CGT	344-6		v	Northumb	Jesmond	1994
	NL	329-6		v	Derbyshire	Nottingham	1993
	T20	210-7		v	Yorkshire	Nottingham	2004
Lowest Total	CGT	123		v	Yorkshire	Scarborough	1969
	NL	66		v	Yorkshire	Bradford	1969
	T20	94		v	Derbyshire	Derby	2003
Highest Innings	CGT	149*	D.W.Randall	v	Devon	Torquay	1988
	NL	167*	P.Johnson	v	Kent	Nottingham	1993
	T20	91	M.A.Ealham	v	Yorkshire	Nottingham	2004
Best Bowling	CGT	6-10	K.P.Evans	v	Northumb	Jesmond	1994
	NL	6-12	R.J.Hadlee	v	Lancashire	Nottingham	1980
	T20	5-26	R.J.Logan	v	Lancashire	Nottingham	2003

SOMERSET

Formation of Present Club: 18 August 1875
Inaugural First-Class Match: 1882
Colours: Black, White and Maroon
Badge: Somerset Dragon
County Champions: (0); best – 2nd (Div 1) 2001
Gillette/NatWest/C & G Trophy Winners: (3) 1979, 1983, 2001
Benson and Hedges Cup Winners: (2) 1981, 1982
National League (Div 1) Winners: (0); best – 4th 2001
Sunday League Winners: (1) 1979
Twenty20 Cup Winners: (1) 2005
Match Awards: CGT 63; BHC 70

Chief Executive: Richard A.Gould, County Ground, Taunton TA1 1JT • Tel: 01823 272946 • Fax: 01823 332395 • Email: enquiries@somersetcountycc.co.uk • Web: www.somersetcountycc.co.uk

First XI Coach: A.Hurry. **Director of Academy**: J.I.D.Kerr. **Captain**: I.D.Blackwell. **Vice-Captain**: M.J.Wood. **Overseas Players**: D.J.Cullen and C.L.White. **2006 Beneficiary**: R.L.Johnson. **Head Groundsman**: P.W.Frost. **Scorer**: G.A.Stickley. ‡ New registration. NQ Not qualified for England.

ANDREW, Gareth Mark (Ansford Community S; Richard Huish C), b Yeovil 27 Dec 1983. 6'0". LHB, RMF. Debut 2003. Somerset 2nd XI debut 1999 when aged 15y 247d. HS 44 and BB 4-63 v SL A (Taunton) 2004. CC HS 32 v Lancs (Taunton) 2005. CC BB 4-134 v Derbys (Taunton) 2005. LO HS 23 v Hants (Southampton) 2003 (NL). LO BB 4-48 v Scot (Taunton) 2004 (NL). T20 HS 12. T20 BB 4-22.

BLACKWELL, Ian David (Brookfield Community S), b Chesterfield, Derbys 10 Jun 1978. 6'2". LHB, SLA. Derbyshire 1997-99. Somerset debut 2000; cap 2001; captain 2006. **LOI**: 28 (2002-03 to 2005-06); HS 82 v I (Colombo) 2002-03; BB 3-26 v A (Adelaide) 2002-03. 1000 runs (2); most – 1256 (2005). HS 247* v Derbys (Taunton) 2003 – off 156 balls and including 204 off 98 balls in reduced post-lunch session. Won Walter Lawrence Trophy 2005 for 67-ball hundred v Derbys (Taunton). BB 7-90 v Glamorgan (Taunton) 2004 and 7-90 v Notts (Nottingham) 2004. Awards: CGT 1; BHC 1. LO HS 134* v Sussex (Taunton) 2005 (NL). LO BB 5-26 v Derbys (Taunton) 2005 (NL) T20 HS 82. T20 BB 4-26.

CADDICK, Andrew Richard (Papanui HS), b Christchurch, NZ 21 Nov 1968. Son of English emigrants – qualified for England 1992. 6'5". RHB, RFM. Debut 1991; cap 1992; benefit 1999. Represented NZ in 1987-88 Youth World Cup. *Wisden* 2000. **ECB contracts 2000-01-02-03**. **Tests**: 62 (1993 to 2002-03); HS 49* v A (Birmingham) 2001; BB 7-46 v SA (Durban) 1999-00. **LOI**: 54 (1993 to 2002-03); HS 36 v A (Oval) 2001; BB 4-19 v SA (Johannesburg) 1999-00. F-c Tours: A 1992-93 (Eng A), 2002-03; SA 1999-00; WI 1993-94, 1997-98; NZ 1996-97, 2001-02; P 2000-01; Z 1996-97. HS 92 v Worcs (Worcester) 1995. 50 wkts (10) inc 100 (1): 105 (1998). BB 9-32 (12-120 match) v Lancs (Taunton) 1993. Awards: CGT 2. LO HS 39 v Hants (Taunton) 1996 (SL). LO BB 6-30 v Glos (Taunton) 1992 (NWT). T20 HS 0. T20 BB 2-12.

‡NQCULLEN, Daniel James, b Woodville, Adelaide, Australia 10 Apr 1984. RHB, OB. S Australia 2004-05 to date. HS 42 S Aus v Tas (Hobart) 2004-05. BB 5-38 S Aus v WA (Perth) 2004-05. LO HS 13* S Aus v WA (Perth) 2004-05. LO BB 3-55 S Aus v Vic (Melbourne) 2004-05. T20 HS 10. T20 BB 2-14.

DURSTON, Wesley John (Millfield S; University C, Worcester), b Taunton 6 Oct 1980. 5'10". RHB, OB. Debut 2002. HS 146* v Derbys (Derby) 2005. BB 3-23 v SL A (Taunton) 2004. CC BB 2-82 v Northants (Taunton) 2005. LO HS 58* v Warwks (Taunton) 2005 (NL). LO BB 2-21 v Durham (Chester-le-St) 2005 (NL). T20 HS 34. T20 BB 3-25.

EDWARDS, Neil James (Cape Cornwall CS; Richard Huish C), b Treliske, Cornwall 14 Oct 1983. 6'3". LHB, RM. Debut 2002. HS 160 v Hants (Taunton) 2003. BB 1-16. T20 HS 1.

FRANCIS, John Daniel (King Edward VI S, Southampton; Durham U; Loughborough U), b Bromley, Kent 13 Nov 1980. Younger brother of S.R.G.Francis. 5'11". LHB, SLA. Hampshire 2001-03. British U 2002-03. Loughborough UCCE 2003. Somerset debut 2004. 1000 (1): 1062 (2005). HS 125* v Yorks (Leeds) 2005 – carrying bat. BB (H) 1-1. Sm BB 1-4. LO HS 103* H v Northants (Southampton) 2002 (NL). T20 HS 49.

FRANCIS, Simon Richard George (Yardley Court, Tonbridge; King Edward VI S, Southampton; Durham U), b Bromley, Kent 15 Aug 1978. Elder brother of J.D.Francis. 6'2". RHB, RMF. Hampshire 1997-2000. British U 1998-99. Somerset debut 2002. F-c Tour (Eng A): I 2003-04. HS 44 v Yorks (Taunton) 2003. BB 5-42 v Glamorgan (Taunton) 2004. Hat-trick 2003. LO HS 33* v Derbys (Taunton) 2003 (NL). LO BB 8-66 v Derbys (Derby) 2004 (CGT) – record l-o Sm analysis. T20 HS 9*. T20 BB 2-22.

GAZZARD, Carl Matthew (Mounts Bay CS, Penzance; Richard Huish C), b Penzance, Cornwall 15 Apr 1982. 6'0". RHB, WK. Debut 2002. Cornwall 1998 to date. HS 74 v Worcester (Worcester) 2005. CC HS 41 v Northants (Taunton) 2003. LO HS 157 v Derbys (Derby) 2004 (NL). T20 HS 39.

HILDRETH, James Charles (Millfield S), b Milton Keynes, Bucks 9 Sep 1984. 5'10". RHB, RMF. Debut 2003. HS 125* v Essex (Colchester) 2005. CC HS 108 v Notts (Nottingham) 2004. BB 2-39 v Hants (Taunton) 2004. LO HS 85 v Notts (Nottingham) 2004 (NL). LO BB (Somerset CB) 1-44 (CGT). T20 HS 71. T20 BB 3-24.

JOHNSON, Richard Leonard (Sunbury Manor S; S Pelthorne C), b Chertsey, Surrey 29 Dec 1974. 6'2". RHB, RFM. Middlesex 1992-2000; cap 1995. Somerset debut/cap 2001; benefit 2006. **Tests**: 3 (2003 to 2003-04); HS 26 v SL (Galle) 2003-04; BB 6-33 v Z (Chester-le-St) 2003 on debut, including wickets with his third and fourth balls. Hit first ball in Test cricket for four. **LOI**: 10 (2003 to 2003-04); HS 10 v SA (Manchester) 2003; BB 3-22 v B (Dhaka) 2003-04. Took wicket with his second ball in LOI. F-c Tours: I 1994-95 (Eng A – part), 2001-02; SL 2003-04, B 2003-04. HS 118 v Glos (Bristol) 2003 (100 off 75 balls). Won Walter Lawrence Trophy 2004 for 63-ball hundred v Durham (Chester-le-St). 50 wkts (4); most – 62 (2001). BB 10-45 M v Derbys (Derby) 1994 (second youngest to take all ten wickets in any f-c match). Sm BB 7-43 (10-75 match) v Hants (Bath) 2002. Award: CGT 1. LO HS 53 v Derbys (Derby) 2003 (NL). LO BB 5-50 M v Kent (Lord's) 1997 (NWT). T20 HS 10. T20 BB 3-21.

^NQ^**McLEAN, Nixon** Alexei McNamara (Crapan SS, St Vincent), b Stubbs, St Vincent 20 Jul 1973. 6'4". LHB, RFM. Windward Is 1991-92 to 2000-01. Hampshire 1998-99; cap 1998. KwaZulu-Natal 2001-02 to 2003-04. Somerset debut/cap 2003. **Tests** (WI): 19 (1997-98 to 2000-01); HS 46 v P (Georgetown) 1999-00; BB 3-53 v SA (Cape Town) 1998-99. **LOI** (WI): 45 (1996-97 to 2002-03); HS 50* v Z (Canterbury) 2000; BB 3-21 v A (Perth) 2000-01. F-c Tours (WI): E 2000; A 1996-97, 2000-01; SA 1997-98 (WI A), 1998-99. HS 76 v Glos (Taunton) 2003. 50 wkts (2): most – 65 (2003). BB 7-28 WI v FS (Bloemfontein) 1998-99. UK BB 6-79 (11-124 match) Sm v Yorks (Scarborough) 2004. LO HS 50* (see LOI). LO BB 5-26 WI Select XI v P (St John's) 1999-00.

MUNDAY, Michael Kenneth (Truro S, Cornwall; Corpus Christi C, Oxford), b Nottingham 22 Oct 1984. 5'7½". RHB, LB. Oxford U 2003-04; blue 2003-4. Somerset debut 2005. Cornwall 2001-03. HS 14 OU v Surrey (Oxford) 2004. Sm HS – . BB 5-83 OU v CU (Cambridge) 2004. Sm BB 1-77. LO HS – and BB 1-39 Cornwall v Sussex (Truro) 2001 (CGT).

PARSONS, Keith Alan (The Castle S, Taunton; Richard Huish C), b Taunton 2 May 1973. Identical twin brother of K.J.Parsons (Somerset staff 1992-94). 6'1". RHB, RM. Debut 1992; cap 1999; benefit 2004. HS 193* v WI (Taunton) 2000. CC HS 139 v Northants (Taunton) 2001. BB 5-13 v Lancs (Taunton) 2000. Awards: CGT 2. LO HS 121 v Worcs (Taunton) 2002 (CGT). LO BB 5-39 v Derbys (Derby) 2004 (NL). T20 HS 57*. T20 BB 3-12.

PARSONS, Michael (Ladymead Community S, Taunton; Richard Huish C), b Taunton 26 Nov 1984. 5'11". RHB, RMF. Debut 2005. HS 6*. LO HS 1* (NL). LO BB 3-70 Somerset CB v Cornwall (Camborne) 2002. T20 HS 0.

NOSUPPIAH, Arul Vivasvan (Exeter U), b Kuala Lumpur, Malaysia 30 Aug 1983. Son of R.Suppiah (Kuala Lumpur). Brother of R.V.Suppiah (Malaysia – vice-captain). 6'0". RHB, SLA. Somerset debut 2002. Malaysia 1999-2001. HS 123 v Derbys (Derby) 2005. CC HS 21 v Lancs (Taunton) 2002 – on debut. BB 3-46 v WI A (Taunton) 2002. CC BB 2-36 v Leics (Leicester) 2004. LO HS 79 v Derbys (Derby) 2005 (NL). LO BB 3-41 v Surrey (Oval) 2005 (NL). T20 HS 18*. T20 BB 1-5.

TREGO, Peter David (Wyvern CS, W-s-M), b Weston-super-Mare 12 Jun 1981. 6'0". RHB, RMF. Somerset 2000-02; 2nd XI debut 1997 when aged 16y 20d. Kent 2003. Middlesex 2005. HS 140 v West Indies A (Taunton) 2002. CC HS 72 M v Glamorgan (Southgate) 2005 – on Middx debut. BB 6-59 M v Notts (Nottingham) 2005. LO HS 31* and BB 4-39 K v Leics (Canterbury) 2003 (NL). T20 HS 11. T20 BB 2-17.

TRESCOTHICK, Marcus Edward (Sir Bernard Lovell S), b Keynsham 25 Dec 1975. 6'2". LHB, RM. Debut 1993; cap 1999; joint captain 2002. PCA 2000. *Wisden* 2004. MBE 2005. **ECB contracts 2001-02-03-04-05. Tests**: 69 (2000 to 2005-06, 2 as captain); HS 219 v SA (Oval) 2003; BB 1-34. **LOI**: 114 (2000 to 2005-06, 10 as captain); HS 137 v P (Lord's) 2001; BB 2-7 v Z (Manchester) 2000. F-c Tours: A 2002-03; SA 1004-05; WI 2003-04; NZ 1999-00 (Eng A), 2001-02; I 2001-02; P 2000-01, 2005-06; SL 2000-01, 2003-04; B 1999-00 (Eng A), 2003-04. HS 219 (*see Tests*). Sm HS 190 v Middx (Taunton) 1999. BB 4-36 (inc hat-trick) v Young A (Taunton) 1995. CC BB 4-82 v Yorks (Leeds) 1998. Hat-trick 1995. Awards: CGT 4; BHC 3. LO HS 137 (*see LOI*). LO BB 4-50 v Northants (Northampton) 2000 (NL). T20 HS 56.

‡**NOWHITE, Cameron** Leon, b Bairnsdale, Victoria, Australia 18 Aug 1983. 6'1½". RHB, LB. Victoria 2000-01 to date. **LOI** (A): 2 (2005-06); HS 0 and BB 1-34 v NZ (Christchurch) 2005-06. HS 119 Vic v Q (Brisbane) 2004-05. BB 6-66 Vic v WA (Perth) 2002-03. LO HS 61 Aus A v WI (Hobart) 2004-05 and Vic v NSW (Sydney) 2004-05. LO BB 4-15 Vic v Tas (Melbourne) 2004-05. T20 HS 58*. T20 BB 3-8.

‡**NOWILLOUGHBY, Charl** Myles (Wynberg BHS; Stellenbosch U), b Cape Town, South Africa 3 Dec 1974. 6'2". LHB, LMF. Boland 1994-95 to 1999-00. W Province 2000-01 to 2003-04. WP-Boland 2000-05. Berkshire 2000. MCC 2001, 2004. Leicestershire 2005 (Kolpak registration). **Tests** (SA): 2 (2002-03); HS – ; BB 1-47 v B (Chittagong) 2002-03 – on debut. **LOI** (SA): 3 (1999-00 to 2002-03); HS 0; BB 2-39 v P (Sharjah) 1999-00 – on debut. F-c Tours (SA): E 2003; WI 1999-00 (SA A); Z 1998-99 (SA Acad), 2004 (SA A); B 2002-03. HS 17* Boland v North West (Paarl) 1999-00. Le HS 16* Le v Worcs (Leicester) 2005. 50 wkts (0+2); most 51 (2004-05). BB 7-56 WP v Northerns (Pretoria) 2003-04. Le BB 4-92 Le v Durham (Chester-le-St) 2005. Award: CGT 1. LO HS 11 Boland v N Transvaal (Pretoria) 1996-97. LO BB 6-16 Le v Somerset (Leicester) 2005 (NL). T20 HS 11. T20 BB 4-9.

WOOD, Matthew James (Exmouth Community C; Exeter U), b Exeter, Devon 30 Sep 1980. 5'11". RHB, OB. Debut 2001; cap 2005. 2nd XI debut 1997 when aged 16y 345d. Devon 1998-2000. 1000 (1): 1058 (2005). HS 297 v Yorks (Taunton) 2005. LO HS 129 v Yorks (Taunton) 2005 (NL). T20 HS 94.

WOODMAN, Robert James (Castle School; Taunton; Richard Huish S); b Taunton 12 Oct 1986. 5'11". LHB, LMF. Debut 2005. HS 46* v Worcs (Worcester) 2005 – on debut. BB 1-78. LO HS – . LO BB 1-38 (NL). T20 HS 1*. T20 BB 2-37.

RELEASED/RETIRED

(Registered players who made a first-class County appearance in 2005)

BURNS, Michael (Walney CS), b Barrow-in-Furness, Lancs 6 Feb 1969. 6'0". RHB, RM, WK. Cumberland 1988-90. Warwickshire 1992-96. Somerset 1997-2005; cap 1999; captain 2003-04. Scored earliest hundred in UK f-c matches (160 v OU (Taunton) on 7 Apr 2000). 1000 runs (2): most – 1133 (2003). HS 221 v Yorks (Bath) 2001. BB 6-54 v Leics (Taunton) 2001. Awards: CGT 1; BHC 1. LO HS 115* v Middx (Taunton) 1997 (SL). LO BB 4-39 v Glos (Taunton) 1997 (SL). T20 HS 36. T20 BB 1-15.

[NQ]**JAYASURIYA, Sanath** Teran (St Servatius C, Matara), b Matara, Ceylon 30 Jun 1969. 5'7". LHB, SLA. Colombo 1988-89 to 1992-93. Southern Districts/Province 1989-90 to 1993-94. Bloomfield 1994-95 to date. Somerset 2005. **Tests** (SL): 100 (1990-91 to 2005-06, 38 as captain); HS 340 v I (Colombo) 1997-98; BB 5-34 v SA (Colombo) 2004. **LOI** (SL): 353 (1989-90 to 2005-06, 118 as captain); HS 189 v I (Sharjah) 2000-01. Scored fastest LOI hundred (48 balls) v P (Singapore) 1995-96. BB 6-29 v E (Moratuwa) 1992-93. F-c Tours (SL) (C=captain): E 1991, 1998, 2002C; A 1995-96, 2004; SA 1992-93 (SL U-24), 1994-95, 1997-98, 2000-01C, 2002-03C; WI 1996-97, 2003; NZ 1990-91, 1994-95, 1996-97, 2004-05; I 1993-94, 1997-98; P 1988-89 (SL B), 1991-92, 1995-96, 1999-00C, 2001-02C, 2004-05; Z 1994-95, 1999-00C, 2003-04. 1000 (0+1): 1229 (2003-04). HS 340 (see Tests). Sm HS 73 v Lancs (Taunton) 2005. BB 5-34 (see Tests). Sm BB 2-2 v Durham (Stockton) 2005. LO HS 189 (see LOI). LO BB 6-29 (see LOI). T20 HS 27*. T20 BB 3-36.

[NQ]**LANGEVELDT, Charl** Kenneth (Luckhoff SS), b Stellenbosch, S Africa 17 Dec 1974. RHB, RFM. Boland 1997-98 to 2003-04. Lions 2004-05. Somerset 2005; cap 2005. **Tests** (SA): 6 (2004-05 to 2005-06); HS 10 v WI (Georgetown) 2004-05; BB 5-46 v E (Cape Town) 2004-05 – on debut. **LOI** (SA): 29 (2001-02 to 2005-06); HS 3; BB 5-62 v WI (Bridgetown) 2004-05. F-c Tour (SA): A 2005-06. HS 56 Boland v E Province (Port Elizabeth) 1999-00. Sm HS 18* and Sm BB 3-67 (twice) v Leics (Taunton) 2005 – on UK debut. BB 5-19 Boland v Free State (Paarl) 2000-01. LO HS 33* S Africa A v SL (Potchefstroom) 2002-03. LO BB 5-7 SA President's XI v B (Pietermaritzburg) 2000-01. T20 HS 2. T20 BB 2-14.

LARAMAN, Aaron William (Enfield GS), b Enfield, Middx 10 Jan 1979. 6'5". RHB, RFM. Middlesex 1998-2002. Somerset 2003-05. HS 148* v Glos (Taunton) 2003. BB 5-58 v Derbys (Taunton) 2004. LO HS 51 v Scot (Edinburgh) 2005 (NL). LO BB 6-42 M v Glamorgan(Cardiff) 2000 (NL). T20 HS 28*. T20 BB 4-15.

[NQ]**SMITH, Graeme** Craig (King Edward VII S, Johannesburg), b Johannesburg. South Africa 1 Feb 1981. 6'3". LHB, OB. UCB Invitation XI 1999-00, scoring 187 on debut v GW (Kimberley). W Province 2000-01 to 2003-04. WP-Boland 2004-05. Gauteng (l-o) 1999-00. Somerset 2005; captain/cap 2005. *Wisden* 2003. **Tests** (SA): 42 (2001-02 to 2005-06, 34 as captain); HS 277 v E (Birmingham) 2003; BB 2-145 v WI (St John's) 2004-05. **LOI** (SA): 85 (2001-02 to 2005-06, 63 as captain); HS 134* v I (Calcutta) 2005-06; BB 3-30 v SL (Perth) 2005-06. F-c Tours (SA) (C=captain): E 2003C; A 2005-06C; WI 2004-05C; NZ 2003-04C; I 2004-05C; P 2003-04C; SL 2004C; B 2002-03C. HS 311 v Leics (Taunton) 2005. BB 2-145 (see Tests). Sm BB 1-34. LO HS 117* WP v N West (Cape Town) 2001-02. LO BB 3-35 WP v FS (Bloemfontein) 2001-02. T20 HS 105. T20 BB 3-23.

TURNER, Robert Julian (Millfield S; Magdalene C, Cambridge), b Malvern, Worcs 25 Nov 1967. 6'1½". RHB, WK. Brother of S.J.Turner (Somerset 1984-85). Cambridge U 1988-91; blue 1988-89-90-91; captain 1991. Somerset 1991-2005; cap 1994; benefit 2002. Cambridgeshire 1990. F-c Tours (Eng A): NZ 1999-00; B 1999-00. Held 7 catches in an innings v Northants (Taunton) 2001. 1000 runs (2); most – 1217 (1999). HS 144 v Kent (Taunton) 1997. Award: BHC 1. LO HS 70 v Glamorgan(Cardiff) 1996 (BHC). T20 HS 11.

SOMERSET 2005

RESULTS SUMMARY

	Place	Won	Lost	Tied	Drew	No Result
County Championship (2nd Division)	8th	4	7		5	
All First-Class Matches		4	7		6	
C & G Trophy	1st Round					
National League (2nd Division)	6th	9	8			1
Twenty20 Cup	Winners					

COUNTY CHAMPIONSHIP AVERAGES

BATTING AND FIELDING

Cap		M	I	NO	HS	Runs	Avge	100	50	Ct/St
2005	G.C.Smith	4	8	1	311	472	67.42	1	1	7
2001	I.D.Blackwell	16	27	4	122	1065	46.30	2	9	5
1999	K.A.Parsons	8	12	3	94	401	44.55	–	2	5
2005	M.J.Wood	12	21	–	297	891	42.42	2	5	4
–	J.D.Francis	16	29	4	125*	936	37.44	3	5	8
–	W.J.Durston	7	11	2	146*	323	35.88	1	–	5
–	J.C.Hildreth	15	27	4	125*	825	35.86	1	6	14
1999	M.Burns	8	15	1	87	456	32.57	–	2	4
–	A.V.Suppiah	7	13	–	123	419	32.23	1	2	1
1994	R.J.Turner	8	12	2	68*	255	25.50	–	1	21/1
–	S.T.Jayasuriya	7	13	–	73	327	25.15	–	3	2
–	C.M.Gazzard	8	10	2	74	190	23.75	–	1	15
–	S.R.G.Francis	6	9	5	29	87	21.75	–	–	6
1992	A.R.Caddick	10	16	3	54	256	19.69	–	1	3
–	R.J.Woodman	3	4	1	46*	54	18.00	–	–	1
1999	M.E.Trescothick	4	6	–	22	96	16.00	–	–	6
–	A.W.Laraman	8	12	–	53	186	15.50	–	1	2
2001	R.L.Johnson	10	15	–	35	218	14.53	–	5	3
–	G.M.Andrew	5	6	1	32	68	13.60	–	–	1
2005	C.K.Langeveldt	6	6	3	18*	38	12.66	–	–	1
2003	N.A.M.McLean	5	7	1	40	59	9.83	–	–	1

Also batted: M.Parsons (2 matches) 6*, 1, 4. M.K.Munday (1) did not bat.

BOWLING

	O	M	R	W	Avge	Best	5wI	10wM
A.R.Caddick	416.1	86	1441	52	27.71	6- 96	4	1
N.A.M.McLean	103	23	435	11	39.54	3-107		
A.W.Laraman	156	20	547	13	42.07	3- 68		
C.K.Langeveldt	215.1	59	637	15	42.46	3- 67		
G.M.Andrew	104.5	14	500	11	45.45	4-134		
R.L.Johnson	262.3	46	987	20	49.35	4-118		
I.D.Blackwell	481.5	98	1474	28	52.64	4- 86		
Also bowled:								
S.T.Jayasuriya	56.1	7	230	5	46.00	2- 2		
K.A.Parsons	112.1	19	428	7	61.14	3- 81		
W.J.Durston	92	8	449	6	74.83	2- 82		
S.R.G.Francis	114.4	16	520	5	104.00	2- 81		

M.Burns 25.5-2-91-2; J.C.Hildreth 11-0-49-0; M.K.Munday 14-0-77-1; M.Parsons 27-3-135-0; G.C.Smith 20-4-71-1; A.V.Suppiah 43.1-8-191-2; R.J.Woodman 66-11-268-2.

The First-Class Averages (pp 129–145) give the records of Somerset players in all first-class matches for the county (Somerset's other opponents being Durham UCCE), with the exception of M.K.Munday and M.E.Trescothick whose full county figures are as above.

SOMERSET RECORDS

FIRST-CLASS CRICKET

Highest Total	For 705-9d		v	Hampshire	Taunton	2003
	V 811		by	Surrey	The Oval	1899
Lowest Total	For 25		v	Glos	Bristol	1947
	V 22		by	Glos	Bristol	1920
Highest Innings	For 322	I.V.A.Richards	v	Warwicks	Taunton	1985
	V 424	A.C.MacLaren	for	Lancashire	Taunton	1895

Highest Partnership for each Wicket

1st	346	H.T.Hewett/L.C.H.Palairet	v	Yorkshire	Taunton	1892
2nd	290	J.C.W.MacBryan/M.D.Lyon	v	Derbyshire	Burton upon T	1924
3rd	319	P.M.Roebuck/M.D.Crowe	v	Leics	Taunton	1984
4th	310	P.W.Denning/I.T.Botham	v	Glos	Taunton	1980
5th	320	J.D.Francis/I.D.Blackwell	v	Durham UCCE	Taunton	2005
6th	265	W.E.Alley/K.E.Palmer	v	Northants	Northampton	1961
7th	279	R.J.Harden/G.D.Rose	v	Sussex	Taunton	1997
8th	172	I.V.A.Richards/I.T.Botham	v	Leics	Leicester	1983
	172	A.R.K.Pierson/P.S.Jones	v	N Zealanders	Taunton	1999
9th	183	C.H.M.Greetham/H.W.Stephenson	v	Leics	Weston-s-Mare	1963
	183	C.J.Tavaré/N.A.Mallender	v	Sussex	Hove	1990
10th	163	I.D.Blackwell/N.A.M.McLean	v	Derbyshire	Taunton	2003

Best Bowling	For 10- 49	E.J.Tyler	v	Surrey	Taunton	1895
(Innings)	V 10- 35	A.Drake	for	Yorkshire	Weston-s-Mare	1914
Best Bowling	For 16- 83	J.C.White	v	Worcs	Bath	1919
(Match)	V 17-137	W.Brearley	for	Lancashire	Manchester	1905

Most Runs – Season	2761	W.E.Alley	(av 58.74)	1961
Most Runs – Career	21142	H.Gimblett	(av 36.96)	1935-54
Most 100s – Season	11	S.J.Cook		1991
Most 100s – Career	49	H.Gimblett		1935-54
Most Wkts – Season	169	A.W.Wellard	(av 19.24)	1938
Most Wkts – Career	2166	J.C.White	(av 18.02)	1909-37
Most Career W-K Dismissals	1007	H.W.Stephenson	(698 ct/309 st)	1948-64
Most Career Catches in the Field	381	J.C.White		1909-37

LIMITED-OVERS CRICKET

Highest Total	CGT	413-4	v	Devon	Torquay	1990
	NL	377-9	v	Sussex	Hove	2003
	T20	228-5	v	Glos	Taunton	2005
Lowest Total	CGT	58	v	Middlesex	Southgate	2000
	NL	58	v	Essex	Chelmsford	1977
	T20	119-9	v	Glos	Taunton	2003
Highest Innings	CGT	162*	C.J.Tavaré	v	Devon	Torquay	1990
	NL	175*	I.T.Botham	v	Northants	Wellingborough	1986
	T20	105	G.C.Smith	v	Northants	Taunton	2005
Best Bowling	CGT	8-66	S.R.G.Francis	v	Derbyshire	Derby	2004
	NL	6-24	I.V.A.Richards	v	Lancashire	Manchester	1983
	T20	4-15	A.W.Laraman	v	Worcs	Taunton	2004

87

SURREY

Formation of Present Club: 22 August 1845
Inaugural First-Class Match: 1864
Colours: Chocolate
Badge: Prince of Wales' Feathers
County Champions (since 1890): (18) 1890, 1891, 1892, 1894, 1895, 1899, 1914, 1952, 1953, 1954, 1955, 1956, 1957, 1958, 1971, 1999, 2000, 2002
Joint Champions: (1) 1950
Gillette/NatWest/C & G Trophy Winners: (1) 1982
Benson and Hedges Cup Winners: (3) 1974, 1997, 2001
National League (Div 1) Winners: (1) 2003
Sunday League Winners: (1) 1996
Twenty20 Cup Winners: (1) 2003
Match Awards: CGT 57; BHC 76

Chief Executive: Paul C.J.Sheldon, Kennington Oval, London, SE11 5SS • Tel: 020 7582 6660 • Fax: 020 7735 7769 • E-mail: enquiries@surreyccc.com • Web: www.surreycricket.com

First XI Coach: A.R.Butcher. **Captain**: M.A.Butcher. **Vice-Captain**: R.Clarke. **Overseas Players**: Azhar Mahmood and A.Kumble. **2006 Beneficiary**: M.P.Bicknell (Testimonial). **Head Groundsman**: W.H.Gordon. **Scorer**: K.R.Booth. ‡ New registration. NQ Not qualified for England.

NQAZHAR MAHMOOD SAGAR (F.G. No. 1 HS, Islamabad), b Multan, Pakistan 28 Feb 1975. 5'11". RHB, RFM. Islamabad 1993-94 to 1997-98, 2001-02. United Bank 1996-97. Rawalpindi 1998-99. PIA 1999-00 to 2001-02. Surrey debut 2002; cap 2004. **Tests** (P): 21 (1997-98 to 2001); HS 136 v SA (Johannesburg) 1997-98; BB 4-50 v E (Lord's) 2001. Scored 128* and 50* v SA (Rawalpindi) 1997-98 on debut. **LOI** (P): 139 (1996-97 to 2004-05); HS 67 v I (Adelaide) 1999-00; BB 6-18 v WI (Sharjah) 1999-00. F-c Tours (P): E 2001; A 1999-00; SA 1997-98; I 1998-99; SL 2000-01; Z 1997-98. HS 204* v Middx (Oval) 2005. 50 wkts (0+1): 59 (1996-97). BB 8-61 v Lancs (Oval) 2002. LO HS 100* P v Aus A (Perth) 1999-00. LO BB 6-18 (*see LOI*). T20 HS 57*. T20 BB 4-20.

BATTY, Jonathan Neil (Wheatley Park S, Oxon; Repton S; Durham U; Keble C, Oxford), b Chesterfield, Derbys 18 Apr 1974. 5'10". RHB, WK. Minor C 1994. Comb U 1995. Oxford U 1996; blue 1996. Surrey debut 1997; cap 2001; captain 2004. Oxfordshire 1993-96. HS 168* v Essex (Chelmsford) 2003. BB 1-21. LO HS 158* v Hants (Oval) 2005 (CGT). T20 HS 39.

BENNING, James Graham Edward (Beacon S; Chesham S; Caterham S), b Mill Hill, N London 4 May 1983. 6'0". RHB, RM. Debut 2003. Buckinghamshire 2000-01. HS 128 v OU (Oxford) 2004. CC HS 57 v Glamorgan (Oval) 2005. BB 3-57 v Kent (Tunbridge Wells) 2005. HS 73 v Hants (Oval) 2005 (CGT). BB 4-43 v Leics (Oval) 2003 (NL). T20 HS 66. T20 BB 1-7.

BICKNELL, Martin Paul (Robert Haining County SS), b Guildford 14 Jan 1969. Younger brother of D.J.Bicknell (*see NOTTINGHAMSHIRE*). 6'3". RHB, RFM. Debut 1986; cap 1989; benefit 1997; Testimonial 2006. *Wisden* 2000. **Tests**: 4 (1993 to 2003); HS 15 v SA (Leeds) 2003; BB 4-84 v SA (Oval) 2003. **LOI**: 7 (1990-91); HS 31* v A (Perth) 1990-91; BB 3-55 v NZ (Christchurch) 1990-91. F-c Tours: A 1990-91; SA 1993-94 (Eng A); Z 1989-90 (Eng A). HS 141 v Essex (Chelmsford) 2003. 50 wkts (11); most – 72 (2001). BB 9-45 v CU (Oval) 1988. CC BB 9-47 (16-119 match) v Leics (Guildford) 2000. Took his 1000th f-c wicket 2004. Awards: BHC 3. LO HS 66* v Northants (Oval) 1991 (NWT). LO BB 7-30 v Glamorgan(Oval) 1999 (NL). T20 HS 10*. T20 BB 2-11.

BROWN, Alistair Duncan (Caterham S), b Beckenham, Kent 11 Feb 1970. 5'10". RHB, occ LB. Debut 1992; cap 1994; benefit 2002. **LOI**: 16 (1996 to 2001); HS 118 v I (Manchester) 1996. 1000 runs (7); most – 1382 (1993). HS 295* v Leics (Oakham) 2000 – record score (all levels) in Rutland. BB 1-11. Awards: CGT 1; BHC 4. LO HS 268 v Glamorgan(Oval) 2002 (CGT) – world record 1-o score (160 balls, 12 sixes, 30 fours). LO BB 3-39 v Notts (Nottingham) 2000 (NL). T20 HS 64.

BUTCHER, Mark Alan (Trinity S; Archbishop Tenison's S, Croydon), b Croydon 23 Aug 1972. Son of A.R.Butcher (Surrey, Glamorgan and England 1972-92); brother of G.P.Butcher (Glamorgan 1994-98; Surrey 1999-2001). 5'11". LHB, RM/OB. Debut 1992; cap 1996; captain 2005-; benefit 2005. **ECB contracts 2002-03-04-05. Tests**: 71 (1997 to 2004-05, 1 as captain); HS 173* v A (Leeds) 2001; BB 4-42 v A (Birmingham) 2001. F-c Tours: A 1996-97 (Eng A), 1998-99, 2002-03; SA 1999-00; WI 1997-98; NZ 2001-02; I 2001-02; SL 2003-04; B 2003-04. 1000 runs (7); most – 1604 (1996). HS 259 v Leics (Leicester) 1999. BB 5-86 v Lancs (Manchester) 2000. Awards: CGT 2; BHC 3. LO HS 104 v Yorks (Oval) 2003 (NL). LO BB 3-23 v Sussex (Oval) 1992 (SL). T20 HS 60.

CLARKE, Rikki (Broadwater SS; Godalming C), b Orsett, Essex 29 Sep 1981. 6'4". RHB, RFM. Debut 2002 – scoring 107* v CU (Cambridge); cap 2005. YC 2002. **Tests**: 2 (2003-04); HS 55 and BB 2-7 v B (Chittagong) 2003-04. **LOI**: 17 (2003 to 2004); HS 37 v SA (Birmingham) 2003; BB 2-28 v B (Dhaka) 2003-04. F-c Tours: WI 2003-04; SL 2002-03 (ECB Acad); B 2003-04. HS 153* v Somerset (Taunton) 2002. BB 4-21 v Leics (Leicester) 2003. Award: CGT 1. LO HS 98* v Derbys (Derby) 2002 (NL). LO BB 4-49 v Warwks (Birmingham) 2005 (NL). T20 HS 52. T20 BB 3-11.

CLINTON, Richard Selvey (Colfes S), b Sidcup, Kent 1 Sep 1981. Son of G.S.Clinton (Kent and Surrey 1974-90). 6'3". LHB, RM. Kent staff 1999-2000 – no f-c appearances. Essex 2001-02. Loughborough U. 2004. Surrey debut 2004. HS 107 Ex v CU (Cambridge) 2002. Sy HS 105 v Kent (Tunbridge Wells) 2005. BB 2-30 Ex v A (Chelmsford) 2001. CC BB – . LO HS 56 Ex v Durham (Ilford) 2001 (NL). LO BB 2-16 v Staffs (Leek) 2005 (CGT).

DERNBACH, Jade Winston (St John the Baptist S), b Johannesburg, South Africa 3 Mar 1986. 6'1½". RHB, RMF. Italian passport. UK resident since 1998. Debut 2003, when aged 17. 'Sir Jack Hobbs Fair Play Award' 2003. HS 3. CC HS 1*. BB 2-66 v Warwks (Birmingham) 2005. LO HS 21 v Warwks (Birmingham) 2005 (NL). LO BB 4-36 v Scot (Oval) 2005 (NL).

DOSHI, Nayan Dilip, b Nottingham 6 Oct 1978. Son of D.R.Doshi (Bengal, Notts, Warwks, Saurashtra, Herts and India 1968-69 to 1986). Saurashtra 2001-02 to 2003-04. Surrey debut 2004. Buckinghamshire 2001. HS 33 v Notts (Oval) 2005. BB 7-110 (10-183 match) v Sussex (Hove) 2004. LO HS 38* Saurashtra v Baroda (Bombay) 2001-02. LO BB 2-28 v Leics (Leicester) 2005 (NL). T20 HS 1*. T20 BB 4-27.

HAMILTON-BROWN, Rory James (Millfield S), b St John's Wood, London 3 Sep 1987. 6'0". RHB,OB. Debut 2005. Awaiting CC debut. HS 9 v Bangladesh A (Oval) 2005. LO HS 20 v Sussex (Guildford) 2005 (NL).

‡NQ**KUMBLE, Anil** (National HS; R.V. Engineering C, Bangalore), b Bangalore, India 17 Oct 1970. 6'1½". RHB, LB. Karnataka 1989-90 to date. Northamptonshire 1995 (cap 1995). Wisden 1995. **Tests** (I): 23 (1990 to 1995-96); HS 88 v SA (Calcutta) 1996-97; BB 10-74 (14-149 match) v P (Delhi) 1998-99. **LOI** (I): 262 (1989-90 to 2005, 1 as captain); HS 26 v A (Perth) 1999-00; BB 6-12 v WI (Calcutta) 1993-94. . F-c Tours (I): E 1990, 1996, 2002; A 1999-00, 2003-04; SA 1992-93, 1996-97, 2001-02; WI 1996-97, 2001-02; NZ 1993-94, 1998-99; P 2003-04, 2005-06; SL 1993-94, 1997-98, 1998-99; Z 1992-93, 1998-99, 2005-06; B 2004-05. HS 154* Karnataka v Kerala (Bijapur) 1991-92. CC HS 40* Nh v Glos (Northampton) 1995. 50 wkts (1+2) inc 100 (1); most – 105 (1995). BB 10-74 (see Tests). CC BB 7-82 Nh v Warwks (Birmingham) 1995. LO HS 30* Karnataka v Wills XI (Bangalore) 1994-95. LO BB 6-12 (see LOI).

89

‡**MILLER, Daniel** James (Ewell Castle S; Kingston-upon-Thames C; Loughborough U), b Hammersmith, London 12 Jun 1983. LHB, RFM. Summer contract 2005. Awaiting f-c debut. LO HS 1 v Northants (Croydon) 2002 (NL).

NQ**MOHAMMAD AKRAM** AWAN, b Islamabad, Pakistan 10 Sep 1972. 6'2". RHB, RFM. Rawalpindi 1992-93 to 1998-99, 2001-02 to date. Allied Bank 1996-97 to 2000-01. Northamptonshire 1997. Essex 2003. Sussex 2004; cap 2004. Surrey debut 2005. Tests (P): 9 (1995-96 to 2001-02); HS 10* and BB 5-138 v A (Perth) 1999-00. LOI (P): 23 (1995-96 to 2000-01); HS 7*; BB 2-28 v I (Toronto) 1997. F-c Tours (P): E 1996; A 1995-96. HS 35* Sx v Warwks (Birmingham) 2004. Sy HS 27* v Notts (Oval) 2005. BB 8-49 (10-142 match) Ex v Surrey (Oval) 2003. Sy BB 5-41 v Hants (Southampton) 2005. LO HS 33 Allied Bank v Faisalabad (Faisalabad) 1998-99. LO BB 4-19 Nh v Surrey (Northampton) 1997 (SL) T20 HS 7*. T20 BB 2-22.

MURTAGH, Timothy James (John Fisher S; St Mary's C), b Lambeth 2 Aug 1981. Nephew of A.J.Murtagh (Hampshire and E Province 1973-7). 6'0". LHB, RFM. British U 2000-03. Surrey debut 2001. HS 74* v Middx (Oval) 2004 and 74* v Warwks (Croydon) 2005. BB 6-86 Brit U v P (Nottingham) 2001. Sy BB 5-39 v Leics (Oval) 2002. LO HS31* v Durham (Oval) 2005 (NL). LO BB 4-14 v Derbys (Derby) 2005 (NL). T20 HS 24*. T20 BB 6-24.

NEWMAN, Scott Alexander (Trinity S, Croydon; Coulsdon C; Brighton U), b Epsom 3 Nov 1979. 6'2". LHB, RM. Debut 2002 – scoring 99 v Hants (Oval) 2002; cap 2005. F-c Tour (Eng A): I 2003-04. 1000 runs (2); most – 1286 (2005). HS 219 (and 117) v Glam (Oval) 2005. LO HS 106 v Essex (Oval) 2004 (NL). T20 HS 59.

ORMOND, James (St Thomas More S, Nuneaton), b Walsgrave, Coventry, Warwks 20 Aug 1977. 6'3". RHB, RFM. Leicestershire 1995-2001; cap 1999. Surrey debut 2002; cap 2003. **Tests**: 2 (2001 to 2001-02); HS 18 v A (Oval) 2001; BB 1-70. F-c Tours: NZ 2001-02; I 2001-02; SL 1997-98 (Eng A); K 1997-98 (Eng A). HS 57 v Glos (Bristol) 2004. Sy HS 47 v Middx (Guildford) 2003. 50 wkts (4); most – 52 (1999, 2004). BB 7-63 v Glamorgan (Cardiff) 2005. Hat-trick (4 wkts in 6 balls) 2003 Awards: BHC 2. LO HS 32 v Somerset (Taunton) 2005 (NL). LO BB 4-12 Le v Middx (Leicester) 1998 (SL). T20 HS 6. T20 BB 5-26.

RAMPRAKASH, Mark Ravin (Gayton HS; Harrow Weald SFC), b Bushey, Herts 5 Sep 1969. 5'9". RHB, RM. Middlesex 1987-2000; cap 1990; captain 1997-99. Surrey debut 2001 – scoring 146 v Kent (Oval); cap 2002. YC 1991. **ECB contract 2000**. **Tests**: 52 (1991 to 2001-02); HS 154 v WI (Bridgetown) 1997-98; BB 1-2. **LOI**: 18 (1991 to 2001-02); HS 51 v WI (Pt-of-Spain) 1997-98; BB 3-28 v Z (Harare) 2001-02. F-c Tours: A 1994-95 (part), 1998-99; SA 1995-96; WI 1991-92 (Eng A), 1993-94, 1997-98; NZ 1991-92, 2001-02; I 1994-95 (Eng A), 2001-02; P 1990-91 (Eng A); SL 1990-91 (Eng A). 1000 runs (15 inc 2000 (1): 2258 (1995). HS 279* v Notts (Croydon) 2003. BB 3-32 M v Glamorgan(Lord's) 1998. Sy BB 2-35 v Northants (Northampton) 2004. Awards: CGT 3; BHC 4. LO HS 147* M v Worcs (Lord's) 1990 (SL). LO BB 5-38 M v Leics (Lord's) 1993 (SL). T20 HS 76*.

SAKER, Neil Clifford (Raynes Park HS; Nescot C), b Tooting, London 20 Sep 1984. 6'4". RHB, RFM. Debut 2004. No f-c appearance 2004. HS 5. BB 1-62. CC BB 1-71. LO HS 2* (NL). LO BB 4-43 v Kent (Canterbury) 2005 (NL).

SALISBURY, Ian David Kenneth (Moulton CS), b Northampton 21 Jan 1970. 5'11". RHB, LBG. Sussex 1989-96; cap 1991. Surrey debut 1997; cap 1998. MCC YC. YC 1992. Wisden 1992. **Tests**: 15 (1992 to 2000-01); HS 50 v P (Manchester) 1992; BB 4-163 v WI (Georgetown) 1993-94. **LOI**: 4 (1992-93 to 1993-94); HS 5; BB 3-41 v WI (Pt-of-Spain) 1993-94. F-c Tours: WI 1991-92 (Eng A), 1993-94; I 1992-93; 1994-95 (Eng A); P 1990-91 (Eng A), 1995-96 (Eng A), 2000-01; SL 1990-91 (Eng A). HS 101* v Leics (Oval) 2003. 50 wkts (6); most – 87 (1992). BB 8-60 (12-91 match) v Somerset (Oval) 2000. Awards: CGT 1; BHC 2. LO HS 59* v Glamorgan(Oval) 2004 (NL). LO BB 5-30 Sx v Leics (Leicester) 1992 (SL). T20 HS 20. T20 BB 2-20.

(Having made a first-class County appearance in 2005)

^{NQ}**HARBHAJAN SINGH** PLAHA, b Jullundur City, India 3 Jul 1980. 6'0". RHB, OB. Punjab 1997-98 to date. Surrey 2005. **Tests** (I): 52 (1997-98 to 2005-06); HS 66 v Z (Bulawayo) 2001; BB 8-84 (15-217 match) v A (Madras) 2000-01. Took 28 wickets, including a hat-trick, in 2 Tests v Australia 2000-01. **LOI** (I): 117 (1997-98 to 2005-06); HS 46 v A (Vishakapatnam) 2000-01; BB 5-43 v E (Bombay) 2001-02. F-c Tours (I): E 2002; A 2003-04; SA 2001-02; WI 2001-02; NZ 1998-99, 2002-03; P 2005-06; SL 1998-99, 2001; Z 1998-99, 2001, 2005-06 ; B 2004-05. HS 84 Punjab v Haryana (Amritsar) 2000-01 and 84 v Glos (Bristol) 2005. UK HS 54 I v E (Nottingham) 2002. 50 wkts (0+2); most – 70 (2000-01). BB 8-84 (15-217 match) (*see Tests*). Hat-trick (India 2000-01). UK BB 7-83 I v Essex (Chelmsford) 2002. Sy BB 6-36 v Hants (Southampton) 2005. LO HS 46 (*see LOI*). LO BB 5-43 (*see LOI*). T20 HS 6. T20 BB 2-22.

HODD, A.J. – *see SUSSEX.*

^{NQ}**SAQLAIN MUSHTAQ** (Govt Muslim League HS, M.A.O. College, Lahore), b Lahore, Pakistan 29 Dec 1976. Brother of Sibtain Mushtaq (Lahore 1988-89). 5'11". RHB, OB. Islamabad 1994-95. PIA 1994-95 to 2001-02. Surrey 1997-2004; cap 1998. *Wisden* 1999. **Tests** (P): 49 (1995-96 to 2003-04); HS 101* v NZ (Christchurch) 2000-01; BB 8-164 v E (Lahore) 2000-01 (all eight wickets to fall). **LOI** (P): 169 (1995-96 to 2003-04); HS 37* v A (Brisbane) 1999-00; BB 5-20 v E (Rawalpindi) 2000-01, 2 hat-tricks. F-c Tours (P): E 1996, 2001; A 1995-96, 1996-97, 1999-00; SA 1997-98, 2002-03; WI 1999-00; NZ 2000-01; I 1998-99, SL 1996-97; Z 1997-98, 2002-03; B 1998-99, 2001-02. HS 101* (*see Tests*). Sy HS 69 v Middx (Lord's) 2003. 50 wkts (5+1); most – 66 (2000). BB 8-65 (11-107 match) v Derbys (Oval) 1988. Took 7-11 (including 7-5 in 34 balls) v Derbys (Oval) 2000. Three hat-tricks, all for Surrey 1997 and 1999 (2). Awards: CGT 2. LO HS 38* v Yorks (Leeds) 2001 (NL). LO BB 5-20 (*see LOI*). T20 HS 5. T20 BB 2-35.

^{NQ}**THORNELY, D.J.** – *see HAMPSHIRE.*

THORPE, Graham Paul (Weydon CS; Farnham SFC), b Farnham 1 Aug 1969. 5'10". LHB, RM. Debut 1988; cap 1991; benefit 2000. *Wisden* 1997. **ECB contracts 2001-02-04-05. Tests**: 98 (1993 to 2004-05); HS 200* v NZ (Christchurch) 2001-02; scored 114* v A (Nottingham) 1993 on debut. **LOI**: 82 (1993 to 2002, 3 as captain); HS 89 v Z (Brisbane) 1994-95 and 89 v H (Peshawar) 1995-96; BB 2-15 v I (Manchester) 1996. F-c Tours: A 1992-93 (Eng A), 1994-95, 1998-99 (*part*); SA 1995-96, 2004-05; WI 1991-92 (Eng A), 1993-94, 1997-98, 2003-04; NZ 1996-97, 2001-02; I 2001-02 (*part*); P 1990-91 (Eng A), 2000-01; SL 1990-91 (Eng A), 2000-01, 2003-04; Z 1989-90 (Eng A), 1996-97; B 2003-04. 1000 runs (9); most – 1895 (1992). HS 223* Eng XI v S Aus (Adelaide) 1998-99. Sy HS 222 v Glamorgan (Oval) 1997. BB 4-40 v A (Oval) 1993. CC BB 2-14 v Derbys (Oval) 1996. Awards: CGT 4; BHC 1. LO HS 145* v Lancs (Oval) 1994 (NWT). LO BB 3-21 v Somerset (Oval) 1991 (SL). T20 HS 50.

P.J.Sampson left the staff without making a first-class appearance in 2005. C.P.Murtagh and S.J.Walters appeared in NL matches.

SURREY 2005

RESULTS SUMMARY

	Place	Won	Lost	Tied	Drew	No Result
County Championship (1st Division)	7th	4	3		9	
All First-Class Matches		4	3		10	
C & G Trophy	Quarter-Finalist					
National League (2nd Division)	7th	7	10			1
Twenty20 Cup	Semi-Finalist					

COUNTY CHAMPIONSHIP AVERAGES
BATTING AND FIELDING

Cap		M	I	NO	HS	Runs	Avge	100	50	Ct/St
2002	M.R.Ramprakash	14	23	2	252	1568	74.66	6	5	8
2004	Azhar Mahmood	9	13	2	204*	582	52.90	1	2	10
2005	S.A.Newman	15	25	–	219	1230	49.20	4	4	14
1994	A.D.Brown	16	26	5	152*	958	45.61	3	2	19
2001	J.N.Batty	16	25	3	124	961	43.68	1	8	50/4
2005	R.Clarke	13	22	4	127*	776	43.11	2	3	16
1989	M.J.Bicknell	8	11	2	76	347	38.55	–	3	4
–	T.J.Murtagh	9	11	3	74*	296	37.00	–	2	4
1991	G.P.Thorpe	8	12	1	95	346	31.45	–	3	1
1996	M.A.Butcher	4	6	–	75	188	31.33	–	1	–
–	Harbhajan Singh	4	5	1	84	124	31.00	–	1	2
–	J.G.E Benning	3	5	–	57	150	30.00	–	2	1
–	R.S.Clinton	12	20	–	105	594	29.70	1	4	8
2003	J.Ormond	9	11	2	35	129	14.33	–	–	2
1998	Saqlain Mushtaq	4	5	1	31	55	13.75	–	–	1
–	N.D.Doshi	10	14	3	33	93	8.45	–	–	1
–	Mohammad Akram	14	15	5	27*	79	7.90	–	–	1

Also batted (2 matches each): J.W.Dernbach 1, 1*, 0* (1 ct); I.D.K.Salisbury (4 – cap 1998) 3, 15, 20 (4 ct); D.J.Thornely (2) 81, 73 (1 ct).

BOWLING

	O	M	R	W	Avge	Best	5wI	10wM
Harbhajan Singh	187.1	42	517	20	25.85	6-36	1	–
J.Ormond	301	65	1001	36	27.80	7-63	1	–
M.J.Bicknell	251.5	55	881	29	30.37	6-56	2	–
Azhar Mahmood	227.2	44	884	26	34.00	5-72	1	–
Mohammad Akram	366.4	54	1542	43	35.86	5-41	2	–
R.Clarke	152.1	16	708	18	39.33	4-91	–	–
Saqlain Mushtaq	154.5	19	506	12	42.16	4-80	–	–
T.J.Murtagh	163.2	30	563	12	46.91	3-71	–	–
N.D.Doshi	270.1	52	987	21	47.00	3-58	–	–
Also bowled:								
J.G.E.Benning	52	3	253	5	50.60	3-57	–	–
I.D.K.Salisbury	82.3	4	359	7	51.28	3-73	–	–

A.D.Brown 5-0-14-0; R.S.Clinton 18.1-2-80-0; J.W.Dernbach 30-3-153-2; S.A.Newman 3-0-17-0; M.R.Ramprakash 2-0-6-0; D.J.Thornely 28-4-108-2.

The First-Class Averages (pp 129–145) give the records of Surrey players in all first-class matches for the county (Surrey's other opponents being Bangladesh A), with the exception of G.P.Thorpe whose full county figures are as above, and:
R.S.Clinton 13-22-0-105-672-30.54-1-5-8ct. 18.1-2-80-0.

SURREY RECORDS

FIRST-CLASS CRICKET

Highest Total	For 811		v	Somerset	The Oval	1899
	V 863		by	Lancashire	The Oval	1990
Lowest Total	For 14		v	Essex	Chelmsford	1983
	V 16		by	MCC	Lord's	1872
Highest Innings	For 357*	R.Abel	v	Somerset	The Oval	1899
	V 366	N.H.Fairbrother	for	Lancashire	The Oval	1990

Highest Partnership for each Wicket

1st	428	J.B.Hobbs/A.Sandham	v	Oxford U	The Oval	1926
2nd	371	J.B.Hobbs/E.G.Hayes	v	Hampshire	The Oval	1909
3rd	413	D.J.Bicknell/D.M.Ward	v	Kent	Canterbury	1990
4th	448	R.Abel/T.W.Hayward	v	Yorkshire	The Oval	1899
5th	318	M.R.Ramprakash/Azhar Mahmood	v	Middlesex	The Oval	2005
6th	298	A.Sandham/H.S.Harrison	v	Sussex	The Oval	1913
7th	262	C.J.Richards/K.T.Medlycott	v	Kent	The Oval	1987
8th	205	I.A.Greig/M.P.Bicknell	v	Lancashire	The Oval	1990
9th	168	E.R.T.Holmes/E.W.J.Brooks	v	Hampshire	The Oval	1936
10th	173	A.Ducat/A.Sandham	v	Essex	Leyton	1921

Best Bowling	For 10-43	T.Rushby	v	Somerset	Taunton	1921
(Innings)	V 10-28	W.P.Howell	for	Australians	The Oval	1899
Best Bowling	For 16-83	G.A.R.Lock	v	Kent	Blackheath	1956
(Match)	V 15-57	W.P.Howell	for	Australians	The Oval	1899

Most Runs – Season	3246	T.W.Hayward	(av 72.13)	1906
Most Runs – Career	43554	J.B.Hobbs	(av 49.72)	1905-34
Most 100s – Season	13	T.W.Hayward		1906
	13	J.B.Hobbs		1925
Most 100s – Career	144	J.B.Hobbs		1905-34
Most Wkts – Season	252	T.Richardson	(av 13.94)	1895
Most Wkts – Career	1775	T.Richardson	(av 17.87)	1892-1904
Most Career W-K Dismissals	1221	H.Strudwick	(1035 ct/186 st)	1902-27
Most Career Catches in the Field	605	M.J.Stewart		1954-72

LIMITED-OVERS CRICKET

Highest Total	CGT	438-5		v	Glamorgan	The Oval	2002
	NL	375-4		v	Yorkshire	Scarborough	1994
	T20	221-8		v	Sussex	Hove	2004
Lowest Total	CGT	74		v	Kent	The Oval	1967
	NL	64		v	Worcs	Worcester	1978
	T20	118		v	Hampshire	The Oval	2005
Highest Innings	CGT	268	A.D.Brown	v	Glamorgan	The Oval	2002
	NL	203	A.D.Brown	v	Hampshire	Guildford	1997
	T20	76*	M.R.Ramprakash	v	Hampshire	The Oval	2004
Best Bowling	CGT	7-33	R.D.Jackman	v	Yorkshire	Harrogate	1970
	NL	7-30	M.P.Bicknell	v	Glamorgan	The Oval	1999
	T20	6-24	T.J.Murtagh	v	Middlesex	Lord's	2005

SUSSEX

Formation of Present Club: 1 March 1839
Substantial Reorganisation: August 1857
Inaugural First-Class Match: 1864
Colours: Dark Blue, Light Blue and Gold
Badge: County Arms of Six Martlets
County Champions: (1) 2003
Gillette/NatWest/C & G Trophy Winners: (4) 1963, 1964, 1978, 1986
Benson and Hedges Cup Winners: (0); best – semi-finalist 1982, 1999
National League (Div 1) Winners: (0); best – 9th 2000
National League (Div 2) Winners: (1) 2005
Sunday League Winners: (1) 1982
Twenty20 Cup Winners: (0); best – 2nd in Group 2003
Match Awards: CGT 63; BHC 64

Chief Executive: Hugh H.Griffiths, County Ground, Eaton Road, Hove BN3 3AN • Tel: 01273 827100 • Fax: 01273 771549 • Email: info@sussexcricket.co.uk • Web: www.sussexcricket.co.uk

Director of Cricket: M.A.Robinson. **First XI Coach**: M.J.G.Davis. **Captain**: C.J.Adams.
Vice-Captain: R.J.Kirtley. **Overseas Players**: Mushtaq Ahmed and Naved-ul-Hasan. **2006
Beneficiary**:. **Head Groundsman**: D.J.Traill. **Scorer**: M.J.Charman. ‡ New registration.
NQ Not qualified for England.

ADAMS, Christopher John (Repton S), b Whitwell, Derbyshire 6 May 1970. 6'0". RHB, RM/OB. Derbyshire 1988-97; cap 1992. Sussex debut/cap 1998; captain 1998 to date; benefit 2003. *Wisden* 2003. Tests: 5 (1999-00); HS 31 v SA (Cape Town) 1999-00; BB 1-42. LOI: 5 (1998 to 1999-00); HS 42 v SA (Cape Town) 1999-00. F-c Tour: SA 1999-00. 1000 runs (7); most – 1742 (1996). HS 239 De v Hants (Southampton) 1996. Sx HS 217 v Lancs (Manchester) 2002. BB 4-28 v Durham (Chester-le-St) 2001. Awards: CGT 4; BHC 6. LO HS 163 v Middx (Arundel) 1999 (NL). LO BB 5-16 v Middx (Hove) 1998 (SL). T20 HS 44.

NQ**GOODWIN, Murray** William (Newton Moore HS, Bunbury, WA), b Salisbury, Rhodesia 11 Dec 1972. Younger brother of D.G.Goodwin (Zimbabwe 1986-97 to 1989-90). 5'9". Emigrated to Australia in Nov 1986. Gained Australian citizenship in Sep 1997. Kolpak registration 2005. RHB, LB. W Australia 1994-95 to 1996-97, 2000-01 to date. Mashonaland 1997-98 to 1998-99. Sussex debut/cap 2001. Holland 1997. Tests (Z): 19 (1997-98 to 2000); HS 166* v P (Bulawayo) 1997-98. LOI (Z): 71 (1997-98 to 2000); HS 112* v WI (Chester-le-St) 2000; BB 1-12. F-c Tours (Z): E 2000, SA 1999-00; WI 1999-00; NZ 1997-98; P 1998-99; SL 1997-98. 1000 runs (4+1); most – 1654 (2001). HS 335* (Sussex record) v Leics (Hove) 2003. BB 2-23 Z v Lahore City (Lahore) 1998-99. Sx BB – . Awards: BHC 2. LO HS 167 WA v NSW (Perth) 2000-01 (MC) – Australian l-o record. LO BB 1-9 Mashonaland v Eng A (Harare) 1998-99. T20 HS 38.

HEATHER, Sean Andrew (Chichester HS), b Chichester 5 Feb 1982. 6'0". RHB, RM. Debut 2005. Awaiting CC debut. HS 7 v B (Hove) 2005.

HODD, Andrew John (Bexhill C), b Chichester, Sussex 12 Jan 1984. RHB, WK. Sussex 2003 (1 match). Surrey 2005 (one match). Awaiting CC debut. HS 57* (and 57) Sy v Bangladesh A (Oval) 2005. LO HS 9 Sy v Somerset (Taunton) 2005 (NL). TO SUSSEX T20 HS – .

HOPKINSON, Carl Daniel (Brighton C), b Brighton 14 Sep 1981. 5'11". RHB, RM. Debut 2002. HS 64 v B (Hove) 2005. CC HS 59 v Glos (Cheltenham) 2005. BB 1-20. CC BB 1-35. Award: CGT 1. LO HS 67* and BB 3-19 v Scot (Edinburgh) 2003 (NL). T20 HS 8.

KIRTLEY, Robert James (Clifton C), b Eastbourne 10 Jan 1975. 6'0". RHB, RFM. Debut 1995; cap 1998; benefit 2006. Mashonaland 1996-97. **Tests**: 4 (2003 to 2003-04); HS 12 v SL (Colombo) 2003-04; BB 6-34 v SA (Nottingham) 2003 on debut. **LOI**: 11 (2001-02 to 2004-05); HS 1 (*twice*); BB 2-33 v Z (Harare) 2001-02 on debut, and 2-33 v B (Dhaka) 2003-04. F-c Tours: NZ 1999-00 (Eng A); SL 2003-04; B 1999-00 (Eng A). HS 59 v Durham (Eastbourne) 1998. 50 wkts (7); most – 75 (2001). BB 7-21 v Hants (Southampton) 1999. Took 5-53 (7-88 match) for Mashonaland v Eng XI (Harare) 1996-97. Award: CGT 1. LO HS 30* v Middx (Lord's) 2003 (CGT). LO BB 5-33 v Essex (Chelmsford) 2002 (BHC). T20 HS 2. T20 BB 2-8.

LEWRY, Jason David (Durrington HS, Worthing), b Worthing 2 Apr 1971. 6'2". LHB, LFM. Debut 1994; cap 1996; benefit 2002. F-c Tour: Z 1998-99 (Eng A). HS 72 v Surrey (Oval) 2004. 50 wkts (4); most – 62 (1998). BB 8-106 v Leics (Hove) 2003. 2 hat-tricks (1998, 2001). LO HS 16* v Yorks (Arundel) 2004 (NL). LO BB 4-29 v Somerset (Bath) 1995 (SL). T20 HS 8*. T20 BB 3-34.

‡**LINLEY,** Timothy Edward (St Mary's RC CS, Menston; Notre Dame SFC; Oxford Brookes U), b Leeds 23 Mar 1982. 6'2". RHB, RFM. Oxford UCCE 2003-04-05. British U 2004. Staff 2006 – awaiting county debut. HS 42 OU v Derbys (Oxford) 2005. BB 3-44 OU v Surrey (Oxford) 2004.

MARTIN-JENKINS, Robin Simon Christopher (Radley C; Durham U), b Guildford, Surrey 28 Oct 1975. Son of C.D.A.Martin-Jenkins (*Times* Chief Cricket Correspondent/ BBC Commentator). 6'5". RHB, RFM. Debut 1995; cap 2000. British U 1996. 1000 runs (1): 1008 (2002). HS 205* v Somerset (Taunton) 2002. BB 7-51 v Leics (Horsham) 2002. Award: BHC 1. LO HS 68* v Northants (Hove) 2003 (NL). LO BB 4-22 v Kent (Canterbury) 2002 (BHC). T20 HS 56*. T20 BB 4-20.

MONTGOMERIE, Richard Robert (Rugby S; Worcester C, Oxford), b Rugby, Warwks 3 Jul 1971. 5'10½". RHB, OB. Oxford U 1991-94; blue 1991-92-93-94; captain 1994; half blues for rackets and real tennis. Northamptonshire 1991-98; cap 1995. Sussex debut/cap 1999. F-c Tour: Z 1994-95 (Nh). 1000 runs (5); most – 1704 (2001). HS 196 v Hants (Hove) 2002. BB 1-0. Award: CGT 1. LO HS 132* v Somerset (Hove) 2005 (NL).

NQ**MUSHTAQ AHMED** (Mahmoodia HS, Sahiwal), b Sahiwal, Pakistan 28 Jun 1970. 5'5". RHB, LBG. Multan 1986-87, 1988-89, 1990-91. United Bank 1987-88 to 1996-97. Islamabad 1994-95. Lahore 1996-97, 2000-01. Peshawar 1998-99. National Bank 1999-00 to date. REDCO 1999-00. Somerset 1993-95, 1997-98; cap 1993. Surrey 2002 (2 matches). Sussex debut/cap 2003. *Wisden* 1996. **Tests** (P): 52 (1989-90 to 2003-04); HS 59 v SA (Rawalpindi) 1997-98; BB 7-56 (10-171 match) v NZ (Christchurch) 1995-96. **LOI** (P): 144 (1988-89 to 2003-014; HS 34* v SA (Colombo) 2000-01; BB 5-36 v I (Toronto) 1996-97. F-c Tours (P): E 1992, 1996; A 1989-90, 1991-92, 1992-93, 1995-96, 1996-97, 1999-00; SA 1997-98; WI 1992-93, 1999-00; NZ 1992-93, 1993-94, 1995-96, 2000-01; I 1998-99; SL 1994-95, 1996-97, 2000-01; Z 1997-98. HS 90* v Kent (Hove) 2005. Sx HS 62 v Warwks (Horsham) 2004. 50 wkts (7+2) inc 100 (1): 103 (2003). Took 1000th f-c wicket 2004. BB 9-93 Multan v Peshawar (Sahiwal) 1990-91. Sx BB 7-73 (13-140 match) v Worcs (Hove) 2004. Awards: NWT 2; BHC 2. LO HS 41 Sm v Durham (Taunton) 1998 (SL). LO BB 7-24 Sm v Ire (Taunton) 1997 (BHC). T20 HS 16. T20 BB 5-11.

NASH, Christopher David (Collyers SFC; Loughborough U), b Cuckfield 19 May 1983. 5'11". RHB, OB. Sussex debut 2002 – no appearances 2003-04. Loughborough UCCE 2003-04. British U 2004. HS 63 LU v Somerset (Taunton) 2004. BB (LU) 1-5. Sx HS 0* and BB 1-81 v Warwks (Birmingham) 2002 – on debut.

^{NQ}**NAVED-UL-HASAN, Rana**, b Sheikhhupura, Pakistan 28 Feb 1978. RHB, RMF. Debut Pakistan A 1995-96. Lahore 1999-00. Customs 2000-01. Sheikhhupura 2000-01 to 2001-02. Allied Bank 2001-02. PCB Blues 2002-03. WAPDA 2002-03 to 2003-04. Sialkot 2002-03 to date. Sussex debut/cap 2005. Herefordshire 2005. **Tests** (P): 8 (2004-05 to 2005-06); HS 42* v E (Lahore) 2005-06; BB 3-30 v E (Faisalabad) 2005-06. **LOI** (P): 39 (2002-03 to 2004-05); HS 29 v A (Melbourne) 2004-05; BB 6-27 v I (Jamshedpur) 2004-05. F-c Tours (P): A 2004-05; WI 2004-05; I 2004-05, 2005-06. HS 139 v Middx (Lord's) 2005. 50 wkts (1+3); most – 91 (2000-01). BB 7-49 Sheikhhupura v Sialkot (Muridke) 2001-02. Sx BB 5-41 v Glamorgan (Hove) 2005. LO HS 70* Lahore v Habib Bank (Sheikhhupura) 1999-00. LO BB 6-27 (*see LOI*). T20 HS 7*. T20 BB 2-17.

PRIOR, Matthew James (Brighton C), b Johannesburg, South Africa 24 Feb 82. 6'2". RHB, WK. Debut 2001; cap 2003. **LOI**: 6 (2004-05 to 2005-06); HS 45 v P (Lahore) 2005-06. F-c Tour (Eng A): I 2003-04. 1000 runs (2); most – 1158 (2004). HS 201* v LU (Hove) 2004. CC HS 153* v Essex (Colchester) 2003. LO HS 144 v Warwks (Hove) 2005 (NL). T20 HS 68*.

TURK, Neil Richard Keith (Sackville S, E Grinstead; Exeter U), b Cuckfield 28 Apr 1983. 6'0". LHB, RM. Awaiting f-c debut. LO HS 36 v Essex (Chelmsford) 2002 (NL).

WRIGHT, Luke (Belvoir HS; Ratcliffe C: Loughborough U), b Grantham, Lincs 7 Mar 1985. 5'11". Younger brother of A.S.Wright (Leicestershire 2001-02). RHB, RM. Leicestershire 2003 (one f-c match). Sussex debut 2004. HS 100 v LU (Hove) 2004 – on Sx debut. CC HS 37 v Kent (Hove) 2005. BB 3-33 v Surrey (Hove) 2005. LO HS 35 v Surrey (Guildford) 2005 (NL). LO BB 4-12 v Middx (Hove) 2004 (NL). T20 HS 18. T20 BB 3-39.

YARDY, Michael Howard (William Parker S, Hastings), b Pembury, Kent 27 Nov 1980. 6'0". LHB, LM. Debut 2000; cap 2005. 1000 (1): 1520 (2005). HS 257 v B (Hove) 2005 – record Sussex score v touring team. CC HS 179 v Middx (Lord's) 2005. BB 5-83 v B (Hove) 2005. CC BB 2-62 v Glamorgan (Swansea) 2005. LO HS 88* v Derbys (Hove) 2004 (NL). LO BB 6-27 v Warwks (Birmingham) 2005 (NL). T20 HS 28.

RELEASED/RETIRED

(Having made a first-class County appearance in 2005)

AMBROSE, T. R. – see WARWICKSHIRE.

DAVIS, Mark Jeffrey Gronow (Grey HS; Pretoria U), b Port Elizabeth, South Africa 10 Oct 1971. British/EU passport. 6'2". RHB, OB. N Transvaal/Northerns 1990-91 to 1999-00. MCC 1999 and 2000. Sussex 2001-05; cap 2002. HS 168 v Middx (Hove) 2003. BB 8-37 (12-84 match) NT B v W Transvaal (Potchefstroom) 1994-95. Sx BB 6-97 v Surrey (Hove) 2002. Award: BHC 1. LO HS 37 v Hants (Hove) 2003 (NL). LO BB 4-14 v Lancs (Manchester) 2003 (NL). Appointed Club Coach 2005. T20 HS 20*. T20 BB 3-13.

^{NQ}**VAN DER WATH, Johannes** Jacobus (Ermelo HS), b Newcastle, Natal, South Africa 10 Jan 1978. RHB, RF. Easterns 1996-97. Free State 1997-98 to date. Eagles 2004-05. Sussex 2005. **LOI** (SA): 6 (2005-06); HS 38* v A (Sydney) 2005-06; BB 2-21 v SA (Melbourne – DS) 2005-06.-on debut. HS 113* FS v KZ-Natal (Bloemfontein) 2001-02. Sx HS 34 v Warwks (Hove) 2005. BB 6-37 FS v Boland (Bloemfontein) 2001-02. Sx BB 3-21 v B (Hove) 2005. CC BB 2-113 v Notts (Nottingham) 2005. LO HS 91 FS v GW (Bloemfontein) 2000-01. LO BB 4-45 FS v Border (E London) 2000-01. LO HS 28*. T20 BB 2-11.

WARD, Ian James (Millfield S), b Plymouth, Devon 30 Sep 1972. 5'8½". LHB, RM. Surrey 1992, 1996-2003; cap 2000. Sussex 2004-05; cap 2004. **Tests**: 5 (2001); HS 39 v P (Lord's) 2001 – on debut. F-c Tours (Eng A): WI 2000-01; NZ 1999-00; B 1999-00. 1000 runs (3); most 1759 (2002) – including 114, 112, 156 and 118 in successive innings. HS 168* Sy v Kent (Canterbury) 2002. Sx HS 160 v Warwks (Horsham) 2004. BB 1-1 (Sy – *twice*). Awards: CGT 2. LO HS 136 v Leics (Horsham) 2004 (NL). LO BB 2-27 Sy v Sussex (Hove) 2002 (BHC). T20 HS 50.

M.J.Nicholson withdrew from his contract because of injury before the start of the season and was replaced as an overseas player by J.J.van der Wath.

SUSSEX 2005

RESULTS SUMMARY

	Place	Won	Lost	Tied	Drew	No Result
County Championship (1st Division)	3rd	7	3		6	
All First-Class Matches		8	3		7	
C & G Trophy	Quarter-Finalist					
National League (2nd Division)	1st	13	4			1
Twenty20 Cup	3rd in South Division					

COUNTY CHAMPIONSHIP AVERAGES
BATTING AND FIELDING

Cap		M	I	NO	HS	Runs	Avge	100	50	Ct/St
2001	M.W.Goodwin	15	25	1	158	1380	57.50	4	7	8
2005	M.H.Yardy	16	28	3	179	1217	48.68	4	6	15
1998	C.J.Adams	16	26	2	120*	1059	44.12	1	9	21
2000	R.S.C.Martin-Jenkins	14	19	4	88	541	36.06	–	2	4
2003	M.J.Prior	15	24	1	109	724	31.47	2	4	44/1
2004	I.J.Ward	9	15	–	100	470	31.33	1	2	3
2005	Naved-ul-Hasan	9	14	2	139	346	28.83	1	–	5
1999	R.R.Montgomerie	16	28	2	184*	662	25.46	1	3	9
–	C.D.Hopkinson	6	11	–	59	246	22.36	–	2	3
1998	R.J.Kirtley	16	22	12	30	192	19.20	–	–	7
2003	Mushtaq Ahmed	16	22	3	90*	360	18.94	–	2	4
2003	T.R.Ambrose	5	8	1	44	128	18.28	–	–	8/1
–	L.J.Wright	5	7	–	37	125	17.85	–	–	3
–	J.J.van der Wath	4	6	1	34	88	17.60	–	–	1
2002	M.J.G.Davis	4	5	–	50	82	16.40	–	1	–
1996	J.D.Lewry	10	15	3	23	90	7.50	–	–	3

BOWLING

	O	M	R	W	Avge	Best	5wI	10wM
Naved-ul-Hasan	313.1	53	1076	54	19.92	5-41	2	–
L.J.Wright	73	14	223	10	22.30	3-33	–	–
J.D.Lewry	301	64	934	40	23.35	6-65	4	–
R.J.Kirtley	498.1	123	1452	59	24.61	6-80	2	–
Mushtaq Ahmed	600.5	82	2139	80	26.73	6-44	4	1
R.S.C.Martin-Jenkins	258.4	61	773	17	45.47	4-31	–	–

Also bowled: C.J.Adams 4-0-17-0; M.J.G.Davis 31-4-94-0; C.D.Hopkinson 4-1-25-0; R.R.Montgomerie 5-0-13-0; J.J.van der Wath 79-16-347-4; I.J.Ward 1-1-0-0; M.H.Yardy 35-2-144-4.

The First-Class Averages (pp 129–145) give the records of Sussex players in all first-class matches for the county (Sussex's other opponents being Bangladesh and Loughborough UCCE), with the exception of:
   M.J.Prior 16-25-1-109-775-32.29-2-5-44ct/1st. Did not bowl.

SUSSEX RECORDS

FIRST-CLASS CRICKET

Highest Total	For 705-8d		v	Surrey	Hastings	1902
	V 726		by	Notts	Nottingham	1895
Lowest Total	For 19		v	Surrey	Godalming	1830
	19		v	Notts	Hove	1873
	V 18		by	Kent	Gravesend	1867
Highest Innings	For 335*	M.W.Goodwin	v	Leics	Hove	2003
	V 322	E.Paynter	for	Lancashire	Hove	1937

Highest Partnership for each Wicket

1st	490	E.H.Bowley/J.G.Langridge	v	Middlesex	Hove	1933
2nd	385	E.H.Bowley/M.W.Tate	v	Northants	Hove	1921
3rd	298	K.S.Ranjitsinhji/E.H.Killick	v	Lancashire	Hove	1901
4th	326*	J.Langridge/G.Cox	v	Yorkshire	Leeds	1949
5th	297	J.H.Parks/H.W.Parks	v	Hampshire	Portsmouth	1937
6th	255	K.S.Duleepsinhji/M.W.Tate	v	Northants	Hove	1930
7th	344	K.S.Ranjitsinhji/W.Newham	v	Essex	Leyton	1902
8th	291	R.S.C.Martin-Jenkins/M.J.G.Davis	v	Somerset	Taunton	2002
9th	178	H.W.Parks/A.F.Wensley	v	Derbyshire	Horsham	1930
10th	156	G.R.Cox/H.R.Butt	v	Cambridge U	Cambridge	1908

Best Bowling	For 10- 48	C.H.G.Bland	v	Kent	Tonbridge	1899
(Innings)	V 9- 11	A.P.Freeman	for	Kent	Hove	1922
Best Bowling	For 17-106	G.R.Cox	v	Warwicks	Horsham	1926
(Match)	V 17- 67	A.P.Freeman	for	Kent	Hove	1922

Most Runs – Season	2850	J.G.Langridge	(av 64.77)	1949
Most Runs – Career	34152	J.G.Langridge	(av 37.69)	1928-55
Most 100s – Season	12	J.G.Langridge		1949
Most 100s – Career	76	J.G.Langridge		1928-55
Most Wkts – Season	198	M.W.Tate	(av 13.47)	1925
Most Wkts – Career	2211	M.W.Tate	(av 17.41)	1912-37
Most Career W-K Dismissals	1176	H.R.Butt	(911 ct/265 st)	1890-1912
Most Career Catches in the Field	779	J.G.Langridge		1928-55

LIMITED-OVERS CRICKET

Highest Total	CGT	384-9		v	Ireland	Belfast	1996
	NL	323-5		v	Leics	Horsham	2004
	T20	180-6		v	Essex	Hove	2003
Lowest Total	CGT	49		v	Derbyshire	Chesterfield	1969
	NL	59		v	Glamorgan	Hove	1996
	T20	67		v	Hampshire	Hove	2004
Highest Innings	CGT	158	R.K.Rao	v	Derbyshire	Derby	1997
	NL	163	C.J.Adams	v	Middlesex	Arundel	1999
	T20	68*	M.J.Prior	v	Essex	Chelmsford	2004
Best Bowling	CGT	6- 9	A.I.C.Dodemaide	v	Ireland	Downpatrick	1990
	NL	7-41	A.N.Jones	v	Notts	Nottingham	1986
	T20	5-11	Mushtaq Ahmed	v	Essex	Hove	2005

WARWICKSHIRE

Formation of Present Club: 8 April 1882
Substantial Reorganisation: 19 January 1884
Inaugural First-Class Match: 1894
Colours: Dark Blue, Gold and Silver
Badge: Bear and Ragged Staff
County Champions: (6) 1911, 1951, 1972, 1994, 1995, 2004
Gillette/NatWest/C & G Trophy Winners: (5) 1966, 1968, 1989, 1993, 1995
Benson and Hedges Cup Winners: (2) 1994, 2002
National League (Div 1) Winners: (0); best – 3rd 2001, 2002
Sunday League Winners: (3) 1980, 1994, 1997
Twenty20 Cup Winners: (0); best – Finalist 2003
Match Awards: CGT 80; BHC 69

Chief Executive: Colin Povey, County Ground, Edgbaston, Birmingham, B5 7QU • Tel: 0121 446 4422 • Fax: 0121 446 4544 • Email: info@edgbaston.com • Web: www.edgbaston.com

Director of Coaching/First XI Coach: M.J.Greatbatch. **Captain**: H.H.Streak.
Vice-Captain: D.R.Brown. **Overseas Player**: H.H.Streak and D.L.Vettori. **2006**
Beneficiary: A.F.Giles. **Head Groundsman**: S.J.Rouse. **Scorer**: D.E.Wainwright. ‡ New registration. ^NQ Not qualified for England.

ALI, Moeen Munir (Moseley S), b Birmingham 18 Jun 1987. Brother of Kadeer Ali (*see GLOUCESTERSHIRE*) and cousin of Kabir Ali (*see WORCESTERSHIRE*) 6'0". LHB, OB. Joined Warwickshire staff 2003 when aged 15. Debut 2005. Awaiting CC debut. HS 57 v CU (Cambridge) 2005.

‡AMBROSE, Timothy Raymond (Merewether HS, NSW; TAFE C), b Newcastle, NSW, Australia 1 Dec 1982. ECB qualified – British/EU passport. 5'7". RHB, WK. Sussex 2001-05; cap 2003. HS 149 Sx v Yorks (Leeds) 2002. Award: CGT 1. LO HS 95 Sx v Bucks (Beaconsfield) 2002 (CGT). T20 HS 54*.

ANYON, James Edward (Garstang HS; Preston C; Loughborough U), b Lancaster, Lancs 5 May 1983. 6'1". LHB, RFM. Loughborough U 2003-04. Warwickshire debut 2005. Cumberland 2003. HS 21 LU v Leics (Leicester) 2003. Wa HS 10 v Hants (Southampton) 2005. BB 4-33 v Sussex (Birmingham) 2005. LO HS 0. BB 3-44 v Surrey (Birmingham) 2005 (NL). T20 HS 8*. T20 BB 3-6.

BELL, Ian Ronald (Princethorpe C), b Walsgrave-on-Sowe 11 Apr 1982. 5'9". RHB, RM. Debut 1999; cap 2001. YC 2004. MBE 2005. **Tests**: 11 (2004 to 2005-06); HS 162* (inc 105* before lunch 2nd day) v B (Chester-le-St) 2005; BB 1-33. **LOI**: 10 (2004-05 t0 2005-06); HS 75 v Z (Harare) 2004-05 – on debut; BB 3-9 v Z (Bulawayo) 2004-05 – taking a wicket with his third ball in LOI. F-c Tours: WI 2000-01 (Eng A-*part*;) P 2005-06; SL 2002-03 (ECB Acad). 1000 runs (2); most – 1714 (2004). Scored 480 runs (avge 80.00) in April 2005 – record f-c UK aggregate before May. HS 262* v Sussex (Horsham) 2004. BB 4-4 v Middx (Lord's) 2004. Awards: CGT 1; BHC 2. LO HS 137 v Yorks (Birmingham) 2005 (NL). LO BB 5-41 v Essex (Chelmsford) 2003 (NL). T20 HS 66*. T20 BB 1-12.

BROWN, Douglas Robert (Alloa Academy; W London IHE), b Stirling, Scotland 29 Oct 1969. 6'2". RHB, RFM. Scotland 1989. Warwickshire debut 1991-92 (SA tour); cap 1995; benefit 2005. Wellington 1995-96. **LOI**: 9 (1997-98); HS 21 v WI (Bridgetown) 1997-98; BB 2-28 v WI (Sharjah) 1997-98. F-c Tours (Wa): SA 1991-92, 1994-95; SL 1997-98 (Eng A). 1000 runs (1): 1028 (2003). HS 203 v Sussex (Hove) 2000. 50 wkts (4); most – 81 (1997). BB 8-89 (11-154 match) F-C Counties XI v Pak A (Chelmsford) 1997. Wa BB 7-66 v Durham (Chester-le-St) 1999. Awards: CGT 1; BHC 1. LO HS 108 v Essex (Birmingham) 2003 (CGT). LO BB 5-31 v Worcs (Worcester) 1997 (BHC). T20 HS 37. T20 BB 3-21.

CARTER, Neil Miller (Hottentots Holland HS; Cape Technicon), b Cape Town, South Africa 29 Jan 1975. British passport. 6'2". LHB, LFM. Boland 1999-00 to 2000-01. Warwickshire debut 2001; cap 2005. HS 103 v Sussex (Hove) 2002 – completed maiden hundred off 67 balls. BB 6-63 Boland v GW (Kimberley) 2000-01. Wa BB 5-75 v Surrey (Birmingham) 2003. Award: CGT 1. LO HS 75 v Leics (Birmingham) 2003 (NL). LO BB 5-31 v Durham (Birmingham) 2002 (NL). T20 HS 47. T20 BB 5-19.

FROST, Tony (James Brinkley HS; Stoke-on-Trent C), b Stoke-on-Trent, Staffs 17 Nov 1975. 5'11". RHB, WK. Debut 1997; cap 1999. HS 135* v Sussex (Horsham) 2004. CC HS 103 v Yorks (Birmingham) 2002. Award: CGT 1. LO HS 47 v Beds (Luton) (CGT). T20 HS 31.

GILES, Ashley Fraser (George Abbot S, Guildford), b Chertsey, Surrey 19 Mar 1973. 6'3". RHB, SLA. Debut 1993; cap 1996; benefit 2006. *Wisden* 2004. MBE 2005. **ECB contracts 2001-02-03-04-05. Tests**: 52 (1998 to 2005-06): HS 59 v A (Oval) 2005; BB 5-57 v WI (Birmingham) 2004. **LOI**: 62 (1997 to 2005); HS 41 v SA (Pretoria) 2004-05; BB 5-57 v I (Delhi) 2001-02. F-c Tours: A 1996-97 (Eng A), 2002-03 (*part*); NZ 2001-02; I 2001-02; P 2000-01; SL 1997-98 (Eng A), 2000-01, 2003-04; B 2003-04; K 1997-98 (Eng A). HS 128* v Sussex (Hove) 2000. 50 wkts (2); most – 64 (1996). BB 8-90 (12-135 match) v Northants (Northampton) 2000. Awards: CGT 2; BHC 1. LO HS 107 v Derbys (Birmingham) 2000 (NWT). LO BB 5-21 v Norfolk (Birmingham) 1997 (NWT). T20 HS 0*. T20 BB 2-21.

HARRISON, Paul William (Forest S, Horsham, Loughborough U), b Cuckfield, Sussex 22 May 1984. RHB, RM. Loughborough UCCE 2004-05. Warwickshire 2005 (one non-CC match). HS 54 LU v Notts (Nottingham) 2005. Wa HS 0* (not CC). T20 HS 3.

KNIGHT, Nicholas Verity (Felsted S; Loughborough U), b Watford, Herts 28 Nov 1969. 6'0". LHB, occ RM. Essex 1991-94; cap 1994. Warwickshire debut 1994-95 (SA tour); cap 1995; captain 2000-05; benefit 2004. **Tests**: 17 (1995 to 2001); HS 113 v P (Leeds) 1996. **LOI**: 100 (1996 to 2002-03); HS 125* v P (Nottingham) 1996. F-c Tours: SA 1994-95 (Wa), 1999-00 (*part*); NZ 1996-97; I 1994-95 (Eng A); SL 1997-98 (Eng A – captain); P 1995-96 (Eng A); Z 1996-97; K 1997-98 (Eng A – captain). 1000 runs (6); most – 1520 (2002). HS 303* v Middx (Lord's) 2004. BB 1-61. Awards: CGT 6; BHC 4. LO HS 151 v Somerset (Birmingham) 1995 (NWT). LO BB 1-14 (SL). T20 HS 89.

LOUDON, Alexander Guy Rushworth (Wellesley House; Eton C; Collingwood C, Durham U), b Westminster, London 6 Sep 1980. Younger brother of H.J.H.Loudon (Durham UCCE 2001). 6'3". RHB, OB. Durham UCCE 2001-03; captain 2003. Kent 2003-04. Warwickshire debut 2005. HS 172 DU (record) v Durham (Chester-le-St) 2003. Wa HS 95* v Middx (Lord's) 2005.llllll BB 6-47 K v Middx (Canterbury) 2004. Wa BB 6-66 v Glos (Birmingham) 2005. LO HS 73* v Kent (Canterbury) 2005 (NL). LO BB 4-48 K v Essex (Colchester) 2004 (NL). T20 HS 25. T20 BB 5-33.

PARKER, Luke Charles, b Coventry 27 Sep 1983. RHB, RM. Oxford UCCE 2004-05. British U 2005. Warwickshire debut 2005. HS 89 OU v Derbys (Oxford) 2005. Wa HS 43 v Middx (Lord's) 2005. BB 2-37 v Glos (Oxford) 2005. LO HS 17 Warwks CB v Cumb (Millom) 2001.

POWELL, Michael James (Lawrence Sheriff S, Rugby), b Bolton, Lancs 5 Apr 1975. 5'11". RHB, RM. Debut 1996; cap 1999; captain 2001-03. Griqualand West 2001-02. F-c Tour (Eng A): WI 2000-01. 1000 runs (1): 1046 (2000). HS 236 v OU (Oxford) 2001. CC HS 146 v Glamorgan (Birmingham) 2005. BB 2-16 v OU (Oxford) 1998. CC BB 2-29 v Somerset (Taunton) 2002. Award: BHC 1. LO HS 101* v Northants (Birmingham) 2002 (BHC). LO BB 5-40 v Kent (Canterbury) 2002 (CGT). T20 HS 40*.

SHANTRY, Adam John (Priory S; Shrewsbury SFC), b Bristol 13 Nov 1982. 6'2½". Son of B.K.Shantry (Gloucestershire 1978-79). LHB, LFM. Northamptonshire 2003-04. Shropshire 2001. Warwickshire staff 2005 – awaiting county f-c debut. HS 38* and BB 3-8 (3 wkts in 5 balls) Nh v Somerset (Northampton) 2003 – on CC debut. LO HS 15 Nh CB v Yorks CB (Northampton) 2002 (CGT). LO BB 5-37 Nh v NZ (Northampton) 2004.

NQSTREAK, Heath Hilton (Falcon C), b Bulawayo, Rhodesia 16 Mar 1974. 6'1". Son of D.H.Streak (Rhodesia 1976-77 to 1978-79). RHB, RFM. Debut for Zimbabwe B v Kent (Harare) 1992-93. Matabeleland 1993-94 to 2003-04. Hampshire 1995. Warwickshire debut 2004; cap 2005; captain 2006. **Tests** (Z): 65 (1993-94 to 2005-06, 21 as captain); HS 127* v WI (Harare) 2003-04. BB 6-73 v I (Harare) 2005-06. **LOI** (Z): 187 (1993-94 to 2005, 68 as captain; HS 79* v NZ (Auckland) 2000-01; BB 5-32 v I (Bulawayo) 1996-97. F-c Tours (Z) (C=captain): E 1993, 2000, 2003C; A 1994-95, 2003-04C; SA 2004-05; 1995-96, 1997-98, 2000-01C; I 2000-01C, 2001-02; P 1993-94, 1998-99; SL 1996-97, 1997-98, 2001-02; B 2001-02. HS 131 Matabeleland v Mashonaland CD (Bulawayo) 1995-96 and 131 v Midlands (Bulawayo) 2003-04. Wa HS 51 and BB 7-80 (13-158 match) v Northants (Birmingham) 2004 – on Wa debut. 50 wkts (1): 53 (1995). BB 7-55 Matabeleland – v Mashonaland (Bulawayo) 2003-04. Award: CGT 1. LO HS 90* Matabeleland v Manicaland (Bulawayo) 2003-04. LO BB 5-32 (*see LOI*). T20 HS 59. T20 BB 3-21.

TAHIR, Naqaash (Moseley S; Spring Hill C), b Birmingham 14 Nov 1983. 5'10", RHB, RFM. Debut 2004. HS 49 v Worcs (Worcester) 2004. BB 4-43 v Worcs (Birmingham) 2004 – on CC debut. LO HS 1* (NL). LO BB 1-23 (NL).

TROTT, Ian Jonathan Leonard (Rondebosch BHC; Stellenbosch U), b Cape Town, South Africa 22 Apr 1981. 6'0". Step brother of K.C.Jackson (WP and Boland 1988-89 to 2001-02). RHB, RM. Boland 2002-01. W Province 2001-02. EU/British passport. Warwickshire debut 2003 scoring 134; cap 2005. Otago 2005-06. 1000 runs (2); most – 1170 (2004). HS 210 v Sussex (Birmingham) 2005. BB 7-39 v Kent (Canterbury) 2003. LO HS 112* v Somerset (Taunton) 2005 (NL). LO BB 3-35 v Hants (Lord's) 2005 (CGT). T20 HS 65*. T20 BB 2-19.

TROUGHTON, Jamie Oliver ('*Jim*') (Trinity S; Leamington Spa; Birmingham U), b Camden, London 2 Mar 1979. Great-grandson of H.T.Crichton (Warwicks 1908). 5'11". LHB, SLA. Debut 2001, cap 2002. **LOI**: 6 (2003); HS 20 v P (Lord's) 2003. F-c Tour (ECB Acad): SL 2002-03. 1000 runs (1): 1067 (2002). HS 131* v Hants (Southampton) 2002. BB 3-1 v CU (Cambridge) 2004. CC BB 2-106 v Glos (Bristol) 2004. Awards: CGT 2. LO HS 115* and BB 4-23 Warwks CB v Cumb (Millom) 2001 (CGT). T20 HS 51. T20 BB 2-10.

‡NQVETTORI, Daniel Luca (St Paul's Collegiate, Hamilton), b Epsom, Auckland, New Zealand 27 Jan 1979. 6'3". LHB, SLA. N Districts 1996-97 to date. **Tests** (NZ): 64 (1996-97 to 2005); HS 137* v P (Hamilton) 2003-04; BB 7-87 (12-149 match) v A (Auckland) 1999-00. **LOI** (NZ): 164 (1996-97 to 2005-06, 8 as captain); HS 83 v A (Christchurch) 2004-05; BB 5-30 v WI (Lord's) 2004. F-c Tours (NZ): E 1999, 2004; A 1997-98, 2001-02, 2004-05; SA 1997-98 (NZ Acad); WI 2001-02; I 1999-00, 2003-04; P 2001-02; SL 1997-98, 2002-03; Z 1997-98, 2000-01, 2005; B 2004-05. HS 137* (*see Tests*). CC HS 0. BB 7-87 (*see Tests*). CC BB 4-74 Nt v Kent (Maidstone) 2003. LO HS 138 ND v Auckland (Auckland) 2004-05. LO BB 5-30 (*see LOI*). T20 HS 5.

101

WAGH, Mark Anant (King Edward's S, Birmingham; Keble C, Oxford), b Birmingham 20 Oct 1976. 6'2". RHB, OB. Oxford U 1996-98; blue 1996-97-98; captain 1997. Warwickshire debut 1997; cap 2000. British U 1998. Mashonaland A 1998-99. F-c Tour (Eng A): I 2003-04. 1000 runs (4); most – 1277 (2001). HS 315 v Middx (Lord's) 2001. BB 7-222 v Lancs (Birmingham) 2003. Award: CGT 1. LO HS 102* v Kent (Birmingham) 2004 (NL). LO BB 4-35 v Glamorgan(Birmingham) 2004 (NL). T20 HS 28. T20 BB 2-16.

WARREN, Nick Alexander (Wheelers Lane S; Solihull SFC), b Moseley, Birmingham 26 Jun 1982. 5'11". RHB, RMF. No appearances 2003. 2nd XI debut 1998 when aged 16y 76d. HS 11 v WI A (Birmingham) 2002. CC HS 5*. BB 3-40 v Glamorgan (Birmingham) 2005. LO HS 2 and LO BB 3-34 v Kent (Canterbury) 2002 (NL). T20 HS 1*. T20 BB 3-25.

WESTWOOD, Ian James (Wheelers Lane S; Solihull SFC), b Birmingham 13 Jul 1982. 5'7½". LHB, OB. Debut 2003. HS 106 v Glamorgan (Colwyn Bay) 2005. BB 1-30. LO HS 55 and BB 1-28 Warwks CB v Cambs (March) 2001 (CGT). T20 HS 4*.

RELEASED/RETIRED

(Having made a first-class County appearance in 2005)

EUSTACE, Stuart Malcolm, b Birmingham 3 May 1979. LHB, WK. Devon.2001. Warwickshire 2005 (one non-CC match). HS –. T20 HS 2*.

MEES, Thomas (Worcester RGS; King Edward VII C, Stourbridge; Brookes U, Oxford), b Wolverhampton, Staffs 8 Jun 1981. 6'3". RHB, RMF. Oxford UCCE 2001-03. British U 2003. Herefordshire 1999. Warwickshire 2005. No CC appearances. HS 36* OU v Hants (Oxford) 2003. Wa HS – . BB 6-64 OU v Middx (Oxford) 2001. Award: CGT 1. LO HS 4* and BB 3-19 Warwks CB v Cambs (March) 2001 (CGT).

[NQ]**NTINI, Makhaya** (Dale C; East London TC), b Mdingi, nr King William's Town, S Africa 6 Jul 1977. 6'0". RHB, RF. Border 1995-96 to date. Warwickshire 2005. **Tests** (SA): (1997-98 to 2005-06); HS 32* v E (Leeds) 2003; BB 7-37 (13-132 match) v WI (Port-of-Spain) 2004-05. **LOI** (SA): 123 (1997-98 to 2005-06); HS 42* v NZ (Napier) 2003-04; BB 5-31 v NZ (Melbourne) 2001-02. F-c Tours (SA): E 1998, 2003; A 2001-02, 2005-06; WI 2000-01, 2004-05; NZ 2003-04; I 2004-05; P 2003-04; SL 2000-01, 2004; Z 2001-02; B 2002-03. HS 34* Border v Gauteng (Johannesburg) 1999-00. Wa HS 27* v Hants (Southampton) 2005. BB 7-37 (see Tests). Wa BB 5-69 v Middx (Lord's) 2005 – on Wa debut. LO HS 42* (see LOI). LO BB 6-22 (see LOI). in ODIs in 2005-06 – best to 2005 is previous ODI best of 5-31 South Africa v New Zealand (Melbourne) 2001-02. T20 HS 6*. T20 BB 2-26.

PIPER, Keith John (Haringey Cricket C), b Leicester 18 Dec 1969. 5'6". RHB, WK. Warwickshire 1989-2005; cap 1992; benefit 2001. No f-c appearances 2004. F-c Tours (Wa): SA 1991-92, 1992-93, 1994-95; I 1994-95 (Eng A); P 1995-96 (Eng A); Z 1993-94. HS 116* v Durham (Birmingham) 1994. BB 1-57. LO HS 38* v Leics (Birmingham) 1999 (NL). T20 HS 1*.

[NQ]**PRETORIUS, Dewald** (Dr Viljoen HS), b Pretoria, South Africa 6 Dec 1977. 6'3". RHB, RF. Free State 1997-98 to 2003-04. Durham 2003. Warwickshire debut 2004; Kolpak registration 2005. **Tests** (SA): 4 (2001-02 to 2003); HS 9; BB 4-115 v E (Birmingham) 2003. F-c Tours (SA): E 2003; Sc/Ire 1999 (SA A). HS 43 FS v WP (Bloemfontein) 1998-99. Wa HS 22 v Notts (Birmingham) 2005. BB 6-49 SA A v Ind A (Bloemfontein) 2001-02. LO HS 4-15 Du v Yorks (Leeds) 2003. Wa HS 4-119 v Sussex (Horsham) 2004. LO HS 7* (twice – FS and Du). LO BB 5-32 v Kent (Canterbury) 2005 (NL). T20 HS 22. T20 BB 2-22.

T.L.Penney left the staff without making a first-class appearance in 2005.

WARWICKSHIRE 2005

RESULTS SUMMARY

		Place	Won	Lost	Tied	Drew	No Result
County Championship (1st Division)		**4th**	8	5		3	
All First-Class Matches			9	6		3	
C & G Trophy		Finalist					
National League (2nd Division)		3rd	10	6			2
Twenty20 Cup		Quarter-Finalist					

COUNTY CHAMPIONSHIP AVERAGES

BATTING AND FIELDING

Cap		M	I	NO	HS	Runs	Avge	100	50	Ct/St
2001	I.R.Bell	7	12	1	231	601	54.63	1	3	6
1995	N.V.Knight	16	29	3	117	1107	42.57	3	5	9
2002	J.O.Troughton	11	17	–	119	583	34.29	1	5	6
–	A.G.R.Loudon	15	26	3	95*	771	33.52	–	5	12
–	L.C.Parker	5	9	3	43	200	33.33	–	–	1
2005	I.J.L.Trott	16	27	–	210	864	32.00	3	–	31
–	I.J.Westwood	10	20	3	106	542	31.88	1	2	6
1999	M.J.Powell	11	18	1	146	508	29.88	1	2	7
1995	D.R.Brown	16	25	1	122	589	24.54	1	2	14
1996	A.F.Giles	4	6	1	62	119	23.80	–	1	–
2005	H.H.Streak	8	11	2	51	194	21.55	–	1	8
–	N.Tahir	4	6	3	22*	63	21.00	–	–	–
2005	N.M.Carter	15	23	3	82	389	19.45	–	1	7
1999	T.Frost	15	24	2	82*	391	17.77	–	1	40/1
–	D.Pretorius	5	6	2	22	56	14.00	–	–	3
–	M.Ntini	6	8	1	27*	74	10.57	–	–	1
–	J.E.Anyon	6	11	7	10	29	7.25	–	–	3
–	N.A.Warren	4	5	3	5*	11	5.50	–	–	–

Also played (1 match each): M.A.Wagh (cap 2000) 28; K.J.Piper (cap 1992) did not bat (2 ct, 2 st).

BOWLING

	O	M	R	W	Avge	Best	5wI	10wM
A.F.Giles	163.5	26	445	24	18.54	6- 44	3	–
H.H.Streak	231.2	64	624	25	24.96	6- 31	2	–
N.Tahir	70	11	264	10	26.40	3- 28	–	–
D.R.Brown	472.3	106	1450	49	29.59	5-128	1	–
M.Ntini	192.1	29	721	22	32.77	5- 69	1	–
N.M.Carter	410.4	83	1378	41	33.60	4- 30	–	–
A.G.R.Loudon	369.2	42	1154	34	33.94	6- 66	2	–
J.E.Anyon	105	15	425	12	35.41	4- 33	–	–
D.Pretorius	120.3	12	446	12	37.16	3- 88	–	–

Also bowled:

	O	M	R	W	Avge	Best	5wI	10wM
I.R.Bell	57	12	202	5	40.40	3- 64		
N.A.Warren	81	15	303	6	50.50	3- 40		
I.J.L.Trott	97.5	11	346	6	57.66	2- 19		

J.O.Troughton 35.2-5-157-3; I.J.Westwood 3-0-30-1.

The First-Class Averages (pp 129–145) give the records of Warwickshire's players in all first-class matches for the county (Warwickshire's other opponents being the MCC and Cambridge UCCE), with the exception of A.F.Giles and L.C.Parker whose full county figures are as below:

I.R.Bell 8-14-1-231-635-48.84-1-3-6ct. 70-14-264-6-44.00-3/64.

P.W.Harrison 1-1-1-0*-0-8 ∞ 0-0-1ct. Did not bowl.

WARWICKSHIRE RECORDS

FIRST-CLASS CRICKET

Highest Total	For 810-4d		v	Durham	Birmingham	1994
	V 887		by	Yorkshire	Birmingham	1896
Lowest Total	For 16		v	Kent	Tonbridge	1913
	V 15		by	Hampshire	Birmingham	1922
Highest Innings	For 501*	B.C.Lara	v	Durham	Birmingham	1994
	V 322	I.V.A.Richards	for	Somerset	Taunton	1985

Highest Partnership for each Wicket

1st	377*	N.F.Horner/K.Ibadulla	v	Surrey	The Oval	1960
2nd	465*	J.A.Jameson/R.B.Kanhai	v	Glos	Birmingham	1974
3rd	327	S.P.Kinneir/W.G.Quaife	v	Lancashire	Birmingham	1901
4th	470	A.I.Kallicharran/G.W.Humpage	v	Lancashire	Southport	1982
5th	322*	B.C.Lara/K.J.Piper	v	Durham	Birmingham	1994
6th	220	H.E.Dollery/J.Buckingham	v	Derbyshire	Derby	1938
7th	289*	I.R.Bell/T.Frost	v	Sussex	Horsham	2004
8th	228	A.J.W.Croom/R.E.S.Wyatt	v	Worcs	Dudley	1925
9th	154	G.W.Stephens/A.J.W.Croom	v	Derbyshire	Birmingham	1925
10th	214	N.V.Knight/A.Richardson	v	Hampshire	Birmingham	2002

Best Bowling	For	10-41	J.D.Bannister	v	Comb Servs	Birmingham	1959
(Innings)	V	10-36	H.Verity	for	Yorkshire	Leeds	1931
Best Bowling	For	15-76	S.Hargreave	v	Surrey	The Oval	1903
(Match)	V	17-92	A.P.Freeman	for	Kent	Folkestone	1932

Most Runs – Season	2417	M.J.K.Smith	(av 60.42)	1959
Most Runs – Career	35146	D.L.Amiss	(av 41.64)	1960-87
Most 100s – Season	9	A.I.Kallicharran		1984
	9	B.C.Lara		1994
Most 100s – Career	78	D.L.Amiss		1960-87
Most Wkts – Season	180	W.E.Hollies	(av 15.13)	1946
Most Wkts – Career	2201	W.E.Hollies	(av 20.45)	1932-57
Most Career W-K Dismissals	800	E.J.Smith	(662 ct/138 st)	1904-30
Most Career Catches in the Field	422	M.J.K.Smith		1956-75

LIMITED-OVERS CRICKET

Highest Total	CGT	392-5		v	Oxfordshire	Birmingham	1984
	NL	310-5		v	Lancs	Birmingham	2004
	T20	205-7		v	Glamorgan	Swansea	2005
		205-2		v	Northants	Birmingham	2005
Lowest Total	CGT	98		v	Leics	Leicester	1998
	NL	59		v	Yorks	Leeds	2001
	T20	115		v	Surrey	Nottingham	2003
Highest Innings	CGT	206	A.I.Kallicharran	v	Oxfordshire	Birmingham	1984
	NL	137	I.R.Bell	v	Yorkshire	Birmingham	2005
	T20	89	N.V.Knight	v	Worcestershire	Worcester	2003
Best Bowling	CGT	6-32	K.Ibadulla	v	Hampshire	Birmingham	1965
		6-32	A.I.Kallicharran	v	Oxfordshire	Birmingham	1984
	NL	6-15	A.A.Donald	v	Yorkshire	Birmingham	1995
	T20	5-19	N.M.Carter	v	Worcestershire	Birmingham	2005

WORCESTERSHIRE

Formation of Present Club: 11 March 1865
Inaugural First-Class Match: 1899
Colours: Dark Green and Black
Badge: Shield Argent a Fess between three Pears Sable
County Championships: (5) 1964, 1965, 1974, 1988, 1989
Gillette/NatWest/C & G Trophy Winners: (1) 1994
Benson and Hedges Cup Winners: (1) 1991
National League (Div 1) Winners: (0); best – 2nd 1999, 2002
Sunday League Winners: (3) 1971, 1987, 1988
Twenty20 Cup Winners: (0); best – Quarter-Finalist 2004
Match Awards: CGT 58; BHC 72

Chief Executive: Mark S.Newton, County Ground, New Road, Worcester, WR2 4QQ • Tel: 01905 748474 • Fax: 01905 748005 • Email: admin@wccc.co.uk • Web: www.wccc.co.uk

Director of Cricket/First XI Coach: S.J.Rhodes. **Captain**: V.S.Solanki. **Vice-Captain**: G.J.Batty. **Overseas Players**: N.W.Bracken and P.A.Jaques. **2006 Beneficiary**: G.A.Hick (Testimonial). **Head Groundsman**: T.Packwood. **Scorer**: N.D.Smith. ‡ New registration. ᴺᑫ Not qualified for England.

Worcestershire revised their capping policy in 2002 and now award players with their County Colours when they make their Championship debut.

ALI, Kabir (Moseley CS and SFC), b Moseley, Birmingham 24 Nov 1980. 6'0". Cousin of Kadeer Ali (*see Gloucestershire*). RHB, RMF. Debut 1999. F-c Tour: SL 2002-03 (ECB Acad). **Tests**: 1 (2003); HS 9 and BB 3-80 v SA (Leeds) 2003 on debut. **LOI**: 9 (2003 to 2005-06); HS 39* v P (Rawalpindi) 2005-06; BB 3-44 v SA (Durban) 2004-05. HS 84* v Durham (Stockton) 2003. 50 wkts (3); most – 71 (2002). BB 8-53 (*before lunch first day*) v Yorks (Scarborough) 2003. Award: BHC 1. LO HS 92 v Essex (Worcester) 2003 (NL). LO BB 5-36 v Yorks (Leeds) 2002 (NL). T20 HS 49. T20 BB 2-25.

BATTY, Gareth Jon (Bingley GS), b Bradford, Yorks 13 Oct 1977. Younger brother of J.D.Batty (Yorkshire and Somerset 1989-96). 5'11". RHB, OB. Yorkshire 1997. Surrey 1999-2001. Worcestershire debut 2002. **Tests**: 7 (2003-04 to 2005); HS 38 v SL (Kandy) 2003-04; BB 3-55 v SL (Galle) 2003-04. Took wicket with his third ball in Test cricket. **LOI**: 6 (2002-03 to 2004-05); HS 3; BB 2-40 v WI (Gros Islet) 2003-04. F-c Tours: WI 2003-04; SL 2002-03 (ECB Acad); SL 2003-04. HS 133 v Surrey (Oval) 2004. 50 wkts (2); most – 60 (2003). BB 7-52 (10-113 match) v Northants (Northampton) 2004. LO HS 83* v Yorks (Oval) 2001 (NL). LO BB 4-36 Sy v Kent (Canterbury) 2001 (NL) and 4-36 v Notts (Nottingham) 2002 (NL). T20 HS 87. T20 BB 3-45.

‡ᴺᑫBRACKEN, Nathan Wade (Springwood HS, NSW), b Penrith, NSW, Australia 12 Sep 1977. 6'5". RHB, LFM. NSW to date. Gloucestershire debut/cap 1998-99. **Tests** (A): 5 (2003-04 to 2005-06); HS 37 and BB 4-48 v WI (Brisbane) 2005-06. **LOI** (A): 28 (2000-01 to 2005-06); HS 21* v NZ (Christchurch) 2005-06; BB 4-29 v I (Bombay) 2003-04. HS 38* NSW v Tas (Hobart) 2002-03. CC HS 13* and CC BB 2-12 Gs v Lancs (Manchester) 2004. BB 7-4 NSW v S Aus (29 all out) (Sydney) 2004-05. LO HS 16* NSW v Tas (Sydney) 2002-03. LO BB 5-38 NSW v Vic (Melbourne) 2001-02. T20 HS 3*. T20 BB 2-9.

DAVIES, Steven Michael (King Charles I S, Kidderminster), b Bromsgrove 17 Jun 1986. 5'10". LHB, WK. Debut 2005. Worcs 2nd XI debut 2001 when 15yr 8d. HS 148 v Somerset (Worcester) 2005. LO HS 43 v Notts (Nottingham) 2005 (NL).

NQDe BRUYN, Zander (Helpmekaar HS; Randburg HS; Rand Afrikaans U, Jo'burg), b Johannesburg, South Africa 5 Jul 1975. 6'0". RHB, RMF. Transvaal B 1995-96 to 1996-97. Gauteng 1996-97 to 2001-02. Easterns 2002-03 to 2003-04. Titans 2004-05. MCC 2000. Worcestershire debut 2005. Kolpak registration. **Tests** (SA): 3 (2004-05); HS 83 v I (Kanpur) 2004-05 – on debut; BB 2-32 v I (Calcutta) 2004-05. F-c Tour (SA): I 2004-05. 1000 (0+1): 1048 (2003-04). HS 266* Easterns v GW (Kimberley) 2003-04. Wo HS 161 v Somerset (Worcester) 2005. BB 6-120 Transvaal B v WP B (Cape Town) 1996-97. Wo BB 1-13. Award: CGT 1. LO HS 113* Surrey CB v Hunts (Cheam) 2001. LO BB 5-44 Easterns v WP (Cape Town) 2003-04. T20 HS 76*. T20 BB 3-27.

HICK, Graeme Ashley (Prince Edward HS, Salisbury), b Salisbury, Rhodesia 23 May 1966. 6'3". RHB, OB. Zimbabwe 1983-84 to 1985-86. Worcestershire debut 1984; cap 1986; benefit 1999; captain 2000-02; Testimonial 2006. N Districts 1987-88 to 1988-89. Queensland 1990-91. *Wisden* 1986. PCA 1988. **ECB contract 2000. Tests**: 65 (1991 to 2000-01); HS 178 v I (Bombay) 1992-93; BB 4-126 v NZ (Wellington) 1991-92. Took wicket with third ball in Test cricket. **LOI**: 120 (1991 to 2000-01); HS 126* v SL (Adelaide) 1998-99; BB 5-33 v Z (Harare) 1999-00. F-c Tours: E 1985 (Z); A 1994-95, 1998-99 (*part*); SA 1995-96, 1999-00 (*part*); WI 1993-94; NZ 1991-92; I 1992-93; P 2000-01; SL 1983-84 (Z), 1992-93, 2000-01; Z 1990-91 (Wo), 1996-97 (Wo). 1000 runs (18+1) inc 2000 (3); most – 2713 (1988); youngest to score 2000 (1986). Scored 1019 runs before June 1988, including a record 410 runs in April. Fewest innings for 10,000 runs in county cricket (179). Youngest (24) to score 50 f-c hundreds. Second-youngest (32) to score 100 f-c hundreds. Scored 645 runs without being dismissed (UK record) in 1990. HS 405* (Worcs record and then second highest in UK f-c matches) v Somerset (Taunton) 1988. BB 5-18 v Leics (Worcester) 1995. Awards: CGT 5; BHC 11. LO HS 172* v Devon (Worcester) 1987 (NWT). LO BB 5-19 E v Pak A (Lahore) 1998-99. T20 HS 116*.

‡NQ JAQUES, Philip Anthony (Fig Tree HS, Wollongong; Australian C of PE, Homebush), b Wollongong, NSW, Australia 3 May 1979. 6'1". LHB, SLC. British passport (English parents). NSW 2000-01 to date. Northamptonshire 2003; cap 2003. Yorkshire 2004-05; cap 2005. **Tests** (A): 1 (2005-06); HS 28 v SA (Melbourne) 2005-06 – on debut. **LOI** (A): 1 (2005-06); HS 94 v SA (Melbourne –DS) 2005-06. 1000 runs (3+1); most – 1409 (2003). HS 243 Y v Hants (Southampton) 2004. First to score 200s for and against Yorks (222 for Northants 2003). LO HS 117 Nh v Hants (Northampton) 2003 (NL). T20 HS 92.

KHALID, Shaftab Ahmad (Dormers Wells HS; W Thames C; Middlesex U), b Lahore, Pakistan 6 Oct 1982. 5'11". RHB, OB. Debut 2003. F-c Tour (Eng A): I 2003-04. HS 20 v LU (Worcester) 2005. CC HS 13 v Glamorgan(Worcester) 2003 – on CC debut. BB 4-131 v Northants (Northampton) 2003. LO HS 9* (CGT). LO BB 2-40 v Essex (Worcester) 2003 (NL).

MALIK Muhammad **Nadeem**, (Wilford Meadows CS; Bilborough C), b Nottingham 6 Oct 1982. 6'5". RHB, RFM. Nottinghamshire 2001-03. Worcestershire debut 2004. Notts 2nd XI debut 1999 when aged 16y 337d. HS 39* v NZ (Worcester) 2004. CC HS 30* Nt v Essex (Nottingham) 2003. BB 5-57 Nt v Derbys (Nottingham) 2001. Wo BB 5-71 v Leics (Leicester) 2005. LO HS 11 Nt v Worcs (Nottingham) 2002 (NL). LO BB 4-42 v Sussex (Worcester) 2004 (NL). T20 HS 3*. T20 BB 3-23.

MASON, Matthew Sean (Mazenod C, Lesmurdie, WA), b Claremont, Perth, Australia 20 Mar 1974. British passport. 6'5". RHB, RFM. W Australia 1996-97 to 1997-98. Worcestershire debut 2002. HS 63 v Warwks (Worcester) 2004. 50 wkts (3); most – 53 (2003, 2005). BB 6-68 v Durham (Worcester) 2003. LO HS 25 v Durham (Worcester) 2004 (NL). LO BB 4-34 v Surrey (Guildford) 2003 (NL). T20 HS 8*. T20 BB 1-21.

MITCHELL, Daryl Keith Henry (Prince Henry's HS; University C, Worcester), b Badsey, near Evesham 25 Nov 1983. 5'10". RHB, RM. Debut 2005. HS 63* v Leics (Leicester) 2005. BB 1-59. LO HS 2. T20 HS 4. T20 BB 2-26.

MOORE, Stephen Colin (St Stithian's C, Johannesburg; Exeter U), b Johannesburg, South Africa 4 Nov 1980. 6'1". RHB, RM. Debut 2003. 1000 runs (2); most – 1399 (2005). HS 246 v Derbys (Worcester) 2005. BB 1-13. LO HS 104 v Glamorgan (Worcester) 2005 (NL). LO BB 1-1 (NL). T20 HS 53.

NQPRICE, Raymond William (Watershed C), b Salisbury, Rhodesia 12 Jun 1976. 6'2". RHB, SLA. Mashonaland CD 1995-96. Zimbabwe Academy 1998-99 to 2000-01. Midlands 1999-00 to date. Worcestershire debut 2004. Kolpak registration 2005. **Tests** (Z): 18 (1999-00 to 2003-04); HS 36 v A (Perth) 2003-04; BB 6-73 (10-161 match) v WI (Harare) 2003-04. **LOI** (Z): 26 (2002-03 to 2003-04); HS 20* v B (Harare) 2003-04; BB 2-16 v WI (Bulawayo) 2003-04. F-c Tours (Z): E 2003; A 2003-04; I 2001-02; SL 1999-00 (Zim A); K 2001-02 (Zim A). HS 117* Midlands v Manicaland (Mutare) 2003-04. Wo HS 76 * v Lancs (Worcester) 2004. BB 8-35 Midlands v CFX Academy) Kwekwe) 2001-02. Wo BB 4-64 v Leics (Leicester) 2005. LO HS 35 Zim A v Eng A (Harare) 1998-99. LO BB 4-21 v Notts (Worcester) 2005 (NL). T20 HS – . T20 BB 1-26.

‡SILLENCE, Roger John (Highbury SS; Salisbury Art C), b Salisbury, Wilts 29 Jun 1977. 6'3". RHB, RMF. Gloucestershire 2001-05, taking 5-97 v Sussex (Hove) on debut; cap 2004. Wiltshire 1996-2001. HS 101 Gs v Derbys (Bristol) 2002. BB 5-63 Gs v Durham (Bristol) 2002. LO HS (Wilts) 82 Gs v Northants CB (Northampton) 1999 (NWT). LO BB 4-35 Gs v WI A (Cheltenham) 2002.

SMITH, Benjamin Francis (Kibworth HS), b Corby, Northants 3 Apr 1972. 5'9". RHB, RM. Leicestershire 1990-2001; cap 1995. Central Districts 2001-02. Worcestershire debut 2002; captain 2003 to 2004 (part). F-c Tour (Le): SA 1996-97. 1000 runs (7); most – 1546 (2005). HS 204 Le v Surrey (Oval) 1998. Wo HS 187 v Glos (Worcester) 2004. BB (Le) 1-5. Wo BB 1-45. Awards: CGT 3. LO HS 115 Le v Somerset (Weston-s-M) 1995 (SL). LO BB 1-2 (CGT). T20 HS 105.

SOLANKI, Vikram Singh (Regis S, Wolverhampton), b Udaipur, India 1 Apr 1976. 6'0". RHB, OB. Debut 1995; cap 1998; captain 2005. F-c Tours (Eng A): SA 1999-00 (Eng – part); WI 2000-01; NZ 1999-00; Z 1996-97 (Wo), 1998-99; B 1999-00. **LOI**: 46 (1999-00 to 2005-06); HS 106 v SA (Oval) 2003. 1000 runs (2); most – 1339 (1999). HS 185 Eng A v Bangladesh (Chittagong) 1999-00. Wo HS 171 v Glos (Cheltenham) 1999. BB 5-40 v Middx (Lord's) 2004. Awards: CGT 5; BHC 1. LO HS 164* v Worcs CB (Worcester) 2003 (CGT). LO BB 2-5 v Middx (Lord's) 2004 (NL). T20 HS 50.

WEDGE, Stuart Andrew (Codsall Community HS), b Wolverhampton, Staffs 24 Oct 1985. 5'10". LHB, LMF. Debut 2005. HS 0*. CC HS – . BB 5-112 v Essex (Worcester) 2005 – on CC debut. T20 HS T20 BB

RELEASED/RETIRED

(Having made a first-class County appearance in 2005)

NQGAYLE, Christopher Henry (Excelsior HS), b Kingston, Jamaica 21 Sep 1979. 6'3". LHB, OB. Jamaica 1998-99 to date. Worcestershire 2005. **Tests** (WI): 54 (1999-00 to 2005-06); HS 317 v SA (St John's) 2004-05; BB 5-34 v E (Birmingham) 2004. **LOI** (WI): 119 (1999 to 2005-06); HS 153* v Z (Bulawayo) 2003-04; BB 5-46 v A (St George's) 2003.F-c Tours (WI): E 2000, 2004; A ; I 2002-03, 2005-06; SA 2003-04; SL 2001-02; Z 2001, 2003-04; B 2002-03. HS 317 (see Tests). Wo HS 57 v Leics (Worcester) 2005. BB 5-34 (see Tests). Wo BB 2-18 v Leics (Worcester) 2005. LO HS 153* (see LOI). LO BB 5-46 (see LOI). T20 HS 11. T20 BB 3-13.

LEATHERDALE, David Anthony (Pudsey Grangefield S), b Bradford, Yorks 26 Nov 1967. 5'10½". RHB, RM. Debut 1988; cap 1994; benefit 2003. No f-c appearances 2004. F-c Tours (Wo): Z 1993-94, 1996-97. 1000 runs (1): 1001 (1998). HS 157 v Somerset (Worcester) 1991. BB 5-20 v Glos (Worcester) 1998. Awards: CGT 1; BHC 1. LO HS 80 v Yorks (Worcester) 2003 (CGT). LO BB 5-9 v Durham (Chester-le-St) 2002 (NL). T20 HS 52*. T20 BB 2-14.

PETERS, S.D. − see NORTHAMPTONSHIRE.

PIPE, D.J. − see DERBYSHIRE.

SHERIYAR, A − see KENT

NQSHOAIB AKHTAR (Elliott HS; Government C, Rawalpindi), b Rawalpindi, Pakistan 13 Aug 1975. 5'11½". RHB, RF. PIA 1994-95 to 1995-96. Rawalpindi 1994-95 to 1998-99. ADBP 1996-97 to 1997-98. KRL 2001-02. Somerset (one match) 2001. Durham 2003-04. Worcestershire 2005. **Tests** (P): 42 (1997-98 to 2005-06); HS 47 v I (Faisalabad) 2005-06; BB 6-11 v NZ (Lahore) 2001-02. **LOI** (P): 124 (1997-98 to 2005-06); HS 43 v E (Cape Town) 2002-03; BB 6-16 v NZ (Karachi) 2002-03. F-c Tours (P): E (Pak A) 1997; A 1999-00, 2004-05; SA 1997-98; NZ 2003-04; I 1998-99; SL 2002-03; Z 1997-98, 2001-02; B 1998-99, 2001-02. HS 59* KRL v PIA (Lahore) 2001-02. CC HS 46 Du v Somerset (Taunton) 2004. Wo HS 35 v Northants (Worcester) 2005. 50 wkts (0+1): 69 (1996-97). BB 6-11 (see Tests). CC BB 6-47 v Northants (Northampton) 2005 − on Wo debut. LO HS 56 KRL v Habib Bank (Lahore) 2002-03. LO BB 6-16 (see LOI) and 6-16 v Glos (Worcester) 2005 (NL). T20 HS 11. T20 BB 5-23.

NQVAAS, Warnakulasooriya Patabendige Ushantha **Chaminda** Joseph, b Mattumagala 27 Jan 1974. LHB, LFM. Colts 1990-91 to date. Hampshire 2003. Worcestershire debut 2005. **Tests**: 82 (1994-95 to 2004-05); HS 74* v Z (Colombo) 2001-02; BB 7-71 (14-191 match) v WI (Colombo) 2001-02. **LOI**: 274 (1993-94 to 2005-06, 1 as captain); HS 50* v P (Sharjah) 2000-01; BB 8-19 v Z (Colombo) 2001-02, including the first of two LOI hat tricks. F-c Tours (SL): E 2002; A 1995-96, 2004; SA 1997-98, 2000-01, 2002-03; WI 2003; NZ 1994-95, 1996-97, 2006-07; I 1997-98, 2005-06; P 1995-96, 1998-99, 1999-00, 2001-02, 2004-05; Z 1994-95, 1999-00, 2003-04. HS 134 Colts v Burgher (Colombo) 2004-05. Wo/CC 45 v Derbys (Worcester) 2005. 50 wkts (0+2); most 62 (2001-02). BB 7-54 W Province v S Province (Colombo) 2004-05. CC BB 4-82 H v Derbys (Southampton) 2003 − on CC debut. Wo BB 3-36 v Durham (Worcester) 2005. LO HS 62* Colts v Sinhalese (Colombo) 1999-00. LO BB 8-19 (see LOI). T20 HS 12.

WIGLEY, D.H. − see NORTHAMPTONSHIRE

WORCESTERSHIRE 2005

RESULTS SUMMARY

		Place	Won	Lost	Tied	Drew	No Result
County Championship	(2nd Division)	6th	5	7		4	
All First-Class Matches			5	8		5	
C & G Trophy		2nd Round					
National League	(1st Division)	8th	5	10			1
Twenty20 Cup		5th in Mid/West/Wales Division					

COUNTY CHAMPIONSHIP AVERAGES

BATTING AND FIELDING

Cap		M	I	NO	HS	Runs	Avge	100	50	Ct/St
2002[c]	B.F.Smith	16	27	3	172	1477	61.54	6	4	18
2003[c]	S.C.Moore	16	30	4	246	1303	50.11	2	5	9
2005[c]	S.M.Davies	10	17	1	148	584	36.50	1	2	11/3
1986	G.A.Hick	15	28	2	176	911	35.03	2	5	35
2005[c]	C.H.Gayle	3	6	–	57	192	32.00	–	2	6
2005[c]	Z.de Bruyn	9	13	–	161	410	31.53	1	1	8
1998	V.S.Solanki	12	20	2	80	549	30.50	–	4	9
2005[c]	W.P.U.C.J.Vaas	7	10	1	45	271	30.11	–	–	3
2005[c]	D.K.H.Mitchell	5‡	8	2	63*	179	29.83	–	2	6
2002[c]	G.J.Batty	13	20	4	57	456	28.50	–	3	10
2002[c]	S.D.Peters	7	13	1	88	274	22.83	–	2	5
2002[c]	Kabir Ali	12	17	2	57	324	21.60	–	2	9
2002[c]	D.J.Pipe	10	16	1	80*	277	18.46	–	1	39/2
2002[c]	M.S.Mason	15	22	5	38	264	15.52	–	–	2
2005[c]	Shoaib Akhtar	4	7	1	35	84	14.00	–	–	1
2003[c]	D.H.Wigley	4	4	3	7*	11	11.00	–	–	2
2004[c]	R.W.Price	8	10	1	20	73	8.11	–	–	6
2004[c]	M.N.Malik	7	11	5	21*	43	7.16	–	–	–

Also batted: D.A.Leatherdale (1 match – cap 1994) 14; A.Sheriyar (2 – cap 1997) 3*, 5, 5. S.A.Wedge (1 – 2005[c]) did not bat.

BOWLING

	O	M	R	W	Avge	Best	5wI	10wM
M.S.Mason	467.4	130	1387	51	27.19	5- 34	1	–
W.P.U.C.J.Vaas	285.4	80	779	28	27.82	3- 36	–	–
Kabir Ali	350.5	55	1420	50	28.40	4- 70	–	–
Shoaib Akhtar	86.3	15	405	14	28.92	6- 47	2	–
M.N.Malik	209.4	39	815	28	29.10	5- 71	1	–
D.H.Wigley	97.1	17	380	13	29.23	4- 68	–	–
R.W.Price	326.3	83	821	26	31.57	4- 64	–	–
G.J.Batty	385	72	1196	32	37.37	5- 87	1	–

Also bowled:

S.A.Wedge	37	6	143	5	28.60	5-112	1	–
A.Sheriyar	58.5	13	181	5	36.20	3- 48	–	–
Z.de Bruyn	149	21	590	5	118.00	1- 13	–	–

C.H.Gayle 33-6-78-3; D.A.Leatherdale 17-4-47-1; D.K.H.Mitchell 15-1-99-1; S.C.Moore 11-1-44-1; B.F.Smith 7-1-41-0; V.S.Solanki 11-0-49-0.

The First-Class Averages (pp 129–145) give the records of Worcestershire's players in all first-class matches for the county (Worcestershire's other opponents being the Australians and Loughborough UCCE), with the exception of G.J.Batty whose full county figures are as above.

2005[c] Denotes awarded Worcestershire 1st XI colours, a system which replaced capping in 2002.

‡ Full substitute for G.J.Batty v Somerset at Bath.

WORCESTERSHIRE RECORDS

FIRST-CLASS CRICKET

Highest Total	For 696-8d		v	Somerset	Worcester	2005
	V 701-4d		by	Leics	Worcester	1906
Lowest Total	For 24		v	Yorkshire	Huddersfield	1903
	V 30		by	Hampshire	Worcester	1903
Highest Innings	For 405*	G.A.Hick	v	Somerset	Taunton	1988
	V 331*	J.D.B.Robertson	for	Middlesex	Worcester	1949

Highest Partnership for each Wicket

1st	309	F.L.Bowley/H.K.Foster	v	Derbyshire	Derby	1901
2nd	300	W.P.C.Weston/G.A.Hick	v	Indians	Worcester	1996
3rd	438*	G.A.Hick/T.M.Moody	v	Hampshire	Southampton	1997
4th	281	J.A.Ormrod/Younis Ahmed	v	Notts	Nottingham	1979
5th	393	E.G.Arnold/W.B.Burns	v	Warwicks	Birmingham	1909
6th	265	G.A.Hick/S.J.Rhodes	v	Somerset	Taunton	1988
7th	256	D.A.Leatherdale/S.J.Rhodes	v	Notts	Nottingham	2002
8th	184	S.J.Rhodes/S.R.Lampitt	v	Derbyshire	Kidderminster	1991
9th	181	J.A.Cuffe/R.D.Burrows	v	Glos	Worcester	1907
10th	119	W.B.Burns/G.A.Wilson	v	Somerset	Worcester	1906

Best Bowling	For 9- 23	C.F.Root	v	Lancashire	Worcester	1931
(Innings)	V 10- 51	J.Mercer	for	Glamorgan	Worcester	1936
Best Bowling	For 15- 87	A.J.Conway	v	Glos	Moreton-in-M	1914
(Match)	V 17-212	J.C.Clay	for	Glamorgan	Swansea	1937

Most Runs – Season	2654	H.H.I.Gibbons	(av 52.03)		1934
Most Runs – Career	34490	D.Kenyon	(av 34.18)		1946-67
Most 100s – Season	10	G.M.Turner			1970
	10	G.A.Hick			1988
Most 100s – Career	98	G.A.Hick			1984-2005
Most Wkts – Season	207	C.F.Root	(av 17.52)		1925
Most Wkts – Career	2143	R.T.D.Perks	(av 23.73)		1930-55
Most Career W-K Dismissals	1095	S.J.Rhodes	(991 ct/104 st)		1985-2004
Most Career Catches in the Field	451	G.A.Hick			1984-2005

LIMITED-OVERS CRICKET

Highest Total	CGT	404-3	v	Devon	Worcester	1987
	NL	307-4	v	Derbyshire	Worcester	1975
	T20	223-9	v	Glamorgan	Worcester	2005
Lowest Total	CGT	98	v	Durham	Chester-le-St	1968
	NL	86	v	Yorkshire	Leeds	1969
	T20	100	v	Glos	Worcester	2005
Highest Innings	CGT	180* T.M.Moody	v	Surrey	The Oval	1994
	NL	160 T.M.Moody	v	Kent	Worcester	1991
	T20	116* G.A.Hicks	v	Northants	Luton	2004
Best Bowling	CGT	7-19 N.V.Radford	v	Beds	Bedford	1991
	NL	6-16 Shoaib Akhtar	v	Glos	Worcester	2005
	T20	3-21 M.Hayward	v	Somerset	Worcester	2003

110

YORKSHIRE

Formation of Present Club: 8 January 1863
Substantial Reorganisation: 10 December 1891
Inaugural First-Class Match: 1864
Colours: Dark Blue, Light Blue and Gold
Badge: White Rose
County Championships (since 1890): (30) 1893, 1896,
1898, 1900, 1901, 1902, 1905, 1908, 1912, 1919, 1922,
1923, 1924, 1925, 1931, 1932, 1933, 1935, 1937, 1938,
1939, 1946, 1959, 1960, 1962, 1963, 1966, 1967, 1968,
2001
Joint Champions: (1) 1949
Gillette/NatWest/C & G Trophy Winners: (3) 1965, 1969,
2002
Benson and Hedges Cup Winners: (1) 1987
National League (Div 1) Winners: (0); best – 2nd 2000
Sunday League Winners: (1) 1983
Twenty20 Cup Winners: (0); best – 2nd in Group 2003
Match Awards: CGT 50; BHC 80

Chief Executive: Stewart M.Regan, Headingley Cricket Ground, Leeds, LS6 3BU • Tel:
0113 278 7394 • Fax: 0113 278 4099 • Email: cricket@yorkshireccc.org.uk • Web:
www.yorkshireccc.org.uk

Director of Cricket: D.Byas. **Batting Coach:** K.Sharp. **Bowling Coach:** S.Oldham.
Captain: C.White. **Vice-Captain:** none. **Overseas Players:** J.N.Gillespie and
D.S.Lehmann. **2006 Beneficiary:**. **Head Groundsman:** A.W.Fogarty. **Scorer:** J.T.Potter.
‡ New registration. ^NQ Not qualified for England.

BLAIN, John Angus Rae (Penicuik HS; Jewel & Esk Valley C), b Edinburgh, Scotland
4 Jan 1979. 6'1". RHB, RMF. Scotland 1996-99. Northamptonshire 1997-2003. Yorkshire
debut 2004. **LOI** (Scot): 5 (1999); HS 9 and BB 4-37 v B (Edinburgh) 1999. HS 34 Nh v
Surrey (Northampton) 2001. Y HS 28* v Notts (Nottingham) 2004 and 28* v Derbys
(Leeds) 2004. BB 6-42 Nh v Kent (Canterbury) 2001. Y BB 4-38 v Derbys (Leeds) 2004.
Award: BHC 1. LO HS 29 Scot v UAE (Dubai) 2003-04. LO BB 5-24 Nh v Derbys (Derby)
1997 (SL).

BLAKEY, Richard John (Rastrick GS), b Huddersfield 15 Jan 1967. 5'9". RHB, WK.
Debut 1985; cap 1987; benefit 1998. YC 1987. No f-c appearances 2004-05. **Tests:** 2
(1992-93); HS 6. **LOI:** 3 (1992 to 1992-93); HS 25 v P (Lord's) 1992 – on debut. F-c Tours:
SA 1991-92 (Y); WI 1986-87 (Y); I 1992-93; P 1990-91 (Eng A); SL 1990-91 (Eng A); Z
1989-90 (Eng A), 1995-96 (Y). 1000 runs (6); most – 1361 (1987). HS 223* v Northants
(Leeds) 2003. BB 1-68. Awards: BHC 2. LO HS 130* v Kent (Scarborough) 1991 (SL). T20
HS 32.

BRESNAN, Timothy Thomas (Castleford HS and TC; Pontefract New C), b Pontefract
28 Feb 1985. 6'0". RHB, RMF. Debut 2003. HS 74 v Somerset (Leeds) 2005. BB 5-42 v
Worcs (Worcester) 2005. LO HS 61 v Leics (Leeds) 2003 (NL). BB 4-25 v Somerset
(Leeds) 2005 (NL). T20 HS 42. T20 BB 3-22.

‡^NQBROPHY, Gerard Louis (Christian Brothers C, Boksburg; Witwatersrand TC), b
Welkom, South Africa 26 Nov 1975. 5'11". British/EU passport. RHB, WK. Transvaal
1996-97 to 1998-99. Free State 1999-00 to 2000-01. Northamptonshire 2002-05. HS 185 SA
Academy v Zim President's XI (Harare) 1998-99. UK HS 181 Nh v Sussex (Hove) 2004.
LO HS Nh 57* v NZ (Northampton) 2004. T20 HS 18.

CLAYDON, Mitchell Eric, b Fairfield, NSW, Australia 25 Nov 1982. LHB, RMF. Debut 2005. Awaiting CC debut. HS – and BB 1-27 v Bangladesh A (Leeds) 2005.

DAWSON, Richard Kevin James (Batley GS; Exeter U), b Doncaster 4 Aug 1980. 6'3". RHB, OB. British U 2000. Yorkshire debut 2001. Cap 2004. Devon 1999-2000. **Tests**: 7 (2000-02 to 2002-03); HS 19* v A (Perth) 2002-03; BB 4-134 v I (Chandigarh) 2001-02 – on debut. F-c Tours: A 2002-03; NZ 2001-02; I 2001-02; SL 2002-03 (ECB Acad). HS 87 v Kent (Canterbury) 2002. BB 6-82 v Glamorgan(Scarborough) 2001. LO HS 41 v Leics (Scarborough) 2002 (NL). LO BB 4-13 v Derbys (Derby) 2002 (BHC). T20 HS 7. T20 BB 2-20.

GALE, Andrew William (Whitcliffe Mount S; Heckmondwike GS), b Dewsbury 28 Nov 1983. 6'2". LHB, LB. Debut 2004. No f-c appearances 2005. HS 29 v Derbys (Leeds) 2004. LO HS 70* v Somerset (Scarborough) 2004 (NL). T20 HS 38.

‡**NO GILLESPIE, Jason** Neil, b Darlinghurst, Sydney, Australia 19 April 1975. RHB, RFM. S Australia 1994-95 to date. **Tests** (A): 69 (1996-97 to 2005); HS 54* v NZ (Brisbane) 2004-05; BB 7-37 v E (Leeds) 1997. **LOI** (A); 97 (1996-97 to 2005); HS 44* v WI (Adelaide) 2004-05; BB 5-22 v P (Nairobi) 2002. F-c Tours (A): E 1997, 2001, 2005; SA 1996-97, 2001-02: WI 1998-99, 2002-03; NZ 2004-05; I 2000-01, 2004-05; P ; SL 1999-00, 2002-03(v P), 2003-04; Z ; B . HS 58 S Aus v WA (Perth) 1996-97. BB 8-50 S Aus v NSW (Sydney) 2001-02. LO HS 44* (see LOI). LO BB 5-22 (see LOI). T20 HS 24. T20 BB 1-49.

GUY, Simon Mark (Wickersley CS), b Rotherham 17 Nov 1978. 5'7". RHB, WK. Debut 2000. HS 42 v Somerset (Taunton) 2000 and 42 v Derbys (Derby) 2005. LO HS 40 v Leics (Leeds) 2005 (NL).

HOGGARD, Matthew James (Grangefield S, Pudsey), b Leeds 31 Dec 1976. 6'2". RHB, RFM. Debut 1996; cap 2000. Free State 1998-99 to 1999-00. MBE 2005. **ECB contracts 2001-02-03-04-05. Tests**: 48 (2000 to 2005-06); HS 38 v WI (Oval) 2004; BB 7-61 (12-205 match) v SA (Johannesburg) 2004-05; hat-trick v WI (Bridgetown) 2003-04. **LOI**: 24 (2001-02 to 2004-05); HS 5; BB 5-49 v Z (Harare) 2001-02. F-c Tours: A 2002-03; SA 2004-05; WI 2003-04; NZ 2001-02; I 2001-02; P 2000-01; SL 2000-01, 2003-04; B 2003-04. HS 89* v Glamorgan(Leeds) 2004. 50 wkts (2); most – 50 (2000, 2005). BB 7-49 v Somerset (Leeds) 2003. Hat-trick 2003-04. LO HS 7* (twice). LO BB 5-28 v Leics (Leicester) 2000 (NL). T20 HS 18. T20 BB 3-23.

NO KRUIS, Gideon Jacobus (St Albans C), b Pretoria 9 May 1974. N Transvaal B 1993-94 to 1995-96. N Transvaal 1995-96 to 1996-97. Griqualand West 1997-98 to 2003-04. Eagles 2004-05. MCC 2000, 2001. Yorkshire debut 2005 (Kolpak registration). HS 59 GW v B (Kimberley) 2000-01. Y HS 37* v Durham (Chester-le-St) 2005. 50 wkts (1): 64 (2005). BB 7-58 GW v Northerns (Pretoria) 1997-98. Y BB 5-59 v Northants (Leeds) 2005. LO HS 28* GW v WP (Kimberley) 2000-01. LO BB 4-26 GW v Boland (Kimberley) 1999-00. T20 HS – . T20 BB 2-15.

LAWSON, Mark Anthony Kenneth (Castle Hall Language C, Mirfield), b Leeds 24 Nov 1985. 5'8". RHB, LB. Debut 2004. HS 20* v Leics (Scarborough) 2005. BB 5-62 v Durham (Scarborough) 2004. LO HS 20 v Warwks (Birmingham) 2005 (NL). LO BB 1-27 (NL). T20 HS 4*. T20 BB 2-34.

NO LEHMANN, Darren Scott (Gawler HS), b Gawler, S Australia 5 Feb 1970. 5'10". LHB, SLA. S Australia 1987-88 to 1989-90, 1993-94 to date; captain 1998-99 to date. Victoria 1990-91 to 1992-93. Yorkshire 1997-98, 2000, 2002, 2003; cap 1997; captain 2002. Wisden 2000. **Tests** (A): 27 (1997-98 to 2004-05); HS 177 v B (Cairns) 2003; BB 3-42 v SL (Colombo) 2003-04. **LOI** (A): 117 (1996-97 to 2004-05); HS 119 v SL (Perth) 2002-03; BB 4-7 v Z (Harare) 2004. F-c Tours (A): E 1991 (Vic); SA 2001-02; WI 2002-03; I 1997-98, 2004-05; P 1998-99; SL 2003-04. 1000 runs (4+5); most – 1575 (1997). HS 255 S Aus v Queensland (Adelaide) 1996-97. Y HS 252 v Lancs (Leeds) 2001. BB 4-35 v Essex (Chelmsford) 2004. Awards: CGT 1; BHC 5. LO HS 191 v Notts (Scarborough) 2001 (NL). LO BB 4-7 (see LOI). T20 HS 1. T20 BB 1-12.

LUMB, Michael John (St Stithians C, Johannesburg), b Johannesburg, South Africa 12 Feb 1980. Son of R.G.Lumb (Yorkshire 1970-84); nephew of A.J.S.Smith (SAU and Natal 1971-72 to 1983-84). 6'0". LHB, RM. Debut 2000; ECB qualified and CC debut 2001; cap 2003. F-c Tour (Eng A): I 2003-04. 1000 runs (1): 1038 (2003). HS 130 v Somerset (Taunton) 2005. BB 2-10 v Kent (Canterbury) 2001. Award: CGT 1. LO HS 92 v Glamorgan(Colwyn Bay) 2003 (NL). T20 HS 55. T20 BB 3-32.

McGRATH, Anthony (Yorkshire Martyrs Collegiate S), b Bradford 6 Oct 1975. 6'2". RHB, RM. Debut 1995; cap 1999; captain 2003. **Tests**: 4 (2003); HS 81 v Z (Chester-le-St) 2003; BB 3-16 v Z (Lord's) 2003 on debut. **LOI**: 14 (2003 to 2004); HS 52 v SA (Manchester) 2003; BB 1-13. F-c Tours (Eng A): A 1996-97; P 1995-96; Z 1995-96 (Y). 1000 (1): 1425 (2005). HS 174 and BB 5-39 v Derbys (Derby) 2004. Awards: CGT 2; BHC 1. LO HS 109* v Minor C (Leeds) 1997 (BHC). LO BB 4-41 v Surrey (Leeds) 2003 (NL). T20 HS 37. T20 BB 3-27.

PATTERSON, Steven Andrew (Malet Lambert CS; St Mary's C, Hull), b Hull 3 Oct 1983. RHB, RMF. Debut 2005. Awaiting CC debut. HS – v Bangladesh A (Leeds) 2005. LO HS 11* v Derbys (Derby) 2005 (NL). LO BB 3-11 Yorks CB v Northants CB (Northampton) 2002.

PYRAH, Richard Michael (Ossett S; Wakefield C), b Dewsbury 1 Nov 1982. 6'0". RHB, RM. Yorkshire 2004. HS 78 v Worcs (Worcester) 2005. BB 1-4. CC BB 1-9. LO HS 42 v Durham (Scarborough) 2004 (NL). LO BB 5-50 Yorks CB v Somerset (Scarborough) 2002 (CGT). T20 HS 33*.

SAYERS, Joseph John (St Mary's RC CS, Menston; Worcester C, Oxford) b Leeds 5 Nov 1983. 6'0". LHB, OB. Oxford U 2002-04; blue 2002-03-04. Yorkshire debut 2004. HS 147 OU v CU (Oxford) 2004. Y HS 104 v Leics (Scarborough) 2005. LO HS 62 v Glos (Leeds) 2003 (NL). LO BB 1-31 (NL). T20 HS 12.

SHAHZAD, Ajmal, Huddersfield 27 Jul 1985. RHB, RMF. First British-born Asian to play for Yorkshire. Yorkshire Academy player awaiting f-c debut. LO HS 5 v Worcs (Leeds) 2004 (NL).

THORNICROFT, Nicholas David (Easingwold S), b York 23 Jan 1985. 5'11". LHB, RMF. Debut 2002. Essex 2005 (on loan – no Yorkshire f-c appearances). HS 30 v Notts (Leeds) 2004. BB 2-27 v Durham (Chester-le-St) 2004. LO HS 8* (NL). LO BB 5-42 v Glos (Leeds) 2003 (NL). T20 HS 0*. T20 BB – .

VAUGHAN, Michael Paul (Silverdale CS, Sheffield), b Manchester, Lancs 29 Oct 1974. 6'2". RHB, OB. Debut 1993; cap 1995; benefit 2005. *Wisden* 2002. PCA 2002. OBE 2005. ECB contracts 2000-01-02-03-04-05. Tests: 64 (1999-00 to 2005-06, 33 as captain); HS 197 and BB 2-71 v I (Nottingham) 2002. Scored Eng record 1,481 runs (avge 61.70) with six hundreds in 2002. LOI: 66 (2000-01 to 2004-05, 40 as captain); HS 90* v Z (Bulawayo) 2004-05; BB 4-22 v SL (Manchester) 2002. F-c Tours (C=captain): A 1996-97 (Eng A), 2002-03; SA 1998-99C (Eng A), 1999-00, 2004-05C; WI 2003-04C; NZ 2001-02; I 1994-95 (Eng A), 2001-02; P 2000-01; SL 2000-01, 2003-04C; Z 1995-96 (Y), 1998-99C (Eng A); B 2003-04C. 1000 runs (4); most – 1244 (1995). HS 197 (see Tests). Y HS 183 v Glamorgan(Cardiff) 1996. BB 4-39 v OU (Oxford) 1994. CC BB 4-47 v Somerset (Taunton) 2001. Awards: CGT 3; BHC 2. LO HS 125* v Somerset (Taunton) 2001 (BHC). LO BB 4-22 (see LOI). T20 HS 0.

WAINWRIGHT, David John (Hemsworth HS and SFC; Loughborough U); b Pontefract 21 Mar 1985. LHB, SLA. Debut 2004. Loughborough UCCE 2005. HS 62 v Bangladesh A (Leeds) 2005. CC HS 5. BB 4-48 LU v Worcs (Worcester) 2005. Y BB 3-22 v Bangladesh A (Leeds) 2005. CC BB 1-86. LO HS – (NL).

WHITE, Craig (Flora Hill HS, Bendigo, Australia; Bendigo HS), b Morley 16 Dec 1969. 6'0". RHB, RFM. Debut 1990; cap 1993; benefit 2002; captain 2004-. Victoria 1990-91 (2 matches). **ECB contracts 2000-01. Tests**: 30 (1994 to 2002-03); HS 121 v I (Ahmedabad) 2001-02; BB 5-32 v WI (Oval) 2000. **LOI**: 51 (1994-95 to 2002 03); HS 57* v A (Melbourne) 2002-03; BB 5-21 v Z (Bulawayo) 1999-00. F-c Tours: A 1994-95, 1996-97 (Eng A), 2002-03; SA 1991-92 (Y), 1992-93 (Y); NZ 1996-97, 2001-02; I 2001-02; P 1995-96 (Eng A), 2000-01; SL 2000-01; Z 1996-97 (*part*). HS 186 v Lancs (Manchester) 2001. BB 8-55 v Glos (Gloucester) 1998 – inc hat-trick. Hat-trick 1998. Awards: CGT 4; BHC 4. LO HS 148 v Leics (Leicester) 1997 (SL). LO BB 5-19 v Somerset (Scarborough) 2002 (NL). T20 HS 55. T20 BB 1-22.

WOOD, Matthew James (Shelley HS & SFC), b Huddersfield 6 Apr 1977. 5'9". RHB, OB. Debut 1997; cap 2001. 1000 runs (4): most – 1432 (2003). HS 207 v Somerset (Taunton) 2003. BB 1-4. Awards: CGT 2; BHC 1. LO HS 160 v Devon (Exmouth) 2004 (CGT). LO BB 3-45 v Cambs (March) 2003 (CGT). T20 HS 96*. T20 BB 1-11.

RELEASED/RETIRED

(Having made a first-class County appearance in 2005)

[NQ]**CLEARY, Mark** Francis, b Moorabbin, Melbourne, Australia 19 Jul 1980. LHB, RFM. South Australia 2002-03 to date. Australia A 2002-03. Leicestershire 2004 (withdrew from 2005 contract through injury). Yorkshire 2005. HS 58 S Aus v Tas (Hobart) 2003-04. CC HS 38 Le v Durham (Leicester) 2004. Y HS 12 and Y BB 3-46 v Derbys (Derby) 2005. BB 7-80 Le v Derbys (Oakham) 2004. LO HS 70 S Aus v NSW (Adelaide) 2003-04. LO BB 4-55 S Aus v Tas (Hobart) 2003-04. T20 HS 24*. T20 BB 3-11.

DAWOOD, Ismail (Batley GS), b Dewsbury, Yorks 23 Jul 1976. 5'8". RHB, WK. Northamptonshire 1994. Worcestershire 1996-97. Glamorgan 1998-99. British U 2004. Yorkshire 2004-05. Hertfordshire 2002 (CGT). HS 102 Gm v Glos (Cardiff) 1999. Y HS 75 v Durham (Scarborough) 2004. LO HS 60 Herts v Warwks CB (Coventry) 2002. T20 HS 15.

[NQ]**HARVEY, Ian** Joseph (Wonthaggi TC), b Wonthaggi, Victoria, Australia 10 Apr 1972. 5'10". RHB, RMF. Victoria 1993-94 to date. Gloucestershire 1999-2003/cap 1999. Yorkshire 2004-05. *Wisden* 2003. **LOI** (A): 73 (1997-98 to 2004); HS 48* v WI (Kingston) 2003; BB 4-16 v B (Darwin) 2003. F-c Tour: NZ 1994-95 (Aus Academy). HS 209* v Somerset (Leeds) 2005. BB 8-101 Aus A v SA A (Adelaide) 2002-03. UK BB 6-19 (10-32 match) Gs v Sussex (Hove) 2000. Y BB 5-40 v Derbys (Derby) 2005. Hat-trick (Victoria 2001-02). Awards: CGT 3; BHC 4. LO HS 96 Gs v Essex (Chelmsford) 2003 (NL). LO BB 5-19 Gs v Northants (Bristol) 2000 (NL). T20 HS 109. T20 BB 3-28.

[NQ]**JAQUES, P.A.** – see WORCESTERSHIRE.

LUCAS, David Scott (Djanogly CTC, Nottingham), b Nottingham 19 Aug 1978. 6'2". RHB, LMF. Nottinghamshire 1999-2002. Yorkshire staff 2005 – no f-c appearances. HS 49 Nt v DU (Nottingham) 2002. CC HS 46* Nt v Middx (Nottingham) 2000. BB 5-49 v Bangladesh A (Leeds) 2005. CC BB 5-104 Nt v Essex (Nottingham) 1999. LO HS 32 v Derbys (Derby) 2005 (NL). LO BB 4-27 Nt v Derbys (Derby) 2000 (NL).

SILVERWOOD, C.E.W. – *see MIDDLESEX.*

TAYLOR., C.R. – see DERBYSHIRE.

YORKSHIRE 2005

RESULTS SUMMARY

	Place	Won	Lost	Tied	Drew	No Result
County Championship (2nd Division)	**3rd**	5	1		10	
All First-Class Matches		5	1		10	
C & G Trophy	Semi-Finalist					
National League (2nd Division)	9th	5	13			
Twenty20 Cup	4th in North Division					

COUNTY CHAMPIONSHIP AVERAGES
BATTING AND FIELDING

Cap		M	I	NO	HS	Runs	Avge	100	50	Ct/St
2005	P.A.Jaques	13	23	2	219	1359	64.71	4	6	14
1999	A.McGrath	16	28	4	173*	1425	59.37	5	5	20
1993	C.White	16	26	8	110*	873	48.50	1	8	10
–	I.J.Harvey	13	20	2	209*	772	42.88	2	4	8
–	J.J.Sayers	9	16	1	104	477	31.80	1	2	9
2004	R.K.J.Dawson	14	18	4	86	430	30.71	–	3	8
2003	M.J.Lumb	10	19	3	130	467	29.18	1	1	7
2001	M.J.Wood	16	29	1	95	803	28.67	–	6	19
1996	C.E.W.Silverwood	6	7	–	80	186	26.57	–	2	3
–	I.Dawood	12	17	2	62*	326	21.73	–	2	34/1
–	S.M.Guy	4	5	1	42	82	20.50	–	–	11
–	T.T.Bresnan	15	20	3	74	339	19.94	–	3	4
2000	M.J.Hoggard	6	7	1	64*	116	19.33	–	1	2
–	G.J.Kruis	16	18	9	37*	174	19.33	–	–	5
–	M.A.K.Lawson	3	4	1	20*	31	10.33	–	–	–

Also batted: M.F.Cleary (2 matches) 11, 12; R.M.Pyrah (1) 78, 0; M.P.Vaughan (2 – cap 1995) 12, 9, 53; D.J.Wainwright (1) 0, 4* (1 ct). J.A.R.Blain (1) did not bat (1 ct).

BOWLING

	O	M	R	W	Avge	Best	5wI	10wM
I.J.Harvey	288.3	83	788	30	26.26	5- 40	1	–
G.J.Kruis	584.3	135	1961	64	30.64	5- 59	4	–
T.T.Bresnan	459	87	1571	47	33.42	5- 42	1	–
M.J.Hoggard	228.5	53	732	20	36.60	3- 68	–	–
R.K.J.Dawson	325.4	46	1098	27	40.66	4- 54	–	–
A.McGrath	231	36	727	16	45.43	3- 35	–	–
Also bowled:								
M.F.Cleary	67	10	250	8	31.25	3- 46	–	–
M.A.K.Lawson	82	9	372	7	53.14	5-155	1	–
C.E.W.Silverwood	142.2	28	479	9	53.22	3- 73	–	–

J.A.R.Blain 19-0-97-0; P.A.Jaques 3-0-19-0; M.J.Lumb 23-2-92-2; R.M.Pyrah 3-1-9-1; J.J.Sayers 5-0-26-0; D.J.Wainwright 29-5-86-1; C.White 12-2-71-1.

The First-Class Averages (pp 129–145) give the records of Yorkshire's players in all first-class matches for the county (Yorkshire's other opponents being Bangladesh A), with the exception of M.J.Hoggard and M.P.Vaughan whose full county figures are as above, N.D.Thornicroft whose only first-class appearance was whilst on loan to Essex, and:
   D.J.Wainwright 2-3-1-62-66-33.00-0-1-2ct. 62-15-164-7-23.42-3/22.

YORKSHIRE RECORDS

FIRST-CLASS CRICKET

Highest Total	For 887		v	Warwicks	Birmingham	1896
	V 681-7d		by	Leics	Bradford	1996
Lowest Total	For 23		v	Hampshire	Middlesbrough	1965
	V 13		by	Notts	Nottingham	1901
Highest Innings	For 341	G.H.Hirst	v	Leics	Leicester	1905
	V 318*	W.G.Grace	for	Glos	Cheltenham	1876

Highest Partnership for each Wicket

1st	555	P.Holmes/H.Sutcliffe	v	Essex	Leyton	1932
2nd	346	W.Barber/M.Leyland	v	Middlesex	Sheffield	1932
3rd	323*	H.Sutcliffe/M.Leyland	v	Glamorgan	Huddersfield	1928
4th	330	M.J.Wood/D.R.Martyn	v	Glos	Leeds	2003
5th	340	E.Wainwright/G.H.Hirst	v	Surrey	The Oval	1899
6th	276	M.Leyland/E.Robinson	v	Glamorgan	Swansea	1926
7th	254	W.Rhodes/D.C.F.Burton	v	Hampshire	Dewsbury	1919
8th	292	R.Peel/Lord Hawke	v	Warwicks	Birmingham	1896
9th	192	G.H.Hirst/S.Haigh	v	Surrey	Bradford	1898
10th	149	G.Boycott/G.B.Stevenson	v	Warwicks	Birmingham	1982

Best Bowling	For 10-10	H.Verity	v	Notts	Leeds	1932
(Innings)	V 10-37	C.V.Grimmett	for	Australians	Sheffield	1930
Best Bowling	For 17-91	H.Verity	v	Essex	Leyton	1933
(Match)	V 17-91	H.Dean	for	Lancashire	Liverpool	1913

Most Runs – Season		2883	H.Sutcliffe	(av 80.08)	1932
Most Runs – Career		38558	H.Sutcliffe	(av 50.20)	1919-45
Most 100s – Season		12	H.Sutcliffe		1932
Most 100s – Career		112	H.Sutcliffe		1919-45
Most Wkts – Season		240	W.Rhodes	(av 12.72)	1900
Most Wkts – Career		3598	W.Rhodes	(av 16.01)	1898-1930
Most Career W-K Dismissals		1186	D.Hunter	(863 ct/323 st)	1888-1909
Most Career Catches in the Field		665	J.Tunnicliffe		1891-1907

LIMITED-OVERS CRICKET

Highest Total	CGT	411-6		v	Devon	Exmouth	2004
	NL	352-6		v	Notts	Scarborough	2001
	T20	211-6		v	Leics	Leeds	2004
Lowest Total	CGT	76		v	Surrey	Harrogate	1970
	NL	54		v	Essex	Leeds	2003
	T20	97		v	Lancashire	Manchester	2005
Highest Innings	CGT	160	M.J.Wood	v	Devon	Exmouth	2004
	NL	191	D.S.Lehmann	v	Notts	Scarborough	2001
	T20	109	I.J.Harvey	v	Derbyshire	Leeds	2005
Best Bowling	CGT	7-27	D.Gough	v	Ireland	Leeds	1997
	NL	7-15	R.A.Hutton	v	Worcs	Leeds	1969
	T20	3-18	A.K.D.Gray	v	Lancashire	Leeds	2004

FIRST-CLASS UMPIRES 2006

† New appointment
  See page ** for key to abbreviations.

†BAILEY, Robert John (Biddulph HS), b Biddulph, Staffs 28 Oct 1963. RHB, OB. Northamptonshire 1982-99; cap 1985; benefit 1993; captain 1996-97. Derbyshire 2000-01; cap 2000. Staffordshire 1980. YC 1984. **Tests:** 4 (1988 to 1989-90); HS 43 v WI (Oval) 1988. **LOI:** 4 (1984-85 to 1989-90); HS 43* v SL (Oval) 1988. Tours: SA 1991-92 (Nh); WI 1989-90; Z 1994-95 (Nh). 1000 runs (13); most – 1987 (1990). HS 224* Nh v Glamorgan (Swansea) 1986. BB 5-54 Nh v Notts (Northampton) 1993. F-c career: 374 matches; 21844 runs @ 40.52, 47 hundreds; 121 wickets @ 42.51; 272 ct. Appointed 2006.

†BAINTON, Neil Laurence, b Romford, Essex 2 October 1970. No f-c appearances. Appointed 2006.

BENSON, Mark Richard (Sutton Valence S), b Shoreham, Sussex 6 Jul 1958. LHB, OB. Kent 1980-95; cap 1981; captain 1991-96 (did not play in 1996); benefit 1991. **Tests:** 1 (1986); HS 30 v I (Birmingham) 1986. **LOI:** 1 (1986; HS 24). 1000 runs (11); most – 1725 (1987). HS 257 K v Hants (Southampton) 1991. BB 2-55 K v Surrey (Dartford) 1986. F-c career: 292 matches; 18387 runs @ 40.23, 48 hundreds; 5 wickets @ 98.60; 140 ct. Appointed 2000. Umpired 6 Tests (2004-05 to 2005-06) and 24 LOI (2004 to 2005-06).

BURGESS, Graham Iefvion (Millfield S), b Glastonbury, Somerset 5 May 1943. RHB, RM. Somerset 1966-79; cap 1968; testimonial 1977. HS 129 Sm v Glos (Taunton) 1973. BB 7-43 (13-75 match) Sm v OU (Oxford) 1975. F-c career: 252 matches; 7129 runs @ 18.90, 2 hundreds; 474 wickets @ 28.57. Appointed 1991.

CONSTANT, David John b Bradford-on-Avon, Wilts 9 Nov 1941. LHB, SLA. Kent 1961-63. Leicestershire 1965-68. HS 80 Le v Glos (Bristol) 1966. BB 1-28. F-c career: 61 matches; 1517 runs @ 19.20; 1 wicket @ 36.00. Appointed 1969. Umpired 36 Tests (1971 to 1988) and 33 LOI (1972 to 2001). Represented Gloucestershire at bowls 1984-86.

COWLEY, Nigel Geoffrey (Dutchy Manor SS, Mere), b Shaftesbury, Dorset 1 Mar 1953. RHB, OB. Dorset 1972. Hampshire 1974-89; cap 1978; benefit 1988. Glamorgan 1990. 1000 runs (1): 1042 (1984). HS 109* H v Somerset (Taunton) 1977. BB 6-48 H v Leics (Southampton) 1982. F-c career: 271 matches; 7309 runs @ 23.35, 2 hundreds; 437 wickets @ 34.04. Appointed 2000.

DUDLESTON, Barry (Stockport S), b Bebington, Cheshire 16 Jul 1945. RHB, SLA. Leicestershire 1966-80; cap 1969; benefit 1980. Gloucestershire 1981-83. Rhodesia 1976-77 to 1979-80. 1000 runs (8); most – 1374 (1970). HS 202 Le v Derbys (Leicester) 1979. BB 4-6 Le v Surrey (Leicester) 1972. F-c career: 295 matches; 14747 runs @ 32.48, 32 hundreds; 47 wickets @ 29.04. Appointed 1984. Umpired 2 Tests (1991 to 1992) and 4 LOI (1992 to 2001).

EVANS, Jeffery Howard, b Llanelli, Carms 7 Aug 1954. No f-c appearances. Appointed 2001.

GOULD, Ian James (Westgate SS, Slough), b Taplow, Bucks 19 Aug 1957. LHB, WK. Middlesex 1975 to 1980-81, 1996; cap 1977. Auckland 1979-80. Sussex 1981-90; cap 1981; captain 1987; benefit 1990. MCC YC. **LOI:** 18 (1982-83 to 1983; HS 42). Tours: A 1982-83; P 1980-81 (Int); Z 1980-81 (M). HS 128 M v Worcs (Worcester) 1978. BB 3-10 Sx v Surrey (Oval) 1989. Middlesex coach 1991-2000. Reappeared in one match (v OU) 1996. F-c career: 298 matches; 8756 runs @ 26.05, 4 hundreds; 7 wickets @ 52.14; 603 dismissals (536 ct, 67 st). Appointed 2002.

HARRIS, Michael John (*'Pasty'*) (Gerrans S, nr Truro), b St Just-in-Roseland, Cornwall 25 May 1944. RHB, LB, WK. Middlesex 1964-68; cap 1967. Nottinghamshire 1969-82; cap 1970; benefit 1977. E Province 1971-72. Wellington 1975-76. 1000 runs (11); most – 2238 (1971). Equalled Notts record with 9 hundreds in 1971. HS 201* Nt v Glamorgan

(Nottingham) 1973. BB 4-16 Nt v Warwks (Nottingham) 1969. F-c career: 344 matches; 19196 runs @ 36.70, 41 hundreds; 79 wickets @ 43.78; 302 dismissals (288 ct, 14 st). Appointed 1998.

HARTLEY, Peter John (Greenhead GS; Bradford C), b Keighley, Yorks 18 Apr 1960. RHB, RMF. Warwickshire 1982. Yorkshire 1985-97; cap 1987; benefit 1996. Hampshire 1998-2000; cap 1998. Tours (Y): SA 1991-92; WI 1986-87; Z 1995-96. HS 127* Y v Lancs (Manchester) 1988. 50 wkts (7); most – 81 (1995). BB 9-41 (inc hat-trick, 4 wkts in 5 balls and 5 in 9; 11-68 match) Y v Derbys (Chesterfield) 1995. Hat-trick 1995. F-c career: 232 matches; 4321 runs @ 19.91, 2 hundreds; 683 wickets @ 30.21. Appointed 2003.

HOLDER, John Wakefield (Combermere S), b St George, Barbados 19 Mar 1945. RHB, RFM. Hampshire 1968-72. HS 33 H v Sussex (Hove) 1971. BB 7-79 H v Glos (Gloucester) 1972. Hat-trick 1972. F-c career: 47 matches; 374 runs @ 10.68; 139 wickets @ 24.56. Appointed 1983. Umpired 11 Tests (1988 to 2001) and 19 LOI (1988 to 2001).

HOLDER, Vanburn Alonza (Richmond SM), b Deans Village, St Michael, Barbados 8 Oct 1945. RHB, RFM. Barbados 1966-67 to 1977-78. Worcestershire 1968-80; cap 1970; benefit 1979. Shropshire 1981. **Tests** (WI): 40 (1969 to 1978-79); 682 runs @ 14.20, HS 42 v NZ (P-o-S) 1971-72; 109 wkts @ 33.27, BB 6-28 v A (P-o-S) 1977-78. **LOI** (WI): 12. Tours (WI): E 1969, 1973, 1976; A 1975-76; I 1974-75, 1978-79; P 1973-74 (RW), 1974-75; SL 1974-75, 1978-79. HS 122 Barbados v Trinidad (Bridgetown) 1973-74. BB 7-40 Wo v Glamorgan (Cardiff) 1974. F-c career: 311 matches; 3559 runs @ 13.03, 1 hundred; 947 wickets @ 24.48. Appointed 1992.

†ILLINGWORTH, Richard Keith (Salts GS), b Bradford, Yorks 23 Aug 1963. RHB, SLA. Worcestershire 1982-2000; cap 1986; benefit 1997. Natal 1988-89. Derbyshire 2001. Wiltshire 2005. **Tests:** 9 (1991 to 1995-96); HS 28 v SA (Pt Elizabeth) 1995-96; BB 4-96 v WI (Nottingham) 1995. Took wicket of P.V.Simmons with his first ball in Tests – v WI (Nottingham) 1991. **LOI:** 25 (1991 to 1995-96); HS 14 v P (Melbourne) 1991-92; BB 3-33 v Z (Albury) 1991-92. Tours: SA 1995-96; NZ 1991-92; P 1990-91 (Eng A); SL 1990-91 (Eng A); Z 1989-90 (Eng A), 1990-91 (Wo), 1993-94 (Wo), 1996-97 (Wo). HS 120* Wo v Warwks (Worcester) 1987 – as night-watchman. Scored 106 for England A v Z (Harare) 1989-90 – also as night-watchman. 50 wkts (5); most – 75 (1990). BB 7-50 Wo v OU (Oxford) 1985. F-c career: 376 matches; 7027 runs @ 22.45, 4 hundreds; 831 wickets @ 31.54; 161 ct. Appointed 2006.

JESTY, Trevor Edward (Privet County SS, Gosport), b Gosport, Hants 2 Jun 1948. RHB, RM. Hampshire 1966-84; cap 1971; benefit 1982. Surrey 1985-87; cap 1985; captain 1985. Lancashire 1987-88 to 1991; cap 1989. Border 1973-74. GW 1974-75 to 1980-81. Canterbury 1979-80. *Wisden* 1982. **LOI:** 10. Tours: WI 1987-88 (La), 1982-83 (Int); Z 1988-89 (La). 1000 runs (10); most – 1645 (1982). HS 248 H v CU (Cambridge) 1984. Scored 122* La v OU (Oxford) 1991 in his final f-c innings. 50 wkts (2); most – 52 (1981). BB 7-75 H v Worcs (Southampton) 1976. F-c career: 490 matches; 21916 runs @ 32.71, 35 hundreds; 585 wickets @ 27.47. Appointed 1994.

JONES, Allan Arthur (St John's C, Horsham), b Horley, Surrey 9 Dec 1947. RHB, RM. Sussex 1966-69. Somerset 1970-75; cap 1972. Middlesex 1976-79; cap 1976. Glamorgan 1980-81. Northern Transvaal 1972-73. Orange Free State 1976-77. HS 33 M v Kent (Canterbury) 1978. BB 9-51 Sm v Sussex (Hove) 1972. F-c career: 214 matches; 799 runs @ 5.39; 549 wickets @ 28.07. Appointed 1985. Umpired 1 LOI (1996).

†KETTLEBOROUGH, Richard Allan (Worksop C), b Sheffield, Yorks 15 Mar 1973. LHB, RM. Yorkshire 1994-97. Middlesex 1998-99. Tour: Z 1995-96 (Y). HS 108 Y v Essex (Leeds) 1996. BB 2-26 Y v Notts (Scarborough) 1996. F-c career: 33 matches; 1258 runs @ 25.16, 1 hundred; 3 wickets @ 81.00. 20 ct. Appointed 2006.

LEADBEATER, Barrie (Harehills SS), b Harehills, Leeds, Yorks 14 Aug 1943. RHB, RM. Yorkshire 1966-79; cap 1969; joint benefit with G.A.Cope 1980. Tour: WI 1969-70 (DN). HS 140* Y v Hants (Portsmouth) 1976. BB 1-1. F-c career: 147 matches; 5373 runs @ 25.34, 1 hundred; 1 wicket @ 5.00. Appointed 1981. Umpired 5 LOI (1983 to 2000).

LLONG, Nigel James (Ashford North S), b Ashford, Kent 11 Feb 1969. LHB, OB. Kent 1990-98; cap 1993. Tour: Z 1992-93 (K). HS 130 K v Hants (Canterbury) 1996. BB 5-21 K v Middx (Canterbury) 1996. F-c career: 68 matches; 3024 runs @ 31.17, 6 hundreds; 35 wickets @ 35.97. Appointed 2002.

LLOYDS, Jeremy William (Blundell's S), b Penang, Malaya 17 Nov 1954. LHB, OB. Somerset 1979-84; cap 1982. Gloucestershire 1985-91; cap 1985. Orange Free State 1983-84 to 1987-88, Tour (Glos): SL 1986-87. 1000 runs (3); most – 1295 (1986). HS 132* Sm v Northants (Northampton) 1982. BB 7-88 Sm v Essex (Chelmsford) 1982. F-c career: 267 matches; 10679 runs @ 31.04, 10 hundreds; 333 wickets @ 38.86; 229 ct. Appointed 1998. Umpired 5 Tests (2003-04 to 2004-05) and 14 LOI (2000 to 2005).

MALLENDER, Neil Alan (Beverley GS), b Kirk Sandall, Yorks 13 Aug 1961. RHB, RFM. Northamptonshire 1980-86 and 1995-96; cap 1984. Somerset 1987-94; cap 1987; benefit 1994. Otago 1983-84 to 1992-93; captain 1990-91 to 1992-93. **Tests:** 2 (1992); 8 runs @ 2.66, HS 4; 10 wkts @ 21.50, BB 5-50 v P (Leeds) 1992 – on debut. Tour: Z 1994-95 (Nh). HS 100* Otago v CD (Palmerston N) 1991-92. UK HS 87* Sm v Sussex (Hove) 1990. 50 wkts; most – 56 (1983). BB 7-27 Otago v Auckland (Auckland) 1984-85. UK BB 7-41 Nh v Derbys (Northampton) 1982. F-c career: 345 matches; 4709 runs @ 17.18, 1 hundred; 937 wickets @ 26.31; 111 ct. Appointed 1999. Umpired 3 Tests (2003-04) and 22 LOI (2001 to 2003-04), including 2002-03 World Cup. **Elite Panel 2004.**

PALMER, Roy (Southbroom SM, Devizes), b Devizes, Wilts 12 Jul 1942. RHB, RFM. Younger brother of K.E.Palmer, MBE (Somerset and England 1955-69). Somerset 1965-70. HS 84 Sm v Leics (Taunton) 1967. BB 6-45 Sm v Middx (Lord's) 1967. F-c career: 74 matches; 1037 runs @ 13.29; 172 wickets @ 31.62. Appointed 1980. Umpired 2 Tests (1992 to 1993) and 8 LOI (1983 to 1995).

SHARP, George (Elwick Road SS, Hartlepool), b West Hartlepool, Co Durham 12 Mar 1950. RHB, WK, occ LM. Northamptonshire 1968-85; cap 1973; benefit 1982. HS 98 Nh v Yorks (Northampton) 1983. BB 1-47. F-c career: 306 matches; 6254 runs @ 19.85; 1 wicket @ 70.00; 655 dismissals (565 ct, 90 st). Appointed 1992. Umpired 15 Tests (1996 to 2001-02) and 31 LOI (1995-96 to 2001-02). International Panel 1996 to 2001-02.

STEELE, John Frederick (Endon SS), b Brown Edge, Staffs 23 Jul 1946. RHB, SLA. Brother of D.S. (Northants, Derbys and England 1963-84). Leicestershire 1970-83; cap 1971; benefit 1983. Glamorgan 1984-86; cap 1984. Natal 1973-74 to 1977-78. Staffordshire 1965-69. Tour: SA 1974-75 (DHR). 1000 runs (5); most – 1347 (1972). HS 195 Le v Derbys (Leicester) 1971. BB 7-29 Natal B v GW (Umzinto) 1973-74 and 7-29 Le v Glos (Leicester) 1980. F-c career: 379 matches; 15054 runs @ 28.95, 21 hundreds; 584 wickets @ 27.04; 413 ct. Appointed 1997.

WILLEY, Peter (Seaham SS), b Sedgefield, Co Durham 6 Dec 1949. RHB, OB. Northamptonshire 1966-83; cap 1971; benefit 1981. Leicestershire 1984-91; cap 1984; captain 1987. E Province 1982-83 to 1984-85. Northumberland 1992. **Tests:** 26 (1976 to 1986); 1184 runs @ 26.90, HS 102* v WI (St John's) 1980-81; 7 wkts @ 65.14, BB 2-73 v WI (Lord's) 1980. **LOI:** 26. Tours: A 1979-80; SA 1972-73 (DHR), 1981-82 (SAB); WI 1980-81, 1985-86; I 1979-80; SL 1977-78 (DHR). 1000 runs (10); most – 1783 (1982). HS 227 Nh v Somerset (Northampton) 1976. 50 wkts (3); most – 52 (1979). BB 7-37 Nh v OU (Oxford) 1975. F-c career: 559 matches; 24361 runs @ 30.56, 44 hundreds; 756 wickets @ 30.95. Appointed 1993. Umpired 25 Tests (1995-96 to 2003-04) and 34 LOI (1996 to 2003), including 1999 and 2002-03 World Cups. International Panel 1996 to 2001-02 and 2003-04.

RESERVE FIRST-CLASS LIST: Martin J.Bodenham, Nicholas G.B.Cook, Stephen A.Garratt, Michael A.Gough, †Darrell B.Hair (69 Tests and 118 LOI), R.Timothy Robinson, Terence J.Urben.

Test Match and LOI statistics to 25 and 14 February 2006 (inclusive) respectively.

119

INTERNATIONAL UMPIRES AND REFEREES 2006

ELITE PANEL OF UMPIRES 2006

The Elite Panel of ICC Umpires and Referees was introduced in April 2002 to raise standards and guarantee impartial adjudication. Two umpires from this panel stand in Test matches while one officiates with a home umpire from the Supplementary International Panel in limited-overs internationals.

Full Names	Birthdate	Birthplace	Tests	Debut	LOI	Debut
ALIM Sarwar DAR	06.06.68	Jhang, Pakistan	27	2003-04	64	1999-00
BOWDEN, Brent Fraser	11.04.63	Auckland, N Zealand	35	1999-00	83	1994-95
BUCKNOR, Stephen Anthony	31.05.46	Montego Bay, Jamaica	108	1988-89	136	1988-89
HAIR, Darrell Bruce	30.09.52	Mudgee, Australia	69	1991-92	118	1991-92
HARPER, Daryl John	23.10.61	Adelaide, Australia	55	1998-99	113	1993-94
KOERTZEN, Rudolf Eric ('Rudi')	26.03.49	Knysna, S Africa	70	1992-93	140	1992-93
TAUFEL, Simon James Arthur	21.01.71	Sydney, Australia	31	2000-01	86	1998-99

ELITE PANEL OF REFEREES 2006

Full Names	Birthdate	Birthplace	Tests	Debut	LOI	Debut
BROAD, Brian Christopher	29.09.57	Bristol, England	17	2003-04	48	2003-04
CROWE, Jeffrey John	14.09.58	Auckland, N Zealand	8	2004-05	50	2003-04
HURST, Alan George	15.07.50	Melbourne, Australia	6	2004-05	19	2004-05
LLOYD, Clive Hubert	31.08.44	Georgetown, Guyana	51	1992-93	110	1992-93
MADUGALLE, Ranjan Senerath	22.04.59	Kandy, Sri Lanka	82	1993-94	172	1993-94
MAHANAMA, Roshan Siriwardena	31.05.66	Colombo, England	7	2004	30	2004
PROCTER, Michael John	15.09.46	Durban, S Africa	37	2001-02	87	2001-02

INTERNATIONAL PANEL OF UMPIRES 2006

Nominated by their respective cricket boards, members from this panel officiate in home LOIs and supplement the Elite panel for Test matches. Specialist third umpires have been selected to undertake adjudication involving television replays.

			Third Umpire
Australia	S.J.Davis	P.D.Parker	R.L.Parry
Bangladesh	A.F.M.Akhtaruddin	Mahbubur Rahman	Nadir Shah
England	M.R.Benson	J.W.Lloyds	N.J.Llong
India	Hariharan Krishna	A.V.Jayaprakash	I.Shivram
New Zealand	G.A.Baxter	A.L.Hill	E.A.Watkin
Pakistan	Asad Rauf	Nadeem Ghauri	Zamir Haider
South Africa	I.L.Howell	B.G.Jerling	K.H.Hurter
Sri Lanka	E.A.R.de Silva	T.H.Wijewardene	P.Manuel
West Indies	B.R.Doctrove	E.A.Nicholls	B.E.W.Morgan
Zimbabwe	K.C.Barbour	R.B.Tiffin	I.D.Robinson

Test Match and LOI statistics to 25 and 14 February 2006 (inclusive) respectively.

UNIVERSITY FIRST-CLASS REGISTER 2005

‡ Represented British Universities v Bangladeshis

CAMBRIDGE († Blue 2005)

Full Names	Birthdate	Birthplace	College	Bat/Bowl	F-C Debut
‡AKRAM, Mohammed Adnan	17.11.83	Leytonstone	(Anglia PU)	RHB/RM	2003
AKRAM, Mohammed Arfan	17.11.83	Leytonstone	(Anglia PU)	RHB/LB	2003
†BANERJEE, Vikram	20.03.84	Bradford	Downing	LHB/SLA	2004
BUCKHAM, Craig Thomas	09.08.83	Ashford (Kent)	(Anglia PU)	RHB/LB	2004
†CHERVAK, James Alexander	07.04.85	Harrogate	Jesus	RHB/LB	2005
EDWARDS, Philip Duncan	16.04.84	Minster, I of Sheppey	(Anglia PU)	RHB/RFM	2004
‡FRIEDLANDER, Matthew James	01.08.79	Durban, S Africa	(Anglia PU)	RHB/RFM	2003-04
†HEATH, Duncan Robert	06.11.81	Grimsby	Pembroke	RHB/RM	2002
HEMBRY, Tobias Digby Charles	16.11.83	Ipswich	(Anglia PU)	LHB	2004
†HEYWOOD, James John Neville	24.09.82	Eastbourne	Homerton	RHB/WK	2003
HOOPER, Matthew Robert	27.03.84	Sidcup	(Anglia PU)	LHB/OB	2005
†JACKLIN, Benjamin David	26.04.84	Leeds	Magdalene	RHB/RM	2005
JAMES, Gareth David	01.12.84	Walthamstow	(Anglia PU)	RHB/LB	2004
†KEMP, Robin Andrew	29.09.84	Luton	St John's	RHB/RM	2005
†MANN, Richard James	26.09.82	Ipswich	St John's	LHB/OB	2003
MOHAMMAD AMIN	19.10.84	Gujranwala, Pakistan	(Anglia PU)	RHB/RMF	2005
‡PALLADINO, Antonio Paul	29.06.83	London	(Anglia PU)	RHB/RMF	2003
PARK, Garry Terence	19.04.83	Empangeni, SA	(Anglia PU)	RHB/RM	2003
†SAVILL, Thomas Edward	16.05.83	Sheffield	Homerton	RHB/RFM	2002
†SHANKAR, Adrian	07.05.82	Ascot	Queens	RHB/OB	2002
SHARIF, Zoheb Khalid	22.02.83	Leytonstone	(Anglia PU)	LHB/LB	2001
†SINGH, Anirudh	28.12.83	Birmingham	Gonville & Caius	RHB/LB	2003
†TIMMS, Richard Thomas	09.09.84	Bristol	Clare	RHB/RFM	2005
WEBLEY, Thomas	02.03.83	Bristol	(Anglia PU)	LHB/SLA	2003
WRIGHT, Christopher Julian Clement	14.07.85	Chipping Norton	(Anglia PU)	RHB/RFM	2004

DURHAM

Full Names	Birthdate	Birthplace	College	Bat/Bowl	F-C Debut
BALCOMBE, David John	24.12.84	City of London	St Hild & St Bede	RHB/RFM	2005
‡BROWN, David Owen	08.12.82	Burnley	Collingwood	RHB/RM	2003
BRUCE, Thomas Oscar	10.02.83	Bampton, Oxon	Hatfield	LHB/SLA	2005
BURNELL, William Fleet	07.01.85	Havering	St Aidan's	RHB/RM	2004
DAGGETT, Lee Martin	01.10.82	Bury	John Snow	RHB/RMF	2003
DALE, Mark Adam Paul	16.03.82	Hucknall	George Stephenson	RHB/RM	2003
HOWELLS, Peter William	09.10.81	Stockton-on-Tees	St Aidan's	RHB/WK	2004
LAMB, Nicholas John	09.11.85	St Albans	Collingwood	RHB/RMF	2005
‡MAIDEN, Alastair Jonathan	15.09.82	Stourbridge	Collingwood	RHB/RM	2002
MORRIS, James Calum	17.01.85	Welwyn Gdn City	University	RHB/LB	2005
PHYTHIAN, Mark John	26.04.85	Peterborough	University	RHB	2005
‡READ, Glen George	04.09.81	Cuckfield	Collingwood	LHB/LM	2004
‡SHILVOCK, Daniel James Francis	22.11.83	Birmingham	St Hild & St Bede	RHB/LB	2005
‡SMITH, Will Rew	28.09.82	Luton	Collingwood	RHB/OB	2002
WOOD, James Robert	08.09.85	Cape Town, SA	Van Mildert	RHB	2005

BRITISH UNIVERSITIES
(Excluding players listed above)

Full Names	Birthdate	Birthplace	University	Bat/Bowl	F-C Debut
‡PANESAR, Mudhsuden Singh	25.04.82	Luton	Loughborough	LHB/SLA	2001

LOUGHBOROUGH

Full Names	Birthdate	Birthplace		Bat/Bowl	F-C Debut
ATRI, Vikram	09.03.83	Hull		RHB/OB	2002
CLARK, Steven George	17.11.82	Doncaster		RHB/RMF	2005
CLEWLEY, Nicholas James	13.06.83	Wolverhampton		RHB/RMF	2005
CLINTON, Richard Selvey	01.09.81	Sidcup		LHB/RM	2001
CUMMINS, Ryan Anthony Gilbert	14.04.84	Sutton, Surrey		RHB/RM	2003
FOSTER, Edward John	21.01.85	Shrewsbury		LHB/RM	2005
GIFFORD, William McLean	10.10.85	Birmingham		RHB/RM	2005
HARRISON, Paul William	22.05.84	Cuckfield		RHB/WK	2004
HOLT, David Robert	29.12.81	Hammersmith		RHB	2005
MURTAGH, Christopher Paul	14.10.84	Lambeth		RHB/LB	2005
SINGH, Krishana Raj	19.12.82	Middlesex Hospital, London		RHB/LB	2005
WAINWRIGHT, David John	21.03.85	Pontefract		LHB/SLA	2004
WILKINSON, Richard Malcolm	24.11.82	Birkenhead		RHB/RM	2004

OXFORD († Blue 2005)

Full Names	Birthdate	Birthplace	College	Bat/Bowl	F-C Debut
AIREY, Stuart James	18.03.83	Cleethorpes	(Brookes U)	RHB/RMF	2003
ANWAR, Omar Sohail	01.07.83	Harrow	(Brookes U)	RHB	2003
†CLINTON, Paul James Selvey	30.08.83	Dartford	Keble	RHB/RM	2004
†DALEY, Stephen Robert	15.04.77	Atherton, Australia	Magdalen	LHB/RMF	2003
†DORAN, Graeme Paul	02.12.79	Liverpool	St Edmund Hall	RHB/WK	2004
†FOX, Daniel Richard	03.03.83	Birmingham	Greyfriars	RHB	2004
‡KNAPPETT, Joshua Philip Thomas	15.04.85	Westminster	(Brookes U)	RHB/WK	2004
LINLEY, Timothy Edward	23.03.82	Leeds	(Brookes U)	RHB/RM	2003
†McMAHON, Paul Joseph	12.03.83	Wigan	Wadham	RHB/OB	2002
MORETON, Stephen John Patrick	09.09.84	Birmingham	(Brookes U)	RHB/LB	2005
†MORSE, Edward James	30.01.86	Stevenage	St Edmund Hall	RHB/RM	2005
†MUNDAY, Michael Kenneth	22.10.84	Nottingham	Corpus Christi	RHB/LB	2003
†OBEROI, Salil	07.12.83	Delhi, India	Merton	RHB, OB	2002-03
‡PARKER, Luke Charles	27.09.83	Coventry	(Brookes U)	RHB/RM	2004
RICHARDS, Mali Alexander	02.09.83	Taunton	(Brookes U)	LHB/RM	2004
†STEARN, Christopher Paul	11.07.80	Luton	Worcester	RHB/RM	2005
†‡SUMAN, Amit Kumar	10.12.80	Sahibganj, India	Pembroke	RHB/LM	1998-99
†WOODS, Nicholas James	02.01.86	Bolton	Queens	RHB/LB	2005

TOURING TEAMS FIRST-CLASS REGISTER 2005

BANGLADESH
† Also member of BANGLADESH A touring team

Full Names	Birthdate	Birthplace	Team/Division	Type	F-C Debut
AFTAB AHMED	10.11.85	Chittagong	Chittagong	RHB/RM	2001-02
ANWAR HOSSAIN Monir	31.12.81	Munshiganj	Biman Bangladesh	RHB/RFM	2000-01
†ENAMUL HAQUE II	05.12.86	Sylhet	Sylhet	LHB/SLA	2001-02
HABIBUL BASHAR	17.08.72	Nagakanda, Kushtia	Biman Bangladesh	RHB/OB	1997-98
JAVED OMAR Belim	25.11.76	Dhaka	Dhaka	RHB/LB	1997-98
KHALED MASUD	08.02.76	Rajshahi	Rajshahi	RHB/WK	1997-98
MASHRAFE Bin MORTAZA	05.10.83	Norail, Khulna	Khulna	RHB/RM	2001-02
MOHAMMED ASHRAFUL	09.09.84	Dhaka	Dhaka	RHB/LB	2000-01
MOHAMMAD RAFIQUE	05.09.70	Dhaka	Sylhet; Dhaka	LHB/SLA	2000-01
†MUSHFIQUR RAHIM	01.09.88	Bogra	Bangladesh U-19	RHB/WK	2004-05
†NAFIS IQBAL	31.01.85	Chittagong	Chittagong	RHB/RM	2000-01
RAJIN SALEH	20.11.83	Sylhet	Sylhet	RHB/OB	2000-01
†SHAHADAT HOSSAIN	07.08.86	Dhaka	Bangladesh A	RHB/RMF	2003-04
†SHAHRIAR NAFIS	25.01.86	Dhaka	Bangladesh A	LHB	2003-04
†TALHA JUBAIR	10.12.85	Faridpur, Dhaka	Dhaka	RHB/RM	2001-02
TAPASH BAISYA	25.12.82	Sylhet	Sylhet	RHB/RFM	2000-01

BANGLADESH A

Full Names	Birthdate	Birthplace	Team/Division	Type	F-C Debut
ABDUR RAZZAK	15.06.82	Khulna	Khulna	RHB/SLA	2001-02
ALOK KAPALI	01.01.84	Sylhet	Sylhet	RHB/LB	2000-01
HASANUZZAMAN Rozel	01.04.77	Rajshahi	Rajshahi	RHB/WK	2001-02
MEHRAB HOSSAIN II	08.07.87	Dhaka	Dhaka	LHB/SLA	2004-05
MUSHFIQUR RAHMAN	01.01.80	Rajshahi	Rajshahi	RHB/RFM	1999-00
NAZIMUDDIN, Mohd	01.10.85		Chittagong	RHB	2002-03
SHAHIN HOSSAIN, Mohd	08.08.84	Dhaka	Barisal	RHB/WK	2000-01
SYED RASEL	03.07.84	Jessore	Khulna	LHB/LMF	2001-02
TUSHAR IMRAN, Sheikh	20.12.83	Jessore	Khulna	RHB	2000-01

AUSTRALIA

Full Names	Birthdate	Birthplace	Team	Type	F-C Debut
CLARKE, Michael John	02.04.81	Liverpool, NSW	NSW	RHB/SLA	1999-00
GILCHRIST, Adam Craig	14.11.71	Bellingen, NSW	WA	LHB/WK	1992-93
GILLESPIE, Jason Neil	19.04.75	Darlinghurst, NSW	SA	RHB/RFM	1994-95
HADDIN, Bradley James	23.10.77	Cowra, NSW	NSW	RHB/WK	1999-00
HAYDEN, Matthew Lawrence	29.10.71	Kingaroy, Q	Q	LHB/RM	1991-92
HODGE, Bradley John	29.12.74	Sandringham, Vic	Vic	RHB/OB	1993-94
KASPROWICZ, Michael Scott	10.02.72	S Brisbane, Q	Q	RHB/RFM	1989-90
KATICH, Simon Mathew	21.08.75	Middle Swan, WA	NSW	LHB/SLC	1996-97
LANGER, Justin Lee	21.11.70	Perth, WA	WA	LHB/WK	1991-92
LEE, Brett	08.11.76	Wollongong, NSW	NSW	RHB/RF	1994-95
MacGILL, Stuart Charles Glyndwr	25.02.71	Mount Lawley, WA	NSW	RHB/LBG	1993-94
McGRATH, Glenn Donald	09.02.70	Dubbo, NSW	NSW	RHB/RFM	1992-93
MARTYN, Damien Richard	21.10.71	Darwin, NT	WA	RHB/RM	1990-91
PONTING, Ricky Thomas	19.12.74	Launceston, Tas	Tas	RHB/OB	1992-93
TAIT, Shaun William	22.02.83	Adelaide	SA	RHB/RFM	2002-03
WARNE, Shane Keith	13.09.69	Ferntree Gully, Vic	Vic	RHB/LBG	1990-91

THE 2005 FIRST-CLASS SEASON
STATISTICAL HIGHLIGHTS

FIRST TO INDIVIDUAL TARGETS

1000 RUNS	E.C.Joyce	Middlesex	18 June
2000 RUNS	–	Most 1728 – O.A.Shah (Middlesex)	
100 WICKETS	–	Most 87 – S.K.Warne (Hampshire and Australia)	

TEAM HIGHLIGHTS

HIGHEST INNINGS TOTALS († *County record;* * *Second innings*)

714-5d†	Hampshire v Nottinghamshire	Southampton
707-7d†	Derbyshire v Somerset	Taunton
696-8d†	Worcestershire v Somerset	Worcester
692-7d	Nottinghamshire v Surrey	The Oval
686-5d	Surrey v Middlesex	The Oval
655-6d	Lancashire v Essex	Manchester
622-8d	Essex v Yorkshire	Leeds
610-5d	Oxford U v Cambridge U	Cambridge
603	Surrey v Gloucestershire	Bristol

HIGHEST FOURTH INNINGS TOTALS

447-9	Kent (set 485) v Hampshire	Canterbury
408-4	Middlesex (set 406) Glamorgan	Southgate
406-4	Yorkshire (set 404) v Leicestershire	Leicester
400-4	Yorkshire (set 397) v Leicestershire	Scarborough

LOWEST INNINGS TOTALS († *One man absent hurt*)

96	Glamorgan v Sussex	Hove
98	Gloucestershire v Kent	Maidstone

MATCH AGGREGATES OF 1500 RUNS

1683-14	Glamorgan (584-3d, 256-3d) v Middlesex (435-4d, 408-4)	Southgate
1606-34	Surrey (452-8d, 350) v Kent (572, 232-6)	Guildford
1547-19	Essex (574, 201-1d) v Worcestershire (424-3d, 348-5)	Worcester
1541-38	Hampshire (328, 461-9d) v Kent (305, 447-9)	Canterbury

BATSMEN'S MATCH (Qualification: 1200 runs average 70 per wicket)

120.21 (1683-14)	Glamorgan (584-3d, 256-3d) v Middx (435-4d, 408-4)	Southgate
102 (1224-12)	Somerset (580-6d, 211-2d) v Durham UCCE (433-4d)	Taunton
81.42 (1547-19)	Essex (574, 201-1d) v Worcs (424-3d, 348-5)	Worcester

SIX OR MORE FIFTIES IN AN INNINGS

7	Surrey (603) v Gloucestershire	Bristol
6	Derbyshire (707-7d) v Somerset	Taunton

FIFTY EXTRAS IN AN INNINGS

B	LB	W	NB	P		
75	10	13	14	38 –	Hampshire (714-5d) v Nottinghamshire	Southampton
57	2	5	2	48 –	Essex (307-4d) v Cambridge UCCE	Cambridge
55	4	11	7	33 –	Durham (505) v Essex	Chester-le-St
55	16	8	7	24 –	Yorkshire (323-6d) v Lancashire	Manchester
50	11	8	–	26 5	Nottinghamshire (692-7d) v Surrey	The Oval
50	4	20	–	26 –	Hampshire (576-6d) v Warwickshire	Southampton
50	8	16	10	16 –	Yorkshire (520) v Derbyshire	Derby

Under ECB regulations Test matches excluded two penalty extras were scored for each no-ball.

BATTING HIGHLIGHTS

TRIPLE HUNDREDS († *County record*)

J.P.Crawley	311*	Hampshire v Nottinghamshire	Southampton
G.C.Smith	311	Somerset v Leicestershire	Taunton

DOUBLE HUNDREDS († *County record*)

Azhar Mahmood	204*	Surrey v Middlesex	The Oval
I.R.Bell	231	Warwickshire v Middlesex	Birmingham
D.D.Cherry	226	Glamorgan v Middlesex	Southgate
M.J.Di Venuto	203	Derbyshire v Durham	Derby
S.P.Fleming	238	Nottinghamshire v Surrey	The Oval
I.J.Harvey	209*	Yorkshire v Somerset	Leeds
D.J.Hussey	232*	Nottinghamshire v Warwickshire	Nottingham
M.E.K.Hussey	253	Durham v Leicestershire	Leicester
P.A.Jaques	219	Yorkshire v Derbyshire	Leeds
M.B.Loye	200	Lancashire v Durham	Chester-le-St
A.J.Maiden	211*	Durham UCCE v Somerset	Taunton
S.C.Moore	246	Worcestershire v Derbyshire	Worcester
S.A.Newman	219	Surrey v Glamorgan	The Oval
S.Oberoi	247	Oxford U v Cambridge U	Cambridge
M.R.Ramprakash	252	Surrey v Middlesex	The Oval
C.J.L.Rogers	209	Leicestershire v Australians	Leicester
C.M.Spearman	216	Gloucestershire v Oxford UCCE	Oxford
D.I.Stevens	208	Kent v Glamorgan	Canterbury
I.J.L.Trott	210	Warwickshire v Sussex	Birmingham
M.van Jaarsveld	262*	Kent v Glamorgan	Cardiff
S.R.Watson	203*	Hampshire v Warwickshire	Southampton
M.J.Wood	297	Somerset v Yorkshire	Taunton
M.J.Wood	202*	Yorkshire v Bangladesh A	Leeds
M.H.Yardy	257	Sussex v Bangladeshis	Hove

HUNDREDS IN THREE CONSECUTIVE INNINGS

U.Afzaal (Northamptonshire)	147	v Lancs	(Northampton)
	112	v Somerset	(Taunton)
	119	v Durham	(Chester-le-St)
B.F.Smith (Worcestershire)	100	v Essex	(Chelmsford)
	123	v Durham	(Worcester)
	140	v Somerset	(Bath)

HUNDRED IN EACH INNINGS OF A MATCH

P.D.Collingwood	181	105*	Durham v Somerset	Taunton
J.Hughes	134*	100*	Glamorgan v Middlesex	Southgate
R.W.T.Key	112	189	Kent v Surrey	Tunbridge W
S.A.Newman	117	219	Surrey v Glamorgan	The Oval
M.van Jaarsveld	118	111	Kent v Warwickshire	Canterbury

FASTEST HUNDRED (WALTER LAWRENCE TROPHY)

I.D.Blackwell (107) 67 balls	Somerset v Derbyshire	Taunton

HUNDRED BEFORE LUNCH

		Day		
I.R.Bell	57*-162*	2	England v Bangladesh	Chester-le-St
A.N.Cook	0*-117	4	Essex v Worcestershire	Worcester
J.P.Crawley	150*-298*	2	Hampshire v Nottinghamshire	Southampton

125

TEN OR MORE SIXES IN AN INNINGS

11   G.C.Smith (311)   Somerset v Leicestershire   Taunton

FOUR SIXES OFF CONSECUTIVE BALLS

C.M.Spearman (off S.J.P.Moreton)   Gloucestershire v Oxford UCCE   Oxford
    He scored 34 (666646) off the over

HUNDRED ON FIRST-CLASS DEBUT IN BRITAIN

Javed Omar	167	Bangladeshis v British Universities	Cambridge
Mohammad Ashraful	102	Bangladeshis v British Universities	Cambridge

CARRYING BAT THROUGH COMPLETED INNINGS († *One man absent*)

Kadeer Ali	55*	Gloucestershire (103) v Nottinghamshire	Nottingham
†J.D.Francis	125*	Somerset (275) v Yorkshire	Leeds
M.E.K.Hussey	144*	Durham (338) v Lancashire	Manchester

NOTABLE PARTNERSHIPS († *County/University record*)

First Wicket

304	W.R.Smith/A.J.Maiden	Durham UCCE v Somerset	Taunton
297	M.L.Love/B.M.Shafayat	Northamptonshire v Derbyshire	Derby
294	I.J.Ward/R.R.Montgomerie	Sussex v Loughborough UCCE	Hove
283	D.P.Fulton/R.W.T.Key	Kent v Middlesex	Canterbury
280	S.A.Newman/R.S.Clinton	Surrey v Kent	Tunbridge W
272	M.J.Wood/J.J.Sayers	Yorkshire v Bangladesh A	Leeds
264	E.T.Smith/O.A.Shah	Middlesex v Glamorgan	Southgate

Second Wicket

283	S.D.Stubbings/M.H.Adnan	Derbyshire v Somerset	Taunton
282	B.L.Hutton/O.A.Shah	Middlesex v Kent	Lord's
255	M.E.Trescothick/M.P.Vaughan	England v Bangladesh (1st Test)	Lord's
254	S.A.Newman/M.R.Ramprakash	Surrey v Glamorgan	The Oval

Third Wicket

408†	S.Oberoi/D.R.Fox	Oxford U v Cambridge U	Cambridge
333	S.C.Moore/B.F.Smith	Worcestershire v Essex	Worcester
323†	R.W.T.Key/M.van Jaarsveld	Kent v Surrey	Tunbridge W
310	A.McGrath/P.A.Jaques	Yorkshire v Derbyshire	Leeds
272	M.J. Di Venuto/M.H.Adnan	Derbyshire v Durham	Derby

Fourth Wicket

307	M.J.Walker/D.I.Stevens	Kent v Warwickshire	Birmingham
270	B.F.Smith/S.M.Davies	Worcestershire v Somerset	Worcester
250†	P.D.Collingwood/D.M.Benkenstein	Durham v Derbyshire	Derby

Fifth Wicket

320†	J.D.Francis/I.D.Blackwell	Somerset v Durham UCCE	Taunton
318†	M.R.Ramprakash/Azhar Mahmood	Surrey v Middlesex	The Oval
235	A.P.R.Gidman/S.J.Adshead	Gloucestershire v Surrey	Bristol
233	M.J.Walker/J.M.Kemp	Kent v Surrey	Guildford
213	A.Flower/R.C.Irani	Essex v Yorkshire	Leeds

Sixth Wicket

267	D.I.Stevens/A.J.Hall	Kent v Glamorgan	Canterbury
254*	J.P.Crawley/A.D.Mascarenhas	Hampshire v Nottinghamshire	Southampton
201	M.J.Wood/K.A.Parsons	Somerset v Yorkshire	Taunton

Seventh Wicket

234*	S.R Watson/A.D.Mascarenhas	Hampshire v Warwickshire	Southampton
228	M.H.Yardy/Naved-ul-Hasan	Sussex v Middlesex	Lord's
139†	M.E.K.Hussey/P.Mustard	Durham v Lancashire	Manchester

Eighth Wicket

257†	N.Pothas/A.J.Bichel	Hampshire v Gloucestershire	Cheltenham

238	I.J.Harvey/T.T.Bresnan	Yorkshire v Somerset	Leeds
170	A.G.Botha/A.K.D.Gray	Derbyshire v Somerset	Derby
164	J.S.Foster/A.R.Adams	Essex v Durham	Chester-le-St
159†	M. van Jaarsveld/M.M.Patel	Kent v Glamorgan	Cardiff
150	M.J.Friedlander/C.J.C.Wright	Cambridge UCCE v Essex	Cambridge

Ninth Wicket

| 173 | S.C.Moore/D.J.Pipe | Worcestershire v Derbyshire | Worcester |

Tenth Wicket

135	J.M.Kemp/A.Khan	Kent v Middlesex	Lord's
118	D.L.Hemp/H.T.Waters	Glamorgan v Kent	Canterbury
101	C.M.W. Read/M.H.A.Footitt	Nottinghamshire v Glamorgan	Nottingham

BOWLING HIGHLIGHTS

EIGHT OR MORE WICKETS IN AN INNINGS

| D.G.Wright | 8-60 | Northamptonshire v Yorkshire | Leeds |

TEN OR MORE WICKETS IN A MATCH

J.F.Brown	(2)	10-135	Northamptonshire v Lancashire	Northampton
		10-160	Northamptonshire v Yorkshire	Northampton
A.R.Caddick		12-204	Somerset v Durham	Stockton
R.D.B.Croft		10-160	Glamorgan v Hampshire	Cardiff
Danish Kaneria		11-176	Essex v Derbyshire	Derby
M.Kartik (on UK debut)		10-168	Lancashire v Essex	Chelmsford
G.Keedy		10-79	Lancashire v Oxford UCCE	Oxford
Mushtaq Ahmed		10-118	Sussex v Glamorgan	Hove
M.S.Panesar		10-128	Northamptonshire v Yorkshire	Northampton
S.B.Styris		10-118	Middlesex v Hampshire	Southampton
Syed Rasel		10-91	Bangladesh A v Kent	Canterbury
S.K.Warne	(2)	10-162	Australia v England (2nd Test)	Birmingham
		12-246	Australia v England (5th Test)	The Oval
A.G.Wharf		11-121	Glamorgan v Gloucestershire	Bristol

HAT-TRICKS

A.R.Adams	Essex v Somerset	Taunton
S.J.Harmison	Durham v Worcestershire	Chester-le-St
C.T.Tremlett	Hampshire v Nottinghamshire	Nottingham

RECORD APRIL AGGREGATE

| 24 wkts (avge 17.00) | A.F.Giles | Warwickshire |

200 RUNS CONCEDED IN AN INNINGS

| Danish Kaneria | 70.2-10-208-0 Essex v Lancashire | Manchester |

30 RUNS CONCEDED IN AN OVER

| S.J.P.Moreton | 1-0-34-0 | Oxford UCCE v Gloucestershire | Oxford |

60 OVERS IN AN INNINGS

| Danish Kaneria | 70.2-10-208-0 Essex v Lancashire | Manchester |
| Danish Kaneria | 60.1-16-111-6 Essex v Derbyshire | Derby |

MATCH DOUBLE (100 RUNS AND 10 WICKETS)

| R.D.B.Croft | 20, 90; 5-103, 5-57 Glamorgan v Hampshire | Cardiff |

SIX OR MORE WICKET-KEEPING DISMISSALS IN AN INNINGS

| J.N.Batty | 6 ct | Surrey v Glamorgan | Cardiff |
| J.P.Crawley | 5 ct, 1 st | Hampshire v Nottinghamshire | Nottingham |

W.K.Hegg	6 ct	Lancashire v Leicestershire	Leicester
G.O.Jones	6 ct	England v Bangladesh (2nd Test)	Chester-le-St
N.J.O'Brien	6 ct	Kent v Gloucestershire	Maidstone
D.J.Pipe	6 ct	Worcestershire v Derbyshire	Derby
B.J.M.Scott	5 ct, 1 st	Middlesex v Cambridge UCCE	Cambridge

NINE OR MORE WICKET-KEEPING DISMISSALS IN A MATCH
J.N.Batty	9 ct	Surrey v Glamorgan	Cardiff
T. Frost	9 ct	Warwickshire v Sussex	Birmingham
G. O. Jones	9 ct	England v Bangladesh (2nd Test)	Chester-le-St
N. J. O'Brien	9 ct	Kent v Gloucestershire	Maidstone

NO BYES CONCEDED IN TOTAL OF 550 OR MORE
603	S.J.Adshead	Gloucestershire v Surrey	Bristol
587	M.A.Wallace	Glamorgan v Kent	Canterbury
574	C.M.Gazzard	Somerset v Northamptonshire	Taunton
564-8d	M.A.Wallace	Glamorgan v Warwickshire	Birmingham
534	M.A.Wallace	Glamorgan v Middlesex	Cardiff
523-8d	P.A.Nixon	Leicestershire v Durham	Leicester
522	B.J.M. Scott	Middlesex v Sussex	Lord's

FIVE CATCHES IN AN INNINGS IN THE FIELD
| G.A.Hick | 5 ct | Worcestershire v Essex | Chelmsford |

SIX OR MORE CATCHES IN A MATCH IN THE FIELD
G.A.Hick	8 ct	Worcestershire v Essex	Chelmsford
D.J.Hussey	6 ct	Nottinghamshire v Glamorgan	Nottingham
M.L.Love	6 ct	Northamptonshire v Worcestershire	Northampton
M.L.Love	6 ct	Northamptonshire v Derbyshire	Northampton

2005 FIRST-CLASS AVERAGES

These averages involve the 508 cricketers who appeared in the 175 first-class matches played by 28 teams in the British Isles during the 2005 season.

'*Cap*' denotes the season in which the player was awarded a 1st XI cap by the county he represented in 2005. For Worcestershire players, 2005^C denotes the award of county colours in 2005. Gloucestershire now cap players on first-class debut.

Team abbreviations: A – Australia (ns); B – Bangladesh (is); BA – Bangladesh 'A'; BU – British Universities; CU – Cambridge University/Cambridge UCCE; De – Derbyshire; Du – Durham; DU – Durham UCCE; E – England; Ex – Essex; Gm – Glamorgan; Gs – Gloucestershire; H – Hampshire; K – Kent; La – Lancashire; Le – Leicestershire; LU – Loughborough UCCE; M – Middlesex; MCC – Marylebone Cricket Club; Nh – Northamptonshire; Nt – Nottinghamshire; OU – Oxford University/Oxford UCCE; Sm – Somerset; Sy – Surrey; Sx – Sussex; Wa – Warwickshire; Wo – Worcestershire; Y – Yorkshire. † Left-handed batsman.

BATTING AND FIELDING

	Cap	M	I	NO	HS	Runs	Avge	100	50	Ct/St
Abdur Razzak (BA)	–	1	2	–	30	56	28.00	–	–	–
Ackerman, H.D.(Le)	2005	17	29	2	125	1040	38.51	2	7	9
Adams, A.R.(Ex)	2004	12	12	1	103	373	33.90	1	–	14
Adams, C.J.(Sx)	1998	17	27	2	120*	1060	42.40	1	9	23
† Adams, J.H.K.(H)	–	8	13	–	71	310	23.84	–	3	8
Adnan, M.Hassan(De)	2004	16	29	1	191	817	29.17	2	3	9
Adshead, S.J.(Gs)	2004	18	33	3	148*	920	30.66	1	5	40/6
Aftab Ahmed(B)	–	4	7	1	82*	190	31.66	–	1	–
† Afzaal, U.(Nh)	2005	17	28	3	168*	1187	47.48	5	1	9
Ahmed, J.S.(Ex)	–	1	1	1	14*	14	–	–	–	–
Airey, S.J.(OU)	–	3	5	2	42*	76	25.33	–	–	1
Akram, M.Adnan(CU/BU)	–	4	6	1	129*	205	41.00	1	–	4
Akram, M.Arfan(CU)	–	3	5	1	45	93	23.25	–	–	–
Ali, Kabir(Wo)	2002^c	13	18	2	57	328	20.50	–	2	9
Ali, Kadeer(Gs)	2005	13	25	2	66	494	21.47	–	4	8
† Ali, M.M.(Wa)	–	1	1	–	57	57	57.00	–	1	2
Alleyne, D.(Nt)	–	1	2	–	40	46	23.00	–	–	5
Alleyne, M.W.(Gs)	1990	1	2	–	51	67	33.50	–	1	–
Alok Kapali(BA)	–	5	8	1	59	175	25.00	–	1	1
Ambrose, T.R.(Sx)	2003	7	10	1	78	244	27.11	–	1	14/2
† Anderson, J.M.(La)	2003	16	19	5	37*	145	10.35	–	–	8
† Andrew, G.M.(Sm)	–	5	6	1	32	68	13.60	–	–	1
Anwar, O.S.(OU)	–	3	5	–	14	38	7.60	–	–	1
Anwar Hossain(B)	–	3	4	2	13	18	9.00	–	–	–
† Anyon, J.E.(Wa)	–	6	11	7	29	29	7.25	–	–	3
Astle, N.J.(Du)	–	5	8	–	65	273	34.12	–	3	3
Atri, V.(LU)	–	3	6	–	67	126	21.00	–	1	3
Averis, J.M.M.(Gs)	2001	10	16	1	33	194	12.93	–	–	2
Azhar Mahmood(Sy)	2004	9	13	2	204*	582	52.90	1	2	10
Baker, T.M.(Nh)	–	1	1	1	0	0	0.00	–	–	1
Balcombe, D.J.(DU)	–	3	3	–	73	89	29.66	–	1	1
Ball, M.C.J.(Gs)	1996	3	6	–	7	10	1.66	–	–	5
Bandara, C.M.(Gs)	2005	8	14	–	70	194	13.85	–	1	6
† Banerjee, V.(CU)	–	1	2	–	29	35	17.50	–	–	–
Bassano, C.W.G.(De)	2002	9	14	–	87	429	30.64	–	2	4
Batty, G.J.(Wo/E)	2002^c	15	20	4	57	456	28.50	–	3	11

129

F-C	Cap	M	I	NO	HS	Runs	Avge	100	50	Ct/St
Batty, J.N.(Sy)	2001	16	25	3	124	961	43.68	1	8	50/4
Bell, I.R.(Wa/E)	2001	15	26	3	231	1033	44.91	2	6	14
Benham, C.C.(H)	–	5	10	–	41	117	11.70	–	–	5
Benkenstein, D.M.(Du)	2005	17	25	4	162*	1236	58.85	4	5	12
Benning, J.G.E.(Sy)	–	4	7	–	124	325	46.42	1	3	1
Betts, M.M.(M)	–	9	10	2	36*	136	17.00	–	–	4
Bichel, A.J.(H)	–	4	3	–	138	227	75.66	1	1	1
† Bicknell, D.J.(Nt)	2000	17	27	3	123	1222	50.91	2	10	3
Bicknell, M.P.(Sy)	1989	8	11	2	76	347	38.55	–	3	4
† Bishop, J.E.(Ex)	–	1	–	–	0	0	0.00	–	–	2
† Blackwell, I.D.(Sm)	2001	17	28	4	191	1256	52.33	3	9	5
Blain, J.A.R.(Y)	–	2	1	1	19*	19	–	–	–	1
Bopara, R.S.(Ex)	2005	17	29	5	105*	880	36.66	1	5	7
Borrington, P.M.(De)	–	2	2	–	28	32	16.00	–	–	5
† Botha, A.G.(De)	2004	17	28	7	156*	808	38.47	1	2	7
Breese, G.R.(Du)	–	17	24	2	79*	715	32.50	–	7	16
Bresnan, T.T.(Y)	–	15	20	3	74	339	19.94	–	3	4
Bridge, G.D.(Du)	–	2	3	2	31*	37	37.00	–	–	2
Brignull, D.S.(Le)	–	1	–	–	0	0	0.00	–	–	–
† Broad, S.C.J.(Le)	–	10	12	2	31	107	10.70	–	–	1
Brophy, G.L.(Nh)	–	3	3	1	52*	52	26.00	–	1	6
Brown, A.D.(Sy)	1994	16	26	5	152*	958	45.61	3	2	19
Brown, D.O.(DU/BU)	–	4	5	–	77	134	26.80	–	1	5
Brown, D.R.(Wa)	1995	17	26	2	122	616	25.66	1	2	14
Brown, J.F.(Nh)	2000	15	16	7	22	47	5.22	–	–	4
Brown, M.J.(H)	–	13	25	1	54	560	23.33	–	3	13
Bruce, J.T.A.(H)	–	4	3	1	2	2	1.00	–	–	3
† Bruce, T.O.(DU)	–	3	4	2	26	86	43.00	–	–	4
Bryant, J.D.C.(De)	–	4	8	1	61	132	18.85	–	1	2
Buckham, C.T.(CU)	–	1	1	1	2*	2	–	–	–	2
Burnell, W.F.(DU)	–	2	2	–	7	7	3.50	–	–	–
Burns, M.(Sm)	1999	9	17	1	87	484	30.25	–	2	4
Burrows, T.G.(H)	–	1	2	–	42	55	27.50	–	–	5
† Butcher, M.A.(Sy)	1996	5	8	–	90	283	35.37	–	2	3
Caddick, A.R.(Sm)	1992	11	16	3	54	256	19.69	–	1	3
† Carberry, M.A.(K)	–	1	2	–	47	47	23.50	–	–	1
† Carter, N.M.(Wa)	2005	15	23	3	82	389	19.45	–	1	7
Chambers, M.A.(Ex)	–	1	1	1	2*	2	–	–	–	–
Chandana, U.D.U.(Gs)	2005	6	10	2	49*	136	17.00	–	–	2
Chapple, G.(La)	1994	14	20	1	82	422	22.21	–	3	5
† Cherry, D.D.(Gm)	–	14	27	–	226	838	31.03	2	1	1
Chervak, J.A.(CU)	–	1	2	–	48	74	37.00	–	–	1
Chilton, M.J.(La)	2002	17	28	3	130	895	35.80	3	2	10
Clark, S.G.(LU)	–	3	3	1	47*	57	28.50	–	–	1
Clark, S.R.(M)	–	4	7	3	17*	47	11.75	–	–	1
Clarke, M.J.(A)	–	7	12	–	91	412	34.33	–	3	3
Clarke, R.(Sy)	2005	13	22	4	127*	776	43.11	2	3	16
† Claydon, M.E.(Y)	–	1	–	–	–	–	–	–	–	–
† Cleary, M.F.(Y)	–	2	2	–	12	23	11.50	–	–	–
Clewley, N.J.(LU)	–	2	2	2	2*	3	–	–	–	1
Clinton, P.J.S.(OU)	–	3	5	–	24	51	10.20	–	–	–
† Clinton, R.S.(LU/Sy)	–	15	26	–	106	811	31.19	2	5	8
Clough, G.D.(Nt)	–	1	2	1	14*	14	14.00	–	–	–
Collingwood, P.D.(Du/E)	1998	14	25	3	190	1120	50.90	6	–	16

F-C	Cap	M	I	NO	HS	Runs	Avge	100	50	Ct/St
Compton, N.R.D.(M)	–	1	2	2	56*	95	–	–	1	–
† Cook, A.N.(Ex/MCC)	2005	17	30	2	195	1466	52.35	5	6	12
Cook, S.J.(K)	–	14	18	2	38	193	12.06	–	–	3
Cork, D.G.(La)	2004	14	19	2	102*	540	31.76	1	5	12
Cosker, D.A.(Gm)	2000	12	20	7	52	304	23.38	–	1	5
Cowan, A.P.(Ex)	1997	1	2	–	27	27	13.50	–	–	1
Crawley, J.P.(H)	2002	16	29	2	311*	1246	46.14	3	4	14/1
Croft, R.D.B.(Gm)	1992	17	30	2	90	743	26.53	–	3	5
Croft, S.J.(La)	–	1	1	–	6	6	6.00	–	–	–
Crook, A.R.(La)	–	2	2	–	88	131	65.50	–	1	4
Crook, S.P.(La/Nh)	–	5	6	2	97	288	72.00	–	3	–
Cross, G.D.(La)	–	2	3	–	22	38	12.66	–	–	9/2
Cummins, R.A.G.(LU/Le)	–	5	5	2	26	32	10.66	–	–	1
Cusden, S.M.J.(K)	–	1	1	1	6*	6	–	–	–	–
Daggett, L.M.(DU)	–	3	3	2	0*	0	0.00	–	–	–
Dale, M.A.P.(DU)	–	2	2	–	44	62	31.00	–	–	–
† Daley, S.R.(OU)	–	1	1	–	12	12	12.00	–	–	1
Dalrymple, J.W.M.(M)	2004	13	23	2	108	721	34.33	1	6	3
Danish Kaneria (Ex)	2004	7	6	5	22	47	47.00	–	–	2
Davies, A.M.(Du)	2005	12	14	5	62	120	13.33	–	1	2
† Davies, A.P.(Gm)	–	7	12	4	41*	172	21.50	–	–	3
† Davies, S.M.(Wo)	2005[c]	11	19	1	148	627	34.83	1	2	11/3
Davis, M.J.G.(Sx)	2002	6	6	–	50	84	14.00	–	1	–
Dawood, I.(Y)	–	12	17	2	62*	326	21.73	–	2	34/1
Dawson, R.K.J.(Y)	2004	14	18	4	86	430	30.71	–	3	8
† Dean, K.J.(De)	1998	6	6	1	12	52	10.40	–	–	–
De Bruyn, Z.(Wo)	2005[c]	11	16	–	161	498	31.12	1	2	10
DeFreitas, P.A.J.(Le)	1986	4	7	–	20	62	8.85	–	–	–
Denly, J.L.(K)	–	1	2	–	10	14	7.00	–	–	–
Dennington, M.J.(K)	–	4	8	1	55	161	23.00	–	2	3
Dernbach, J.W.(Sy)	–	3	3	2	1*	2	2.00	–	–	1
Dexter, N.J.(K)	–	3	6	1	79*	176	35.20	–	2	4
† Di Venuto, M.J.(De)	2000	13	26	2	203	1193	49.70	3	5	12
Dixey, P.G.(K)	–	1	2	1	24	40	40.00	–	–	3
Doran, G.P.(OU)	–	1	–	–	0	0	0.00	–	–	3
Doshi, N.D.(Sy)	–	11	14	3	33	93	8.45	–	–	1
Durston, W.J.(Sm)	–	7	11	2	146*	323	35.88	1	–	5
Ealham, M.A.(Nt)	2004	15	19	3	72	484	30.25	–	3	5
† Edwards, N.J.(Sm)	–	1	1	–	42	42	42.00	–	–	–
Edwards, P.D.(CU)	–	2	3	2	11*	31	31.00	–	–	1
† Elliott, M.T.G.(Gm)	2000	7	14	–	162	746	53.28	2	5	6
Enamul Haque(B/BA)	–	6	7	2	10	27	5.40	–	–	1
† Ervine, S.M.(H)	2005	16	28	1	75	821	30.40	–	7	8
† Eustace, S.M.(Wa)	–	1	–	–	0	0	0.00	–	–	1
Ferley, R.S.(K)	–	1	2	–	23	33	16.50	–	–	–
Finn, S.T.(M)	–	1	–	–	0	0	0.00	–	–	–
† Fisher, I.D.(Gs)	2004	9	17	2	43	310	20.66	–	–	8
† Fleming, S.P.(Nt)	2005	11	16	1	238	908	60.53	4	2	14
Flintoff, A.(La/E)	1998	11	16	1	102	586	39.06	1	5	8
† Flower, A.(Ex/MCC)	2002	16	25	6	188	1349	71.00	6	4	11
Flower, G.W.(Ex)	2005	12	19	–	115	397	20.89	1	3	5
Footitt, M.H.A.(Nt)	–	2	3	1	19*	35	17.50	–	–	1
† Foster, E.J.(LU)	–	1	1	–	83	105	105.00	–	1	–
Foster, J.S.(Ex)	2001	17	25	4	107*	771	36.71	1	5	35/6

131

F-C	Cap	M	I	NO	HS	Runs	Avge	100	50	Ct/St
Fox, D.R.(OU)	–	2	3	–	184	191	63.66	1	–	1
† France, B.J.(De)	–	7	13	–	56	189	14.53	–	1	3
† Francis, J.D.(Sm)	–	17	31	5	125*	1062	40.84	4	5	8
Francis, S.R.G.(Sm)	–	6	9	5	29	87	21.75	–	–	6
† Franks, P.J.(Nt)	1999	5	6	3	104*	195	65.00	1	–	–
Friedlander, M.J.(CU/BU/Nh)	–	4	5	–	81	113	22.60	–	1	2
Friend, T.J.(De)	–	3	6	–	82	120	20.00	–	1	2
† Frost, T.(Wa)	1999	16	25	2	91	482	20.95	–	2	42/1
Fulton, D.P.(K)	1998	16	29	1	110	833	29.75	1	5	16
Gallian, J.E.R.(Nt)	1998	17	27	4	199	1220	53.04	3	5	14
† Ganguly, S.C.(Gm)	–	5	9	2	142	438	62.57	1	3	2
† Gayle, C.H.(Wo)	2005c	6	–	57	192	32.00	–	2	6	
Gazzard, C.M.(Sm)	–	8	10	2	74	190	23.75	–	1	15
Gibson, O.D.(Le)	–	15	24	4	91	379	18.95	–	2	2
Gidman, A.P.R.(Gs)	2004	16	30	3	142	1012	37.48	3	4	14
Gifford, W.M.(LU)	–	3	5	1	33	78	19.50	–	–	3
† Gilchrist, A.C.(A)	–	6	10	1	49*	207	23.00	–	–	20/1
Giles, A.F.(Wa/E)	–	9	16	3	62	274	21.07	–	2	5
Gillespie, J.N.(A)	–	5	8	2	53*	149	24.83	–	1	1
† Godleman, B.A.(M)	–	1	1	1	69*	69	–	–	1	–
† Golwalker, Y.A.(M)	–	2	2	–	3	5	2.50	–	–	–
Goodwin, M.W.(Sx)	2001	15	25	1	158	1380	57.50	4	7	8
Gough, D.(Ex)	2004	10	10	2	93	296	37.00	–	2	1
Grant, R.N.(Gm)	–	4	7	1	33	103	17.16	–	–	1
Gray, A.K.D.(De)	–	8	13	5	77*	237	29.62	–	1	9
Greenidge, C.G.(Gs)	2005	4	7	2	25	72	14.40	–	–	–
Guy, S.M.(Y)	–	5	6	1	42	117	23.40	–	–	13/1
† Habib, A.(Le)	1998	13	21	2	153*	705	37.10	1	3	8
Habibul Bashar (B)	–	4	7	1	75	193	32.16	–	2	1
Hadden, B.J.(A)	–	1	1	–	94	94	94.00	–	1	2
Hall, A.J.(K)	2005	11	16	2	133	538	38.42	1	2	9
Hamilton-Brown, R.J.(Sy)	–	1	2	–	9	14	7.00	–	–	1
Hancock, T.H.C.(Gs)	1998	5	9	1	41*	141	17.62	–	–	11
Harbhajan Singh (Sy)	–	4	5	1	84	124	31.00	–	1	2
Hardinges, M.A.(Gs)	2004	13	25	2	58*	404	17.56	–	1	10
Harmison, S.J.(Du/E)	1999	11	11	3	20*	61	7.62	–	–	3
Harris, A.J.(Nt)	2000	12	12	4	35	75	9.37	–	–	4
Harrison, A.J.(Gm)	–	1	1	–	0	0	0.00	–	–	–
Harrison, D.S.(Gm/MCC)	–	17	29	2	75*	318	11.77	–	1	9
Harrison, P.W.(LU/Wa)	–	4	6	2	54	143	35.75	–	1	5
Harvey, I.J.(Y)	–	13	20	2	209*	772	42.88	2	4	8
Hasanuzzaman (BA)	–	1	1	–	0	0	0.00	–	–	2
† Havell, P.M.R.(De)	–	3	5	4	6*	10	10.00	–	–	–
† Hayden, M.L.(A)	–	7	12	1	138	472	42.90	1	2	14
Hayward, M.(M)	–	4	5	3	12*	20	10.00	–	–	1
Heath, D.R.(CU)	–	1	2	–	54	64	32.00	–	1	–
Heather, S.A.(Sx)	–	1	1	–	7	7	7.00	–	–	–
Hegg, W.K.(La)	1989	15	21	6	77*	502	33.46	–	3	41/5
† Hembry, T.D.C.(CU)	–	1	1	–	72	72	72.00	–	1	1
† Hemp, D.L.(Gm)	1994	16	32	1	171*	1369	44.16	3	8	9
Henderson, C.W.(Le)	–	15	21	4	55	413	24.29	–	2	6
Heywood, J.J.N.(CU)	–	1	2	1	19*	19	19.00	–	–	2
Hick, G.A.(Wo)	1986	16	29	2	176	932	34.51	2	5	36
Hildreth, J.C.(Sm)	–	16	29	4	125*	937	37.48	2	6	15

132

F-C	Cap	M	I	NO	HS	Runs	Avge	100	50	Ct/St
Hodd, A.J.(Sy)	–	1	2	2	57*	112	–	–	2	1
Hodge, B.J.(La/A)	–	8	13	1	110*	390	32.50	1	1	7
Hodnett, G.P.(Gs)	2005	1	2	–	49	59	29.50	–	–	1
† Hogg, K.W.(La)	–	2	4	–	9	18	4.50	–	–	2
Hoggard, M.J.(Y/E)	2000	13	16	3	64*	161	12.38	–	1	4
Holt, D.R.(LU)	–	1	1	–	5	5	5.00	–	–	1
† Hooper, M.R.(CU)	–	1	1	–	2	2	2.00	–	–	1
Hopkinson, C.D.(Sx)	–	8	13	–	64	341	26.23	–	3	3
Horton, P.J.(La)	–	6	9	–	99	350	38.88	–	2	2/1
Howells, P.W.(DU)	–	1	2	1	51*	53	53.00	–	1	2
Huggins, T.B.(Nh)	–	1	1	–	8	8	8.00	–	–	1
Hughes, J.(Gm)	–	13	25	2	134*	511	22.21	2	–	10
Hunter, I.D.(De)	–	13	20	6	40	212	15.14	–	–	5
Hussey, D.J.(Nt)	2004	16	21	2	232*	1293	68.05	3	8	30
† Hussey, M.E.K.(Du)	2005	10	18	4	253	1074	76.71	3	5	19
† Hutchison, P.M.(M)	–	2	3	1	26*	28	14.00	–	–	2
† Hutton, B.L.(M)	2003	17	31	2	152	1010	34.82	2	4	24
Irani, R.C.(Ex)	1994	16	23	2	103	1202	57.23	1	10	5
Jacklin, B.D.(CU)	–	1	2	1	4	4	4.00	–	–	–
James, G.D.(CU)	–	2	4	–	17	26	6.50	–	–	–
† Jaques, P.A.(Y)	2005	13	23	2	219	1359	64.71	4	6	14
Javed Omar (B)	–	4	7	–	167	365	52.14	1	1	1
† Jayasuriya, S.T.(Sm)	–	7	13	–	73	327	25.15	–	3	2
Jefferson, W.I.(Ex)	2002	15	26	2	149	938	39.08	2	4	11
Johnson, R.L.(Sm)	2001	11	15	–	35	218	14.53	–	–	5
Jones, C.M.P.(M)	–	1	–	–	0	0	0.00	–	–	–
Jones, G.O.(K/E)	2003	10	16	2	85	330	23.57	–	1	41/2
Jones, K.J.F.(K)	–	1	2	–	14	14	7.00	–	–	1
Jones, P.S.(Nh)	–	6	6	–	51	78	13.00	–	1	–
† Jones, S.P.(Gm/E)	2002	9	12	8	20*	85	21.25	–	–	3
Joseph, R.H.(K)	–	2	3	1	12	12	6.00	–	–	1
Joyce, E.C.(M)	2002	16	29	2	192	1668	61.77	3	13	15
† Kartik, M.(La)	–	2	3	–	7	11	3.66	–	–	1
Kasprowicz, M.S.(A)	2002	4	5	–	20	52	10.40	–	–	5
† Katich, S.M.(H/A)	2003	14	24	1	128	863	37.52	1	6	12
† Keedy, G.(La)	2000	9	10	7	34	47	15.66	–	–	4
Keegan, C.B.(M)	2003	2	3	–	28	48	16.00	–	–	1
Kemp, J.M.(K)	–	8	12	2	124	527	52.70	2	2	8
Kemp, R.A.(CU)	–	1	2	–	1	1	0.50	–	–	–
Kenway, D.A.(H)	2001	1	2	–	20	20	10.00	–	–	3
Key, R.W.T.(K)	2001	15	27	1	189	1556	59.84	4	8	8
Khalid Masud (B)	–	4	6	–	44	146	24.33	–	–	7
Khalid, S.A.(Wo)	2003ᶜ	1	2	–	20	20	10.00	–	–	–
Khan, A.(K)	–	14	17	9	58*	170	21.25	–	1	2
Killeen, N.(Du)	1999	5	5	1	23	39	9.75	–	–	3
King, R.E.(Nh)	–	1	–	–	0	0	0.00	–	–	–
Kirby, S.P.(Gs)	2005	13	21	11	15*	105	10.50	–	–	4
Kirtley, R.J.(Sx)	1998	17	23	13	30	194	19.40	–	–	7
Knappett, J.P.(OU/BU)	–	4	6	1	73	232	46.40	–	2	10/1
† Knight, N.V.(Wa)	1995	17	30	3	117	1222	45.25	4	5	9
Krejza, J.J.(Le)	–	1	2	–	38	57	28.50	–	–	–
Kruis, G.J.(Y)	–	16	18	9	37*	174	19.33	–	–	5
Lamb, G.A.(H)	–	9	15	–	75	250	16.66	–	2	13
Lamb, N.J.(DU)	–	2	3	–	23	31	10.33	–	–	–

133

F-C	Cap	M	I	NO	HS	Runs	Avge	100	50	Ct/St
† Langer, J.L.(A)	–	7	13	2	115	574	52.18	2	3	3
Langeveldt, C.K.(Sm)	2005	6	6	3	18*	38	12.66	–	–	–
Laraman, A.W.(Sm)	–	9	13	1	53	236	19.66	–	2	2
Law, S.G.(La)	2002	15	24	2	143	858	39.00	3	2	18
Lawson, M.A.K.(Y)	–	3	4	1	20*	31	10.33	–	–	–
Leatherdale, D.A.(Wo)	1994	1	1	–	14	14	14.00	–	–	–
Lee, B.(A)	–	6	10	3	47	164	23.42	–	–	2
Lewis, J.(Gs/MCC)	1998	12	19	6	55	324	24.92	–	1	5
Lewis, J.J.B.(Du)	1998	10	17	1	68	495	30.93	–	3	8
Lewis, M.L.(Du)	–	5	6	1	20	44	8.80	–	–	2
† Lewry, J.D.(Sx)	1996	12	16	3	23	90	6.92	–	–	3
Liddle, C.J.(Le)	–	1	–	–	0	0	0.00	–	–	–
Linley, T.E.(OU)	–	2	3	–	42	52	17.33	–	–	1
Logan, R.J.(H)	–	6	9	2	28	61	8.71	–	–	–
Loudon, A.G.R.(Wa)	–	17	30	4	95*	834	32.07	–	5	12
Louw, J.(Nh)	–	15	20	3	64	277	16.29	–	2	2
Love, M.L.(Nh)	–	15	25	1	177	1345	56.04	4	6	36
Lowe, J.A.(Du)	–	1	2	–	26	40	20.00	–	–	–
Loye, M.B.(La)	2003	16	25	1	200	1198	49.91	4	3	11
Lucas, D.S.(Y)	–	1	–	–	0	0	0.00	–	–	–
† Lumb, M.J.(Y)	2003	11	21	4	130	584	34.35	2	1	10
† Lungley, T.(De)	–	3	3	–	36	41	13.66	–	–	1
MacGill, S.C.G.(A)	–	2	–	–	0	0	0.00	–	–	1
McGrath, A.(Y)	1999	16	28	4	173*	1425	59.37	5	5	20
McGrath, G.D.(A)	–	3	5	4	20*	36	36.00	–	–	1
McLean, J.J.(H)	–	6	9	1	68	242	30.25	–	3	4
† McLean, N.A.M.(Sm)	2003	6	7	1	40	59	9.83	–	–	1
McMahon, P.J.(OU)	–	3	3	1	62*	79	39.50	–	1	5
McMillan, C.D.(H)	–	4	8	1	52	169	24.14	–	1	–
Maddy, D.L.(Le)	1996	15	25	–	124	660	26.40	1	1	17
† Maher, J.P.(Du)	–	2	4	–	9	18	4.50	–	–	3
Mahmood, S.I.(La/MCC)	–	8	10	–	57	177	17.70	–	1	–
Maiden, A.J.(DU/BU)	–	4	5	1	211*	291	72.75	1	–	1
Malik, M.N.(Wo)	2004c	9	14	5	21*	61	6.77	–	–	–
† Mann, R.J.(CU)	–	1	2	–	5	9	4.50	–	–	–
Marshall, S.J.(La)	–	4	6	3	35*	104	34.66	–	–	1
Martin-Jenkins, R.S.C.(Sx)	2000	15	20	4	88	586	36.62	–	2	4
Martyn, D.R.(A)	–	6	10	1	154*	332	36.88	1	1	4
Mascarenhas, A.D.(H)	1998	11	18	7	103*	540	49.09	2	1	5
Mashrafe Mortaza (B)	–	4	7	–	21	39	5.57	–	–	–
Mason, M.S.(Wo)	2002c	16	23	5	38	267	14.83	–	–	2
Masters, D.D.(Le)	–	13	16	6	36	195	19.50	–	–	4
† Maunders, J.K.(Le)	–	16	27	–	148	759	28.11	1	3	7
Maynard, M.P.(Gm)	1987	1	2	–	20	20	10.00	–	–	1
Mees, T.(Wa)	–	1	–	–	0	0	0.00	–	–	–
Mehrab Hossain (BA)	–	4	6	1	30*	60	12.00	–	–	3
Middlebrook, J.D.(Ex)	2003	16	23	5	71	609	33.83	–	3	9
Mitchell, D.K.H.(Wo)	2005c	6	10	2	63*	196	24.50	–	2	6
Mohammad Akram (Sy)	–	14	15	5	27*	79	7.90	–	–	1
Mohammad Amin (CU)	–	1	1	–	1	1	1.00	–	–	–
Mohammad Ashraful(B)	–	5	9	1	102	169	21.12	1	–	3
† Mohammad Rafique(B)	–	4	6	–	54	84	14.00	–	1	1
† Mongia, D.(Le)	–	11	17	–	164	684	40.23	1	5	5
Montgomerie, R.R.(Sx)	1999	18	30	2	184*	851	30.39	2	3	11

F-C	Cap	M	I	NO	HS	Runs	Avge	100	50	Ct/St
Moore, S.C.(Wo)	2003c	18	33	4	246	1399	48.24	2	6	11
Moreton S.J.P.(OU)	–	3	5	–	74	139	27.80	–	1	1
Morris, J.C.(DU)	–	1	2	–	21	34	17.00	–	–	1
Morse, E.J.(OU)	–	2	2	1	7*	7	7.00	–	–	–
Moss, J. (De)	2004	17	31	1	109*	1021	34.03	2	7	11
Muchall, G.J.(Du)	2005	17	29	4	123	764	30.56	1	3	6
Munday, M.K.(OU/Sm)	–	4	2	2	1*	1	–	–	–	3
Muralitharan, M.(La)	1999	6	8	2	24*	78	13.00	–	–	3
Murtagh, C.P.(LU)	–	3	5	2	37*	52	17.33	–	–	2
† Murtagh, T.J.(Sy)	–	9	11	3	74*	296	37.00	–	2	4
Mushfiqur Rahim (B/BA)	–	4	7	1	115*	248	41.33	1	1	2
Mushfiqur Rahman (BA)	–	1	2	–	15	19	9.50	–	–	1
Mushtaq Ahmed (Sx)	2003	16	22	3	90*	360	18.94	–	2	4
† Mustard, P.(Du)	–	17	23	1	80	578	26.27	–	3	45/3
Nafis Iqbal (B/BA)	–	9	16	–	46	250	15.62	–	–	1
Napier, G.R.(Ex)	2003	8	7	–	55	153	21.85	–	2	2
Nash, C.D.(Sx)	–	1	–	–	0	0	0.00	–	–	1
Nash, D.C.(M)	2000	1	2	–	12	12	6.00	–	–	–
Naved-ul-Hasan (Sx)	2005	9	14	2	139	346	28.83	1	–	5
Nazimuddin (BA)	–	5	7	–	60	190	27.14	–	2	3
Needham, J.(De)	–	1	2	1	6	7	7.00	–	–	–
Nel, A.(Ex)	–	1	–	–	0	0	0.00	–	–	1
† New, T.J.(Le)	–	7	11	1	89	329	32.90	–	2	7/1
Newby, O.J.(Nt)	–	2	3	1	38*	49	24.50	–	–	–
† Newman, S.A.(Sy)	2005	16	27	–	219	1286	47.62	4	4	10
† Nixon, P.A.(Le)	1994	16	27	7	85	708	35.40	–	6	40/4
Noffke, A.A.(Du)	–	6	8	2	65	138	23.00	–	1	1
† North, M.J.(La)	–	3	4	–	60	101	25.25	–	1	2
Ntini, M.(Wa)	–	6	8	1	27*	74	10.57	–	–	1
Oberoi, S.(OU)	–	2	3	–	247	324	108.00	1	–	2
† O'Brien, N.J.(K)	–	14	22	4	64	442	24.55	–	3	46/5
Onions, G.(Du)	–	4	4	2	9*	13	6.50	–	–	1
Ormond, J.(Sy)	2003	9	11	2	35	129	14.33	–	–	2
O'Shea, M.P.(Gm)	–	3	5	–	24	52	10.40	–	–	1
Palladino, A.P.(CU/BU/Ex)	–	8	11	5	30	106	17.66	–	–	3
† Panesar, M.S.(BU/Nh)	–	9	12	4	39*	75	9.37	–	–	2
Park, G.T.(CU)	–	3	4	1	48*	112	37.33	–	–	5
Parker, L.C.(OU/BU/Wa)	–	9	15	3	89	440	36.66	–	2	5
Parsons, K.A.(Sm)	1999	8	12	3	94	401	44.55	–	2	5
Parsons, M.(Sm)	–	2	3	1	6*	11	5.50	–	–	–
Patel, M.M.(K)	1994	16	21	4	87	487	28.64	–	4	3
Patel, S.R.(Nt)	–	3	4	–	12	27	6.75	–	–	–
† Pathan, I.K.(M)	–	3	4	2	68	126	63.00	–	1	1
Patterson, S.A.(Y)	–	1	–	–	–	–	–	–	–	1
† Pearson, J.A.(Gs)	2004	5	10	1	68	206	22.88	–	2	2
Peng, N.(Du)	2001	10	15	–	87	282	18.80	–	1	–
Peploe, C.T.(M)	–	7	10	2	42	147	18.37	–	–	2
Peters, S.D.(Wo)	2002c	9	16	1	88	282	18.80	–	2	6
Pettini, M.L.(MCC)	–	1	1	1	41*	41	–	–	–	2
Phillips, B.J.(Nh)	2005	13	20	6	58	447	31.92	–	2	2
† Phillips, T.J.(Ex)	–	3	4	2	89	116	58.00	–	1	–
Phythian, M.J.(DU)	–	2	1	–	0	0	0.00	–	–	6
† Pietersen, C.(Nh)	–	4	3	–	1	1	0.33	–	–	2
Pietersen, K.P.(H/E)	2005	11	21	1	158	897	44.85	3	4	4

135

	F-C Cap	M	I	NO	HS	Runs	Avge	100	50	Ct/St
Pipe, D.J.(Wo)	2002ᶜ	12	19	2	80*	326	19.17	–	1	43/2
Piper, K.J.(Wa)	1992	1	–	–	0	0	0.00	–	–	2/2
Plunkett, L.E.(Du)	–	14	19	4	74*	256	17.06	–	1	6
Ponting, R.T.(A)	–	7	12	1	156	557	50.63	2	2	5
Pothas, N.(H)	2003	15	24	5	139	973	51.21	3	5	48/3
Powell, M.J.(Gm/MCC)	2000	17	32	2	111	1044	34.80	1	6	10
Powell, M.J.(Wa)	1999	13	22	2	146	608	30.40	1	2	8
Poynter, A.D.(M)	–	1	1	–	1	1	1.00	–	–	2
Pretorius, D.(Wa)	–	6	6	2	22	56	14.00	–	–	3
Price, R.W.(Wo)	2004ᶜ	10	13	1	20	101	8.41	–	–	6
Prior, M.J.(Sx/MCC)	2003	17	27	1	109	874	33.61	2	6	45/1
Pyrah, R.M.(Y)	–	2	3	–	78	78	26.00	–	1	1
Rajin Saleh (B)	–	4	7	1	30*	71	11.83	–	–	2
Ramprakash, M.R.(Sy)	2002	14	23	2	252	1568	74.66	6	5	8
Read, C.M.W.(Nt)	1999	16	21	4	103*	756	44.47	1	7	62/2
† Read, G.G.(DU/BU)	–	4	4	1	25	42	14.00	–	–	4
† Richards, M.A.(OU)	–	2	3	–	43	57	19.00	–	–	2
Richardson, A.(M)	2005	13	16	5	25	137	12.45	–	–	2
Roberts, T.W.(Nh)	–	3	5	–	53	114	22.80	–	1	–
Robinson, D.D.J.(Le)	–	16	27	1	139	1108	42.61	4	4	13
† Rogers, C.J.L.(Le)	–	3	6	–	209	441	73.50	1	2	4
Rudge, W.D.(Gs)	2005	5	8	1	15	35	5.00	–	–	2
† Sadler, J.L.(Le)	–	6	10	4	82*	302	50.33	–	3	4
Saggers, M.J.(K)	2001	9	13	5	45	216	27.00	–	–	5
Saker, N.C.(Sy)	–	1	1	–	0	0	0.00	–	–	–
Sales, D.J.G.(Nh)	1999	16	27	2	190	1171	46.84	3	6	20
Salisbury, I.D.K.(Sy)	1998	5	5	2	59*	141	47.00	–	1	4
Saqlain Mushtaq (Sy)	1998	5	5	1	31	55	13.75	–	–	3
Sarwan, R.R.(Gs)	2005	7	14	–	117	442	31.57	1	2	9
Savill, T.E.(CU)	–	2	3	1	59	72	36.00	–	1	3
† Sayers, J.J.(Y)	–	10	17	1	115	592	37.00	2	3	11
Scott, B.J.M.(M)	–	16	23	5	64*	442	24.55	–	3	44/6
Scott, G.M.(Du)	–	7	13	2	61*	307	27.90	–	1	2
Shafayat, B.M.(Nt)	–	17	28	–	161	1058	37.78	2	6	21
Shah, O.A.(M/MCC)	2000	17	31	5	173*	1728	66.46	7	8	22
Shahadat Hossain(B/BA)	–	8	12	6	19*	52	8.66	–	–	1
Shahin Hossain(Ba)	–	4	5	2	12	33	11.00	–	–	11/1
† Shahriar Nafis(B/BA)	–	7	13	1	63	408	34.00	–	4	1
Shankar, A.(CU)	–	2	4	–	27	52	13.00	–	–	–
† Sharif, Z.K.(CU)	–	2	4	1	54*	64	21.33	–	1	1
† Sheikh, M.A.(De)	–	5	8	–	55	137	17.12	–	1	–
Sheriyar, A.(Wo)	–	2	3	1	5	13	6.50	–	–	–
Shilvock, D.J.F.(DU)	–	1	1	–	0	0	0.00	–	–	–
Shoaib Akhtar (Wo)	2005ᶜ	4	7	1	35	84	14.00	–	–	1
† Sidebottom, R.J.(Nt)	2004	15	15	4	31	129	11.72	–	–	6
Sillence, R.J.(Gs)	2004	1	2	–	12	12	6.00	–	–	–
Silverwood, C.E.W.(Y)	1996	6	7	–	80	186	26.57	–	2	3
Singh, A.(CU)	–	1	2	–	75	78	39.00	–	1	–
Singh, A.(Nt)	–	7	10	–	131	301	30.10	1	1	2
Singh, K.R.(LU)	–	3	5	1	29*	54	13.50	–	–	3
Smith, B.F.(Wo)	2002ᶜ	18	30	3	172	1546	57.25	6	5	20
Smith, E.T.(M)	2005	17	32	–	145	1274	39.81	2	7	12
† Smith, G.C.(Sm)	2005	4	8	1	311	472	67.42	1	1	7
Smith, G.J.(Nt)	2001	15	16	3	26	137	10.53	–	–	4

136

F-C	Cap	M	I	NO	HS	Runs	Avge	100	50	Ct/St
† Smith, T.C.(La)	–	1	1	–	–	0	0.00	–	–	1
Smith, W.R.(DU/BU/Nt)	–	7	10	1	156	332	36.88	1	1	4
Snape, J.N.(Le)	–	2	4	–	31	101	25.25	–	–	–
Snell, S.D.(Gs)	2005	2	4	1	83*	141	47.00	–	1	4
Solanki, V.S.(Wo)	1998	13	21	2	80	585	30.78	–	4	9
Spearman, C.M.(Gs)	2002	14	27	–	216	930	34.44	1	3	13
Stearn, C.P.(OU)	–	1	1	1	33*	33	–	–	–	1
Stephenson, J.P.(MCC)	–	1	–	–	0	0	0.00	–	–	–
Stevens, D.I.(K)	2005	16	27	1	208	1277	49.11	4	6	13
Steyn, D.W.(Ex)	–	6	7	2	82	94	18.80	–	1	2
Stiff, D.A.(K)	–	1	2	2	15*	27	–	–	–	–
† Strauss, A.J.(M/E)	2001	11	20	–	129	588	29.40	2	1	12
Streak, H.H.(Wa)	2005	9	11	2	51	194	21.55	–	1	8
† Stubbings, S.D.(De)	2001	16	29	1	151	1126	40.21	2	8	9
Styris, S.B. (M)	–	9	17	1	100*	484	30.25	1	3	4
Suman, A.K.(OU/BU)	–	4	3	–	39	39	13.00	–	–	4
Suppiah, A.V.(Sm)	–	7	13	–	123	419	32.23	1	2	1
† Sutcliffe, I.J.(La)	2003	15	25	3	153	1046	47.54	2	7	15
Sutton, L.D.(De)	2002	17	29	4	95	833	33.32	–	4	52
Swann, G.P.(Nt/MCC)	–	16	17	2	63	322	21.46	–	2	7
† Syed Rasel(BA)	–	5	7	–	33	76	10.85	–	–	1
Symonds, A.(La)	2005	7	10	–	146	623	62.30	3	1	4
Tahir, N.(Wa)	–	5	7	3	32	95	23.75	–	–	–
Tait, S.W.(A)	–	3	4	2	22	30	15.00	–	–	–
Talha Jubair (B/BA)	–	6	9	–	37	54	6.00	–	–	4
Tapash Baisya(B)	–	3	4	2	18	40	20.00	–	–	–
† Taylor, B.V.(H)	–	8	14	6	24	66	8.25	–	–	–
Taylor, C.G.(Gs)	2001	9	17	1	176	563	35.18	1	2	5
Taylor, C.R.(Y)	–	1	2	1	14*	14	14.00	–	–	1
Ten Doeschate, R.N.(Ex)	–	2	1	–	98	98	98.00	–	1	1
† Thomas, I.J.(Gm)	–	4	8	–	40	129	16.12	–	–	2
† Thomas, S.D.(Gm)	1997	7	14	–	63	274	19.57	–	1	–
Thornely, D.J.(Sy)	–	2	2	–	81	154	77.00	–	2	1
Thornicroft, N.D.(Ex)	–	1	2	1	4*	4	4.00	–	–	–
Thorp, C.D.(Du)	–	5	6	–	23	49	8.16	–	–	3
† Thorpe, G.P.(Sy/E)	1991	10	14	3	95	454	41.27	–	4	5
Timms, R.T.(CU)	–	3	6	–	57	105	17.50	–	1	–
† Tredwell, J.C.(K)	–	3	5	–	27	55	11.00	–	–	1
Trego, P.D.(M)	–	7	10	1	72	234	26.00	–	2	2
Tremlett, C.T.(H)	2004	11	14	5	64	219	24.33	–	1	3
† Trescothick, M.E.(Sm/E)	1999	11	18	–	194	872	48.44	2	3	13
Trott, I.J.L.(Wa)	2005	18	30	2	210	1161	41.46	4	2	32
† Troughton, J.O.(Wa)	2002	12	18	–	119	583	32.38	1	5	6
Tudor, A.J.(Ex)	–	3	2	–	57	86	43.00	–	1	2
Turner, M.L.(Du)	–	2	2	1	18	19	19.00	–	–	1
Turner, R.J.(Sm)	1994	9	13	3	68*	277	27.70	–	1	22/1
Tushar Imran(BA)	–	5	9	1	119	467	58.37	2	2	–
Udal, S.D.(H)	1992	11	14	4	47*	196	19.60	–	–	7
† Vaas, W.P.U.C.J.(Wo)	2005[c]	7	10	1	45	271	30.11	–	3	3
Van der Wath, J.J.(Sx)	–	5	7	2	34	104	20.80	–	–	1
Van Jaarsveld, M.(K)	2005	16	28	1	262*	1198	44.37	4	4	18
Vaughan, M.P.(Y/E)	1995	9	15	–	166	564	37.60	2	2	2
Wagh, M.A.(Wa)	2000	2	2	–	66	94	47.00	–	1	–
† Wainwright, D.J.(LU/Y)	–	5	6	2	62	153	38.25	–	1	4

137

F-C	Cap	M	I	NO	HS	Runs	Avge	100	50	Ct/St
† Walker, M.J.(K)	2000	16	28	3	173	993	39.72	3	4	8
Walker, N.G.E.(De)	–	10	14	3	79	156	14.18	–	1	4
† Wallace, M.A.(Gm)	2003	17	30	2	96	746	26.64	–	6	31/4
† Ward, I.J.(Sx)	2004	10	16	–	150	620	38.75	2	2	3
Warne, S.K.(H/A)	2000	16	27	3	107*	742	30.91	2	2	18
Warren, N.A.(Wa)	–	6	5	3	5*	11	5.50	–	–	–
† Warren, R.J.(Nt)	2004	9	13	1	60*	351	29.25	–	3	6
Waters, H.T.(Gm)	–	7	13	7	34	41	6.83	–	–	–
† Watkins, R.E.(Gm)	–	5	9	–	41	131	14.55	–	–	–
Watson, S.R.(H)	2005	5	8	1	203*	540	77.14	1	3	10
† Webley, T.(CU)	–	3	5	–	88	232	46.40	–	2	3
† Wedge, S.A.(Wo)	2005ᶜ	2	2	2	0*	0	–	–	–	–
† Weekes, P.N.(M)	1993	16	26	7	128*	842	44.31	1	5	7
Welch, G.(De)	2001	17	29	3	112	818	31.46	1	4	9
Wessels, M.H.(Nh)	–	14	23	3	107	613	30.65	3	2	23/4
Westfield, M.S.(Ex)	–	1	2	–	0	0	0.00	–	–	–
† Weston, W.P.C.(Gs)	2004	13	24	–	103	710	29.58	1	5	4
† Westwood, I.J.(Wa)	–	11	22	4	106	624	34.66	1	3	6
Wharf, A.G.(Gm)	2000	12	21	–	113	430	20.47	1	1	10
Whelan, C.D.(M)	–	2	2	1	9*	10	10.00	–	–	–
White, A.R.(Nh)	–	2	3	1	30*	36	18.00	–	–	1
White, C.(Y)	1993	16	26	8	110*	873	48.50	1	8	10
White, R.A.(Nh)	–	15	24	2	95	644	29.27	–	2	10
White, W.A.(De)	–	2	2	–	6	8	4.00	–	–	–
Wigley, D.H.(Wo)	–	4	4	3	7*	11	11.00	–	–	2
Wilkinson, R.M.(LU)	–	3	4	–	33	50	12.50	–	–	5
Williams, B.A.(Du)	–	3	4	3	22*	51	51.00	–	–	1
† Willoughby, C.M.(Le)	–	14	17	5	16*	68	5.66	–	–	2
Windows, M.G.N.(Gs)	1998	11	22	1	65*	479	22.80	–	2	2
Wolstenholme, J.P.(Nh)	–	1	–	–	0	0	0.00	–	–	2
Wood, J.R.(DU)	–	1	2	–	29	29	14.50	–	–	–
Wood, M.J.(Sm)	2005	13	23	1	297	1058	48.09	2	7	4
Wood, M.J.(Y)	2001	17	30	2	202*	1005	35.89	1	6	20
† Woodman, R.J.(Sm)	–	3	4	1	46*	54	18.00	–	–	–
Woods, N.J.(OU)	–	4	6	1	26	101	20.20	–	–	1
Wright, C.J.C.(CU/M)	–	5	6	–	76	161	26.83	–	1	1
Wright, D.G.(Nh)	–	16	25	2	85	609	26.47	–	4	6
Wright, L.J.(Sx)	–	7	8	–	37	126	15.75	–	–	5
† Yardy, M.H.(Sx)	2005	18	30	3	257	1520	56.29	5	6	16
Younis Khan (Nt)	–	5	7	1	53	131	21.83	–	1	4

BOWLING

See BATTING and FIELDING section for details of matches, caps and teams

	Cat	O	M	R	W	Avge	Best	5wI	10wM
Abdur Razzak	SLA	29	2	119	0			–	–
Adams, A.R.	RMF	391.3	111	1218	36	33.83	5- 60	1	–
Adams, C.J.	RM/OB	6	0	21	0			–	–
Adams, J.H.K.	LM	6	1	26	0			–	–
Adnan, M.Hassan	OB	15	0	52	0				
Aftab Ahmed	RM	33	3	161	3	53.66	2- 50	–	–
Afzaal, U.	SLA	23	5	94	1	94.00	1- 10	–	–
Ahmed, J.S.	RMF	27	4	141	1	141.00	1- 90	–	–
Airey, S.J.	RMF	54	7	257	2	128.50	1- 35	–	–
Akram, M.Adnan	RM	1.5	0	29	0				
Akram, M.Arfan	LB	4	0	19	0				
Ali, Kabir	RMF	376.5	59	1578	51	30.94	4- 70	–	–
Ali, Kadeer	LB	24	4	69	2	34.50	1- 4	–	–
Ali, M.M.	OB	2	0	15	0				
Alleyne, M.W.	RM	24	3	84	1	84.00	1- 84	–	–
Alok Kapali	LB	5	1	9	0				
Anderson, J.M.	RFM	512.4	99	1813	60	30.21	5- 79	1	–
Andrew, G.M.	RMF	104.5	14	500	11	45.45	4-134	–	–
Anwar, O.S.	RSM	0.3	0	1	0				
Anwar Hossain	RFM	57	3	325	4	81.25	4-113	–	–
Anyon, J.E.	RFM	105	15	425	12	35.41	4- 33	–	–
Astle, N.J.	RM	52.4	17	117	3	39.00	3- 20	–	–
Atri, V.	OB	1	0	6	0				
Averis, J.M.M.	RMF	236	50	865	20	43.25	3- 11	–	–
Azhar Mahmood	RMF	227.2	44	884	26	34.00	5- 72	1	–
Baker, T.M.	RM	13	2	55	1	55.00	1- 55	–	–
Balcombe, D.J.	RFM	92.1	13	391	8	48.87	5-112	1	–
Ball, M.C.J.	OB	149	38	400	6	66.66	3- 99	–	–
Bandara, C.M.	LBG	352.4	69	1087	45	24.15	5- 45	2	–
Banerjee, V.	SLA	48	8	181	2	90.50	2-181	–	–
Batty, G.J.	OB	400	74	1240	33	37.57	5- 87	1	–
Bell, I.R.	RM	77	16	284	6	47.33	3- 64	–	–
Benkenstein, D.M.	RM/OB	91.4	20	333	12	27.75	4- 29	–	–
Benning, J.G.E.	RM	59	3	293	6	48.83	3- 57	–	–
Betts, M.M.	RFM	229.1	45	838	22	38.09	4- 58	–	–
Bichel, A.J.	RFM	120.4	25	441	14	31.50	4-122	–	–
Bicknell, D.J.	SLA	15	2	87	0				
Bicknell, M.P.	RFM	251.5	55	881	29	30.37	6- 56	2	–
Bishop, J.E.	LMF	16.5	3	51	2	25.50	1- 19	–	–
Blackwell, I.D.	SLA	517.5	107	1569	28	56.03	4- 86	–	–
Blain, J.A.R.	RMF	44	5	201	3	67.00	2- 40	–	–
Bopara, R.S.	RMF	214.2	26	959	20	47.95	4- 93	–	–
Botha, A.G.	SLA	473.4	109	1506	33	45.63	6-104	1	–
Breese, G.R.	OB	332.1	61	1080	31	34.83	5- 83	2	–
Bresnan, T.T.	RMF	459	87	1571	47	33.42	5- 42	1	–
Bridge, G.D.	SLA	38	7	108	4	27.00	4- 54	–	–
Brignull, D.S.	RMF	13.2	4	36	3	12.00	3- 36	–	–
Broad, S.C.J.	RMF	214.1	37	831	30	27.70	4- 64	–	–
Brown, A.D.	LB	5	0	14	0				
Brown, D.O.	RM	78	10	357	4	89.25	2-119	–	–
Brown, D.R.	RFM	495.3	110	1540	50	30.80	5-128	1	–

F-C	Cat	O	M	R	W	Avge	Best	5wI	10wM
Brown, J.F.	OB	629.4	184	1551	55	28.20	6-112	6	2
Bruce, J.T.A.	RMF	91	13	324	14	23.14	3- 42	–	–
Buckham, C.T.	LB	8	1	61	0				
Burnell, W.F.	RM	4	0	12	0				
Burns, M.	RM	40.3	5	142	3	47.33	2- 12	–	–
Butcher, M.A.	RM/OB	3	0	11	0				
Caddick, A.R.	RFM	443.1	94	1501	54	27.79	6- 96	4	1
Carter, N.M.	LFM	410.4	83	1378	41	33.60	4- 30	–	–
Chambers, M.A.	RFM	16	1	84	1	84.00	1- 73	–	–
Chandana, U.D.U.	LB	239.1	38	740	16	46.25	5-117	1	–
Chapple, G.	RFM	383.1	98	1010	47	21.48	5- 22	2	–
Cherry, D.D.	RM	3	1	9	0				
Chilton, M.J.	RM	5	1	9	1	9.00	1- 9	–	–
Clark, S.G.	RMF	84.2	20	254	11	23.09	5- 29	1	–
Clark, S.R.	RFM	120.4	22	412	15	27.46	5- 61	1	–
Clarke, M.J.	SLA	7	0	42	0				
Clarke, R.	RFM	152.1	16	708	18	39.33	4- 91	–	–
Claydon, M.E.	RMF	24	5	92	1	92.00	1- 27	–	–
Cleary, M.F.	RFM	67	10	250	8	31.25	3- 46	–	–
Clewley, N.J.	RMF	74	16	257	3	85.66	2-132	–	–
Clinton, R.S.	RM	20.1	2	92	0				
Clough, G.D.	RM	24	2	84	1	84.00	1- 39	–	–
Collingwood, P.D.	RMF	185.3	28	687	21	32.71	5- 52	1	–
Cook, A.N.	OB	18	1	80	3	26.66	3- 13	–	–
Cook, S.J.	RM	397.1	103	1247	41	30.41	5- 44	2	–
Cork, D.G.	RFM	395.3	98	1118	43	26.00	4- 27	–	–
Cosker, D.A.	SLA	395.4	60	1405	28	50.17	4- 57	–	–
Cowan, A.P.	RFM	25	6	99	1	99.00	1- 59	–	–
Crawley, J.P.	RM	2.5	0	7	1	7.00	1- 7	–	–
Croft, R.D.B.	OB	577.4	77	2134	43	49.62	5- 57	2	1
Croft, S.J.	RMF	11	1	49	0				
Crook, A.R.	OB	35	7	132	4	33.00	3- 71	–	–
Crook, S.P.	RFM	83.3	14	286	4	71.50	3- 54	–	–
Cummins, R.A.G.	RM	150	38	468	14	33.42	3- 32	–	–
Cusden, S.M.J.	RFM	28	1	107	3	35.66	2- 50	–	–
Daggett, L.M.	RMF	64	13	254	2	127.00	1- 66	–	–
Dalrymple, J.W.M.	OB	248.4	25	940	23	40.86	4- 53	–	–
Danish Kaneria	LB	394.4	86	1069	32	33.40	6- 74	3	1
Davies, A.M.	RM	296.4	94	810	49	16.53	6- 32	2	–
Davies, A.P.	RMF	168.1	30	664	13	51.07	3-121	–	–
Davis, M.J.G.	OB	74.2	16	177	3	59.00	2- 52	–	–
Dawson, R.K.J.	OB	325.4	46	1098	27	40.66	4- 54	–	–
Dean, K.J.	LMF	104.5	22	319	6	53.16	3- 36	–	–
De Bruyn, Z.	RMF	192	27	780	8	97.50	1- 13	–	–
DeFreitas, P.A.J.	RFM	111	21	406	12	33.83	4- 76	–	–
Dennington, M.J.	RFM	62.1	15	206	7	29.42	3- 23	–	–
Dernbach, J.W.	RMF	48.2	5	261	4	65.25	2- 66	–	–
Dexter, N.J.	RM	32	3	161	2	80.50	1- 42	–	–
Doshi, N.D.	SLA	294.1	58	1087	23	47.26	3- 58	–	–
Durston, W.J.	OB	92	8	449	6	74.83	2- 82	–	–
Ealham, M.A.	RMF	390.5	90	1165	56	20.80	5- 31	1	–
Edwards, P.D.	RFM	35	6	154	2	77.00	1- 31	–	–
Elliott, M.T.G.	LM/SLC	5	0	20	0				
Enamul Haque	SLA	149.5	19	585	8	73.12	3-174	–	–

F-C	Cat	O	M	R	W	Avge	Best	5wI	10wM
Ervine, S.M.	RM	374.1	79	1360	42	32.38	5- 60	3	–
Ferley, R.S.	SLA	8	1	26	1	26.00	1- 26	–	–
Finn, S.T.	RMF	20	6	53	2	26.50	1- 16	–	–
Fisher, I.D.	SLA	255.4	47	849	19	44.68	4- 89	–	–
Flintoff, A.	RFM	250.5	43	852	34	25.05	5- 78	1	–
Flower, G.W.	SLA	131.3	32	393	9	43.66	3-112	–	–
Footitt, M.H.A.	LFM	43.3	6	260	6	43.33	4- 45	–	–
France, B.J.	RM	16	3	70	1	70.00	1- 37	–	–
Francis, S.R.G.	RMF	114.4	16	520	5	104.00	2- 81	–	–
Franks, P.J.	RMF	107	17	453	9	50.33	2- 37	–	–
Friedlander, M.J.	RFM	64	7	345	8	43.12	3- 67	–	–
Fulton, D.P.	SLA	2	0	5	0				
Gallian, J.E.R.	RM	30	4	180	0				
Ganguly, S.C.	RM	38	4	148	3	49.33	3- 68	–	–
Gayle, C.H.	OB	33	6	78	3	26.00	2- 18	–	–
Gibson, O.D.	RFM	498.3	84	1682	45	37.37	6- 56	1	–
Gidman, A.P.R.	RM	124.1	11	508	13	39.07	4- 47	–	–
Giles, A.F.	SLA	323.5	44	1023	34	30.08	6- 44	3	–
Gillespie, J.N.	RFM	110	16	445	7	63.57	2- 40	–	–
Golwalker, Y.A.	LB	104.4	25	329	7	47.00	3- 41	–	–
Gough, D.	RF	291.5	72	839	27	31.07	5- 85	1	–
Grant, R.N.	RM	3	0	18	0				
Gray, A.K.D.	OB	174.4	28	565	12	47.08	3- 56	–	–
Greenidge, C.G.	RMF	79.5	17	284	6	47.33	2- 78	–	–
Hall, A.J.	RFM	347.5	71	1028	40	25.70	4- 32	–	–
Hancock, T.H.C.	RM	7	2	31	1	31.00	1- 14	–	–
Harbhajan Singh	OB	187.1	42	517	20	25.85	6- 36	1	–
Hardinges, M.A.	RMF	259.5	53	915	32	28.59	5- 51	1	–
Harmison, S.J.	RF	346.1	54	1142	54	21.14	6- 52	4	–
Harris, A.J.	RM	325.2	54	1293	49	26.38	6- 76	3	–
Harrison, A.J.	RMF	15	2	54	1	54.00	1- 54	–	–
Harrison, D.S.	RM	417.3	71	1649	31	53.19	5-117	1	–
Harvey, I.J.	RM	288.3	83	788	30	26.26	5- 40	1	–
Havell, P.M.R.	RFM	81.5	9	385	6	64.16	3-106	–	–
Hayward, M.	RF	94	9	380	8	47.50	2- 23	–	–
Heath, D.R.	RM	14	5	48	1	48.00	1- 48	–	–
Henderson, C.W.	SLA	537.2	121	1416	33	42.90	5- 63	1	–
Hildreth, J.C.	RMF	15	0	73	0				
Hodge, B.J.	OB	17	3	35	1	35.00	1- 14	–	–
Hogg, K.W.	RFM	34.2	9	113	3	37.66	2- 40	–	–
Hoggard, M.J.	RFM	401.1	83	1386	50	27.72	5- 73	1	–
Hooper, M.R.	OB	15	0	81	0				
Hopkinson, C.D.	RM	12	1	42	0				
Hunter, I.D.	RMF	382.3	56	1506	34	44.29	5- 63	1	–
Hussey, D.J.	RM/OB	71	11	304	8	38.00	4-105	–	–
Hussey, M.E.K.	RM	12	0	59	1	59.00	1- 36	–	–
Hutchinson, P.M.	LFM	53.4	3	255	5	51.00	2- 43	–	–
Hutton, B.L.	RMF	93	10	394	1	394.00	1- 31	–	–
Jacklin, B.D.	RM	19	2	87	0				
Jaques, P.A.	SLC	3	0	19	0				
Jayasuriya, S.T.	SLA	56.1	7	230	5	46.00	2- 2	–	–
Jefferson, W.I.	RMF	20	6	60	1	60.00	1- 16	–	–
Johnson, R.L.	RFM	287.3	52	1048	20	52.40	4-118	–	–
Jones, C.M.P.	RMF	30.2	6	90	3	30.00	2- 26	–	–

141

F-C	Cat	O	M	R	W	Avge	Best	5wI	10wM
Jones, P.S.	RMF	144	34	474	9	52.66	4- 74	–	–
Jones, S.P.	RF	230.4	46	808	33	24.48	6- 53	2	–
Joseph, R.H.	RF	41.4	7	179	9	19.88	5- 19	1	–
Joyce, E.C.	RM	32.3	1	204	3	68.00	1- 4	–	–
Kartik, M.	SLA	90	21	260	16	16.25	5- 75	2	1
Kasprowicz, M.S.	RFM	99	15	417	10	41.70	5- 67	1	–
Katich, S.M.	SLC	37	5	136	5	27.20	2- 25	–	–
Keedy, G.	SLA	265.3	67	753	33	22.81	6- 33	2	1
Keegan, C.B.	RFM	70	18	233	1	233.00	1- 78	–	–
Kemp, J.M.	RMF	109.5	14	359	11	32.63	3- 53	–	–
Kemp, R.A.	RM	23	1	86	2	43.00	2- 86	–	–
Key, R.W.T.	RM/OB	1	0	5	0			–	–
Khalid, S.A.	OB	16	3	39	0				
Khan, A.	RFM	415.2	80	1555	55	28.27	6- 73	1	–
Killeen, N.	RFM	122.5	37	357	8	44.62	3- 40	–	–
King, R.E.	LMF	7	2	32	1	32.00	1- 32	–	–
Kirby, S.P.	RFM	349.5	79	1170	45	26.00	4- 20	–	–
Kirtley, R.J.	RFM	525.1	130	1533	63	24.33	6- 80	2	–
Krejza, J.J.	OB	25	0	136	0			–	–
Kruis, G.J.	RFM	584.3	135	1961	64	30.64	5- 59	4	–
Lamb, G.A.	OB	36.4	5	145	3	48.33	2- 30	–	–
Lamb, N.J.	RMF	38	9	107	3	35.66	1- 6	–	–
Langeveldt, C.K.	RFM	215.1	59	637	15	42.46	3- 67	–	–
Laraman, A.W.	RFM	177	21	602	13	46.30	3- 68	–	–
Lawson, M.A.K.	LB	82	9	372	7	53.14	5-155	1	–
Leatherdale, D.A.	RM	17	4	47	1	47.00	1- 18	–	–
Lee, B.	RF	218.1	30	953	25	38.12	4- 53	–	–
Lewis, J.	RMF	426.3	106	1309	43	30.44	5- 57	2	–
Lewis, M.L.	RFM	169	27	614	26	23.61	5- 80	1	–
Lewry, J.D.	LFM	350	80	1044	48	21.75	6- 65	4	–
Liddle, C.J.	LFM	14	2	45	0			–	–
Linley, T.E.	RMF	36	9	130	4	32.50	3- 86	–	–
Logan, R.J.	RMF	128.4	15	572	7	81.71	3- 59	–	–
Loudon, A.G.R.	OB	416.2	48	1356	37	36.64	6- 66	2	–
Louw, J.	RFM	415.5	94	1424	44	32.36	6- 51	2	–
Lucas, D.S.	LMF	29.4	4	84	8	10.50	5- 49	1	–
Lumb, M.J.	RM	23	2	92	2	46.00	1- 7	–	–
Lungley, T.	RM	79	12	320	5	64.00	2- 54	–	–
MacGill, S.C.G.	LBG	44	6	207	7	29.57	4-122	–	–
McGrath, A.	RM	231	36	727	16	45.43	3- 35	–	–
McGrath, G.D.	RFM	134	22	440	19	23.15	5- 53	2	–
McLean, N.A.M.	RFM	123	27	507	12	42.25	3-107	–	–
McMahon, P.J.	OB	137.5	46	332	12	27.66	5- 30	1	–
McMillan, C.D.	RM	41	7	150	3	50.00	2- 49	–	–
Maddy, D.L.	RM/OB	181	36	568	13	43.69	4- 65	–	–
Mahmood, S.I.	RMF	141.2	22	521	14	37.21	3- 21	–	–
Malik, M.N.	RFM	270.3	58	1002	36	27.83	5- 71	1	–
Marshall, S.J.	LB	94.3	15	266	7	38.00	2- 23	–	–
Martin-Jenkins, R.S.C.	RFM	283.4	71	824	20	41.20	4- 31	–	–
Mascarenhas, A.D.	RMF	273.4	65	801	34	23.55	5- 55	2	–
Mashrafe Mortaza	RM	95	19	346	6	57.66	2- 52	–	–
Mason, M.S.	RFM	496.4	137	1486	53	28.03	5- 34	1	–
Masters, D.D.	RMF	305.2	85	903	34	26.55	6- 74	1	–
Maunders, J.K.	RM	105	16	384	14	27.42	4- 28	–	–

142

F-C	Cat	O	M	R	W	Avge	Best	5wI	10wM
Mees, T.	RMF	10	2	49	0				
Mehrab Hossain	RM	45	3	182	0				
Middlebrook, J.D.	OB	467.3	97	1417	32	44.28	5- 54	1	–
Mitchell, D.K.H.	RM	15	1	99	1	99.00	1- 59	–	–
Mohammad Akram	RFM	366.4	54	1542	43	35.86	5- 41	2	–
Mohammad Amin	RMF	25	3	112	2	56.00	2- 70	–	–
Mohammad Ashraful	LB	3	0	16	0				
Mohammad Rafique	SLA	85.5	7	331	3	110.33	2- 47	–	–
Mongia, D.	SLA	76.2	14	209	5	41.80	2- 8	–	–
Montgomerie, R.R.	OB	6	1	13	0				
Moore, S.C.	RM	11	1	44	1	44.00	1- 36	–	–
Moreton, S.J.P.	LB	14	1	81	0				
Morris, J.C.	LB	11	2	32	3	10.66	2- 29	–	–
Morse, E.J.	RM	46.1	6	158	7	22.57	4- 78	–	–
Moss, J.	RM	326.1	98	944	25	37.76	4- 40	–	–
Muchall, G.J.	RM	7	0	18	0				
Munday, M.K.	LB	89.3	13	360	8	45.00	2- 45	–	–
Muralitharan, M.	OB	233.2	69	540	36	15.00	6- 50	4	–
Murtagh, T.J.	RFM	163.2	30	563	12	46.91	3- 71	–	–
Mushfiqur Rahman	RFM	13	3	74	3	24.66	2- 43	–	–
Mushtaq Ahmed	LBG	600.5	82	2139	80	26.73	6- 44	4	1
Napier, G.R.	RM	166.2	32	634	14	45.28	3- 25	–	–
Naved-ul-Hasan	RFM	313.1	53	1076	54	19.92	5- 41	2	–
Needham, J.	OB	15	4	68	2	34.00	2- 42	–	–
Nel, A.	RFM	23	3	88	4	22.00	2- 12	–	–
Newby, O.J.	RMF	47	10	223	5	44.60	2- 78	–	–
Newman, S.A.	RM	3	0	17	0				
Noffke, A.	RFM	168	45	489	16	30.56	4- 19	–	–
North, M.J.	OB	56	10	176	2	88.00	1- 16	–	–
Ntini, M.	RF	192.1	29	721	22	32.77	5- 69	1	–
Oberoi, S.	OB	18	0	61	3	20.33	3- 49	–	–
Onions, G.	RMF	67	8	309	4	77.25	2- 83	–	–
Ormond, J.	RFM	301	65	1001	36	27.80	7- 63	1	–
Palladino, A.P.	RMF	162	36	584	13	44.92	4- 74	–	–
Panesar, M.S.	SLA	429.2	106	1146	51	22.47	7-181	4	1
Parker, L.C.	RM	36	4	131	4	32.75	2- 37	–	–
Parsons, K.A.	RM	112.1	19	428	7	61.14	3- 81	–	–
Parsons, M.	RM	27	3	135	0				
Patel, M.M.	SLA	598.4	132	1626	59	27.55	6- 53	3	–
Patel, S.R.	SLA	77.1	17	218	6	36.33	3- 73	–	–
Pathan, I.K.	LFM	89	13	324	5	64.80	4- 81	–	–
Patterson, S.A.	RMF	18	0	53	0				
Peploe, C.T.	SLA	249	57	801	18	44.50	3- 77	–	–
Phillips, B.J.	RFM	254	73	728	21	34.66	3- 42	–	–
Phillips, T.J.	SLA	81	13	322	6	53.66	3- 24	–	–
Pietersen, C.	LMF	48	1	204	4	51.00	3- 74	–	–
Pietersen, K.P.	OB	2	1	7	0				
Plunkett, L.E.	RMF	423	80	1573	51	30.84	5- 43	2	–
Ponting, R.T.	RM/OB	6	2	9	1	9.00	1- 9	–	–
Powell, M.J.(Wa)	RM	11	4	30	1	30.00	1- 16	–	–
Pretorius, D.	RFM	126.3	13	464	12	38.66	3- 88	–	–
Price, R.W.	SLA	372.3	90	964	30	32.13	4- 64	–	–
Pyrah, R.M.	RM	10	2	34	3	11.33	1- 4	–	–
Rajin Saleh	OB	2	0	12	0				

143

F-C	Cat	O	M	R	W	Avge	Best	5wI	10wM
Ramprakash, M.R.	RM	2	0	6	0			–	–
Read, G.G.	LM	145.5	42	450	9	50.00	3- 66	–	–
Richards, M.A.	RMF	25	3	134	1	134.00	1- 38	–	–
Richardson, A.	RMF	471.4	109	1438	57	25.22	7-113	3	–
Robinson, D.D.J.	RMF	2	0	3	0				
Rogers, C.J.L.	LBG	5	0	14	0				
Rudge, W.D.	RM	110.1	21	505	14	36.07	3- 46	–	–
Saggers, M.J.	RMF	258.3	55	854	20	42.70	5- 48	1	–
Saker, N.C.	RFM	22	3	93	1	93.00	1- 62	–	–
Salisbury, I.D.K.	LBG	82.3	4	359	7	51.28	3- 73	–	–
Saqlain Mushtaq	OB	189.5	28	593	16	37.06	4- 80	–	–
Sarwan, R.R.	LB	32	5	99	2	49.50	2- 38	–	–
Savill, T.E.	RFM	46.2	8	170	0				
Sayers, J.J.	OB	7	0	35	0				
Scott, G.M.	OB	10	1	48	0				
Shafayat, B.M.	RMF	20.5	2	61	0				
Shah, O.A.	OB	48.3	3	220	3	73.33	2- 95	–	–
Shahadat Hossain	RFM	178.5	16	813	19	42.78	4- 33	–	–
Shahriar Nafis	–	1	0	6	0				
Sharif, Z.K.	LB	28	4	108	2	54.00	1- 33	–	–
Sheikh, M.A.	RM	175.5	44	498	13	38.30	4- 67	–	–
Sheriyar, A.	LFM	58.5	13	181	5	36.20	3- 48	–	–
Shilvock, D.J.F.	LB	16	0	114	3	38.00	2- 77	–	–
Shoaib Akhtar	RF	86.3	15	405	14	28.92	6- 47	2	–
Sidebottom, R.J.	LFM	433.4	130	1132	50	22.64	5- 61	1	–
Sillence, R.J.	RMF	30	3	144	2	72.00	2- 90	–	–
Silverwood, C.E.W.	RFM	142.2	28	479	9	53.22	3- 73	–	–
Singh, A.(Nt)	OB	1	0	13	0				
Smith, B.F.	RM	7	1	41	0				
Smith, G.C.	OB	20	4	71	1	71.00	1- 34	–	–
Smith, G.J.	LFM	393.5	97	1314	51	25.76	5- 19	1	–
Smith, T.C.	RMF	20	8	46	1	46.00	1- 24	–	–
Smith, W.R.	OB	60.3	4	321	4	80.25	3- 34	–	–
Snape, J.N.	OB	11	1	39	1	39.00	1- 23	–	–
Solanki, V.S.	OB	11	0	49	0				
Stephenson, J.P.	RM	14	1	74	1	74.00	1- 42	–	–
Stevens, D.I.	RM	199.4	28	655	17	38.52	3- 19	–	–
Steyn, D.W.	RF	199.2	38	838	14	59.85	3- 69	–	–
Stiff, D.A.	RFM	17	1	85	2	42.50	1- 41	–	–
Streak, H.H.	RFM	254.2	67	708	26	27.23	6- 31	2	–
Styris, S.B.	RMF	230.5	44	730	31	23.54	6- 73	2	1
Suman, A.K.	LM	158	45	451	15	30.06	4- 59	–	–
Suppiah, A.V.	SLA	43.1	8	191	2	95.50	1- 28	–	–
Swann, G.P.	OB	413.2	89	1307	33	39.60	6- 57	1	–
Syed Rasel	LMF	136.2	24	520	20	26.00	7- 50	1	1
Symonds, A.	RMF/OB	177	37	484	16	30.25	3- 80	–	–
Tahir, N.	RFM	83	11	313	11	28.45	3- 28	–	–
Tait, S.W.	RFM	61	9	261	7	37.28	3- 97	–	–
Talha Jubair	RM	117.5	11	608	13	46.76	4- 99	–	–
Tapash Baisya	RFM	39	4	202	3	67.33	2- 69	–	–
Taylor, B.V.	RMF	187.4	34	587	19	30.89	6- 45	1	–
Taylor, C.G.	OB	13	1	43	1	43.00	1- 26	–	–
Ten Doeschate, R.N.	RFM	19	2	118	0				
Thomas, S.D.	RFM	122.3	9	611	9	67.88	3- 63	–	–

F-C	Cat	O	M	R	W	Avge	Best	5wI	10wM
Thornely, D.J.	RM	28	4	108	2	54.00	2- 40	–	–
Thornicroft, N.D.	RMF	22	6	70	1	70.00	1- 70	–	–
Thorp, C.D.	RMF	71	13	227	4	56.75	3- 10	–	–
Timms, R.T.	RFM	16	0	75	0				
Tredwell, J.C.	OB	36.5	8	146	3	48.66	2- 37	–	–
Trego, P.D.	RMF	131	21	576	16	36.00	6- 59	1	–
Tremlett, C.T.	RMF	334	57	1232	46	26.78	6- 44	2	–
Trott, I.J.L.	RM	129.5	15	449	9	49.88	2- 19	–	–
Troughton, J.O.	SLA	44.2	6	220	5	44.00	2- 63	–	–
Tudor, A.J.	RF	56	13	165	8	20.62	2- 30	–	–
Turner, M.L.	RMF	49	5	166	2	83.00	1- 47	–	–
Tushar Imran	RM	16.5	2	102	2	51.00	1- 21	–	–
Udal, S.D.	OB	274.3	54	832	44	18.90	6- 44	3	–
Vaas, W.P.U.C.J.	LFM	285.4	80	779	28	27.82	3- 36	–	–
Van der Wath, J.J.	RFM	104	24	399	10	39.90	3- 21	–	–
Van Jaarsveld, M.	OB	35	11	82	3	27.33	1- 7	–	–
Vaughan, M.P.	OB	5	0	21	0				
Wainwright, D.J.	SLA	142	34	416	18	23.11	4- 48	–	–
Walker, M.J.	RM	35	1	164	4	41.00	1- 6	–	–
Walker, N.G.E.	RFM	209.5	27	892	17	52.47	4- 69	–	–
Ward, I.J.	RM	1	1	0	0				
Warne, S.K.	LBG	650.3	98	1958	87	22.50	6- 46	4	2
Warren, N.A.	RMF	119	20	478	9	53.11	3- 40	–	–
Waters, H.T.	RMF	100	15	332	11	30.18	4- 75	–	–
Watkins, R.E.	RM	37	5	125	3	41.66	2- 14	–	–
Watson, S.R.	RM	112	20	372	9	41.33	2- 33	–	–
Wedge, S.A.	LMF	54.2	8	211	5	42.20	5-112	1	–
Weekes, P.N.	OB	237.5	33	765	14	54.64	3- 83	–	–
Welch, G.	RM	549.3	139	1559	60	25.98	5- 63	3	–
Westfield, M.S.	RFM	18	0	90	1	90.00	1- 90	–	–
Westwood, I.J.	OB	3	0	30	1	30.00	1- 30	–	–
Wharf, A.G.	RMF	297.2	40	1245	28	44.46	6- 59	2	1
Whelan, C.D.	RMF	41.4	8	182	7	26.00	2- 34	–	–
White, A.R.	OB	15	1	82	0				
White, C.	RFM	17	2	71	1	71.00	1- 21	–	–
White, R.A.	LB	20	3	66	0				
White, W.A.	RMF	58.5	8	280	5	56.00	4- 77	–	–
Wigley, D.H.	RFM	97.1	17	380	13	29.23	4- 68	–	–
Wilkinson, R.M.	RM	49	9	188	4	47.00	2- 24	–	–
Williams, B.A.	RFM	83.2	12	335	7	47.85	3- 73	–	–
Willoughby, C.M.	LMF	429.5	97	1385	33	41.96	4- 92	–	–
Wolstenholme, J.P.	RFM	9	3	14	0				
Woodman, R.J.	LMF	66	11	268	2	134.00	1- 78	–	–
Woods, N.J.	SLA	41	9	155	0				
Wright, C.J.C.	RFM	119.4	14	538	6	89.66	2- 36	–	–
Wright, D.G.	RMF	480	139	1398	53	26.37	8- 60	2	–
Wright, L.J.	RMF	111	23	329	13	25.30	3- 33	–	–
Yardy, M.H.	LM	67.2	10	252	9	28.00	5- 83	1	–
Younis Khan	LB	37.1	1	151	4	37.75	2- 21	–	–

145

COUNTY CHAMPIONSHIP 2005
FRIZZELL FINAL TABLES

DIVISION 1

	P	W	L	T	D	Bonus Points Bat	Bonus Points Bowl	Deduct Points	Total Points
1 NOTTINGHAMSHIRE (-)	16	9	3	–	4	50	44	–	236.0
2 Hampshire (-)	16	9	3	–	4	46	46	0.5	233.5
3 Sussex (5)	16	7	3	–	6	57	45	–	224.0
4 Warwickshire (1)	16	8	5	–	3	42	44	0.5	209.5
5 Kent (2)	16	6	3	–	7	57	42	8.5	202.5
6 Middlesex (4)	16	4	'5	–	7	56	42	0.5	181.5
7 Surrey (3)	16	4	3	–	9	53	44	8.5	180.5
8 Gloucestershire (6)	16	1	10	–	5	26	46	2.0	104.0
9 Glamorgan (-)	16	1	14	–	1	33	38	0.5	88.5

DIVISION 2

	P	W	L	T	D	Bonus Points Bat	Bonus Points Bowl	Deduct Points	Total Points
1 LANCASHIRE (-)	16	7	3	–	6	43	47	–	212.0
2 Durham (9)	16	6	2	–	8	45	44	–	205.0
3 Yorkshire (7)	16	5	1	–	10	49	42	0.5	200.5
4 Northamptonshire (-)	16	5	3	–	8	45	46	–	193.0
5 Essex (5)	16	5	4	–	7	51	36	–	185.0
6 Worcestershire (-)	16	5	7	–	4	53	46	5.5	179.5
7 Leicestershire (6)	16	3	6	–	7	45	45	0.5	159.5
8 Somerset (4)	16	4	7	–	5	42	37	–	155.0
9 Derbyshire (8)	16	1	8	–	7	31	43	–	116.0

2004 final positions for that division are shown in brackets.

SCORING OF CHAMPIONSHIP POINTS 2005

(a) For a win, 14 points, plus any points scored in the first innings.

(b) In a tie, each side to score seven points, plus any points scored in the first innings.

(c) In a drawn match, each side to score four points, plus any points scored in the first innings (see also paragraph (f) below).

(d) If the scores are equal in a drawn match, the side batting in the fourth innings to score seven points plus any points scored in the first innings, and the opposing side to score four points plus any points scored in the first innings.

(e) First Innings Points (awarded only for performances **in the first 130 overs** of each first innings and retained whatever the result of the match).
   • A maximum of five batting points to be available as under:-
     200 to 249 runs – 1 point; 250 to 299 runs – 2 points; 300 to 349 runs – 3 points;
     350 to 399 runs – 4 points; 400 runs or over – 5 points.
   • A maximum of three bowling points to be available as under:-
     3 to 5 wickets taken – 1 point; 6 to 8 wickets taken – 2 points; 9 to 10 wickets taken – 3 points.

(f) If play starts when fewer than eight hours' playing time remains (in which event a one innings match shall be played as provided for in First-Class Playing Condition 18), no first innings points shall be scored. The side winning on the one innings to score 14 points. In a tie, each side to score seven points. In a drawn match, each side to score four points. If the scores are equal in a drawn match, the side batting in the second innings to score seven points and the opposing side to score four points.

(g) If a match is abandoned without a ball being bowled, each side to score four points.

(h) The side which has the highest aggregate of points gained at the end of the season shall be the Champion County of their respective Division. Should any sides in the Championship table be equal on points, the following tie-breakers will be applied in the order stated: most wins, least losses, team achieving most points in contests between teams level on points, most wickets taken, most runs scored. At the end of the season, the top three teams from the Second Division will be promoted and the bottom three teams from the First Division will be relegated.

COUNTY CHAMPIONS

The English County Championship was not officially constituted until December 1889. Prior to that date there was no generally accepted method of awarding the title; although the 'least matches lost' method existed, it was not consistently applied. Rules governing playing qualifications were agreed in 1873 and the first unofficial points system 15 years later.

Research has produced a list of champions dating back to 1826, but at least seven different versions exist for the period from 1864 to 1889 (see *The Wisden Book of Cricket Records*). Only from 1890 can any authorised list of county champions commence.

That first official Championship was contested between eight counties: Gloucestershire, Kent, Lancashire, Middlesex, Nottinghamshire, Surrey, Sussex and Yorkshire. The remaining counties were admitted in the following seasons: 1891 – Somerset, 1895 – Derbyshire, Essex, Hampshire, Leicestershire and Warwickshire, 1899 – Worcestershire, 1905 – Northamptonshire, 1921 – Glamorgan, and 1992 – Durham.

The Championship pennant was introduced by the 1951 champions, Warwickshire, and the Lord's Taverners' Trophy was first presented in 1973. The first sponsors, Schweppes (1977 to 1983), were succeeded by Britannic Assurance (1984 to 1998), PPP Healthcare (1999-2000), CricInfo (2001) and Frizzell (2002 to 2005). Based on their previous season's positions, the 18 counties were separated into two divisions in 2001.

1890	Surrey	1931	Yorkshire	1972	Warwickshire
1891	Surrey	1932	Yorkshire	1973	Hampshire
1892	Surrey	1933	Yorkshire	1974	Worcestershire
1893	Yorkshire	1934	Lancashire	1975	Leicestershire
1894	Surrey	1935	Yorkshire	1976	Middlesex
1895	Surrey	1936	Derbyshire	1977	{ Kent
1896	Yorkshire	1937	Yorkshire		Middlesex
1897	Lancashire	1938	Yorkshire	1978	Kent
1898	Yorkshire	1939	Yorkshire	1979	Essex
1899	Surrey	1946	Yorkshire	1980	Middlesex
1900	Yorkshire	1947	Middlesex	1981	Nottinghamshire
1901	Yorkshire	1948	Glamorgan	1982	Middlesex
1902	Yorkshire	1949	{ Middlesex	1983	Essex
1903	Middlesex		Yorkshire	1984	Essex
1904	Lancashire	1950	{ Lancashire	1985	Middlesex
1905	Yorkshire		Surrey	1986	Essex
1906	Kent	1951	Warwickshire	1987	Nottinghamshire
1907	Nottinghamshire	1952	Surrey	1988	Worcestershire
1908	Yorkshire	1953	Surrey	1989	Worcestershire
1909	Kent	1954	Surrey	1990	Middlesex
1910	Kent	1955	Surrey	1991	Essex
1911	Warwickshire	1956	Surrey	1992	Essex
1912	Yorkshire	1957	Surrey	1993	Middlesex
1913	Kent	1958	Surrey	1994	Warwickshire
1914	Surrey	1959	Yorkshire	1995	Warwickshire
1919	Yorkshire	1960	Yorkshire	1996	Leicestershire
1920	Middlesex	1961	Hampshire	1997	Glamorgan
1921	Middlesex	1962	Yorkshire	1998	Leicestershire
1922	Yorkshire	1963	Yorkshire	1999	Surrey
1923	Yorkshire	1964	Worcestershire	2000	Surrey
1924	Yorkshire	1965	Worcestershire	2001	Yorkshire
1925	Yorkshire	1966	Yorkshire	2002	Surrey
1926	Lancashire	1967	Yorkshire	2003	Sussex
1927	Lancashire	1968	Yorkshire	2004	Warwickshire
1928	Lancashire	1969	Glamorgan	2005	Nottinghamshire
1929	Nottinghamshire	1970	Kent		
1930	Lancashire	1971	Surrey		

COUNTY CHAMPIONSHIP RESULTS 2005

DIVISION 1

	GLAM	GLOS	HANTS	KENT	MIDDX	NOTTS	SURREY	SUSSEX	WARWKS
GLAM	–	Cardiff Gs 7w	Cardiff H 75	Cardiff K 10w	Cardiff M I/23	Cardiff Nt 8w	Cardiff Sy 5w	Swansea Drawn	Col Bay Wa 10w
GLOS	Bristol Gm 322	–	Chelt H 178	Bristol Drawn	Bristol Drawn	Bristol Nt I/27	Bristol Drawn	Chelt Sx 226	Glos Wa I/2
HANTS	So'ton H 9w	So'ton H 48	–	So'ton Drawn	So'ton H 64	So'ton H I/188	So'ton Sy I/55	So'ton H 35	So'ton H I/86
KENT	Cant K I/124	Maidstone K 7w	Cant Drawn	–	Cant Drawn	Cant Nt 214	Tun W Drawn	Cant Sx 66	Cant Drawn
MIDDX	Southgate M 6w	Lord's M 340	Southgate M 2w	Lord's Drawn	–	Lord's Drawn	Lord's Drawn	Lord's Sx I/232	Lord's Wa 3w
NOTTS	N'ham Nt 10w	N'ham Nt I/64	N'ham H 14	N'ham K 196	N'ham Drawn	–	N'ham Drawn	N'ham Nt 10w	N'ham Nt I/151
SURREY	Oval Sy 276	Oval Drawn	Oval Drawn	Guildford K 4w	Oval Sy I/39	Oval Nt I/71	–	Oval Drawn	Croydon Drawn
SUSSEX	Hove Sx 9w	Hove Drawn	Hove Drawn	Hove Sx 8w	Hove Drawn	Arundel Drawn	Hove Sx 5w	–	Hove Sx I/87
WARWKS	B'ham Wa I/43	B'ham Wa 181	Stratford Wa 10w	B'ham K I/164	B'ham Wa 7w	B'ham Nt 10w	B'ham Drawn	B'ham Wa 101	–

DIVISION 2

	DERBYS	DURHAM	ESSEX	LANCS	LEICS	N'HANTS	SOM'T	WORCS	YORKS
DERBYS	–	Derby Drawn	Derby Ex 5w	Derby La 1w	Derby Le 4w	Derby Drawn	Derby Sm 5	Derby Wo 10w	Derby Drawn
DURHAM	C-le-St Drawn	–	C-le-St Du I/19	C-le-St La I/228	C-le-St Drawn	C-le-St Drawn	C-le-St Du 4w	C-le-St Du 7w	C-le-St Drawn
ESSEX	Chelms Drawn	Southend Ex 2w	–	Chelms La 8w	Chelms Ex 6w	Chelms Ex 10w	Colchester Sm 5w	Chelms Wo 8w	Chelms Drawn
LANCS	Man La I/72	Man Du 9w	Man Drawn	–	Man Le 4	Man Drawn	Man Drawn	Blackpool La I/73	Man Drawn
LEICS	Leics Drawn	Leics Du I/216	Leics Drawn	Leics La 234	–	Leics Drawn	Oakham Drawn	Leics Le 12	Leics Y 6w
N'HANTS	No'ton Nh 182	No'ton Drawn	No'ton Drawn	No'ton Nh 285	No'ton Drawn	–	No'ton Sm 6w	No'ton Nh 82	No'ton Nh I/21
SOM'T	Taunton De I/18	Taunton Du 207	Taunton Ex 9w	Taunton Drawn	Taunton Sm 10w	Taunton Drawn	–	Bath Wo 8w	Taunton Drawn
WORCS	Worcs Wo 9w	Worcs Drawn	Worcs Drawn	Worcs La 76	Worcs Drawn	Worcs Nh 137	Worcs Wo I/56	–	Worcs Y 3w
YORKS	Leeds Drawn	Scar Drawn	Leeds Drawn	Leeds Drawn	Scar Y 6w	Leeds Y 10w	Leeds Y I/44	Leeds Drawn	–

COUNTY CHAMPIONSHIP RESULTS 2006

KEEP YOUR OWN RECORD (see page 148)

DIVISION 1

	DURHAM	HANTS	KENT	LANCS	MIDDX	NOTTS	SUSSEX	WARWKS	YORKS
DURHAM	–	C-le-St	tba	C-le-St	C-le-St	C-le-St	C-le-St	C-le-St	C-le-St
HANTS	So'ton	–	So'ton	So'ton	So'ton	So'ton	So'ton	So'ton	So'ton
KENT	Cant	Cant	–	Cant	Cant	Cant	Cant	Tun W	Cant
LANCS	Man	Man	Man	–	Man	Man	L'pool	B'pool	Man
MIDDX	Lord's	Lord's	Lord's	Lord's	–	Lord's	Southgate	Lord's	Southgate
NOTTS	N'ham	N'ham	N'ham	N'ham	N'ham	–	N'ham	N'ham	N'ham
SUSSEX	Hove	Hove	Hove	Hove	Horsham	Hove	–	Hove	Arundel
WARWKS	B'ham	B'ham	B'ham	B'ham	B'ham	B'ham	B'ham	–	B'ham
YORKS	Leeds	Leeds	Leeds	Leeds	Scar	Leeds	Leeds	Scar	–

DIVISION 2

	DERBYS	ESSEX	GLAM	GLOS	LEICS	N'HANTS	SOM'T	SURREY	WORCS
DERBYS	–	Derby	Derby	Derby	Derby	Derby	Derby	Derby	Ch'field
ESSEX	Chelms	–	Chelms	Chelms	Chelms	Chelms	Southend	Colchester	Chelms
GLAM	Cardiff	Cardiff	–	Cardiff	Cardiff	Cardiff	Swansea	tba	Col Bay
GLOS	Bristol	Bristol	Chelt	–	Chelt	Bristol	Bristol	Bristol	Glos
LEICS	Leics	Leics	Leics	Leics	–	Oakham	Leics	Leics	Leics
N'HANTS	No'ton	No'ton	No'ton	No'ton	No'ton	–	No'ton	No'ton	No'ton
SOM'T	Taunton	Taunton	Taunton	Taunton	Taunton	Taunton	–	Bath	Taunton
SURREY	Oval	Croydon	Oval	Oval	Oval	Oval	Guildford	–	Oval
WORCS	Worcs	Worcs	Worcs	Worcs	Worcs	Worcs	Worcs	Worcs	–

UNIVERSITY MATCH RESULTS

Played: 160. Wins: Cambridge 56; Oxford 52. Drawn: 52. Abandoned: 1

In 2001, for the very first time, Cambridge hosted the University Match, cricket's oldest surviving first-class fixture, after the ECB's re-organisation of university cricket around six centres of excellence had removed it from Lord's. Dating from 1827 it has, wartime interruptions apart, been played annually since 1838. With the exception of five matches played in the area of Oxford (1829, 1843, 1846, 1848 and 1850), all the previous fixtures had been staged at Lord's. Since 2001 it has been played over four days rather than three.

In 2003, Oxford (with Brookes), Cambridge (with Anglia) and Durham were joined by Loughborough in playing three first-class matches against counties. The other two centres – Cardiff (with UWIC and Glamorgan), and Leeds (with Bradford and Leeds Metropolitan) – also play three counties apiece but without first-class status.

Year	Result	Year	Result	Year	Result	Year	Result
1827	Drawn	1876	Cambridge	1921	Cambridge	1968	Drawn
1829	Oxford	1877	Oxford	1922	Cambridge	1969	Drawn
1836	Oxford	1878	Cambridge	1923	Oxford	1970	Drawn
1838	Oxford	1879	Cambridge	1924	Cambridge	1971	Drawn
1839	Cambridge	1880	Cambridge	1925	Drawn	1972	Cambridge
1840	Cambridge	1881	Oxford	1926	Cambridge	1973	Drawn
1841	Cambridge	1882	Cambridge	1927	Cambridge	1974	Drawn
1842	Cambridge	1883	Cambridge	1928	Drawn	1975	Drawn
1843	Cambridge	1884	Oxford	1929	Drawn	1976	Oxford
1844	Drawn	1885	Cambridge	1930	Cambridge	1977	Drawn
1845	Cambridge	1886	Oxford	1931	Oxford	1978	Drawn
1846	Oxford	1887	Oxford	1932	Drawn	1979	Cambridge
1847	Cambridge	1888	Drawn	1933	Drawn	1980	Drawn
1848	Oxford	1889	Cambridge	1934	Drawn	1981	Drawn
1849	Cambridge	1890	Cambridge	1935	Cambridge	1982	Cambridge
1850	Oxford	1891	Cambridge	1936	Cambridge	1983	Drawn
1851	Cambridge	1892	Oxford	1937	Oxford	1984	Oxford
1852	Oxford	1893	Cambridge	1938	Drawn	1985	Drawn
1853	Oxford	1894	Oxford	1939	Oxford	1986	Cambridge
1854	Oxford	1895	Cambridge	1946	Oxford	1987	Drawn
1855	Oxford	1896	Oxford	1947	Drawn	1988	Abandoned
1856	Cambridge	1897	Cambridge	1948	Oxford	1989	Drawn
1857	Oxford	1898	Oxford	1949	Cambridge	1990	Drawn
1858	Oxford	1899	Drawn	1950	Drawn	1991	Drawn
1859	Cambridge	1900	Drawn	1951	Oxford	1992	Cambridge
1860	Cambridge	1901	Drawn	1952	Drawn	1993	Oxford
1861	Cambridge	1902	Cambridge	1953	Cambridge	1994	Drawn
1862	Cambridge	1903	Oxford	1954	Drawn	1995	Drawn
1863	Oxford	1904	Drawn	1955	Drawn	1996	Drawn
1864	Oxford	1905	Cambridge	1956	Drawn	1997	Drawn
1865	Oxford	1906	Cambridge	1957	Cambridge	1998	Cambridge
1866	Oxford	1907	Cambridge	1958	Cambridge	1999	Drawn
1867	Cambridge	1908	Oxford	1959	Oxford	2000	Drawn
1868	Cambridge	1909	Drawn	1960	Drawn	2001	Oxford
1869	Cambridge	1910	Oxford	1961	Drawn	2002	Drawn
1870	Cambridge	1911	Oxford	1962	Drawn	2003	Oxford
1871	Oxford	1912	Cambridge	1963	Drawn	2004	Oxford
1872	Cambridge	1913	Cambridge	1964	Drawn	2005	Oxford
1873	Oxford	1914	Oxford	1965	Drawn		
1874	Oxford	1919	Oxford	1966	Oxford		
1875	Oxford	1920	Drawn	1967	Drawn		

CAMBRIDGE UNIVERSITY RECORDS
ALL FIRST-CLASS MATCHES

Highest Total	For 703-9d		v	Sussex	Hove	1890
	V 730-3		by	W Indians	Cambridge	1950
Lowest Total	For 30		v	Yorkshire	Cambridge	1928
	V 32		by	Oxford U	Lord's	1878
Highest Innings	For 254*	K.S.Duleepsinhji	v	Middlesex	Cambridge	1927
	V 304*	E.de C.Weekes	for	W Indians	Cambridge	1950
Highest Partnership						
(2nd wicket)	429*	J.G.Dewes/G.H.G.Doggart	v	Essex	Cambridge	1949
Best Innings Bowling	10-69	S.M.J.Woods	v	Thornton's XI	Cambridge	1890
Best Match Bowling	15-88	S.M.J.Woods	v	Thornton's XI	Cambridge	1890
Most Runs – Season	1581	D.S.Sheppard		(av 79.05)		1952
Most Runs – Career	4310	J.M.Brearley		(av 38.48)		1961-68
Most 100s – Season	7	D.S.Sheppard				1952
Most 100s – Career	14	D.S.Sheppard				1950-52
Most Wkts – Season	80	O.S.Wheatley		(av 17.63)		1958
Most Wkts – Career	208	G.Goonesena		(av 21.82)		1954-57

UNIVERSITY MATCH RECORDS

Highest Total	604		Oxford	2002
Lowest Total	39		Lord's	1858
Highest Innings	211	G.Goonesena	Lord's	1957
Best Innings Bowling	8-44	G.E.Jeffery	Lord's	1873
Best Match Bowling	13-73	A.G.Steel	Lord's	1878

Hat Tricks: F.C.Cobden (1870), A.G.Steel (1879), P.H.Morton (1880), J.F.Ireland (1911), R.G.H.Lowe (1926).

OXFORD UNIVERSITY RECORDS
ALL FIRST-CLASS MATCHES

Highest Total	For 651		v	Sussex	Hove	1895
	V 679-7d		by	Australians	Oxford	1938
Lowest Total	For 12		v	MCC	Oxford	1877
	V 24		by	MCC	Oxford	1846
Highest Innings	For 281	K.J.Key	v	Middlesex	Chiswick Park	1887
	V 338	W.W.Read	for	Surrey	The Oval	1888
Highest Partnership						
(3rd wicket)	408	S.Oberoi/D.R.Fox	v	Cambridge U	Oxford	2005
Best Innings Bowling	10-38	S.E.Butler	v	Cambridge U	Lord's	1871
Best Match Bowling	15-65	B.J.T.Bosanquet	v	Sussex	Oxford	1900
Most Runs – Season	1307	Nawab of Pataudi sr		(av 93.35)		1931
Most Runs – Career	3319	N.S.Mitchell-Innes		(av 47.41)		1934-37
Most 100s – Season	6	Nawab of Pataudi sr				1931
Most 100s – Career	9	A.M.Crawley				1927-30
	9	Nawab of Pataudi sr				1928-31
	9	N.S.Mitchell-Innes				1934-37
	9	M.P.Donnelly				1946-47
Most Wkts – Season	70	I.A.R.Peebles		(av 18.15)		1930
Most Wkts – Career	182	R.H.B.Bettington		(av 19.38)		1920-23

UNIVERSITY MATCH RECORDS

Highest Total	610-5d		Cambridge	2005
Lowest Total	32		Lord's	1878
Highest Innings	247	S.Oberoi	Cambridge	2005
Best Innings Bowling	10-38	S.E.Butler	Lord's	1871
Best Match Bowling	15-95	S.E.Butler	Lord's	1871

Match Doubles: P.R.le Couteur (160 and 11-66 in 1910); G.J.Toogood (149 and 10-93 in 1985)

NATWEST TRIANGULAR SERIES 2005

Kennington Oval, London 16 June. Toss: England. **ENGLAND** beat **Bangladesh** by ten wickets. Bangladesh 190 (45.2; Aftab Ahmed 51; S.J.Harmison 4-39, J.Lewis 3-32). England 192-0 (24.5; M.E.Trescothick 100*, A.J.Strauss 82*). Award: M.E.Trescothick.

Sophia Gardens, Cardiff 18 June. Toss: Australia. **BANGLADESH** beat **Australia** by five wickets. Australia 249-5 (D.R.Martyn 77, M.J.Clarke 54; Tapash Baisya 3-69). Bangladesh 250-5 (49.2; Mohammad Ashraf 100). Award: Mohammad Ashraful.

County Ground, Bristol 19 June. Toss: Australia. **ENGLAND** beat **Australia** by three wickets. Australia 252-9 (50; M.E.K.Hussey 84; S.J.Harmison 5-33). England 253-7 (47.3; K.P.Pietersen 91*, M.P.Vaughan 57; G.B.Hogg 3-42). Award: K.P.Pietersen.

Trent Bridge, Nottingham 21 June (floodlit). Toss: England. **ENGLAND** beat **Bangladesh** by 168 runs. England 391-4 (England record and second-highest total in 2,251 LOI matches) (A.J.Strauss 152, P.D.Collingwood 112, M.E.Trescothick 85; Nazmul Hossain 3-83). Bangladesh 223 (45.2; Mohammad Ashraful 94, Javed Omar 59; P.D.Collingwood 6-31, C.T.Tremlett 4-32). Award: P.D.Collingwood (returned England's best analysis and became the first to score a hundred and take six wickets in an LOI).

Riverside, Chester-le-Street 23 June (floodlit). Toss: England. **AUSTRALIA** beat **England** by 57 runs. Australia 266-5 (50; A.Symonds 73, D.R.Martyn 68*). England 209-9 (50). Award: A.Symonds.

Old Trafford, Manchester 25 June. Toss: Australia. **AUSTRALIA** beat **Bangladesh** by ten wickets. Bangladesh 139 (35.2; Mohammad Ashraful 58; A.Symonds 5-18). Australia 140-0 (19; A.C.Gilchrist 66*, M.L.Hayden 66*). Award: A.Symonds.

Headingley, Leeds 26 June. Toss: Bangladesh. **ENGLAND** beat **Bangladesh** by five wickets. Bangladesh 208-7 (50: Javed Omar 81; A.Flintoff 4-29). England 209-5 (38.5; A.J.Strauss 98; Manjural Rana 3-57). Award: A.J.Strauss.

Edgbaston, Birmingham 28 June (floodlit). Toss: Australia. **England** v **Australia** – no result (rain). Australia 261-9 (50; A.Symonds 74; D.Gough 3-70). England 37-1 (6). No award.

St Lawrence Ground, Canterbury 30 June. Toss: Australia. **AUSTRALIA** beat **Bangladesh** by six wickets. Bangladesh 250-8 (50; Shahriar Nafiz 75, Khaled Masud 71*; S.R.Watson 3-43). Australia 254-4 (48.1; M.J.Clarke 80*, R.T.Ponting 66). Award: Shahriar Nafiz.

	Played	Won	Lost	No Result	Bonus	Points	NRR
England	6	4	1	1	3	26	1.38
Australia	6	3	2	1	2	22	0.88
Bangladesh	6	1	5	–	–	6	–2.00

Final – Lord's 2 July

Toss: England. **ENGLAND TIED WITH AUSTRALIA**. Australia 196 (48.5; M.E.K.Hussey 62*; A.Flintoff 3-23, S.J.Harmison 3-27). England 196-9 (50; G.O.Jones 71, P.D.Collingwood 53; G.D.McGrath 3-25). Award: G.O.Jones. Series Award: A.Symonds.

NATWEST CHALLENGE 2005

Headingley, Leeds 7 July. Toss: England. **ENGLAND** beat **Australia** by nine wickets. Australia 219-7 (50; P.D.Collingwood 4-34). England 221-1 (46; M.E.Trescothick 104*, M.P.Vaughan 59*). Award: M.E.Trescothick.

This was the first international to feature an experimental rule involving 'supersubs' and 'powerplays'. S.P.Jones was the first player to be substituted out of an LOI (by V.S.Solanki). Caps were awarded to all the original XI, plus the 'supersub' but only if he was officially substituted into the match.

Lord's, London 10 July. Toss: Australia. **AUSTRALIA** beat **England** by seven wickets. England 223-8 (50; A.Flintoff 87; B.Lee 5-41). Australia 224-3 (R.T.Ponting 111); Award: B.Lee.

Kennington Oval, London 12 July. Toss: Australia. **AUSTRALIA** beat **England** by eight wickets. England 228-7 (50; K.P.Pietersen 74, V.S.Solanki 53*; J.N.Gillespie 3-44). Australia 229-2 (34.5; A.C.Gilchrist 121*). Award: A.C.Gilchrist. Series Award: R.T.Ponting.

TWENTY20 INTERNATIONAL 2005

Rose Bowl, Southampton 13 June. Toss: England. **ENGLAND** beat **Australia** by 100 runs. England 179-8 (20; P.D.Collingwood 46, M.E.Trescothick 41, K.P.Pietersen 34; G.D.McGrath 3-31). Australia 79 (14.3; J.Lewis 4-24; D.Gough 3-16). Award: K.P.Pietersen (34 off 18 balls).

This was the first Twenty20 international in Britain.

CHELTENHAM & GLOUCESTER TROPHY 2005 RESULTS CHART

FIRST ROUND 3, 4, 5 May	SECOND ROUND 17, 18 May	QUARTER-FINALS 15, 16 July	SEMI-FINALS 20 August	FINAL 3 September
Shropshire†				
HAMPSHIRE	HAMPSHIRE			
Suffolk†		HAMPSHIRE		
GLAMORGAN	Glamorgan†			
Staffordshire†			HAMPSHIRE†	
SURREY	SURREY			
Berkshire†		Surrey†		
GLOUCESTERSHIRE	Gloucestershire†			
Ireland†				HAMPSHIRE
YORKSHIRE	YORKSHIRE†			
Scotland†		YORKSHIRE†		
WORCESTERSHIRE	Worcestershire			
Denmark†			Yorkshire	
NORTHAMPTONSHIRE	NORTHAMPTONSHIRE			
Northumberland†		Northamptonshire		
MIDDLESEX	Middlesex†			
Buckinghamshire†				
LANCASHIRE	LANCASHIRE†			
Devon†		LANCASHIRE†		
ESSEX	Essex			
Bedfordshire†			Lancashire	
SUSSEX	SUSSEX†			
Wales MC†		Sussex		
NOTTINGHAMSHIRE	Nottinghamshire			
Wiltshire†				Warwickshire
KENT	KENT			
Durham†		Kent		
DERBYSHIRE	Derbyshire†			
Somerset			WARWICKSHIRE†	
LEICESTERSHIRE†	Leicestershire			
Holland†		WARWICKSHIRE†		
WARWICKSHIRE	WARWICKSHIRE†			

† Home team. Winning teams are in capitals.

154

2005 C & G TROPHY FINAL

HAMPSHIRE v WARWICKSHIRE

At Lord's, London on 3 September.
Result: **HAMPSHIRE** won by 18 runs.
Toss: Warwickshire. Award: S.M.Ervine.

HAMPSHIRE		Runs	Balls	4/6	Fall
J.P.Crawley	c Frost b Carter	29	44	5	1- 57
† N.Pothas	c Frost b Carter	68	99	5/1	2-191
S.M.Ervine	c Troughton b Trott	104	93	12	5-253
K.P.Pietersen	c Giles b Trott	5	10	–	3-206
S.R.Watson	c Troughton b Trott	25	28	2	4-249
A.D.Mascarenhas	c Bell b Carter	8	6	1	6-265
A.J.Bichel	c Bell b Carter	16	13	3	9-282
G.A.Lamb	run out	4	4	–	7-282
* S.D.Udal	c Bell b Carter	0	1	–	8-282
K.J.Latouf	not out	0	–	–	
C.T.Tremlett	run out	7	2	–/1	10-290
Extras	(LB 4, W 20)	24			
Total	(50 overs; 208 minutes)	**290**			

WARWICKSHIRE		Runs	Balls	4/6	Fall
N.M.Carter	run out	32	23	4/1	1- 44
* N.V.Knight	c Latouf b Bichel	118	127	10	7-251
I.R.Bell	c Tremlett b Watson	54	82	3	2-166
J.O.Troughton	b Bichel	10	18	–	3-198
T.L.Penney	c Pothas b Bichel	4	9	–	4-207
I.J.L.Trott	run out	3	3	–	5-215
A.G.R.Loudon	b Tremlett	7	14	–	6-237
D.R.Brown	b Watson	15	11	1	8-260
A.F.Giles	b Watson	6	5	1	9-265
† T.Frost	not out	2	3	–	
M.Ntini	b Tremlett	0	2	–	10-266
Extras	(B 1, LB 2, W 10, NB 2, Pen 6)	21			
Total	(49.2 overs; 228 minutes)	**272**			

WARWICKS	O	M	R	W	HAMPSHIRE	O	M	R	W
Ntini	10	2	43	0	Bichel	10	0	57	3
Brown	8	0	50	0	Tremlett	9.2	0	48	2
Carter	10	0	66	5	Ervine	6	0	43	0
Bell	3	0	18	0	Mascarenhas	10	0	44	0
Giles	10	0	50	0	Udal	6	0	37	0
Loudon	4	0	24	0	Watson	8	0	34	3
Trott	5	0	35	3					

Scores after 15 overs: Hampshire 61-1; Warwickshire 93-1.

Umpires: A.A.Jones and N.A.Mallender.

CHELTENHAM & GLOUCESTER TROPHY

PRINCIPAL RECORDS 1963-2005
(Including Gillette Cup and NatWest Trophy Matches)

Highest Total	438-5	Surrey v Glamorgan	The Oval	2002
Highest Total in a Final	322-5	Warwicks v Sussex	Lord's	1993
Highest Total Batting Second	429	Glamorgan v Surrey	The Oval	2002
Highest Total to Win Batting Second	359-8	Hampshire v Surrey	The Oval	2005
Lowest Total	39	Ireland v Sussex	Hove	1985
Lowest Total in a Final	57	Essex v Lancashire	Lord's	1996
Lowest Total to Win Batting First	98	Worcs v Durham	Chester-le-St	1968

Highest Score	268	A.D.Brown	Surrey v Glamorgan	The Oval	2002
Fastest Hundred	36 balls	G.D.Rose	Somerset v Devon	Torquay	1990
Most Hundreds	8	R.A.Smith	Hampshire		1985-03
Most Runs	2547	(av 48.98)	G.A.Gooch	Essex	1973-96

Highest Partnership for each Wicket

1st	311	A.J.Wright/N.J.Trainor	Glos v Scotland	Bristol	1997
2nd	286	I.S.Anderson/A.Hill	Derbys v Cornwall	Derby	1986
3rd	309*	T.S.Curtis/T.M.Moody	Worcs v Surrey	The Oval	1994
4th	234*	D.Lloyd/C.H.Lloyd	Lancashire v Glos	Manchester	1978
5th	166	M.A.Lynch/G.R.J.Roope	Surrey v Durham	The Oval	1982
6th	226	N.J.Llong/M.V.Fleming	Kent v Cheshire	Bowdon	1999
7th	170	D.R.Brown/A.F.Giles	Warwicks v Essex	Birmingham	2003
8th	112	A.L.Penberthy/J.E.Emburey	Northants v Lancs	Manchester	1996
9th	87	M.A.Nash/A.E.Cordle	Glamorgan v Lincs	Swansea	1974
10th	81	S.Turner/R.E.East	Essex v Yorkshire	Leeds	1982

Best Bowling	8-21	M.A.Holding	Derbys v Sussex	Hove	1988
Most Wickets	88	(av 14.35)	A.A.Donald	Warwks/Worcs	1987-02

Most Wicket-Keeping Dismissals in an Innings

8 (8ct)	D.J.Pipe	Worcs v Herts	Hertford	2001

Most Match Wins: 91 – Lancashire; Warwickshire.   **Most Cup/Trophy Wins:** 7 – Lancashire

GILLETTE CUP WINNERS

1963	Sussex	1970	Lancashire	1977	Middlesex
1964	Sussex	1971	Lancashire	1978	Sussex
1965	Yorkshire	1972	Lancashire	1979	Somerset
1966	Warwickshire	1973	Gloucestershire	1980	Middlesex
1967	Kent	1974	Kent		
1968	Warwickshire	1975	Lancashire		
1969	Yorkshire	1976	Northamptonshire		

NATWEST TROPHY WINNERS

1981	Derbyshire	1988	Middlesex	1995	Warwickshire
1982	Surrey	1989	Warwickshire	1996	Lancashire
1983	Somerset	1990	Lancashire	1997	Essex
1984	Middlesex	1991	Hampshire	1998	Lancashire
1985	Essex	1992	Northamptonshire	1999	Gloucestershire
1986	Sussex	1993	Warwickshire	2000	Gloucestershire
1987	Nottinghamshire	1994	Worcestershire		

CHELTENHAM & GLOUCESTER TROPHY WINNERS

2001	Somerset	2003	Gloucestershire	2005	Hampshire
2002	Yorkshire	2004	Gloucestershire		

BENSON AND HEDGES CUP

PRINCIPAL RECORDS 1972-2002

Highest Total		388-7	Essex v Scotland	Chelmsford	1992
Highest Total Batting Second		318-5	Lancashire v Leics	Manchester	1995
Lowest Total		50	Hampshire v Yorks	Leeds	1991
Largest Victory (Runs)		172	Essex v Scotland	Chelmsford	1992
Highest Score	198*	G.A.Gooch	Essex v Sussex	Hove	1982
Fastest Hundred	62 min	M.A.Nash	Glamorgan v Hants	Swansea	1976

Highest Partnership for each Wicket

1st	252	V.P.Terry/C.L.Smith	Hants v Combined U	Southampton	1990
2nd	285*	C.G.Greenidge/D.R.Turner	Hants v Minor C (S)	Amersham	1973
3rd	271	C.J.Adams/M.G.Bevan	Sussex v Essex	Chelmsford	2000
4th	207	R.C.Russell/A.J.Wright	Glos v British U	Bristol	1998
5th	160	A.J.Lamb/D.J.Capel	Northants v Leics	Northampton	1986
6th	167*	M.G.Bevan/R.J.Blakey	Yorkshire v Lancs	Manchester	1996
7th	149*	J.D.Love/C.M.Old	Yorks v Scotland	Bradford	1981
8th	112	D.C.Nash/A.A.Noffke	Middlesex v Sussex	Lord's	2002
9th	83	P.G.Newman/M.A.Holding	Derbyshire v Notts	Nottingham	1985
10th	80*	D.L.Bairstow/M.Johnson	Yorkshire v Derbys	Derby	1981

Best Bowling	7-12	W.W.Daniel	Middx v Minor C (E)	Ipswich	1978
	7-22	J.R.Thomson	Middx v Hampshire	Lord's	1981
	7-24	Mushtaq Ahmed	Somerset v Ireland	Taunton	1997
	7-32	R.G.D.Willis	Warwicks v Yorks	Birmingham	1981
Four Wickets in Four Balls		S.M.Pollock	Warwicks v Leics	Birmingham	1996

Most Wicket-Keeping Dismissals in an Innings

8 (8ct)	D.J.S.Taylor	Somerset v Combined U	Taunton	1982

Most Catches in an Innings

5	V.J.Marks	Combined U v Kent	Oxford	1976

BENSON AND HEDGES CUP WINNERS

1972	Leicestershire	1983	Middlesex	1994	Warwickshire
1973	Kent	1984	Lancashire	1995	Lancashire
1974	Surrey	1985	Leicestershire	1996	Lancashire
1975	Leicestershire	1986	Middlesex	1997	Surrey
1976	Kent	1987	Yorkshire	1998	Essex
1977	Gloucestershire	1988	Hampshire	1999	Gloucestershire
1978	Kent	1989	Nottinghamshire	2000	Gloucestershire
1979	Essex	1990	Lancashire	2001	Surrey
1980	Northamptonshire	1991	Worcestershire	2002	Warwickshire
1981	Somerset	1992	Hampshire		
1982	Somerset	1993	Derbyshire		

TOTESPORT NATIONAL LEAGUE 2005

FIRST DIVISION

		P	W	L	T	NR	Pts	NRR
1	ESSEX (6)	16	13	1	–	2	56	7.28
2	Middlesex (-)	16	10	5	–	1	42	5.54
3	Northamptonshire (4)	16	7	7	–	2	32	-0.13
4	Glamorgan (1)	16	6	6	–	4	32	-0.24
5	Nottinghamshire (-)	16	6	7	–	3	30	5.83
6	Lancashire (2)	16	6	9	–	1	26	-0.69
7	Gloucestershire (5)	16	6	9	–	1	26	-8.39
8	Worcestershire (-)	16	5	10	–	1	22	-2.53
9	Hampshire (3)	16	5	10	–	1	22	-6.23

SECOND DIVISION

		P	W	L	T	NR	Pts	NRR
1	SUSSEX (5)	18	13	4	–	1	54	13.94
2	Durham (6)	18	12	4	–	2	52	11.21
3	Warwickshire (-)	18	10	6	–	2	44	6.00
4	Leicestershire (7)	18	10	7	–	1	42	5.54
5	Derbyshire (9)	18	9	7	1	1	40	-4.10
6	Somerset (8)	18	9	8	–	1	38	0.85
7	Surrey (-)	18	7	10	–	1	30	-5.09
8	Kent (-)	18	6	10	–	2	28	0.68
9	Yorkshire (4)	18	5	13	–	–	20	-8.63
10	Scotland (10)	18	2	14	1	1	12	-16.68

Win = 4 points. Tie (T)/No Result (NR) = 2 points. Positions of counties finishing equal on points are decided by most wins or, if equal, by higher net run-rate (NRR – overall run-rate in all matches, i.e. total runs scored times 100 divided by balls received, minus the run-rate of its opponents in those same matches). Horizontal rules segregate the counties relegated and promoted for the 2005 competition. 2004 final positions for that division are shown in brackets.

HIGHEST BATTING AGGREGATE– Div 1   785 (av 52.33) P.N.Weekes   Middlesex
   – Div 2   753 (av 47.06) M.J.Di Venuto   Derbyshire
HIGHEST BOWLING AGGREGATE – Div 1   26 (av 22.07) D.G.Wright   Northamptonshire
   – Div 2   31 (av 19.12) R.J.Kirtley   Sussex

SUNDAY LEAGUE CHAMPIONS

1969	Lancashire	1979	Somerset	1989	Lancashire
1970	Lancashire	1980	Warwickshire	1990	Derbyshire
1971	Worcestershire	1981	Essex	1991	Nottinghamshire
1972	Kent	1982	Sussex	1992	Middlesex
1973	Kent	1983	Yorkshire	1993	Glamorgan
1974	Leicestershire	1984	Essex	1994	Warwickshire
1975	Hampshire	1985	Essex	1995	Kent
1976	Kent	1986	Hampshire	1996	Surrey
1977	Leicestershire	1987	Worcestershire	1997	Warwickshire
1978	Hampshire	1988	Worcestershire	1998	Lancashire

NATIONAL LEAGUE CHAMPIONS

1999	Lancashire	2002	Glamorgan	2005	Essex
2000	Gloucestershire	2003	Surrey		
2001	Kent	2004	Glamorgan		

SCOTLAND
NATIONAL LEAGUE REGISTER 2005

Full Names	Birthdate	Birthplace	Bat/Bowl	F-C Debut
ASIM BUTT	24.10.67	Lahore, Pakistan	RHB/LMF	1983-84
BEUKES, Jonathan Alan	15.03.79	Kimberley, S Africa	LHB/OB	1997-98
DRAKES, Vasbert Conniel	05.08.69	St Andrew, Barbados	RHB, RFM	1991-92
ENGLISH, Cedric Vaughan	13.09.73	Kimberley, S Africa	RHB/RFM	1990-91
GOUDIE, Gordon	12.08.87	Aberdeen	RHB/RFM	2005

Full Names	Birthdate	Birthplace	Bat/Bowl	F-C Debut
HAMILTON, Gavin Mark	16.09.74	Broxburn	LHB/RMF	1993
HAQ, Rana Majid Khan	11.12.83	Paisley	LHB/OB	2004
HOFFMAN, Paul Jacob Christopher	14.01.70	Rockhampton, Australia	RHB/RMF	2004
HUSSAIN, Rana Omer	03.12.84	Paisley	LHB	–
KNOX, Steven Thomas	16.02.74	Barrow-in-Furness	RHB/RM	2004
LOCKHART, Douglas Ross	19.01.76	Glasgow	RHB/WK	1996
LYONS, Ross Thomas	08.12.84	Greenock	LHB/SLA	–
MAIDEN, Gregor Ian	22.07.79	Glasgow	RHB/OB	1999
NEL, Johann Dewald	06.06.80	Klerksdorp, S Africa	RHB/RMF	2004
SHEIKH, Mohammad Qasim	30.10.84	Glasgow	LHB/LM	2005
SMITH, Colin John Ogilvie	27.09.72	Aberdeen	RHB/WK	1999
STANGER, Ian Michael	05.10.71	Glasgow	RHB/RMF	1997
WATSON, Ryan Robert	12.11.76	Salisbury, Rhodesia	RHB/RM	2004
WATTS, David Fraser	05.06.79	King's Lynn, Norfolk	RHB/RMF	1999
WEERARATNA, Sean Dinesh	21.11.85	Morija, Lesotho	RHB/RMF	2005
WILLIAMSON, John Greig	20.12.68	Glasgow	RHB/RM	1994
WRIGHT, Craig McIntyre	28.04.74	Paisley	RHB/RMF	1997
YASIR ARAFAT Satti	12.03.82	Rawalpindi, Pakistan	RHB/RMF	1997-98

NATIONAL (SUNDAY) LEAGUE 1969-2005

PRINCIPAL RECORDS

Highest Total		377-9	Somerset v Sussex	Hove	2003
Highest Total Batting Second		323-5	Sussex v Leics	Horsham	2004
Lowest Total		23	Middlesex v Yorks	Leeds	1974
Largest Victory (Runs)		220	Somerset v Glamorgan	Neath	1990
Highest Scores	203	A.D.Brown	Surrey v Hampshire	Guildford	1997
	191	D.S.Lehmann	Yorks v Notts	Scarborough	2001
	176	G.A.Gooch	Essex v Glamorgan	Southend	1983
	175*	I.T.Botham	Somerset v Northants	Wellingborough	1986
Fastest Hundred	44 balls	M.A.Ealham	Kent v Derbyshire	Maidstone	1995
Most Sixes (Inns)	13	I.T.Botham	Somerset v Northants	Wellingborough	1986

Highest Partnership for each Wicket

1st	239	G.A.Gooch/B.R.Hardie	Essex v Notts	Nottingham	1985
2nd	273	G.A.Gooch/K.S.McEwan	Essex v Notts	Nottingham	1983
3rd	228*	M.W.Goodwin/C.J.Adams	Sussex v Middlesex	Hove	2003
4th	219	C.G.Greenidge/C.L.Smith	Hampshire v Surrey	Southampton	1987
5th	220*	C.C.Lewis/P.A.Nixon	Leics v Kent	Canterbury	1999
6th	167	C.L.Cairns/C.M.W.Read	Notts v Sussex	Nottingham	2003
7th	164	J.N.Snape/M.A.Hardinges	Glos v Notts	Nottingham	2003
8th	116*	N.D.Burns/P.A.J.DeFreitas	Leics v Northants	Leicester	2001
9th	105	D.G.Moir/R.W.Taylor	Derbyshire v Kent	Derby	1984
10th	82	G.Chapple/P.J.Martin	Lancashire v Worcs	Manchester	1996

Best Bowling	8-26	K.D.Boyce	Essex v Lancashire	Manchester	1971
	7-15	R.A.Hutton	Yorkshire v Worcs	Leeds	1969
	7-16	S.D.Thomas	Glamorgan v Surrey	Swansea	1998
	7-30	M.P.Bicknell	Surrey v Glamorgan	The Oval	1999
	7-39	A.Hodgson	Northants v Somerset	Northampton	1976
	7-41	A.N.Jones	Sussex v Notts	Nottingham	1986
Four Wkts in Four Balls		A.Ward	Derbyshire v Sussex	Derby	1970
		V.C.Drakes	Notts v Derbys	Nottingham	1999

Most Economical Analysis

8-8-0-0		B.A.Langford	Somerset v Essex	Yeovil	1969

Most Expensive Analysis

9-0-99-1		M.R.Strong	Northants v Glos	Cheltenham	2001

Most Wicket-Keeping Dismissals in an Innings

7 (6ct, 1st)		R.W.Taylor	Derbyshire v Lancs	Manchester	1975

Most Catches in an Innings by a Fielder

5		J.M.Rice	Hampshire v Warwicks	Southampton	1978

TWENTY20 CUP 2005

GROUP TABLES

MIDLANDS/WALES/WEST	P	W	L	T	NR	Pts	NRR
1 NORTHAMPTONSHIRE	8	4	2	–	2	10	1.17
2 WARWICKSHIRE	8	4	3	–	1	9	0.79
3 SOMERSET	8	4	3	–	1	9	1.09
4 Gloucestershire	8	3	3	–	2	8	-1.44
5 Worcestershire	8	3	4	–	1	7	-0.46
6 Glamorgan	8	2	5	–	1	5	-1.09

NORTH	P	W	L	T	NR	Pts	NRR
1 LANCASHIRE	8	6	1	–	1	13	1.77
2 LEICESTERSHIRE	8	5	2	–	1	11	0.26
3 DERBYSHIRE	8	4	3	–	1	9	-0.45
4 Yorkshire	8	3	5	–	–	6	-0.71
5 Durham	8	2	5	–	1	5	-0.87
6 Nottinghamshire	8	2	6	–	–	4	0.14

SOUTH	P	W	L	T	NR	Pts	NRR
1 SURREY	8	5	3	–	–	10	0.64
2 MIDDLESEX	8	4	3	–	1	9	0.16
3 Sussex	8	3	2	–	3	9	0.14
4 Hampshire	8	3	2	–	3	9	0.20
5 Essex	8	3	3	–	2	8	-0.07
6 Kent	8	2	5	–	1	5	-1.02

QUARTER-FINALS: LANCASHIRE beat Derbyshire by 17 runs at Manchester
LEICESTERSHIRE beat Middlesex by 19 runs at Leicester
SOMERSET beat Northamptonshire by 4 wickets at Northampton
SURREY tied with Warwickshire at The Oval (won bowl-out 4-3)

SEMI-FINALS: LANCASHIRE beat Surrey by 22 runs at The Oval
SOMERSET beat Leicestershire by 4 runs at The Oval

LEADING AVERAGES 2005

BATTING (Qual: 4 Inns, Avge 45)		M	I	NO	HS	Runs	Avge	100	50	SR
B.J.Hodge	Lancashire	6	6	2	90*	330	82.50	–	3	153.48
M.A.Carberry	Kent	7	6	3	59*	242	80.66	–	2	141.52
S.D.Udal	Hampshire	7	5	4	34*	60	60.00	–	–	113.20
O.A.Shah	Middlesex	9	9	2	79	410	58.57	–	5	159.53
W.P.C.Weston	Gloucestershire	7	5	2	73*	167	55.66	–	1	126.51
M.J.Prior	Sussex	6	4	1	66*	159	53.00	–	2	144.54
S.J.Law	Lancashire	9	9	1	101	387	48.37	1	3	151.76
Azhar Mahmood	Surrey	7	7	3	40*	188	47.00	–	–	163.47
J.S.Foster	Essex	7	5	3	62*	91	45.50	–	1	151.66
G.J.Muchall	Durham	7	7	2	64*	227	45.40	–	1	120.10

BOWLING (Qual: 10 wkts, Avge 15.00)		O	M	R	W	Avge	BB	4w	R/Over
Mushtaq Ahmed	Sussex	21.3	1	115	14	8.21	5-11	1	5.34
M.Muralitharan	Lancashire	17	1	90	10	9.00	4-19	1	5.29
B.J.Hodge	Lancashire	19	–	137	13	10.23	4-17	2	7.21
I.K.Pathan	Middlesex	24	–	153	12	12.75	4-27	1	6.37
N.D.Doshi	Surrey	29	–	230	17	13.52	4-27	1	7.93
G.M.Andrew	Somerset	24	–	182	13	14.00	4-22	1	7.58
J.N.Snape	Leicestershire	23	1	156	11	14.18	3-18	–	6.78
I.D.Blackwell	Somerset	35	–	228	16	14.25	4-26	1	6.51
N.M.Carter	Warwickshire	29.5	–	222	15	14.80	5-19	1	7.44
J.C.Hildreth	Somerset	18.4	–	148	10	14.80	3-24	–	7.92
R.Clarke	Surrey	17.5	1	150	10	15.00	3-11	–	8.41

TWENTY20 CUP FINAL 2005

LANCASHIRE v SOMERSET

At Kennington Oval, London, on 30 July.
Result: **SOMERSET** won by seven wickets
Toss: Lancashire. Award: G.C.Smith.

LANCASHIRE		Runs	Balls	4/6	Fall
M.B.Loye	c Johnson b Caddick	5	5	1	1- 6
S.G.Law	run out	59	45	8	8-114
A.Flintoff	c Blackwell b Caddick	2	3	–	2- 15
A.Symonds	run out	12	7	2	3- 40
D.G.Cork	c Trescothick b Johnson	1	3	–	4- 41
G.Chapple	b Johnson	0	1	–	5- 41
* M.J.Chilton	b Blackwell	9	12	1	6- 69
A.R.Crook	c Gazzard b Johnson	15	15	1	7-101
† W.K.Hegg	not out	6	5	1	
J.M.Anderson					
G.Keedy					
Extras	(LB 2, W 3)	5			
Total	(16 overs; 8 wickets)	**114**			

SOMERSET		Runs	Balls	4/6	Fall
* G.C.Smith	not out	64	47	5/2	
M.E.Trescothick	c Hegg b Flintoff	10	8	2	1-28
M.J.Wood	b Flintoff	22	13	5	2-60
I.D.Blackwell	c Law b Keedy	3	3	–	3-65
J.C.Hildreth	not out	16	14	1	
† C.M.Gazzard					
K.A.Parsons					
R.L.Johnson					
W.J.Durston					
A.R.Caddick					
C.K.Langeveldt					
Extras	(LB 1, W 2)	3			
Total	(14.1 overs; 3 wickets)	**118**			

SOMERSET	O	M	R	W	LANCASHIRE	O	M	R	W
Caddick	4	0	21	2	Cork	2	0	12	0
Langeveldt	3	0	28	0	Anderson	1.1	0	14	0
Johnson	3	0	26	3	Flintoff	4	0	33	2
Parsons	3	0	13	0	Chapple	2	0	23	0
Blackwell	3	0	24	1	Keedy	3	0	21	1
					Symonds	2	0	14	0

Umpires: I.J.Gould and P.Willey

ECB TWENTY20 COUNTY COMPETITION 2003-05

PRINCIPAL RECORDS

Highest Total		228-5	Somerset v Glos	Taunton	2005
Lowest Total		67	Sussex v Hampshire	Hove	2004
Hundreds	116*	G.A.Hick	Worcs v Northants	Luton	2004
	116*	I.J.Thomas	Glamorgan v Somerset	Taunton	2004
	112	A.Symonds	Kent v Middlesex	Maidstone	2004
	111	D.L.Maddy	Leics v Yorks	Leeds	2004
	109	I.J.Harvey	Yorkshire v Derbys	Leeds	2005
	108*	I.J.Harvey	Yorkshire v Lancs	Leeds	2004
	105	B.F.Smith	Worcs v Glamorgan	Worcester	2004
	105	G.C.Smith	Somerset v Northants	Taunton	2005
	101	S.G.Law	Lancs v Yorkshire	Manchester	2005
	100*	I.J.Harvey	Glos v Warwicks	Birmingham	2005
	100	M.B.Loye	Lancs v Durham	Manchester	2005

Highest Partnership for each Wicket

1st	167	B.J.Hodge/D.L.Maddy	Leics v Yorkshire	Leeds	2004
2nd	160	M.B.Loye/B.J.Hodge	Lancs v Durham	Manchester	2005
3rd	120	M.J.Wood/C.M.Gazzard	Somerset v Worcs	Taunton	2005
4th	95	A.Flower/A.P.Grayson	Essex v Leics	Leicester	2004
5th	101*	D.A.Leatherdale/A.J.Bichel	Worcs v Somerset	Taunton	2004
6th	90*	M.R.Ramprakash/A.J.Hollioake	Surrey v Hampshire	The Oval	2004
7th	63	J.S.Foster/A.R.Adams	Essex v Middlesex	Southgate	2004
8th	68	M.W.Alleyne/J.Lewis	Glos v Glamorgan	Cardiff	2005
9th	59*	G.Chapple/P.J.Martin	Lancs v Leics	Leicester	2004
10th	59	H.H.Streak/J.E.Anyon	Warwicks v Worcs	Birmingham	2005

Best Bowling

Best Bowling	6-24	T.J.Murtagh	Surrey v Middlesex	Lord's	2005
	5-11	Mushtaq Ahmed	Sussex v Essex	Hove	2005
	5-14	A.D.Mascarenhas	Hampshire v Sussex	Hove	2004
	5-19	N.N.Carter	Warwicks v Worcs	Birmingham	2005
	5-21	A.J.Hollioake	Surrey v Hampshire	Southampton	2003
	5-24	C.O.Obuya	Warwicks v Glamorgan	Birmingham	2005
	5-26	R.J.Logan	Notts v Lancs	Nottingham	2003
	5-26	J.Ormond	Surrey v Middlesex	The Oval	2005
	5-27	J.F.Brown	Northants v Somerset	Northampton	2003
	5-33	A.G.R.Loudon	Warwicks v Glamorgan	Swansea	2005
	5-34	A.J.Hollioake	Surrey v Hampshire	The Oval	2004

Hat-Tricks

Hat-Tricks	J.E.Anyon	Warwicks v Somerset	Birmingham	2005
	D.G.Cork	Lancs v Notts	Manchester	2004
	A.D.Mascarenhas	Hampshire v Sussex	Hove	2004

Most Economical Analyses

Most Economical Analyses	4-1-6-2	J.Louw	Northants v Warwicks	Birmingham	2005
	4-0-6-1	M.W.Alleyne	Glos v Worcs	Worcester	2005
	4-1-7-1	R.S.C.Martin-Jenkins	Sussex v Hampshire	Hove	2004
	4-1-7-4	N.Killeen	Durham v Leics	Leicester	2004
	4-1-8-2	R.J.Kirtley	Sussex v Hampshire	Hove	2004

Most Expensive Analyses

Most Expensive Analyses	4-0-65-2	M.J.Hoggard	Yorkshire v Lancs	Leeds	2005
	4-0-63-1	R.J.Kirtley	Sussex v Surrey	Hove	2004
	4-0-60-0	S.P.Kirby	Yorks v Lancs	Leeds	2004

MINOR COUNTIES CHAMPIONSHIP

FINAL TABLES 2005

	P	W	L	D	Bonus Points Bat	Bowl	Total Points
EASTERN DIVISION							
SUFFOLK	6	4	1	1	19	23	110
Cambridgeshire	6	4	1	1	12	19	99
Norfolk	6	3	2	1	18	19	93
Northumberland	6	3	0	3	19	19	86
Staffordshire*	6	3	1	2	18	14	82
Buckinghamshire	6	2	2	2	13	19	72
Cumberland	6	2	1	3	6	23	65
Lincolnshire	6	2	1	3	20	17	63
Hertfordshire	6	1	0	5	15	20	51
Bedfordshire	6	0	3	3	11	16	39
WESTERN DIVISION							
CHESHIRE	6	3	3	0	17	23	100
Devon	6	3	2	1	14	21	91
Berkshire	6	2	4	0	19	24	91
Cornwall	6	2	3	1	18	24	86
Oxfordshire	6	2	2	2	15	23	78
Shropshire	6	1	3	2	22	21	71
Wales	6	1	3	2	14	21	63
Herefordshire*	6	1	3	2	12	19	57
Wiltshire*	6	1	2	3	11	22	55
Dorset	6	0	3	3	18	13	43

* Indicates a 2 point deduction for slow over rate. Win = 16 points. Draw/Tie = 4 points.

2005 CHAMPIONSHIP FINAL

At Ransomes and Reavals, Ipswich on 11, 12, 13 September. Toss: Cheshire. **SUFFOLK drew with CHESHIRE – TITLE SHARED.** Cheshire 148 (D.B.Pennett 41, A.C.McGarry 4-40) and 279 (N.R.C.Dumelow 80, A.J.Hall 61). Suffolk 201-9 closed (50 overs; P.J.Caley 51*; C.P.Schofield 6-78). *Rain prevented play on the first day.*

MCCA KNOCK-OUT TROPHY FINAL

At Slough CC on 31 August. Toss: Wiltshire. **NORFOLK beat WILTSHIRE by six wickets.** Wiltshire 134 (45.1; Baqar Rizvi 39; P.J.Bradshaw 3-16, M.W.Thomas 3-21, C.J.Rogers 3-23). Norfolk 135-4 (27; C.R.Borrett 37; R.D.Bedbrook 3-37). *The scheduled final at Lord's on 22 August was abandoned without a ball bowled because of rain.*

MINOR COUNTIES RECORDS

Highest Total	621		Surrey II v Devon	The Oval	1928
Lowest Total	14		Cheshire v Staffs	Stoke	1909
Highest Score	282	E.Garnett	Berkshire v Wiltshire	Reading	1908
Most Runs – Season	1212	A.F.Brazier	Surrey II		1949
Record Partnership:					
2nd wkt	388*	T.H.Clark/A.F.Brazier	Surrey II v Sussex II	The Oval	1949
Best Bowling – Innings	10- 11	S.Turner	Cambs v Cumberland	Penrith	1987
– Match	18-100	N.W.Harding	Kent II v Wiltshire	Swindon	1937
Most Wickets – Season	119	S.F.Barnes	Staffordshire		1906

MINOR COUNTIES CHAMPIONS

	Norfolk	1933	*Undecided*	1976	Durham
1895	Durham	1934	Lancashire II	1977	Suffolk
	Worcestershire	1935	Middlesex II	1978	Devon
1896	Worcestershire	1936	Hertfordshire	1979	Suffolk
1897	Worcestershire	1937	Lancashire II	1980	Durham
1898	Worcestershire	1938	Buckinghamshire	1981	Durham
1899	Northamptonshire	1939	Surrey II	1982	Oxfordshire
	Buckinghamshire	1946	Suffolk	1983	Hertfordshire
	Glamorgan	1947	Yorkshire II	1984	Durham
1900	Durham	1948	Lancashire II	1985	Cheshire
	Northamptonshire	1949	Lancashire II	1986	Cumberland
1901	Durham	1950	Surrey II	1987	Buckinghamshire
1902	Wiltshire	1951	Kent II	1988	Cheshire
1903	Northamptonshire	1952	Buckinghamshire	1989	Oxfordshire
1904	Northamptonshire	1953	Berkshire	1990	Hertfordshire
1905	Norfolk	1954	Surrey II	1991	Staffordshire
1906	Staffordshire	1955	Surrey II	1992	Staffordshire
1907	Lancashire II	1956	Kent II	1993	Staffordshire
1908	Staffordshire	1957	Yorkshire II	1994	Devon
1909	Wiltshire	1958	Yorkshire II	1995	Devon
1910	Norfolk	1959	Warwickshire II	1996	Devon
1911	Staffordshire	1960	Lancashire II	1997	Devon
1912	*In abeyance*	1961	Somerset II	1998	Staffordshire
1913	Norfolk	1962	Warwickshire II	1999	Cumberland
1920	Staffordshire	1963	Cambridgeshire	2000	Dorset
1921	Staffordshire	1964	Lancashire II	2001	Cheshire
1922	Buckinghamshire	1965	Somerset II		Lincolnshire
1923	Buckinghamshire	1966	Lincolnshire	2002	Herefordshire
1924	Berkshire	1967	Cheshire		Norfolk
1925	Buckinghamshire	1968	Yorkshire II	2003	Lincolnshire
1926	Durham	1969	Buckinghamshire	2004	Bedfordshire
1927	Staffordshire	1970	Bedfordshire		Devon
1928	Berkshire	1971	Yorkshire II	2005	Cheshire
1929	Oxfordshire	1972	Bedfordshire		Suffolk
1930	Durham	1973	Shropshire		
1931	Leicestershire II	1974	Oxfordshire		
1932	Buckinghamshire	1975	Hertfordshire		

LEADING CHAMPIONSHIP AGGREGATES 2005

BATTING

		M	I	NO	HS	Runs	Ave	100	50
C.J.Rogers	Norfolk	6	11	2	141*	779	86.55	3	4
S.A.Selwood	Dorset	5	9	1	204*	640	80.00	2	3
S.P.Naylor	Berkshire	6	11	2	113*	630	70.00	1	5
G.M.Fellows	Shropshire	6	11	3	182*	624	78.00	2	4
B.Parker	Northumberland	6	11	1	173	579	57.90	1	4
D.G.Shurben	Northumberland	6	11	·0	153	553	50.27	1	4
A.J.Hall	Cheshire	7	14	1	106	548	42.15	1	6
A.R.Roberts	Bedfordshire	6	9	2	154*	538	76.85	2	3
N.R.C.Dumelow	Cheshire	7	13	1	114*	537	44.75	2	2
C.Amos	Norfolk	6	11	0	157	529	48.09	1	4
D.C.Shirazi	Wiltshire	5	10	1	106	491	54.55	1	4
R.P.Harvey	Staffordshire	6	10	2	163	489	61.12	2	2
S.Mason	Lincolnshire	6	12	0	112	479	39.91	1	3
K.J.Barnett	Staffordshire	6	9	3	133	478	79.66	2	2
T.D.Fray	Berkshire	2	3	2	201*	466	466.00	3	–
D.M.Ward	Hertfordshire	6	10	0	119	456	45.60	1	4

		M	I	NO	HS	Runs	Ave	100	50
S.A.Richardson	Cumberland	4	8	0	126	447	55.87	3	–
M.C.Dobson	Lincolnshire	6	12	1	122	447	40.63	2	2
D.N.Catterall	Shropshire	6	10	2	70	444	55.50	–	4
C.M.Mole	Devon	6	12	2	104*	441	44.10	1	3
C.P.Schofield	Cheshire	6	11	0	100	438	39.81	1	3
A.L.Penberthy	Cornwall	6	10	1	150	434	48.22	2	–
M.P.O'Shea	Wales MC	5	10	2	115	429	53.62	2	2
R.P.Lane	Buckinghamshire	6	11	0	106	428	38.90	1	3
R.D.King	Staffordshire	6	12	1	75	426	38.72	–	3
M.P.Dowman	Lincolnshire	6	12	0	114	421	35.08	1	3
M.S.Coles	Wiltshire	6	10	0	119	419	41.90	2	1
T.G.Sharp	Cornwall	5	7	0	156	412	58.85	1	3
C.Jones	Cambridgeshire	6	12	1	72	412	37.45	–	4
R.I.Dawson	Devon	6	11	2	130	408	45.33	1	2
C.W.Boroughs	Herefordshire	6	10	3	115*	406	58.00	1	2
B.H.D.Mordt	Berkshire	6	11	0	89	405	36.81	–	4
C.S.Knightley	Oxfordshire	5	9	0	133	403	44.77	2	1
R.W.Cook	Lincolnshire	6	11	2	101*	390	43.33	1	1
B.J.Frazer	Hertfordshire	6	11	1	77	377	37.70	–	4
C.P.Martin	Shropshire	6	11	0	71	376	34.18	–	5
A.P.Cook	Oxfordshire	4	8	1	118	375	53.57	1	3
D.G.Brandy	Cambridgeshire	5	10	1	80*	374	41.55	–	4
M.H.Steed	Bedfordshire	4	8	1	76	371	53.00	–	3
K.D.Bell	Staffordshire	3	6	1	118*	367	73.40	2	1
C.J.Warn	Suffolk	7	9	2	165*	361	51.57	1	2
S.A.Kellett	Cambridgeshire	6	12	0	105	357	29.75	1	1
B.J.Wright	Wales MC	6	10	0	101	353	35.30	1	2
A.D.Mawson	Suffolk	5	9	2	96	350	50.00	–	3

BOWLING

		O	M	R	W	Ave	BB	5w	10w
C.Brown	Norfolk	288.5	64	804	44	18.27	8-65	3	1
A.C.McGarry	Suffolk	247.5	45	803	34	23.61	6-38	1	–
A.J.Procter	Devon	279.2	58	871	33	26.39	5-50	2	–
N.R.C.Dumelow	Cheshire	180	48	510	31	16.45	5-52	3	1
K.A.Arnold	Oxfordshire	230.4	62	600	31	19.35	5-65	1	–
S.Humble	Northumberland	132.4	26	465	30	15.50	6-37	3	1
M.A.Sharp	Cumberland	155.2	68	280	29	9.65	7-19	3	1
D.J.Edwards	Staffordshire	201.5	42	743	29	25.62	5-78	2	–
T.L.Lambert	Berkshire	189.1	45	617	28	22.03	5-35	1	–
C.P.Schofield	Cheshire	151.4	25	539	27	19.96	6-78	2	–
T.M.Smith	Suffolk	198	36	701	27	25.96	7-42	1	–
P.J.Bradshaw	Norfolk	194.4	40	538	26	20.69	4-25	–	–
D.N.Catterall	Shropshire	147.3	24	587	25	23.48	5-30	1	–
J.J.Newell	Buckinghamshire	233.2	64	608	25	24.32	7-99	2	–
A.Jones	Devon	263.1	78	747	25	29.88	5-61	1	–
P.D.King	Suffolk	137	22	518	24	21.58	4-35	–	–
A.R.Roberts	Bedfordshire	163	46	530	24	22.08	5-48	1	–
C.A.Hunkin	Cornwall	183.5	39	596	24	24.83	5-68	2	–
C.D.Crowe	Berkshire	190.1	55	602	24	25.08	8-100	1	1
E.J.Wilson	Lincolnshire	185.2	36	699	22	31.77	5-23	1	–
J.P.Hewitt	Oxfordshire	136.4	18	602	21	28.66	6-86	2	–
R.C.Driver	Cornwall	144	41	450	20	22.50	6-89	1	–
C.M.Roberts	Wales MC	196.5	31	708	20	35.40	7-102	1	–
S.F.Stanway	Buckinghamshire	232	52	707	20	35.35	6-68	1	–

SECOND XI CHAMPIONSHIP 2005
FINAL TABLE

	P	W	L	D	Deduct	Bat	Bowl	Total Points	Avge
1 KENT (13)	6	4	–	2	2	21	17	100	16.67
2 Gloucestershire (9)	9	5	–	4	–	24	30	140	15.56
3 Hampshire (10)	11	5	3	3	1	30	39	150	13.64
4 Lancashire (3)	13	6	3	4	–	32	44	176	13.54
5 Durham (17)	8	3	2	3	1	25	26	104	13.00
6 Essex (6)	9	2	1	6	1	26	28	108	12.00
7 Surrey (15)	13	4	4	5	–	37	36	149	11.46
8 Somerset (1)	6	2	1	3	–	11	15	66	11.00
9 Leicestershire (7)	10	2	2	6	–	30	27	109	10.90
10 Yorkshire (8)	12	2	4	6	–	36	41	129	10.75
11 Derbyshire (11)	12	2	3	7	2	30	39	123	10.25
12 Nottinghamshire (5)	13	2	4	7	–	35	39	130	10.00
13 Sussex (2)	10	2	4	4	–	24	28	96	9.60
14 MCC YC (-)	10	1	2	7	–	27	25	94	9.40
14 Northamptonshire (14)	10	1	–	9	–	21	23	94	9.40
16 Middlesex (12)	6	–	2	4	–	22	15	53	8.83
16 Worcestershire (18)	6	–	2	4	–	15	22	53	8.83
18 Glamorgan (16)	8	–	2	6	–	22	21	67	8.38
19 Warwickshire (4)	10	1	5	4	–	24	28	82	8.20

Win = 14 points, plus any first-innings points.
Draw = 4 points, plus any first-innings points.
2004 final positions are shown in brackets.

SECOND XI CHAMPIONS

1959	Gloucestershire	1975	Surrey	1991	Yorkshire
1960	Northamptonshire	1976	Kent	1992	Surrey
1961	Kent	1977	Yorkshire	1993	Middlesex
1962	Worcestershire	1978	Sussex	1994	Somerset
1963	Worcestershire	1979	Warwickshire	1995	Hampshire
1964	Lancashire	1980	Glamorgan	1996	Warwickshire
1965	Glamorgan	1981	Hampshire	1997	Lancashire
1966	Surrey	1982	Worcestershire	1998	Northamptonshire
1967	Hampshire	1983	Leicestershire	1999	Middlesex
1968	Surrey	1984	Yorkshire	2000	Middlesex
1969	Kent	1985	Nottinghamshire	2001	Hampshire
1970	Kent	1986	Lancashire	2002	Kent
1971	Hampshire	1987	Kent/Yorkshire	2003	Yorkshire
1972	Nottinghamshire	1988	Surrey	2004	Somerset
1973	Essex	1989	Middlesex	2005	Kent
1974	Middlesex	1990	Sussex		

SECOND XI TROPHY 2005

Semi-Finals: NOTTS beat YORKSHIRE by three wickets at Headingley.
SUSSEX beat WARWICKSHIRE by seven wickets at Knowle and Dorridge.

Final: SUSSEX beat ESSEX by eight wickets at Horsham.

YOUNG CRICKETER OF THE YEAR

This annual award, made by The Cricket Writers' Club, which celebrates its 60th anniversary this year, is currently restricted to players qualified for England, Andrew Symonds meeting that requirement at the time of his award, and under the age of 23 on 1st May. In 1986 their ballot resulted in a dead heat. Up to 28 February 2006 their selections have gained a tally of 1,864 international Test match caps (shown in brackets).

1950	R.Tattersall (16)	1979	P.W.G.Parker (1)
1951	P.B.H.May (66)	1980	G.R.Dilley (41)
1952	F.S.Trueman (67)	1981	M.W.Gatting (79)
1953	M.C.Cowdrey (114)	1982	N.G.Cowans (19)
1954	P.J.Loader (13)	1983	N.A.Foster (29)
1955	K.F.Barrington (82)	1984	R.J.Bailey (4)
1956	B.Taylor	1985	D.V.Lawrence (5)
1957	M.J.Stewart (8)	1986 {	A.A.Metcalfe
1958	A.C.D.Ingleby-Mackenzie		J.J.Whitaker (1)
1959	G.Pullar (28)	1987	R.J.Blakey (2)
1960	D.A.Allen (39)	1988	M.P.Maynard (4)
1961	P.H.Parfitt (37)	1989	N.Hussain (96)
1962	P.J.Sharpe (12)	1990	M.A.Atherton (115)
1963	G.Boycott (108)	1991	M.R.Ramprakash (52)
1964	J.M.Brearley (39)	1992	I.D.K.Salisbury (15)
1965	A.P.E.Knott (95)	1993	M.N.Lathwell (2)
1966	D.L.Underwood (86)	1994	J.P.Crawley (37)
1967	A.W.Greig (58)	1995	A.Symonds (7-Australia)
1968	R.M.H.Cottam (4)	1996	C.E.W.Silverwood (6)
1969	A.Ward (5)	1997	B.C.Hollioake (2)
1970	C.M.Old (46)	1998	A.Flintoff (55)
1971	J.Whitehouse	1999	A.J.Tudor (10)
1972	D.R.Owen-Thomas	2000	P.J.Franks
1973	M.Hendrick (30)	2001	O.A.Shah
1974	P.H.Edmonds (51)	2002	R.Clarke (2)
1975	A.Kennedy	2003	J.M.Anderson (12)
1976	G.Miller (34)	2004	I.R.Bell (11)
1977	I.T.Botham (102)	2005	A.N.Cook
1978	D.I.Gower (117)		

THE PROFESSIONAL CRICKETERS' ASSOCIATION
PLAYER OF THE YEAR

Founded in 1967, the Professional Cricketers' Association introduced this award, decided by their membership, in 1970. Since 1998 it has been presented at their Annual Awards Dinner at the Royal Albert Hall. Only John Lever and Andrew Flintoff won the award in successive years.

1970 {	M.J.Procter	1982	M.D.Marshall	1995	D.G.Cork
	J.D.Bond	1983	K.S.McEwan	1996	P.V.Simmons
1971	L.R.Gibbs	1984	R.J.Hadlee	1997	S.P.James
1972	A.M.E.Roberts	1985	N.V.Radford	1998	M.B.Loye
1973	P.G.Lee	1986	C.A.Walsh	1999	S.G.Law
1974	B.Stead	1987	R.J.Hadlee	2000	M.E.Trescothick
1975	Zaheer Abbas	1988	G.A.Hick	2001	D.P.Fulton
1976	P.G.Lee	1989	S.J.Cook	2002	M.P.Vaughan
1977	M.J.Procter	1990	G.A.Gooch	2003	Mushtaq Ahmed
1978	J.K.Lever	1991	Waqar Younis	2004	A.Flintoff
1979	J.K.Lever	1992	C.A.Walsh	2005	A.Flintoff
1980	R.D.Jackman	1993	S.L.Watkin		
1981	R.J.Hadlee	1994	B.C.Lara		

FIRST–CLASS CAREER RECORDS

Compiled by **Philip Bailey**

The following career records are for all players who appeared in first–class cricket during the 2005 season, and are complete to the end of that season. Some players who did not appear in 2005 but may do so in 2006 are included.

BATTING AND FIELDING

'1000' denotes instances of scoring 1000 runs in a season. Where these have been achieved outside the British Isles they are shown after a plus sign.

	M	I	NO	HS	Runs	Avge	100	50	1000	Ct/St
Abdur Razzak	31	48	7	83	840	20.48	–	4	–	11
Ackerman, H.D.	135	221	22	202*	8432	42.37	22	47	1+1	102
Adams, A.R.	54	70	2	124	1570	23.08	2	8	–	37
Adams, C.J.	290	474	35	239	16813	38.29	42	81	7	336
Adams, J.H.K.	36	64	5	107	1570	26.61	1	8	–	19
Adnan, M.Hassan	98	163	20	191	5919	41.39	9	41	1	58
Adshead, S.J.	36	61	11	148*	1631	32.62	1	10	–	86/10
Aftab Ahmed	19	35	3	129	956	29.87	1	4	–	16
Afzaal, U.	164	282	28	168*	9244	36.39	22	45	5	81
Ahmed, J.S.	1	1	1	14*	14	–	–	–	–	–
Airey, S.J.	9	12	4	72	272	34.00	–	1	–	3
Akram, M. Adnan	9	13	1	129*	515	42.91	2	1	–	4
Akram, M. Arfan	8	14	3	110	308	28.00	1	–	–	3
Ali, Kabir	69	93	17	84*	1506	19.81	–	7	–	21
Ali, Kadeer	38	68	3	99	1304	20.06	–	9	–	18
Ali, M.M.	1	1	–	57	57	57.00	–	1	–	2
Ali, S. Mohd H.	84	112	26	92	1247	14.50	–	5	–	26
Alleyne, D.	10	13	3	49*	306	30.60	–	–	–	28
Alleyne, M.W.	328	537	52	256	14943	30.81	22	72	6	272/3
Alok Kapali	49	86	3	85	1659	19.98	–	9	–	23
Ambrose, T.R.	47	76	5	149	2322	32.70	2	15	–	76/10
Anderson, J.M.	50	59	30	37*	290	10.00	–	–	–	19
Andrew, G.M.	11	14	1	44	163	12.53	–	–	–	5
Anwar, O.S.	10	12	–	99	264	22.00	–	2	–	2
Anwar Hossain	24	35	13	28	158	7.18	–	–	–	6
Anyon, J.E.	11	15	8	21	52	7.42	–	–	–	5
Astle, N.J.	149	238	22	223	8298	38.41	18	43	–	121
Atri, V.	12	22	3	98	548	28.84	–	4	–	8
Averis, J.M.M.	66	86	17	48*	856	12.40	–	–	–	14
Azhar Mahmood	119	185	22	204*	4966	30.46	5	27	–	98
Baker, T.M.	1	1	–	0	0	0.00	–	–	–	–
Balcombe, D.J.	3	3	–	73	89	29.66	–	1	–	1
Ball, M.C.J.	183	280	53	75	4418	19.46	–	15	–	217
Bandara, C.M.	89	121	26	79	1733	18.24	–	8	–	57
Banerjee, V.	2	4	–	29	67	16.75	–	–	–	–
Bassano, C.W.G.	59	101	9	186*	3132	34.04	5	20	1	34
Batty, G.J.	76	116	18	133	2290	23.36	1	11	–	54
Batty, J.N.	127	189	27	168*	5245	32.37	10	24	–	334/42
Bell, I.R.	84	142	13	262*	5553	43.04	13	28	2	51
Benham, C.C.	9	16	1	74	319	21.26	–	1	–	5
Benkenstein, D.M.	130	188	21	259	7423	44.44	18	40	1	94

F-C	M	I	NO	HS	Runs	Avge	100	50	1000	Ct/St
Benning, J.G.E.	12	21	1	128	677	33.85	2	3	–	4
Betts, M.M.	115	164	37	73	1879	14.79	–	5	–	37
Bichel, A.J.	147	191	18	142	4237	24.49	6	15	–	77
Bicknell, D.J.	306	531	43	235*	19080	39.09	46	87	9	105
Bicknell, M.P.	288	352	85	141	6584	24.65	3	25	–	101
Bishop, J.E.	25	33	5	66	433	15.46	–	4	–	7
Blackwell, I.D.	111	172	13	247*	6232	39.19	16	29	2	44
Blain, J.A.R.	33	38	16	34	272	12.36	–	–	–	7
Bond, S.E.	42	48	18	100	587	19.56	1	2	–	20
Bopara, R.S.	30	51	10	105*	1364	33.26	1	5	–	21
Borrington, P.M.	2	2	–	28	32	16.00	–	–	–	–
Botha, A.G.	72	116	19	156*	2419	24.93	2	8	–	48
Bracken, N.W.	49	66	25	38*	716	17.46	–	–	–	13
Breese, G.R.	83	129	18	165*	3216	28.97	2	24	–	66
Bresnan, T.T.	29	39	6	74	563	17.06	–	4	–	8
Bridge, G.D.	39	64	12	52	918	17.65	–	3	–	20
Brignull, D.S.	5	6	2	46	58	14.50	–	–	–	–
Broad, S.C.J.	10	12	2	31	107	10.70	–	–	–	1
Brophy, G.L.	53	86	14	185	2508	34.83	5	12	–	125/7
Brown, A.D.	215	338	35	295*	13164	43.44	39	53	7	226/1
Brown, D.O.	10	16	–	77	442	27.62	–	4	–	7
Brown, D.R.	196	296	38	203	8083	31.32	10	42	1	124
Brown, J.F.	90	104	46	38	423	7.29	–	–	–	18
Brown, M.J.	41	73	7	109*	1892	28.66	2	13	–	37
Bruce, J.T.A.	22	25	8	21*	107	6.29	–	–	–	8
Bruce, T.O.	3	4	2	26	86	43.00	–	–	–	4
Bryant, J.D.C.	83	150	17	234*	4288	32.24	8	20	–	55
Buckham, C.T.	2	3	2	8	14	14.00	–	–	–	2
Burnell, W.F.	4	6	–	49	64	10.66	–	–	–	–
Burns, M.	154	248	14	221	7648	32.68	8	51	2	142/7
Burrows, T.G.	1	2	–	42	55	27.50	–	–	–	5
Butcher, M.A.	238	410	30	259	14881	39.16	29	82	7	218
Caddick, A.R.	228	303	58	92	3616	14.75	–	7	–	78
Cairns, C.L.	216	340	38	158	10680	35.36	13	71	1	78
Carberry, M.A.	35	59	6	153*	2044	38.56	4	11	–	16
Carter, N.M.	58	76	15	103	1201	19.68	1	3	–	19
Chambers, M.A.	1	1	1	2*	2	–	–	–	–	–
Chandana, U.D.U.	141	191	16	194	5434	31.05	8	29	–	110
Chapple, G.	190	262	53	155	5105	24.42	6	22	–	62
Cherry, D.D.	24	42	1	226	1094	26.68	2	1	–	5
Chervak, J.A.	1	2	–	48	74	37.00	–	–	–	1
Chilton, M.J.	113	184	13	130	5583	32.64	15	19	1	90
Clark, S.	3	3	1	47*	57	28.50	–	–	–	1
Clark, S.R.	56	79	23	35	710	12.67	–	–	–	14
Clarke, M.J.	68	117	6	151	4208	37.90	13	17	–	67
Clarke, R.	51	84	9	153*	2818	37.57	7	12	–	60
Claydon, M.E.	1									
Cleary, M.F.	30	44	10	58	615	18.08	–	1	–	14
Clewley, N.J.	2	2	2	2*	3	–	–	–	–	1
Clinton, P.J.S.	5	6	–	24	57	9.50	–	–	–	1
Clinton, R.S.	35	61	3	107	1601	27.60	3	9	–	22
Clough, G.D.	10	15	2	55	147	11.30	–	1	–	3
Coetzer, K.J.	8	13	3	133*	358	35.80	1	1	–	–
Collingwood, P.D.	119	207	14	190	6464	33.49	14	31	2	125

F-C	M	I	NO	HS	Runs	Avge	100	50	1000	Ct/St
Compton, N.R.D.	5	9	4	56*	206	41.20	–	1	–	3
Cook, A.N.	36	64	5	195	2567	43.50	6	15	1	40
Cook, S.J.	80	105	13	93*	1540	16.73	–	3	–	26
Cork, D.G.	251	373	48	200*	8282	25.48	7	49	–	185
Cosker, D.A.	121	150	48	52	1319	12.93	–	1	–	83
Cowan, A.P.	106	158	30	94	2268	17.71	–	9	–	52
Crawley, J.P.	303	500	50	311*	21034	46.74	46	116	9	199/1
Croft, R.D.B.	318	471	85	143	10121	26.22	6	45	–	150
Croft, S.J.	1	1	–	6	6	6.00	–	–	–	–
Crook, A.R.	5	7	–	88	200	28.57	–	1	–	4
Crook, S.P.	11	12	2	97	472	47.20	–	4	–	2
Cross, G.D.	2	3	–	22	38	12.66	–	–	–	9/2
Cullen, D.J.	10	18	5	42	219	16.84	–	–	–	5
Cummins, R.A.G.	8	8	4	26	35	8.75	–	–	–	1
Cusden, S.M.J.	5	7	5	12*	28	14.00	–	–	–	2
Daggett, L.M.	9	11	6	7	21	4.20	–	–	–	–
Dale, M.A.P.	6	10	1	48	241	26.77	–	–	–	–
Daley, S.R.	2	1	–	12	12	12.00	–	–	–	1
Dalrymple, J.W.M.	49	83	10	244	2664	36.49	5	12	–	28
Danish Kaneria	85	104	53	47	445	8.72	–	–	–	30
Davies, A.M.	41	63	23	62	478	11.95	–	1	–	7
Davies, A.P.	30	40	8	41*	436	13.62	–	–	–	7
Davies, S.M.	11	19	1	148	627	34.83	1	2	–	11/3
Davis, M.J.G.	127	187	30	168	2941	18.73	2	8	–	68
Dawood, I.	39	61	10	102	1122	22.00	1	4	–	94/6
Dawson, R.K.J.	80	119	14	87	2369	22.56	–	10	–	44
Dean, K.J.	100	136	42	54*	1111	11.81	–	2	–	20
De Bruyn, Z.	73	125	15	266*	4651	42.28	10	23	0+1	46
DeFreitas, P.A.J.	372	533	50	123*	10991	22.75	10	54	–	127
Denly, J.L.	2	3	–	10	14	4.66	–	–	–	–
Dennington, M.J.	11	17	3	55	269	19.21	–	3	–	5
Dernbach, J.W.	4	4	2	3	5	2.50	–	–	–	1
Dexter, N.J.	3	6	1	79*	176	35.20	–	2	–	4
Di Venuto, M.J.	209	371	19	230	15013	42.65	32	91	5	229
Dixey, P.G.	1	2	1	24	40	40.00	–	–	–	3
Doran, G.P.	2	1	1	9*	9	–	–	–	–	6/2
Doshi, N.D.	30	43	7	33	299	8.30	–	–	–	4
Durston, W.J.	12	20	3	146*	538	31.64	1	1	–	18
Ealham, M.A.	223	343	52	153	9495	32.62	10	59	1	114
Edwards, N.J.	17	31	–	160	997	32.16	1	3	–	13
Edwards, P.D.	5	8	5	43	96	32.00	–	–	–	1
Elliott, M.T.G.	190	349	26	203	16141	49.97	50	76	3+5	206
Enamul Haque	24	37	19	18	114	6.33	–	–	–	8
Ervine, S.M.	46	76	7	126	2331	33.78	4	15	–	44
Eustace, S.M.	1									1
Ferley, R.S.	23	31	7	78*	466	19.41	–	2	–	8
Finn, S.T.	1									–
Fisher, I.D.	70	104	17	103*	1962	22.55	1	7	–	25
Fleming, S.P.	200	332	29	274*	12941	42.70	27	74	1	261
Flintoff, A.	141	218	15	167	7347	36.19	15	41	–	149
Flower, A.	206	345	63	232*	14843	52.63	42	72	4	343/21
Flower, G.W.	161	278	22	243*	9704	37.90	20	54	–	144
Footitt, M.H.A.	2	3	1	19*	35	17.50	–	–	–	1
Foster, E.J.	1	2	1	83	105	105.00	–	1	–	–

F-C	M	I	NO	HS	Runs	Avge	100	50	1000	Ct/St
Foster, J.S.	89	133	17	212	3766	32.46	6	16	1	211/25
Fox, D.R.	3	4	–	184	295	73.75	2	–	–	1
France, B.J.	11	20	–	56	315	15.75	–	2	–	5
Francis, J.D.	49	87	8	125*	2507	31.73	6	14	1	27
Francis, S.R.G.	55	72	32	44	424	10.60	–	–	–	17
Franks, P.J.	121	177	37	123*	3781	27.00	3	17	–	43
Friedlander, M.J.	6	9	–	81	164	18.22	–	1	–	2
Friend, T.J.	44	66	9	183	1791	31.42	3	7	–	33
Frost, T.	84	121	16	135*	2747	26.16	3	12	–	205/16
Fulton, D.P.	185	326	19	208*	11156	36.33	26	47	3	259
Gallian, J.E.R.	204	350	35	312	12554	39.85	32	60	6	174
Ganguly, S.C.	192	300	37	200*	11544	43.89	22	69	–	141
Gayle, C.H.	118	212	16	317	8860	45.20	22	43	0+1	111
Gazzard, C.M.	14	20	4	74	427	26.68	–	1	–	26/1
Gibson, O.D.	149	222	30	101*	4430	23.07	1	23	–	57
Gidman, A.P.R.	52	90	7	142	2867	34.54	4	19	1	40
Gifford, W.M.	3	5	1	33	78	19.50	–	–	–	3
Gilchrist, A.C.	164	244	44	204*	9268	46.34	28	36	–	645/46
Giles, A.F.	173	239	44	128*	5133	26.32	3	22	–	77
Gillespie, J.N.	118	154	39	58	1816	15.79	–	6	–	46
Godleman, B.A.	1	1	1	69*	69	–	–	1	–	–
Golwalkar, Y.A.	30	43	11	41*	282	8.81	–	–	–	13
Goodwin, M.W.	175	306	23	335*	13434	47.46	40	58	4+1	110
Gough, D.	219	293	54	121	4067	17.01	1	17	–	44
Grant, R.N.	4	7	1	33	103	17.16	–	–	–	1
Gray, A.K.D.	26	39	8	104	886	28.58	1	3	–	25
Greenidge, C.G.	36	41	7	46	306	9.00	–	–	–	12
Guy, S.M.	26	37	4	42	462	14.00	–	–	–	71/7
Habib, A.	158	240	29	215	8869	42.03	21	46	2	79
Habibul Bashar	63	118	4	224	3930	34.47	6	27	–	28
Haddin, B.J.	61	104	12	154	3445	37.44	4	22	–	163/16
Hall, A.J.	106	156	20	163	4586	33.72	5	31	–	77
Hamilton-Brown, R.J.	1	2	–	9	14	7.00	–	–	–	1
Hancock, T.H.C.	185	322	21	220*	8485	28.18	7	51	1	124
Harbhajan Singh	100	132	26	84	1955	18.44	–	6	–	48
Hardinges, M.A.	24	37	4	172	731	22.15	1	2	–	16
Harmison, S.J.	116	157	43	42	1038	9.10	–	–	–	21
Harris, A.J.	104	141	37	41*	911	8.75	–	–	–	32
Harrison, A.J.	2	2	1	34*	34	34.00	–	–	–	–
Harrison, D.S.	55	82	11	88	1060	14.92	–	3	–	20
Harrison, P.W.	7	10	3	54	220	31.42	–	1	–	9
Harvey, I.J.	149	246	23	209*	7428	33.30	11	43	–	103
Hasanuzzaman	33	54	5	109	1353	27.61	2	10	–	24/1
Havell, P.M.R.	16	21	15	13*	52	8.66	–	–	–	4
Hayden, M.L.	256	443	44	380	21380	53.58	69	88	3+4	244
Hayward, M.	114	129	47	55*	926	11.29	–	1	–	32
Heath, D.R.	9	16	1	75	256	17.06	–	2	–	6
Heather, S.A.	1	1	–	7	7	7.00	–	–	–	–
Hegg, W.K.	348	504	99	134	11302	27.90	7	55	–	857/94
Hembry, T.D.C.	3	5	–	72	128	25.60	–	1	–	1
Hemp, D.L.	218	370	34	186*	12066	35.91	22	69	5	142
Henderson, C.W.	146	196	48	71	2486	16.79	–	7	–	56
Heywood, J.J.N.	4	6	2	19*	30	7.50	–	–	–	6
Hick, G.A.	486	806	78	405*	38437	52.79	128	147	18+1	632

171

F-C	M	I	NO	HS	Runs	Avge	100	50	1000	Ct/St
Hildreth, J.C.	30	51	6	125*	1706	37.91	4	11	–	27
Hodd, A.J.	2	2	2	57*	112	–	–	2	–	3
Hodge, B.J.	162	289	26	302*	12317	46.83	37	45	2+2	91
Hodnett, G.P.	1	2	–	49	59	29.50	–	–	–	1
Hogg, K.W.	21	29	1	53	448	16.00	–	3	–	9
Hoggard, M.J.	123	154	52	89*	946	9.27	–	2	–	36
Holt, D.R.	1	1	–	5	5	5.00	–	–	–	1
Hooper, M.R.	1	1	–	2	2	2.00	–	–	–	1
Hopkinson, C.D.	11	18	1	64	403	23.70	–	3	–	5
Horton, P.J.	8	11	1	99	374	37.40	–	2	–	3/1
Howells, P.W.	4	7	3	51*	111	27.75	–	1	–	9
Huggins, T.B.	11	17	2	82*	403	26.86	–	2	–	4
Hughes, J.	42	69	3	134*	1556	23.57	3	4	–	27
Hunter, I.D.	35	54	10	65	795	18.06	–	2	–	9
Hussey, D.J.	55	79	9	232*	3892	55.60	15	15	2	69
Hussey, M.E.K.	173	311	26	331*	15094	52.96	38	66	4	194
Hutchison, P.M.	62	66	31	30	305	8.71	–	–	–	14
Hutton, B.L.	95	162	14	152	4933	33.33	15	17	2	116
Irani, R.C.	212	344	42	207*	11932	39.50	23	66	6	74
Jacklin, B.D.	1	2	1	4	4	4.00	–	–	–	–
James, G.D.	4	8	1	33*	89	12.71	–	–	–	–
Jaques, P.A.	64	112	5	243	5877	54.92	16	27	3+1	52
Javed Omar	63	119	1	167	3170	26.86	5	16	–	22
Jayasuriya, S.T.	238	377	33	340	13805	40.13	29	65	0+1	150
Jefferson, W.I.	66	119	11	222	4295	39.76	11	17	1	58
Johnson, M.G.	6	8	3	51*	152	30.40	–	1	–	–
Johnson, R.L.	154	211	27	118	3286	17.85	2	7	–	60
Jones, C.M.P.	1	–	–	–	–	–	–	–	–	–
Jones, G.O.	53	75	10	108*	2316	35.63	4	13	–	160/12
Jones, K.J.F.	1	2	–	14	14	7.00	–	–	–	1
Jones, P.S.	83	99	24	105	1322	17.62	1	4	–	17
Jones, S.P.	74	88	29	46	712	12.06	–	–	–	17
Joseph, R.H.	10	13	5	26	89	11.12	–	–	–	4
Joyce, E.C.	78	130	13	192	5533	47.29	14	31	4	65
Kartik, M.	87	102	11	79	1671	18.36	–	10	–	45
Kasprowicz, M.S.	225	303	63	92	4173	17.38	–	11	–	91
Katich, S.M.	143	246	33	228*	10514	49.36	28	55	2+3	137
Keedy, G.	132	151	78	57	816	11.17	–	1	–	37
Keegan, C.B.	40	47	5	44	496	11.80	–	–	–	11
Kemp, J.M.	76	124	14	188	4033	36.66	8	19	–	84
Kemp, R.A.	1	2	–	1	1	0.50	–	–	–	–
Kenway, D.A.	93	163	15	166	4382	29.60	7	20	1	85/1
Key, R.W.T.	144	249	12	221	9694	40.90	28	39	4	90
Khaled Masud	68	122	15	201*	2812	26.28	3	12	–	110/13
Khalid, S.A.	10	9	2	20	64	9.14	–	–	–	3
Khan, A.	48	55	16	78	726	18.61	–	3	–	8
Killeen, N.	89	131	27	48	1225	11.77	–	–	–	23
King, R.E.	4	5	–	17	19	3.80	–	–	–	–
Kirby, S.P.	61	84	25	57	447	7.57	–	1	–	13
Kirtley, R.J.	150	208	68	59	1760	12.57	–	3	–	50
Klusener, L.	134	186	39	174	5303	36.07	8	29	–	74
Knappett, J.P.T.	6	8	1	73	277	39.57	–	2	–	12/1
Knight, N.V.	223	379	42	303*	15102	44.81	38	71	6	270
Krejza, J.J.	10	15	2	63	271	20.84	–	2	–	9

172

F-C	M	I	NO	HS	Runs	Avge	100	50	1000	Ct/St
Kruis, G.J.	92	134	36	59	1406	14.34	–	2	–	39
Kumble, A.	196	254	53	154*	4618	22.97	6	15	–	91
Lamb, G.A.	26	40	4	100*	842	23.38	1	5	–	22
Lamb, N.J.	2	3	–	23	31	10.33	–	–	–	–
Langer, J.L.	277	486	47	274*	22410	51.04	71	86	3+6	225
Langeveldt, C.K.	56	68	23	56	666	14.80	–	1	–	14
Laraman, A.W.	47	56	11	148*	1378	30.62	1	7	–	17
Law, S.G.	322	531	58	263	23957	50.64	71	109	7+2	362
Lawson, M.A.K.	6	9	2	20*	64	9.14	–	–	–	1
Leatherdale, D.A.	215	347	41	157	10017	32.73	14	54	1	151
Lee, B.	76	87	16	79	1297	18.26	–	4	–	21
Lehmann, D.S.	248	420	28	255	21991	56.09	70	100	4+5	129
Lewis, J.	145	205	45	62	2244	14.02	–	4	–	34
Lewis, J.J.B.	196	349	26	210*	10466	32.40	16	64	4	112
Lewis, M.L.	54	71	18	54*	479	9.03	–	1	–	27
Lewry, J.D.	136	186	42	72	1520	10.55	–	2	–	31
Liddle, C.J.	1	–	–	–	–	–	–	–	–	–
Linley, T.E.	7	7	–	42	75	10.71	–	–	–	1
Logan, R.J.	43	61	13	37*	486	10.12	–	–	–	14
Loudon, A.G.R.	39	65	5	172	1954	32.56	1	12	–	28
Louw, J.	56	82	11	124	1450	20.42	1	7	–	23
Love, M.L.	184	320	30	300*	14620	50.41	36	68	2+3	234
Lowe, J.A.	4	8	–	80	211	26.37	–	1	–	2
Loye, M.B.	196	312	27	322*	11543	40.50	32	46	5	98
Lucas, D.S.	23	28	8	49	436	21.80	–	–	–	3
Lumb, M.J.	65	116	10	130	3323	31.34	6	18	1	38
Lungley, T.	22	35	5	47	397	13.23	–	–	–	7
MacGill, S.C.G.	150	178	46	53	1288	9.75	–	1	–	66
McGrath, A.	155	266	20	174	8523	34.64	18	37	1	104
McGrath, G.D.	176	180	62	61	928	7.86	–	2	–	50
McLean, J.J.	12	17	1	68	404	25.25	–	4	–	11
McLean, N.A.M.	145	216	32	76	2458	13.35	–	3	–	41
McMahon, P.J.	17	21	3	99	340	18.88	–	2	–	11
McMillan, C.D.	125	205	23	168*	7131	39.18	13	42	–	51
Maddy, D.L.	203	331	20	229*	10135	32.58	19	49	4	212
Maher, J.P.	151	268	27	217	10024	41.59	21	49	1+2	159/2
Mahmood, S.I.	29	37	6	94	540	17.41	–	2	–	4
Maiden, A.J.	10	14	1	211*	468	36.00	1	2	–	3
Malik, M.N.	31	39	14	39*	208	8.32	–	–	–	3
Mann, R.J.	5	9	–	63	216	24.00	–	2	–	5
Marshall, H.J.H.	56	92	5	160	2587	29.73	3	12	–	29
Marshall, S.J.	16	26	6	126*	733	36.65	1	3	–	4
Martin-Jenkins, R.S.C.	116	180	22	205*	4765	30.15	3	24	1	33
Martyn, D.R.	194	324	44	238	14144	50.51	43	71	–	150/2
Mascarenhas, A.D.	130	196	24	104	4295	24.97	6	16	–	54
Mashrafe Mortaza	24	43	6	132*	622	16.81	1	2	–	7
Mason, M.S.	58	76	18	63	839	14.46	–	3	–	11
Masters, D.D.	64	78	19	119	734	12.44	1	1	–	20
Maunders, J.K.	40	73	2	171	2010	28.30	4	8	–	17
Maynard, M.P.	395	643	60	243	24799	42.53	59	131	13	372/7
Mees, T.	9	12	2	36*	110	11.00	–	–	–	1
Mehrab Hossain	12	19	2	103*	300	17.64	1	1	–	9
Middlebrook, J.D.	89	131	15	115	2718	23.43	2	10	–	41
Mitchell, D.K.H.	6	10	2	63*	196	24.50	–	2	–	6

F-C	M	I	NO	HS	Runs	Avge	100	50	1000	Ct/St
Mohammad Akram	108	138	39	35*	863	8.71	–	–	–	27
Mohammad Amin	1	1	–	1	1	1.00	–	–	–	–
Mohammad Ashraful	58	108	4	158*	2986	28.71	8	14	–	25
Mohammad Asif	44	63	27	42	349	9.69	–	–	–	21
Mohammad Rafique	38	63	9	111	1135	21.01	1	6	–	16
Mongia, D.	100	148	13	308*	6664	49.36	21	26	0+1	108
Montgomerie, R.R.	217	376	32	196	12303	35.76	26	66	5	200
Moore, S.C.	37	66	8	246	2500	43.10	5	10	2	20
Moreton, S.J.P.	3	5	–	74	139	27.80	–	1	–	1
Morgan, E.J.G.	3	6	–	151	250	41.66	1	1	–	–
Morris, J.C.	1	2	–	21	34	17.00	–	–	–	1
Morse, E.J.	2	2	1	7*	7	7.00	–	–	–	–
Moss, J.	66	112	8	172*	3905	37.54	7	26	1	33
Muchall, G.J.	64	115	6	142*	3231	29.64	5	16	–	40
Munday, M.K.	12	8	5	14	16	5.33	–	–	–	5
Muralitharan, M.	183	224	65	67	1869	11.75	–	1	–	100
Murtagh, C.P.	3	5	2	37*	52	17.33	–	–	–	2
Murtagh, T.J.	35	50	20	74*	851	28.36	–	6	–	15
Mushfiqur Rahim	7	13	3	115	448	44.80	2	2	–	9/1
Mushfiqur Rahman	30	54	5	115	1161	23.69	1	6	–	18
Mushtaq Ahmed	269	337	45	90*	4649	15.92	–	19	–	110
Mustard, P.	34	52	2	80	1287	25.74	–	6	–	98/6
Nafis Iqbal	38	66	5	147	1893	31.03	3	10	–	7
Napier, G.R.	65	95	17	106*	2298	29.46	2	14	–	29
Nash, C.D.	9	13	2	63	363	33.00	–	4	–	5
Nash, D.C.	116	164	33	114	4295	32.78	7	20	–	239/19
Naved-ul-Hasan	72	104	13	139	2202	24.19	2	7	–	42
Nazimuddin	25	40	3	204	1384	37.40	4	6	–	12
Needham, J.	1	2	1	6	7	7.00	–	–	–	–
Nel, A.	73	77	29	44	718	14.95	–	–	–	24
New, T.J.	12	18	4	89	423	30.21	–	3	–	18/2
Newby, O.J.	4	4	2	38*	49	24.50	–	–	–	–
Newman, S.A.	41	72	2	219	3045	43.50	8	15	2	32
Nicholson, M.J.	63	94	17	101*	1518	19.71	1	3	–	34
Nixon, P.A.	281	414	91	134*	10227	31.66	14	46	1	743/62
Noffke, A.A.	70	86	18	114*	1704	25.05	1	6	–	24
North, M.J.	71	123	10	219	4467	39.53	9	27	0+1	45
Ntini, M.	122	137	41	34*	943	9.82	–	–	–	30
Oberoi, S.	7	11	–	247	557	50.63	1	2	–	5
O'Brien, N.J.	30	45	5	176	1192	33.11	2	6	–	88/10
Onions, G.	12	16	7	20*	89	9.88	–	–	–	3
Ormond, J.	119	144	34	57	1682	15.29	–	2	–	26
O'Shea, M.P.	3	5	–	24	52	10.40	–	–	–	1
Padget, C.D.	4	4	2	7	7	3.50	–	–	–	–
Palladino, A.P.	17	18	8	41	171	17.10	–	–	–	5
Panesar, M.S.	28	34	14	39*	156	7.80	–	–	–	9
Park, G.T.	9	13	2	68	331	30.09	–	1	–	15
Parker, L.C.	12	18	3	89	472	31.46	–	2	–	6
Parsons, K.A.	120	194	21	193*	4813	27.82	5	26	–	106
Parsons, M.	2	3	1	6*	11	5.50	–	–	–	–
Patel, M.M.	189	254	49	87	3650	17.80	–	15	–	92
Patel, S.R.	5	7	–	55	126	18.00	–	1	–	1
Pathan, I.K.	48	59	15	68	935	21.25	–	4	–	16
Patterson, S.A.	1	–	–	–	–	–	–	–	–	1

174

F-C	M	I	NO	HS	Runs	Avge	100	50	1000	Ct/St
Pearson, J.A.	8	16	2	68	320	22.85	–	3	–	4
Peng, N.	68	116	2	158	2732	23.96	4	12	–	35
Peploe, C.T.	17	24	5	42	300	15.78	–	–	–	7
Peters, S.D.	116	193	17	165	5278	29.98	9	27	1	86
Pettini, M.L.	11	19	2	78	516	30.35	–	5	–	9
Phillips, B.J.	63	89	15	100*	1494	20.18	1	7	–	13
Phillips, T.J.	20	29	5	89	504	21.00	–	2	–	7
Phythian, M.J.	2	1	–	0	0	0.00	–	–	–	6
Pietersen, C.	18	28	7	45	327	15.57	–	–	–	4
Pietersen, K.P.	83	134	12	254*	6409	52.53	22	28	3	80
Pipe, D.J.	31	47	5	104*	781	18.59	1	2	–	81/7
Piper, K.J.	200	275	44	116*	4618	19.99	2	14	–	504/36
Plunkett, L.E.	31	47	13	74*	722	21.23	–	2	–	10
Ponting, R.T.	187	313	45	257	15640	58.35	56	62	–	190
Pothas, N.	146	227	36	165	7102	37.18	15	35	–	398/36
Powell, M.J. (Gm)	138	233	20	200*	8118	38.11	17	42	4	87
Powell, M.J. (Wa)	125	208	9	236	6511	32.71	12	35	1	89
Poynter, A.D.	1	1	–	1	1	1.00	–	–	–	2
Pratt, A.J.	47	84	1	150	2217	26.71	1	14	1	32
Pretorius, D.	67	71	19	43	508	9.76	–	–	–	16
Price, R.W.	71	114	20	117*	1502	15.97	1	6	–	25
Prior, M.J.	88	138	13	201*	4742	37.93	11	25	2	190/7
Pyrah, R.M.	6	10	1	78	236	26.22	–	1	–	1
Rajin Saleh	45	80	8	130*	2546	35.36	6	10	–	41
Ramprakash, M.R.	371	612	77	279*	26355	49.26	79	121	15	209
Read, C.M.W.	155	233	36	160	5838	29.63	5	33	–	442/22
Read, G.G.	5	6	2	25	52	13.00	–	–	–	4
Richards, M.A.	4	4	–	43	62	15.50	–	–	–	3
Richardson, A.	77	78	30	91	529	11.02	–	1	–	20
Roberts, T.W.	32	51	2	89	1235	25.20	–	9	–	21
Robinson, D.D.J.	168	295	14	200	9344	33.25	20	46	3	142
Rogers, C.J.L.	52	94	6	209	4040	45.90	11	19	–	50
Rudge, W.D.	5	8	1	15	35	5.00	–	–	–	2
Rudolph, J.A.	74	131	9	222*	4972	40.75	13	23	–	53
Sadler, J.L.	27	46	7	145	1302	33.38	2	7	–	16
Saggers, M.J.	93	117	31	64	1008	11.72	–	2	–	26
Saker, N.C.	3	4	–	5	6	1.50	–	–	–	–
Sales, D.J.G.	138	216	19	303*	7718	39.17	15	41	3	117
Salisbury, I.D.K.	289	372	75	101*	6082	20.47	2	21	–	184
Sampson, P.J.	5	9	4	42	91	18.20	–	–	–	–
Saqlain Mushtaq	176	242	54	101*	3111	16.54	1	12	–	64
Sarwan, R.R.	140	237	18	261*	8258	37.70	18	47	–	104
Savill, T.E.	14	19	4	59	206	13.73	–	1	–	10
Sayers, J.J.	26	44	2	147	1505	35.83	4	8	–	14
Scott, B.J.M.	25	39	10	101*	757	26.10	1	4	–	58/9
Scott, G.M.	8	15	2	61*	340	26.15	–	1	–	3
Shafayat, B.M.	44	76	1	161	2390	31.86	4	13	1	31/1
Shah, O.A.	149	251	23	203	9528	41.78	26	50	5	114
Shahadat Hossain	12	18	10	19*	88	11.00	–	–	–	1
Shahin Hossain	33	55	5	119*	1262	25.24	2	7	–	83/17
Shahriar Nafis	12	23	1	97	758	34.45	–	7	–	6
Shankar, A.	12	20	–	143	384	19.20	1	–	–	5
Shantry, A.J.	5	6	4	38*	62	31.00	–	–	–	2
Sharif, Z.K.	9	14	2	67	322	26.83	–	3	–	3

175

F-C	M	I	NO	HS	Runs	Avge	100	50	1000	Ct/St
Sheikh, M.A.	38	53	13	58*	968	24.20	–	3	–	4
Sheriyar, A.	152	165	65	21	829	8.29	–	–	–	22
Shilvock, D.J.F.	1	–	–	–	–	–	–	–	–	–
Shoaib Akhtar	114	160	45	59*	1326	11.53	–	1	–	35
Shreck, C.E.	19	21	10	67	19	6.09	–	–	–	3
Sidebottom, R.J.	85	104	30	54	802	10.83	–	1	–	32
Sillence, R.J.	13	18	–	101	379	21.05	1	1	–	3
Silverwood, C.E.W.	148	197	38	80	2511	15.79	–	8	–	34
Singh, A. (CU)	5	10	1	75	176	19.55	–	1	–	–
Singh, A. (Nt)	107	175	7	187	5437	32.36	11	24	2	42
Singh, K.R.	3	5	1	29*	54	13.50	–	–	–	3
Smith, B.F.	266	414	48	204	15320	41.85	38	74	7	150
Smith, E.T.	151	259	14	213	9964	40.66	24	44	6	61
Smith, G.C.	74	127	10	311	6270	53.58	19	21	–	102
Smith, G.J.	141	173	56	68	1598	13.65	–	2	–	29
Smith, G.M.	9	18	1	56*	311	18.29	–	2	–	1
Smith, T.C.	1	1	–	0	0	0.00	–	–	–	1
Smith, W.R.	15	23	3	156	548	27.40	1	1	–	10
Snape, J.N.	113	169	30	131	3975	28.59	3	22	–	71
Snell, S.D.	2	4	1	83*	141	47.00	–	1	–	4
Solanki, V.S.	184	299	21	185	9767	35.13	15	56	2	219
Spearman, C.M.	163	294	15	341	10584	37.93	22	49	2	153
Stearn, C.P.	1	1	1	33*	33	–	–	–	–	1
Stephenson, J.P.	303	510	56	202*	14772	32.53	25	78	5	182
Stevens, D.I.	96	161	9	208	4819	31.70	8	29	1	77
Steyn, D.W.	18	22	8	82	167	11.92	–	1	–	6
Stiff, D.A.	7	6	3	18	57	19.00	–	–	–	/
Strauss, A.J.	106	187	12	176	7436	42.49	18	34	3	71
Streak, H.H.	145	217	39	131	4839	27.18	6	23	–	53
Stubbings, S.D.	88	159	7	151	4823	31.73	8	27	2	36
Styris, S.B.	88	148	15	212*	4131	31.06	7	19	–	63
Suman, A.K.	16	15	6	39	112	12.44	–	–	–	8
Suppiah, A.V.	12	21	–	123	506	24.09	1	2	–	3
Sutcliffe, I.J.	162	258	22	203	8250	34.95	13	46	3	91
Sutton, L.D.	87	154	20	140*	4098	30.58	5	14	–	181/7
Swann, G.P.	126	181	10	183	4386	25.64	4	20	–	85
Syed Rasel	26	36	9	33	307	11.37	–	–	–	6
Symonds, A.	187	313	28	254*	12269	43.04	37	49	2	133
Tahir, N.	17	19	8	49	245	22.27	–	–	–	1
Tait, S.W.	29	45	19	58	282	10.84	–	1	–	6
Talha Jubair	22	35	9	50	207	7.96	–	1	–	6
Tapash Baisya	44	75	13	66	827	13.33	–	3	–	15
Taylor, B.V.	47	62	23	40	426	10.92	–	–	–	5
Taylor, C.G.	68	121	7	196	3897	34.18	10	12	1	43
Taylor, C.R.	16	27	3	52*	416	17.33	–	2	–	8
Ten Doeschate, R.N.	8	7	–	98	237	33.85	–	2	–	4
Thomas, I.J.	32	54	4	82	1070	21.40	–	6	–	21
Thomas, S.D.	169	234	44	138	3977	20.93	2	18	–	56
Thompson, G.J.	5	4	2	35	43	21.50	–	–	–	3
Thornely, D.J.	20	34	3	261*	1562	50.38	5	9	0+1	12
Thornicroft, N.D.	7	12	5	30	54	7.71	–	–	–	1
Thorp, C.D.	11	14	–	26	115	8.21	–	–	–	5
Thorpe, G.P.	341	567	80	223*	21937	45.04	49	122	9	291
Timms, R.T.	3	6	–	57	105	17.50	–	1	–	–

F-C	M	I	NO	HS	Runs	Avge	100	50	1000	Ct/St
Tomlinson, J.A	15	24	11	23	73	5.61	–	–	–	5
Tredwell, J.C.	32	45	6	61	827	21.20	–	3	–	34
Trego, P.D.	22	32	4	140	768	27.42	1	3	–	8
Tremlett, C.T.	52	70	21	64	939	19.16	–	2	–	16
Trescothick, M.E.	192	332	18	219	11362	36.18	21	61	–	214
Trott, I.J.L.	62	108	11	210	3894	40.14	7	24	2	61
Troughton, J.O.	55	86	7	131*	3177	40.21	9	18	1	25
Tudor, A.J.	95	122	27	116	2127	22.38	1	7	–	29
Turner, M.L.	2	2	1	18	19	19.00	–	–	–	–
Turner, R.J.	250	380	70	144	9519	30.70	10	46	2	703/50
Tushar Imran	40	72	5	119	1914	28.56	5	9	–	18
Udal, S.D.	240	341	65	117*	6465	23.42	1	28	–	112
Vaas, W.P.U.C.J.	152	202	39	134	3659	22.44	3	13	–	46
Van der Wath, J.J.	48	73	14	113*	1570	26.61	2	8	–	19
Van Jaarsveld, M.	125	214	20	262*	8617	44.41	24	36	1+1	142
Vaughan, M.P.	224	395	24	197	14272	38.46	39	58	4	105
Vettori, D.L.	103	142	21	137*	2794	23.09	2	15	–	46
Wagg, G.G.	10	15	2	74	284	21.84	–	2	–	2
Wagh, M.A.	127	210	18	315	7429	38.69	18	33	4	69
Wainwright, D.J.	6	7	2	62	158	31.60	–	1	–	4
Walker, M.J.	149	247	28	275*	7522	34.34	17	30	2	106
Walker, N.G.E.	18	23	6	80	377	22.17	–	3	–	7
Wallace, M.A.	86	141	12	121	3542	27.45	4	18	–	232/13
Ward, I.J.	138	230	17	168*	8575	40.25	23	43	3	72
Warne, S.K.	250	341	41	107*	5676	18.92	2	21	–	212
Warren, N.A.	8	8	4	11	24	6.00	–	–	–	–
Warren, R.J.	141	230	26	201*	7636	37.43	15	40	1	125/5
Waters, H.T.	7	13	7	34	41	6.83	–	–	–	–
Watkins, R.E.	5	9	–	41	131	14.55	–	–	–	–
Watson, S.R.	43	74	8	203*	3197	48.43	9	16	–	28
Webley, T.	15	26	2	104	833	34.70	1	5	–	7
Wedge, S.A.	2	2	2	0*	0	–	–	–	–	–
Weekes, P.N.	228	357	51	171*	10712	35.00	19	55	2	210
Welch, G.	156	242	38	115*	4722	23.14	2	19	–	65
Wessels, M.H.	15	25	3	107	648	29.45	3	2	–	27/5
Westfield, M.S.	1	2	–	0	0	0.00	–	–	–	–
Weston, W.P.C.	215	378	33	205	11680	33.85	22	58	4	121
Westwood, I.J.	13	25	4	106	684	32.57	1	3	–	6
Wharf, A.G.	84	125	18	113	2126	19.86	3	9	–	43
Whelan, C.D.	2	2	1	9*	10	10.00	–	–	–	–
White, A.R.	7	9	3	152*	313	52.16	1	1	–	4
White, C.	250	397	56	186	11090	32.52	17	57	–	158
White, C.L.	37	58	6	119	1443	27.75	1	8	–	44
White, R.A.	33	58	3	277	1656	30.10	1	8	–	20
White, W.A.	2	2	–	6	8	4.00	–	–	–	–
Wigley, D.H.	11	13	5	23*	102	12.75	–	–	–	4
Wilkinson, R.M.	5	6	–	49	119	19.83	–	–	–	5
Williams, B.A.	66	83	24	41*	793	13.44	–	–	–	25
Willoughby, C.M.	111	125	51	17*	330	4.45	–	–	–	29
Windows, M.G.N.	165	293	20	184	8976	32.87	16	47	3	90
Wolstenholme, J.P.	1	–	–	–	–	–	–	–	–	2
Wood, J.R.	1	2	–	29	29	14.50	–	–	–	–
Wood, M.J. (Sm)	58	102	6	297	3698	38.52	9	22	1	17
Wood, M.J. (Y)	122	213	20	207	6620	34.30	16	29	4	107

177

F-C	M	I	NO	HS	Runs	Avge	100	50	1000	Ct/St
Woodman, R.J.	3	4	1	46*	54	18.00	–	–	–	–
Woods, N.J.	4	6	1	26	101	20.20	–	–	–	1
Wright, C.J.C.	9	11	–	76	257	23.36	–	2	–	4
Wright, D.G.	78	119	19	111	2415	24.15	1	12	–	36
Wright, L.J.	10	13	1	100	255	21.25	1	–	–	6
Yardy, M.H.	56	96	11	257	3245	38.17	6	14	1	43
Younis Khan	87	138	14	267	5965	48.10	20	24	0+1	92
Yousuf Youhana, Mohd	96	157	14	204*	6497	45.43	17	37	–	69

BOWLING

'50wS' denotes instances of taking 50 or more wickets in a season. Where these have been achieved outside the British Isles they are shown after a plus sign.

	Runs	Wkts	Avge	Best	5wI	10wM	50wS
Abdur Razzak	3080	110	28.00	7- 11	4	1	–
Ackerman, H.D.	57	0					
Adams, A.R.	4978	201	24.76	6- 25	8	1	–
Adams, C.J.	1911	41	46.60	4- 28	–	–	–
Adams, J.H.K.	249	6	41.50	2- 16	–	–	–
Adnan, M.Hassan	281	3	93.66	1- 4	–	–	–
Akram, Adnan M.	192	3	64.00	2- 85	–	–	–
Akram, Arfan M.	132	5	26.40	3- 41	–	–	–
Aftab Ahmed	448	18	24.88	7- 39	1	–	–
Afzaal, U.	3637	71	51.22	4-101	–	–	–
Ahmed, J.S.	141	1	141.00	1- 90	–	–	–
Airey, S.J.	626	6	104.33	2- 32	–	–	–
Ali, Kabir	7120	256	27.81	8- 53	10	2	3
Ali, Kadeer	232	3	77.33	1- 4	–	–	–
Ali, M.M.	15	0					
Ali, S.Mohammad H.	8607	264	32.60	6- 37	11	2	0+1
Alleyne, M.W.	13656	415	32.90	6- 49	9	–	1
Alok Kapali	2061	80	25.76	7- 33	4	1	–
Ambrose, T.R.	1	0					
Anderson, J.M.	5072	184	27.56	6- 23	8	1	2
Andrew, G.M.	989	28	35.32	4- 63	–	–	–
Anwar, O.S.	1	0					
Anwar Hossain	2039	69	29.55	7- 81	2	–	–
Anyon, J.E.	919	19	48.36	4- 33	–	–	–
Astle, N.J.	4389	134	32.75	6- 22	2	–	–
Atri, V.	6	0					
Averis, J.M.M.	6273	146	42.96	6- 32	5	–	–
Azhar Mahmood	10505	412	25.49	8- 61	15	3	0+1
Baker, T.M.	55	1	55.00	1- 55	–	–	–
Balcombe, D.J.	391	8	48.87	5-112	1	–	–
Ball, M.C.J.	13752	362	37.98	8- 46	12	1	–
Bandara, C.M.	5837	233	25.05	8- 49	9	2	–
Banerjee, V.	288	2	144.00	2-181	–	–	–
Bassano, C.W.G.	11	0					
Batty, G.J.	7161	229	31.27	7- 52	8	1	2
Batty, J.N.	61	1	61.00	1- 21	–	–	–
Bell, I.R.	1323	41	32.26	4- 4	–	–	–
Benkenstein, D.M.	1752	51	34.35	4- 29	–	–	–
Benning, J.G.E.	466	8	58.25	3- 57	–	–	–
Betts, M.M.	10635	343	31.00	9- 64	14	2	–

178

F-C	Runs	Wkts	Avge	Best	5wI	10wM	50wS
Bichel, A.J.	15514	598	25.94	9- 93	29	6	1+2
Bicknell, D.J.	1015	29	35.00	3- 7	–	–	–
Bicknell, M.P.	26286	1054	24.93	9- 45	43	4	11
Bishop, J.E.	2248	57	39.43	5-148	1	–	–
Blackwell, I.D.	7959	184	43.25	7- 90	7	–	–
Blain, J.A.R.	3420	92	37.17	6- 42	2	–	–
Bond, S.E.	3731	137	27.23	5- 37	6	–	–
Bopara, R.S.	1263	23	54.91	4- 93	–	–	–
Botha, A.G.	5960	176	33.86	8- 53	4	1	–
Bracken, N.W.	4158	155	26.82	7- 4	7	–	–
Breese, G.R.	6116	221	27.67	7- 60	11	3	–
Bresnan, T.T.	2387	71	33.61	5- 42	1	–	–
Bridge, G.D.	3068	88	34.86	6- 84	1	–	–
Brignull, D.S.	392	12	32.66	3- 36	–	–	–
Broad, S.C.J.	831	30	27.70	4- 64	–	–	–
Brophy, G.L.	1	0					
Brown, A.D.	518	2	259.00	1- 11	–	–	–
Brown, D.O.	649	10	64.90	2- 48	–	–	–
Brown, D.R.	15159	527	28.76	8- 89	20	4	4
Brown, J.F.	10210	339	30.11	7- 69	20	5	3
Bruce, J.T.A.	1917	47	40.78	3- 42	–	–	–
Bryant, J.D.C.	37	1	37.00	1- 22	–	–	–
Buckham, C.T.	140	0					
Burnell, W.F.	12	0					
Burns, M.	2885	68	42.42	6- 54	1	–	–
Butcher, M.A.	4201	124	33.87	5- 86	1	–	–
Caddick, A.R.	25823	1007	25.64	9- 32	69	16	10
Cairns, C.L.	18278	643	28.43	8- 47	30	6	3
Carberry, M.A.	251	3	83.66	1- 45	–	–	–
Carter, N.M.	5472	145	37.73	6- 63	4	–	–
Chambers, M.A.	84	1	84.00	1- 73	–	–	–
Chandana, U.D.U.	9489	378	25.10	7- 80	16	1	–
Chapple, G.	16201	563	28.77	6- 30	23	1	4
Cherry, D.D.	9	0					
Chilton, M.J.	599	8	74.87	1- 1	–	–	–
Clark, S.	254	11	23.09	5- 29	1	–	–
Clark, S.R.	5737	183	31.34	6- 84	8	–	–
Clarke, M.J.	613	15	40.86	6- 9	1	–	–
Clarke, R.	2868	67	42.80	4- 21	–	–	–
Claydon, M.E.	92	1	92.00	1- 27	–	–	–
Cleary, M.F.	2795	89	31.40	7- 80	3	–	–
Clewley, N.J.	257	3	85.66	2-132	–	–	–
Clinton, R.S.	152	2	76.00	2- 30	–	–	–
Clough, G.D.	628	10	62.80	3- 69	–	–	–
Coetzer, K.J.	3	0					
Collingwood, P.D.	3808	98	38.85	5- 52	1	–	–
Cook, A.N.	103	3	34.33	3- 13	–	–	–
Cook, S.J.	6657	209	31.85	8- 63	6	–	–
Cork, D.G.	21195	803	26.39	9- 43	31	5	7
Cosker, D.A.	10816	285	37.95	6-140	2	–	–
Cowan, A.P.	9335	284	32.86	6- 47	8	–	1
Crawley, J.P.	232	2	116.00	1- 7	–	–	–
Croft, R.D.B.	32212	882	36.52	8- 66	38	7	7
Croft, S.J.	49	0					

F-C	Runs	Wkts	Avge	Best	5wI	10wM	50wS
Crook, A.R.	509	7	72.71	3- 71	–	–	–
Crook, S.P.	750	12	62.50	3- 54	–	–	–
Cullen, D.J.	1306	43	30.37	5- 38	2	–	–
Cummins, R.A.G.	825	16	51.56	3- 32	–	–	–
Cusden, S.M.J.	511	16	31.93	4- 68	–	–	–
Daggett, L.M.	807	17	47.47	8- 94	1	–	–
Dale, M.A.P.	66	1	66.00	1- 34	–	–	–
Daley, S.R.	31	0					
Dalrymple, J.W.M.	3597	79	45.53	5- 49	1	–	–
Danish Kaneria	10722	420	25.52	7- 39	33	5	1+1
Davies, A.M.	3199	146	21.91	6- 32	7	–	1
Davies, A.P.	2456	58	42.34	5- 79	1	–	–
Davis, M.J.G.	8368	232	36.06	8- 37	5	1	–
Dawson, R.K.J.	6945	173	40.14	6- 82	5	–	–
Dean, K.J.	9185	358	25.65	8- 52	15	4	2
De Bruyn, Z.	3737	97	38.52	6-120	1	–	–
DeFreitas, P.A.J.	34809	1248	27.89	7- 21	61	6	14
Dennington, M.J.	574	16	35.87	3- 23	–	–	–
Dernbach, J.W.	335	5	67.00	2- 66	–	–	–
Dexter, N.J.	161	2	80.50	1- 42	–	–	–
Di Venuto, M.J.	480	5	96.00	1- 0	–	–	–
Doshi, N.D.	2617	70	37.38	7-110	4	2	–
Durston, W.J.	754	14	53.85	3- 23	–	–	–
Ealham, M.A.	14250	507	28.10	8- 36	20	1	1
Edwards, N.J.	181	2	90.50	1- 16	–	–	–
Edwards, P.D.	495	5	99.00	1- 31	–	–	–
Elliott, M.T.G.	754	13	58.00	3- 68	–	–	–
Enamul Haque	2510	87	28.85	7- 47	6	2	–
Ervine, S.M.	3551	97	36.60	6- 82	5	–	–
Ferley, R.S.	1890	45	42.00	4- 76	–	–	–
Finn, S.T.	53	2	26.50	1- 16	–	–	–
Fisher, I.D.	5798	145	39.98	5- 30	7	1	–
Fleming, S.P.	129	0					
Flintoff, A.	7381	229	32.23	5- 24	3	–	–
Flower, A.	250	6	41.66	1- 1	–	–	–
Flower, G.W.	5260	154	34.15	7- 31	3	–	–
Footitt, M.H.A.	260	6	43.33	4- 45	–	–	–
Foster, J.S.	6	0					
France, B.J.	90	1	90.00	1- 37	–	–	–
Francis, J.D.	155	4	38.75	1- 1	–	–	–
Francis, S.R.G.	5284	131	40.33	5- 42	3	–	–
Franks, P.J.	10335	345	29.95	7- 56	11	–	2
Friedlander, M.J.	497	10	49.70	3- 67	–	–	–
Friend, T.J.	3154	79	39.92	5- 16	2	–	–
Frost, T.	15	0					
Fulton, D.P.	117	1	117.00	1- 37	–	–	–
Gallian, J.E.R.	4099	95	43.14	6-115	1	–	–
Ganguly, S.C.	4898	125	39.18	6- 46	3	–	–
Gayle, C.H.	3123	83	37.62	5- 34	2	–	–
Gibson, O.D.	15201	530	28.68	7- 55	23	5	2
Gidman, A.P.R.	2263	48	47.14	4- 47	–	–	–
Giles, A.F.	15394	530	29.04	8- 90	26	3	2
Gillespie, J.N.	10785	424	25.43	8- 50	15	1	0+1
Golwalkar, Y.A.	3166	91	34.79	8-127	4	1	–

F-C	Runs	Wkts	Avge	Best	5wI	10wM	50wS
Goodwin, M.W.	357	7	51.00	2- 23	–	–	–
Gough, D.	21089	784	26.89	7- 28	29	3	5
Grant, R.N.	18	0					
Gray, A.K.D.	1924	42	45.80	4-128	–	–	–
Greenidge, C.G.	3687	103	35.79	6- 40	4	–	1
Guy, S.M.	8	0					
Habib, A.	80	1	80.00	1- 10	–	–	–
Habibul Bashar	491	8	61.37	2- 28	–	–	–
Hall, J.W.	8372	324	25.83	6- 77	11	1	–
Hancock, T.H.C.	1816	47	38.63	3- 5	–	–	–
Harbhajan Singh	11272	428	26.33	8- 84	27	4	0+2
Hardinges, M.A.	1652	46	35.91	5- 51	1	–	–
Harmison, S.J.	11660	403	28.93	7- 12	13	–	3
Harris, A.J.	10804	349	30.95	7- 54	15	3	2
Harrison, A.J.	162	4	40.50	2- 65	–	–	–
Harrison, D.S.	4813	135	35.65	5- 48	5	–	1
Harvey, I.J.	11099	405	27.40	8-101	15	2	–
Hasanuzzaman	32	1	32.00	1- 1	–	–	–
Havell, P.M.R.	1713	41	41.78	4- 75	–	–	–
Hayden, M.L.	671	17	39.47	3- 10	–	–	–
Hayward, M.	11082	388	28.56	6- 31	9	2	1
Heath, D.R.	424	8	53.00	3- 28	–	–	–
Hegg, W.K.	7	0					
Hemp, D.L.	778	17	45.76	3- 23	–	–	–
Henderson, C.W.	15447	507	30.46	7- 57	16	–	1
Hick, G.A.	10308	232	44.43	5- 18	5	1	–
Hildreth, J.C.	149	2	74.50	2- 39	–	–	–
Hodge, B.J.	2551	61	41.81	4- 17	–	–	–
Hogg, K.W.	1509	39	38.69	5- 48	1	–	–
Hoggard, M.J.	11862	441	26.89	7- 49	14	1	2
Hooper, M.R.	81	0					
Hopkinson, C.D.	119	2	59.50	1- 20	–	–	–
Hunter, I.D.	3452	82	42.09	5- 63	1	–	–
Hussey, D.J.	679	12	56.58	4-105	–	–	–
Hussey, M.E.K.	693	18	38.50	3- 34	–	–	–
Hutchison, P.M.	5256	184	28.56	7- 31	7	1	1
Hutton, B.L.	1948	32	60.87	4- 37	–	–	–
Irani, R.C.	10007	339	29.51	6- 71	9	–	1
Jacklin, B.D.	87	0					
Jaques, P.A.	72	0					
Javed Omar	145	2	72.50	2- 75	–	–	–
Jayasuriya, S.T.	6003	187	32.10	5- 34	2	–	–
Jefferson, W.I.	60	1	60.00	1- 16	–	–	–
Johnson, M.G.	600	17	35.29	3- 23	–	–	–
Johnson, R.L.	13993	500	27.98	10- 45	19	3	4
Jones, C.M.P.	90	3	30.00	2- 26	–	–	–
Jones, G.O.	4	0					
Jones, P.S.	8179	207	39.51	6- 67	5	1	1
Jones, S.P.	6804	216	31.50	6- 45	11	1	–
Joseph, R.H.	883	29	30.44	5- 19	1	–	–
Joyce, E.C.	768	9	85.33	2- 34	–	–	–
Kartik, M.	7538	294	25.63	9- 70	17	3	–
Kasprowicz, M.S.	23651	892	26.51	9- 36	49	6	4+3
Katich, S.M.	2951	78	37.83	7-130	3	–	–

F-C	Runs	Wkts	Avge	Best	5wI	10wM	50wS
Keedy, G.	12640	396	31.91	7- 95	20	5	2
Keegan, C.B.	4151	121	34.30	6-114	5	–	1
Kemp, J.M.	4218	159	26.52	6- 56	4	–	–
Kemp, R.A.	86	2	43.00	2- 86	–	–	–
Kenway, D.A.	159	4	39.75	1- 5	–	–	–
Key, R.W.T.	49	0					
Khaled Masud	14	0					
Khalid, S.A.	712	14	50.85	4-131	–	–	–
Khan, A.	5158	156	33.06	6- 52	5	–	2
Killeen, N.	7362	229	32.14	7- 70	7	–	1
King, R.E.	345	2	172.50	1- 32	–	–	–
Kirby, S.P.	6401	229	27.95	8- 80	9	3	1
Kirtley, R.J.	14977	576	26.00	7- 21	29	4	7
Klusener, L.	11033	399	27.65	8- 34	15	4	–
Knight, N.V.	230	1	230.00	1- 61	–	–	–
Krejza, J.J.	625	12	52.08	2- 11	–	–	–
Kruis, G.J.	9334	316	29.53	7- 58	16	1	1
Kumble, A.	22776	924	24.64	10- 74	63	17	1+2
Lamb, G.A.	719	29	24.79	7- 73	1	–	–
Lamb, N.J.	107	3	35.66	1- 6	–	–	–
Langer, J.L.	204	5	40.80	2- 17	–	–	–
Langeveldt, C.K.	4641	163	28.47	5- 19	5	1	–
Laraman, A.W.	3214	92	34.93	5- 58	1	–	–
Law, S.G.	4165	82	50.79	5- 39	1	–	–
Lawson, M.A.K.	680	16	42.50	5- 62	2	–	–
Leatherdale, D.A.	4158	132	31.50	5- 20	2	–	–
Lee, B.	8666	315	27.51	7-114	13	2	–
Lehmann, D.S.	3359	96	34.98	4- 35	–	–	–
Lewis, J.	13898	514	27.03	8- 95	26	3	5
Lewis, J.J.B.	121	1	121.00	1- 73	–	–	–
Lewis, M.L.	5509	194	28.39	6- 59	7	–	–
Lewry, J.D.	12727	480	26.51	8-106	29	4	4
Liddle, C.J.	45	0					
Linley, T.E.	480	13	36.92	3- 44	–	–	–
Logan, R.J.	4295	114	37.67	6- 93	4	–	–
Loudon, A.G.R.	2561	67	38.22	6- 47	4	–	–
Louw, J.	5274	173	30.48	6- 51	6	–	1
Love, M.L.	11	1	11.00	1- 5	–	–	–
Loye, M.B.	61	1	61.00	1- 8	–	–	–
Lucas, D.S.	1993	60	33.21	5- 49	2	–	–
Lumb, M.J.	206	6	34.33	2- 10	–	–	–
Lungley, T.	1654	47	35.19	4-101	–	–	–
MacGill, S.C.G.	19046	647	29.43	8-111	38	6	0+3
McGrath, A.	2489	77	32.32	5- 39	1	–	–
McGrath, G.D.	16179	786	20.58	8- 24	41	7	1+1
McLean, N.A.M.	13649	496	27.51	7- 28	19	3	2
McMahon, P.J.	1581	44	35.93	5- 30	1	–	–
McMillan, C.D.	2894	81	35.72	6- 71	1	–	–
Maddy, D.L.	5170	162	31.91	5- 37	4	–	–
Maher, J.P.	504	10	50.40	3- 11	–	–	–
Mahmood, S.I.	2376	67	35.46	5- 37	2	–	–
Malik, M.N.	2986	95	31.43	5- 57	4	–	–
Marshall, H.J.H.	113	2	56.50	1- 12	–	–	–
Marshall, S.J.	1729	24	72.04	6-128	1	–	–

F-C	Runs	Wkts	Avge	Best	5wI	10wM	50wS
Martin-Jenkins, R.S.C.	8555	249	34.35	7- 51	5	–	–
Martyn, D.R.	1535	36	42.63	4- 30	–	–	–
Mascarenhas, A.D.	8668	306	28.32	6- 25	12	–	1
Mashrafe Mortaza	2115	64	33.04	4- 60	–	–	–
Mason, M.S.	5074	184	27.57	6- 68	5	–	3
Masters, D.D.	5321	163	32.64	6- 27	5	–	–
Maunders, J.K.	506	16	31.62	4- 28	–	–	–
Maynard, M.P.	895	6	149.16	3- 21	–	–	–
Mees, T.	966	20	48.30	6- 64	1	–	–
Mehrab Hossain	661	16	41.31	6- 80	1	1	–
Middlebrook, J.D.	8049	209	38.51	6- 82	6	1	1
Mitchell, D.K.H.	99	1	99.00	1- 59	–	–	–
Mohammad Akram	10433	368	28.35	8- 49	16	1	–
Mohammad Amin	112	2	56.00	2- 70	–	–	–
Mohammad Ashraful	2195	68	32.27	7- 99	4	–	–
Mohammad Asif	4182	158	26.46	7- 35	6	1	–
Mohammad Rafique	3878	155	25.01	7- 52	9	2	–
Mongia, D.	995	26	38.26	4- 34	–	–	–
Montgomerie, R.R.	147	2	73.50	1- 0	–	–	–
Moore, S.C.	171	4	42.75	1- 13	–	–	–
Moreton, S.J.P.	81	0					
Morgan, E.J.G.	14	0					
Morris, J.C.	32	3	10.66	2- 29	–	–	–
Morse, E.J.	158	7	22.57	4- 78	–	–	–
Moss, J.	3218	96	33.52	4- 40	–	–	–
Muchall, G.J.	589	15	39.26	3- 26	–	–	–
Munday, M.K.	922	32	28.81	5- 83	1	–	–
Muralitharan, M.	20103	1068	18.82	9- 51	93	26	2+3
Murtagh, T.J.	2595	69	37.60	6- 86	3	–	–
Mushfiqur Rahman	2095	62	33.79	4- 45	–	–	–
Mushtaq Ahmed	30754	1179	26.08	9- 93	82	24	7+2
Nafis Iqbal	33	0					
Napier, G.R.	5196	131	39.66	5- 56	2	–	–
Nash, C.D.	457	5	91.40	1- 5	–	–	–
Nash, D.C.	52	1	52.00	1- 8	–	–	–
Naved-ul-Hasan	7876	334	23.58	7- 49	18	2	1+3
Nazimuddin	41	1	41.00	1- 9	–	–	–
Needham, J.	68	2	34.00	2- 42	–	–	–
Nel, A.	6503	268	24.26	6- 25	12	1	–
Newby, O.J.	412	8	51.50	2- 32	–	–	–
Newman, S.A.	22	0					
Nicholson, M.J.	6481	236	27.46	7- 77	8	–	–
Nixon, P.A.	22	0					
Noffke, A.A.	7131	230	31.00	8- 24	9	1	–
North, M.J.	1647	36	45.75	4- 16	–	–	–
Ntini, M.	12206	409	29.84	7- 37	14	2	–
Oberoi, S.	61	3	20.33	3- 49	–	–	–
Onions, G.	902	13	69.38	3-110	–	–	–
Ormond, J.	12049	417	28.89	7- 63	20	1	4
Padget, C.D.	206	3	68.66	3- 63	–	–	–
Palladino, A.P.	1445	27	53.51	6- 41	1	–	–
Panesar, M.S.	3021	107	28.23	7-181	5	1	1
Park, G.T.	261	0					
Parker, L.C.	144	4	36.00	2- 37	–	–	–

183

F-C	Runs	Wkts	Avge	Best	5wI	10wM	50wS
Parsons, K.A.	4286	95	45.11	5- 13	2	–	–
Parsons, M.	135	0					
Patel, M.M.	17526	578	30.32	8- 96	28	9	4
Patel, S.R.	228	6	38.00	3- 73	–	–	–
Pathan, I.K.	4843	147	32.94	6- 31	6	2	–
Patterson, S.A.	53	0					
Peng, N.	2	0					
Peploe, C.T.	1785	37	48.24	4- 65	–	–	–
Peters, S.D.	31	1	31.00	1- 19	–	–	–
Phillips, B.J.	4258	142	29.98	5- 47	3	–	–
Phillips, T.J.	2026	38	53.31	4- 42	–	–	–
Pietersen, C.	1604	40	40.10	6- 43	1	–	–
Pietersen, K.P.	2605	55	47.36	4- 31	–	–	–
Piper, K.J.	60	1	60.00	1- 57	–	–	–
Plunkett, L.E.	3209	101	31.77	6- 74	4	–	1
Ponting, R.T.	750	14	53.57	2- 10	–	–	–
Pothas, N.	5	0					
Powell, M.J. (Gm)	132	2	66.00	2- 39	–	–	–
Powell, M.J. (Wa)	657	11	59.72	2- 16	–	–	–
Pratt, G.J.	19	0					
Pretorius, D.	6330	231	27.40	6- 49	7	–	–
Price, R.W.	8170	255	32.03	8- 35	15	3	–
Pyrah, R.M.	36	3	12.00	1- 4	–	–	–
Rajin Saleh	542	5	108.40	2- 44	–	–	–
Ramprakash, M.R.	2178	34	64.05	3- 32	–	–	–
Read, C.M.W.	25	0					
Read, G.G.	495	10	49.50	3- 66	–	–	–
Richards, M.A.	196	1	196.00	1- 38	–	–	–
Richardson, A.	6857	223	30.74	8- 46	7	1	1
Roberts, T.W.	20	1	20.00	1- 10	–	–	–
Robinson, D.D.J.	282	1	282.00	1- 7	–	–	–
Rogers, C.J.L.	26	0					
Rudge, W.D.	505	14	36.07	3- 46	–	–	–
Rudolph, J.A.	1594	43	37.06	5- 87	2	–	–
Sadler, J.L.	98	1	98.00	1- 22	–	–	–
Saggers, M.J.	8520	347	24.55	7- 79	16	–	4
Saker, N.C.	272	2	136.00	1- 62	–	–	–
Sales, D.J.G.	169	9	18.77	4- 25	–	–	–
Salisbury, I.D.K.	25523	780	32.72	8- 60	34	6	6
Sampson, P.J.	415	17	24.41	5-121	1	–	–
Saqlain Mushtaq	18026	775	23.25	8- 65	56	15	5+1
Sarwan, R.R.	1657	45	36.82	6- 62	1	–	–
Savill, T.E.	1487	26	57.19	3- 86	–	–	–
Sayers, J.J.	47	0					
Scott, G.M.	59	0					
Shafayat, B.M.	253	1	253.00	1- 22	–	–	–
Shah, O.A.	992	21	47.23	3- 33	–	–	–
Shahadat Hossain	1208	36	33.55	5- 53	2	–	–
Shahin Hossain	61	2	30.50	2- 25	–	–	–
Shahriar Nafis	6	0					
Shantry, A.J.	263	10	26.30	3- 8	–	–	–
Sharif, Z.K.	640	11	58.18	4- 98	–	–	–
Sheikh, M.A.	2834	75	37.78	4- 9	–	–	–
Sheriyar, A.	15085	503	29.99	7-130	23	3	4

F-C	Runs	Wkts	Avge	Best	5wI	10wM	50wS
Shilvock, D.J.F.	114	3	38.00	2- 77	–	–	–
Shoaib Akhtar	10623	407	26.10	6- 11	27	2	0+1
Shreck, C.E.	1701	54	31.50	6- 46	3	–	–
Sidebottom, R.J.	6420	259	24.78	7- 97	10	1	1
Sillence, R.J.	1236	34	36.35	5- 63	2	–	–
Silverwood, C.E.W.	12768	470	27.16	7- 93	20	1	2
Singh, A. (CU)	19	0					
Singh, A. (Nt).	124	0					
Smith, B.F.	391	3	130.33	1- 5	–	–	–
Smith, E.T.	59	0					
Smith, G.C.	858	10	85.80	2-145	–	–	–
Smith, G.J.	12233	445	27.48	8- 53	17	2	3
Smith, G.M.	251	6	41.83	2- 60	–	–	–
Smith, T.C.	46	1	46.00	1- 24	–	–	–
Smith, W.R.	448	6	74.66	3- 34	–	–	–
Snape, J.N.	5400	110	49.09	5- 65	1	–	–
Solanki, V.S.	3606	78	46.23	5- 40	4	1	–
Spearman, C.M.	55	1	55.00	1- 37	–	–	–
Stephenson, J.P.	12856	393	32.71	7- 44	11	1	–
Stevens, D.I.	1068	23	46.43	3- 19	–	–	–
Steyn, D.W.	2141	53	40.39	5- 30	1	–	–
Stiff, D.A.	504	9	56.00	3- 88	–	–	–
Strauss, A.J.	58	1	58.00	1- 27	–	–	–
Streak, H.H.	11850	433	27.36	7- 55	14	2	1
Stubbings, S.D.	77	0					
Styris, S.B.	5062	174	29.09	6- 32	8	1	–
Suman, A.K.	1259	38	33.13	4- 59	–	–	–
Suppiah, A.V.	395	10	39.50	3- 46	–	–	–
Sutcliffe, I.J.	329	9	36.55	2- 21	–	–	–
Swann, G.P.	10504	327	32.12	7- 33	14	2	1
Syed Rasel	2088	72	29.00	8- 67	3	2	–
Symonds, A.	7208	197	36.58	6-105	2	–	–
Tahir, N.	1104	39	28.30	4- 43	–	–	–
Tait, S.W.	3156	125	25.24	7- 99	5	–	0+1
Talha Jubair	2095	49	42.75	4- 36	–	–	–
Tapash Baisya	3462	93	37.22	5- 30	1	–	–
Taylor, B.V.	4119	123	33.48	6- 45	3	–	–
Taylor, C.G.	265	4	66.25	3-126	–	–	–
Ten Doeschate, R.N.	446	10	44.60	3- 29	–	–	–
Thomas, I.J.	38	1	38.00	1- 26	–	–	–
Thomas, S.D.	16023	504	31.79	8- 50	18	1	5
Thompson, G.J.	281	7	40.14	1- 7	–	–	–
Thornely, D.J.	478	9	53.11	3- 52	–	–	–
Thornicroft, N.D.	543	11	49.36	2- 27	–	–	–
Thorp, C.D.	758	14	54.14	3- 10	–	–	–
Thorpe, G.P.	1378	26	53.00	4- 40	–	–	–
Timms, R.T.	75	0					
Tomlinson, J.A.	1585	30	52.83	6- 63	1	–	–
Tredwell, J.C.	2825	65	43.46	5-101	1	–	–
Trego, P.D.	1848	45	41.06	6- 59	1	\	–
Tremlett, C.T.	4766	180	26.47	6- 44	5	–	–
Trescothick, M.E.	1541	36	42.80	4- 36	–	–	–
Trott, I.J.L.	980	23	42.60	7- 39	1	–	–
Troughton, J.O.	764	11	69.45	3- 1	–	–	–

185

F-C	Runs	Wkts	Avge	Best	5wI	10wM	50wS
Tudor, A.J.	8073	288	28.03	7- 48	13	–	–
Turner, M.L.	166	2	83.00	1- 47	–	–	–
Turner, R.J.	58	0					
Tushar Imran	296	8	37.00	3- 22	–	–	–
Udal, S.D.	22156	687	32.25	8- 50	33	4	7
Vaas, W.P.U.C.J.	13569	559	24.27	7- 54	25	3	0+2
Van der Wath, J.J.	4037	146	27.65	6- 37	7	–	–
Van Jaarsveld, M.	540	12	45.00	2- 30	–	–	–
Vaughan, M.P.	5142	114	45.10	4- 39	–	–	–
Vettori, D.L.	11012	338	32.57	7- 87	22	2	–
Wagg, G.G.	726	23	31.56	4- 43	–	–	–
Wagh, M.A.	4553	98	46.45	7-222	2	–	–
Wainwright, D.J.	421	18	23.38	4- 48	–	–	–
Walker, M.J.	955	19	50.26	2- 21	–	–	–
Walker, N.G.E.	1559	35	44.54	5- 68	1	–	–
Ward, I.J.	197	3	65.66	1- 1	–	–	–
Warne, S.K.	28266	1100	25.69	8- 71	53	10	5+1
Warren, N.A.	628	14	44.85	3- 40	–	–	–
Warren, R.J.	0	0					
Waters, H.T.	332	11	30.18	4- 75	–	–	–
Watkins, R.E.	125	3	41.66	2- 14	–	–	–
Watson, S.R.	2441	81	30.13	6- 32	2	1	–
Webley, T.	357	6	59.50	2- 57	–	–	–
Wedge, S.A.	211	5	42.20	5-112	1	–	–
Weekes, P.N.	12421	299	41.54	8- 39	5	–	–
Welch, G.	13836	441	31.37	6- 30	17	1	4
Westfield, M.S.	90	1	90.00	1- 90	–	–	–
Weston, W.P.C.	658	5	131.60	2- 39	–	–	–
Westwood, I.J.	87	1	87.00	1- 30	–	–	–
Wharf, A.G.	7647	216	35.40	6- 59	5	1	1
Whelan, C.D.	182	7	26.00	2- 34	–	–	–
White, A.R.	326	8	40.75	3- 24	–	–	–
White, C.	11174	391	28.57	8- 55	11	–	–
White, C.L.	3102	88	35.25	6- 66	1	1	–
White, R.A.	385	9	42.77	2- 30	–	–	–
White, W.A.	280	5	56.00	4- 77	–	–	–
Wigley, D.H.	1126	28	40.21	4- 68	–	–	–
Wilkinson, R.M.	321	5	64.20	2- 24	–	–	–
Williams, B.A.	7119	222	32.06	6- 74	10	–	0+1
Willoughby, C.M.	10191	403	25.28	7- 56	13	3	0+2
Windows, M.G.N.	131	2	65.50	1- 6	–	–	–
Wolstenholme, J.P.	14	0					
Wood, M.J. (Sm)	68	0					
Wood, M.J. (Y)	39	2	19.50	1- 4	–	–	–
Woodman, R.J.	268	2	134.00	1- 78	–	–	–
Woods, N.J.	155	0					
Wright, C.J.C.	917	12	76.41	2- 36	–	–	–
Wright, D.G.	7672	246	31.18	8- 60	7	–	1
Wright, L.J.	528	14	37.71	3- 33	–	–	–
Yardy, M.H.	862	13	66.30	5- 83	1	–	–
Younis Khan	651	12	54.25	3- 24	–	–	–
Yousuf Youhana, Mohd	24	0					

LIMITED-OVERS 'LIST A' CAREER RECORDS

Compiled by **PHILIP BAILEY**

The following career records, to the end of the 2005 season, include all players currently registered with first-class counties. These records are restricted to performances in limited-overs matches of 'List A' status as defined by the Association of Cricket Statisticians and Historians. The following matches qualify for List A status and are included in the figures that follow: limited-overs internationals; other international matches (e.g. Commonwealth Games, 'A' team internationals); premier domestic limited-overs tournaments in Test status countries; official tourist matches against the main first-class teams.

The following matches do NOT qualify for inclusion: World Cup warm-up games; tourist matches against first-class teams outside the major domestic competitions (e.g. universities, Minor Counties, etc.); festival, pre-season friendly games and Twenty20 Cup matches).

Editor's note: I have deducted from Philip's match totals for A.R.Adams, S.P.Fleming, H.J.H.Marshall and D.L.Vettori the LOI scheduled between New Zealand and West Indies at Southampton on 8 July 2004. Although the ICC ruled that this should count as a match because the toss was made, Law 16 clearly states that the umpire's call of 'play' heralds the start of a match and not the toss.

	M	Runs	Avge	HS	100	50	Wkts	Avge	Best	Ct/St
Ackerman, H.D.	147	3968	33.34	114*	–	28	0	–	–	53
Adams, A.R.	92	970	18.65	90*	–	1	125	27.52	5- 7	22
Adams, C.J.	331	10608	40.80	163	19	67	32	38.03	5-16	156
Adams, J.H.K.	7	102	14.57	40	–	–	0	–	–	4
Adnan, M. Hassan	57	1542	33.52	113*	2	13	5	25.80	2-13	18
Adshead, S.J.	40	525	17.50	77*	–	2		–	–	50/16
Afzaal, U.	133	3776	36.66	122*	3	28	39	24.00	3- 4	35
Ali, Kabir	109	672	14.29	92	–	2	166	23.16	5-36	20
Ali, Kadeer	25	600	25.00	66	–	5	1	45.00	1- 4	1
Ali, S. Mohd H.	49	114	8.76	19	–	–	57	31.14	4-34	6
Allenby, J.	2	11	11.00	7*	–	–	0	–	–	1
Alleyne, D.	32	259	10.79	58	–	1				22/6
Alleyne, M.W.	436	8308	27.23	134*	5	33	415	29.55	5-27	176/1
Ambrose, T.R.	51	1106	25.13	95	–	6		–	–	54/5
Anderson, J.M.	76	121	10.08	13*	–	–	115	24.29	4-25	13
Andrew, G.M.	30	113	8.69	23	–	–	32	34.71	4-48	10
Anyon, J.E.	15	0	0.00	0	–	–	11	44.18	3-44	3
Averis, J.M.M.	136	360	10.58	23*	–	–	204	24.09	6-23	17
Azhar Mahmood	234	2949	20.47	100*	1	11	244	32.80	6-18	68
Baker, T.M.	6	66	33.00	63	–	1	5	38.80	2-13	3
Ball, M.C.J.	269	1745	14.18	51	–	1	265	31.51	5-33	127
Barrick, D.J.	1	24	–	24*	–	–	0	–	–	1
Batty, G.J.	110	1229	17.81	83*	–	4	89	36.13	4-36	42
Batty, J.N.	133	1729	20.83	158*	1	7		–	–	130/20
Bell, I.R.	93	2818	35.22	137	2	24	30	34.66	5-41	33
Benham, C.C.	1	0	0.00	0	–	–		–	–	1
Benkenstein, D.M.	186	4147	33.44	107*	1	22	58	23.68	4-16	66
Benning, J.G.E.	35	934	27.47	73	–	7	25	30.52	4-43	8
Betts, M.M.	95	358	9.94	21	–	–	116	29.75	4-15	16
Bichel, A.J.	197	2032	20.32	100	1	4	260	26.60	7-20	61
Bicknell, D.J.	235	7469	37.34	135*	10	51	3	27.33	1-11	55
Bicknell, M.P.	334	1589	15.57	66*	–	2	429	25.15	7-30	78
Blackwell, I.D.	180	4140	27.60	134*	3	25	132	35.62	5-26	44
Blain, J.A.R.	52	135	10.38	29	–	–	74	25.39	5-24	13
Bond, S.E.	54	296	17.41	40	–	–	78	24.79	6-23	11
Bopara, R.S.	38	731	29.24	96*	–	3	20	30.95	2-10	12

L-O	M	Runs	Avge	HS	100	50	Wkts	Avge	Best	Ct/St
Botha, A.G.	77	723	18.07	60*	–	2	77	27.22	4-44	33
Bracken, N.W.	81	118	7.37	16*	–	–	108	26.96	5-38	14
Breese, G.R.	66	655	17.23	52*	–	1	61	30.59	3-24	29
Bresnan, T.T.	79	621	15.52	61	–	1	67	38.68	4-25	25
Bridge, G.D.	48	332	15.09	50*	–	1	54	27.72	4-20	8
Broad, S.C.J.	1	–	–	–	–	–	2	17.50	2-35	–
Brophy, G.L.	55	829	23.02	57*	–	4	–	–	–	51/11
Brown, A.D.	339	9831	31.71	268	17	45	11	35.54	3-39	118
Brown, D.R.	290	4568	23.42	108	1	22	346	26.40	5-31	73
Brown, J.F.	114	98	5.44	16	–	–	105	37.12	5-19	25
Brown, M.J.	5	78	15.60	35	–	–	–	–	–	2
Bruce, J.T.A.	9	22	22.00	10*	–	–	8	34.25	3-45	1
Burrows, T.G.	1	1	1.00	1	–	–	–	–	–	1
Butcher, M.A.	160	3192	27.51	104	1	17	49	45.10	3-23	54
Caddick, A.R.	240	758	10.52	39	–	–	311	26.45	6-30	36
Cairns, C.L.	406	9999	32.46	143	9	54	426	28.09	6-12	114
Carberry, M.A.	48	827	20.17	79	–	6	1	41.00	1-21	18
Carter, N.M.	103	1386	18.23	75	–	4	144	25.45	5-31	12
Chapple, G.	230	1633	17.37	81*	–	8	256	29.33	6-18	54
Cherry, D.D.	12	232	21.09	42	–	–	0	–	–	3
Chilton, M.J.	131	3233	29.93	115	4	16	41	24.19	5-26	43
Clarke, R.	85	1541	24.85	98*	–	8	56	36.75	4-49	35
Clinton, R.S.	16	174	17.40	56	–	1	2	29.00	2-16	3
Clough, G.D.	73	499	18.48	42*	–	–	66	33.50	4-32	24
Coetzer, K.J.	9	86	12.28	30	–	–	0	–	–	3
Collingwood, P.D.	235	5639	31.50	118*	4	32	138	33.65	6-31	109
Compton, N.R.D.	15	214	23.77	86*	–	1	0	–	–	2
Cook, A.N.	20	398	22.11	94	–	2	0	–	–	7
Cook, S.J.	125	1001	16.96	67*	–	2	154	27.81	6-37	16
Cork, D.G.	259	3704	20.92	93	–	19	319	27.60	6-21	101
Cosker, D.A.	135	297	7.42	27*	–	–	141	32.81	5-54	49
Cowan, A.P.	148	1042	14.27	45	–	–	178	28.22	5-14	49
Crawley, J.P.	271	7524	31.61	114	6	48	0	–	–	81/4
Croft, R.D.B.	359	5927	24.39	143	4	30	372	32.18	6-20	85
Croft, S.J.	3	11	5.50	7	–	–	1	34.00	1-27	1
Crook, A.R.	14	288	28.80	162*	1	–	10	31.90	3-32	4
Crook, S.P.	13	97	10.77	21	–	–	8	53.75	2-47	3
Cross, G.D.	5	53	13.25	21	–	–	–	–	–	6/4
Cullen, D.J.	6	33	11.00	13*	–	–	9	24.55	3-55	2
Cusden, S.M.J.	5	5	2.50	3	–	–	3	53.66	1-29	–
Dalrymple, J.W.M.	70	1383	30.73	107	2	7	50	34.12	4-14	29
Davies, A.M.	63	164	7.45	31*	–	–	60	29.53	4-13	9
Davies, A.P.	84	158	10.53	24	–	–	121	25.69	5-19	10
Davies, S.M.	11	150	25.00	43	–	–	–	–	–	7/3
Dawson, R.K.J.	87	428	10.19	41	–	–	97	26.83	4-13	28
Dean, K.J.	124	235	9.03	16*	–	–	138	29.79	5-32	24
Denly, J.L.	7	78	13.00	49	–	–	–	–	–	–
Dennington, M.J.	16	99	12.37	26*	–	–	7	81.57	3-53	3
Dernbach, J.W.	7	22	11.00	21	–	–	10	25.00	4-36	2
Dexter, N.J.	2	5	2.50	5	–	–	3	22.66	2-33	–
Di Venuto, M.J.	224	6941	34.02	173*	11	35	5	36.20	1-10	86
Doshi, N.D.	37	145	14.50	38*	–	–	26	51.61	2-28	6
Durston, W.J.	21	429	39.00	58*	–	3	10	41.80	2-21	4
Ealham, M.A.	374	5954	24.91	112	1	25	418	27.35	6-53	99

188

L-O	M	Runs	Avge	HS	100	50	Wkts	Avge	Best	Ct/St
Elliott, M.T.G.	134	4947	44.16	156	13	29	0	–	–	52
Ervine, S.M.	88	1844	29.26	104	3	7	95	32.31	5-50	16
Ferley, R.S.	28	200	16.66	42	–	–	32	30.40	3-36	10
Fisher, I.D.	43	117	7.31	23	–	–	49	24.57	3-18	13
Fleming, S.P.	377	11137	34.26	139*	16	66	2	15.50	1- 3	181
Flintoff, A.	223	5387	30.26	143	6	29	207	22.42	4-11	85
Flower, A.	366	11970	38.36	145	12	92	1	103.00	1-21	250/48
Flower, G.W.	305	9195	34.18	148*	11	58	170	34.39	4-32	121
Footitt, M.H.A.	1						0	–	–	–
Foster, J.S.	85	940	20.00	56*	–	2	–	–	–	108/22
France, B.J.	3	52	17.33	31	–	–	–	–	–	–
Francis, J.D.	61	1656	33.79	103*	1	11	–	–	–	13
Francis, S.R.G.	69	240	12.63	33*	–	–	77	33.80	8-66	15
Franks, P.J.	125	1420	21.84	84*	–	4	155	26.58	6-27	20
Frost, T.	73	414	17.25	47	–	–	–	–	–	70/18
Fulton, D.P.	108	1962	20.87	82	–	7	0	–	–	46
Gale, A.W.	17	304	19.00	70*	–	1	–	–	–	6
Gallian, J.E.R.	206	5755	30.77	134	8	35	55	32.87	5-15	68
Gazzard, C.M.	38	833	26.87	157	1	4	–	–	–	33/5
Gibson, O.D.	184	2396	21.39	102*	1	5	263	24.52	5-19	52
Gidman, A.P.R.	71	1320	24.00	73	–	6	17	52.52	3-26	27
Giles, A.F.	224	2089	20.89	107	1	5	272	25.59	5-21	73
Gillespie, J.N.	131	379	11.84	44*	–	–	193	25.22	5-22	14
Goodwin, M.W.	258	7730	34.35	167	10	49	7	43.71	1- 9	83
Gough, D.	377	1830	13.16	72*	–	1	540	24.30	7-27	61
Grant, R.N.	14	183	18.30	29	–	–	2	79.50	1-18	3
Gray, A.K.D.	44	148	9.86	30*	–	–	40	29.45	4-34	12
Greenidge, C.G.	51	88	6.28	20	–	–	56	35.78	3-22	15
Guy, S.M.	16	184	20.44	40	–	–	–	–	–	15/5
Habib, A.	168	3212	26.32	111	1	14	2	29.00	2- 5	57
Hall, A.J.	183	3788	30.79	129*	3	22	193	27.06	4-26	50
Hamilton-Brown, R.J.	2	20	20.00	20	–	–	–	–	–	–
Hardinges, M.A.	49	611	16.07	111*	1	2	35	40.40	4-19	19
Harmison, B.W.	1	0	0.00	0	–	–	1	51.00	1-51	1
Harmison, S.J.	88	105	5.52	13*	–	–	112	30.73	5-33	15
Harris, A.J.	122	160	6.40	16*	–	–	159	28.91	5-35	26
Harrison, D.S.	47	242	12.10	37*	–	–	53	28.16	5-26	5
Hemp, D.L.	227	4664	26.95	121	5	23	11	16.18	4-32	83
Henderson, C.W.	164	641	16.43	32	–	–	207	24.77	6-29	42
Hick, G.A.	610	20806	41.11	172*	39	133	225	29.55	5-19	269
Hildreth, J.C.	44	974	28.64	85	–	4	1	61.00	1-44	16
Hodd, A.J.	3	13	4.33	9	–	–	–	–	–	3
Hodge, B.J.	153	5035	37.57	164	10	27	30	35.13	5-28	61
Hogg, K.W.	63	443	17.72	41*	–	–	62	29.24	4-20	13
Hoggard, M.J.	118	54	3.37	7*	–	–	172	23.54	5-28	12
Hopkinson, C.D.	47	596	18.62	67*	–	2	14	36.14	3-19	25
Horton, P.J.	9	141	28.20	46	–	–	–	–	–	–
Hunter, I.D.	68	268	8.12	39	–	–	74	32.54	4-29	14
Hussey, D.J.	64	1826	36.52	128	3	7	9	41.88	3-48	27
Hussey, M.E.K.	198	6844	44.73	123	9	53	19	35.68	3-52	92
Hutton, B.L.	109	1432	19.88	77	–	7	48	31.62	5-45	53
Irani, R.C.	295	6921	29.70	158*	5	40	309	25.22	5-26	77
Jaques, P.A.	68	2507	39.79	117	3	19	–	–	–	19
Jefferson, W.I.	64	2141	36.28	132	4	11	2	4.50	2- 9	30

189

L-O	M	Runs	Avge	HS	100	50	Wkts	Avge	Best	Ct/St
Johnson, M.G.	6	35	17.50	27	–	–	10	28.70	4-37	1
Johnson, R.L.	176	1075	12.07	53	–	1	195	32.13	5-50	19
Jones, G.O.	80	1278	23.23	80	–	6	–	–	–	94/13
Jones, P.S.	143	423	11.43	27	–	–	195	28.42	6-56	26
Jones, S.P.	21	27	9.00	12*	–	–	16	51.00	3-19	2
Joseph, R.H.	11	23	11.50	15	–	–	12	28.25	2-21	2
Joyce, E.C.	103	2931	37.57	115*	3	19	2	76.00	2-10	34
Kasprowicz, M.S.	209	944	14.52	40	–	–	279	26.46	5-45	46
Keedy, G.	24	19	6.33	10*	–	–	23	34.00	5-30	1
Keegan, C.B.	72	530	17.09	50	–	1	110	24.16	6-33	17
Kemp, J.M.	155	3411	36.67	107*	2	24	159	28.54	6-20	65
Key, R.W.T.	124	3191	29.00	114	1	22	–	–	–	18
Khalid, S.A.	10	13	6.50	9*	–	–	4	71.00	2-40	1
Khan, A.	41	254	12.09	65*	–	1	44	31.88	4-26	10
Killeen, N.	183	595	9.29	32	–	–	258	23.22	6-31	35
King, R.E.	3	2	1.00	2	–	–	2	46.00	2-39	1
Kirby, S.P.	32	39	4.33	15	–	–	25	47.12	3-27	7
Kirtley, R.J.	182	344	9.82	30*	–	–	266	23.25	5-33	53
Klusener, L.	263	5278	38.52	142*	3	27	283	30.30	6-49	65
Knight, N.V.	401	13037	38.57	151	29	66	2	44.50	1-14	169
Kruis, G.J.	94	352	11.35	28*	–	–	114	30.39	4-26	24
Kumble, A.	369	1420	11.36	30*	–	–	501	27.45	6-12	121
Lamb, G.A.	31	583	24.29	100*	1	2	6	36.16	3-24	14
Laraman, A.W.	45	412	14.71	51	–	2	48	30.20	6-42	11
Latouf, K.J.	9	66	11.00	25	–	–	–	–	–	6
Law, S.G.	360	10890	34.24	163	20	55	90	35.17	5-26	146
Lawson, M.A.K.	2	23	11.50	20	–	–	1	53.00	1-27	1
Lehmann, D.S.	335	11718	45.41	191	17	84	152	25.46	4- 7	97
Lewis, J.	148	549	10.98	40	–	–	193	26.86	5-19	28
Lewis, J.J.B.	229	4506	27.30	102	1	20	0	–	–	39
Lewis, M.L.	59	78	8.66	19	–	–	85	24.77	5-48	17
Lewry, J.D.	74	217	7.48	16*	–	–	97	27.15	4-29	13
Logan, R.J.	55	202	11.22	28*	–	–	61	34.49	5-24	19
Loudon, A.G.R.	41	826	24.29	73*	–	7	28	29.53	4-48	15
Louw, J.	65	749	19.20	72	–	3	103	22.65	5-27	7
Lowe, J.A.	1	36	36.00	36	–	–	–	–	–	–
Loye, M.B.	245	7153	34.06	124*	8	47	–	–	–	60
Lumb, M.J.	93	2296	28.00	92	–	16	0	–	–	25
Lungley, T.	52	337	14.04	45	–	–	57	27.50	4-28	10
McGrath, A.	217	5396	31.01	109*	3	31	56	33.85	4-41	68
McLean, J.J.	10	56	14.00	36	–	–	–	–	–	6
McLean, N.A.M.	182	1318	13.44	50*	–	1	226	26.98	5-26	32
McMahon, P.J.	1	0	0.00	0	–	–	0	–	–	–
Maddy, D.L.	279	6823	29.92	151	7	42	166	28.52	4-16	100
Mahmood, S.I.	52	199	8.29	29	–	–	72	25.51	4-39	4
Malik, M.N.	43	80	11.42	11	–	–	41	35.48	4-42	6
Marshall, H.J.H.	119	2870	28.98	111	2	21	1	72.00	1-14	50
Marshall, S.J.	4	15	3.75	8	–	–	0	–	–	–
Martin-Jenkins, R.S.C.	163	1457	13.87	68*	–	3	182	27.73	4-22	38
Mascarenhas, A.D.	165	2655	22.31	79	–	18	209	23.69	5-27	43
Mason, M.S.	57	138	7.66	25	–	–	71	27.36	4-34	10
Masters, D.D.	67	242	11.52	27	–	–	49	43.73	5-20	7
Maunders, J.K.	15	201	13.40	49	–	–	2	17.00	2-16	3
Middlebrook, J.D.	91	735	17.50	47	–	–	76	31.72	4-33	25

L-O	M	Runs	Avge	HS	100	50	Wkts	Avge	Best	Ct/St
Mitchell, D.K.H.	1	2	2.00	2	–	–	–	–	–	–
Mohammad Akram	112	224	8.00	33	–	–	123	32.12	4-19	22
Mohammad Asif	22	55	27.50	12*	–	–	26	33.34	4-30	11
Mongia, D.	160	4222	33.50	159*	8	19	76	26.63	4-12	72
Montgomerie, R.R.	172	5388	36.16	132*	5	37	0	–	–	43
Moore, S.C.	38	1072	32.48	104	1	6	1	33.00	1- 1	10
Morgan, E.J.G.	10	237	39.50	93	–	2	0	–	–	4
Muchall, G.J.	55	1313	33.66	101*	1	7	1	137.00	1-15	12
Munday, M.K.	1	–	–	–	–	–	1	39.00	1-39	–
Murtagh, C.P.	2	34	–	30*	–	–	–	–	–	2
Murtagh, T.J.	50	272	12.95	31*	–	–	72	28.13	4-14	9
Mushtaq Ahmed	358	1554	11.34	41	–	–	433	28.70	7-24	57
Mustard, P.	42	389	14.40	53*	–	1	–	–	–	47/7
Napier, G.R.	113	1361	17.67	79	–	7	109	22.23	6-29	28
Nash, D.C.	112	1321	20.64	67	–	5	–	–	–	88/15
Naved-ul-Hasan	86	1028	22.34	70*	–	4	137	25.08	6-27	29
Needham, J.	4	9	9.00	9*	–	–	2	51.00	1-35	1
New, T.J.	12	236	21.45	47	–	–	–	–	–	1
Newby, O.J.	6	16	16.00	7*	–	–	6	44.16	2-37	1
Newman, S.A.	37	774	22.11	106	1	2	–	–	–	8
Nicholson, M.J.	29	155	11.07	25	–	–	31	34.58	3-34	9
Nixon, P.A.	325	5333	24.24	101	1	21	0	–	–	342/78
O'Brien, N.J.	27	222	14.80	43	–	–	–	–	–	19/7
Onions, G.	15	11	5.50	5	–	–	16	28.43	3-39	1
Ormond, J.	115	356	9.12	32	–	–	142	26.93	4-12	23
O'Shea, M.P.	1	0	0.00	0	–	–	–	–	–	1
Palladino, A.P.	11	17	5.66	16	–	–	14	24.71	3-32	1
Panesar, M.S.	5	24	24.00	16*	–	–	6	23.00	5-20	1
Park, G.T.	1	32	32.00	32	–	–	–	–	–	1
Parker, L.C.	2	23	23.00	17	–	–	0	–	–	1
Parsons, K.A.	225	4812	29.88	121	2	27	133	35.88	5-39	91
Parsons, M.	10	1	0.25	1*	–	–	8	54.00	3-70	3
Patel, M.M.	78	255	9.80	27*	–	–	78	31.98	3-22	23
Patel, S.R.	28	447	29.80	82	–	2	12	32.75	2-14	4
Patterson, S.A.	6	19	19.00	11*	–	–	5	42.60	3-11	1
Peng, N.	93	2245	25.80	121	3	12	–	–	–	19
Peploe, C.T.	8	17	5.66	14*	–	–	11	23.63	4-38	2
Peters, S.D.	115	1853	18.71	82	–	9	–	–	–	30
Pettini, M.L.	39	635	21.16	92*	–	4	–	–	–	9
Phillips, B.J.	70	555	15.41	44*	–	–	83	29.84	4-25	21
Phillips, T.J.	12	53	13.25	24*	–	–	15	25.60	3-31	3
Pietersen, C.	20	38	12.66	14*	–	–	27	29.00	7-10	3
Pietersen, K.P.	121	3860	45.95	147	8	22	34	49.55	3-14	56
Pipe, D.J.	30	390	22.94	56	–	2	–	–	–	26/12
Plunkett, L.E.	27	154	17.11	21	–	–	33	29.54	4-28	5
Pothas, N.	175	3500	36.84	114*	2	19	–	–	–	165/38
Powell, M.J. (Gm)	158	3683	28.33	91	–	21	1	26.00	1-26	62
Powell, M.J. (Wa)	100	1809	26.21	101*	1	5	25	29.08	5-40	46
Pratt, G.J.	70	1617	33.00	101*	1	11	–	–	–	30
Pretorius, D.	56	38	2.53	7*	–	–	95	21.56	5-32	8
Price, R.W.	75	252	8.40	35	–	–	71	34.67	4-21	12
Prior, M.J.	101	2094	24.63	144	2	12	–	–	–	78/15
Pyrah, R.M.	16	240	17.14	42	–	–	10	22.20	5-50	5
Ramprakash, M.R.	357	11336	38.82	147*	11	75	46	29.43	5-38	121

L-O	M	Runs	Avge	HS	100	50	Wkts	Avge	Best	Ct/St
Read, C.M.W.	191	2977	26.34	119*	1	6	–	–	–	204/46
Richardson, A.	57	102	10.20	21*	–	–	53	36.37	5-35	11
Robinson, D.D.J.	179	4078	26.14	137*	4	20	1	26.00	1- 7	46
Rogers, C.J.L.	39	1040	31.51	117*	1	5	–	–	–	16
Rudge, W.D.	2	4	4.00	3	–	–	0	–	–	–
Rudolph, J.A.	80	2846	46.66	134*	3	17	0	–	0- 8	23
Sadler, J.L.	45	750	20.83	88	–	2	–	–	–	7
Saggers, M.J.	110	289	9.32	34*	–	–	146	25.70	5-22	21
Saker, N.C.	12	6	6.00	2*	–	–	12	38.83	4-43	2
Sales, D.J.G.	187	4797	31.76	133*	2	32	0	–	–	84
Salisbury, I.D.K.	244	1521	13.46	59*	–	1	239	33.32	5-30	86
Sampson, P.J.	24	51	6.37	16	–	–	23	39.34	3-42	6
Sayers, J.J.	9	199	28.42	62	–	2	1	71.00	1-31	–
Scott, B.J.M.	40	214	15.28	50*	–	1	–	–	–	36/12
Scott, G.M.	4	130	43.33	100	1	–	4	26.75	2-32	3
Shafayat, B.M.	62	1198	22.18	97*	–	4	17	29.47	4-33	22/1
Shah, O.A.	204	5252	31.07	134	7	30	9	34.88	2- 2	67
Shantry, A.J.	4	25	8.33	15	–	–	7	17.00	5-37	4
Sheikh, M.A.	103	429	11.59	50*	–	1	103	29.99	4-17	16
Shreck, C.E.	9	14	7.00	9	–	–	18	21.94	5-19	3
Sidebottom, R.J.	126	320	11.42	32	–	–	130	29.73	6-40	27
Sillence, R.J.	7	102	17.00	82	–	1	10	13.60	4-35	1
Silverwood, C.E.W.	180	954	14.45	61	–	4	241	23.60	5-28	27
Singh, A. (Nt)	113	2941	27.74	123	1	19	–	–	–	28
Smith, B.F.	334	8301	29.96	115	2	53	2	52.50	1- 2	111
Smith, E.T.	97	2772	32.23	122	2	19	–	–	–	19
Smith, G.C.	118	4742	43.90	117*	8	34	33	35.21	3-35	53
Smith, G.J.	129	204	8.16	17*	–	–	183	24.07	5-11	18
Smith, G.M.	7	99	16.50	53	–	1	1	121.00	1-23	3
Smith, T.C.	1	8	8.00	8	–	–	0	–	–	–
Smith, W.R.	14	128	11.63	36	–	–	–	–	–	2
Snape, J.N.	247	3398	23.43	104*	1	11	199	29.33	5-32	85
Snell, S.D.	8	29	4.83	17	–	–	–	–	–	9
Solanki, V.S.	272	6704	29.79	164*	11	36	13	39.53	2- 5	102
Spearman, C.M.	243	6812	29.11	153	7	43	0	–	–	91
Stephenson, J.P.	319	7252	29.36	142	8	38	270	26.40	6-33	122
Stevens, D.I.	146	3415	27.10	133	3	20	25	34.16	5-32	62
Stiff, D.A.	1	–	–	–	–	–	1	27.00	1-27	–
Strauss, A.J.	140	3734	30.60	152	4	24	0	–	–	30
Streak, H.H.	274	3710	25.76	90*	–	14	352	28.13	5-32	69
Stubbings, S.D.	85	1743	23.87	98*	–	8	–	–	–	10
Suppiah, A.V.	19	438	24.33	79	–	2	11	34.45	3-41	6
Sutcliffe, I.J.	122	3220	29.54	105*	4	20	–	–	–	27
Sutton, L.D.	108	1506	19.30	83	–	5	–	–	–	108/10
Swann, G.P.	146	2074	19.56	83	–	11	141	28.87	5-35	41
Symonds, A.	334	8532	32.94	146	5	48	235	31.41	6-14	140
Tahir, N.	6	2	2.00	1*	–	–	1	139.00	1-23	1
Taylor, B.V.	96	156	6.24	21*	–	–	127	24.67	5-28	17
Taylor, C.G.	98	1449	19.84	93	–	6	4	18.50	2- 5	32/1
Taylor, C.R.	4	57	19.00	28	–	–	–	–	–	–
Ten Doeschate, R.N.	21	431	71.83	89*	–	3	19	17.57	4-18	9
Thomas, S.D.	138	1256	16.31	71*	–	1	171	26.91	7-16	25
Thompson, G.J.	1	0	0.00	0	–	–	1	2.00	1- 2	–
Thornely, D.J.	38	707	22.80	78	–	4	25	36.08	3-32	16

L-O	M	Runs	Avge	HS	100	50	Wkts	Avge	Best	Ct/St
Thornicroft, N.D.	8	8	–	8*	–	–	11	24.63	5-42	1
Thorp, C.D.	15	73	18.25	52	–	1	19	29.26	4-46	2
Timms, R.T.	1	38	–	38*	–	–	–	–	–	–
Tomlinson, J.A.	14	14	2.80	6	–	–	12	38.25	2-35	1
Tredwell, J.C.	72	685	15.93	71	–	2	65	31.89	4-16	34
Trego, P.D.	35	275	11.95	31*	–	–	34	30.00	4-39	7
Tremlett, C.T.	76	328	10.25	38*	–	–	116	22.17	4-25	15
Trescothick, M.E.	257	8183	36.86	137	20	38	57	28.70	4-50	98
Trott, I.J.L.	76	2121	36.56	112*	3	14	20	27.00	3-35	24
Troughton, J.O.	76	1770	29.01	115*	2	8	15	28.06	4-23	26
Tudor, A.J.	71	428	12.58	56	–	1	103	23.39	4-26	21
Udal, S.D.	338	2330	15.74	78	–	8	386	29.89	5-43	111
Van Jaarsveld, M.	164	5101	39.54	123	7	33	8	54.00	1- 0	91
Vaughan, M.P.	256	6424	28.93	125*	3	40	73	32.46	4-22	76
Vettori, D.L.	209	1880	18.80	138	2	5	211	31.95	5-30	58
Wagg, G.G.	27	323	17.00	45	–	–	19	34.05	4-50	8
Wagh, M.A.	68	1449	24.55	102*	1	8	25	34.48	4-35	12
Wainwright, D.J.	2	–	–	–	–	–	0	–	–	–
Walker, M.J.	219	4933	28.18	117	3	30	30	24.66	4-24	59
Walker, N.G.E.	16	109	9.08	43	–	–	9	29.55	3-24	7
Wallace, M.A.	82	737	16.37	48	–	–	–	–	–	89/19
Walters, J.	6	134	33.50	32*	–	–	–	–	–	4
Warne, S.K.	283	1722	11.95	55	–	1	428	24.92	5-33	114
Warren, A.C.	1	3	3.00	3	–	–	1	35.00	1-35	–
Warren, N.A.	5	2	1.00	2	–	–	3	63.00	3-34	2
Warren, R.J.	176	3359	24.69	100*	1	15	–	–	–	133/11
Waters, H.T.	1	8	8.00	8	–	–	0	–	–	–
Watkins, R.E.	4	52	13.00	26	–	–	3	41.00	2-33	–
Watson, S.R.	85	1838	34.67	132	2	11	55	43.07	3-27	20
Weekes, P.N.	311	7463	31.62	143*	9	45	324	28.87	4-17	135
Welch, G.	214	2404	19.54	82	–	7	197	34.12	6-31	31
Wessels, M.H.	16	251	20.88	80	–	1	–	–	–	17
Weston, W.P.C.	181	3910	25.55	134	4	20	1	2.00	1- 2	43
Westwood, I.J.	10	112	28.00	55	–	1	2	69.50	1-28	2
Wharf, A.G.	117	1026	17.68	72	–	1	139	29.70	6- 5	31
Whelan, C.D.	1	6	6.00	6	–	–	0	–	–	–
White, A.R.	13	173	21.62	45	–	–	8	37.12	3-17	6
White, C.	327	6413	25.65	148	3	24	337	24.90	5-19	92
White, C.L.	35	480	19.20	61	–	3	31	35.93	4-15	9
White, R.A.	28	496	19.84	101	1	1	2	23.00	2-18	6
Wigley, D.H.	9	5	1.00	2	–	–	10	32.10	4-37	1
Willoughby, C.M.	138	82	4.31	11	–	–	171	27.27	6-16	19
Windows, M.G.N.	217	4850	27.24	117	3	25	0	–	–	69
Wolstenholme, J.P.	1	10	10.00	10	–	–	–	–	–	–
Wood, M.J. (Sm)	55	1245	25.40	129	1	7	–	–	–	10
Wood, M.J. (Y)	135	3096	27.89	160	5	14	3	25.33	3-45	51
Woodman, R.J.	4	–	–	–	–	–	1	136.00	1-38	2
Wright, C.J.C.	5	0	0.00	0*	–	–	2	101.50	1-34	–
Wright, D.G.	69	831	18.06	55	–	4	110	27.20	5-37	20
Wright, L.J.	37	288	14.40	35	–	–	34	30.70	4-12	7
Yardy, M.H.	81	1186	18.82	88*	–	6	40	32.77	6-27	33
Yousuf Youhana, Mohd	226	7343	40.12	141*	11	47	0	–	–	53

LIMITED-OVERS INTERNATIONALS CAREER RECORDS

These records, complete to 14 February 2006, include all players registered for county cricket in 2006 at the time of going to press, plus those who have appeared in LOI matches since the final of the Champions Trophy on 25 September 2004. For reasons outlined in the Preface, they exclude all matches involving multinational teams, as well as the NatWest Series match between West Indies and New Zealand at Southampton in 2004 that was abandoned without a ball bowled after the toss.

ENGLAND – BATTING AND FIELDING

	M	I	NO	HS	Runs	Avge	100	50	Ct/St
C.J.Adams	5	4	–	42	71	17.75	–	–	3
Kabir Ali	9	5	2	39*	91	30.33	–	–	1
J.M.Anderson	44	14	5	11	52	5.77	–	–	9
G.J.Batty	6	4	1	3	4	1.33	–	–	4
I.R.Bell	10	8	2	75	226	37.66	–	2	2
I.D.Blackwell	28	23	1	82	344	15.63	–	1	5
A.D.Brown	16	16	–	118	354	22.12	1	1	6
D.R.Brown	9	8	4	21	99	24.75	–	–	1
A.R.Caddick	54	38	18	36	249	12.45	–	–	9
R.Clarke	17	10	–	37	99	9.90	–	–	11
P.D.Collingwood	85	75	19	112*	1791	31.98	2	8	44
D.G.Cork	32	21	3	31*	180	10.00	–	–	8
J.P.Crawley	13	12	1	73	235	21.36	–	2	1/1
R.D.B.Croft	50	36	12	32	345	14.37	–	–	11
M.A.Ealham	64	45	4	45	716	17.46	–	–	9
A.Flintoff	95	83	12	123	2500	35.21	3	15	31
J.S.Foster	11	6	3	13	41	13.66	–	–	13/7
P.J.Franks	1	1	–	4	4	4.00	–	–	1
A.F.Giles	62	35	13	41	385	17.50	–	–	22
D.Gough	156	85	38	46*	590	12.55	–	–	24
S.J.Harmison	38	17	10	13*	55	7.85	–	–	8
G.A.Hick	120	118	15	126*	3846	37.33	5	27	64
M.J.Hoggard	24	5	2	5	10	3.33	–	–	3
R.C.Irani	31	30	5	53	360	14.40	–	1	6
R.L.Johnson	10	4	1	10	16	5.33	–	–	–
G.O.Jones	38	30	6	80	565	23.54	–	3	58/3
S.P.Jones	8	5	–	1	1	1.00	–	–	–
R.W.T.Key	5	5	–	19	54	10.80	–	–	–
R.J.Kirtley	11	2	–	1	2	1.00	–	–	5
N.V.Knight	100	100	10	125*	3637	40.41	5	25	44
J.Lewis	3	1	1	7*	7	–	–	–	–
A.McGrath	14	12	2	52	166	16.60	–	1	4
D.L.Maddy	8	6	–	53	113	18.83	–	1	1
S.I.Mahmood	1	1	–	1	1	1.00	–	–	–
K.P.Pietersen	23	17	6	116	870	79.09	3	5	14
L.E.Plunkett	5	4	1	56	94	31.33	–	1	1
M.J.Prior	6	6	–	45	129	21.50	–	1	6
M.R.Ramprakash	18	18	4	51	376	26.85	–	1	8
C.M.W.Read	28	17	6	30*	239	21.72	–	–	36/2
I.D.K.Salisbury	4	2	1	5	7	7.00	–	–	1
O.A.Shah	15	15	2	62	283	21.76	–	2	6
R.J.Sidebottom	2	1	1	2*	2	–	–	–	–
C.E.W.Silverwood	7	4	–	12	17	4.25	–	–	–
J.N.Snape	10	7	3	38	118	29.50	–	–	5
V.S.Solanki	46	41	4	106	1014	27.40	2	5	12
A.J.Strauss	44	42	6	152	1371	38.08	2	7	11

ENGLAND – BATTING AND FIELDING (continued)

	M	I	NO	HS	Runs	Avge	100	50	Ct/St
G.P.Swann	1	–	–	–	–	–	–	–	–
C.T.Tremlett	3	1	–	8	8	8.00	–	–	–
M.E.Trescothick	114	113	6	137	3923	36.66	10	20	47
J.O.Troughton	6	5	1	20	36	9.00	–	–	1
A.J.Tudor	3	2	1	6	9	9.00	–	–	1
S.D.Udal	11	7	4	11*	35	11.66	–	–	1
M.P.Vaughan	74	71	10	90*	1730	28.36	–	15	20
A.G.Wharf	13	5	3	9	19	9.50	–	–	1
C.White	51	41	5	57*	568	15.77	–	1	12

ENGLAND – BOWLING

	O	M	R	W	Avge	Best	4wI	R/Over
Kabir Ali	72.3	3	391	15	26.06	3-44	–	5.39
J.M.Anderson	352.3	35	1683	66	25.50	4-25	5	4.77
G.J.Batty	52	1	253	4	63.25	2-40	–	4.86
I.R.Bell	3.4	0	9	3	3.00	3-9	–	2.45
I.D.Blackwell	146	6	647	19	34.05	3-26	–	4.43
A.D.Brown	1	0	5	0	–	–	–	5.00
D.R.Brown	54	3	305	7	43.57	2-28	–	5.64
A.R.Caddick	489.3	66	1965	69	28.47	4-19	3	4.01
R.Clarke	67.2	3	351	10	35.10	2-28	–	5.21
P.D.Collingwood	315.3	5	1606	42	38.23	6-31	3	5.09
D.G.Cork	295.2	17	1368	41	33.36	3-27	–	4.63
R.D.B.Croft	411	25	1743	45	38.73	3-51	–	4.24
M.A.Ealham	537.5	32	2197	67	32.79	5-15	3	4.08
A.Flintoff	590.4	50	2538	103	24.64	4-14	4	4.29
P.J.Franks	9	0	48	0	–	–	–	5.33
A.F.Giles	476	17	2069	55	37.61	5-57	1	4.34
D.Gough	1391.4	120	6082	234	25.99	5-44	12	4.37
S.J.Harmison	336.2	23	1634	53	30.83	5-33	3	4.85
G.A.Hick	206	6	1026	30	34.20	5-33	1	4.98
M.J.Hoggard	200.4	13	1034	32	32.31	5-49	1	5.15
R.C.Irani	213.5	5	989	24	41.20	5-26	2	4.62
R.L.Johnson	67	9	239	11	21.72	3-22	–	3.56
S.P.Jones	58	9	275	7	39.28	2-43	–	4.74
R.J.Kirtley	91.3	4	481	9	53.44	2-33	–	5.25
J.Lewis	25	1	124	4	31.00	3-32	–	4.96
A.McGrath	38	2	175	4	43.75	1-13	–	4.60
S.I.Mahmood	7	0	56	0	–	–	–	8.00
K.P.Pietersen	2	0	22	0	–	–	–	11.00
L.E.Plunkett	40	0	265	7	37.85	3-51	–	6.62
M.R.Ramprakash	22	0	108	4	27.00	3-28	–	4.90
I.D.K.Salisbury	31	1	177	5	35.40	3-41	–	5.70
R.J.Sidebottom	14	0	84	2	42.00	1-42	–	6.00
C.E.W.Silverwood	51	0	244	6	40.66	3-43	–	4.78
J.N.Snape	88.1	2	403	13	31.00	3-43	–	4.57
V.S.Solanki	7	0	37	0	–	–	–	5.28
A.J.Strauss	1	0	3	0	–	–	–	3.00
G.P.Swann	5	0	24	0	–	–	–	4.80
C.T.Tremlett	24.2	1	111	5	22.20	4-32	–	4.56
M.E.Trescothick	38.4	0	219	4	54.75	2-7	–	5.66
A.J.Tudor	21.1	1	136	4	34.00	2-30	–	6.42
S.D.Udal	102	4	400	9	44.44	2-37	–	3.92
M.P.Vaughan	110.4	2	562	12	46.83	4-22	1	5.07
A.G.Wharf	97.2	10	428	18	23.77	4-24	1	4.39
C.White	394	25	1725	65	26.53	5-21	2	4.37

LOI

AUSTRALIA – BATTING AND FIELDING

	M	I	NO	HS	Runs	Avge	100	50	Ct/St
N.W.Bracken	28	6	5	21*	49	49.00	–	–	6
S.R.Clark	10	1	–	15	15	15.00	–	–	4
M.J.Clarke	71	64	18	105*	2211	48.06	2	15	26
M.J.Di Venuto	9	9	–	89	241	26.77	–	2	1
B.R.Dorey	3	1	–	2	2	2.00	–	–	–
M.T.G.Elliott	1	1	–	1	1	1.00	–	–	–
A.C.Gilchrist	230	224	9	172	7781	36.19	13	43	331/41
J.N.Gillespie	97	39	16	44*	289	12.56	–	–	10
B.J.Haddin	13	11	–	41	200	18.18	–	–	13/4
M.L.Hayden	118	114	12	146	4129	40.48	5	26	46
B.J.Hodge	5	5	–	59	79	15.80	–	1	1
G.B.Hogg	79	45	21	71*	530	22.08	–	2	22
J.R.Hopes	8	3	–	43	84	28.00	–	–	3
M.E.K.Hussey	29	22	14	88*	795	99.37	–	6	14
P.A.Jaques	1	1	–	94	94	94.00	–	1	–
M.G.Johnson	1	–	–	–	–	–	–	–	–
M.S.Kasprowicz	43	13	9	28*	72	18.00	–	–	13
S.M.Katich	30	28	4	107*	849	35.37	1	7	11
S.G.Law	54	51	5	110	1237	26.89	1	7	12
B.Lee	125	53	19	57	596	17.52	–	2	30
D.S.Lehmann	117	101	22	119	3078	38.96	4	17	26
M.L.Lewis	4	–	–	–	–	–	–	–	1
G.D.McGrath	218	59	32	11	104	3.85	–	–	31
D.R.Martyn	192	167	49	144*	4889	41.43	5	32	61
R.T.Ponting	243	237	29	145	8686	41.75	18	49	98
A.Symonds	138	109	19	156	3423	38.03	4	17	59
S.K.Warne	193	106	28	55	1016	13.02	–	1	80
S.R.Watson	37	23	10	77*	380	29.23	–	1	10
C.L.White	2	1	–	0	0	0.00	–	–	2

AUSTRALIA – BOWLING

	O	M	R	W	Avge	Best	4wI	R/Over
N.W.Bracken	236.5	25	1001	48	20.85	4-29	2	4.22
S.R.Clark	90	4	430	17	25.29	4-55	1	4.77
M.J.Clarke	138.5	2	731	20	36.55	5-35	2	5.26
B.R.Dorey	23	1	134	1	134.00	1-51	–	5.82
J.N.Gillespie	857.2	79	3611	142	25.42	5-22	6	4.21
M.L.Hayden	1	0	18	0	–	–	–	18.00
B.J.Hodge	3	0	16	0	–	–	–	5.33
G.B.Hogg	616	19	2790	95	29.36	5-32	2	4.52
J.R.Hopes	51	4	261	3	87.00	1-16	–	5.11
M.E.K.Hussey	15	0	92	1	92.00	1-31	–	6.13
M.G.Johnson	9	0	64	0	–	–	–	7.11
M.S.Kasprowicz	370.5	28	1674	67	24.98	5-45	3	4.51
S.G.Law	134.3	3	635	12	52.91	2-22	–	4.72
B.Lee	1065	83	4962	219	22.65	5-22	13	4.65
D.S.Lehmann	298.5	3	1445	52	27.78	4-7	1	4.83
M.L.Lewis	33.5	1	215	5	43.00	3-56	–	6.35
G.D.McGrath	1907.1	257	7349	327	22.47	7-15	16	3.85
D.R.Martyn	132.2	2	704	12	58.66	2-21	–	5.32
R.T.Ponting	25	0	104	3	34.66	1-12	–	4.16
A.Symonds	804.1	27	3949	107	36.90	5-18	3	4.91
S.K.Warne	1766.4	110	7514	291	25.82	5-33	13	4.25
S.R.Watson	239.5	11	1125	25	45.00	3-27	–	4.69
C.L.White	5	0	38	1	38.00	1-34	–	7.60

LOI	SOUTH AFRICA – BATTING AND FIELDING								
	M	I	NO	HS	Runs	Avge	100	50	Ct/St
A.M.Bacher	13	13	–	56	270	20.76	–	1	4
D.M.Benkenstein	23	20	3	69	305	17.94	–	1	3
N.Boje	113	69	18	129	1410	27.64	2	4	33
J.Botha	11	6	3	46	98	32.66	–	–	6
M.V.Boucher	210	151	38	76	2997	26.52	–	18	286/16
A.B.de Villiers	12	12	–	30	158	13.16	–	–	4
H.H.Dippenaar	91	79	13	125*	3031	45.92	3	24	28
H.H.Gibbs	180	179	13	153	5859	35.29	15	24	76
A.J.Hall	63	42	10	81	745	23.28	–	2	22
C.W.Henderson	4	–	–	–	–	–	–	–	–
J.H.Kallis	224	214	39	139	7926	45.29	13	56	89
J.M.Kemp	46	34	10	80	799	33.29	–	6	22
L.Klusener	171	137	50	103*	3576	41.10	2	19	35
G.J.P.Kruger	3	2	1	0*	0	0.00	–	–	1
C.K.Langeveldt	29	5	1	3	7	1.75	–	–	1
J.A.Morkel	8	6	1	23*	63	12.60	–	–	1
A.Nel	43	7	5	4*	12	6.00	–	–	11
M.Ntini	123	28	14	42*	145	10.35	–	–	24
J.L.Ontong	20	11	1	32	98	9.80	–	–	10
R.J.Peterson	23	8	1	36	91	13.00	–	–	3
S.M.Pollock	249	162	57	75	2542	24.20	–	9	93
N.Pothas	3	1	–	24	24	24.00	–	–	4/1
A.G.Prince	34	30	10	89*	792	39.60	–	2	20
A.G.Puttick	1	1	–	0	0	0.00	–	–	1
J.A.Rudolph	43	37	6	81	1157	37.32	–	7	11
G.C.Smith	85	84	4	134*	3145	39.31	5	18	36
D.W.Steyn	2	–	–	–	–	–	–	–	–
J.J.van der Wath	6	5	2	38*	46	15.33	–	–	2
M.van Jaarsveld	11	7	1	45	124	20.66	–	–	4
C.M.Willoughby	3	2	–	0	0	0.00	–	–	–
M.Zondeki	9	2	2	3*	4	–	–	–	3

	SOUTH AFRICA – BOWLING							
	O	M	R	W	Avge	Best	4wI	R/Over
A.M.Bacher	18	0	64	3	21.33	2-36	–	3.55
D.M.Benkenstein	10.5	1	44	4	11.00	3-5	–	4.06
N.Boje	742.5	21	3352	95	35.28	5-21	3	4.51
J.Botha	73	1	361	7	51.57	2-49	–	4.94
A.J.Hall	357.1	18	1620	60	27.00	4-23	2	4.53
C.W.Henderson	36.1	2	132	7	18.85	4-17	1	3.64
J.H.Kallis	1325.4	60	6336	197	32.16	5-30	4	4.77
J.M.Kemp	141.5	9	653	19	34.36	3-20	–	4.60
L.Klusener	1222.4	48	5751	192	29.95	6-49	7	4.70
G.J.P.Kruger	23	1	139	2	69.50	1-43	–	6.04
C.K.Langeveldt	224.5	12	1102	38	29.00	5-62	2	4.90
J.A.Morkel	44	1	212	7	30.28	2-23	–	4.81
A.Nel	346	32	1624	55	29.52	4-39	1	4.69
M.Ntini	1023.3	87	4464	194	23.01	5-31	8	4.36
J.L.Ontong	89.4	3	396	9	44.00	3-30	–	4.41
R.J.Peterson	130	1	626	9	69.55	2-26	–	4.81
S.M.Pollock	2168.4	243	8136	337	24.14	6-35	15	3.75
J.A.Rudolph	4	0	26	0	–	–	–	6.50
G.C.Smith	101.2	0	564	10	56.40	3-30	–	5.56
D.W.Steyn	8	0	90	1	90.00	1-58	–	11.25
J.J.van der Wath	52.4	2	323	10	32.30	2-21	–	6.13

SOUTH AFRICA – BOWLING (continued)

	O	M	R	W	Avge	Best	4wI	R/Over
M.van Jaarsveld	5.1	1	18	2	9.00	1-0	–	3.48
C.M.Willoughby	28	2	148	2	74.00	2-39	–	5.28
M.Zondeki	67	4	350	8	43.75	2-46	–	5.22

WEST INDIES – BATTING AND FIELDING

† Excluding match abandoned without a ball bowled after toss

	M	I	NO	HS	Runs	Avge	100	50	Ct/St
O.A.C.Banks	5	5	–	33	83	16.60	–	–	–
T.L.Best	10	7	3	24	44	11.00	–	–	3
I.D.R.Bradshaw	30	17	4	34*	153	11.76	–	–	2
D.J.J.Bravo†	31	23	6	41*	313	18.41	–	–	11
C.O.Browne	46	32	8	46*	415	17.29	–	–	59/9
D.C.Butler	3	3	2	13*	22	22.00	–	–	–
S.Chanderpaul†	177	166	21	150	5281	36.42	3	35	54
P.T.Collins	30	12	5	10*	30	4.28	–	–	8
C.D.Collymore	64	26	12	13*	72	5.14	–	–	10
N.Deonarine	4	4	–	41	91	22.75	–	–	–
M.Dillon	108	51	20	21*	227	7.32	–	–	20
F.H.Edwards	6	2	2	4*	4	–	–	–	–
C.H.Gayle†	119	117	6	153*	4361	39.28	11	23	53
O.D.Gibson	15	11	1	52	141	14.10	–	1	3
W.W.Hinds	98	94	7	127*	2627	30.19	5	13	27
S.C.Joseph	13	11	1	58	161	16.10	–	1	4
R.D.King	50	23	14	12*	65	7.22	–	–	4
B.C.Lara†	254	248	26	169	9302	41.90	19	56	106
J.J.C.Lawson†	12	5	2	8	18	6.00	–	–	–
X.M.Marshall	10	10	–	26	98	9.80	–	–	6
R.S.Morton	7	7	–	84	199	28.42	–	2	3
D.B.Powell	9	5	1	6	14	3.50	–	–	1
R.L.Powell†	108	100	16	124	2085	24.82	1	8	43
R.Ramdass	1	1	–	1	1	1.00	–	–	–
D.Ramdin	4	3	1	74*	127	63.50	–	1	3/1
M.N.Samuels	57	54	8	108*	1448	31.47	1	10	17
R.R.Sarwan†	88	82	20	104*	2761	44.53	2	16	25
D.R.Smith†	6	6	1	44	129	25.80	–	–	3

WEST INDIES – BOWLING

	O	M	R	W	Avge	Best	4wI	R/Over
O.A.C.Banks	45	1	189	7	27.00	2-24	–	4.20
T.L.Best	74.2	3	357	12	29.75	4-35	1	4.80
I.D.R.Bradshaw	246	23	1064	38	28.00	3-15	–	4.32
D.J.J.Bravo	209.3	6	1132	31	36.51	3-26	–	5.40
D.C.Butler	25	3	94	3	31.33	1-25	–	3.76
S.Chanderpaul	119.2	0	617	14	44.07	3-18	–	5.17
P.T.Collins	262.5	18	1212	39	31.07	5-43	1	4.61
C.D.Collymore	521.4	31	2300	68	33.82	5-51	2	4.40
N.Deonarine	22	0	142	5	28.40	2-18	–	6.45
M.Dillon	913.2	67	4217	130	32.43	5-29	6	4.61
F.H.Edwards	43	1	195	12	16.25	6-22	1	4.53
C.H.Gayle	655.2	24	3093	100	30.93	5-46	4	4.71
O.D.Gibson	123.1	8	621	34	18.26	5-40	4	5.04
W.W.Hinds	133.3	3	693	25	27.72	3-24	–	5.19
R.D.King	433.5	41	1807	76	23.77	4-25	2	4.16
B.C.Lara	8.1	0	61	4	15.25	2-5	–	7.46

WEST INDIES – BOWLING (continued)

	O	M	R	W	Avge	Best	4wI	R/Over
J.J.C.Lawson	93	5	498	17	29.29	4-57	1	5.35
R.S.Morton	1	0	2	0	–	–	–	2.00
D.B.Powell	76	7	337	5	67.40	2-28	–	4.43
R.L.Powell	78.5	3	491	11	44.63	2-5	–	6.22
M.N.Samuels	281	6	1414	35	40.40	3-25	–	5.03
R.R.Sarwan	56.4	1	336	7	48.00	3-31	–	5.92
D.R.Smith	113.2	3	561	11	51.00	3-24	–	4.95

NEW ZEALAND – BATTING AND FIELDING

† Excluding match abandoned without a ball bowled after toss

	M	I	NO	HS	Runs	Avge	100	50	Ct/St
A.R.Adams†	38	31	10	45	409	19.47	–	–	7
N.J.Astle†	206	202	13	145*	6595	34.89	15	38	77
S.E.Bond	40	17	9	31*	147	18.37	–	–	9
I.G.Butler†	14	6	4	3	6	3.00	–	–	6
C.L.Cairns	214	192	25	115	4881	29.22	4	25	66
T.K.Canning	4	4	1	23*	52	17.33	–	–	1
C.D.Cumming	12	12	1	45*	161	14.63	–	–	6
S.P.Fleming†	246	237	19	134*	6985	32.04	6	41	115
J.E.C.Franklin	37	21	4	29*	180	10.58	–	–	10
P.G.Fulton	5	5	1	112	273	68.25	1	2	5
L.J.Hamilton	2	2	2	2	3	–	–	–	–
C.Z.Harris†	249	213	62	130	4379	29.00	1	16	96
J.M.How	4	3	–	58	75	25.00	–	1	2
B.B.McCullum	79	60	14	56*	1029	22.36	–	4	98/5
C.D.McMillan†	174	164	13	105	4148	27.47	2	25	43
H.J.H.Marshall†	50	47	7	101*	1239	30.97	1	11	16
J.A.H.Marshall	5	5	–	14	30	6.00	–	–	–
C.S.Martin	9	6	1	3	6	1.20	–	–	3
K.D.Mills	58	33	16	44*	228	13.41	–	–	17
J.D.P.Oram	83	62	6	81·	1034	18.46	–	3	21
M.H.W.Papps	6	6	2	92*	207	51.75	–	2	1
J.S.Patel	4	–	–	–	–	–	–	–	1
M.S.Sinclair	45	44	2	118*	1180	28.09	2	7	15
C.M.Spearman	51	50	–	86	936	18.72	–	5	15
S.B.Styris†	110	94	12	141	2361	28.79	3	13	41
D.R.Tuffey†	75	40	20	20*	146	7.30	–	–	19
D.L.Vettori†	164	102	31	83	938	13.21	–	1	39
L.Vincent	79	76	9	172	1734	25.88	1	7	30
J.W.Wilson	6	6	1	44*	103	20.60	–	–	4

NEW ZEALAND – BOWLING

	O	M	R	W	Avge	Best	4wI	R/Over
A.R.Adams	288.1	15	1494	52	28.73	5-22	3	5.18
N.J.Astle	782.4	28	3677	97	37.90	4-43	1	4.69
S.E.Bond	339.4	41	1434	77	18.62	6-19	7	4.22
I.G.Butler	98.5	1	558	14	39.85	3-41	–	5.64
C.L.Cairns	1355.2	80	6557	200	32.78	5-42	4	4.83
T.K.Canning	34	1	203	5	40.60	2-30	–	5.97
S.P.Fleming	4.5	0	28	1	28.00	1-8	–	5.79
J.E.C.Franklin	251	14	1323	34	38.91	5-42	1	5.27
L.J.Hamilton	18	0	143	1	143.00	1-76	–	7.94
C.Z.Harris	1777.5	81	7613	203	37.50	5-42	3	4.28
C.D.McMillan	256.5	6	1397	39	35.82	3-20	–	5.43

NEW ZEALAND – BOWLING (continued)

	O	M	R	W	Avge	Best	4wI	R/Over
C.S.Martin	73	4	397	11	36.09	3-62	–	5.43
K.D.Mills	480.2	39	2240	74	30.27	4-14	2	4.66
J.D.P.Oram	612.4	54	2812	94	29.91	5-26	4	4.58
J.S.Patel	36	0	178	6	29.66	2-23	–	4.94
C.M.Spearman	0.3	0	6	0	–	–	–	12.00
S.B.Styris	686.3	33	3199	104	30.75	6-25	4	4.65
D.R.Tuffey	578.2	63	2693	90	29.92	4-24	2	4.65
D.L.Vettori	1249.5	49	5300	153	34.64	5-30	4	4.24
L.Vincent	0.2	0	3	0	–	–	–	9.00
J.W.Wilson	40.2	0	260	4	65.00	2-21	–	6.44

INDIA – BATTING AND FIELDING

	M	I	NO	HS	Runs	Avge	100	50	Ct/St
A.B.Agarkar	153	94	26	95	1122	16.50	–	3	45
L.Balaji	29	15	6	21*	113	12.55	–	–	11
M.S.Dhoni	33	29	8	183*	1054	50.19	2	5	18/8
R.Dravid	274	253	33	153	8817	40.07	11	65	165/14
G.Gambhir	12	12	–	103	296	24.66	1	1	2
S.C.Ganguly	278	269	21	183	10101	40.72	22	60	96
Harbhajan Singh	117	59	18	46	525	12.80	–	–	36
M.Kaif	106	93	22	111*	2444	34.42	2	14	50
M.Kartik	31	11	4	32*	89	12.71	–	–	10
Z.Khan	102	55	22	34*	420	12.72	–	–	24
A.Kumble	262	129	45	26	895	10.65	–	–	84
V.V.S.Laxman	85	82	7	131	2338	31.17	6	10	39
D.Mongia	51	45	6	159*	1073	27.51	1	3	21
A.Nehra	69	25	14	24	86	7.81	–	–	9
I.K.Pathan	51	35	10	83	678	27.12	–	4	7
R.R.Powar	3	2	1	18*	32	32.00	–	–	–
S.K.Raina	11	5	1	39*	89	22.25	–	–	2
V.Sehwag	134	131	7	130	4047	32.63	7	20	54
J.Sharma	3	2	2	29*	34	–	–	–	3
R.P.Singh	2	–	–	–	–	–	–	–	–
S.Sreesanth	7	1	1	0*	0	–	–	–	1
S.Sriram	8	7	1	57	81	13.50	–	1	1
S.R.Tendulkar	361	352	33	186*	14146	44.34	39	72	107
Y.Venugopal Rao	11	8	1	38	136	19.42	–	–	3
J.P.Yadav	12	7	3	69	81	20.25	–	1	3
Yuvraj Singh	140	126	18	139	3637	33.67	5	22	48

INDIA – BOWLING

	O	M	R	W	Avge	Best	4wI	R/Over
A.B.Agarkar	1262.5	78	6456	236	27.35	6-42	11	5.11
L.Balaji	236.1	11	1312	34	38.58	4-48	1	5.55
R.Dravid	31	1	170	4	42.50	2-43	–	5.48
S.C.Ganguly	687.1	28	3470	93	37.31	5-16	3	5.04
Harbhajan Singh	1049.1	48	4322	138	31.31	5-43	3	4.11
M.Kartik	255	14	1312	27	48.59	6-27	1	5.14
Z.Khan	840.3	50	4124	143	28.83	4-19	6	4.90
A.Kumble	2332.5	106	10010	326	30.70	6-12	10	4.29
V.V.S.Laxman	7	0	40	0	–	–	–	5.71
D.Mongia	66.4	1	370	8	46.25	3-31	–	5.54
A.Nehra	577	38	2777	90	30.85	6-23	4	4.81
I.K.Pathan	439.5	27	2193	85	25.80	5-27	3	4.98
R.R.Powar	10	0	52	0	–	–	–	5.20

LOI **INDIA – BOWLING (continued)**

	O	M	R	W	Avge	Best	4wI	R/Over
S.K.Raina	4.2	0	27	1	27.00	1-23	–	6.23
V.Sehwag	481.2	12	2556	65	39.32	3-25	–	5.31
J.Sharma	21	3	99	1	99.00	1-28	–	4.71
R.P.Singh	13.4	1	77	1	77.00	1-58	–	5.63
S.Sreesanth	61.4	2	396	5	79.20	2-39	–	6.42
S.Sriram	54	1	274	9	30.44	3-43	–	5.07
S.R.Tendulkar	1215.5	24	6167	141	43.73	5-32	6	5.07
J.P.Yadav	66	4	326	6	54.33	2-32	–	4.93
Yuvraj Singh	268.3	10	1351	34	39.73	4-6	1	5.03

PAKISTAN – BATTING AND FIELDING

	M	I	NO	HS	Runs	Avge	100	50	Ct/St
Abdul Razzaq	200	174	43	112	3982	30.39	2	21	29
Arshad Khan	58	29	18	20	133	12.09	–	–	10
Azhar Mahmood	139	107	25	67	1492	18.19	–	3	37
Bazid Khan	3	3	–	66	78	26.00	–	1	1
Danish Kaneria	15	8	6	3*	6	3.00	–	–	2
Iftikhar Anjum	12	6	6	19*	41	–	–	–	1
Inzamam-ul-Haq	351	327	48	137*	11143	39.93	10	82	103
Kamran Akmal	37	31	5	124	809	31.11	3	–	30/4
Misbah-ul-Haq	12	11	2	50*	305	33.88	–	2	5
Mohammad Akram	23	9	7	7*	14	7.00	–	–	8
Mohammad Asif	4	1	–	2	2	2.00	–	–	–
Mohammad Hafeez	30	30	–	69	543	18.10	–	3	13
Mohammad Khalil	3	1	1	0*	0	–	–	–	2
Mohammad Sami	74	39	19	23	214	10.70	–	–	17
Moin Khan	219	183	41	72*	3266	23.00	–	12	214/73
Mushtaq Ahmed	144	76	34	34*	399	9.50	–	–	30
Naved-ul-Hasan	39	27	10	29	234	13.76	–	–	9
Salman Butt	29	29	1	108*	918	32.78	3	3	9
Shabbir Ahmed	32	11	5	2	10	1.66	–	–	10
Shahid Afridi	214	205	9	109	4782	24.39	4	26	80
Shoaib Akhtar	124	59	29	43	299	9.96	–	–	16
Shoaib Malik	110	95	11	143	2932	34.90	5	18	38
Taufiq Umar	19	19	1	81*	447	24.83	–	3	9
Umar Gul	18	2	1	17*	19	19.00	–	–	1
Yasir Arafat	4	3	1	6	11	5.50	–	–	1
Yasir Hamid	48	48	1	127*	1805	38.40	3	10	11
Younis Khan	126	121	15	144	3296	31.09	1	22	70
M.Yousuf Youhana	206	196	28	141*	6953	41.38	11	46	45

PAKISTAN – BOWLING

	O	M	R	W	Avge	Best	4wI	R/Over
Abdul Razzaq	1460.2	83	6699	225	29.77	6-35	10	4.58
Azhar Mahmood	1024.4	57	4740	122	38.85	6-18	5	4.62
Bazid Khan	2	0	11	0	–	–	–	5.50
Danish Kaneria	121.2	9	555	12	46.25	3-31	–	4.57
Iftikhar Anjum	97	6	472	8	59.00	2-67	–	4.86
Inzamam-ul-Haq	9.4	1	64	3	21.33	1-0	–	6.61
Mohammad Akram	164.5	6	790	19	41.57	2-28	–	4.79
Mohammad Asif	32.4	4	119	7	17.00	3-30	–	3.64
Mohammad Hafeez	188.3	8	841	27	31.14	3-17	–	4.46
Mohammad Khalil	24	0	144	5	28.80	2-55	–	6.00
Mohammad Sami	609.3	36	2986	105	28.43	5-10	4	4.89
Mushtaq Ahmed	1257.1	51	5361	161	33.29	5-36	4	4.26

LOI PAKISTAN – BOWLING (continued)

	O	M	R	W	Avge	Best	4wI	R/Over
Naved-ul-Hasan	326.1	12	1770	68	26.02	6-27	4	5.42
Salman Butt	6	0	42	0	–	–	–	7.00
Shabbir Ahmed	273.4	26	1192	33	36.12	3-32	–	4.35
Shahid Afridi	1400.2	45	6514	177	36.80	5-11	4	4.65
Shoaib Akhtar	967.3	78	4470	193	23.16	6-16	8	4.62
Shoaib Malik	711.2	21	3148	91	34.59	4-19	1	4.42
Taufiq Umar	12	0	85	1	85.00	1-49	–	7.08
Umar Gul	134.2	8	645	20	32.25	5-17	1	4.80
Yasir Arafat	26	0	149	3	49.66	1-28	–	5.73
Yasir Hamid	3	0	26	0	–	–	–	8.66
Younis Khan	15.1	0	101	1	101.00	1-24	–	6.65
M.Yousuf Youhana	0.1	0	1	0	–	–	–	6.00

SRI LANKA – BATTING AND FIELDING

	M	I	NO	HS	Runs	Avge	100	50	Ct/St
R.P.Arnold	157	137	37	103	3660	36.60	1	26	45
M.S.Atapattu	252	246	28	132*	8233	37.76	11	59	69
C.M.Bandara	11	4	–	12	23	5.75	–	–	1
U.D.U.Chandana	146	110	17	89	1626	17.48	–	5	76
L.H.D.Dilhara	8	8	–	29	77	9.62	–	–	3
T.M.Dilshan	82	72	16	82*	1538	27.46	–	6	43/1
C.R.D.Fernando	85	31	19	13*	97	8.08	–	–	12
W.C.A.Ganegama	4	2	–	7	7	3.50	–	–	1
D.A.Gunawardana	61	61	1	132	1708	28.46	1	12	13
W.S.Jayantha	17	17	2	74*	400	26.66	–	2	5
P.S.Jayaprakashdaran	1	–	–	–	–	–	–	–	–
S.T.Jayasuriya	353	344	15	189	10484	31.86	19	59	106
D.P.M.deS.Jayawardena	205	191	18	128	5379	31.09	6	31	97
S.H.T.Kandamby	4	4	–	13	23	5.75	–	–	–
C.K.Kapugedera	5	5	–	38	73	14.60	–	–	–
M.D.N.Kulasekera	14	7	4	4*	8	2.66	–	–	3
K.S.Lokuarachchi	12	10	2	28	91	11.37	–	–	2
M.F.Maharoof	33	21	7	38	229	16.35	–	–	8
S.L.Malinga	5	3	3	5*	7	–	–	–	–
J.Mubarak	18	17	–	61	309	18.17	–	2	6
M.Muralitharan	263	123	47	27	451	5.93	–	–	105
P.D.R.L.Perera	11	4	1	3	4	1.33	–	–	1
T.T.Samaraweera	17	13	1	33	199	16.58	–	–	4
K.C.Sangakkara	153	141	18	138*	4282	34.81	4	27	126/35
W.U.Tharanga	17	17	–	105	467	27.47	2	1	4
W.P.U.C.J.Vaas	274	190	62	50*	1777	13.88	–	1	54
M.G.Vandort	1	1	–	48	48	48.00	–	–	–
D.N.T.Zoysa	94	47	21	47*	343	13.19	–	–	13

SRI LANKA – BOWLING

	O	M	R	W	Avge	Best	4wI	R/Over
R.P.Arnold	348.2	8	1689	37	45.64	3-47	–	4.84
M.S.Atapattu	8.3	0	41	0	–	–	–	4.82
C.M.Bandara	78.2	0	382	15	25.46	4-31	2	4.87
U.D.U.Chandana	1015.4	20	4781	151	31.66	5-61	5	4.70
L.H.D.Dilhara	47	3	221	6	36.83	2-30	–	4.70
T.M.Dilshan	255.4	6	1222	29	42.13	4-29	1	4.77
C.R.D.Fernando	609.5	31	3209	100	32.09	4-48	1	5.26

LOI **SRI LANKA – BOWLING (continued)**

	O	M	R	W	Avge	Best	4wI	R/Over
W.C.A.Ganegama	11	0	88	2	44.00	2-27	–	8.00
W.S.Jayantha	9.1	0	46	0	–	–	–	5.01
P.S.Jayaprakashdaran	6	1	21	1	21.00	1-21	–	3.50
S.T.Jayasuriya	2083.4	36	9961	269	37.02	6-29	10	4.78
D.P.M.deS.Jayawardena	94.4	1	539	7	77.00	2-56	–	5.69
M.D.N.Kulasekera	95.1	7	416	8	52.00	2-19	–	4.37
K.S.Lokuarachchi	91	4	383	14	27.35	3-37	–	4.20
M.F.Maharoof	218.2	18	1043	37	28.18	4-20	1	4.77
S.L.Malinga	40	3	203	4	50.75	2-56	–	5.07
J.Mubarak	8	0	49	1	49.00	1-10	–	6.12
M.Muralitharan	2398.3	171	9214	400	23.03	7-30	18	3.84
P.D.R.L.Perera	93	4	537	12	44.75	3-55	–	5.77
T.T.Samaraweera	112	2	509	10	50.90	3-34	–	4.54
W.P.U.C.J.Vaas	2246.3	232	9433	351	26.87	8-19	13	4.19
D.N.T.Zoysa	709.5	60	3213	108	29.75	5-26	3	4.52

ZIMBABWE – BATTING AND FIELDING

	M	I	NO	HS	Runs	Avge	100	50	Ct/St
A.M.Blignaut	51	40	8	63*	625	19.53	–	5	11
S.V.Carlisle	111	107	8	121*	2740	27.67	3	9	39
C.J.Chibhabha	1	1	–	0	0	0.00	–	–	1
E.Chigumbura	21	20	2	77	414	23.00	–	3	5
C.K.Coventry	5	5	–	74	137	27.40	–	1	1
K.M.Dabengwa	1	–	–	–	–	–	–	–	1
D.D.Ebrahim	82	76	6	121	1443	20.61	1	4	23
S.M.Ervine	42	34	7	100	698	25.85	1	2	5
G.M.Ewing	7	7	–	46	97	13.85	–	–	3
A.Flower	213	208	16	145	6786	35.34	4	55	141/32
G.W.Flower	219	212	18	142*	6536	33.69	6	40	86
M.W.Goodwin	71	70	3	112*	1818	27.13	2	8	20
D.T.Hondo	56	29	12	17	127	7.47	–	–	15
A.J.Ireland	4	1	1	1*	1	–	–	–	–
N.B.Mahwire	7	6	2	8*	28	7.00	–	–	3
A.Maregwede	11	11	1	37	124	12.40	–	–	2
H.Masakadza	17	17	–	66	278	16.35	–	2	8
S.Matsikenyeri	45	43	2	73	658	16.04	–	2	14
C.B.Mpofu	11	6	4	3*	9	4.50	–	–	–
T.Mupariwa	6	6	2	12*	28	7.00	–	–	3
M.L.Nkala	47	32	5	47	288	10.66	–	1	8
T.Panyangara	23	19	4	16*	90	6.00	–	–	3
R.W.Price	26	12	5	20*	90	12.85	–	–	1
E.C.Rainsford	5	5	1	5	13	3.25	–	–	–
B.G.Rogers	15	15	–	84	478	31.86	–	5	7
V.Sibanda	27	26	–	58	300	11.53	–	2	7
H.H.Streak	187	157	55	79*	2901	28.44	–	13	45
T.Taibu	83	70	15	96*	1400	25.45	–	7	73/8
B.R.M.Taylor	29	29	–	74	684	23.58	–	5	6
P.Utseya	26	23	10	31	149	11.46	–	–	7
M.A.Vermeulen	32	32	4	79	583	20.82	–	4	9
S.C.Williams	4	4	1	33*	54	18.00	–	–	1
C.B.Wishart	90	82	8	172*	1719	23.22	2	5	26

ZIMBABWE – BOWLING

	O	M	R	W	Avge	Best	4wI	R/Over
A.M.Blignaut	378.2	11	2020	49	41.22	4-43	2	5.33
E.Chigumbura	76.3	4	551	10	55.10	3-37	–	7.20
D.D.Ebrahim	0.5	0	11	0	–	–	–	13.20
S.M.Ervine	274.5	10	1561	41	38.07	3-29	–	5.67
G.M.Ewing	52	0	236	5	47.20	3-31	–	4.53
A.Flower	5	0	23	0	–	–	–	4.60
G.W.Flower	903.1	11	4187	104	40.25	4-32	2	4.63
M.W.Goodwin	41.2	1	210	4	52.50	1-12	–	5.08
D.T.Hondo	396.5	21	2171	61	35.59	4-37	3	5.47
A.J.Ireland	37	0	226	8	28.25	3-54	–	6.10
N.B.Mahwire	30.5	3	202	4	50.50	2-40	–	6.55
H.Masakadza	8.2	0	49	1	49.00	1-45	–	5.88
S.Matsikenyeri	106	2	554	11	50.36	2-33	–	5.22
C.B.Mpofu	80.5	1	444	10	44.40	3-59	–	5.49
T.Mupariwa	53.3	1	272	10	27.20	2-25	–	5.08
M.L.Nkala	259.5	8	1557	22	70.77	3-12	–	5.99
T.Panyangara	177	15	956	26	36.76	3-28	–	5.40
R.W.Price	221.2	9	917	15	61.13	2-16	–	4.14
E.C.Rainsford	42	1	185	4	46.25	2-29	–	4.40
B.G.Rogers	54	0	321	6	53.50	2-55	–	5.94
V.Sibanda	15	0	87	2	43.50	1-12	–	5.80
H.H.Streak	1569	114	7066	237	29.81	5-32	8	4.50
T.Taibu	14	1	61	2	30.50	2-42	–	4.35
B.R.M.Taylor	35	0	224	8	28.00	3-54	–	6.40
P.Utseya	197.5	6	821	12	68.41	3-40	–	4.15
C.B.Wishart	2	0	12	0	–	–	–	6.00

BANGLADESH – BATTING AND FIELDING

	M	I	NO	HS	Runs	Avge	100	50	Ct/St
Abdur Razzaq	6	6	2	21	39	9.75	–	–	–
Aftab Ahmed	22	22	2	81*	442	22.10	–	3	3
Alok Kapali	45	43	2	89*	818	19.95	–	4	17
Enamul Haque II	3	2	1	4*	4	4.00	–	–	5
Habibul Bashar	72	72	2	74	1379	19.70	–	9	12
Hasibul Hossain	32	26	6	21*	172	8.60	–	–	6
Javed Omar	44	44	3	85*	951	23.19	–	8	9
Khaled Mahmud	76	71	3	50	955	14.04	–	1	17
Khaled Masud	102	94	22	71*	1536	21.33	–	7	68/25
Manjural Rana	23	20	5	63	308	20.53	–	1	5
Mashrafe Mortaza	24	21	4	39	218	12.82	–	–	7
Mohammad Ashraful	57	56	2	100	1053	19.50	1	6	5
Mohammad Rafique	82	78	13	77	872	13.41	–	2	20
Mushfiqur Rahman	28	25	3	49	360	16.36	–	–	6
Nafis Iqbal	16	16	–	58	309	19.31	–	2	2
Nazmul Hossain	16	11	7	6*	30	7.50	–	–	4
Rajin Saleh	31	31	–	82	710	22.90	–	5	7
Shahriar Nafiz	7	7	–	75	254	36.28	–	2	3
Syed Rasel	3	2	–	15	17	8.50	–	–	2
Tapash Baisya	51	39	12	35*	318	11.77	–	–	6
Tushar Imran	33	32	–	65	523	16.34	–	2	5

BANGLADESH – BOWLING

	O	M	R	W	Avge	Best	4wI	R/Over
Abdur Razzaq	53	5	214	7	30.57	3-17	–	4.03
Aftab Ahmed	82.4	0	411	9	45.66	5-31	1	4.97
Alok Kapali	143.3	6	712	11	64.72	2-40	–	4.96
Enamul Haque II	30	1	129	4	32.25	2-37	–	4.30
Habibul Bashar	29.1	0	142	1	142.00	1-31	–	4.86
Hasibul Hossain	229.1	13	1338	29	46.13	4-56	1	5.83
Khaled Mahmud	562.1	30	2850	67	42.53	4-19	1	5.06
Manjural Rana	160	9	655	23	28.47	4-34	2	4.09
Mashrafe Mortaza	203.1	16	1037	22	47.13	2-26	–	5.10
Mohammad Ashraful	50.3	1	309	8	38.62	3-26	–	6.11
Mohammad Rafique	681.2	36	3175	71	44.71	4-33	2	4.66
Mushfiqur Rahman	221.5	19	978	19	51.47	2-21	–	4.40
Nazmul Hossain	120.3	9	672	17	39.52	4-40	1	5.57
Rajin Saleh	66.2	1	333	9	37.00	3-48	–	5.02
Syed Rasel	25	1	120	3	40.00	2-42	–	4.80
Tapash Baisya	397.5	17	2224	56	39.71	4-16	2	5.59
Tushar Imran	3	0	26	0	–	–	–	8.66

SCOTLAND – BATTING AND FIELDING

	M	I	NO	HS	Runs	Avge	100	50	Ct/St
J.A.R.Blain	5	5	1	9	15	3.75	–	–	1

SCOTLAND – BOWLING

	O	M	R	W	Avge	Best	4wI	R/Over
J.A.R.Blain	37.1	1	210	10	21.00	4-37	1	5.64

TEST MATCH CAREER RECORDS

These records, complete to 26 February 2006, contain all players registered for county cricket in 2006 at the time of going to press, plus those who have played Test cricket since 1 October 2004 (Test No. 1713 onwards). For reasons outlined in the Preface, they exclude any match involving a multinational team.

ENGLAND – BATTING AND FIELDING

	M	I	NO	HS	Runs	Avge	100	50	Ct/St
C.J.Adams	5	8	–	31	104	13.00	–	–	6
U.Afzaal	3	6	1	54	83	16.60	–	1	–
K.Ali	1	2	–	9	10	5.00	–	–	–
J.M.Anderson	12	16	12	21*	68	17.00	–	–	4
G.J.Batty	7	8	1	38	144	20.57	–	–	3
I.R.Bell	11	19	2	162*	781	45.94	2	6	14
M.P.Bicknell	4	7	–	15	45	6.42	–	–	2
R.J.Blakey	2	4	–	6	7	1.75	–	–	2
M.A.Butcher	71	131	7	173*	4288	34.58	8	23	61
A.R.Caddick	62	95	12	49*	861	10.37	–	–	21
R.Clarke	2	3	–	55	96	32.00	–	1	1
P.D.Collingwood	5	10	–	96	295	29.50	–	2	7
D.G.Cork	37	56	8	59	864	18.00	–	3	18
J.P.Crawley	37	61	9	156*	1800	34.61	4	9	29
R.D.B.Croft	21	34	8	37*	421	16.19	–	–	10
R.K.J.Dawson	7	13	3	19*	114	11.40	–	–	3
M.A.Ealham	8	13	3	53*	210	21.00	–	2	4
A.Flintoff	55	88	3	167	2766	32.54	5	18	37
J.S.Foster	7	12	3	48	226	25.11	–	–	17/1
J.E.R.Gallian	3	6	–	28	74	12.33	–	–	1
A.F.Giles	52	77	12	59	1347	20.72	–	4	32
D.Gough	58	86	18	65	855	12.57	–	2	13
A.Habib	2	3	–	19	26	8.66	–	–	–
S.J.Harmison	38	50	15	42	376	10.74	–	–	5
G.A.Hick	65	114	6	178	3383	31.32	6	18	90
M.J.Hoggard	48	64	24	38	323	8.07	–	–	18
R.C.Irani	3	5	–	41	86	17.20	–	–	2
R.L.Johnson	3	4	–	26	59	14.75	–	–	–
G.O.Jones	23	35	3	100	952	29.75	1	5	82/3
S.P.Jones	18	18	5	44	205	15.76	–	–	4
R.W.T.Key	15	26	1	221	775	31.00	1	3	11
R.J.Kirtley	4	7	1	12	32	5.33	–	–	3
N.V.Knight	17	30	–	113	719	23.96	1	4	26
A.McGrath	4	5	–	81	201	40.20	–	2	3
D.L.Maddy	3	4	–	24	46	11.50	–	–	4
J.Ormond	2	4	1	18	38	12.66	–	–	–
M.M.Patel	2	2	–	27	45	22.50	–	–	2
K.P.Pietersen	8	16	1	158	674	44.93	2	3	3
L.E.Plunkett	1	2	–	9	9	4.50	–	–	1
M.R.Ramprakash	52	92	6	154	2350	27.32	2	12	39
C.M.W.Read	11	16	3	38*	199	15.30	–	–	31/4
M.J.Saggers	3	3	–	1	1	0.33	–	–	1
I.D.K.Salisbury	15	25	3	50	368	16.72	–	1	5
R.J.Sidebottom	1	1	–	4	4	4.00	–	–	–
C.E.W.Silverwood	6	7	3	10	29	7.25	–	–	2
E.T.Smith	3	5	–	64	87	17.40	–	1	5
A.J.Strauss	21	40	2	147	1760	46.31	7	5	26
M.E.Trescothick	69	131	10	219	5502	45.47	13	28	81
A.J.Tudor	10	16	4	99*	229	19.08	–	1	3
S.D.Udal	3	5	1	33*	86	21.50	–	–	1
M.P.Vaughan	64	115	8	197	4595	42.94	15	14	37
C.White	30	50	7	121	1052	24.46	1	5	14

ENGLAND – BOWLING

	O	M	R	W	Avge	Best	5wI	10wM
C.J.Adams	20	5	59	1	59.00	1- 42	–	–
U.Afzaal	9	0	49	1	49.00	1- 49	–	–
K.Ali	36	5	136	5	27.20	3- 80	–	–
J.M.Anderson	339	70	1274	35	36.40	5- 73	2	–
G.J.Batty	232.2	34	733	11	66.63	3- 55	–	–
I.R.Bell	16	3	62	1	62.00	1- 33	–	–
M.P.Bicknell	180	39	543	14	38.78	4- 84	–	–
M.A.Butcher	150.1	27	541	15	36.06	4- 42	–	–
A.R.Caddick	2259.4	501	6999	234	29.91	7- 46	13	1
R.Clarke	29	11	60	4	15.00	2- 7	–	–
P.D.Collingwood	30	4	91	0				
D.G.Cork	1279.4	306	3906	131	29.81	7- 43	5	–
R.D.B.Croft	769.5	195	1825	49	37.24	5- 95	1	–
R.K.J.Dawson	186	20	677	11	61.54	4-134	–	–
M.A.Ealham	176.4	43	488	17	28.70	4- 21	–	–
A.Flintoff	1688.5	357	5030	156	32.24	5- 58	2	–
J.E.R.Gallian	14	1	62	0				
A.F.Giles	1948	388	5544	140	39.60	5- 57	5	–
D.Gough	1970.1	370	6503	229	28.39	6- 42	9	–
S.J.Harmison	1386	278	4321	150	28.80	7- 12	6	–
G.A.Hick	509.3	128	1306	23	56.78	4-126	–	–
M.J.Hoggard	1647.1	344	5533	184	30.07	7- 61	5	1
R.C.Irani	32	10	112	3	37.33	1- 22	–	–
R.L.Johnson	91.1	25	275	16	17.18	6- 33	2	–
S.P.Jones	470.1	78	1666	59	28.23	6- 53	3	–
R.J.Kirtley	179.5	50	561	19	29.52	6- 34	1	–
A.McGrath	17	1	56	4	14.00	3- 16	–	–
D.L.Maddy	14	1	40	0				
J.Ormond	62	12	185	2	92.50	1- 70	–	–
M.M.Patel	46	8	180	1	180.00	1-101	–	–
L.E.Plunkett	28.2	1	125	2	62.50	2-125	–	–
M.R.Ramprakash	149.1	16	477	4	119.25	1- 2	–	–
M.J.Saggers	82.1	20	247	7	35.28	2- 29	–	–
I.D.K.Salisbury	415.2	50	1539	20	76.95	4-163	–	–
R.J.Sidebottom	20	2	64	0				
C.E.W.Silverwood	138	27	444	11	40.36	5- 91	1	–
M.E.Trescothick	50	6	155	1	155.00	1- 34	–	–
A.J.Tudor	252	51	963	28	34.39	5- 44	1	–
S.D.Udal	74	8	277	3	92.33	1- 31	–	–
M.P.Vaughan	156	20	537	6	89.50	2- 71	–	–
C.White	659.5	119	2220	59	37.62	5- 32	3	–

AUSTRALIA – BATTING AND FIELDING

	M	I	NO	HS	Runs	Avge	100	50	Ct/St
N.W.Bracken	5	6	2	37	70	17.50	–	–	2
M.J.Clarke	19	29	2	151	1028	38.07	2	4	17
M.T.G.Elliott	21	36	1	199	1172	33.48	3	4	14
A.C.Gilchrist	79	114	18	204*	4823	50.23	15	21	299/31
J.N.Gillespie	69	90	26	54*	987	15.42	–	2	25
N.M.Hauritz	1	2	–	15	15	7.50	–	–	1
M.L.Hayden	78	139	12	380	6800	53.54	24	23	94
B.J.Hodge	5	9	2	203*	409	58.42	1	1	1
M.E.K.Hussey	6	11	3	137	640	80.00	3	1	1
P.A.Jaques	1	2	–	28	30	15.00	–	–	–
M.S.Kasprowicz	35	50	10	25	423	10.57	–	–	15
S.M.Katich	22	36	3	125	1258	38.12	2	8	14
J.L.Langer	96	166	9	250	7249	46.17	22	29	61

207

AUSTRALIA – BATTING AND FIELDING (continued)

	M	I	NO	HS	Runs	Avge	100	50	Ct/St
S.G.Law	1	1	1	54*	54	–	–	1	1
B.Lee	48	52	10	62*	897	21.35	–	2	11
D.S.Lehmann	27	42	2	177	1798	44.95	5	10	11
S.C.G.MacGill	37	42	8	43	347	10.20	–	–	16
G.D.McGrath	118	131	49	61	629	7.67	–	1	37
D.R.Martyn	61	98	12	165	4125	47.96	12	22	30
M.J.Nicholson	1	2	–	9	14	7.00	–	–	–
R.T.Ponting	99	164	23	257	8153	57.82	28	31	115
A.Symonds	7	11	–	72	185	16.81	–	1	7
S.W.Tait	2	3	2	4	8	8.00	–	–	–
S.K.Warne	134	186	16	99	2853	16.78	–	11	118
S.R.Watson	2	2	–	31	47	23.50	–	–	–

AUSTRALIA – BOWLING

	O	M	R	W	Avge	Best	5wI	10wM
N.W.Bracken	185	53	505	12	42.08	4-48	–	–
M.J.Clarke	22.2	2	68	8	8.50	6- 9	1	–
M.T.G.Elliott	2	1	4	0				
J.N.Gillespie	2329.2	617	6680	251	26.61	7-37	8	–
N.M.Hauritz	27	4	103	5	20.60	3-16	–	–
M.L.Hayden	9	0	40	0				
B.J.Hodge	2	0	8	0				
M.E.K.Hussey	2	0	12	0				
M.S.Kasprowicz	1112.4	240	3424	106	32.30	7-36	4	–
S.M.Katich	109.5	10	406	12	33.83	6-65	1	–
J.L.Langer	1	0	3	0				
S.G.Law	3	1	9	0				
B.Lee	1668.4	336	6022	190	31.69	5-30	6	–
D.S.Lehmann	162.2	36	412	15	27.46	3-42	–	–
S.C.G.MacGill	1586.5	328	5004	173	28.92	7-50	10	2
G.D.McGrath	4647.3	1399	11642	539	21.59	8-24	28	3
D.R.Martyn	58	15	168	2	84.00	1- 0	–	–
M.J.Nicholson	25	4	115	4	28.75	3-56	–	–
R.T.Ponting	85.5	22	224	5	44.80	1- 0	–	–
A.Symonds	107	26	295	8	36.87	3-50	–	–
S.W.Tait	48	5	210	5	42.00	3-97	–	–
S.K.Warne	6296.4	1679	16503	653	25.27	8-71	34	10
S.R.Watson	25	5	85	2	42.50	1-25	–	–

SOUTH AFRICA – BATTING AND FIELDING

	M	I	NO	HS	Runs	Avge	100	50	Ct/St
H.M.Amla	3	6	–	25	62	10.33	–	–	2
N.Boje	36	49	8	85	1048	25.56	–	4	13
J.Botha	1	1	1	20*	20	–	–	–	–
M.V.Boucher	87	119	16	125	3126	30.34	4	19	321/14
Z.de Bruyn	3	5	1	83	155	38.75	–	1	–
A.B.de Villiers	14	25	1	178	1119	46.62	3	6	16/1
H.H.Dippenaar	33	53	5	177*	1511	31.47	3	6	23
H.H.Gibbs	73	123	6	228	5478	46.82	14	20	61
A.J.Hall	15	23	3	163	559	27.95	1	2	12
C.W.Henderson	7	7	–	30	65	9.28	–	–	2
J.H.Kallis	95	159	27	189*	7530	57.04	23	38	90
J.M.Kemp	4	6	–	55	80	13.33	–	1	3
L.Klusener	49	69	11	174	1906	32.86	4	8	34
C.K.Langeveldt	6	4	2	10	16	8.00	–	–	2
A.Nel	18	16	5	14	64	5.81	–	–	5
M.Ntini	61	64	18	32*	479	10.41	–	–	16
J.L.Ontong	2	4	1	32	57	19.00	–	–	1

	M	I	NO	HS	Runs	Avge	100	50	Ct/St
R.J.Peterson	5	6	1	61	159	31.80	–	1	4
S.M.Pollock	97	137	34	111	3315	32.18	2	16	65
A.G.Prince	15	21	1	139*	728	36.40	3	–	7
J.A.Rudolph	30	53	7	222*	1756	38.17	5	7	20
G.C.Smith	42	73	5	277	3596	52.88	11	12	53
D.W.Steyn	3	5	3	8	25	12.50	–	–	1
T.L.Tsolekile	3	5	–	22	47	9.40	–	–	6
M.van Jaarsveld	9	15	2	73	397	30.53	–	3	11
C.M.Willoughby	2	–	–	–	–	–	–	–	–
M.Zondeki	5	4	–	59	82	20.50	–	1	1

SOUTH AFRICA – BOWLING

	O	M	R	W	Avge	Best	5wI	10wM
N.Boje	1181.2	250	3423	88	38.89	5- 62	3	–
J.Botha	19.3	2	103	2	51.50	1- 26	–	–
M.V.Boucher	1.2	0	6	1	6.00	1- 6	–	–
Z.de Bruyn	36	7	92	3	30.66	2- 32	–	–
A.B.de Villiers	28	6	65	2	32.50	2- 49	–	–
H.H.Dippenaar	2	1	1	0				
H.H.Gibbs	1	0	4	0				
A.J.Hall	365.1	73	1153	31	37.19	3- 1	–	–
C.W.Henderson	327	79	928	22	42.18	4-116	–	–
J.H.Kallis	2142.4	583	5943	188	31.61	6- 54	4	–
J.M.Kemp	79.5	20	222	9	24.66	3- 33	–	–
L.Klusener	1147.5	319	3033	80	37.91	8- 64	1	–
C.K.Langeveldt	166.3	27	593	16	37.06	5- 46	1	–
A.Nel	673	159	1993	76	26.22	6- 32	3	1
M.Ntini	2141.4	490	6721	230	29.22	7- 37	10	2
J.L.Ontong	30.5	2	133	1	133.00	1- 79	–	–
R.J.Peterson	130.5	37	403	8	50.37	3- 46	–	–
S.M.Pollock	3695.2	1123	8764	385	22.76	7- 87	16	1
A.G.Prince	9	1	22	0				
J.A.Rudolph	103.4	13	387	4	96.75	1- 1	–	–
G.C.Smith	187.5	24	652	8	81.50	2-145	–	–
D.W.Steyn	100.2	16	416	8	52.00	2- 26	–	–
M.van Jaarsveld	7	0	28	0				
C.M.Willoughby	50	18	125	1	125.00	1- 47	–	–
M.Zondeki	115.2	21	438	16	27.37	6- 39	1	–

WEST INDIES – BATTING AND FIELDING

	M	I	NO	HS	Runs	Avge	100	50	Ct/St
O.A.C.Banks	10	16	4	50*	318	26.50	–	1	6
T.L.Best	12	19	2	27	174	10.23	–	–	1
D.J.J.Bravo	9	17	–	113	611	35.94	2	3	8
G.R.Breese	1	2	–	5	5	2.50	–	–	1
C.O.Browne	20	30	6	68	387	16.12	–	1	79/2
S.Chanderpaul	91	155	21	203*	6156	45.94	14	35	38
P.T.Collins	29	43	7	24	231	6.41	–	–	5
C.D.Collymore	19	34	18	16*	146	9.12	–	–	5
N.Deonarine	4	6	1	40	107	21.40	–	–	2
F.H.Edwards	20	33	8	20	111	4.44	–	–	5
D.Ganga	31	54	–	117	1230	22.77	2	5	19
C.H.Gayle	54	95	3	317	3569	38.79	7	20	61
O.D.Gibson	2	4	–	37	93	23.25	–	–	–
R.O.Hinds	9	16	1	84	363	24.20	–	2	4
W.W.Hinds	45	80	1	213	2608	33.01	5	14	33
S.C.Joseph	4	8	–	45	133	16.62	–	–	2
R.D.King	19	27	8	12*	66	3.47	–	–	5

WEST INDIES – BATTING AND FIELDING (continued)

	M	I	NO	HS	Runs	Avge	100	50	Ct/St
B.C.Lara	120	212	6	400*	11163	54.18	31	46	148
J.J.C.Lawson	13	21	6	14	52	3.46	–	–	3
N.A.M.McLean	19	32	2	46	368	12.26	–	–	5
X.M.Marshall	2	4	–	10	17	4.25	–	–	1
R.S.Morton	2	4	–	43	53	13.25	–	–	5
D.J.Pagon	2	3	–	35	37	12.33	–	–	–
D.B.Powell	15	24	–	16	134	5.58	–	–	1
R.Ramdass	1	2	–	23	26	13.00	–	–	2
D.Ramdin	5	10	1	71	279	31.00	–	2	13
M.N.Samuels	21	37	4	104	930	28.18	1	6	9
R.R.Sarwan	58	104	7	261*	3884	40.04	8	23	43
D.R.Smith	8	12	1	105*	282	25.63	1	–	9
D.S.Smith	16	30	1	108	735	25.34	1	3	14
D.M.Washington	1	1	1	7*	7	–	–	–	3

WEST INDIES – BOWLING

	O	M	R	W	Avge	Best	5wI	10wM
O.A.C.Banks	400.1	62	1367	28	48.82	4- 87	–	–
T.L.Best	308.3	38	1171	26	45.03	4- 46	–	–
D.J.J.Bravo	289.4	52	939	28	33.53	6- 55	2	–
G.R.Breese	31.2	3	135	2	67.50	2-108	–	–
S.Chanderpaul	260	52	769	8	96.12	1- 2	–	–
P.T.Collins	1044.1	196	3277	96	34.13	6- 53	3	–
C.D.Collymore	645	141	1882	60	31.36	7- 57	3	1
N.Deonarine	56.5	17	151	2	75.50	1- 5	–	–
F.H.Edwards	598.1	65	2400	53	45.28	5- 36	3	–
D.Ganga	27	2	86	0				
C.H.Gayle	594.1	129	1530	41	37.31	5- 34	2	–
O.D.Gibson	78.4	9	275	3	91.66	2- 81	–	–
R.O.Hinds	166.2	42	390	5	78.00	2- 83	–	–
W.W.Hinds	187.1	41	590	16	36.87	3- 79	–	–
S.C.Joseph	2	0	8	0				
R.D.King	573.4	119	1733	53	32.69	5- 51	1	–
B.C.Lara	10	1	28	0				
J.J.C.Lawson	394	55	1512	51	29.64	7- 78	2	–
N.A.M.McLean	549.5	85	1873	44	42.56	3- 53	–	–
R.S.Morton	5	0	15	0				
D.B.Powell	495.3	89	1652	39	42.35	5- 25	1	–
M.N.Samuels	191	28	625	5	125.00	2- 49	–	–
R.R.Sarwan	269.1	33	872	20	43.60	4- 37	–	–
D.R.Smith	73.3	12	229	4	57.25	1- 5	–	–
D.M.Washington	29	4	93	0				

NEW ZEALAND – BATTING AND FIELDING

	M	I	NO	HS	Runs	Avge	100	50	Ct/St
A.R.Adams	1	2	–	11	18	9.00	–	–	1
N.J.Astle	73	124	10	222	4386	38.47	11	21	67
S.E.Bond	12	12	6	41*	102	17.00	–	–	4
I.G.Butler	8	10	2	26	76	9.50	–	–	4
C.L.Cairns	62	104	5	158	3320	33.53	5	22	14
C.D.Cumming	5	9	1	74	208	26.00	–	1	2
S.P.Fleming	96	165	10	274*	6050	39.03	8	40	140
J.E.C.Franklin	13	17	2	55	230	15.33	–	1	4
B.B.McCullum	17	27	2	143	893	35.72	2	5	42/4
C.D.McMillan	55	91	10	142	3116	38.46	6	19	22
H.J.H.Marshall	9	13	1	160	583	48.58	2	2	–
J.A.H.Marshall	5	7	–	52	166	23.71	–	1	3
C.S.Martin	25	34	17	7	46	2.70	–	–	8

	M	I	NO	HS	Runs	Avge	100	50	Ct/St
K.D.Mills	4	7	1	31	98	16.33	–	–	1
I.E.O'Brien	2	3	–	5	10	3.33	–	–	1
J.D.P.Oram	17	29	6	126*	1002	43.56	2	4	12
M.H.Richardson	38	65	3	145	2776	44.77	4	19	26
M.S.Sinclair	25	42	5	214	1365	36.89	3	4	22
C.M.Spearman	19	37	2	112	922	26.34	1	3	21
S.B.Styris	21	35	2	170	1285	38.93	4	5	17
D.L.Vettori	64	92	15	137*	1855	24.09	2	9	33
L.Vincent	22	38	1	224	1295	35.00	3	9	19
P.J.Wiseman	25	34	8	36	366	14.07	–	–	11

NEW ZEALAND – BOWLING

	O	M	R	W	Avge	Best	5wI	10wM
A.R.Adams	31.4	5	105	6	17.50	3- 44	–	–
N.J.Astle	885	296	2016	46	43.82	3- 27	–	–
S.E.Bond	348.3	78	1165	56	20.80	6- 51	3	1
I.G.Butler	228	37	884	24	36.83	6- 46	1	–
C.L.Cairns	1949.4	412	6410	218	29.40	7- 27	13	1
J.E.C.Franklin	351.4	66	1274	47	27.10	6-119	2	–
C.D.McMillan	417	101	1257	28	44.89	3- 48	–	–
H.J.H.Marshall	1	0	4	0				
C.S.Martin	785	176	2831	82	34.52	6- 54	6	1
K.D.Mills	86	26	273	3	91.00	2- 34	–	–
I.E.O'Brien	43	7	197	2	98.50	1- 73	–	–
J.D.P.Oram	487.4	124	1269	35	36.25	4- 41	–	–
M.H.Richardson	11	0	21	1	21.00	1- 16	–	–
M.S.Sinclair	4	0	13	0				
S.B.Styris	279.3	66	874	16	54.62	3- 28	–	–
D.L.Vettori	2672.5	680	7140	207	34.49	7- 87	12	3
L.Vincent	1	0	2	0				
P.J.Wiseman	943.2	208	2903	61	47.59	5- 82	2	–

INDIA – BATTING AND FIELDING

	M	I	NO	HS	Runs	Avge	100	50	Ct/St
A.B.Agarkar	26	39	5	109*	571	16.79	1	–	6
L.Balaji	8	9	–	31	51	5.66	–	–	1
A.Chopra	10	19	–	60	437	23.00	–	2	15
M.S.Dhoni	6	8	1	148	328	46.85	1	1	12/2
R.Dravid	96	161	20	270	8221	58.30	22	39	130
G.Gambhir	13	21	2	139	684	36.00	1	3	12
S.C.Ganguly	88	140	12	173	5221	40.78	12	25	59
Harbhajan Singh	52	71	15	66	879	15.69	–	2	27
M.Kaif	8	15	1	64	307	21.92	–	2	12
K.D.Karthik	10	13	–	93	245	18.84	–	1	29/4
M.Kartik	8	10	1	43	88	9.77	–	–	2
Z.Khan	42	54	14	75	507	12.67	–	1	10
A.Kumble	103	131	27	88	1764	16.96	–	3	46
V.V.S.Laxman	72	115	13	281	4441	43.53	9	24	79
P.A.Patel	19	28	7	69	669	31.85	–	4	39/7
I.K.Pathan	21	26	2	93	695	28.95	–	5	6
V.Sehwag	41	66	2	309	3531	55.17	11	9	35
R.P.Singh	2	3	2	6	6	6.00	–	–	–
S.R.Tendulkar	129	206	21	248*	10386	56.14	35	41	81
Yuvraj Singh	13	19	3	122	662	41.37	2	3	13

INDIA – BOWLING

	O	M	R	W	Avge	Best	5wI	10wM
A.B.Agarkar	809.3	168	2745	58	47.32	6-41	1	–
L.Balaji	292.4	64	1004	27	37.18	5-76	1	–
M.S.Dhoni	1	0	13	0				
R.Dravid	20	4	39	1	39.00	1-18	–	–
S.C.Ganguly	419.2	86	1419	26	54.57	3-28	–	–
Harbhajan Singh	2306.5	480	6460	219	29.49	8-84	17	4
M.Kaif	3	0	4	0				
M.Kartik	322	74	820	24	34.16	4-44	–	–
Z.Khan	1326.5	266	4398	121	36.34	5-29	3	–
A.Kumble	5391.3	1308	14203	494	28.75	10-74	31	8
V.V.S.Laxman	42	10	100	1	100.00	1-32	–	–
I.K.Pathan	719.2	158	2394	81	29.55	7-59	7	2
V.Sehwag	108.3	12	405	3	135.00	1-17	–	–
R.P.Singh	87	8	345	9	38.33	4-89	–	–
S.R.Tendulkar	553	75	1882	37	50.86	3-10	–	–
Yuvraj Singh	23	1	89	1	89.00	1-25	–	–

PAKISTAN – BATTING AND FIELDING

	M	I	NO	HS	Runs	Avge	100	50	Ct/St
Abdul Razzaq	39	65	6	134	1727	29.27	3	6	9
Arshad Khan	9	8	2	9*	31	5.16	–	–	–
Asim Kamal	12	20	1	99	717	37.73	–	8	10
Azhar Mahmood	21	34	4	136	900	30.00	3	1	14
Bazid Khan	1	2	–	23	32	16.00	–	–	2
Danish Kaneria	34	46	23	15	122	5.30	–	–	11
Faisal Iqbal	11	20	1	139	547	28.78	1	3	8
Hasan Raza	7	10	1	68	235	26.11	–	2	5
Imran Farhat	16	30	–	128	920	30.66	2	5	20
Inzamam-ul-Haq	106	175	19	329	8171	52.37	25	42	76
Kamran Akmal	21	36	2	154	1068	31.41	4	2	70/14
Mohammad Akram	9	15	6	10*	24	2.66	–	–	4
Mohammad Asif	3	5	3	12*	18	9.00	–	–	2
Mohammad Khalil	2	4	1	5	9	3.00	–	–	–
Mohammad Sami	25	38	11	49	317	11.74	–	–	3
Moin Khan	69	104	8	137	2741	28.55	4	15	128/20
Mushtaq Ahmed	52	72	16	59	656	11.71	–	2	23
Naved-ul-Hasan	8	13	3	42*	176	17.60	–	–	3
Riaz Afridi	1	1	–	9	9	9.00	–	–	–
Salman Butt	12	22	–	122	731	33.22	2	4	5
Shabbir Ahmed	10	15	5	24*	88	8.80	–	–	3
Shahid Afridi	23	42	1	156	1620	39.51	5	8	10
Shoaib Akhtar	42	62	12	47	537	10.74	–	–	11
Shoaib Malik	14	22	3	64	637	33.52	–	4	5
Taufiq Umar	24	44	2	135	1711	40.73	4	9	32
Yasir Hamid	17	33	3	170	1168	38.93	2	7	13
Younis Khan	42	74	3	267	3439	48.43	11	13	43
M.Yousuf Youhana	65	108	8	223	5075	50.75	16	25	57

PAKISTAN – BOWLING

	O	M	R	W	Avge	Best	5wI	10wM
Abdul Razzaq	1014.4	192	3176	86	36.93	5-35	–	–
Arshad Khan	423	119	960	32	30.00	5-38	1	–
Azhar Mahmood	502.3	109	1402	39	35.94	4-50	–	–
Danish Kaneria	1539	294	4679	148	31.61	7-77	11	2
Faisal Iqbal	1	0	7	0				
Hasan Raza	1	0	1	0				
Imran Farhat	38.1	3	182	3	60.66	2-69	–	–
Inzamam-ul-Haq	1.3	0	8	0				

TEST **PAKISTAN – BOWLING (continued)**

	O	M	R	W	Avge	Best	5wI	10wM
Mohammad Akram	246.1	36	859	17	50.52	5-138	1	–
Mohammad Asif	83.1	11	317	8	39.62	4- 78	–	–
Mohammad Khalil	48.2	3	200	0				
Mohammad Sami	887.3	149	3065	65	47.15	5- 36	2	–
Mushtaq Ahmed	2088.4	406	6100	185	32.97	7- 56	10	3
Naved-ul-Hasan	236.5	31	931	16	58.18	3- 30	–	–
Riaz Afridi	31	10	87	2	43.50	2- 42	–	–
Shabbir Ahmed	429.2	97	1175	51	23.03	5- 48	2	–
Shahid Afridi	432.5	68	1373	42	32.69	5- 52	1	–
Shoaib Akhtar	1248.2	218	4240	165	25.69	6- 11	12	2
Shoaib Malik	202.1	30	700	12	58.33	4- 42	–	–
Taufiq Umar	11	2	36	0				
Yasir Hamid	1	0	5	0				
Younis Khan	44	7	169	2	84.50	1- 24	–	–
M.Yousuf Youhana	1	0	3	0				

SRI LANKA – BATTING AND FIELDING

	M	I	NO	HS	Runs	Avge	100	50	Ct/St
M.S.Atapattu	88	152	15	249	5330	38.90	16	15	57
C.M.Bandara	4	6	2	28*	40	10.00	–	–	2
U.D.U.Chandana	16	24	1	92	616	26.78	–	2	7
T.M.Dilshan	30	48	6	168	1629	38.78	4	6	35
C.R.D.Fernando	20	28	10	15	97	5.38	–	–	7
D.A.Gunawardena	6	11	–	43	181	16.45	–	–	2
M.R.K.B.Herath	12	16	2	33*	123	8.78	–	–	2
S.T.Jayasuriya	100	170	14	340	6580	42.17	14	29	73
D.P.M.deS.Jayawardena	74	120	9	242	5306	47.80	13	27	99
S.Kalavitigoda	1	2	–	7	8	4.00	–	–	2
R.S.Kaluwitharana	49	78	4	132*	1933	26.12	3	9	93/26
M.D.N.Kulasekara	1	1	–	0	0	0.00	–	–	1
M.F.Maharoof	6	9	2	40	108	15.42	–	–	2
S.L.Malinga	11	13	7	6*	16	2.66	–	–	5
J.Mubarak	7	12	1	48	230	20.90	–	–	10
M.Muralitharan	98	125	43	67	1040	12.68	–	1	52
W.M.G.Ramyakumara	2	3	–	14	38	12.66	–	–	–
T.T.Samaraweera	33	48	8	142	1857	46.42	5	10	27
K.C.Sangakkara	53	87	5	270	3822	46.60	8	18	126/18
W.U.Tharanga	1	2	–	47	49	24.50	–	–	1
W.P.U.C.J.Vaas	90	128	22	74*	2251	21.23	–	9	28

SRI LANKA – BOWLING

	O	M	R	W	Avge	Best	5wI	10wM
M.S.Atapattu	8	0	24	1	24.00	1- 9	–	–
C.M.Bandara	113	17	375	9	41.66	3- 84	–	–
U.D.U.Chandana	447.3	64	1535	37	41.48	6-179	3	1
T.M.Dilshan	74	19	204	6	34.00	2- 4	–	–
C.R.D.Fernando	495.2	71	1889	56	33.73	5- 42	3	–
M.R.K.B.Herath	399.1	80	1204	35	34.40	4- 38	–	–
S.T.Jayasuriya	1232.5	294	3016	92	32.78	5- 34	2	–
D.P.M.deS.Jayawardena	76.2	17	228	4	57.00	2- 32	–	–
M.D.N.Kulasekara	35	9	89	1	89.00	1- 70	–	–
M.F.Maharoof	146	41	451	8	56.37	2- 52	–	–
S.L.Malinga	320.1	44	1244	41	30.34	5- 80	1	–
J.Mubarak	13	2	42	0				
M.Muralitharan	5475	1440	12971	579	22.40	9- 51	48	14
W.M.G.Ramyakumara	19	4	66	2	33.00	2- 49	–	–

213

TEST **SRI LANKA – BOWLING (continued)**

	O	M	R	W	Avge	Best	5wI	10wM
T.T.Samaraweera	214.1	36	671	14	47.92	4-49	–	–
K.C.Sangakkara	1	0	4	0				
W.P.U.C.J.Vaas	3264.4	753	8673	301	28.81	7-71	11	2

ZIMBABWE – BATTING AND FIELDING

	M	I	NO	HS	Runs	Avge	100	50	Ct/St
A.M.Blignaut	19	36	3	92	886	26.84	–	6	13
S.V.Carlisle	37	66	6	118	1615	26.91	2	8	34
E.Chigumbura	6	12	–	71	187	15.58	–	1	2
C.K.Coventry	2	4	–	37	88	22.00	–	–	3
A.G.Cremer	6	12	1	12	29	2.63	–	–	3
K.M.Dabengwa	3	6	–	35	90	15.00	–	–	1
T.Duffin	2	4	–	56	80	20.00	–	1	1
D.D.Ebrahim	29	55	1	94	1225	22.68	–	10	16
S.M.Ervine	5	8	–	86	261	32.62	–	3	7
G.M.Ewing	3	6	–	71	108	18.00	–	1	1
N.R.Ferreira	1	2	–	16	21	10.50	–	–	–
A.Flower	63	112	19	232*	4794	51.54	12	27	151/9
G.W.Flower	67	123	6	201*	3457	29.54	6	15	43
M.W.Goodwin	19	37	4	166*	1414	42.84	3	8	10
D.T.Hondo	9	15	6	19	83	9.22	–	–	5
N.B.Mahwire	10	17	6	50*	147	13.36	–	1	1
H.Masakadza	15	30	1	119	785	27.06	1	3	8
S.Matsikenyeri	8	16	1	57	351	23.40	–	2	7
C.B.Mpofu	6	12	6	7	17	2.83	–	–	–
W.Mwayenga	1	2	1	14*	15	15.00	–	–	–
M.L.Nkala	10	15	2	47	187	14.38	–	–	4
T.Panyangara	3	6	2	40*	128	32.00	–	–	–
R.W.Price	18	30	7	36	224	9.73	–	–	3
B.G.Rogers	4	8	–	29	90	11.25	–	–	1
V.Sibanda	3	6	–	18	48	8.00	–	–	4
H.H.Streak	65	107	18	127*	1990	22.35	1	11	17
T.Taibu	24	46	3	153	1273	29.60	1	9	48/4
B.R.M.Taylor	10	20	–	78	422	21.10	–	3	7
C.B.Wishart	27	50	1	114	1098	22.40	1	5	15

ZIMBABWE – BOWLING

	O	M	R	W	Avge	Best	5wI	10wM
A.M.Blignaut	528.5	101	1964	53	37.05	5- 73	3	–
E.Chigumbura	138.1	22	498	9	55.33	5- 54	1	–
A.G.Cremer	145	16	595	13	45.76	3- 86	–	–
K.M.Dabengwa	73	10	249	5	49.80	3-127	–	–
S.M.Ervine	95	18	388	9	43.11	4-146	–	–
G.M.Ewing	71	11	260	2	130.00	1- 27	–	–
A.Flower	0.3	0	4	0				
G.W.Flower	563	122	1537	25	61.48	4- 41	–	–
M.W.Goodwin	19.5	3	69	0				
D.T.Hondo	247.4	50	774	21	36.85	6- 59	1	–
N.B.Mahwire	214.3	35	915	18	50.83	4- 92	–	–
H.Masakadza	21	4	39	2	19.50	1- 9	–	–
S.Matsikenyeri	80.3	6	345	2	172.50	1- 58	–	–
C.B.Mpofu	138.2	22	556	8	69.50	4-109	–	–
W.Mwayenga	21	6	79	1	79.00	1- 79	–	–
M.L.Nkala	242	54	727	11	66.09	3- 82	–	–
T.Panyangara	89.1	21	286	8	35.75	3- 28	–	–
R.W.Price	855.5	198	2475	69	35.86	6- 73	5	1
B.G.Rogers	3	0	17	0				
H.H.Streak	2259.5	595	6079	216	28.14	6- 73	7	–

TEST   ZIMBABWE – BOWLING (continued)

	O	M	R	W	Avge	Best	5wI	10wM
T.Taibu	8	1	27	1	27.00	1-27	–	–
B.R.M.Taylor	7	0	38	0				

BANGLADESH – BATTING AND FIELDING

	M	I	NO	HS	Runs	Avge	100	50	Ct/St
Aftab Ahmed	8	16	1	82*	313	20.86	–	1	4
Alok Kapali	16	32	1	85	559	18.03	–	2	5
Anwar Hossain Monir	3	6	3	13	22	7.33	–	–	–
Enamul Haque II	7	12	9	9	18	6.00	–	–	1
Habibul Bashar	38	75	1	113	2514	33.97	3	21	19
Hannan Sarkar	17	33	–	76	662	20.06	–	5	7
Javed Omar	31	62	1	119	1376	22.55	1	6	6
Khaled Masud	37	71	8	103*	1260	20.00	1	3	68/8
Manjural Rana	6	11	1	69	257	25.70	–	1	3
Mashrafe Mortaza	18	33	4	48	272	9.37	–	–	5
Mohammad Ashraful	29	57	3	158*	1269	23.50	2	6	8
Mohammad Rafique	22	42	5	111	725	19.59	1	2	6
Mushfiqur Rahim	1	2	–	19	22	11.00	–	–	–
Mushfiqur Rahman	10	19	2	46*	232	13.64	–	–	6
Nafis Iqbal	9	18	–	121	450	25.00	1	2	1
Nazmul Hossain	1	2	1	8*	8	8.00	–	–	–
Rajin Saleh	15	29	1	89	754	26.92	–	4	11
Shahadat Hossain	3	6	2	7	21	5.25	–	–	–
Shahriar Nafis	2	4	–	51	72	18.00	–	1	1
Syed Rasel	2	4	–	19	26	6.50	–	–	–
Talha Jubair	7	14	6	31	52	6.50	–	–	1
Tapash Baisya	21	40	6	66	384	11.29	–	2	6
Tareq Aziz	3	6	4	10*	22	11.00	–	–	1
Tushar Imran	4	8	–	28	55	6.87	–	–	1

BANGLADESH – BOWLING

	O	M	R	W	Avge	Best	5wI	10wM
Aftab Ahmed	28	3	148	2	74.00	1- 33	–	–
Alok Kapali	180.5	15	697	6	116.16	3- 3	–	–
Anwar Hossain Monir	58	5	307	0				
Enamul Haque II	280.2	62	819	24	34.12	7- 95	3	1
Habibul Bashar	39	1	195	0				
Javed Omar	1	0	12	0				
Manjural Rana	124.5	19	401	5	80.20	3- 84	–	–
Mashrafe Mortaza	523.2	121	1650	47	35.10	4- 60	–	–
Mohammad Ashraful	129	7	563	8	70.37	2- 42	–	–
Mohammad Rafique	1008.4	229	2659	73	36.42	6- 77	6	–
Mushfiqur Rahman	227.3	45	823	13	63.30	4- 65	–	–
Nazmul Hossain	25.5	4	114	2	57.00	2-114	–	–
Rajin Saleh	58	4	207	2	103.50	1- 9	–	–
Shahadat Hossain	52	3	284	6	47.33	4-108	–	–
Syed Rasel	40.5	4	196	6	32.66	4-129	–	–
Talha Jubair	181.4	21	771	14	55.07	3-135	–	–
Tapash Baisya	562.4	93	2137	36	59.36	4- 72	–	–
Tareq Aziz	60	7	261	1	261.00	1- 76	–	–

FIRST-CLASS CRICKET RECORDS

To the end of the 2005 season

TEAM RECORDS
HIGHEST INNINGS TOTALS

1107	Victoria v New South Wales	Melbourne	1926-27
1059	Victoria v Tasmania	Melbourne	1922-23
952-6d	Sri Lanka v India	Colombo	1997-98
951-7d	Sind v Baluchistan	Karachi	1973-74
944-6d	Hyderabad v Andhra	Secunderabad	1993-94
918	New South Wales v South Australia	Sydney	1900-01
912-8d	Holkar v Mysore	Indore	1945-46
910-6d	Railways v Dera Ismail Khan	Lahore	1964-65
903-7d	England v Australia	The Oval	1938
887	Yorkshire v Warwickshire	Birmingham	1896
863	Lancashire v Surrey	The Oval	1990
860-6d	Tamil Nadu v Goa	Panjim	1988-89

Excluding penalty runs in India, there have been 30 innings totals of 800 runs or more in first-class cricket. Tamil Nadu's total of 860-6d was boosted to 912 by 52 penalty runs.

HIGHEST SECOND INNINGS TOTAL

770	New South Wales v South Australia	Adelaide	1920-21

HIGHEST FOURTH INNINGS TOTAL

654-5	England v South Africa	Durban	1938-39

HIGHEST MATCH AGGREGATE

2376-37	Maharashtra v Bombay	Poona	1948-49

RECORD MARGIN OF VICTORY

Innings and 851 runs: Railways v Dera Ismail Khan   Lahore   1964-65

MOST RUNS IN A DAY

721	Australians v Essex	Southend	1948

MOST HUNDREDS IN AN INNINGS

6	Holkar v Mysore	Indore	1945-46

LOWEST INNINGS TOTALS

12	†Oxford University v MCC and Ground	Oxford	1877
12	Northamptonshire v Gloucestershire	Gloucester	1907
13	Auckland v Canterbury	Auckland	1877-78
13	Nottinghamshire v Yorkshire	Nottingham	1901
14	Surrey v Essex	Chelmsford	1983
15	MCC v Surrey	Lord's	1839
15	†Victoria v MCC	Melbourne	1903-04
15	†Northamptonshire v Yorkshire	Northampton	1908
15	Hampshire v Warwickshire	Birmingham	1922

† Batted one man short

There have been 27 instances of a team being dismissed for under 20.

| 34 (16 and 18) | Border v Natal | East London | 1959-60 |

LOWEST COMPLETED MATCH AGGREGATE BY BOTH TEAMS

| 105 | MCC v Australians | Lord's | 1878 |

FEWEST RUNS IN AN UNINTERRUPTED DAY'S PLAY

| 95 | Australia (80) v Pakistan (15-2) | Karachi | 1956-57 |

TIED MATCHES

Before 1949 a match was considered to be tied if the scores were level after the fourth innings, even if the side batting last had wickets in hand when play ended. Law 22 was amended in 1948 and since then a match has been tied only when the scores are level after the fourth innings has been completed. There have been 56 tied first-class matches, five of which would not have qualified under the current law. The most recent are:

| Warwickshire (446-7d & forfeit) v Essex (66-0d & 380) | Birmingham | 2003 |
| Worcestershire (262 & 247) v Zimbabweans (334 & 175) | Worcester | 2003 |

BATTING RECORDS
HIGHEST INDIVIDUAL INNINGS

501*	B.C.Lara	Warwickshire v Durham	Birmingham	1994
499	Hanif Mohammed	Karachi v Bahawalpur	Karachi	1958-59
452*	D.G.Bradman	New South Wales v Queensland	Sydney	1929-30
443*	B.B.Nimbalkar	Maharashtra v Kathiawar	Poona	1948-49
437	W.H.Ponsford	Victoria v Queensland	Melbourne	1927-28
429	W.H.Ponsford	Victoria v Tasmania	Melbourne	1922-23
428	Aftab Baloch	Sind v Baluchistan	Karachi	1973-74
424	A.C.MacLaren	Lancashire v Somerset	Taunton	1895
405*	G.A.Hick	Worcestershire v Somerset	Taunton	1988
400*	B.C.Lara	West Indies v England	St John's	2003-04
394	Naved Latif	Sargodha v Gujranwala	Gujranwala	2000-01
385	B.Sutcliffe	Otago v Canterbury	Christchurch	1952-53
383	C.W.Gregory	New South Wales v Queensland	Brisbane	1906-07
380	M.L.Hayden	Australia v Zimbabwe	Perth	2003-04
377	S.V.Manjrekar	Bombay v Hyderabad	Bombay	1990-91
375	B.C.Lara	West Indies v England	St John's	1993-94
369	D.G.Bradman	South Australia v Tasmania	Adelaide	1935-36
366	N.H.Fairbrother	Lancashire v Surrey	The Oval	1990
366	M.V.Sridhar	Hyderabad v Andhra	Secunderabad	1993-94
365*	C.Hill	South Australia v NSW	Adelaide	1900-01
365*	G.St A.Sobers	West Indies v Pakistan	Kingston	1957-58
364	L.Hutton	England v Australia	The Oval	1938
359*	V.M.Merchant	Bombay v Maharashtra	Bombay	1943-44
359	R.B.Simpson	New South Wales v Queensland	Brisbane	1963-64
357*	R.Abel	Surrey v Somerset	The Oval	1899
357	D.G.Bradman	South Australia v Victoria	Melbourne	1935-36
356	B.A.Richards	South Australia v W Australia	Perth	1970-71
355*	G.R.Marsh	W Australia v S Australia	Perth	1989-90
355	B.Sutcliffe	Otago v Auckland	Dunedin	1949-50
353	V.V.S.Laxman	Hyderabad v Karnataka	Bangalore	1999-00
352	W.H.Ponsford	Victoria v New South Wales	Melbourne	1926-27
350	Rashid Israr	Habib Bank v National Bank	Lahore	1976-77

There have been 148 triple hundreds in first-class cricket, W.V.Raman (313) and Arjan Kripal Singh (302*) for Tamil Nadu v Goa at Panjim in 1988-89 providing the only instance of two batsmen scoring 300 in the same innings.

MOST HUNDREDS IN SUCCESSIVE INNINGS

6	C.B.Fry	Sussex and Rest of England	1901
6	D.G.Bradman	South Australia and D.G.Bradman's XI	1938-39
6	M.J.Procter	Rhodesia	1970-71

TWO DOUBLE HUNDREDS IN A MATCH

244	202*	A.E.Fagg	Kent v Essex	Colchester	1938

TRIPLE HUNDRED AND HUNDRED IN A MATCH

333	123	G.A.Gooch	England v India	Lord's	1990

DOUBLE HUNDRED AND HUNDRED IN A MATCH MOST TIMES

4	Zaheer Abbas	Gloucestershire	1976-81

TWO HUNDREDS IN A MATCH MOST TIMES

8	Zaheer Abbas	Gloucestershire and PIA	1976-82
7	W.R.Hammond	Gloucestershire, England and MCC	1927-45

MOST HUNDREDS IN A SEASON

18	D.C.S.Compton	1947	16 J.B.Hobbs	1925

100 HUNDREDS IN A CAREER

	Total		100th Hundred	
	Hundreds	Inns	Season	Inns
J.B.Hobbs	197	1315	1923	821
E.H.Hendren	170	1300	1928-29	740
W.R.Hammond	167	1005	1935	679
C.P.Mead	153	1340	1927	892
G.Boycott	151	1014	1977	645
H.Sutcliffe	149	1088	1932	700
F.E.Woolley	145	1532	1929	1031
L.Hutton	129	814	1951	619
G.A.Hick	128	806	1998	574
G.A.Gooch	128	990	1992-93	820
W.G.Grace	126	1493	1895	1113
D.C.S.Compton	123	839	1952	552
T.W.Graveney	122	1223	1964	940
D.G.Bradman	117	338	1947-48	295
I.V.A.Richards	114	796	1988-89	658
Zaheer Abbas	108	768	1982-83	658
A.Sandham	107	1000	1935	871
M.C.Cowdrey	107	1130	1973	1035
T.W.Hayward	104	1138	1913	1076
G.M.Turner	103	792	1982	779
J.H.Edrich	103	979	1977	945
L.E.G.Ames	102	951	1950	915
G.E.Tyldesley	102	961	1934	919
D.L.Amiss	102	1139	1986	1081

MOST 400s: 2 – B.C.Lara, W.H.Ponsford

MOST 300s or more: 6 – D.G.Bradman; 4 – W.R.Hammond, W.H.Ponsford

MOST 200s or more: 37 – D.G.Bradman; 36 – W.R.Hammond; 22 – E.H.Hendren

MOST RUNS IN A MONTH

1294 (avge 92.42)   L.Hutton   Yorkshire   June 1949

MOST RUNS IN A SEASON

Runs			I	NO	HS	Avge	100	Season
3816	D.C.S.Compton	Middlesex	50	8	246	90.85	18	1947
3539	W.J.Edrich	Middlesex	52	8	267*	80.43	12	1947
3518	T.W.Hayward	Surrey	61	8	219	66.37	13	1906

The feat of scoring 3000 runs in a season has been achieved 28 times, the most recent instance being by W.E.Alley (3019) in 1961. The highest aggregate in a season since 1969 is 2755 by S.J.Cook in 1991.

1000 RUNS IN A SEASON MOST TIMES

28   W.G.Grace (Gloucestershire), F.E.Woolley (Kent)

HIGHEST BATTING AVERAGE IN A SEASON

(Qualification: 12 innings)

Avge			I	NO	HS	Runs	100	Season
115.66	D.G.Bradman	Australians	26	5	278	2429	13	1938
104.66	D.R.Martyn	Australians	14	5	176*	942	5	2001
102.53	G.Boycott	Yorkshire	20	5	175*	1538	6	1979
102.00	W.A.Johnston	Australians	17	16	28*	102	–	1953
101.70	G.A.Gooch	Essex	30	3	333	2746	12	1990
100.12	G.Boycott	Yorkshire	30	5	233	2503	13	1971

FASTEST HUNDRED AGAINST AUTHENTIC BOWLING

35 min   P.G.H.Fender   Surrey v Northamptonshire   Northampton   1920

FASTEST DOUBLE HUNDRED

113 min   R.J.Shastri   Bombay v Baroda   Bombay   1984-85

FASTEST TRIPLE HUNDRED

181 min   D.C.S.Compton   MCC v NE Transvaal   Benoni   1948-49

MOST SIXES IN AN INNINGS

16   A.Symonds   Gloucestershire v Glamorgan   Abergavenny   1995

MOST SIXES IN A MATCH

20   A.Symonds   Gloucestershire v Glamorgan   Abergavenny   1995

MOST SIXES IN A SEASON

80   I.T.Botham   Somerset and England   1985

MOST FOURS IN AN INNINGS

72   B.C.Lara   Warwickshire v Durham   Birmingham   1994

MOST RUNS OFF ONE OVER

36   G.St A.Sobers   Nottinghamshire v Glamorgan   Swansea   1968
36   R.J.Shastri   Bombay v Baroda   Bombay   1984-85

Both batsmen hit for six all six balls of overs bowled by M.A.Nash and Tilak Raj respectively.

MOST RUNS IN A DAY

390*   B.C.Lara   Warwickshire v Durham   Birmingham   1994

There have been 19 instances of a batsman scoring 300 or more runs in a day.

LONGEST INNINGS

1015 min R.Nayyar (271)   Himachal Pradesh v Jammu & Kashmir Chamba   1999-00

HIGHEST PARTNERSHIPS FOR EACH WICKET

First Wicket

561	Waheed Mirza/Mansoor Akhtar	Karachi W v Quetta	Karachi	1976-77
555	P.Holmes/H.Sutcliffe	Yorkshire v Essex	Leyton	1932
554	J.T.Brown/J.Tunnicliffe	Yorkshire v Derbys	Chesterfield	1898

Second Wicket

576	S.T.Jayasuriya/R.S.Mahanama	Sri Lanka v India	Colombo (RPS)	1997-98
475	Zahir Alam/L.S.Rajput	Assam v Tripura	Gauhati	1991-92
465*	J.A.Jameson/R.B.Kanhai	Warwickshire v Glos	Birmingham	1974

Third Wicket

467	A.H.Jones/M.D.Crowe	N Zealand v Sri Lanka	Wellington	1990-91
456	Khalid Irtiza/Aslam Ali	United Bank v Multan	Karachi	1975-76
451	Mudassar Nazar/Javed Miandad	Pakistan v India	Hyderabad	1982-83
445	P.E.Whitelaw/W.N.Carson	Auckland v Otago	Dunedin	1936-37
438*	G.A.Hick/T.M.Moody	Worcestershire v Hants	Southampton	1997

Fourth Wicket

577	V.S.Hazare/Gul Mahomed	Baroda v Holkar	Baroda	1946-47
574*	C.L.Walcott/F.M.M.Worrell	Barbados v Trinidad	Port-of-Spain	1945-46
502*	F.M.M.Worrell/J.D.C.Goddard	Barbados v Trinidad	Bridgetown	1943-44
470	A.I.Kallicharran/G.W.Humpage	Warwickshire v Lancs	Southport	1982

Fifth Wicket

464*	M.E.Waugh/S.R.Waugh	NSW v W Australia	Perth	1990-91
405	S.G.Barnes/D.G.Bradman	Australia v England	Sydney	1946-47
401	M.B.Loye/D.Ripley	Northants v Glamorgan	Northampton	1998

Sixth Wicket

487*	G.A.Headley/C.C.Passailaigue	Jamaica v Tennyson's	Kingston	1931-32
428	W.W.Armstrong/M.A.Noble	Australians v Sussex	Hove	1902
411	R.M.Poore/E.G.Wynyard	Hampshire v Somerset	Taunton	1899

Seventh Wicket

460	Bhupinder Singh jr/P.Dharmani	Punjab v Delhi	Delhi	1994-95
347	D.St E.Atkinson/C.C.Depeiza	W Indies v Australia	Bridgetown	1954-55
344	K.S.Ranjitsinhji/W.Newham	Sussex v Essex	Leyton	1902

Eighth Wicket

433	V.T.Trumper/A.Sims	Australians v C'bury	Christchurch	1913-14
313	Wasim Akram/Saqlain Mushtaq	Pakistan v Zimbabwe	Sheikhupura	1996-97
292	R.Peel/Lord Hawke	Yorkshire v Warwicks	Birmingham	1896

Ninth Wicket

283	J.Chapman/A.Warren	Derbys v Warwicks	Blackwell	1910
268	J.B.Commins/N.Boje	SA 'A' v Mashonaland	Harare	1994-95
251	J.W.H.T.Douglas/S.N.Hare	Essex v Derbyshire	Leyton	1921

Tenth Wicket

307	A.F.Kippax/J.E.H.Hooker	NSW v Victoria	Melbourne	1928-29
249	C.T.Sarwate/S.N.Banerjee	Indians v Surrey	The Oval	1946
239	Aqil Arshad/Ali Raza	Lahore Whites v Hyderabad	Lahore	2004-05
235	F.E.Woolley/A.Fielder	Kent v Worcs	Stourbridge	1909

35000 RUNS IN A CAREER

	Career	I	NO	HS	Runs	Avge	100
J.B.Hobbs	1905-34	1315	106	316*	**61237**	50.65	197
F.E.Woolley	1906-38	1532	85	305*	**58969**	40.75	145
E.H.Hendren	1907-38	1300	166	301*	**57611**	50.80	170
C.P.Mead	1905-36	1340	185	280*	**55061**	47.67	153
W.G.Grace	1865-1908	1493	105	344	**54896**	39.55	126
W.R.Hammond	1920-51	1005	104	336*	**50551**	56.10	167
H.Sutcliffe	1919-45	1088	123	313	**50138**	51.95	149
G.Boycott	1962-86	1014	162	261*	**48426**	56.83	151
T.W.Graveney	1948-71/72	1223	159	258	**47793**	44.91	122
G.A.Gooch	1973-2000	990	75	333	**44846**	49.01	128
T.W.Hayward	1893-1914	1138	96	315*	**43551**	41.79	104
D.L.Amiss	1960-87	1139	126	262*	**43423**	42.86	102
M.C.Cowdrey	1950-76	1130	134	307	**42719**	42.89	107
A.Sandham	1911-37/38	1000	79	325	**41284**	44.82	107
L.Hutton	1934-60	814	91	364	**40140**	55.51	129
M.J.K.Smith	1951-75	1091	139	204	**39832**	41.84	69
W.Rhodes	1898-1930	1528	237	267*	**39802**	30.83	58
J.H.Edrich	1956-78	979	104	310*	**39790**	45.47	103
R.E.S.Wyatt	1923-57	1141	157	232	**39405**	40.04	85
D.C.S.Compton	1936-64	839	88	300	**38942**	51.85	123
G.E.Tyldesley	1909-36	961	106	256*	**38874**	45.46	102
G.A.Hick	1983/84-2005	806	78	405*	**38437**	52.79	128
J.T.Tyldesley	1895-1923	994	62	295*	**37897**	40.60	86
K.W.R.Fletcher	1962-88	1167	170	228*	**37665**	37.77	63
C.G.Greenidge	1970-92	889	75	273*	**37354**	45.88	92
J.W.Hearne	1909-36	1025	116	285*	**37252**	40.98	96
L.E.G.Ames	1926-51	951	95	295	**37248**	43.51	102
D.Kenyon	1946-67	1159	59	259	**37002**	33.63	74
W.J.Edrich	1934-58	964	92	267*	**36965**	42.39	86
J.M.Parks	1949-76	1227	172	205*	**36673**	34.76	51
M.W.Gatting	1975-98	861	123	258	**36549**	49.52	94
D.Denton	1894-1920	1163	70	221	**36479**	33.37	69
G.H.Hirst	1891-1929	1215	151	341	**36323**	34.13	60
I.V.A.Richards	1971/72-93	796	63	322	**36212**	49.40	114
A.Jones	1957-83	1168	72	204*	**36049**	32.89	56
W.G.Quaife	1894-1928	1203	185	255*	**36012**	35.37	72
R.E.Marshall	1945/46-72	1053	59	228*	**35725**	35.94	68
G.Gunn	1902-32	1061	82	220	**35208**	35.96	62

BOWLING RECORDS

ALL TEN WICKETS IN AN INNINGS

This feat has been achieved 78 times in first-class matches (excluding 12-a-side fixtures).
Three Times: A.P.Freeman (1929, 1930, 1931)
Twice: V.E.Walker (1859, 1865); H.Verity (1931, 1932); J.C.Laker (1956)

Instances since 1945:

W.E.Hollies	Warwickshire v Notts	Birmingham	1946
J.M.Sims	East v West	Kingston on Thames	1948
J.K.R.Graveney	Gloucestershire v Derbyshire	Chesterfield	1949
T.E.Bailey	Essex v Lancashire	Clacton	1949
R.Berry	Lancashire v Worcestershire	Blackpool	1953
S.P.Gupte	President's XI v Combined XI	Bombay	1954-55
J.C.Laker	Surrey v Australians	The Oval	1956

K.Smales	Nottinghamshire v Glos	Stroud	1956
G.A.R.Lock	Surrey v Kent	Blackheath	1956
J.C.Laker	England v Australia	Manchester	1956
P.M.Chatterjee	Bengal v Assam	Jorhat	1956-57
J.D.Bannister	Warwicks v Combined Services	Birmingham (M & B)	1959
A.J.G.Pearson	Cambridge U v Leicestershire	Loughborough	1961
N.I.Thomson	Sussex v Warwickshire	Worthing	1964
P.J.Allan	Queensland v Victoria	Melbourne	1965-66
I.J.Brayshaw	Western Australia v Victoria	Perth	1967-68
Shahid Mahmood	Karachi Whites v Khairpur	Karachi	1969-70
E.E.Hemmings	International XI v W Indians	Kingston	1982-83
P.Sunderam	Rajasthan v Vidarbha	Jodhpur	1985-86
S.T.Jefferies	Western Province v OFS	Cape Town	1987-88
Imran Adil	Bahawalpur v Faisalabad	Faisalabad	1989-90
G.P.Wickremasinghe	Sinhalese v Kalutara	Colombo	1991-92
R.L.Johnson	Middlesex v Derbyshire	Derby	1994
Naeem Akhtar	Rawalpindi B v Peshawar	Peshawar	1995-96
A.Kumble	India v Pakistan	Delhi	1998-99
D.S.Mohanty	East Zone v South Zone	Agartala	2000-01

MOST WICKETS IN A MATCH

| 19 | J.C.Laker | England v Australia | Manchester | 1956 |

MOST WICKETS IN A SEASON

Wkts		Season	Matches	Overs	Mdns	Runs	Avge
304	A.P.Freeman	1928	37	1976.1	423	5489	18.05
298	A.P.Freeman	1933	33	2039	651	4549	15.26

The feat of taking 250 wickets in a season has been achieved on 12 occasions, the last instance being by A.P.Freeman in 1933. 200 or more wickets in a season have been taken on 59 occasions, the last being by G.A.R.Lock (212 wickets, average 12.02) in 1957.

The highest aggregates of wickets taken in a season since the reduction of County Championship matches in 1969 are as follows:

Wkts		Season	Matches	Overs	Mdns	Runs	Avge
134	M.D.Marshall	1982	22	822	225	2108	15.73
131	L.R.Gibbs	1971	23	1024.1	295	2475	18.89
125	F.D.Stephenson	1988	22	819.1	196	2289	18.31
121	R.D.Jackman	1980	23	746.2	220	1864	15.40

Since 1969 there have been 50 instances of bowlers taking 100 wickets in a season.

MOST HAT-TRICKS IN A CAREER

7	D.V.P.Wright
6	T.W.J.Goddard, C.W.L.Parker
5	S.Haigh, V.W.C.Jupp, A.E.G.Rhodes, F.A.Tarrant

2000 WICKETS IN A CAREER

	Career	Runs	Wkts	Avge	100w
W.Rhodes	1898-1930	69993	**4187**	16.71	23
A.P.Freeman	1914-36	69577	**3776**	18.42	17
C.W.L.Parker	1903-35	63817	**3278**	19.46	16
J.T.Hearne	1888-1923	54352	**3061**	17.75	15
T.W.J.Goddard	1922-52	59116	**2979**	19.84	16
W.G.Grace	1865-1908	51545	**2876**	17.92	10
A.S.Kennedy	1907-36	61034	**2874**	21.23	15
D.Shackleton	1948-69	53303	**2857**	18.65	20
G.A.R.Lock	1946-70/71	54709	**2844**	19.23	14

	Career	Runs	Wkts	Avge	100w
F.J.Titmus	1949-82	63313	**2830**	22.37	16
M.W.Tate	1912-37	50571	**2784**	18.16	13+1
G.H.Hirst	1891-1929	51282	**2739**	18.72	15
C.Blythe	1899-1914	42136	**2506**	16.81	14
D.L.Underwood	1963-87	49993	**2465**	20.28	10
W.E.Astill	1906-39	57783	**2431**	23.76	9
J.C.White	1909-37	43759	**2356**	18.57	14
W.E.Hollies	1932-57	48656	**2323**	20.94	14
F.S.Trueman	1949-69	42154	**2304**	18.29	12
J.B.Statham	1950-68	36999	**2260**	16.37	13
R.T.D.Perks	1930-55	53771	**2233**	24.07	16
J.Briggs	1879-1900	35431	**2221**	15.95	12
D.J.Shepherd	1950-72	47302	**2218**	21.32	12
E.G.Dennett	1903-26	42571	**2147**	19.82	12
T.Richardson	1892-1905	38794	**2104**	18.43	10
T.E.Bailey	1945-67	48170	**2082**	23.13	9
R.Illingworth	1951-83	42023	**2072**	20.28	10
F.E.Woolley	1906-38	41066	**2068**	19.85	8
N.Gifford	1960-88	48731	**2068**	23.56	4
G.Geary	1912-38	41339	**2063**	20.03	11
D.V.P.Wright	1932-57	49307	**2056**	23.98	10
J.A.Newman	1906-30	51111	**2032**	25.15	9
A.Shaw	1864-97	24580	**2026**+1	12.12	9
S.Haigh	1895-1913	32091	**2012**	15.94	11

ALL-ROUND RECORDS

THE 'DOUBLE'

3000 runs and 100 wickets: J.H.Parks (1937)

2000 runs and 200 wickets: G.H.Hirst (1906)

2000 runs and 100 wickets: F.E.Woolley (4), J.W.Hearne (3), W.G.Grace (2), G.H.Hirst (2), W.Rhodes (2), T.E.Bailey, D.E.Davies, G.L.Jessop, V.W.C.Jupp, J.Langridge, F.A.Tarrant, C.L.Townsend, L.F.Townsend

1000 runs and 200 wickets: M.W.Tate (3), A.E.Trott (2), A.S.Kennedy

Most Doubles: 16 – W.Rhodes; 14 – G.H.Hirst; 10 – V.W.C.Jupp

Double in Debut Season: D.B.Close (1949) – aged 18, the youngest to achieve this feat.
    The feat of scoring 1000 runs and taking 100 wickets in a season has been achieved on 305 occasions, R.J.Hadlee (1984) and F.D.Stephenson (1988) being the only players to complete the 'double' since the reduction of County Championship matches in 1969.

WICKET-KEEPING RECORDS

EIGHT DISMISSALS IN AN INNINGS

9	(8ct, 1st)	Tahir Rashid	Habib Bank v PACO	Gujranwala	1992-93
9	(7ct, 2st)	W.R.James	Matabeleland v Mashonaland CD	Bulawayo	1995-96
8	(8ct)	A.T.W.Grout	Queensland v W Australia	Brisbane	1959-60
8	(8ct)	D.E.East	Essex v Somerset	Taunton	1985
8	(8ct)	S.A.Marsh	Kent v Middlesex	Lord's	1991
8	(6ct, 2st)	T.J.Zoehrer	Australians v Surrey	The Oval	1993
8	(7ct, 1st)	D.S.Berry	Victoria v South Australia	Melbourne	1996-97
8	(7ct, 1st)	Y.S.S.Mendis	Bloomfield v Kurunegala Youth	Colombo	2000-01
8	(7ct, 1st)	S.Nath	Assam v Tripura (*on debut*)	Gauhati	2001-02
8	(8ct)	J.N.Batty	Surrey v Kent	The Oval	2004

TWELVE DISMISSALS IN A MATCH

13	(11ct, 2st)	W.R.James	Matabeleland v Mashonaland CD Bulawayo	1995-96
12	(8ct, 4st)	E.Pooley	Surrey v Sussex The Oval	1868
12	(9ct, 3st)	D.Tallon	Queensland v NSW Sydney	1938-39
12	(9ct, 3st)	H.B.Taber	NSW v South Australia Adelaide	1968-69

MOST DISMISSALS IN A SEASON

128 (79ct, 49st) L.E.G.Ames   1929

1000 DISMISSALS IN A CAREER

	Career	Dismissals	Ct	St
R.W.Taylor	1960-88	1649	1473	176
J.T.Murray	1952-75	1527	1270	257
H.Strudwick	1902-27	1497	1242	255
A.P.E.Knott	1964-85	1344	1211	133
R.C.Russell	1981-2004	1320	1192	128
F.H.Huish	1895-1914	1310	933	377
B.Taylor	1949-73	1294	1083	211
S.J.Rhodes	1981-2004	1263	1139	124
D.Hunter	1889-1909	1253	906	347
H.R.Butt	1890-1912	1228	953	275
J.H.Board	1891-1914/15	1207	852	355
H.Elliott	1920-47	1206	904	302
J.M.Parks	1949-76	1181	1088	93
R.Booth	1951-70	1126	948	178
L.E.G.Ames	1926-51	1121	703	418
D.L.Bairstow	1970-90	1099	961	138
G.Duckworth	1923-47	1096	753	343
H.W.Stephenson	1948-64	1082	748	334
J.G.Binks	1955-75	1071	895	176
T.G.Evans	1939-69	1066	816	250
A.Long	1960-80	1046	922	124
G.O.Dawkes	1937-61	1043	895	148
R.W.Tolchard	1965-83	1037	912	125
W.L.Cornford	1921-47	1017	675	342

FIELDING RECORDS

MOST CATCHES IN AN INNINGS

7	M.J.Stewart	Surrey v Northamptonshire	Northampton	1957
7	A.S.Brown	Gloucestershire v Nottinghamshire	Nottingham	1966

MOST CATCHES IN A MATCH

10	W.R.Hammond	Gloucestershire v Surrey	Cheltenham	1928

MOST CATCHES IN A SEASON

78	W.R.Hammond	1928	77 M.J.Stewart	1957

750 CATCHES IN A CAREER

1018	F.E.Woolley	1906-38	784	J.G.Langridge	1928-55
887	W.G.Grace	1865-1908	764	W.Rhodes	1898-1930
830	G.A.R.Lock	1946-70/71	758	C.A.Milton	1948-74
819	W.R.Hammond	1920-51	754	E.H.Hendren	1907-38
813	D.B.Close	1949-86			

LIMITED–OVERS INTERNATIONALS RESULTS

1970–71 to 14 February 2006

For reasons outlined in the Preface these records exclude all matches involving multinational teams and the NatWest Series match between West Indies and New Zealand at Southampton in 2004 that was abandoned without a ball bowled after the toss.

	Opponents	Matches	E	A	SA	WI	NZ	I	P	SL	Z	B	Ass	Tied	NR
England	Australia	85	34	47	–	–	–	–	–	–	–	–	–	2	2
	South Africa	34	11	–	21	–	–	–	–	–	–	–	–	1	1
	West Indies	70	29	–	–	37	–	–	–	–	–	–	–	–	4
	New Zealand	54	25	–	–	–	25	–	–	–	–	–	–	1	3
	India	51	25	–	–	–	–	24	–	–	–	–	–	–	2
	Pakistan	58	33	–	–	–	–	–	24	–	–	–	–	–	1
	Sri Lanka	32	19	–	–	–	–	–	–	13	–	–	–	–	–
	Zimbabwe	30	21	–	–	–	–	–	–	–	8	–	–	–	1
	Bangladesh	7	7	–	–	–	–	–	–	–	–	0	–	–	–
	Associates	7	7	–	–	–	–	–	–	–	–	–	0	–	–
Australia	South Africa	60	–	32	25	–	–	–	–	–	–	–	–	3	–
	West Indies	108	–	49	–	55	–	–	–	–	–	–	–	2	2
	New Zealand	100	–	70	–	–	27	–	–	–	–	–	–	–	3
	India	80	–	49	–	–	–	27	–	–	–	–	–	–	4
	Pakistan	74	–	43	–	–	–	–	27	–	–	–	–	1	3
	Sri Lanka	62	–	41	–	–	–	–	–	19	–	–	–	–	2
	Zimbabwe	27	–	25	–	–	–	–	–	–	1	–	–	–	1
	Bangladesh	9	–	8	–	–	–	–	–	–	–	1	–	–	–
	Associates	9	–	9	–	–	–	–	–	–	–	–	0	–	–
S Africa	West Indies	38	–	–	26	11	–	–	–	–	–	–	–	–	1
	N Zealand	45	–	–	27	–	14	–	–	–	–	–	–	–	4
	India	50	–	–	30	–	–	18	–	–	–	–	–	–	2
	Pakistan	41	–	–	28	–	–	–	13	–	–	–	–	–	–
	Sri Lanka	43	–	–	20	–	–	–	–	21	–	–	–	1	1
	Zimbabwe	21	–	–	18	–	–	–	–	–	2	–	–	–	1
	Bangladesh	7	–	–	7	–	–	–	–	–	–	0	–	–	–
	Associates	11	–	–	11	–	–	–	–	–	–	–	0	–	–
W Indies	New Zealand	39	–	–	–	22	13	–	–	–	–	–	–	–	4
	India	78	–	–	–	46	–	30	–	–	–	–	–	1	1
	Pakistan	105	–	–	–	62	–	–	41	–	–	–	–	2	–
	Sri Lanka	41	–	–	–	24	–	–	–	16	–	–	–	–	1
	Zimbabwe	24	–	–	–	17	–	–	–	–	7	–	–	–	–
	Bangladesh	11	–	–	–	9	–	–	–	–	–	0	–	–	2
	Associates	8	–	–	–	7	–	–	–	–	–	–	1	–	–
N Zealand	India	75	–	–	–	–	35	36	–	–	–	–	–	–	4
	Pakistan	77	–	–	–	–	28	–	47	–	–	–	–	1	1
	Sri Lanka	60	–	–	–	–	32	–	–	25	–	–	–	1	2
	Zimbabwe	28	–	–	–	–	19	–	–	–	7	–	–	1	1
	Bangladesh	7	–	–	–	–	7	–	–	–	–	0	–	–	–
	Associates	6	–	–	–	–	6	–	–	–	–	–	0	–	–
India	Pakistan	104	–	–	–	–	–	37	63	–	–	–	–	–	4
	Sri Lanka	89	–	–	–	–	–	47	–	35	–	–	–	–	7
	Zimbabwe	49	–	–	–	–	–	39	–	–	8	–	–	2	–
	Bangladesh	14	–	–	–	–	–	13	–	–	–	1	–	–	–
	Associates	18	–	–	–	–	–	16	–	–	–	–	2	–	–
Pakistan	Sri Lanka	103	–	–	–	–	–	–	62	38	–	–	–	1	2
	Zimbabwe	34	–	–	–	–	–	–	30	–	2	–	–	1	1
	Bangladesh	18	–	–	–	–	–	–	17	–	–	1	–	–	–
	Associates	14	–	–	–	–	–	–	14	–	–	–	0	–	–
Sri Lanka	Zimbabwe	36	–	–	–	–	–	–	–	29	6	–	–	–	1
	Bangladesh	14	–	–	–	–	–	–	–	14	–	0	–	–	–
	Associates	8	–	–	–	–	–	–	–	7	–	–	1	–	–
Zimbabwe	Bangladesh	18	–	–	–	–	–	–	–	–	14	4	–	–	–
	Associates	18	–	–	–	–	–	–	–	–	15	–	1	–	2
Bangladesh	Associates	10	–	–	–	–	–	–	–	–	–	3	7	–	–
Associates	Associates	3	–	–	–	–	–	–	–	–	–	–	3	–	–
		2322	211	373	213	290	206	287	338	217	70	10	15	21	71

MERIT TABLE OF ALL L-O INTERNATIONALS
1970-71 to 14 February 2006

	Matches	Won	Lost	Tied	No Result	% Won (exc NR)
South Africa	350	213	122	5	10	62.64
Australia	614	373	216	8	17	62.47
West Indies	522	290	212	5	15	57.19
Pakistan	628	338	272	6	12	54.87
England	428	211	199	4	14	50.96
India	608	287	294	3	24	49.14
Sri Lanka	488	217	252	3	16	45.97
New Zealand	491	206	259	4	22	43.92
Zimbabwe	285	70	203	4	8	25.27
Bangladesh	115	10	103	–	2	8.84
Associate Members	115	15	98	–	2	13.27

TEAM RECORDS
HIGHEST TOTALS

398-5	(50 overs)	Sri Lanka v Kenya	Kandy	1995-96
397-5	(44 overs)	New Zealand v Zimbabwe	Bulawayo	2005
391-4	(50 overs)	England v Bangladesh	Nottingham	2005
376-2	(50 overs)	India v New Zealand	Hyderabad, India	1999-00
373-6	(50 overs)	India v Sri Lanka	Taunton	1999
371-9	(50 overs)	Pakistan v Sri Lanka	Nairobi	1996-97
368-5	(50 overs)	Australia v Sri Lanka	Sydney	2005-06
363-3	(50 overs)	South Africa v Zimbabwe	Bulawayo	2001-02
363-7	(55 overs)	England v Pakistan	Nottingham	1992
360-4	(50 overs)	West Indies v Sri Lanka	Karachi	1987-88
359-2	(50 overs)	Australia v India	Johannesburg	2002-03
359-5	(50 overs)	Australia v India	Sydney	2003-04
356-9	(50 overs)	India v Pakistan	Vishakhapatnam	2004-05
354-3	(50 overs)	South Africa v Kenya	Cape Town	2001-02
353-5	(50 overs)	India v New Zealand	Hyderabad, India	2003-04
353-6	(50 overs)	Pakistan v England	Karachi	2005-06
351-3	(50 overs)	India v Kenya	Paarl	2001-02

The highest for Zimbabwe 340-2 (v Namibia, Harare, 2002-03), and for Bangladesh 272-8 (v Z, Bulawayo, 2000-01).

HIGHEST TOTALS BATTING SECOND

WINNING:	332-8	(49.0 overs)	New Zealand v Australia	Christchurch	2005-06
LOSING:	344-8	(50.0 overs)	Pakistan v India	Karachi	2003-04

HIGHEST MATCH AGGREGATE

693-15	(100.0 overs)	India (349-7) v Pakistan (344-8)	Karachi	2003-04

LARGEST RUNS MARGINS OF VICTORY

256 runs	Australia beat Namibia	Potschefstroom	2002-03
245 runs	Sri Lanka beat India	Sharjah	2000-01
233 runs	Pakistan v Bangladesh	Dhaka	1999-00
232 runs	Australia beat Sri Lanka	Adelaide	1984-85
224 runs	Australia beat Pakistan	Nairobi	2002
217 runs	Pakistan beat Sri Lanka	Sharjah	2001-02
210 runs	New Zealand beat USA	The Oval	2004
209 runs	South Africa beat West Indies	Cape Town	2003-04
208 runs	South Africa beat Kenya	Cape Town	2001-02
208 runs	Australia beat India	Sydney	2003-04
206 runs	New Zealand beat Australia	Adelaide	1985-86
206 runs	Sri Lanka beat Holland	Colombo (RPS)	2002-03
202 runs	England beat India	Lord's	1975
202 runs	South Africa beat Kenya	Nairobi	1996-97
202 runs	Zimbabwe beat Kenya	Dhaka	1998-99
200 runs	India beat Bangladesh	Dhaka	2002-03

226

LOWEST TOTALS (Excluding reduced innings)

35	18.0 overs)	Zimbabwe v Sri Lanka	Harare	2003-04
36	(18.4 overs)	Canada v Sri Lanka	Paarl	2002-03
38	(15.4 overs)	Zimbabwe v Sri Lanka	Colombo (SSC)	2001-02
43	(19.5 overs)	Pakistan v West Indies	Cape Town	1992-93
45	(40.3 overs)	Canada v England	Manchester	1979
45	(14.0 overs)	Namibia v Australia	Potschefstroom	2002-03
54	(26.3 overs)	India v Sri Lanka	Sharjah	2000-01
54	(23.2 overs)	West Indies v South Africa	Cape Town	2003-04
55	(28.3 overs)	Sri Lanka v West Indies	Sharjah	1986-87
63	(25.5 overs)	India v Australia	Sydney	1980-81
64	(35.5 overs)	New Zealand v Pakistan	Sharjah	1985-86
65	(24.0 overs)	USA v Australia	Southampton	2004
65	(24.3 overs)	Zimbabwe v India	Harare	2005
68	(31.3 overs)	Scotland v West Indies	Leicester	1999
69	(28.0 overs)	South Africa v Australia	Sydney	1993-94
70	(25.2 overs)	Australia v England	Birmingham	1977
70	(26.3 overs)	Australia v New Zealand	Adelaide	1985-86

The lowest for England is 86 (v A, Manchester, 2001), and for Bangladesh 76 (v SL, Colombo (SSC), 2002, and v I, Dhaka, 2002-03).

LOWEST MATCH AGGREGATES

73-11	(23.2 overs)	Canada (36) v Sri Lanka (37-1)	Paarl	2002-03
75-11	(27.2 overs)	Zimbabwe (35) v Sri Lanka (40-1)	Harare	2003-04
78-11	(20.0 overs)	Zimbabwe (38) v Sri Lanka (40-1)	Colombo (SSC)	2001-02

BATTING RECORDS
HIGHEST INDIVIDUAL INNINGS

194	Saeed Anwar	Pakistan v India	Madras	1996-97
189*	I.V.A.Richards	West Indies v England	Manchester	1984
189	S.T.Jayasuriya	Sri Lanka v India	Sharjah	2000-01
188*	G.Kirsten	South Africa v UAE	Rawalpindi	1995-96
186*	S.R.Tendulkar	India v New Zealand	Hyderabad	1999-00
183*	M.S.Dhoni	India v Sri Lanka	Jaipur	2005-06
183	S.C.Ganguly	India v Sri Lanka	Taunton	1999
181	I.V.A.Richards	West Indies v Sri Lanka	Karachi	1987-88
175*	Kapil Dev	India v Zimbabwe	Tunbridge Wells	1983
173	M.E.Waugh	Australia v West Indies	Melbourne	2000-01
172*	C.B.Wishart	Zimbabwe v Namibia	Harare	2002-03
172	A.C.Gilchrist	Australia v Zimbabwe	Hobart	2003-04
172	L.Vincent	New Zealand v Zimbabwe	Bulawayo	2005
171*	G.M.Turner	New Zealand v East Africa	Birmingham	1975
169*	D.J.Callaghan	South Africa v New Zealand	Pretoria	1994-95
169	B.C.Lara	West Indies v Sri Lanka	Sharjah	1995-96
167*	R.A.Smith	England v Australia	Birmingham	1993
161	A.C.Hudson	South Africa v Holland	Rawalpindi	1995-96
159*	D.Mongia	India v Zimbabwe	Gauhati	2001-02
158	D.I.Gower	England v New Zealand	Brisbane	1982-83
156	B.C.Lara	West Indies v Pakistan	Adelaide	2004-05
156	A.Symonds	Australia v New Zealand	Wellington	2005-06
154	A.C.Gilchrist	Australia v Sri Lanka	Melbourne	1998-99
153*	I.V.A.Richards	West Indies v Australia	Melbourne	1979-80
153*	M.Azharuddin	India v Zimbabwe	Cuttack	1997-98
153*	S.C.Ganguly	India v New Zealand	Gwalior	1999-00
153*	C.H.Gayle	West Indies v Zimbabwe	Bulawayo	2003-04
153	B.C.Lara	West Indies v Pakistan	Sharjah	1993-94
153	R.Dravid	India v New Zealand	Hyderabad	1999-00
153	H.H.Gibbs	South Africa v Bangladesh	Potchefstroom	2002-03
152*	D.L.Haynes	West Indies v India	Georgetown	1988-89
152*	C.H.Gayle	West Indies v South Africa	Johannesburg	2003-04
152	C.H.Gayle	West Indies v Kenya	Nairobi	2001-02
152	S.R.Tendulkar	India v Namibia	Pietermaritzburg	2002-03
152	A.J.Strauss	England v Bangladesh	Nottingham	2005

151*	S.T.Jayasuriya	Sri Lanka v India	Bombay	1996-97
151	A.Symonds	Australia v Sri Lanka	Sydney	2005-06
150	S.Chanderpaul	West Indies v South Africa	East London	1998-99

The highest for Bangladesh is 101 by Mehrab Hossain (v Z, Dhaka, 1998-99).

HUNDRED ON DEBUT

D.L.Amiss	103	England v Australia	Manchester	1972
D.L.Haynes	148	West Indies v Australia	St John's	1977-78
A.Flower	115*	Zimbabwe v Sri Lanka	New Plymouth	1991-92
Salim Elahi	102*	Pakistan v Sri Lanka	Gujranwala	1995-96

Shahid Afridi scored 102 for P v SL, Nairobi, 1996-97, in his second match having not batted in his first.

| Fastest 100 | 37 balls | Shahid Afridi (102) | P v SL | Nairobi | 1996-97 |
| Fastest 50 | 17 balls | S.T.Jayasuriya (76) | SL v P | Singapore | 1995-96 |

CARRYING BAT THROUGH INNINGS (SIDE ALL OUT)

G.W.Flower	84*	Zimbabwe (205) v England	Sydney	1994-95
Saeed Anwar	103*	Pakistan (219) v Zimbabwe	Harare	1994-95
N.V.Knight	125*	England (246) v Pakistan	Nottingham	1996
R.D.Jacobs	49*	West Indies (110) v Australia	Manchester	1999
D.R.Martyn	116*	Australia (191) v New Zealand	Auckland	1999-00
H.H.Gibbs	59*	South Africa (101) v Pakistan	Sharjah	1999-00
A.J.Stewart	100*	England (192) v West Indies	Nottingham	2000
Javed Omar	33*	Bangladesh (103) v Zimbabwe	Harare	2000-01

5000 RUNS IN A CAREER

		LOI	I	NO	HS	Runs	Avge	100	50
S.R.Tendulkar	I	361	352	33	186*	14146	44.34	39	72
Inzamam-ul-Haq	P	351	327	48	137*	11143	39.94	10	82
S.T.Jayasuriya	SL	353	344	15	189	10484	31.87	19	59
S.C.Ganguly	I	278	269	21	183	10101	40.73	22	60
M.Azharuddin	I	334	308	54	153*	9378	36.92	7	58
B.C.Lara	WI	254	248	26	169	9302	41.90	19	56
P.A.de Silva	SL	308	296	30	145	9284	34.90	11	64
Saeed Anwar	P	247	244	19	194	8823	39.21	20	43
R.Dravid	I	274	253	33	153	8817	40.08	11	65
R.T.Ponting	A	243	237	29	145	8686	41.76	18	49
D.L.Haynes	WI	238	237	28	152*	8648	41.37	17	57
M.E.Waugh	A	244	236	20	173	8500	39.35	18	50
M.S.Atapattu	SL	252	246	28	132*	8233	37.77	11	59
J.H.Kallis	SA	224	214	39	139	7926	45.29	13	56
A.C.Gilchrist	A	230	224	9	172	7781	36.19	13	43
S.R.Waugh	A	325	288	58	120*	7569	32.90	3	45
A.Ranatunga	SL	269	255	47	131*	7454	35.83	4	49
Javed Miandad	P	233	218	41	119*	7381	41.70	8	50
Salim Malik	P	283	256	38	102	7171	32.89	5	47
S.P.Fleming	NZ	246	237	19	134*	6985	32.04	6	41
M.Yousuf Youhana	P	206	196	28	141*	6953	41.39	11	46
M.G.Bevan	A	232	196	67	108*	6912	53.58	6	46
G.Kirsten	SA	185	185	19	188*	6798	40.95	13	45
A.Flower	Z	213	208	16	145	6786	35.34	4	55
I.V.A.Richards	WI	187	167	24	189*	6721	47.00	11	45
N.J.Astle	NZ	206	202	13	145*	6595	34.89	15	38
Ijaz Ahmed	P	250	232	29	139*	6564	32.33	10	37
G.W.Flower	Z	219	212	18	142*	6536	33.69	6	40
A.R.Border	A	273	252	39	127*	6524	30.62	3	39
R.B.Richardson	WI	224	217	30	122	6248	33.41	5	44
D.M.Jones	A	164	161	25	145	6068	44.61	7	46
D.C.Boon	A	181	177	16	122	5964	37.04	5	37
J.N.Rhodes	SA	245	220	51	121	5935	35.11	2	33

		LOI	I	NO	HS	Runs	Avge	100	50
H.H.Gibbs	SA	180	179	13	153	5859	35.30	15	24
Ramiz Raja	P	198	197	15	119*	5841	32.09	9	31
C.L.Hooper	WI	227	206	43	113*	5761	35.34	7	29
W.J.Cronje	SA	188	175	31	112	5565	38.64	2	39
D.P.M.deS.Jayawardena	SL	205	191	18	128	5379	31.09	6	31
A.Jadeja	I	196	179	36	119	5359	37.47	6	30
S.Chanderpaul	WI	177	166	21	150	5281	36.42	3	35
A.D.R.Campbell	Z	188	184	14	131*	5185	30.50	7	30
R.S.Mahanama	SL	213	198	23	119*	5162	29.49	4	35
C.G.Greenidge	WI	128	127	13	133*	5134	45.03	11	31

The most for England is 4677 in 162 innings by A.J.Stewart, and for Bangladesh 1536 (102) by Khaled Masud.

15 HUNDREDS

		Inns	100	E	A	SA	WI	NZ	I	P	SL	Z	B	Ass
S.R.Tendulkar	I	352	39	1	7	3	2	4	–	5	7	5	–	5
S.C.Ganguly	I	269	22	1	1	3	–	3	–	2	4	3	1	4
Saeed Anwar	P	244	20	–	1	–	2	4	4	–	7	2	–	
B.C.Lara	WI	248	19	1	3	3	–	2	–	5	2	1	1	1
S.T.Jayasuriya	SL	344	19	2	2	–	–	4	5	3	–	1	2	–
M.E.Waugh	A	236	18	1	–	2	3	3	3	1	1	3	–	1
R.T.Ponting	A	237	18	3	–	1	1	2	4	1	4	1	1	–
D.L.Haynes	WI	237	17	2	6	–	–	2	2	4	1	–	–	
H.H.Gibbs	SA	179	15	2	1	–	4	1	2	1	1	1	1	1
N.J.Astle	NZ	202	15	1	2	1	–	–	5	2	–	3	–	1

The most for England is 10 by M.E.Trescothick (113), for Zimbabwe 7 by A.D.R.Campbell (184), and for Bangladesh 1 by Mehrab Hossain (18) and 1 by Mohammad Ashraful (56).

HIGHEST PARTNERSHIP FOR EACH WICKET

1st	258	S.C.Ganguly/S.R.Tendulkar	India v Kenya	Paarl	2001-02
2nd	331	S.R.Tendulkar/R.Dravid	India v New Zealand	Hyderabad (Ind)	1999-00
3rd	237*	R.Dravid/S.R.Tendulkar	India v Kenya	Bristol	1999
4th	275*	M.Azharuddin/A.Jadeja	India v Zimbabwe	Cuttack	1997-98
5th	223	M.Azharuddin/A.Jadeja	India v Sri Lanka	Colombo (RPS)	1997-98
6th	161	M.O.Odumbe/A.V.Vadher	Kenya v Sri Lanka	Southampton	1999
7th	130	A.Flower/H.H.Streak	Zimbabwe v England	Harare	2001-02
8th	119	P.R.Reiffel/S.K.Warne	Australia v South Africa	Port Elizabeth	1993-94
9th	126*	Kapil Dev/S.M.H.Kirmani	India v Zimbabwe	Tunbridge Wells	1983
10th	106*	I.V.A.Richards/M.A.Holding	West Indies v England	Manchester	1984

BOWLING RECORDS
SIX WICKETS IN AN INNINGS

8-19	W.P.U.C.J Vaas	Sri Lanka v Zimbabwe	Colombo (SSC)	2001-02
7-15	G.D.McGrath	Australia v Namibia	Potchefstroom	2002-03
7-20	A.J.Bichel	Australia v England	Port Elizabeth	2002-03
7-30	M.Muralitharan	Sri Lanka v India	Sharjah	2000-01
7-36	Waqar Younis	Pakistan v England	Leeds	2001
7-37	Aqib Javed	Pakistan v India	Sharjah	1991-92
7-51	W.W.Davis	West Indies v Australia	Leeds	1983
6-12	A.Kumble	India v West Indies	Calcutta	1993-94
6-14	G.J.Gilmour	Australia v England	Leeds	1975
6-14	Imran Khan	Pakistan v India	Sharjah	1984-85
6-15	C.E.H.Croft	West Indies v England	Kingstown	1980-81
6-16	Shoaib Akhtar	Pakistan v New Zealand	Karachi	2001-02
6-18	Azhar Mahmood	Pakistan v West Indies	Sharjah	1999-00
6-19	H.K.Olonga	Zimbabwe v England	Cape Town	1999-00
6-19	S.E.Bond	New Zealand v Zimbabwe	Harare	2005
6-20	B.C.Strang	Zimbabwe v Bangladesh	Nairobi	1997-98
6-22	F.H.Edwards	West Indies v Zimbabwe	Harare	2003-04
6-23	A.A.Donald	South Africa v Kenya	Nairobi	1996-97
6-23	A.Nehra	India v England	Durban	2002-03

6-23	S.E.Bond	New Zealand v Australia		Port Elizabeth	2002-03
6-25	S.B.Styris	New Zealand v West Indies		Port-of-Spain	2002
6-25	W.P.U.C.J Vaas	Sri Lanka v Bangladesh		Pietermaritzburg	2002-03
6-26	Waqar Younis	Pakistan v Sri Lanka		Sharjah	1989-90
6-27	Naved-ul-Hasan	Pakistan v India		Jamshedpur	2004-05
6-28	H.K.Olonga	Zimbabwe v Kenya		Bulawayo	2002-03
6-29	B.P.Patterson	West Indies v India		Nagpur	1987-88
6-29	S.T.Jayasuriya	Sri Lanka v England		Moratuwa	1992-93
6-30	Waqar Younis	Pakistan v New Zealand		Auckland	1993-94
6-31	P.D.Collingwood	England v Bangladesh		Nottingham	2005
6-35	S.M.Pollock	South Africa v West Indies		East London	1998-99
6-35	Abdul Razzaq	Pakistan v Bangladesh		Dhaka	2001-02
6-39	K.H.MacLeay	Australia v India		Nottingham	1983
6-41	I.V.A.Richards	West Indies v India		Delhi	1989-90
6-42	A.B.Agarkar	India v Australia		Melbourne	2003-04
6-44	Waqar Younis	Pakistan v New Zealand		Sharjah	1996-97
6-49	L.Klusener	South Africa v Sri Lanka		Lahore	1997-98
6-50	A.H.Gray	West Indies v Australia		Port-of-Spain	1990-91
6-59	Waqar Younis	Pakistan v Australia		Nottingham	2001
6-59	A.Nehra	India v Sri Lanka		Colombo (RPS)	2005

The best for Bangladesh 5-31 is by Aftab Ahmed (v NZ, Dhaka, 2004-05).

150 WICKETS IN A CAREER

		LOI	Balls	R	W	Avge	Best	4w	R/Over
Wasim Akram	P	356	18186	11812	502	23.52	5-15	23	3.89
Waqar Younis	P	262	12698	9919	416	23.84	7-36	27	4.68
M.Muralitharan	SL	263	14391	9214	400	23.03	7-30	18	3.84
W.P.U.C.J.Vaas	SL	274	13479	9433	351	26.87	8-19	13	4.19
S.M.Pollock	SA	249	13012	8136	337	24.14	6-35	15	3.75
G.D.McGrath	A	218	11443	7349	327	22.47	7-15	16	3.85
A.Kumble	I	262	13997	10010	326	30.70	6-12	10	4.29
J.Srinath	I	229	11935	8847	315	28.08	5-23	10	4.44
S.K.Warne	A	193	10600	7514	291	25.82	5-33	13	4.25
Saqlain Mushtaq	P	169	8770	6275	288	21.78	5-20	17	4.29
A.A.Donald	SA	164	8561	5926	272	21.78	6-23	13	4.15
S.T.Jayasuriya	SL	353	12499	9961	269	37.02	6-29	10	4.78
Kapil Dev	I	225	11202	6945	253	27.45	5-43	4	3.72
H.H.Streak	Z	187	9414	7066	237	29.81	5-32	8	4.50
A.B.Agarkar	I	153	7577	6456	236	27.35	6-42	11	5.11
D.Gough	E	156	8350	6082	234	25.99	5-44	12	4.37
C.A.Walsh	WI	205	10822	6915	227	30.46	5- 1	7	3.83
Abdul Razzaq	P	200	8762	6699	225	29.77	6-35	10	4.58
C.E.L.Ambrose	WI	176	9353	5430	225	24.13	5-17	10	3.48
B.Lee	A	125	6390	4962	219	22.65	5-22	13	4.65
C.J.McDermott	A	138	7460	5018	203	24.71	5-44	5	4.03
C.Z.Harris	NZ	249	10667	7613	203	37.50	5-42	3	4.28
C.L.Cairns	NZ	214	8132	6557	200	32.78	5-42	4	4.83
J.H.Kallis	SA	224	7954	6336	197	32.16	5-30	4	4.77
B.K.V.Prasad	I	161	8129	6332	196	32.30	5-27	4	4.67
S.R.Waugh	A	325	8883	6764	195	34.68	4-33	3	4.56
M.Ntini	SA	123	6141	4464	194	23.01	5-31	8	4.36
Shoaib Akhtar	P	124	5805	4470	193	23.16	6-16	8	4.62
C.L.Hooper	WI	227	9573	6957	193	36.04	4-34	3	4.36
L.Klusener	SA	171	7336	5751	192	29.95	6-49	7	4.70
Aqib Javed	P	163	8012	5721	182	31.43	7-37	6	4.28
Imran Khan	P	175	7462	4845	182	26.62	6-14	4	3.90
Shahid Afridi	P	214	8402	6514	177	36.80	5-11	4	4.65
Mushtaq Ahmed	P	144	7543	5361	161	33.29	5-36	4	4.26
R.J.Hadlee	NZ	115	6182	3407	158	21.56	5-25	6	3.31
M.Prabhakar	I	130	6360	4534	157	28.87	5-33	6	4.27
M.D.Marshall	WI	136	7175	4233	157	26.96	4-18	6	3.54
D.L.Vettori	NZ	164	7499	5300	153	34.64	5-30	4	4.24
U.D.U.Chandana	SL	146	6094	4781	151	31.66	5-61	5	4.70

The most for Bangladesh is 71 by Mohammad Rafique (82 LOI).

HAT-TRICKS

Jalaluddin	Pakistan v Australia	Hyderabad	1982-83
B.A.Reid	Australia v New Zealand	Sydney	1985-86
C.Sharma	India v New Zealand	Nagpur	1987-88
Wasim Akram	Pakistan v West Indies	Sharjah	1989-90
Wasim Akram	Pakistan v Australia	Sharjah	1989-90
Kapil Dev	India v Sri Lanka	Calcutta	1990-91
Aqib Javed	Pakistan v India	Sharjah	1991-92
D.K.Morrison	New Zealand v India	Napier	1993-94
Waqar Younis	Pakistan v New Zealand	East London	1994-95
Saqlain Mushtaq	Pakistan v Zimbabwe	Peshawar	1996-97
E.A.Brandes	Zimbabwe v England	Harare	1996-97
A.M.Stuart	Australia v Pakistan	Melbourne	1996-97
Saqlain Mushtaq	Pakistan v Zimbabwe	The Oval	1999
W.P.U.C.J Vaas	Sri Lanka v Zimbabwe	Colombo (SSC)	2001-02
Mohammad Sami	Pakistan v West Indies	Sharjah	2001-02
W.P.U.C.J Vaas[1]	Sri Lanka v Bangladesh	Pietermaritzburg	2002-03
B.Lee	Australia v Kenya	Durban	2002-03
J.M.Anderson	England v Pakistan	The Oval	2003
S.J.Harmison	England v India	Nottingham	2004
C.K.Langeveldt	South Africa v West Indies	Bridgetown	2004-05

[1] The first three balls of the match. Took four wickets in opening over (W W W 4 wide W 0).

WICKET-KEEPING RECORDS
SIX DISMISSALS IN AN INNINGS

6	(6ct)	A.C.Gilchrist	Australia v South Africa	Cape Town	1999-00
6	(6ct)	A.J.Stewart	England v Zimbabwe	Manchester	2000
6	(5ct/1st)	R.D.Jacobs	West Indies v Sri Lanka	Colombo (RPS)	2001-02
6	(5ct/1st)	A.C.Gilchrist	Australia v England	Sydney	2002-03
6	(6ct)	A.C.Gilchrist	Australia v Namibia	Potchefstroom	2002-03
6	(6ct)	A.C.Gilchrist	Australia v Sri Lanka	Colombo (RPS)	2003-04

100 DISMISSALS IN A CAREER

Total			LOI	Ct	St
372‡	A.C.Gilchrist	Australia	225	331	41
302	M.V.Boucher	South Africa	210	286	16
287‡	Moin Khan	Pakistan	211	214	73
233	I.A.Healy	Australia	168	194	39
220‡	Rashid Latif	Pakistan	164	182	38
207‡	R.S.Kaluwitharana	Sri Lanka	187	132	75
204‡	P.J.L.Dujon	West Indies	167	183	21
187	R.D.Jacobs	West Indies	146	159	28
165	D.J.Richardson	South Africa	122	148	17
165†‡	A.Flower	Zimbabwe	185	133	32
163†‡	A.J.Stewart	England	138	148	15
154‡	N.R.Mongia	India	139	110	44
142†‡	K.C.Sangakkara	Sri Lanka	110	107	35
136†‡	A.C.Parore	New Zealand	148	111	25
124	R.W.Marsh	Australia	92	120	4
103	Salim Yousuf	Pakistan	86	81	22
101†‡	B.B.McCullum	New Zealand	71	96	5

The most for Bangladesh is 92 by Khaled Masud (100 LOI).
† Excluding catches taken in the field. ‡ Excluding matches when not wicket-keeper.

FIELDING RECORDS
FIVE CATCHES IN AN INNINGS

100 CATCHES IN A CAREER

Total			LOI
156	M.Azharuddin	India	334
127	A.R.Border	Australia	273
120	C.L.Hooper	West Indies	227
115	S.P.Fleming	New Zealand	246
111	S.R.Waugh	Australia	325
109	R.S.Mahanama	Sri Lanka	213
108	M.E.Waugh	Australia	244
107	S.R.Tendulkar	India	361
106	B.C.Lara	West Indies	254
106	S.T.Jayasuriya	Sri Lanka	353
105	J.N.Rhodes	South Africa	245
105	M.Muralitharan	Sri Lanka	263
103	Inzamam-ul-Haq	Pakistan	351
101	I.V.A.Richards	West Indies	187

The most for England is 64 by G.A.Hick (120 LOI), for Zimbabwe 86 by GW Flower (219), and for Bangladesh 20 by Mohammad Rafique (82).

ALL-ROUND RECORDS
50 RUNS AND 5 WICKETS IN A MATCH

I.V.A.Richards	119	5-41	West Indies v New Zealand	Dunedin	1986-87
K.Srikkanth	70	5-27	India v New Zealand	Vishakhapatnam	1988-89
M.E.Waugh	57	5-24	Australia v West Indies	Melbourne	1992-93
L.Klusener	54	6-49	South Africa v Sri Lanka	Lahore	1997-98
Abdul Razzaq	70*	5-48	Pakistan v India	Hobart	1999-00
G.A.Hick	80	5-33	England v Zimbabwe	Harare	1999-00
Shahid Afridi	61	5-40	Pakistan v England	Lahore	2000-01
S.C.Ganguly	71*	5-34	India v Zimbabwe	Kanpur	2000-01
S.B.Styris	63*	6-25	New Zealand v West Indies	Port-of-Spain	2002
R.C.Irani	53	5-26	England v India	The Oval	2002
C.H.Gayle	60	5-46	West Indies v Australia	St George's	2002-03
P.D.Collingwood	112*	6-31	England v Bangladesh	Nottingham	2005

1000 RUNS AND 100 WICKETS

England	I.T.Botham (2113/145), A.Flintoff (2500/103).
Australia	S.P.O'Donnell (1242/108); A.Symonds (3423/107); S.K.Warne (1016/291); S.R.Waugh (7569/195)
South Africa	W.J.Cronje (5565/114); J.H.Kallis (7926/197); L.Klusener (3576/192); S.M.Pollock (2542/337)
West Indies	C.H.Gayle (4361/100); C.L.Hooper (5761/193); I.V.A.Richards (6721/118)
New Zealand	C.L.Cairns (4881/200); R.J.Hadlee (1751/158); C.Z.Harris (4379/203); S.B.Styris (2361/104)
India	A.B.Agarkar (1122/236); Kapil Dev (3782/253); M.Prabhakar (1858/157); R.J.Shastri (3108/129); S.R.Tendulkar (14146/141)
Pakistan	Abdul Razzaq (3982/225); Azhar Mahmood (1492/122); Imran Khan (3709/182); Mudassar Nazar (2654/111); Shahid Afridi (4782/177); Wasim Akram (3717/502)
Sri Lanka	U.D.U.Chandana (1626/151); P.A.de Silva (9284/106); H.D.P.K.Dharmasena (1222/138); S.T.Jayasuriya (10484/269); W.P.U.C.J.Vaas (1777/351)
Zimbabwe	G.W.Flower (6536/104); H.H.Streak (2901/237)

APPEARANCE RECORDS
250 MATCHES

361	S.R.Tendulkar	India	274	W.P.U.C.J.Vaas	Sri Lanka
356	Wasim Akram	Pakistan	273	A.R.Border	Australia
353	S.T.Jayasuriya	Sri Lanka	269	A.Ranatunga	Sri Lanka
351	Inzamam-ul-Haq	Pakistan	263	M.Muralitharan	Sri Lanka
334	M.Azharuddin	India	262	Waqar Younis	Pakistan
325	S.R.Waugh	Australia	262	A.Kumble	India
308	P.A.de Silva	Sri Lanka	254	B.C.Lara	West Indies
283	Salim Malik	Pakistan	252	M.S.Atapattu	Sri Lanka
278	S.C.Ganguly	India	250	Ijaz Ahmed	Pakistan
274	R.Dravid	India			

The most for England is 170 by A.J.Stewart, for South Africa 249 by S.M.Pollock, for New Zealand 249 by C.Z.Harris, for Zimbabwe 219 by G.W.Flower, and for Bangladesh 102 by Khaled Masud. The most consecutive appearances is 172 by A.Flower for Zimbabwe (Feb 1992-Apr 2001).

100 MATCHES AS CAPTAIN

LOI			W	L	T	NR	% Won (exc NR)
193	A.Ranatunga	Sri Lanka	89	95	1	8	48.10
184	S.P.Fleming	New Zealand	80	92	1	11	46.24
178	A.R.Border	Australia	107	67	1	3	61.14
174	M.Azharuddin	India	90	76	2	6	53.57
146	S.C.Ganguly	India	76	65	–	5	53.90
139	Imran Khan	Pakistan	75	59	1	4	55.55
138	W.J.Cronje	South Africa	99	35	1	3	73.33
118	S.T.Jayasuriya	Sri Lanka	66	47	2	3	57.39
112	R.T.Ponting	Australia	84	21	2	5	78.50
109	Wasim Akram	Pakistan	66	41	2	–	60.55
108	I.V.A.Richards	West Indies	68	36	–	4	65.38
106	S.R.Waugh	Australia	67	35	3	1	63.80

The most for England is 56 by N.Hussain, for Zimbabwe 86 by A.D.R.Campbell, and for Bangladesh 30 by Habibul Bashar.

100 LOI UMPIRING APPEARANCES

172	D.R.Shepherd	England	09.06.1983	to	12.07.2005
140	R.E.Koertzen	South Africa	09.12.1992	to	21.12.2005
136	S.A.Bucknor	Jamaica	18.03.1989	to	06.11.2005
118	D.B.Hair	Australia	14.12.1991	to	08.01.2006
113	D.J.Harper	Australia	14.01.1994	to	14.02.2006
107	D.L.Orchard	South Africa	02.12.1994	to	07.12.2003
100	R.S.Dunne	New Zealand	06.02.1989	to	26.02.2002

WOMEN'S TEST CRICKET RECORDS

1934-35 to 8 April 2006

RESULTS SUMMARY

	Opponents	Tests	E	A	NZ	SA	WI	I	P	SL	Ire	Drawn
England	Australia	42	7	10	–	–	–	–	–	–	–	25
	New Zealand	23	6	–	0	–	–	–	–	–	–	17
	South Africa	6	2	–	–	0	–	–	–	–	–	4
	West Indies	3	2	–	–	–	0	–	–	–	–	1
	India	10	1	–	–	–	–	0	–	–	–	9
Australia	New Zealand	13	–	4	1	–	–	–	–	–	–	8
	West Indies	2	–	0	–	–	0	–	–	–	–	2
	India	9	–	4	–	–	–	0	–	–	–	5
New Zealand	South Africa	3	–	–	1	0	–	–	–	–	–	2
	India	6	–	–	0	–	–	0	–	–	–	6
South Africa	India	1	–	–	–	0	–	1	–	–	–	–
West Indies	India	6	–	–	–	–	1	1	–	–	–	4
	Pakistan	1	–	–	–	–	0	–	0	–	–	1
Pakistan	Sri Lanka	1	–	–	–	–	–	–	0	1	–	–
	Ireland	1	–	–	–	–	–	–	0	–	1	–
		127	18	18	2	0	1	2	0	1	1	84

	Tests	Won	Lost	Drawn	Toss Won
England	84	18	10	56	50
Australia	66	18	8	40	22
New Zealand	45	2	10	33	21
South Africa	10	–	4	6	6
West Indies	12	1	3	8	6†
India	32	2	6	24	15†
Pakistan	3	–	2	1	1
Sri Lanka	1	1	–	–	1
Ireland	1	1	–	–	–

† *Results of tosses in five of the six India v West Indies Tests in 1976-77 are not known*

TEAM RECORDS
HIGHEST INNINGS TOTALS

569-6d	Australia v England	Guildford	1998
525	Australia v India	Ahmedabad	1983-84
517-8	New Zealand v England	Scarborough	1996
503-5d	England v New Zealand	Christchurch	1934-35
497	England v South Africa	Shenley	2003
467	India v England	Taunton	2002
455	England v South Africa	Taunton	2003
440	West Indies v Pakistan	Karachi	2003-04
427-4d	Australia v England	Worcester	1998
426-7d	Pakistan v West Indies	Karachi	2003-04
426-9d	India v England	Blackpool	1986
414	England v New Zealand	Scarborough	1996
414	England v Australia	Guildford	1998
404-9d	India v South Africa	Paarl	2001-02
403-8d	New Zealand v India	Nelson	1994-95

The highest totals for countries not included above are:

316	South Africa v England	Shenley	2003
193-3d	Ireland v Pakistan	Dublin	2000

LOWEST INNINGS TOTALS

35	England v Australia	Melbourne	1957-58
38	Australia v England	Melbourne	1957-58
44	New Zealand v England	Christchurch	1934-35
47	Australia v England	Brisbane	1934-35
53	Pakistan v Ireland	Dublin	2000

The lowest innings totals for countries not included above are:

67	West Indies v England	Canterbury	1979
89	South Africa v New Zealand	Durban	1971-72
65	India v West Indies	Jammu	1976-77

BATTING RECORDS
1000 RUNS IN TESTS

			M	I	NO	HS	Avge	100	50
1935	J.A.Brittin	England	27	44	5	167	49.61	5	11
1594	R.Heyhoe-Flint	England	22	38	3	179	45.54	3	10
1301	D.A.Hockley	New Zealand	19	29	4	126*	52.04	4	7
1164	C.A.Hodges	England	18	31	2	158*	40.13	2	6
1110	S.Agarwal	India	13	23	1	190	50.45	4	4
1078	E.Bakewell	England	12	22	4	124	59.88	4	7
1058	C.M.Edwards	England	14	25	1	117	44.08	2	6
1007	M.E.Maclagan	England	14	25	1	119	41.95	2	6

HIGHEST INDIVIDUAL INNINGS ‡ *On debut*

242	Kiran Baluch	P v WI	Karachi	2003-04
214	M.Raj	I v E	Taunton	2002
209*	K.L.Rolton	A v E	Leeds	2001
204	K.E.Flavell	NZ v E	Scarborough	1996
204‡	M.A.J.Goszko	A v E	Shenley	2001
200	J.Broadbent	A v E	Guildford	1998
193	D.A.Annetts	A v E	Collingham	1987
190	S.Agarwal	I v E	Worcester	1986
189	E.A.Snowball	E v NZ	Christchurch	1934-35
179	R.Heyhoe-Flint	E v A	The Oval	1976
177	S.C.Taylor	E v SA	Shenley	2003
176*	K.L.Rolton	A v E	Worcester	1998
167	J.A.Brittin	E v A	Harrogate	1998
161*	E.C.Drumm	E v A	Christchurch	1994-95
160	B.A.Daniels	E v NZ	Scarborough	1996
158*	C.A.Hodges	E v NZ	Canterbury	1984
155*	P.F.McKelvey	NZ v E	Wellington	1968-69

5 HUNDREDS

							Opponents					
		M	I	E	A	NZ	SA	WI	IND	P	SL	IRE
5	J.A.Brittin (E)	27	44	–	3	1	–	–	1	–	–	–

HIGHEST PARTNERSHIP FOR EACH WICKET

1st	241	Kiran Baluch/Sajjida Shah	P v WI	Karachi	2003-04
2nd	235	E.A.Snowball/M.E.Hide	E v NZ	Christchurch	1934-35
3rd	309	L.A.Reeler/D.A.Annetts	A v E	Collingham	1987
4th	253	K.L.Rolton/L.C.Broadfoot	A v E	Leeds	2001
5th	138	J.Logtenberg/C.van der Westhuizen	SA v E	Shenley	2003
6th	132	B.A.Daniels/K.M.Leng	E v NZ	Scarborough	1996
7th	157	M.Raj/J.Goswami	I v E	Taunton	2002
8th	181	S.J.Griffiths/D.L.Wilson	A v NZ	Auckland	1989-90
9th	107	B.Botha/M.Payne	SA v NZ	Cape Town	1971-72
10th	119	S.Nitschke/C.R.Smith	A v E	Hove	2005

BOWLING RECORDS
50 WICKETS IN TESTS

Wkts			M	Balls	Runs	Avge	Best	5wI	10wM
77	M.B.Duggan	E	17	3734	1039	13.49	7- 6	5	–
68	E.R.Wilson	A	11	2885	803	11.80	7- 7	4	2
63	D.F.Edulji	I	20	5098†	1624	25.77	6- 64	1	–
60	M.E.Maclagan	E	14	3432	935	15.58	7- 10	3	–
60	C.L.Fitzpatrick	A	13	3603	1147	19.11	5-292	1	–
57	R.H.Thompson	A	16	4304	1040	18.24	5- 33	1	–
56	S.Kulkarni	I	18	3320	1599	28.55	6- 99	5	–
55	J.Lord	NZ	15	3108	1049	19.07	6-119	4	1
50	E.Bakewell	E	12	2697	831	16.62	7- 61	3	1

† Excludes balls bowled in Sixth Test v West Indies 1976-77

TEN WICKETS IN A TEST

13-226	Shaiza Khan	P v WI	Karachi	2003-04
11- 16	E.R.Wilson	A v E	Melbourne	1957-58
11- 63	J.M.Greenwood	E v WI	Canterbury	1979
11-107	L.C.Pearson	E v A	Sydney	2002-03
10- 65	E.R.Wilson	A v NZ	Wellington	1947-48
10- 75	E.Bakewell	E v WI	Birmingham	1979
10-107	K.Price	A v I	Lucknow	1983-84
10-118	D.A.Gordon	A v E	Melbourne	1968-69
10-137	J.Lord	NZ v A	Melbourne	1978-79

SEVEN WICKETS IN AN INNINGS

8-53	N.David	I v E	Jamshedpur	1995-96
7- 6	M.B.Duggan	E v A	Melbourne	1957-58
7- 7	E.R.Wilson	A v E	Melbourne	1957-58
7-10	M.E.Maclagan	E v A	Brisbane	1934-35
7-18	A.Palmer	A v E	Brisbane	1934-35
7-24	L.Johnston	A v NZ	Melbourne	1971-72
7-34	G.E.McConway	E v I	Worcester	1986
7-41	J.A.Burley	NZ v E	The Oval	1966
7-51	L.C.Pearson	E v A	Sydney	2002-03
7-59	Shaiza Khan	P v WI	Karachi	2003-04
7-61	E.Bakewell	E v WI	Birmingham	1979

HAT-TRICKS

E.R.Wilson	Australia v England	Melbourne	1957-58
Shaiza Khan	Pakistan v West Indies	Karachi	2003-04

WICKET-KEEPING, FIELDING AND APPEARANCE RECORDS
25 DISMISSALS IN TESTS

Total			Tests	Ct	St
58	C.Matthews	Australia	20	46	12
37	J.Smit	England	19	33	4
36	S.A.Hodges	England	11	19	17
28	B.A.Brentnall	New Zealand	10	16	12

EIGHT DISMISSALS IN A TEST

9 (8ct, 1st)	C.Matthews	A v I	Adelaide	1990-91
8 (6ct, 2st)	L.Nye	E v NZ	New Plymouth	1991-92

SIX DISMISSALS IN AN INNINGS

8 (6ct, 2st)	L.Nye	E v NZ	New Plymouth	1991-92
6 (2ct, 4st)	B.A.Brentnall	NZ v SA	Johannesburg	1971-72

20 CATCHES IN THE FIELD IN TESTS

Total			Tests
25	C.A.Hodges	England	18
21	S.Shah	India	20
20	L.A.Fullston	Australia	12

25 TEST MATCH APPEARANCES

27	J.A.Brittin	England	1979-98

TEST MATCHES RESULTS SUMMARY

Matches completed before 26 February 2006

Opponents	Tests	Won by										Tied	Drawn
		E	A	SA	WI	NZ	I	P	SL	Z	B		
England Australia	311	97	126	–	–	–	–	–	–	–	–		88
South Africa	130	54	–	26	–	–	–	–	–	–	–		50
West Indies	134	38	–	–	52	–	–	–	–	–	–		44
New Zealand	88	41	–	–	–	7	–	–	–	–	–		40
India	91	33	–	–	–	–	16	–	–	–	–		42
Pakistan	63	16	–	–	–	–	–	12	–	–	–		35
Sri Lanka	15	7	–	–	–	–	–	–	4	–	–		4
Zimbabwe	6	3	–	–	–	–	–	–	–	0	–		3
Bangladesh	4	4	–	–	–	–	–	–	–	–	0		–
Australia South Africa	74	–	41	15	–	–	–	–	–	–	–		18
West Indies	102	–	48	–	32	–	–	–	–	–	–	1	21
New Zealand	46	–	22	–	–	7	–	–	–	–	–		17
India	68	–	32	–	–	–	15	–	–	–	–	1	20
Pakistan	52	–	24	–	–	–	–	11	–	–	–		17
Sri Lanka	18	–	11	–	–	–	–	–	1	–	–		6
Zimbabwe	3	–	3	–	–	–	–	–	–	0	–		–
Bangladesh	2	–	2	–	–	–	–	–	–	–	0		–
South Africa West Indies	19	–	–	12	2	–	–	–	–	–	–		5
New Zealand	30	–	–	16	–	4	–	–	–	–	–		10
India	16	–	–	7	–	–	3	–	–	–	–		6
Pakistan	11	–	–	5	–	–	–	2	–	–	–		4
Sri Lanka	15	–	–	8	–	–	–	–	2	–	–		5
Zimbabwe	7	–	–	6	–	–	–	–	–	0	–		1
Bangladesh	4	–	–	4	–	–	–	–	–	–	0		–
West Indies New Zealand	32	–	–	–	10	7	–	–	–	–	–		15
India	78	–	–	–	30	–	10	–	–	–	–		38
Pakistan	41	–	–	–	14	–	–	13	–	–	–		14
Sri Lanka	10	–	–	–	2	–	–	–	5	–	–		2
Zimbabwe	6	–	–	–	4	–	–	–	–	0	–		2
Bangladesh	4	–	–	–	3	–	–	–	–	–	0		1
New Zealand India	44	–	–	–	–	9	14	–	–	–	–		21
Pakistan	45	–	–	–	–	6	–	21	–	–	–		18
Sri Lanka	22	–	–	–	–	8	–	–	4	–	–		10
Zimbabwe	13	–	–	–	–	7	–	–	–	0	–		6
Bangladesh	4	–	–	–	–	4	–	–	–	–	0		–
India Pakistan	56	–	–	–	–	–	8	12	–	–	–		36
Sri Lanka	26	–	–	–	–	–	10	–	3	–	–		13
Zimbabwe	11	–	–	–	–	–	7	–	–	2	–		2
Bangladesh	3	–	–	–	–	–	3	–	–	–	0		–
Pakistan Sri Lanka	30	–	–	–	–	–	–	14	7	–	–		9
Zimbabwe	14	–	–	–	–	–	–	8	–	2	–		4
Bangladesh	6	–	–	–	–	–	–	6	–	–	0		–
Sri Lanka Zimbabwe	15	–	–	–	–	–	–	–	10	0	–		5
Bangladesh	5	–	–	–	–	–	–	–	5	–	0		–
Zimbabwe Bangladesh	8	–	–	–	–	–	–	–	–	4	1		3
	1782	293	309	99	149	59	86	99	41	8	1	2	636

237

	Tests	Won	Lost	Drawn	Tied	Toss Won
England	842	293	243	306	–	404
Australia	676	309	178	187	2	340
South Africa	306	99	108	99	–	143
West Indies	426	149	133	143	1	229
New Zealand	324	59	128	137	–	166
India	393	86	128	178	1	201
Pakistan	318	99	82	137	–	150
Sri Lanka	156	41	60	55	–	82
Zimbabwe	83	8	49	26	–	49
Bangladesh	40	1	35	4	–	18

TEST CRICKET RECORDS

(To 26 February 2006)

TEAM RECORDS

HIGHEST INNINGS TOTALS

952-6d	Sri Lanka v India	Colombo (RPS)	1997-98
903-7d	England v Australia	The Oval	1938
849	England v West Indies	Kingston	1929-30
790-3d	West Indies v Pakistan	Kingston	1957-58
758-8d	Australia v West Indies	Kingston	1954-55
751-5d	West Indies v England	St John's	2003-04
747	West Indies v South Africa	St John's	2004-05
735-6d	Australia v Zimbabwe	Perth	2003-04
729-6d	Australia v England	Lord's	1930
713-3d	Sri Lanka v Zimbabwe	Bulawayo	2003-04
708	Pakistan v England	The Oval	1987
705-7d	India v Australia	Sydney	2003-04
701	Australia v England	The Oval	1934
699-5	Pakistan v India	Lahore	1989-90
695	Australia v England	The Oval	1930
692-8d	West Indies v England	The Oval	1995
687-8d	West Indies v England	The Oval	1976
682-6d	South Africa v England	Lord's	2003
681-8d	West Indies v England	Port-of-Spain	1953-54
679-7d	Pakistan v India	Lahore	2005-06
676-7	India v Sri Lanka	Kanpur	1986-87
675-5d	India v Pakistan	Multan	2003-04
674-6	Pakistan v India	Faisalabad	1984-85
674	Australia v India	Adelaide	1947-48
671-4	New Zealand v Sri Lanka	Wellington	1990-91
668	Australia v West Indies	Bridgetown	1954-55
660-5d	West Indies v New Zealand	Wellington	1994-95
659-8d	Australia v England	Sydney	1946-47
658-8d	England v Australia	Nottingham	1938
658-9d	South Africa v West Indies	Durban	2003-04
657-7d	India v Australia	Calcutta	2000-01
657-8d	Pakistan v West Indies	Bridgetown	1957-58
656-8d	Australia v England	Manchester	1964
654-5	England v South Africa	Durban	1938-39
653-4d	England v India	Lord's	1990
653-4d	Australia v England	Leeds	1993
652-7d	England v India	Madras	1984-85

652-7d	Australia v South Africa	Johannesburg	2001-02
652-8d	West Indies v England	Lord's	1973
652	Pakistan v India	Faisalabad	1982-83
650-6d	Australia v West Indies	Bridgetown	1964-65

The highest for Zimbabwe is 563-9d (v WI, Harare, 2001), and for Bangladesh 488 (v Z, Chittagong, 2004-05).

LOWEST INNINGS TOTALS

26	New Zealand v England	Auckland	1954-55
30	South Africa v England	Port Elizabeth	1895-96
30	South Africa v England	Birmingham	1924
35	South Africa v England	Cape Town	1898-99
36	Australia v England	Birmingham	1902
36	South Africa v Australia	Melbourne	1931-32
42	Australia v England	Sydney	1887-88
42	New Zealand v Australia	Wellington	1945-46
42	India v England	Lord's	1974
43	South Africa v England	Cape Town	1888-89
44	Australia v England	The Oval	1896
45	England v Australia	Sydney	1886-87
45	South Africa v Australia	Melbourne	1931-32
46	England v West Indies	Port-of-Spain	1993-94
47	South Africa v England	Cape Town	1888-89
47	New Zealand v England	Lord's	1958
47	West Indies v England	Kingston	2003-04

The lowest for Pakistan is 53 (v A, Sharjah, 2002-03), for Sri Lanka 71 (v P, Kandy, 1994-95), for Zimbabwe 54 (v SA, Cape Town, 2004-05), and for Bangladesh 86 (v SL, Colombo RPS, 2005-06).

BATTING RECORDS

4000 RUNS IN A TEST CAREER

Runs			M	I	NO	HS	Avge	100	50
11174	A.R.Border	A	156	265	44	205	50.56	27	63
11163	B.C.Lara	WI	120	212	6	400*	54.18	31	46
10927	S.R.Waugh	A	168	260	46	200	51.06	32	50
10386	S.R.Tendulkar	I	129	206	21	248*	56.14	35	41
10122	S.M.Gavaskar	I	125	214	16	236*	51.12	34	45
8900	G.A.Gooch	E	118	215	6	333	42.58	20	46
8832	Javed Miandad	P	124	189	21	280*	52.57	23	43
8540	I.V.A.Richards	WI	121	182	12	291	50.23	24	45
8463	A.J.Stewart	E	133	235	21	190	39.54	15	45
8231	D.I.Gower	E	117	204	18	215	44.25	18	39
8221	R.Dravid	I	96	161	20	270	58.30	22	39
8171	Inzamam-ul-Haq	P	106	175	19	329	52.37	25	42
8153	R.T.Ponting	A	99	164	23	257	57.82	28	31
8114	G.Boycott	E	108	193	23	246*	47.72	22	42
8032	G.St A.Sobers	WI	93	160	21	365*	57.78	26	30
8029	M.E.Waugh	A	128	209	17	153*	41.81	20	47
7728	M.A.Atherton	E	115	212	7	185*	37.70	16	46
7624	M.C.Cowdrey	E	114	188	15	182	44.06	22	38
7558	C.G.Greenidge	WI	108	185	16	226	44.72	19	34
7530	J.H.Kallis	SA	95	159	27	189*	57.04	23	38
7525	M.A.Taylor	A	104	186	13	334*	43.49	19	40

Runs			M	I	NO	HS	Avge	100	50
7515	C.H.Lloyd	WI	110	175	14	242*	46.67	19	39
7487	D.L.Haynes	WI	116	202	25	184	42.29	18	39
7422	D.C.Boon	A	107	190	20	200	43.65	21	32
7289	G.Kirsten	SA	101	176	15	275	45.27	21	34
7249	W.R.Hammond	E	85	140	16	336*	58.45	22	24
7249	J.L.Langer	A	96	166	9	250	46.17	22	29
7110	G.S.Chappell	A	87	151	19	247*	53.86	24	31
6996	D.G.Bradman	A	52	80	10	334	99.94	29	13
6971	L.Hutton	E	79	138	15	364	56.67	19	33
6868	D.B.Vengsarkar	I	116	185	22	166	42.13	17	35
6806	K.F.Barrington	E	82	131	15	256	58.67	20	35
6800	M.L.Hayden	A	78	139	12	380	53.54	24	23
6744	G.P.Thorpe	E	100	179	28	200*	44.66	16	39
6580	S.T.Jayasuriya	SL	100	170	14	340	42.17	14	29
6361	P.A.de Silva	SL	93	159	11	267	42.97	20	22
6227	R.B.Kanhai	WI	79	137	6	256	47.53	15	28
6215	M.Azharuddin	I	99	147	9	199	45.03	22	21
6156	S.Chanderpaul	WI	91	155	21	203*	45.94	14	35
6149	R.N.Harvey	A	79	137	10	205	48.41	21	24
6080	G.R.Viswanath	I	91	155	10	222	41.93	14	35
6050	S.P.Fleming	NZ	96	170	10	274*	39.03	8	40
5949	R.B.Richardson	WI	86	146	12	194	44.39	16	27
5807	D.C.S.Compton	E	78	131	15	278	50.06	17	28
5768	Salim Malik	P	103	154	22	237	43.69	15	29
5764	N.Hussain	E	96	171	16	207	37.19	14	33
5762	C.L.Hooper	WI	102	173	15	233	36.46	13	27
5502	M.E.Trescothick	E	69	131	10	219	45.47	13	28
5478	H.H.Gibbs	SA	73	123	6	228	46.82	14	20
5444	M.D.Crowe	NZ	77	131	11	299	45.36	17	18
5410	J.B.Hobbs	E	61	102	7	211	56.94	15	28
5357	K.D.Walters	A	74	125	14	250	48.26	15	33
5345	I.M.Chappell	A	75	136	10	196	42.42	14	26
5334	J.G.Wright	NZ	82	148	7	185	37.82	12	23
5330	M.S.Atapattu	SL	88	152	15	249	38.90	16	15
5312	M.J.Slater	A	74	131	7	219	42.84	14	21
5306	D.P.M.deS.Jayawardena	SL	74	120	9	242	47.80	13	27
5248	Kapil Dev	I	131	184	15	163	31.05	8	27
5234	W.M.Lawry	A	67	123	12	210	47.15	13	27
5215	S.C.Ganguly	I	88	140	12	173	40.74	12	25
5200	I.T.Botham	E	102	161	6	208	33.54	14	22
5138	J.H.Edrich	E	77	127	9	310*	43.54	12	24
5105	A.Ranatunga	SL	93	155	12	135*	35.69	4	38
5075	Mohd Yousuf Youhana	P	65	108	8	223	50.75	16	25
5062	Zaheer Abbas	P	78	124	11	274	44.79	12	20
4882	T.W.Graveney	E	79	123	13	258	44.38	11	20
4869	R.B.Simpson	A	62	111	7	311	46.81	10	27
4823	A.C.Gilchrist	A	79	114	18	204*	50.24	15	21
4794	A.Flower	Z	63	112	19	232*	51.54	12	27
4737	I.R.Redpath	A	66	120	11	171	43.45	8	31
4656	A.J.Lamb	E	79	139	10	142	36.09	14	18
4587	M.P.Vaughan	E	64	115	9	197	43.27	15	14
4555	H.Sutcliffe	E	54	84	9	194	60.73	16	23
4554	D.J.Cullinan	SA	70	115	12	275*	44.21	14	20
4545	H.P.Tillekeratne	SL	83	131	25	204*	42.87	11	20
4537	P.B.H.May	E	66	106	9	285*	46.77	13	22
4502	E.R.Dexter	E	62	102	8	205	47.89	9	27

Runs			M	I	NO	HS	Avge	100	50
4455	E.de C.Weekes	WI	48	81	5	207	58.61	15	19
4447	V.V.S.Laxman	I	72	115	13	280	43.59	9	24
4415	K.J.Hughes	A	70	124	6	213	37.41	9	22
4409	M.W.Gatting	E	79	138	14	207	35.55	10	21
4399	A.I.Kallicharran	WI	66	109	10	187	44.43	12	21
4389	A.P.E.Knott	E	95	149	15	135	32.75	5	30
4386	N.J.Astle	NZ	73	124	10	222	38.47	11	21
4378	M.Amarnath	I	69	113	10	138	42.50	11	24
4356	I.A.Healy	A	119	182	23	161*	27.39	4	22
4334	R.C.Fredericks	WI	59	109	7	169	42.49	8	26
4288	M.A.Butcher	E	71	131	7	173*	34.58	8	23
4236	R.A.Smith	E	62	112	15	175	43.67	9	28
4125	D.R.Martyn	A	61	98	12	165	47.96	12	22
4114	Mudassar Nazar	P	76	116	8	231	38.09	10	17
4052	Saeed Anwar	P	55	91	2	188*	45.52	11	25

The most for Bangladesh is 2514 by Habibul Bashar (75 innings).

750 RUNS IN A SERIES

Runs			Series	M	I	NO	HS	Avge	100	50
974	D.G.Bradman	A v E	1930	5	7	–	334	139.14	4	–
905	W.R.Hammond	E v A	1928-29	5	9	1	251	113.12	4	–
839	M.A.Taylor	A v E	1989	6	11	1	219	83.90	2	5
834	R.N.Harvey	A v SA	1952-53	5	9	–	205	92.66	4	3
829	I.V.A.Richards	WI v E	1976	4	7	–	291	118.42	3	2
827	C.L.Walcott	WI v A	1954-55	5	10	–	155	82.70	5	2
824	G.St A.Sobers	WI v P	1957-58	5	8	2	365*	137.33	3	3
810	D.G.Bradman	A v E	1936-37	5	9	–	270	90.00	3	1
806	D.G.Bradman	A v SA	1931-32	5	5	1	299*	201.50	4	–
798	B.C.Lara	WI v E	1993-94	5	8	–	375	99.75	2	2
779	E.de C.Weekes	WI v I	1948-49	5	7	–	194	111.28	4	2
774	S.M.Gavaskar	I v WI	1970-71	4	8	3	220	154.80	4	3
765	B.C.Lara	WI v E	1995	6	10	1	179	85.00	3	3
761	Mudassar Nazar	P v I	1982-83	6	8	2	231	126.83	4	1
758	D.G.Bradman	A v E	1934	5	8	–	304	94.75	2	1
753	D.C.S.Compton	E v SA	1947	5	8	–	208	94.12	4	2
752	G.A.Gooch	E v I	1990	3	6	–	333	125.33	3	2

HIGHEST INDIVIDUAL INNINGS

400*	B.C.Lara	WI v E	St John's	2003-04
380	M.L.Hayden	A v Z	Perth	2003-04
375	B.C.Lara	WI v E	St John's	1993-94
365*	G.St A.Sobers	WI v P	Kingston	1957-58
364	L.Hutton	E v A	The Oval	1938
340	S.T.Jayasuriya	SL v I	Colombo (RPS)	1997-98
337	Hanif Mohammed	P v WI	Bridgetown	1957-58
336*	W.R.Hammond	E v NZ	Auckland	1932-33
334*	M.A.Taylor	A v P	Peshawar	1998-99
334	D.G.Bradman	A v E	Leeds	1930
333	G.A.Gooch	E v I	Lord's	1990
329	Inzamam-ul-Haq	P v NZ	Lahore	2001-02
325	A.Sandham	E v WI	Kingston	1929-30
317	C.H.Gayle	WI v SA	St John's	2004-05
311	R.B.Simpson	A v E	Manchester	1964

310*	J.H.Edrich	E v NZ	Leeds	1965
309	V.Sehwag	I v P	Multan	2003-04
307	R.M.Cowper	A v E	Melbourne	1965-66
304	D.G.Bradman	A v E	Leeds	1934
302	L.G.Rowe	WI v E	Bridgetown	1973-74
299*	D.G.Bradman	A v SA	Adelaide	1931-32
299	M.D.Crowe	NZ v SL	Wellington	1990-91
291	I.V.A.Richards	WI v E	The Oval	1976
287	R.E.Foster	E v A	Sydney	1903-04
285*	P.B.H.May	E v WI	Birmingham	1957
281	V.V.S.Laxman	I v A	Calcutta	2000-01
280*	Javed Miandad	P v I	Hyderabad	1982-83
278	D.C.S.Compton	E v P	Nottingham	1954
277	B.C.Lara	WI v A	Sydney	1992-93
277	G.C.Smith	SA v E	Birmingham	2003
275*	D.J.Cullinan	SA v NZ	Auckland	1998-99
275	G.Kirsten	SA v E	Durban	1999-00
274*	S.P.Fleming	NZ v SL	Colombo (SSC)	2002-03
274	R.G.Pollock	SA v A	Durban	1969-70
274	Zaheer Abbas	P v E	Birmingham	1971
271	Javed Miandad	P v NZ	Auckland	1988-89
270*	G.A.Headley	WI v E	Kingston	1934-35
270	D.G.Bradman	A v E	Melbourne	1936-37
270	R.Dravid	I v P	Rawalpindi	2003-04
270	K.C.Sangakkara	SL v Z	Bulawayo	2003-04
268	G.N.Yallop	A v P	Melbourne	1983-84
267*	B.A.Young	NZ v SL	Dunedin	1996-97
267	P.A.de Silva	SL v NZ	Wellington	1990-91
267	Younis Khan	P v I	Bangalore	2004-05
266	W.H.Ponsford	A v E	The Oval	1934
266	D.L.Houghton	Z v SL	Bulawayo	1994-95
262*	D.L.Amiss	E v WI	Kingston	1973-74
261*	R.R.Sarwan	WI v B	Kingston	2004
261	F.M.M.Worrell	WI v E	Nottingham	1950
260	C.C.Hunte	WI v P	Kingston	1957-58
260	Javed Miandad	P v E	The Oval	1987
259	G.M.Turner	NZ v WI	Georgetown	1971-72
259	G.C.Smith	SA v E	Lord's	2003
258	T.W.Graveney	E v WI	Nottingham	1957
258	S.M.Nurse	WI v NZ	Christchurch	1968-69
257*	Wasim Akram	P v Z	Sheikhupura	1996-97
257	R.T.Ponting	A v I	Melbourne	2003-04
256	R.B.Kanhai	WI v I	Calcutta	1958-59
256	K.F.Barrington	E v A	Manchester	1964
255*	D.J.McGlew	SA v NZ	Wellington	1952-53
254	D.G.Bradman	A v E	Lord's	1930
254	V.Sehwag	I v P	Lahore	2005-06
253	S.T.Jayasuriya	SL v P	Faisalabad	2004-05
251	W.R.Hammond	E v A	Sydney	1928-29
250	K.D.Walters	A v NZ	Christchurch	1976-77
250	S.F.A.F.Bacchus	WI v I	Kanpur	1978-79
250	J.L.Langer	A v E	Melbourne	2002-03

The highest for Bangladesh is 158* by Mohammad Ashraful (v I, Chittagong, 2004-05).

20 HUNDREDS

			200	Inn	Opponents									
					E	A	SA	WI	NZ	I	P	SL	Z	B
35	S.R.Tendulkar	I	4	206	6	7	3	3	3	–	2	7	3	1
34	S.M.Gavaskar	I	4	214	4	8	–	13	2	–	5	2	–	–
32	S.R.Waugh	A	1	260	10	–	2	7	2	2	3	3	1	2
31	B.C.Lara	WI	8	212	7	9	4	–	1	1	2	5	1	1
29	D.G.Bradman	A	12	80	19	–	4	2	–	4	–	–	–	–
28	R.T.Ponting	A	4	164	5	–	5	6	2	4	4	1	1	–
27	A.R.Border	A	2	265	8	–	–	3	5	4	6	1	–	–
26	G.St A.Sobers	WI	2	160	10	4	–	–	1	8	3	–	–	–
25	Inzamam-ul-Haq	P	2	175	5	1	–	4	3	3	–	5	2	2
24	M.L.Hayden	A	2	139	4	–	5	5	1	3	1	3	2	–
24	G.S.Chappell	A	4	151	9	–	–	5	3	1	6	–	–	–
24	I.V.A.Richards	WI	3	182	8	5	–	–	1	8	2	–	–	–
23	J.H.Kallis	SA	–	159	5	2	–	7	3	1	1	–	3	1
23	Javed Miandad	P	6	189	2	6	–	2	7	5	–	1	–	–
22	W.R.Hammond	E	7	140	–	9	6	1	4	2	–	–	–	–
22	M.Azharuddin	I	–	147	6	2	4	–	2	–	3	5	–	–
22	R.Dravid	I	5	161	3	2	1	2	4	–	5	1	3	1
22	J.L.Langer	A	3	166	4	–	2	3	4	3	4	2	–	–
22	M.C.Cowdrey	E	–	188	–	5	3	6	2	3	3	–	–	–
22	G.Boycott	E	1	193	–	7	1	5	2	4	3	–	–	–
21	R.N.Harvey	A	2	137	6	–	8	3	–	4	–	–	–	–
21	G.Kirsten	SA	3	176	5	2	–	3	2	3	2	1	1	2
21	D.C.Boon	A	2	190	7	–	3	3	6	1	1	1	–	–
20	K.F.Barrington	E	1	131	–	5	2	3	3	3	4	–	–	–
20	P.A.de Silva	SL	2	159	2	1	–	2	5	8	–	1	1	1
20	M.E.Waugh	A	–	209	6	–	4	5	4	1	3	1	–	–
20	G.A.Gooch	E	2	215	–	4	–	5	4	5	1	1	–	–

The most for New Zealand is 17 by M.D.Crowe (131 innings), for Zimbabwe 12 by A.Flower (112), and for Bangladesh 3 by Habibul Bashar (75).

The most double hundreds by batsmen not included above is 6 by M.S.Atapattu (16 hundreds for Sri Lanka), 4 by L.Hutton (19 for England), 4 by C.G.Greenidge (19 for West Indies) and 4 by Zaheer Abbas (12 for Pakistan).

HIGHEST PARTNERSHIP FOR EACH WICKET

1st	413	V.Mankad/Pankaj Roy	I v NZ	Madras	1955-56
2nd	576	S.T.Jayasuriya/R.S.Mahanama	SL v I	Colombo (RPS)	1997-98
3rd	467	A.H.Jones/M.D.Crowe	NZ v SL	Wellington	1990-91
4th	411	P.B.H.May/M.C.Cowdrey	E v WI	Birmingham	1957
5th	405	S.G.Barnes/D.G.Bradman	A v E	Sydney	1946-47
6th	346	J.H.W.Fingleton/D.G.Bradman	A v E	Melbourne	1936-37
7th	347	D.St E.Atkinson/C.C.Depeiza	WI v A	Bridgetown	1954-55
8th	313	Wasim Akram/Saqlain Mushtaq	P v Z	Sheikhupura	1996-97
9th	195	M.V.Boucher/P.L.Symcox	SA v P	Johannesburg	1997-98
10th	151	B.F.Hastings/R.O.Collinge	NZ v P	Auckland	1972-73
	151	Azhar Mahmood/Mushtaq Ahmed	P v SA	Rawalpindi	1997-98

BOWLING RECORDS
200 WICKETS IN TESTS

Wkts			M	Balls	Runs	Avge	5 wI	10 wM
653	S.K.Warne	A	134	37780	16503	25.27	34	10
579	M.Muralitharan	SL	98	32850	12971	22.40	48	14
539	G.D.McGrath	A	118	27885	11642	21.59	28	3
519	C.A.Walsh	WI	132	30019	12688	24.45	22	3
494	A.Kumble	I	103	32349	14203	28.75	31	8
434	Kapil Dev	I	131	27740	12867	29.64	23	2
431	R.J.Hadlee	NZ	86	21918	9612	22.30	36	9
414	Wasim Akram	P	104	22627	9779	23.62	25	5
405	C.E.L.Ambrose	WI	98	22104	8500	20.98	22	3
385	S.M.Pollock	SA	97	22172	8764	22.76	16	1
383	I.T.Botham	E	102	21815	10878	28.40	27	4
376	M.D.Marshall	WI	81	17584	7876	20.94	22	4
373	Waqar Younis	P	87	16224	8788	23.56	22	5
362	Imran Khan	P	88	19458	8258	22.81	23	6
355	D.K.Lillee	A	70	18467	8493	23.92	23	7
330	A.A.Donald	SA	72	15519	7344	22.25	20	3
325	R.G.D.Willis	E	90	17357	8190	25.20	16	–
309	L.R.Gibbs	WI	79	27115	8989	29.09	18	2
307	F.S.Trueman	E	67	15178	6625	21.57	17	3
301	W.P.U.C.J.Vaas	SL	90	19588	8673	28.81	11	2
297	D.L.Underwood	E	86	21862	7674	25.83	17	6
291	C.J.McDermott	A	71	16586	8332	28.63	14	2
266	B.S.Bedi	I	67	21364	7637	28.71	14	1
259	J.Garner	WI	58	13169	5433	20.97	7	–
252	J.B.Statham	E	70	16056	6261	24.84	9	1
251	J.N.Gillespie	A	69	13976	6680	26.61	8	–
249	M.A.Holding	WI	60	12680	5898	23.68	13	2
248	R.Benaud	A	63	19108	6704	27.03	16	1
246	G.D.McKenzie	A	60	17681	7328	29.78	16	3
242	B.S.Chandrasekhar	I	58	15963	7199	29.74	16	2
236	A.V.Bedser	E	51	15918	5876	24.89	15	5
236	Abdul Qadir	P	67	17126	7742	32.80	15	5
236	J.Srinath	I	67	15104	7196	30.49	10	1
235	G.St A.Sobers	WI	93	21599	7999	34.03	6	–
234	A.R.Caddick	E	62	13558	6999	29.91	13	1
230	M.Ntini	SA	61	12850	6721	29.22	10	2
229	D.Gough	E	58	11821	6503	28.39	9	–
228	R.R.Lindwall	A	61	13650	5251	23.03	12	–
219	Harbhajan Singh	I	52	13841	6460	29.49	17	4
218	C.L.Cairns	NZ	62	11698	6410	29.40	13	1
216	C.V.Grimmett	A	37	14513	5231	24.21	21	7
216	H.H.Streak	Z	65	13559	6079	28.14	7	–
212	M.G.Hughes	A	53	12285	6017	28.38	7	1
208	Saqlain Mushtaq	P	49	14070	6206	29.83	13	3
207	D.L.Vettori	NZ	64	16037	7140	34.49	12	2
206	A.M.E.Roberts	WI	47	11136	5174	25.61	11	2
202	J.A.Snow	E	49	12021	5387	26.66	8	1
200	J.R.Thomson	A	51	10535	5601	28.00	8	–

The most for Bangladesh 73 in 22 Tests by Mohammad Rafique.

35 WICKETS IN A SERIES

Wkts			Series	M	Balls	Runs	Avge	5 wI	10 wM
49	S.F.Barnes	E v SA	1913-14	4	1356	536	10.93	7	3
46	J.C.Laker	E v A	1956	5	1703	442	9.60	4	2
44	C.V.Grimmett	A v SA	1935-36	5	2077	642	14.59	5	3
42	T.M.Alderman	A v E	1981	6	1950	893	21.26	4	–
41	R.M.Hogg	A v E	1978-79	6	1740	527	12.85	5	2
41	T.M.Alderman	A v E	1989	6	1616	712	17.36	6	1
40	Imran Khan	P v I	1982-83	6	1339	558	13.95	4	2
40	S.K.Warne	A v V	2005	5	1517	797	19.92	3	2
39	A.V.Bedser	E v A	1953	5	1591	682	17.48	5	1
39	D.K.Lillee	A v E	1981	6	1870	870	22.30	2	1
38	M.W.Tate	E v A	1924-25	5	2528	881	23.18	5	1
37	W.J.Whitty	A v SA	1910-11	5	1395	632	17.08	2	–
37	H.J.Tayfield	SA v E	1956-57	5	2280	636	17.18	4	1
36	A.E.E.Vogler	SA v E	1909-10	5	1349	783	21.75	4	1
36	A.A.Mailey	A v E	1920-21	5	1465	946	26.27	4	2
36	G.D.McGrath	A v E	1997	6	1499	701	19.47	2	–
35	G.A.Lohmann	E v SA	1895-96	3	520	203	5.80	4	2
35	B.S.Chandrasekhar	I v E	1972-73	5	1747	662	18.91	4	–
35	M.D.Marshall	WI v E	1988	5	1219	443	12.65	3	1

The most for New Zealand is 33 by R.J.Hadlee (3 Tests v A, 1985-86), for Sri Lanka 30 by M.Muralitharan (3 Tests v Z, 2001-02), for Zimbabwe 22 by H.H.Streak (3 Tests v P, 1994-95), and for Bangladesh 18 by Enamul Haque II (2 Tests v Z, 2004-05).

15 WICKETS IN A TEST (*† On debut*)

19- 90	J.C.Laker	E v A	Manchester	1956
17-159	S.F.Barnes	E v SA	Johannesburg	1913-14
16-136†	N.D.Hirwani	I v WI	Madras	1987-88
16-137†	R.A.L.Massie	A v E	Lord's	1972
16-220	M.Muralitharan	SL v E	The Oval	1998
15- 28	J.Briggs	E v SA	Cape Town	1888-89
15- 45	G.A.Lohmann	E v SA	Port Elizabeth	1895-96
15- 99	C.Blythe	E v SA	Leeds	1907
15-104	H.Verity	E v A	Lord's	1934
15-123	R.J.Hadlee	NZ v A	Brisbane	1985-86
15-124	W.Rhodes	E v A	Melbourne	1903-04
15-217	Harbhajan Singh	I v A	Madras	2000-01

The best analysis for South Africa is 13-132 by M.Ntini (v WI, Port-of-Spain, 2004-05), for West Indies 14-149 by M.A.Holding (v E, The Oval, 1976), for Pakistan 14-116 by Imran Khan (v SL, Lahore, 1981-82), for Zimbabwe 11-257 by A.G.Huckle (v NZ, Bulawayo, 1997-98), and for Bangladesh 12-200 by Enamul Haque II (v Z, Dhaka, 2004-05).

NINE WICKETS IN AN INNINGS

10-53	J.C.Laker	E v A	Manchester	1956
10-74	A.Kumble	I v P	Delhi	1998-99
9-28	G.A.Lohmann	E v SA	Johannesburg	1895-96
9-37	J.C.Laker	E v A	Manchester	1956
9-51	M.Muralitharan	SL v Z	Kandy	2001-02
9-52	R.J.Hadlee	NZ v A	Brisbane	1985-86
9-56	Abdul Qadir	P v E	Lahore	1987-88
9-57	D.E.Malcolm	E v SA	The Oval	1994
9-65	M.Muralitharan	SL v E	The Oval	1998
9-69	J.M.Patel	I v A	Kanpur	1959-60

9- 83	Kapil Dev	I v WI	Ahmedabad	1983-84
9- 86	Sarfraz Nawaz	P v A	Melbourne	1978-79
9- 95	J.M.Noreiga	WI v I	Port-of-Spain	1970-71
9-102	S.P.Gupte	I v WI	Kanpur	1958-59
9-103	S.F.Barnes	E v SA	Johannesburg	1913-14
9-113	H.J.Tayfield	SA v E	Johannesburg	1956-57
9-121	A.A.Mailey	A v E	Melbourne	1920-21

The best analysis for Zimbabwe is 8-109 by P.A.Strang (v NZ, Bulawayo, 2000-01), and for Bangladesh 7-95 by Enamul Haque II (v Z, Dhaka, 2004-05).

HAT-TRICKS

F.R.Spofforth	Australia v England	Melbourne	1878-79
W.Bates	England v Australia	Melbourne	1882-83
J.Briggs	England v Australia	Sydney	1891-92
G.A.Lohmann	England v South Africa	Port Elizabeth	1895-96
J.T.Hearne	England v Australia	Leeds	1899
H.Trumble	Australia v England	Melbourne	1901-02
H.Trumble	Australia v England	Melbourne	1903-04
T.J.Matthews (2)[2]	Australia v South Africa	Manchester	1912
M.J.C.Allom[1]	England v New Zealand	Christchurch	1929-30
T.W.J.Goddard	England v South Africa	Johannesburg	1938-39
P.J.Loader	England v West Indies	Leeds	1957
L.F.Kline	Australia v South Africa	Cape Town	1957-58
W.W.Hall	West Indies v Pakistan	Lahore	1958-59
G.M.Griffin	South Africa v England	Lord's	1960
L.R.Gibbs	West Indies v Australia	Adelaide	1960-61
P.J.Petherick[1]	New Zealand v Pakistan	Lahore	1976-77
C.A.Walsh[3]	West Indies v Australia	Brisbane	1988-89
M.G.Hughes[3]	Australia v West Indies	Perth	1988-89
D.W.Fleming[1]	Australia v Pakistan	Rawalpindi	1994-95
S.K.Warne	Australia v England	Melbourne	1994-95
D.G.Cork	England v West Indies	Manchester	1995
D.Gough	England v Australia	Sydney	1998-99
Wasim Akram[4]	Pakistan v Sri Lanka	Lahore	1998-99
Wasim Akram[4]	Pakistan v Sri Lanka	Dhaka	1998-99
D.N.T.Zoysa[5]	Sri Lanka v Zimbabwe	Harare	1999-00
Abdul Razzaq	Pakistan v Sri Lanka	Galle	2000-01
G.D.McGrath	Australia v West Indies	Perth	2000-01
Harbhajan Singh	India v Australia	Calcutta	2000-01
Mohammad Sami	Pakistan v Sri Lanka	Lahore	2001-02
J.J.C.Lawson	West Indies v Australia	Bridgetown	2002-03
Alok Kapali	Bangladesh v Pakistan	Peshawar	2003
A.M.Blignaut	Zimbabwe v Bangladesh	Harare	2003-04
M.J.Hoggard	England v West Indies	Bridgetown	2003-04
J.E.C.Franklin	New Zealand v Bangladesh	Dhaka	2004-05
I.K.Pathan[6]	India v Pakistan	Karachi	2005-06

[1] On debut. [2] Hat-trick in each innings. [3] Involving both innings. [4] In successive Tests. [5] His first 3 balls (second over of the match). [6] The fourth, fifth and sixth balls of the match.

WICKET-KEEPING RECORDS
100 DISMISSALS IN TESTS†

Total			Tests	Ct	St
395	I.A.Healy	Australia	119	366	29
355	R.W.Marsh	Australia	96	343	12
335	M.V.Boucher	South Africa	87	321	14
330	A.C.Gilchrist	Australia	79	299	31
270†	P.J.L.Dujon	West Indies	79	265	5
269	A.P.E.Knott	England	95	250	19
241†	A.J.Stewart	England	82	227	14
228	Wasim Bari	Pakistan	81	201	27
219	R.D.Jacobs	West Indies	65	207	12
219	T.G.Evans	England	91	173	46
201†	A.C.Parore	New Zealand	67	194	7
198	S.M.H.Kirmani	India	88	160	38
189	D.L.Murray	West Indies	62	181	8
187	A.T.W.Grout	Australia	51	163	24
176	I.D.S.Smith	New Zealand	63	168	8
174	R.W.Taylor	England	57	167	7
165	R.C.Russell	England	54	153	12
152	D.J.Richardson	South Africa	42	150	2
151†	A.Flower	Zimbabwe	55	142	9
147†	Moin Khan	Pakistan	66	127	20
141	J.H.B.Waite	South Africa	49	124	17
130	Rashid Latif	Pakistan	37	119	11
130	K.S.More	India	49	110	20
130	W.A.S.Oldfield	Australia	54	78	52
127†	K.C.Sangakkara	Sri Lanka	40	109	18
119	R.S.Kaluwitharana	Sri Lanka	49	93	26
112†	J.M.Parks	England	43	101	11
107	N.R.Mongia	India	44	99	8
104	Salim Yousuf	Pakistan	32	91	13
101†	J.R.Murray	West Indies	31	98	3

The most for Bangladesh is 76 (68 ct, 8 st) by Khaled Masud in 37 Tests.

† Excluding catches taken in the field

25 DISMISSALS IN A SERIES

28	R.W.Marsh	Australia v England	1982-83
27 (inc 2st)	R.C.Russell	England v South Africa	1995-96
27 (inc 2st)	I.A.Healy	Australia v England (6 Tests)	1997
26 (inc 3st)	J.H.B.Waite	South Africa v New Zealand	1961-62
26	R.W.Marsh	Australia v West Indies (6 Tests)	1975-76
26 (inc 5st)	I.A.Healy	Australia v England (6 Tests)	1993
26 (inc 1st)	M.V.Boucher	South Africa v England	1998
26 (inc 2st)	A.C.Gilchrist	Australia v England	2001
25 (inc 2st)	I.A.Healy	Australia v England	1994-95
25 (inc 2st)	A.C.Gilchrist	Australia v England	2002-03

TEN DISMISSALS IN A TEST

11	R.C.Russell	England v South Africa	Johannesburg	1995-96
10	R.W.Taylor	England v India	Bombay	1979-80
10	A.C.Gilchrist	Australia v New Zealand	Hamilton	1999-00

SEVEN DISMISSALS IN AN INNINGS

7	Wasim Bari	Pakistan v New Zealand	Auckland	1978-79
7	R.W.Taylor	England v India	Bombay	1979-80
7	I.D.S.Smith	New Zealand v Sri Lanka	Hamilton	1990-91
7	R.D.Jacobs	West Indies v Australia	Melbourne	2000-01

FIVE STUMPINGS IN AN INNINGS

5	K.S.More	India v West Indies	Madras	1987-88

FIELDING RECORDS
100 CATCHES IN TESTS

Total			Tests	Total			Tests
181	M.E.Waugh	Australia	128	115	R.T.Ponting	Australia	99
157	M.A.Taylor	Australia	104	115	C.L.Hooper	West Indies	102
156	A.R.Border	Australia	156	112	S.R.Waugh	Australia	168
148	B.C.Lara	West Indies	120	110	R.B.Simpson	Australia	62
140	S.P.Fleming	New Zealand	96	110	W.R.Hammond	England	85
130	R.Dravid	India	96	109	G.St A.Sobers	West Indies	93
122	G.S.Chappell	Australia	87	108	S.M.Gavaskar	India	125
122	I.V.A.Richards	West Indies	121	105	I.M.Chappell	Australia	75
120	I.T.Botham	England	102	105	M.Azharuddin	India	99
120	M.C.Cowdrey	England	114	105	G.P.Thorpe	England	100
118	S.K.Warne	Australia	134	103	G.A.Gooch	England	118

The most for South Africa is 90 by J.H.Kallis (95 Tests), for Pakistan 93 by Javed Miandad (124), for Sri Lanka 99 by D.P.M.de.S.Jayawardena (74), for Zimbabwe 60 by A.D.R.Campbell (60) and for Bangladesh 19 by Habibul Bashar (38).

15 CATCHES IN A SERIES

15	J.M.Gregory	Australia v England		1920-21

SEVEN CATCHES IN A TEST

7	G.S.Chappell	Australia v England	Perth	1974-75
7	Yajurvindra Singh	India v England	Bangalore	1976-77
7	H.P.Tillekeratne	Sri Lanka v New Zealand	Colombo (SSC)	1992-93
7	S.P.Fleming	New Zealand v Zimbabwe	Harare	1997-98
7	M.L.Hayden	Australia v Sri Lanka	Galle	2003-04

FIVE CATCHES IN AN INNINGS

5	V.Y.Richardson	Australia v South Africa	Durban	1935-36
5	Yajurvindra Singh	India v England	Bangalore	1976-77
5	M.Azharuddin	India v Pakistan	Karachi	1989-90
5	K.Srikkanth	India v Australia	Perth	1991-92
5	S.P.Fleming	New Zealand v Zimbabwe	Harare	1997-98

APPEARANCE RECORDS
100 TEST MATCH APPEARANCES

168	S.R.Waugh	Australia		116	D.B.Vengsarkar	India
156	A.R.Border	Australia		115	M.A.Atherton	England
134	S.K.Warne	Australia		114	M.C.Cowdrey	England
133	A.J.Stewart	England		110	C.H.Lloyd	West Indies
132	C.A.Walsh	West Indies		108	G.Boycott	England
131	Kapil Dev	India		108	C.G.Greenidge	West Indies
129	S.R.Tendulkar	India		107	D.C.Boon	Australia
128	M.E.Waugh	Australia		106	Inzamam-ul-Haq	Pakistan
125	S.M.Gavaskar	India		104	M.A.Taylor	Australia
124	Javed Miandad	Pakistan		104	Wasim Akram	Pakistan
121	I.V.A.Richards	West Indies		103	A.Kumble	India
120	B.C.Lara	West Indies		103	Salim Malik	Pakistan
119	I.A.Healy	Australia		102	I.T.Botham	England
118	G.A.Gooch	England		102	C.L.Hooper	West Indies
118	G.D.McGrath	Australia		101	G.Kirsten	South Africa
117	D.I.Gower	England		100	S.T.Jayasuriya	Sri Lanka
116	D.L.Haynes	West Indies		100	G.P.Thorpe	England

The most for New Zealand is 96 by S.P.Fleming, for Zimbabwe 67 by G.W.Flower, and for Bangladesh 38 by Habibul Bashar.

100 CONSECUTIVE TEST APPEARANCES

153	A.R.Border	Australia	March 1979 to March 1994
107	M.E.Waugh	Australia	June 1993 to October 2002
106	S.M.Gavaskar	India	January 1975 to February 1987

50 TESTS AS CAPTAIN

93	A.R.Border	Australia		54	M.A.Atherton	England
74	C.H.Lloyd	West Indies		53	W.J.Cronje	South Africa
72	S.P.Fleming	New Zealand		50	I.V.A.Richards	West Indies
57	S.R.Waugh	Australia		50	M.A.Taylor	Australia
56	A.Ranatunga	Sri Lanka				

The most for India is 49 by S.C.Ganguly, for Pakistan 48 by Imran Khan, for Zimbabwe 21 by A.D.R.Campbell and H.H.Streak, and for Bangladesh 12 by Habibul Bashar and Khaled Masud.

50 TEST UMPIRING APPEARANCES

108	S.A.Bucknor	(Jamaica)	28.04.1989 to 30.12.2005
92	D.R.Shepherd	(England)	01.08.1985 to 07.06.2005
73	S.Venkataraghavan	(India)	29.01.1993 to 20.01.2004
70	R.E.Koertzen	(South Africa)	26.12.1992 to 25.01.2006
69	D.B.Hair	(Australia)	25.01.1992 to 17.01.2006
66	H.D.Bird	(England)	05.07.1973 to 24.06.1996
55	D.J.Harper	(Australia)	28.11.1998 to 01.02.2006

TEST MATCH SCORES AND SERIES AVERAGES
SOUTH AFRICA v ZIMBABWE (1st Test)

At Newlands, Cape Town, on 4, 5 March 2005.
Toss: Zimbabwe. Result: **SOUTH AFRICA** won by an innings and 21 runs.
Debuts: None.

ZIMBABWE

S.Matsikenyeri	c De Villiers b Ntini	12	c Rudolph b Ntini		13
B.G.Rogers	c Boucher b Pollock	1	c Boucher b Ntini		28
D.D.Ebrahim	b Ntini	3	lbw b Langeveldt		72
H.Masakadza	lbw b Kallis	6	c Gibbs b Boje		46
B.R.M.Taylor	c Boucher b Ntini	2	c Langeveldt b Boje		9
*†T.Taibu	c De Villiers b Kallis	7	c sub ‡ b Langeveldt		9
E.Chigumbura	c Smith b Kallis	2	b Boje		0
H.H.Streak	c Boucher b Pollock	9	c Gibbs b Kallis		12
A.M.Blignaut	c Boje b Kallis	8	st Boucher b Boje		61
A.G.Cremer	c Kallis b Pollock	0	run out		2
C.B.Mpofu	not out	0	not out		0
Extras	(NB 4)	4	(B 2, LB 7, W 2, NB 2)		13
Total		**54**			**265**

SOUTH AFRICA

*G.C.Smith	c Masakadza b Cremer	121
A.B.de Villiers	c Blignaut b Cremer	98
J.A.Rudolph	not out	49
J.H.Kallis	c Blignaut b Cremer	54
H.H.Gibbs	not out	8
A.G.Prince		
†M.V.Boucher		
S.M.Pollock		
N.Boje		
M.Ntini		
C.K.Langeveldt		
Extras	(LB 1, W 1, NB 8)	10
Total	(3 wickets declared)	**340**

SOUTH AFRICA	O	M	R	W		O	M	R	W
Pollock	8	4	9	3		5	1	14	0
Ntini	10	2	23	3		16	2	68	2
Langeveldt	6	2	9	0		9.3	3	27	2
Kallis	7.2	3	13	4		17.3	7	40	1
Boje						26.2	5	106	4
Rudolph						1	0	1	0

ZIMBABWE	O	M	R	W
Streak	13	0	90	0
Mpofu	12	2	53	0
Blignaut	6	0	44	0
Chigumbura	8	0	53	0
Cremer	9	0	86	3
Matsikenyeri	1	0	6	0
Taylor	1	0	7	0

FALL OF WICKETS

	Z	SA	Z
Wkt	1st	1st	2nd
1st	2	217	25
2nd	13	234	59
3rd	20	328	157
4th	22	–	173
5th	33	–	183
6th	36	–	186
7th	37	–	186
8th	50	–	214
9th	50	–	247
10th	54	–	265

‡ (W.E.September)

Umpires: B.F.Bowden (*New Zealand*) (24) and B.R.Doctrove (*West Indies*) (3).
Referee: A.G.Hurst (*Australia*) (3).   **Test No. 1737/7 (SA298/Z78)**

SOUTH AFRICA v ZIMBABWE (2nd Test)

At Centurion Park, (Verwoerdburg), Pretoria, on 11, 12, 13 March 2005.
Toss: South Africa. Result: **SOUTH AFRICA** won by an innings and 62 runs.
Debuts: None.

ZIMBABWE

S.Matsikenyeri	c Smith b Langeveldt	12	b Zondeki		5
B.G.Rogers	c Boucher b Nel	7	c Boucher b Zondeki		0
D.D.Ebrahim	b Kallis	37	c Smith b Nel		1
H.Masakadza	c Smith b Zondeki	26	c Boucher b Zondeki		47
B.R.M.Taylor	b Kallis	4	lbw b Zondeki		6
*†T.Taibu	c Gibbs b Zondeki	14	c Boucher b Zondeki		13
E.Chigumbura	c sub (A.M.Phangiso) b Kallis	0	(8) c Boucher b Boje		44
H.H.Streak	b Kallis	85	(7) c Gibbs b Kallis		16
A.M.Blignaut	c Smith b Zondeki	52	c Boucher b Kallis		0
A.G.Cremer	c Boucher b Nel	12	c Boucher b Zondeki		0
C.B.Mpofu	not out	1	not out		0
Extras	(B 4, LB 8, W 4, NB 3)	19	(B 4, LB 10, NB 3)		17
Total		**269**			**149**

SOUTH AFRICA

A.B.de Villiers	c Masakadza b Mpofu	47
*G.C.Smith	c Rogers b Chigumbura	41
J.A.Rudolph	b Cremer	12
H.H.Gibbs	c Taibu b Streak	47
A.G.Prince	not out	139
†M.V.Boucher	c Masakadza b Cremer	18
J.H.Kallis	b Streak	58
N.Boje	b Cremer	82
M.Zondeki		
A.Nel		
C.K.Langeveldt		
Extras	(B 4, LB 5, W 5, NB.22)	36
Total	(7 wickets declared)	**480**

SOUTH AFRICA	O	M	R	W		O	M	R	W
Nel	12	7	17	2		16	6	42	1
Zondeki	21	7	66	3		14.3	2	39	6
Langeveldt	5	1	19	1					
Kallis	13	4	33	4	(3)	12	5	20	2
Smith	7	2	39	0					
Boje	18	1	62	0	(4)	15	7	25	1
De Villiers	7	0	16	0					
Rudolph	2	0	5	0		2	1	9	0

ZIMBABWE	O	M	R	W
Streak	20	1	78	2
Mpofu	21	1	110	1
Chigumbura	25	1	97	1
Cremer	26.5	4	106	3
Blignaut	16	0	74	0
Taylor	1	0	6	0

FALL OF WICKETS

	Z	SA	Z
Wkt	1st	1st	2nd
1st	15	93	6
2nd	22	106	13
3rd	71	133	18
4th	80	197	29
5th	115	219	76
6th	115	338	85
7th	115	480	143
8th	191	–	147
9th	264	–	149
10th	269	–	149

Umpires: B.R.Doctrove (*West Indies*) (4) and D.J.Harper (*Australia*) (49).
Referee: A.G.Hurst (*Australia*) (4).   **Test No. 1738/8 (SA299/Z79)**

INDIA v PAKISTAN (1st Test)

At Punjab C.A. Stadium, Mohali, Chandigarh, on 8, 9, 10, 11, 12 March 2005.
Toss: India. Result: **MATCH DRAWN**.
Debuts: None.

PAKISTAN

Salman Butt	b Pathan	5	c Karthik b Pathan		5
Taufiq Umar	b Balaji	44	c and b Balaji		4
Younis Khan	lbw b Khan	9	b Balaji		1
*Inzamam-ul-Haq	lbw b Kumble	57	(5) lbw b Kumble		86
Yousuf Youhana	c Karthik b Pathan	6	(4) b Kumble		68
Asim Kamal	b Balaji	91	lbw b Balaji		48
Abdul Razzaq	c Karthik b Balaji	26	c Dravid b Kumble		71
†Kamran Akram	c Dravid b Kumble	15	c sub (Harbhajan Singh) b Balaji		109
Mohammad Sami	b Balaji	20	c and b Kumble		10
Naved-ul-Hasan	lbw b Balaji	11	not out		38
Danish Kaneria	not out	8	not out		4
Extras	(B 11, LB 5, W 1, NB 3)	20	(B 17, LB 20, W 13, NB 2)		52
Total		**312**	(9 wickets declared)		**496**

INDIA

G.Gambhir	c Naved b Kaneria	41	not out	32
V.Sehwag	c Yousuf Razzaq	173	st Akmal b Younis	36
R.Dravid	c Kamal b Sami	50		
S.R.Tendulkar	c Kamal b Naved	94		
*S.C.Ganguly	c Butt b Kaneria	21		
V.V.S.Laxman	b Kaneria	58		
†K.D.Karthik	c Naved b Sami	6		
I.K.Pathan	st Akmal b Kaneria	13		
L.Balaji	c Akmal b Kaneria	31		
A.Kumble	not out	1		
Z.Khan	c and b Kaneria	0		
Extras	(B 1, LB 5, W 1, NB 21)	28	(B 5, LB 8, NB 4)	17
Total		**516**	(1 wicket)	**85**

INDIA	O	M	R	W		O	M	R	W	FALL OF WICKETS			
Pathan	23	5	68	2		27	7	70	1		P	I	P	I
Khan	17	2	70	1	(4)	22	0	93	0	*Wkt*	*1st*	*1st*	*2nd*	*2nd*
Balaji	20.4	5	76	5	(2)	30	5	95	4	1st	11	113	6	85
Kumble	22	6	76	2	(3)	54	16	160	4	2nd	30	216	10	–
Ganguly	2	0	3	0						3rd	89	334	10	–
Sehwag	2	1	3	0		3	1	11	0	4th	104	381	149	–
Tendulkar					(5)	8	0	30	0	5th	156	417	193	–
										6th	191	444	243	–
PAKISTAN										7th	239	465	427	–
Mohammad Sami	36	6	120	2		7	0	25	0	8th	282	507	436	–
Naved-ul-Hasan	32	1	133	1		2	0	6	0	9th	303	516	467	–
Abdul Razzaq	26	1	107	1						10th	312	516	–	–
Danish Kaneria	53.4	12	150	6	(3)	6	2	17	0					
Younis Khan					(4)	2	0	24	0					

Umpires: D.B.Hair (*Australia*) (59) and R.E.Koertzen (*South Africa*) (0).
Referee: B.C.Broad (*England*) (10).   Test No. 1739/51 (I383/P308)

INDIA v PAKISTAN (2nd Test)

At Eden Gardens, Calcutta, on 16, 17, 18, 19, 20 March 2005.
Toss: India. Result: **INDIA** won by 195 runs.
Debuts: None.

INDIA

V.Sehwag	c Inzamam b Afridi	81		b Sami	15
G.Gambhir	lbw Kaneria	29		b Sami	1
R.Dravid	c Akmal b Kaneria	110		c Kamal b Kaneria	135
S.R.Tendulkar	c Akmal b Afridi	52		c Akmal b Razzaq	52
*S.C.Ganguly	c Akmal b Razzaq	12		c and b Sami	12
V.V.S.Laxman	lbw b Razzaq	0		st Akmal b Kaneria	24
†K.D.Karthik	run out	28		b Kaneria	93
I.K.Pathan	c Younis b Kaneria	8		not out	38
L.Balaji	b Afridi	3	(10)	c Akmal b Razzaq	0
Harbhajan Singh	lbw b Razzaq	27	(9)	b Razzaq	0
A.Kumble	not out	21		not out	14
Extras	(B 2, LB 12, W 6, NB 16)	36		(B 5, LB 5, W 1, NB 12)	23
Total		**407**		**(9 wickets declared)**	**407**

PAKISTAN

Taufiq Umar	c Harbhajan b Balaji	18		c Sehwag b Balaji	35
Shahid Afridi	c Tendulkar b Pathan	29		c Ganguly b Kumble	59
Younis Khan	c Laxman b Kumble	147		st Karthik b Kumble	0
Yousuf Youhana	lbw b Balaji	104	(5)	c Gambhir b Kumble	22
*Inzamam-ul-Haq	c Karthik b Pathan	30	(4)	b Kumble	13
Asim Kamal	run out	6		c sub (M.Kaif) b Kumble	50
Abdul Razzaq	c Dravid b Kumble	17		b Kumble	6
†Kamran Akram	c Tendulkar b Harbhajan	0		b Harbhajan	7
Mohammad Sami	c Ganguly b Harbhajan	7		lbw b Kumble	9
Mohammad Khalil	c Sehwag b Kumble	4		not out	0
Danish Kaneria	not out	3		b Harbhajan	3
Extras	(B 5, LB 13, W 2, NB 8)	28		(B 17, LB 3, W 1, NB 2)	22
Total		**393**			**226**

PAKISTAN	O	M	R	W		O	M	R	W		FALL OF WICKETS				
Mohammad Sami	22	3	76	0	(2)	23	5	82	3			I	P	I	P
Mohammad Khalil	11	3	39	0	(1)	12	0	64	0		Wkt	1st	1st	2nd	2nd
Danish Kaneria	35	1	136	3		34	7	123	3		1st	80	35	14	93
Abdul Razzaq	22.1	4	62	3	(5)	19	3	80	3		2nd	156	70	23	95
Shahid Afridi	21	0	80	3	(4)	15	2	47	0		3rd	278	281	121	115
Younis Khan						1	0	1	0		4th	298	331	154	115
INDIA											5th	298	347	321	178
Pathan	23	6	90	2		7	1	32	0		6th	344	361	331	188
Balaji	21	1	81	2		16	4	60	1		7th	345	362	377	203
Kumble	37.1	11	98	3		38	16	63	7		8th	357	378	378	214
Ganguly	2	0	12	0							9th	363	378	378	223
Harbhajan Singh	30	5	94	3	(4)	30.3	16	51	2		10th	407	393	–	226

Umpires: S.A.Bucknor (*West Indies*) (100) and D.B.Hair (*Australia*) (60).
Referee: B.C.Broad (*England*) (11).   Test No. 1740/52 (1384/P309)

INDIA v PAKISTAN (3rd Test)

At Chinnaswamy Stadium, Bangalore, on 24, 25, 26, 27, 28 March 2005.
Toss: Pakistan. Result: **PAKISTAN** won by 168 runs.
Debuts: None.

PAKISTAN

Yasir Hamid	c Karthik b Pathan	6	lbw b Kumble	76
Shahid Afridi	c Dravid b Balaji	0	st Karthik b Tendulkar	58
Younis Khan	c Pathan b Harbhajan	267	not out	84
*Inzamam-ul-Haq	lbw b Balaji	184	not out	31
Yousuf Youhana	c Karthik b Harbhajan	37		
Asim Kamal	c Ganguly b Harbhajan	4		
Abdul Razzaq	c and b Harbhajan	5		
†Kamran Akram	b Harbhajan	28		
Mohammad Sami	run out	17		
Arshad Khan	not out	1		
Danish Kaneria	c Laxman b Harbhajan	0		
Extras	(B 8, LB 5, W 4, NB 4)	21	(B 4, LB 1, W 5, NB 2)	12
Total		**570**	(2 wickets declared)	**261**

INDIA

G.Gambhir	c Younis b Sami	24	lbw b Sami	52
V.Sehwag	c and b Kaneria	201	run out	38
R.Dravid	lbw b Kaneria	22	– c Younis b Arshad	16
S.R.Tendulkar	c Younis b Afridi	41	c Akmal b Afridi	16
V.V.S.Laxman	not out	79	lbw b Afridi	5
*S.C.Ganguly	st Akmal b Kaneria	1	b Afridi	2
†K.D.Karthik	c Kamal b Sami	10	b Sami	9
I.K.Pathan	c Yousuf b Sami	5	(9) c Yousuf b Arshad	0
Harbhajan Singh	c Razzaq b Kaneria	1	(10) c Younis b Kaneria	8
L.Balaji	c Akmal b Kaneria	2	(11) lbw b Kaneria	0
A.Kumble	b Afridi	22	(8) not out	37
Extras	(B 9, LB 13, W 1, NB 18)	41	(B 8, LB 8, W 10, NB 5)	31
Total		**449**		**214**

INDIA	O	M	R	W		O	M	R	W
Pathan	34	4	105	1		5	0	45	0
Balaji	29	4	114	2		3	0	26	0
Kumble	46	8	159	0		21	1	88	1
Harbhajan Singh	51.5	9	152	6	(5)	6	0	35	0
Tendulkar	3	0	14	0	(4)	15	1	62	1
Ganguly	4	0	13	0					
PAKISTAN									
Mohammad Sami	34	5	106	3		21	5	84	2
Abdul Razzaq	17	0	77	0		13	3	34	0
Danish Kaneria	39	7	127	5		25	11	46	2
Arshad Khan	28	3	87	0	(5)	14	8	21	2
Shahid Afridi	10.4	3	30	2	(4)	17	7	13	3

FALL OF WICKETS				
	P	I	P	I
Wkt	1st	1st	2nd	2nd
1st	4	98	91	87
2nd	7	172	183	108
3rd	331	257	–	118
4th	415	337	–	127
5th	428	343	–	135
6th	446	374	–	164
7th	504	386	–	164
8th	565	388	–	189
9th	569	396	–	210
10th	570	449	–	214

Umpires: B.F.Bowden (*New Zealand*) (25) and S.J.A.Taufel (*Australia*) (22).
Referee: B.C.Broad (*England*) (12).   Test No. 1741/53 (I385/P310)

254

INDIA v PAKISTAN 2004-05

INDIA – BATTING AND FIELDING

	M	I	NO	HS	Runs	Avge	100	50	Ct/St
A.Kumble	3	5	4	37*	95	95.00	–	–	1
V.Sehwag	3	6	–	201	544	90.66	2	1	2
R.Dravid	3	5	–	135	333	66.60	2	1	4
S.R.Tendulkar	3	5	–	94	255	51.00	–	3	2
V.V.S.Laxman	3	5	1	79*	166	41.50	–	2	2
G.Gambhir	3	6	1	52	179	35.80	–	1	1
K.D.Karthik	3	5	–	93	146	29.20	–	1	6/2
I.K.Pathan	3	5	1	38*	64	16.00	–	–	1
S.C.Ganguly	3	5	–	21	48	9.60	–	–	3
Harbhajan Singh	2	4	–	27	36	9.00	–	–	2
L.Balaji	3	5	–	31	36	7.20	–	–	1

Played in one Test: Z.Khan 0.

INDIA – BOWLING

	O	M	R	W	Avge	Best	5wI	10wM
L.Balaji	119.4	19	452	14	32.28	5- 76	1	–
Harbhajan Singh	118.2	31	332	10	33.20	6-152	1	–
A.Kumble	218.1	58	644	17	37.88	7- 63	1	–
I.K.Pathan	119	23	410	6	68.33	2- 68	–	–

Also bowled: S.C.Ganguly 8-0-28-0; Z.Khan 39-2-163-1; V.Sehwag 5-2-14-0; S.R.Tendulkar 26-1-106-1.

PAKISTAN – BATTING AND FIELDING

	M	I	NO	HS	Runs	Avge	100	50	Ct/St
Younis Khan	3	6	1	267	508	101.60	2	1	5
Inzamam-ul-Haq	3	6	1	184	401	80.20	1	2	1
Yousuf Youhana	3	5	–	104	237	47.40	1	1	3
Asim Kamal	3	5	–	91	199	39.80	–	2	5
Shahid Afridi	2	4	–	59	146	36.50	–	2	–
Kamran Akmal	3	5	–	109	159	31.80	1	–	7/4
Taufiq Umar	2	4	–	44	101	25.25	–	–	–
Abdul Razzaq	3	5	–	71	125	25.00	–	1	1
Mohammad Sami	3	5	–	20	63	12.60	–	–	1
Danish Kaneria	3	5	3	8*	18	9.00	–	–	2

Played in one Test: Arshad Khan 1*; Mohammad Khalil 4, 0*; Naved-ul-Hasan 11, 38* (2 ct); Salman Butt 5, 5 (1 ct); Yasir Hamid 6, 76.

PAKISTAN – BOWLING

	O	M	R	W	Avge	Best	5wI	10wM
Shahid Afridi	63.4	12	170	8	21.25	3- 13	–	–
Danish Kaneria	192.4	40	599	19	31.52	6-150	2	–
Mohammad Sami	143	24	493	10	49.30	3- 82	–	–
Abdul Razzaq	97.1	11	360	7	51.42	3- 62	–	–
Arshad Khan	42	11	108	2	54.00	2- 21	–	–

Also bowled: Mohammad Khalil 23-3-103-0; Naved-ul-Hasan 34-1-139-1; Younis Khan 3-0-25-1.

NEW ZEALAND v AUSTRALIA (1st Test)

At Lancaster Park, Christchurch, on 10, 11, 12, 13 March 2005.
Toss: Australia. Result: **AUSTRALIA** won by nine wickets.
Debuts: New Zealand – C.D.Cumming, I.E.O'Brien.

NEW ZEALAND

C.D.Cumming	c Gillespie b Kasprowicz	74	lbw b Gillespie		7
*S.P.Fleming	lbw b Warne	18	lbw b McGrath		17
H.J.H.Marshall	b Warne	146	b Warne		22
L.Vincent	lbw b Clarke	27	lbw b Gillespie		4
N.J.Astle	lbw b McGrath	74	b Kasprowicz		21
C.D.McMillan	lbw b Gillespie b McGrath	13	c Katich b Warne		5
†B.B.McCullum	c Langer b McGrath	29	lbw b Gillespie		24
D.L.Vettori	not out	24	lbw b Warne		23
J.E.C.Franklin	lbw b McGrath	0	not out		5
I.E.O'Brien	c Gilchrist b McGrath	5	lbw b Warne		0
C.S.Martin	c Gilchrist b McGrath	1	lbw b Warne		0
Extras	(B 4, LB 14, W 2, NB 2)	22	(B 1, LB 1, NB 1)		3
Total		**433**			**131**

AUSTRALIA

J.L.Langer	b Franklin	23	not out		72
M.L.Hayden	c Astle b O'Brien	35	c Cumming b Vettori		15
*R.T.Ponting	c McCullum b Martin	46	not out		47
D.R.Martyn	lbw b Vettori	32			
J.N.Gillespie	c Cumming b Vettori	12			
M.J.Clarke	c McCullum b Franklin	8			
S.M.Katich	c Vincent b Astle	118			
†A.C.Gilchrist	c O'Brien b Vettori	121			
S.K.Warne	c Astle b Vettori	2			
M.S.Kasprowicz	not out	13			
G.D.McGrath	lbw b Vettori	0			
Extras	(B 2, LB 13, W 3, NB 4)	22	(NB 1)		1
Total		**432**	(1 wicket)		**135**

AUSTRALIA	O	M	R	W	O	M	R	W	FALL OF WICKETS				
										NZ	A	NZ	A
McGrath	42	9	115	6	14	7	19	1	Wkt	1st	1st	2nd	2nd
Gillespie	29	5	87	0	12	2	38	3	1st	56	48	20	25
Kasprowicz	25	6	85	1	10	3	33	1	2nd	153	75	30	
Warne	40	6	112	2	14	3	39	5	3rd	199	140	34	
Clarke	5	0	16	1					4th	330	147	71	
									5th	355	160	78	
NEW ZEALAND									6th	388	201	87	
Martin	29	6	104	1	8	0	27	0	7th	403	413	121	
Franklin	26	5	102	2	5	1	26	0	8th	403	418	127	
O'Brien	14	3	73	1	(4) 5	0	27	0	9th	415	426	131	
Vettori	40.2	13	106	5	(3) 13.3	5	55	1	10th	433	432	131	
Astle	14	6	32	1									

Umpires: Alim Dar (*Pakistan*) (18) and D.R.Shepherd (*England*) (87).
Referee: C.H.Lloyd (*West Indies*) (44).   **Test No. 1742/44 (NZ318/A663)**

NEW ZEALAND v AUSTRALIA (2nd Test)

At Basin Reserve, Wellington, on 18, 19, 20, 21, 22 March 2005.
Toss: New Zealand. Result: **MATCH DRAWN**.
Debuts: None.

AUSTRALIA

J.L.Langer	c McCullum b Vettori	46
M.L.Hayden	c Vincent b Franklin	61
*R.T.Ponting	lbw b Vettori	9
D.R.Martyn	c McCullum b O'Brien	165
M.J.Clarke	c Fleming b Astle	8
S.M.Katich	c McCullum b Franklin	35
†A.C.Gilchrist	c and b Franklin	162
S.K.Warne	not out	50
J.N.Gillespie	b Franklin	2
M.S.Kasprowicz	not out	2
G.D.McGrath		
Extras	(B 4, LB 8, W 2, NB 16)	30
Total	(8 wickets declared)	**570**

NEW ZEALAND

C.D.Cumming	b Kasprowicz	37	not out		10
*S.P.Fleming	lbw b McGrath	0	lbw b McGrath		1
H.J.H.Marshall	c Gillespie b McGrath	18	lbw b McGrath		0
L.Vincent	c Gilchrist b Kasprowicz	63	b Kasprowicz		24
N.J.Astle	c Warne b Clarke	9	not out		4
J.E.C.Franklin	c Gilchrist b Kasprowicz	26			
C.D.McMillan	b Warne	20			
†B.B.McCullum	c Clarke b Warne	3			
D.L.Vettori	c Martyn b Warne	45			
I.E.O'Brien	b Gillespie	5			
C.S.Martin	not out	0			
Extras	(B 4, LB 8, W 1, NB 5)	18	(B 3, LB 5, NB 1)		9
Total		**244**	(3 wickets)		**48**

NEW ZEALAND	O	M	R	W	O	M	R	W		FALL OF WICKETS		
											A	NZ	NZ
Martin	28	6	123	0						Wkt	1st	1st	2nd
Franklin	28	4	128	4						1st	82	9	3
O'Brien	24	4	97	1						2nd	100	55	3
Vettori	47	5	170	2						3rd	146	78	37
Astle	13	2	40	1						4th	163	108	–
										5th	247	166	–
AUSTRALIA										6th	503	180	–
McGrath	14	3	50	2	6	3	10	2		7th	557	184	–
Gillespie	20	4	63	1	5	2	5	0		8th	559	201	–
Kasprowicz	16	2	42	3	(4) 3	0	11	1		9th	–	212	–
Warne	28.1	7	69	3	(3) 3.2	0	14	0		10th	–	244	–
Clarke	3	1	8	1									

Umpires: R.E.Koertzen (*Pakistan*) (61) and D.R.Shepherd (*England*) (88).
Referee: C.H.Lloyd (*West Indies*) (45).   **Test No. 1743/45 (NZ319/A664)**

NEW ZEALAND v AUSTRALIA (3rd Test)

At Eden Park, Auckland, on 26, 27, 28, 29 March 2005.
Toss: New Zealand. Result: **AUSTRALIA** won by nine wickets.
Debuts: New Zealand – J.A.H.Marshall.

NEW ZEALAND

C.D.Cumming	lbw b Gillespie	5	lbw b McGrath		0
J.A.H.Marshall	c Hayden b McGrath	29	c Langer b McGrath		3
H.J.H.Marshall	c Ponting b Warne	76	c Gilchrist b McGrath		7
*S.P.Fleming	b Kasprowicz	65	c and b Gillespie		3
N.J.Astle	c Langer b McGrath	19	c Katich b Warne		69
L.Vincent	b Gillespie	2	run out		40
†B.B.McCullum	c Gilchrist b McGrath	25	lbw b Warne		0
D.L.Vettori	not out	41	c McGrath b Warne		65
J.E.C.Franklin	c Katich b Warne	3	c Ponting b Warne		23
P.J.Wiseman	c Gillespie b Warne	8	b McGrath		23
C.S.Martin	c Clarke b Kasprowicz	0	not out		4
Extras	(B 4, LB 13, NB 2)	19	(B 1, LB 14, NB 2)		17
Total		**292**			**254**

AUSTRALIA

J.L.Langer	b Franklin	6	not out		59
M.L.Hayden	lbw b Franklin	38	run out		9
*R.T.Ponting	c McCullum b Astle	105	not out		86
D.R.Martyn	b Wiseman	38			
M.J.Clarke	run out	22			
J.N.Gillespie	c McCullum b Martin	35			
S.M.Katich	c Wiseman b Franklin	35			
†A.C.Gilchrist	not out	60			
S.K.Warne	c Fleming b Franklin	1			
M.S.Kasprowicz	b Franklin	23			
G.D.McGrath	c McCullum b Franklin	0			
Extras	(B 4, LB 7, NB 9)	20	(LB 10, NB 2)		12
Total		**383**	(1 wicket)		**166**

AUSTRALIA	O	M	R	W	O	M	R	W		FALL OF WICKETS			
											NZ	A	NZ	A
McGrath	34	20	49	6	16.2	5	40	4						
Gillespie	25	8	64	2	16	4	63	1		*Wkt*	*1st*	*1st*	*2nd*	*2nd*
Kasprowicz	30.2	7	89	2	14	2	59	0		1st	15	8	0	18
Warne	23	4	63	3	23	5	77	4		2nd	53	84	9	–
Ponting	4	1	10	0						3rd	179	187	15	–
										4th	183	215	23	–
NEW ZEALAND										5th	194	226	93	–
Martin	21	4	92	1	8	1	51	0		6th	228	297	93	–
Franklin	26.1	3	119	6	7	0	40	0		7th	247	297	174	–
Astle	21	7	50	1	(4)	7	0	33	0	8th	262	303	220	–
Vettori	19	4	47	0	(3)	4	0	19	0	9th	288	377	227	–
Wiseman	31	7	64	1	3.3	0	13	0		10th	292	383	254	–

Umpires: R.E.Koertzen (*South Africa*) (62) and J.W.Lloyds (*England*) (5).
Referee: C.H.Lloyd (*West Indies*) (46).   **Test No. 1744/46 (NZ320/A665)**

258

NEW ZEALAND v AUSTRALIA 2004-05

NEW ZEALAND – BATTING AND FIELDING

	M	I	NO	HS	Runs	Avge	100	50	Ct/St
D.L.Vettori	3	5	2	65	198	66.00	–	1	–
H.J.H.Marshall	3	6	–	146	269	44.83	1	1	–
N.J.Astle	3	6	1	74	196	39.20	–	2	2
L.Vincent	3	6	–	63	160	26.66	–	2	2
C.D.Cumming	3	6	1	74	133	26.60	–	1	2
S.P.Fleming	3	6	–	65	104	17.33	–	1	2
B.B.McCullum	3	5	–	29	81	16.20	–	–	8
J.E.C.Franklin	3	5	1	26	57	14.25	–	–	1
C.D.McMillan	2	3	–	20	38	12.66	–	–	–
I.E.O'Brien	2	3	–	5	10	3.33	–	–	1
C.S.Martin	3	5	2	4*	5	1.66	–	–	–

Played in one Test: J.A.H.Marshall 29, 3; P.J.Wiseman 8, 23 (1 ct).

NEW ZEALAND – BOWLING

	O	M	R	W	Avge	Best	5wI	10wM
J.E.C.Franklin	92.1	13	415	12	34.58	6-119	1	–
D.L.Vettori	123.5	22	397	8	49.62	5-106	1	–
N.J.Astle	55	15	155	3	51.66	1- 32	–	–
I.E.O'Brien	43	7	197	2	98.50	1- 73	–	–
C.S.Martin	94	17	397	2	198.50	1- 92	–	–

Also bowled: P.J.Wiseman 34.3-7-77-1.

AUSTRALIA – BATTING AND FIELDING

	M	I	NO	HS	Runs	Avge	100	50	Ct/St
A.C.Gilchrist	3	3	1	162	343	171.50	2	1	7
R.T.Ponting	3	5	2	105	293	97.66	1	1	2
D.R.Martyn	3	3	–	165	235	78.33	1	–	4
J.L.Langer	3	5	2	72*	206	68.66	–	2	3
S.M.Katich	3	3	–	118	188	62.66	1	–	3
M.S.Kasprowicz	3	3	2	23	38	38.00	–	–	–
M.L.Hayden	3	5	–	61	158	31.60	–	1	1
S.K.Warne	3	3	1	50*	53	26.50	–	1	1
J.N.Gillespie	3	3	–	35	49	16.33	–	–	4
M.J.Clarke	3	3	–	22	38	12.66	–	–	2
G.D.McGrath	3	2	–	0	0	0.00	–	–	1

AUSTRALIA – BOWLING

	O	M	R	W	Avge	Best	5wI	10wM
M.J.Clarke	8	1	24	2	12.00	1- 8	–	–
G.D.McGrath	126.2	47	283	18	15.72	6-115	1	–
S.K.Warne	131.3	25	374	17	22.00	5- 39	1	–
M.S.Kasprowicz	98.2	20	319	8	39.87	3- 42	–	–
J.N.Gillespie	107	25	320	7	45.71	3- 38	–	–

Also bowled: R.T.Ponting 4-1-10-0.

WEST INDIES v SOUTH AFRICA (1st Test)

At Bourda, Georgetown, Guyana, on 31 March, 1, 2, 3, 4 April 2005.
Toss: West Indies. Result: **MATCH DRAWN**.
Debuts: West Indies – N.Deonarine, D.J.Pagon.

WEST INDIES

W.W.Hinds	c Boucher b Langeveldt	213	
D.S.Smith	c Boucher b Nel	11	
D.Ganga	c Boucher b Nel	0	
D.J.Pagon	c Kallis b Nel	35	
*S.Chanderpaul	not out	203	
R.O.Hinds	c Kallis b Boje	48	
N.Deonarine	not out	15	
†C.O.Browne			
DB.Powell			
P.T.Collins			
R.D.King			
Extras	(LB 8, W 2, NB 8)	18	
Total	(5 wickets declared)	**543**	

SOUTH AFRICA

*G.C.Smith	c Browne b Collins	2	(2) b Collins	34
A.B.de Villiers	c Browne b King	41	(1) b King	20
J.A.Rudolph	c R.O.Hinds b Powell	0	lbw b Deonarine	24
J.H.Kallis	b Powell	0	not out	109
H.H.Gibbs	lbw b Collins	5	b R.O.Hinds	49
†M.V.Boucher	c Chanderpaul b Collins	41	not out	4
A.J.Hall	c Collins b King	2		
N.Boje	b King	34		
M.Ntini	lbw b Powell	8		
C.K.Langeveldt	c R.O.Hinds b Deonarine	10		
A.Nel	not out	6		
Extras	(LB 6, W 2, NB 31)	39	(B 16, LB 2, W 2, NB 9)	29
Total		**188**	(4 wickets)	**269**

SOUTH AFRICA	O	M	R	W		O	M	R	W
Ntini	23	5	98	0					
Nel	33	8	93	3					
Langeveldt	27	5	65	1					
Hall	16	4	53	0					
Kallis	14	3	70	0					
Boje	29.1	2	106	1					
Smith	10	0	50	0					

WEST INDIES	O	M	R	W		O	M	R	W
Collins	18	5	39	3		24	10	44	1
Powell	18	2	61	3		28	15	46	0
King	16	2	48	3		24	5	54	1
R.O.Hinds	13	5	29	0	(5)	27	13	27	1
Deonarine	1.5	0	5	1	(6)	30	15	35	1
W.W.Hinds					(4)	14	5	16	0
Chanderpaul						13	6	25	0
Ganga						1	0	4	0

FALL OF WICKETS			
	WI	SA	SA
Wkt	1st	1st	2nd
1st	24	15	46
2nd	24	16	68
3rd	106	16	119
4th	390	30	258
5th	506	71	–
6th	–	95	–
7th	–	158	–
8th	–	169	–
9th	–	172	–
10th	–	188	–

Umpires: Alim Dar (*Pakistan*) (19) and D.R.Shepherd (*England*) (89).
Referee: J.J.Crowe (*New Zealand*) (6). **Test No. 1745/16 (WI/416/SA300)**

WEST INDIES v SOUTH AFRICA (2nd Test)

At Queen's Park Oval, Port-of-Spain, Trinidad, on 8, 9, 10, 11, 12, April.
Toss: West Indies. Result: **SOUTH AFRICA** won by eight wickets.
Debuts: None.

WEST INDIES

W.W.Hinds	c Smith b Ntini	32	lbw b Boje		22
C.H.Gayle	c Boucher b Ntini	6	c De Villiers b Ntini		1
R.R.Sarwan	c Nel b Ntini	5	not out		107
B.C.Lara	b Nel	196	b Boje		4
*S.Chanderpaul	c and b Boje	35	lbw b Ntini		1
D.J.Pagon	b Ntini	0	b Ntini		2
D.J.J.Bravo	b Nel	5	c Boucher b Ntini		33
†C.O.Browne	c Rudolph b Ntini	26	lbw b Ntini		2
D.B.Powell	b Ntini	15	c Kallis b Nel		1
P.T.Collins	lbw b Nel	2	b Ntini		0
R.D.King	not out	1	b Ntini		0
Extras	(B 4, LB 8, W 2, NB 5, Pen 5)	24	(B 6, LB 10, W 1, NB 4)		21
Total		**347**			**194**

SOUTH AFRICA

*G.C.Smith	lbw b Hinds	148	(2) c Gayle b Bravo		41
A.B.de Villiers	c Chanderpaul b King	33	(1) b Powell		62
J.A.Rudolph	c Browne b Bravo	8	not out		7
J.H.Kallis	lbw b Bravo	39	not out		19
M.Zondeki	b Collins	14			
H.H.Gibbs	b Collins	34			
A.G.Prince	c Chanderpaul b Gayle	45			
†M.V.Boucher	c and b Gayle	28			
N.Boje	not out	13			
M.Ntini	b Gayle	4			
A.Nel	b Gayle	6			
Extras	(B 2, LB 2, W 2, NB 20)	26	(B 5, LB 2, W 3, NB 7)		17
Total		**398**	(2 wickets)		**146**

SOUTH AFRICA	O	M	R	W		O	M	R	W	FALL OF WICKETS				
											WI	SA	WI	SA
Nel	28.4	7	71	3		21	6	42	1	Wkt	1st	1st	2nd	2nd
Ntini	28	3	95	6		19.5	7	37	7	1st	7	70	14	117
Kallis	13	4	41	9	(5)	11	33	29	0	2nd	13	86	79	119
Zondeki	15	0	71	0	(3)	11	4	24	0	3rd	108	181	85	–
Boje	20	2	52	1	(4)	20	6	37	2	4th	203	222	86	–
Smith						7	1	9	0	5th	204	274	92	–
										6th	225	303	180	–
WEST INDIES										7th	299	374	188	–
Collins	29	5	78	2		4	0	27	0	8th	318	375	189	–
Powell	22	3	86	0		10	2	27	1	9th	325	384	190	–
King	26	7	50	1	(4)	11.5	1	28	0	10th	347	398	194	–
Bravo	37	8	98	2	(5)	6	2	27	1					
Gayle	37.5	18	50	4	(3)	11	3	16	0					
Chanderpaul	2	0	6	0										
Hinds	8	5	9	1	(6)	2	0	14	0					
Sarwan	5	0	17	0										

Umpires: Alim Dar (*Pakistan*) (20) and D.R.Shepherd (*England*) (90).
Referee: J.J.Crowe (*New Zealand*) (7).   **Test No. 1746/17 (WI417/SA301)**

WEST INDIES v SOUTH AFRICA (3rd Test)

At Kensington Oval, Bridgetown, Barbados, on 21, 22, 23, 24 April.
Toss: West Indies. Result: **SOUTH AFRICA** won by an innings and 86 runs.
Debuts: None.

WEST INDIES

W.W.Hinds	c Smith b Ntini	1	(2)	c Gibbs b Nel	11
C.H.Gayle	c Boucher b Nel	0	(1)	c Smith b Ntini	5
R.R.Sarwan	c Prince b Nell	10		c Gibbs b Ntini	0
B.C.Lara	b Nel	176		lbw b Nel	13
*S.Chanderpaul	c Boucher b Zondeki	53		lbw b Nel	31
R.O.Hinds	c Boucher b Kallis	10	(7)	c Kallis b Boje	15
D.J.J.Bravo	c Smith b Zondeki	26	(6)	c Boucher b Kallis	6
†C.O.Browne	c Zondeki b Nel	5		c Dippenaar b Nel	68
DB.Powell	c Boucher b Zondeki	3		lbw b Nel	5
F.H.Edwards	c Dippenaar b Zondeki	2		c Ntini b Nel	2
R.D.King	not out	0		not out	3
Extras	(B 1, LB 3, W 1, NB 5)	10		(B 1, LB 2, NB 4)	7
Total		**296**			**166**

SOUTH AFRICA

*G.C.Smith	c W.W.Hinds b Gayle	104
A.B.de Villiers	c Browne b King	178
H.H.Dippenaar	run out	71
J.H.Kallis	c sub (D.R.Smith) b W.W.Hinds	78
H.H.Gibbs	c Bravo b Gayle	8
A.G.Prince	c Bravo b Gayle	23
†M.V.Boucher	b Powell	28
N.Boje	not out	20
M.Zondeki	c Chanderpaul b Powell	2
M.Ntini	c Bravo b Powell	16
A.Nel	not out	4
Extras	(B 1, LB 2, NB 13)	16
Total	(9 wickets declared)	**548**

SOUTH AFRICA	O	M	R	W		O	M	R	W
Nel	21.2	3	56	4		16.2	3	32	6
Ntini	17	2	61	1		11	2	40	2
Kallis	14	6	37	1	(5)	6	3	7	1
Zondeki	16	1	50	4	(3)	8	3	43	0
Smith	8	1	23	0	(6)	2	0	8	0
Boje	16	2	65	0	(4)	11	1	33	1

WEST INDIES	O	M	R	W
Edwards	32.5	3	112	0
King	30	5	80	1
Powell	31	2	103	3
Bravo	29	3	73	0
R.O.Hinds	18	1	67	0
Gayle	27	3	85	3
W.W.Hinds	9	2	18	1
Sarwan	1	0	7	0

FALL OF WICKETS			
	WI	SA	WI
Wkt	1st	1st	2nd
1st	2	191	17
2nd	12	334	17
3rd	12	392	17
4th	150	410	54
5th	171	450	63
6th	286	496	71
7th	288	502	107
8th	292	504	130
9th	296	542	143
10th	296	–	166

Umpires: B.F.Bowden (*New Zealand*) (26) and S.J.A.Taufel (*Australia*) (23).
Referee: J.J.Crowe (*New Zealand*) (8).   **Test No. 1747/18 (WI418/SA302)**

WEST INDIES v SOUTH AFRICA (4th Test)

At Recreation Ground, St John's, Antigua, on 29, 30 April, 1, 2, 3 May.
Toss: South Africa. Result: **MATCH DRAWN**.
Debuts: West Indies – D.M.Washington.

SOUTH AFRICA

A.B.de Villiers	c Browne b Best	114	(2) c Washington b Best		12
*G.C.Smith	c Washington b Powell	126	(1) not out		50
H.H.Dippenaar	run out	5	not out		56
J.H.Kallis	c Washington b Powell	147			
H.H.Gibbs	c Deonarine b Gayle	23			
A.G.Prince	c Browne b Bravo	131			
†M.V.Boucher	not out	11			
S.M.Pollock	not out	13			
M.Zondeki					
M.Ntini					
N.Boje					
Extras	(B 4, LB 1, W 5, NB 8)	18	(W 3, NB 6)		9
Total	(6 wickets declared)	**588**	(1 wicket)		**127**

WEST INDIES

C.H.Gayle	c Smith b Zondeki	317
W.W.Hinds	c and b Ntini	0
R.R.Sarwan	c Prince b Zondeki	127
B.C.Lara	c Boucher b Zondeki	4
*S.Chanderpaul	run out	127
N.Deonarine	c Boucher b Smith	4
D.J.J.Bravo	c Prince b Boucher	107
†C.O.Browne	lbw b Smith	0
DB.Powell	b De Villiers	12
T.L.Best	c Gibbs b De Villiers	5
D.M.Washington	not out	7
Extras	(B 2, LB 9, W 3, NB 23)	37
Total		**747**

WEST INDIES	O	M	R	W		O	M	R	W		FALL OF WICKETS			
Powell	32	3	137	2	(2)	6	2	15	0			SA	WI	SA
Best	26	4	116	1	(1)	5	0	32	1		*Wkt*	*1st*	*1st*	*2nd*
Washington	22	3	73	0		7	1	20	0		1st	245	14	14
Bravo	27	4	97	1		5	0	24	0		2nd	245	345	–
Gayle	31	11	65	1	(8)	1	0	3	0		3rd	251	363	–
Hinds	6	0	24	0	(5)	3	1	10	0		4th	295	512	–
Deonarine	18	1	69	0	(6)	3	1	20	0		5th	562	535	–
Sarwan	1	0	2	0	(7)	1	0	3	0		6th	563	665	–
SOUTH AFRICA											7th	–	665	–
Pollock	34	5	111	0							8th	–	700	–
Ntini	33	3	106	1							9th	–	712	–
Zondeki	25	4	120	3							10th	–	747	–
Kallis	36	6	96	0										
Boje	30	6	76	0										
Smith	43	3	145	2										
De Villiers	21	6	49	2										
Prince	9	1	22	0										
Dippenaar	2	1	1	0										
Boucher	1.2	0	6	1										
Gibbs	1	0	4	0										

Umpires: B.F.Bowden (*New Zealand*) (27) and S.J.A.Taufel (*Australia*) (24).
Referee: J.J.Crowe (*New Zealand*) (9).   **Test No. 1748/19 (WI419/SA303)**

WEST INDIES v SOUTH AFRICA 2005

WEST INDIES – BATTING AND FIELDING

	M	I	NO	HS	Runs	Avge	100	50	Ct/St
S.Chanderpaul	4	6	1	203*	450	90.00	2	1	4
B.C.Lara	3	5	–	196	393	78.60	2	–	–
C.H.Gayle	3	5	–	317	329	65.80	1	–	2
R.R.Sarwan	3	5	1	127	249	62.25	2	–	–
W.W.Hinds	4	6	–	213	279	46.50	1	1	2
D.J.J.Bravo	3	5	–	107	177	35.40	1	–	3
R.O.Hinds	2	3	–	48	73	24.33	–	–	2
C.O.Browne	4	5	–	68	101	20.20	–	1	6
N.Deonarine	2	2	1	15*	19	19.00	–	–	1
D.J.Pagon	2	3	–	35	37	12.33	–	–	–
D.B.Powell	4	5	–	15	36	7.20	–	–	–
R.D.King	3	4	3	3*	4	4.00	–	–	–
P.T.Collins	2	2	–	2	2	1.00	–	–	1

Played in one Test: T.L.Best 5; F.H.Edwards 2, 2; D.Ganga 0; D.S.Smith 11; D.M.Washington 7* (3 ct).

WEST INDIES – BOWLING

	O	M	R	W	Avge	Best	5wI	10wM
C.H.Gayle	107.5	35	219	8	27.37	4-50	–	–
P.T.Collins	75	20	188	6	31.33	3-39	–	–
R.D.King	107.5	20	260	6	43.33	3-48	–	–
D.B.Powell	147	29	475	9	52.77	3-61	–	–
D.J.J.Bravo	104	17	319	4	79.75	2-98	–	–

Also bowled: T.L.Best 31-4-148-2; S.Chanderpaul 15-6-31-0; N.Deonarine 52.5-17-129-2; F.H.Edwards 32.5-3-112-0; D.Ganga 1-0-4-0; R.O.Hinds 58-19-123-1; W.W.Hinds 42-13-91-2; R.R.Sarwan 8-0-29-0; D.M.Washington 29-4-93-0.

SOUTH AFRICA – BATTING AND FIELDING

	M	I	NO	HS	Runs	Avge	100	50	Ct/St
J.H.Kallis	4	6	2	147	392	98.00	2	1	4
G.C.Smith	4	7	1	148	505	84.16	3	1	5
N.Boje	4	3	2	34	67	67.00	–	–	1
A.G.Prince	3	3	–	131	199	66.33	1	–	3
H.H.Dippenaar	2	3	1	71	132	66.00	–	2	2
A.B.de Villiers	4	7	1	178	460	65.71	2	1	1
M.V.Boucher	4	5	2	41	112	37.33	–	–	12
H.H.Gibbs	4	5	–	49	119	23.80	–	–	3
A.Nel	3	3	2	6*	16	16.00	–	–	1
J.A.Rudolph	2	4	1	24	39	13.00	–	–	1
M.Ntini	4	3	–	16	28	9.33	–	–	2
M.Zondeki	2	2	–	14	16	8.00	–	–	1

Played in one Test: A.J.Hall 2; C.K.Langeveldt 10; S.M.Pollock 13*.

SOUTH AFRICA – BOWLING

	O	M	R	W	Avge	Best	5wI	10wM
A.Nel	120.2	27	294	17	17.29	6-32	1	1
M.Ntini	131.5	22	437	17	25.70	7-37	2	1
M.Zondeki	75	12	308	7	44.00	4-50	–	–
N.Boje	126.1	19	369	5	73.80	2-37	–	–

Also bowled: M.V.Boucher 1.2-0-6-1; A.B.de Villiers 21-6-49-2; H.H.Dippenaar 2-1-1-0; H.H.Gibbs 1-0-4-0; A.J.Hall 16-4-53-0; J.H.Kallis 94-25-280-2; C.K.Langeveldt 27-5-65-1; S.M.Pollock 34-5-111-0; A.G.Prince 9-1-22-0; G.C.Smith 70-5-235-2.

NEW ZEALAND v SRI LANKA (1st Test)

At McLean Park, Napier, on 4, 5, 6, 7, 8 April 2005.
Toss: New Zealand. Result: **MATCH DRAWN**.
Debuts: Sri Lanka – M.D.N. Kulasekara.

NEW ZEALAND

C.D.Cumming	lbw b Vaas	12		lbw b Malinga	16
J.A.H.Marshall	c Samaraweera b Chandana	52		lbw b Jayasuriya	39
H.J.H.Marshall	c Vaas b Malinga	160		lbw b Malinga	6
*S.P.Fleming	b Malinga	16	(5)	c Kulasekara b Malinga	41
N.J.Astle	c Jayasuriya b Vaas	114	(6)	run out	19
L.Vincent	c Dilshan b Kulasekara	0	(7)	b Chandana	52
†B.B.McCullum	lbw b Malinga	99	(8)	c Samaraweera b Jayasuriya	7
J.E.C.Franklin	c Malinga b Herath	55	(9)	b Malinga	7
K.D.Mills	b Malinga	4	(10)	c Jayasuriya b Herath	22
P.J.Wiseman	c Atapattu b Herath	27	(4)	lbw b Malinga	0
C.S.Martin	not out	1		not out	4
Extras	(B 5, LB 4, W 2, NB 10)	21		(B 6, LB 7, W 2, NB 10)	25
Total		**561**			**238**

SRI LANKA

*M.S.Atapattu	c Fleming b Astle	127	not out	2
S.T.Jayasuriya	lbw b Martin	48	not out	5
†K.C.Sangakkara	b Martin	5		
D.P.M.deS.Jayawardena	c McCullum b Franklin	141		
T.T.Samaraweera	c Fleming b Martin	88		
T.M.Dilshan	c Vincent b Martin	28		
W.P.U.C.J.Vaas	c Astle b Wiseman	17		
U.D.U.Chandana	c Martin b Franklin	19		
M.R.K.B.Herath	b Franklin	0		
M.D.N.Kulasekara	c Fleming b Franklin	0		
S.L.Malinga	not out	0		
Extras	(B 1, LB 6, W 6, NB 12)	25		
Total		**498**	(0 wickets)	**7**

SRI LANKA	O	M	R	W		O	M	R	W
Vaas	33	5	125	2		17	4	38	0
Malinga	35	5	130	4		24.4	4	80	5
Kulasekara	24	7	70	1		11	2	19	0
Herath	30.1	5	91	2		11	4	29	1
Chandana	33	4	123	1	(7)	7	2	12	1
Jayasuriya	3	1	8	0	(5)	21	8	41	2
Dilshan	1	0	5	0					
Samaraweera					(6)	1	0	6	0
NEW ZEALAND									
Martin	37	9	132	4		1	0	1	0
Franklin	32.1	7	126	4		0.3	0	6	0
Wiseman	38	7	128	1					
Mills	23	6	59	0					
Astle	18	6	46	1					

	FALL OF WICKETS			
	NZ	SL	NZ	SL
Wkt	1st	1st	2nd	2nd
1st	35	95	51	
2nd	142	101	64	
3rd	187	285	69	
4th	312	407	85	
5th	317	452	115	
6th	446	463	128	
7th	487	488	148	
8th	497	491	181	
9th	540	497	222	
10th	561	498	238	

Umpires: S.A.Bucknor (*West Indies*) (101) and D.B.Hair (*Australia*) (61).
Referee: M.J.Procter (*South Africa*) (29).   Test No. 1749/21 (NZ321/SL148)

NEW ZEALAND v SRI LANKA (2nd Test)

At Basin Reserve, Wellington, on 11, 12, 13, 14 April 2005.
Toss: New Zealand. Result: **NEW ZEALAND** won by an innings and 38 runs.
Debuts: Sri Lanka – S.Kalavitigoda.

SRI LANKA

*M.S.Atapattu	c Vincent b Martin	0	(2) c Fleming b Franklin	16
S.T.Jayasuriya	c Astle b Martin	22	(1) c Vincent b Martin	2
†K.C.Sangakkara	c J.A.H.Marshall b Martin	16	(4) b Franklin	45
D.P.M.deS.Jayawardena	lbw b Martin	1	(5) c McCullum b Franklin	13
T.T.Samaraweera	lbw b Astle	73	(6) c Fleming b Astle	17
T.M.Dilshan	c McCullum b Martin	9	(7) b Astle	73
S.Kalavitigoda	c Vincent b Martin	7	(8) c McCullum b Mills	1
W.P.U.C.J.Vaas	b Franklin	5	(9) b Franklin	38
U.D.U.Chandana	lbw b Astle	41	(10) b Astle	8
M.F.Maharoof	c sub (J.M.How) b Astle	12	(3) c Astle b Mills	36
S.L.Malinga	not out	4	not out	0
Extras	(B 4, LB 5, W 1, NB 11)	21	(B 4, LB 10, W 2, NB 8)	24
Total		**211**		**273**

NEW ZEALAND

C.D.Cumming	lbw b Vaas	47
J.A.H.Marshall	lbw b Vaas	28
H.J.H.Marshall	c Jayawardena b Vaas	6
L.Vincent	run out	224
N.J.Astle	c Kalavitigoda b Vaas	0
*S.P.Fleming	c Kalavitigoda b Vaas	88
†B.B.McCullum	c and b Vaas	0
J.E.C.Franklin	lbw b Malinga	15
K.D.Mills	c Jayawardena b Malinga	31
P.J.Wiseman	not out	32
C.S.Martin	not out	4
Extras	(B 11, LB 23, W 1, NB 12)	47
Total	(9 wickets declared)	**522**

NEW ZEALAND	O	M	R	W	O	M	R	W
Martin	20	7	54	6	18	4	50	1
Franklin	11	1	51	1	(6) 23.5	4	71	4
Mills	20	6	50	0	(2) 11	4	34	2
Astle	12.1	2	35	4	(4) 13	4	27	3
Wiseman	2	0	12	0	(5) 26	7	75	0
Vincent					(3) 1	0	2	0

SRI LANKA	O	M	R	W
Vaas	40	12	108	6
Malinga	34	2	124	2
Maharoof	28	10	96	0
Jayawardena	6	2	14	0
Chandana	28	4	97	0
Jayasuriya	9	2	34	0
Dilshan	1	0	15	0

FALL OF WICKETS

	SL	NZ	SL
Wkt	1st	1st	2nd
1st	0	61	6
2nd	34	70	47
3rd	36	153	95
4th	41	153	117
5th	60	294	137
6th	80	294	164
7th	86	342	177
8th	175	440	255
9th	200	499	267
10th	211	–	273

Umpires: S.A.Bucknor (*West Indies*) (102) and D.B.Hair (*Australia*) (62).
Referee: M.J.Procter (*South Africa*) (30).   **Test No. 1750/22 (NZ322/SL149)**

ENGLAND v BANGLADESH (1st Test)

At Lord's, London, on 26, 27, 28 May 2005.
Toss: England. Result: **ENGLAND** won by an innings and 261 runs.
Debuts: Bangladesh – Mushfiqur Rahim, Shahadat Hossain.

BANGLADESH

Javed Omar	c Trescothick b S.P.Jones	22	c Thorpe b S.P.Jones	25
Nafis Iqbal	c Trescothick b Harmison	8	c Flintoff b Hoggard	3
*Habibul Bashar	c G.O.Jones b Hoggard	3	c Hoggard b S.P.Jones	16
Aftab Ahmed	c Strauss b Flintoff	20	lbw b Hoggard	32
Mohammad Ashraful	lbw b Flintoff	6	c Harmison b Flintoff	2
Mushfiqur Rahim	b Hoggard	19	c G.O.Jones b Flintoff	3
†Khaled Masud	lbw b Hoggard	6	c Thorpe b Flintoff	44
Mohammad Rafique	run out	1	c G.O.Jones b Harmison	0
Mashrafe Mortaza	b Harmison	0	b Harmison	0
Anwar Hossain	not out	5	c Trescothick b S.P.Jones	13
Shahadat Hossain	c G.O.Jones b Hoggard	4	not out	2
Extras	(B 1, LB 1, NB 12)	14	(B 1, LB 4, NB 14)	19
Total		**108**		**159**

ENGLAND

M.E.Trescothick	c Masud b Rafique	194
A.J.Strauss	lbw b Mortaza	69
*M.P.Vaughan	c Masud b Mortaza	120
I.R.Bell	not out	65
G.P.Thorpe	not out	42
A.Flintoff		
†G.O.Jones		
G.J.Batty		
M.J.Hoggard		
S.J.Harmison		
S.P.Jones		
Extras	(B 4, LB 11, W 3, NB 20)	38
Total	(3 wickets declared)	**528**

ENGLAND	O	M	R	W	O	M	R	W
Hoggard	13.2	5	42	4	9	1	42	2
Harmison	14	3	38	2	10	0	39	2
Flintoff	5	0	22	2	9.5	0	44	3
S.P.Jones	6	4	4	1	11	3	29	3

BANGLADESH	O	M	R	W
Mashrafe Mortaza	29	6	107	2
Shahadat Hossain	12	0	101	0
Anwar Hossain	22	0	110	0
Mohammad Rafique	41	3	150	1
Aftab Ahmed	8	1	45	0

FALL OF WICKETS

	B	E	B
Wkt	1st	1st	2nd
1st	31	148	15
2nd	34	403	47
3rd	65	415	57
4th	65	–	60
5th	71	–	65
6th	89	–	96
7th	94	–	97
8th	98	–	97
9th	98	–	155
10th	108	–	159

Umpires: D.J.Harper (*Australia*) (50) and K.Hariharan (*India*) (1).
Referee: A.J.Hurst (*Australia*) (5).   **Test No. 1751/3 (E833/B37)**

ENGLAND v BANGLADESH (2nd Test)

At Riverside, Chester-le-Street, Durham on 3, 4, 5 June 2005.
Toss: England. Result: **ENGLAND** won by an innings and 27 runs.
Debuts: Nil.

BANGLADESH

Javed Omar	c G.O.Jones b Hoggard	37	c G.O.Jones b Harmison		71
Nafis Iqbal	c Strauss b Harmison	7	c G.O.Jones b Flintoff		15
*Habibul Bashar	b Harmison	6	(5) lbw b Flintoff		63
Mohammad Ashraful	G.O.Jones b S.P.Jones	3	c Hoggard b Batty		12
Rajin Saleh	c Thorpe b Flintoff	2	(3) c Strauss b Flintoff		7
Aftab Ahmed	c G.O.Jones b Harmison	6	(7) not out		82
†Khaled Masud	c G.O.Jones b Harmison	22	(6) lbw b Hoggard		25
Mohammad Rafique	c Batty b Hoggard	9	b Hoggard		2
Tapash Baisya	c G.O.Jones b Hoggard	0	(10) c G.O.Jones b Hoggard		18
Mashrafe Mortaza	c G.O.Jones b Harmison	1	(11) c Trescothick b Hoggard		0
Anwar Hossain	not out	0	(9) c Thorpe b Hoggard		0
Extras	(LB 2, W 5, NB 4)	11	(LB 6, W 1, NB 14)		21
Total		**104**			**316**

ENGLAND

M.E.Trescothick	c Ashraful b Aftab	151
A.J.Strauss	lbw b Mortaza	8
*M.P.Vaughan	c Masud b Mortaza	44
I.R.Bell	not out	162
G.P.Thorpe	not out	66
A.Flintoff		
†G.O.Jones		
G.J.Batty		
M.J.Hoggard		
S.J.Harmison		
S.P.Jones		
Extras	(B 1, LB 10, W 2, NB 3)	16
Total	(3 wickets declared)	**447**

ENGLAND	O	M	R	W	O	M	R	W		FALL OF WICKETS			
											B	E	B
Hoggard	12	6	24	3	15.5	3	73	5					
Harmison	12.5	2	38	5	17	1	86	1	*Wkt*	*1st*	*1st*	*2nd*	
S.P.Jones	8	2	26	1	10	1	49	0	1st	17	18	50	
Flintoff	7	3	14	1	15	2	58	3	2nd	27	105	75	
Batty					15	2	44	1	3rd	34	260	101	
										4th	42	–	125
BANGLADESH										5th	59	–	195
Mashrafe Mortaza	22	4	91	2						6th	69	–	235
Tapash Baisya	15	2	80	0						7th	87	–	245
Mohammad Rafique	18	0	107	0						8th	87	–	251
Anwar Hossain	15	1	102	0						9th	93	–	311
Aftab Ahmed	8	0	56	1						10th	104	–	316

Umpires: D.J.Harper (*Australia*) (51) and A.L.Hill (*New Zealand*) (2).
Referee: A.J.Hurst (*Australia*) (6).   Test No. 1752/4 (E834/B38)

WEST INDIES v PAKISTAN (1st Test)

At Kensington Oval, Bridgetown, Barbados, on 26, 27, 28, 29 May 2005.
Toss: West Indies. Result: **WEST INDIES** won by 276 runs.
Debut: Pakistan – Bazid Khan.

WEST INDIES

C.H.Gayle	c Razzaq b Shabbir	4	c Kamal b Kaneria		50
D.S.Smith	c Hamid b Razzaq	19	c Akmal b Razzaq		10
R.R.Sarwan	c Bazid b Shabbir	6	c Akmal b Afridi		1
B.C.Lara	b Kaneria	130	st Akmal b Afridi		48
*S.Chanderpaul	c Bazid b Kaneria	92	not out		153
W.W.Hinds	run out	28	b Kaneria		52
†C.O.Browne	c Akmal b Shabbir	12	c Akmal b Afridi		1
D.B.Powell	b Razzaq	10	b Naved		5
F.H.Edwards	c Hamid b Kaneria	3	c Akmal b Shabbir		20
R.D.King	c Akmal b Razzaq	3	b Shabbir		5
C.D.Collymore	not out	0	lbw b Razzaq		0
Extras	(B 3, LB 6, W 2, NB 27)	38	(B 4, LB 9, W 2, NB 11)		26
Total		**345**			**371**

PAKISTAN

Salman Butt	c Browne b Collymore	27	c Gayle b Edwards		0
Shahid Afridi	c Smith b Edwards	16	(6) c Chanderpaul b Powell		122
Yasir Hamid	b Edwards	12	(2) c Browne b Powell		11
*Younis Khan	c Collymore b Edwards	31	(3) run out		0
Bazid Khan	c Browne b Collymore	9	(4) lbw b Collymore		23
Asim Kamal	c Sarwan b King	0	(5) c Smith b Gayle		55
Abdul Razzaq	lbw b Edwards	10	st Browne b Gayle		41
†Kamran Akmal	c Hinds b King	4	b Gayle		21
Naved-ul-Haq	c Sarwan b Collymore	17	c Lara b Gayle		6
Shabbir Ahmed	b Edwards	6	not out		0
Danish Kaneria	not out	4	c Browne b Gayle		0
Extras	(B 4, NB 4)	8	(LB 7, NB 10)		17
Total		**144**			**296**

PAKISTAN	O	M	R	W		O	M	R	W		FALL OF WICKETS			
												WI	P	WI	P
Naved-ul-Hasan	18	2	66	0		24	7	88	1					
Shabbir Ahmed	18	4	66	3		20	2	70	2		*Wkt*	*1st*	*1st*	*2nd*	*2nd*
Abdul Razzaq	17	3	58	3	(4)	15	4	36	2		1st	12	26	59	0
Danish Kaneria	24.3	1	114	3	(3)	26	4	115	2		2nd	25	54	64	1
Shahid Afridi	6	0	32	0		17	3	49	3		3rd	45	76	65	16
											4th	214	96	137	47
WEST INDIES											5th	263	96	271	162
Edwards	14	1	38	5		1.2	1	0	1		6th	287	100	274	257
Powell	10	4	36	0		11	1	47	2		7th	336	113	307	277
King	11	1	46	2		11.4	0	70	0		8th	336	120	353	295
Collymore	8.4	3	20	3		19	2	80	1		9th	343	132	367	296
Gayle						18.3	3	91	5		10th	345	144	371	296
Hinds						1	0	1	0						

Umpires: D.B.Hair (*Australia*) (63) and D.R.Shepherd (*England*) (91).
Referee: R.S.Madugalle (*Sri Lanka*) (73).   **Test No. 1753/40 (WI/420/P311)**

WEST INDIES v PAKISTAN (2nd Test)

At Sabina Park, Kingston, Jamaica, on 3, 4, 5, 6, 7 June.
Toss: Pakistan. Result: **PAKISTAN** won by 136 runs.
Debuts: None.

PAKISTAN

Shoaib Malik	c Browne b Collymore	13		c Browne b Collymore	64
Yasir Hamid	c Gayle b Powell	14		c Smith b Collymore	26
Younis Khan	c Hinds b Collymore	106		c and b Gayle	43
*Inzamam-ul-Haq	c Smith b Gayle	50	(5)	not out	117
Asim Kamal	b Collymore	51	(4)	lbw b Collymore	0
Shahid Afridi	c Browne b Collymore	33		c Smith b Best	43
Abdul Razzaq	lbw b Collymore	19		b Best	2
†Kamran Akmal	lbw b Powell	49		c Browne b Best	1
Naved-ul-Haq	not out	7		b King	0
Shabbir Ahmed	c Browne b Collymore	0		c Browne b Best	0
Danish Kaneria	b Collymore	6		c and b Collymore	0
Extras	(B 4, LB 3, W 2, NB 17)	26		(LB 2, W 3, NB 8)	13
Total		**374**			**309**

WEST INDIES

C.H.Gayle	c Akmal b Razzaq	33		c Hamid b Shabbir	15
D.S.Smith	b Razzaq	25		c Akmal b Shabbir	49
R.R.Sarwan	c Kaneria b Shabbir	55		hit wicket b Kaneria	8
B.C.Lara	c Akmal b Shabbir	153		c Akmal b Kaneria	0
*S.Chanderpaul	c Akmal b Kaneria	28		lbw b Kaneria	0
W.W.Hinds	c Hamid b Afridi	63		c Younis b Razzaq	19
†C.O.Browne	c Akmal b Shabbir	0		c Akmal b Shabbir	10
D.B.Powell	c Akmal b Shabbir	14		c Hamid b Kaneria	12
T.L.Best	b Afridi	18		c Afridi b Shabbir	4
R.D.King	lbw b Afridi	0		c Akmal b Shabbir	4
C.D.Collymore	not out	2		not out	7
Extras	(B 3, LB 7, W 1, NB 2)	13		(LB 5, NB 10)	15
Total		**404**			**143**

WEST INDIES	O	M	R	W		O	M	R	W	FALL OF WICKETS				
											P	WI	P	WI
Powell	21	4	69	2		22	0	100	0					
Best	12	1	59	0		13	1	46	4	*Wkt*	*1st*	*1st*	*2nd*	*2nd*
Collymore	27.3	5	78	7	(4)	16.5	2	56	4	1st	16	48	66	27
King	13	1	65	0	(3)	16	1	70	1	2nd	43	59	119	48
Gayle	25	1	85	1		10	2	35	1	3rd	130	205	119	48
Sarwan	2	0	11	0						4th	247	275	194	56
										5th	260	326	267	94
PAKISTAN										6th	298	326	273	100
Naved-ul-Hasan	6	0	50	0						7th	336	356	279	126
Shabbir Ahmed	22	4	64	4		18.5	4	55	4	8th	360	385	280	126
Abdul Razzaq	23	4	83	2		14	5	37	1	9th	374	393	295	130
Danish Kaneria	28.5	7	94	1		20	8	46	5	10th	374	404	309	143
Shahid Afridi	13.1	3	51	3										
Shoaib Malik	19	2	5	0										

Umpires: D.B.Hair (*Australia*) (64) and D.R.Shepherd (*England*) (92).
Referee: R.S.Madugalle (*Sri Lanka*) (74). Test No. 1754/41 (**WI/421/P312**)

SRI LANKA v WEST INDIES (1st Test)

At Sinhalese Sports Club, Colombo, on 13, 14, 15, 16 July.
Toss: West Indies. Result: **SRI LANKA** won by six wickets.
Debuts: Sri Lanka – W.M.G.Ramyakumara; West Indies – X.M.Marshall, R.S.Morton, D.Ramdin.

WEST INDIES

S.C.Joseph	lbw b Ramyakumara	28	c Jayawardena b Muralitharan		2
X.M.Marshall	lbw b Vaas	10	lbw b Vaas		24
R.S.Morton	b Muralitharan	43	lbw b Vaas		0
N.Deonarine	c Sangakkara b Malinga	12	lbw b Vaas		7
*S.Chanderpaul	lbw b Vaas	69	not out		48
D.R.Smith	lbw b Malinga	4	lbw b Vaas		0
†D.Ramdin	b Ramyakumara	56	lbw b Muralitharan		11
O.A.C.Banks	b Malinga	32	c Dilshan b Muralitharan		3
D.B.Powell	c Jayawardena b Malinga	3	c Jayawardena b Muralitharan		4
T.L.Best	b Vaas	4	st Sangakkara b Muralitharan		27
J.J.C.Lawson	not out	4	c sub‡ b Muralitharan		0
Extras	(LB 7, NB 13)	20	(B 8, NB 1)		9
Total		**285**			**113**

SRI LANKA

*M.S.Atapattu	b Powell	1	(2) c Ramdin b Lawson		28
S.T.Jayasuriya	c Smith b Lawson	3	(1) c Marshall b Lawson		15
†K.C.Sangakkara	c Ramdin b Banks	34	c Joseph b Lawson		0
D.P.M.deS.Jayawardena	c Morton b Powell	3	not out		41
T.T.Samaraweera	c and b Lawson	11	lbw b Lawson		51
T.M.Dilshan	c Smith b Banks	32	not out		27
W.P.U.C.J.Vaas	b Smith	49			
W.M.G.Ramyakumara	c Joseph b Best	12			
M.R.K.B.Herath	c Ramdin b Lawson	24			
M.Muralitharan	b Lawson	36			
S.L.Malinga	not out	5			
Extras	(LB 6, NB 11)	17	(LB 6, W 2, NB 2)		10
Total		**227**	(4 wickets)		**172**

SRI LANKA	O	M	R	W	O	M	R	W		FALL OF WICKETS			
Vaas	16.4	4	35	3	18	9	15	4		WI	SL	WI	SL
Malinga	14	1	71	4	12	5	22	0	Wkt	1st	1st	2nd	2nd
Ramyakumara	10	1	49	2					1st	14	4	3	34
Muralitharan	29	8	56	1	(3) 21	8	36	6	2nd	72	7	3	34
Herath	14	1	52	0	3	0	12	0	3rd	95	32	15	49
Jayasuriya	5	1	15	0	(4) 6	1	20	0	4th	109	47	21	135
									5th	113	91	21	–
WEST INDIES									6th	192	93	48	–
Powell	13	4	31	2	8	0	44	0	7th	273	113	69	–
Lawson	14.3	3	59	4	12	1	43	4	8th	276	149	69	–
Best	11	1	47	1	8.3	1	37	0	9th	281	215	113	–
Banks	16	3	70	2	7	0	31	0	10th	285	227	113	–
Deonarine	1	0	9	0									
Smith	2	0	5	1	3	1	11	0	‡ (U.D.U.Chandana)				

Umpires: Nadim Ghauri (*Pakistan*) (2) and S.J.Taufel (*Australia*) (25).
Referee: M.J.Procter (*South Africa*) (31).　　　　Test No. 1755/9 (SL150/WI422)

SRI LANKA v WEST INDIES (2nd Test)

At Asgiriya Stadium, Kandy, on 22, 23, 24, 25 July.
Toss: West Indies. Result: **SRI LANKA** won by 240 runs.
Debuts: West Indies – R. Ramdass.

SRI LANKA

*M.S.Atapattu	b Best	17	(2) c Banks b Powell		19
S.T.Jayasuriya	c Ramdin b Powell	2	(1) c Morton b Lawson		36
†K.C.Sangakkara	c Morton b Powell	6	not out		157
D.P.M.deS.Jayawardena	c Morton b Best	6	b Lawson		43
T.T.Samaraweera	c Deonarine b Banks	37	c Ramdin b Lawson		0
T.M.Dilshan	run out	36	c Morton b Banks		49
W.P.U.C.J.Vaas	c Ramdass b Best	6	(8) b Banks		19
W.M.G.Ramyakumara	c Ramdass b Powell	14	(7) b Powell		12
M.R.K.B.Herath	c Ramdin b Powell	1	not out		15
M.Muralitharan	not out	18			
S.L.Malinga	c Ramdin b Powell	0			
Extras	(LB 6, NB 1)	7	(B 4, LB 6, W 6, NB 9)		25
Total		**150**	(7 wickets declared)		**375**

WEST INDIES

X.M.Marshall	c Atapattu b Vaas	4	lbw b Malinga	1
R.Ramdass	run out	3	c Jayawardena b Muralitharan	23
R.S.Morton	b Vaas	1	lbw b Muralitharan	9
*S.Chanderpaul	lbw b Vaas	13	c Jayawardena b Herath	24
S.C.Joseph	c Dilshan b Vaas	18	c Jayawardena b Muralitharan	0
N.Deonarine	c and b Jayasuriya	40	b Muralitharan	29
†D.Ramdin	lbw b Vaas	13	b Muralitharan	28
O.A.C.Banks	c Dilshan b Muralitharan	17	c Sangakkara b Muralitharan	1
D.B.Powell	b Vaas	0	c Jayawardena b Muralitharan	1
T.L.Best	not out	26	b Muralitharan	8
J.J.C.Lawson	b Muralitharan	3	not out	1
Extras	(B4, LB 2, NB 4)	10	(B 4, LB 2, W 2, NB 5)	13
Total		**148**		**137**

WEST INDIES	O	M	R	W		O	M	R	W
Powell	13.1	3	25	5		28	4	89	2
Lawson	10	0	29	0		29	1	104	3
Best	10	1	50	3		20	3	84	0
Banks	13	1	40	1		19	5	47	2
Deonarine						3	0	13	0
Morton						5	0	15	0
Chanderpaul						3	1	13	0

SRI LANKA	O	M	R	W		O	M	R	W
Vaas	15	6	22	6					
Malinga	9	3	22	0	(1) 12	2	48	1
Ramyakumara	5	2	9	0	(2) 4	1	8	0
Muralitharan	9.1	0	37	2	(3) 16.2	4	46	8
Herath	9	0	26	0	(4) 9	2	29	1
Jayasuriya	11	3	26	1				

	FALL OF WICKETS			
	SL	WI	SL	WI
Wkt	1st	1st	2nd	2nd
1st	3	9	55	2
2nd	17	9	57	38
3rd	35	12	155	49
4th	42	27	155	49
5th	98	75	264	77
6th	107	97	278	105
7th	127	101	321	111
8th	130	101	–	119
9th	143	122	–	131
10th	150	148	–	137

Umpires: A.L.Hill (*New Zealand*) (3) and S.J.Taufel (*Australia*) (26).
Referee: M.J.Procter (*South Africa*) (32).   Test No. 1756/10 (**SL151/WI423**)

272

ENGLAND v AUSTRALIA (1st Test)

At Lord's, London, on 21, 22, 23, 24 July 2005.
Toss: Australia. Result: **AUSTRALIA** won by 239 runs.
Debuts: England – K.P.Pietersen.

AUSTRALIA

J.L.Langer	c Harmison b Flintoff	40	run out		6
M.L.Hayden	b Hoggard	12	b Flintoff		34
*R.T.Ponting	c Strauss b Harmison	9	c sub (J.C.Hildreth) b Hoggard		42
D.R.Martyn	c G.O.Jones b S.P.Jones	2	lbw b Harmison		65
M.J.Clarke	lbw b S.P.Jones	11	b Hoggard		91
S.M.Katich	c G.O.Jones b Harmison	27	c S.P.Jones b Harmison		67
†A.C.Gilchrist	c G.O.Jones b Flintoff	26	b Flintoff		10
S.K.Warne	b Harmison	28	c Giles b Harmison		2
B.Lee	c G.O.Jones b Harmison	3	run out		8
J.N.Gillespie	lbw b Harmison	1	b S.P.Jones		13
G.D.McGrath	not out	10	not out		20
Extras	(B 5, LB 4, W 1, NB 11)	21	(B 10, LB 8, NB 8)		26
Total		**190**			**384**

ENGLAND

M.E.Trescothick	c Langer b McGrath	4	c Hayden b Warne		44
A.J.Strauss	c Warne b McGrath	2	c and b Lee		37
*M.P.Vaughan	b McGrath	3	b Lee		4
I.R.Bell	b McGrath	6	lbw b Warne		8
K.P.Pietersen	c Martyn b Warne	57	not out		64
A.Flintoff	b McGrath	0	c Gilchrist b Warne		3
†G.O.Jones	c Gilchrist b Lee	30	c Gillespie b McGrath		6
A.F.Giles	c Gilchrist b Lee	11	c Hayden b McGrath		0
M.J.Hoggard	c Hayden b Warne	0	lbw b McGrath		0
S.J.Harmison	c Martyn b Lee	11	lbw b Warne		0
S.P.Jones	not out	20	c Warne b McGrath		0
Extras	(B 1, LB 5, NB 5)	11	(B 6, LB 5, NB 3)		14
Total		**155**			**180**

ENGLAND	O	M	R	W	O	M	R	W	FALL OF WICKETS			
										A	E	A	E
Harmison	11.2	0	43	5	27.4	6	54	3	*Wkt*	*1st*	*1st*	*2nd*	*2nd*
Hoggard	8	0	40	1	16	1	56	2	1st	35	10	18	80
Flintoff	11	2	50	2	27	4	123	2	2nd	55	11	54	96
S.P.Jones	10	0	48	2	18	1	69	1	3rd	66	18	100	104
Giles					11	1	56	0	4th	66	19	255	112
Bell					1	0	8	0	5th	87	21	255	119
									6th	126	79	274	158
AUSTRALIA									7th	175	92	279	158
McGrath	18	5	53	5	17.1	2	29	4	8th	178	101	289	164
Lee	15.1	5	47	3	15	3	58	2	9th	178	122	341	167
Gillespie	8	1	30	0	6	0	18	0	10th	190	155	384	180
Warne	7	2	19	2	20	2	64	4					

Umpires: Alim Dar (*Pakistan*) (21) and R.E.Koertzen (*South Africa*) (63).
Referee: R.S.Madugalle (*Sri Lanka*) (75). **Test No. 1757/307 (E835/A666)**

ENGLAND v AUSTRALIA (2nd Test)

At Edgbaston, Birmingham, on 4, 5, 6, 7 August 2005.
Toss: Australia. Result: **ENGLAND** won by two runs.
Debuts: None.

ENGLAND

M.E.Trescothick	c Gilchrist b Kasprowicz	90		c Gilchrist b Lee	21
A.J.Strauss	b Warne	48		b Warne	6
*M.P.Vaughan	c Lee b Gillespie	24	(4)	b Lee	1
I.R.Bell	c Gilchrist b Kasprowicz	6	(5)	c Gilchrist b Warne	21
K.P.Pietersen	c Katich b Lee	71	(6)	c Gilchrist b Warne	20
A.Flintoff	c Gilchrist b Gillespie	68	(7)	b Warne	73
†G.O.Jones	c Gilchrist b Kasprowicz	1	(8)	c Ponting b Lee	9
A.F.Giles	lbw b Warne	23	(9)	c Hayden b Warne	8
M.J.Hoggard	lbw b Warne	16	(3)	c Hayden b Lee	1
S.J.Harmison	b Warne	17		c Ponting b Warne	0
S.P.Jones	not out	19		not out	12
Extras	(LB 9, W 1, NB 14)	24		(LB 1, NB 9)	10
Total		**407**			**182**

AUSTRALIA

J.L.Langer	lbw b S.P.Jones	82		b Flintoff	28
M.L.Hayden	c Strauss b Hoggard	0		c Trescothick b S.P.Jones	31
*R.T.Ponting	c Vaughan b Giles	61		c G.O.Jones b Flintoff	0
D.R.Martyn	run out	20		c Bell b Hoggard	28
M.J.Clarke	c G.O.Jones b Giles	40		b Harmison	30
S.M.Katich	c G.O.Jones b Flintoff	4		c Trescothick b Giles	16
†A.C.Gilchrist	not out	49		c Flintoff b Giles	1
S.K.Warne	b Giles	8	(9)	hit wicket b Flintoff	42
B.Lee	c Flintoff b S.P.Jones	6	(10)	not out	43
J.N.Gillespie	lbw b Flintoff	7	(8)	lbw b Flintoff	0
M.S.Kasprowicz	lbw b Flintoff	0		c G.O.Jones b Harmison	20
Extras	(B 13, LB 7, W 1, NB 10)	31		(B 13, LB 8, W 1, NB 18)	40
Total		**308**			**279**

AUSTRALIA	O	M	R	W		O	M	R	W		FALL OF WICKETS			
Lee	17	1	111	1		18	1	82	4			E	A	E	A
Gillespie	22	3	91	2		8	0	24	0		Wkt	1st	1st	2nd	2nd
Kasprowicz	15	3	80	3		3	0	29	0		1st	112	0	25	47
Warne	25.2	4	116	4		23.1	7	46	6		2nd	164	88	27	48
											3rd	170	118	29	82
ENGLAND											4th	187	194	31	107
Harmison	11	1	48	0		17.3	3	62	2		5th	290	208	72	134
Hoggard	8	0	41	1		5	0	26	1		6th	293	262	75	136
S.P.Jones	16	2	69	2	(5)	5	1	23	1		7th	342	273	101	137
Flintoff	15	1	52	3		22	3	79	4		8th	348	282	131	175
Giles	26	2	78	3	(3)	15	3	68	2		9th	375	308	131	220
											10th	407	308	182	279

Umpires: B.F.Bowden (*New Zealand*) (28) and R.E.Koertzen (*South Africa*) (64).
Referee: R.S.Madugalle (*Sri Lanka*) (76).   **Test No. 1758/308 (E836/A667)**

ENGLAND v AUSTRALIA (3rd Test)

At Old Trafford, Manchester, on 11, 12, 13, 14, 15 August 2005.
Toss: England. Result: **MATCH DRAWN**.
Debuts: None.

ENGLAND

M.E.Trescothick	c Gilchrist b Warne	63	b McGrath		41
A.J.Strauss	b Lee	6	c Martyn b McGrath		106
*M.P.Vaughan	c McGrath b Katich	166	c sub (B.J.Hodge) b Lee		14
I.R.Bell	c Gilchrist b Lee	59	c Katich b McGrath		65
K.P.Pietersen	c sub (B.J.Hodge) b Lee	21	lbw b McGrath		0
M.J.Hoggard	b Lee	4			
A.Flintoff	c Langer b Warne	46	(6) b McGrath		4
†G.O.Jones	b Gillespie	42	(7) not out		27
A.F.Giles	c Hayden b Warne	4	(8) not out		0
S.J.Harmison	not out	10			
S.P.Jones	b Warne	0			
Extras	(B 4, LB 5, W 3, NB 15)	27	(B 5, LB 3, W 1, NB 14)		23
Total		**444**	(6 wickets declared)		**280**

AUSTRALIA

J.L.Langer	c Bell b Giles	31	c G.O.Jones b Hoggard		14
M.L.Hayden	lbw b Giles	34	b Flintoff		36
*R.T.Ponting	c Bell b S.P.Jones	7	c G.O.Jones b Harmison		156
D.R.Martyn	b Giles	20	lbw b Harmison		19
S.M.Katich	b Flintoff	17	c Giles b Flintoff		12
†A.C.Gilchrist	c G.O.Jones b S.P.Jones	30	c Bell b Flintoff		4
S.K.Warne	c Giles b S.P.Jones	90	(9) c G.O.Jones b Flintoff		34
M.J.Clarke	c Flintoff b S.P.Jones	7	(7) b S.P.Jones		39
J.N.Gillespie	lbw b S.P.Jones	26	(8) lbw b Hoggard		0
B.Lee	c Trescothick b S.P.Jones	1	not out		18
G.D.McGrath	not out	1	not out		5
Extras	(B 8, LB 7, W 8, NB 15)	38	(B 5, LB 8, W 2, NB 19)		34
Total		**302**	(9 wickets)		**371**

AUSTRALIA	O	M	R	W		O	M	R	W		FALL OF WICKETS				
McGrath	25	6	86	0		20.5	1	115	5			E	A	E	A
Lee	27	6	100	4		12	0	60	1		*Wkt*	*1st*	*1st*	*2nd*	*2nd*
Gillespie	19	2	114	1	(4)	4	0	23	0		1st	26	58	64	25
Warne	33.2	5	99	4	(3)	25	3	74	0		2nd	163	73	97	96
Katich	9	1	36	1							3rd	290	86	224	129
ENGLAND											4th	333	119	225	165
Harmison	10	0	47	0		22	4	67	2		5th	341	133	248	182
Hoggard	6	2	22	0		13	0	49	2		6th	346	186	264	263
Flintoff	20	1	65	1	(5)	25	6	71	4		7th	433	201	–	264
S.P.Jones	17.5	6	53	6	(6)	17	3	57	1		8th	434	287	–	340
Giles	31	4	100	3	(3)	26	4	93	0		9th	438	293	–	354
Vaughan					(4)	5	0	21	0		10th	444	302	–	–

Umpires: B.F.Bowden (*New Zealand*) (29) and S.A.Bucknor (*West Indies*) (103).
Referee: R.S.Madugalle (*Sri Lanka*) (77).　　　　Test No. 1759/309 (E837/A668)

ENGLAND v AUSTRALIA (4th Test)

At Trent Bridge, Nottingham, on 25, 26, 27, 28 August 2005.
Toss: England. Result: **ENGLAND** won by three wickets.
Debuts: Australia – S.W.Tait.

ENGLAND

M.E.Trescothick	b Tait	65	c Ponting b Warne	27
A.J.Strauss	c Hayden b Warne	35	c Clarke b Warne	23
*M.P.Vaughan	c Gilchrist b Ponting	58	c Hayden b Warne	0
I.R.Bell	c Gilchrist b Tait	3	c Kasprowicz b Lee	3
K.P.Pietersen	c Gilchrist b Lee	45	c Gilchrist b Lee	23
A.Flintoff	lbw b Tait	102	b Lee	26
†G.O.Jones	c and b Kasprowicz	85	c Kasprowicz b Warne	3
A.F.Giles	lbw b Warne	15	not out	7
M.J.Hoggard	c Gilchrist b Warne	10	not out	8
S.J.Harmison	st Gilchrist b Warne	2		
S.P.Jones	not out	15		
Extras	(B 1, LB 15, W 1, NB 25)	42	(LB 4, NB 5)	9
Total		**477**	(7 wickets)	**129**

AUSTRALIA

J.L.Langer	c Bell b Hoggard	27	c Bell b Giles	61
M.L.Hayden	lbw b Hoggard	7	c Giles b Flintoff	26
*R.T.Ponting	lbw b S.P.Jones	1	run out	48
D.R.Martyn	lbw b Hoggard	1	c G.O.Jones b Flintoff	13
M.J.Clarke	lbw b Harmison	36	c G.O.Jones b Hoggard	56
S.M.Katich	c Strauss b S.P.Jones	45	lbw b Harmison	59
†A.C.Gilchrist	c Strauss b Flintoff	27	lbw b Hoggard	11
S.K.Warne	c Bell b S.P.Jones	0	st G.O.Jones b Giles	45
B.Lee	c Bell b S.P.Jones	47	not out	26
M.S.Kasprowicz	b S.P.Jones	5	c G.O.Jones b Harmison	19
S.W.Tait	not out	3	b Harmison	4
Extras	(LB 2, W 1, NB 16)	19	(B 1, LB 4, NB 14)	19
Total		**218**		**387**

AUSTRALIA	O	M	R	W		O	M	R	W
Lee	32	2	131	1		12	0	51	3
Kasprowicz	32	3	122	1		2	0	19	0
Tait	24	4	97	3	(4)	4	0	24	0
Warne	29.1	4	102	4	(3)	13.5	2	31	4
Ponting	6	2	9	1					

ENGLAND									
Harmison	9	1	48	1	(3)	30	5	93	3
Hoggard	15	3	70	3	(1)	27	7	72	2
S.P.Jones	14.1	4	44	5	(2)	4	0	15	0
Flintoff	11	1	54	1		29	4	83	2
Giles						28	3	107	2
Bell						6	2	12	0

FALL OF WICKETS

	E	A	A	E
Wkt	1st	1st	2nd	2nd
1st	105	20	50	32
2nd	137	21	129	36
3rd	146	22	155	57
4th	213	58	161	57
5th	241	99	261	103
6th	418	157	277	111
7th	450	157	314	116
8th	450	163	342	–
9th	454	175	373	–
10th	477	218	387	–

Umpires: Alim Dar (*Pakistan*) (22) and S.A.Bucknor (*West Indies*) (104).
Referee: R.S.Madugalle (*Sri Lanka*) (78).   **Test No. 1760/310 (E838/A669)**

ENGLAND v AUSTRALIA (5th Test)

At Kennington Oval, London, on 8, 9, 10, 11, 12 September 2005.
Toss: England. Result: **MATCH DRAWN**.
Debuts: None.

ENGLAND

M.E.Trescothick	c Hayden b Warne	43	lbw b Warne		33
A.J.Strauss	c Katich b Warne	129	c Katich b Warne		1
*M.P.Vaughan	c Clarke b Warne	11	c Gilchrist b McGrath		45
I.R.Bell	lbw b Warne	0	c Warne b McGrath		0
K.P.Pietersen	b Warne	14	b McGrath		158
A.Flintoff	c Warne b McGrath	72	c and b Warne		8
P.D.Collingwood	lbw b Tait	7	c Ponting b Warne		10
†G.O.Jones	b Lee	25	b Tait		1
A.F.Giles	lbw b Warne	32	b Warne		59
M.J.Hoggard	c Martyn b McGrath	2	not out		4
S.J.Harmison	not out	20	c Hayden b Warne		0
Extras	(B 4, LB 6, W 1, NB 7)	18	(B 4, W 7, NB 5)		16
Total		**373**			**335**

AUSTRALIA

J.L.Langer	b Harmison	105	not out	0
M.L.Hayden	lbw b Flintoff	138	not out	0
*R.T.Ponting	c Strauss b Flintoff	35		
D.R.Martyn	c Collingwood b Flintoff	10		
M.J.Clarke	lbw b Hoggard	25		
S.M.Katich	lbw b Flintoff	1		
†A.C.Gilchrist	lbw b Hoggard	23		
S.K.Warne	c Vaughan b Flintoff	0		
B.Lee	c Giles b Hoggard	6		
G.D.McGrath	c Strauss b Hoggard	0		
S.W.Tait	not out	1		
Extras	(B 4, LB 8, W 2, NB 9)	23	(LB 4)	4
Total		**367**	(0 wickets)	**4**

AUSTRALIA	O	M	R	W		O	M	R	W	FALL OF WICKETS				
											E	A	E	A
McGrath	27	5	72	2		26	3	85	3	Wkt	1st	1st	2nd	2nd
Lee	23	3	94	1		20	4	88	0	1st	82	185	2	–
Tait	15	1	61	1	(5)	5	0	28	1	2nd	102	264	67	–
Warne	37.3	5	122	6	(3)	38.3	3	124	6	3rd	104	281	67	–
Katich	3	0	14	0						4th	131	323	109	–
Clarke					(4)	2	0	6	0	5th	274	329	126	–
										6th	289	356	186	–
ENGLAND										7th	297	359	199	–
Harmison	22	2	87	1		0.4	0	0	0	8th	325	363	308	–
Hoggard	24.1	2	97	4						9th	345	363	335	–
Flintoff	34	10	78	5						10th	373	367	335	–
Giles	23	1	76	0										
Collingwood	4	0	17	0										

Umpires: B.F.Bowden (New Zealand) (30) and R.E.Koertzen (*South Africa*) (65).
Referee: R.S.Madugalle (*Sri Lanka*) (79).   **Test No. 1761/311 (E839/A670)**

ENGLAND v AUSTRALIA 2005

ENGLAND – BATTING AND FIELDING

	M	I	NO	HS	Runs	Avge	100	50	Ct/St
K.P.Pietersen	5	10	1	158	473	52.55	1	3	–
M.E.Trescothick	5	10	–	90	431	43.10	–	3	3
A.Flintoff	5	10	–	102	402	40.20	1	3	3
A.J.Strauss	5	10	–	129	393	39.30	2	–	6
S.P.Jones	4	6	4	20*	66	33.00	–	–	1
M.P.Vaughan	5	10	–	166	326	32.60	1	1	2
G.O.Jones	5	10	1	85	229	25.44	–	1	15/1
A.F.Giles	5	10	2	59	155	19.37	–	1	5
I.R.Bell	5	10	–	65	171	17.10	–	2	8
S.J.Harmison	5	8	2	20*	60	10.00	–	–	1
M.J.Hoggard	5	9	2	16	45	6.42	–	–	–

Played in one Test: P.D.Collingwood 7, 10 (1 ct).

ENGLAND – BOWLING

	O	M	R	W	Avge	Best	5wI	10wM
S.P.Jones	102	17	378	18	21.00	6-53	2	–
A.Flintoff	194	32	655	24	27.29	5-78	1	–
M.J.Hoggard	122.1	15	473	16	29.56	4-97	–	–
S.J.Harmison	161.1	22	549	17	32.29	5-43	1	–
A.F.Giles	160	18	578	10	57.80	3-78	–	–

Also bowled: I.R.Bell 7-2-20-0; P.D.Collingwood 4-0-17-0; M.P.Vaughan 5-0-21-0.

AUSTRALIA – BATTING AND FIELDING

	M	I	NO	HS	Runs	Avge	100	50	Ct/St
J.L.Langer	5	10	1	105	394	43.77	1	2	2
R.T.Ponting	5	9	–	156	359	39.88	1	1	4
M.J.Clarke	5	9	–	91	335	37.22	–	2	2
G.D.McGrath	3	5	4	20*	36	36.00	–	–	1
M.L.Hayden	5	10	1	138	318	35.33	1	–	10
S.K.Warne	5	9	–	90	249	27.66	–	1	5
S.M.Katich	5	9	–	67	248	27.55	–	2	4
B.Lee	5	9	3	47	158	26.33	–	–	2
A.C.Gilchrist	5	9	1	49*	181	22.62	–	–	18/1
D.R.Martyn	5	9	–	65	178	19.77	–	1	4
M.S.Kasprowicz	2	4	–	20	44	11.00	–	–	3
S.W.Tait	2	3	2	4	8	8.00	–	–	–
J.N.Gillespie	3	6	–	26	47	7.83	–	–	1

AUSTRALIA – BOWLING

	O	M	R	W	Avge	Best	5wI	10wM
S.K.Warne	252.5	37	797	40	19.92	6-46	3	2
G.D.McGrath	134	22	440	19	23.15	5-53	2	–
B.Lee	191.1	25	822	20	41.10	4-82	–	–
S.W.Tait	48	5	210	5	42.00	3-97	–	–
M.S.Kasprowicz	52	6	250	4	62.50	3-80	–	–
J.N.Gillespie	67	6	300	37	100.00	2-91	–	–

Also bowled: M.J.Clarke 2-0-6-0; S.M.Katich 12-1-50-1; R.T.Ponting 6-2-9-1.

ZIMBABWE v NEW ZEALAND (1st Test)

At Harare Sports Club on 7, 8 August 2005.
Toss: Zimbabwe. Result: **NEW ZEALAND** won by an innings and 294 runs.
Debuts: Zimbabwe – N.R.Ferreira.

NEW ZEALAND

J.A.H.Marshall	c Taibu b Mahwire	5
L.Vincent	c Carlisle b Mahwire	13
H.J.H.Marshall	lbw b Mpofu	20
*S.P.Fleming	c Carlisle b Mpofu	73
N.J.Astle	c Taylor b Streak	23
S.B.Styris	run out	7
†B.B.McCullum	c Cremer b Mahwire	111
D.L.Vettori	b Streak	127
J.E.C.Franklin	b Cremer	13
S.E.Bond	not out	41
C.S.Martin	not out	4
Extras	(B 1, LB 7, W 2, NB 5)	15
Total	**(9 wickets declared)**	**452**

ZIMBABWE

N.R.Ferreira	c McCullum b Franklin	5	c Fleming b Franklin	16
B.R.M.Taylor	run out	10	c Vettori b Franklin	0
D.D.Ebrahim	lbw b Franklin	0	b Martin	8
H.Masakadza	lbw b Franklin	0	c and b Vettori	42
C.B.Wishart	b Bond	0	c Fleming b Bond	5
S.V.Carlisle	not out	20	c Fleming b Bond	0
*†T.Taibu	lbw b Martin	5	c Fleming b Martin	4
H.H.Streak	c McCullum b Martin	0	lbw b Vettori	3
N.B.Mahwire	lbw b Martin	4	not out	4
A.G.Cremer	c Martin b Vettori	1	c J.A.H.Marshall b Vettori	3
C.B.Mpofu	st McCullum b Vettori	0	st McCullum b Vettori	0
Extras	(LB 6, W 1, NB 7)	14	(LB 8, NB 6)	14
Total		**59**		**99**

ZIMBABWE	O	M	R	W		O	M	R	W
Streak	23.4	5	102	2					
Mahwire	26	4	115	3					
Mpofu	16.2	1	100	2					
Cremer	22	0	113	1					
Taylor	1	0	14	0					

NEW ZEALAND	O	M	R	W		O	M	R	W
Bond	5	1	11	1		11	8	10	2
Franklin	5	0	11	3		10	2	19	2
Martin	10	1	21	3	(4)	8	5	16	2
Styris	7	4	9	0	(3)	2	0	3	0
Vettori	2.4	2	1	2		13.5	4	28	4
Astle						5	0	15	0

FALL OF WICKETS			
	NZ	Z	Z
Wkt	1st	1st	2nd
1st	21	9	5
2nd	24	9	14
3rd	63	10	53
4th	104	11	76
5th	113	28	80
6th	233	46	84
7th	309	46	90
8th	369	51	90
9th	432	53	99
10th	–	59	99

Umpires: M.R.Benson (*England*) (4) and D.B.Hair (*Australia*) (65).
Referee: B.C.Broad (*England*) (13). **Test No. 1762/12 (Z80/NZ323)**

ZIMBABWE v NEW ZEALAND (2nd Test)

At Queens Sports Club, Bulawayo, on 15, 16, 17 August 2005.
Toss: Zimbabwe. Result: **NEW ZEALAND** won by an innings and 46 runs.
Debuts: Zimbabwe – K.M.Dabengwa.

ZIMBABWE

D.D.Ebrahim	lbw b Bond	0	c Styris b Bond	2
B.R.M.Taylor	c McCullum b Bond	37	c Vettori b Bond	77
S.V.Carlisle	lbw b Bond	1	run out	10
H.Masakadza	c Martin b Bond	0	b Vettori	28
C.B.Wishart	c Astle b Franklin	30	run out	0
*†T.Taibu	c Vettori b Bond	76	lbw b Vettori	25
H.H.Streak	c McCullum b Bond	0	c McCullum b Bond	2
K.M.Dabengwa	b Martin	17	c McCullum b Bond	4
N.B.Mahwire	c Astle b Vettori	42	not out	50
A.G.Cremer	not out	7	lbw b Vettori	1
C.B.Mpofu	c J.A.H.Marshall b Vettori	7	run out	3
Extras	(LB 4, NB 10)	14	(LB 2, NB 3)	5
Total		**231**		**207**

NEW ZEALAND

J.A.H.Marshall	c Carlisle b Streak	10
L.Vincent	b Streak	92
H.J.H.Marshall	run out	13
*S.P.Fleming	c Taibu b Mahwire	65
N.J.Astle	b Streak	128
S.B.Styris	c Taibu b Mahwire	45
†B.B.McCullum	c Taylor b Debengwa	24
D.L.Vettori	c Taibu b Dabengwa	48
J.E.C.Franklin	lbw b Streak	19
S.E.Bond	b Mahwire	8
C.S.Martin	not out	0
Extras	(B 6, LB 6, W 2, NB 18)	32
Total		**484**

NEW ZEALAND	O	M	R	W		O	M	R	W
Bond	17	4	51	6		14	1	48	4
Franklin	12	3	43	1		10	3	24	0
Martin	13	4	42	1		12	2	47	0
Styris	4	2	9	0	(5)	3	0	20	0
Vettori	27	9	56	2	(4)	22.1	8	66	3
Astle	6	2	26	0					

ZIMBABWE	O	M	R	W
Streak	22	6	73	4
Mahwire	25.1	2	121	3
Mpofu	15	1	80	0
Cremer	24	1	111	0
Dabengwa	25	2	87	2

FALL OF WICKETS			
	Z	NZ	Z
Wkt	1st	1st	2nd
1st	0	34	4
2nd	3	48	19
3rd	7	185	69
4th	65	205	69
5th	74	292	146
6th	74	346	146
7th	123	439	153
8th	211	475	164
9th	217	484	173
10th	231	484	207

Umpires: M.R.Benson (*England*) (5) and D.B.Hair (*Australia*) (66).
Referee: B.C.Broad (*England*) (14).   **Test No. 1763/13 (Z81/NZ324)**

SRI LANKA v BANGLADESH (1st Test)

At R.Premadasa Stadium, Khettarama, Colombo, on 12, 13, 14 September 2005.
Toss: Sri Lanka. Result: **SRI LANKA** won by an innings and 96 runs.
Debuts: Bangladesh – Shahriar Nafis, Syed Rasel.

BANGLADESH

Javed Omar	c Sangakkara b Fernando	30	c Sangakkara b Malinga		9
Shahriar Nafis	b Malinga	3	b Muralitharan		13
*Habibul Bashar	run out	84	c Sangakkara b Vaas		15
Mohammad Ashraful	c Fernando b Herath	17	lbw b Muralitharan		0
Tushar Imran	b Herath	0	b Muralitharan		0
Aftab Ahmed	c Samaraweera b Herath	0	c Samaraweera b Muralitharan		8
†Khaled Masud	c Samaraweera b Muralitharan	2	b Malinga		15
Mohammad Rafique	lbw b Muralitharan	9	c Samaraweera b Muralitharan		4
Syed Rasel	st Sangakkara b Herath	19	b Malinga		1
Shahadat Hossain	lbw b Muralitharan	2	not out		0
Enamul Haque II	not out	0	st Sangakkara b Muralitharan		2
Extras	(B 8, LB 2, W 1, NB 11)	22	(B 4, W 5, NB 2)		11
Total		**188**			**86**

SRI LANKA

S.T.Jayasuriya	c Aftab b Shahadat	46
*M.S.Atapattu	lbw b Rasel	18
†K.C.Sangakkara	c Ashraful b Rafique	30
T.T.Samaraweera	c Masud b Shahadat	78
D.P.M.deS.Jayawardena	c Masud b Rafique	63
T.M.Dilshan	b Rasel	86
W.P.U.C.J.Vaas	lbw b Rafique	5
M.R.K.B.Herath	c Masud b Rafique	13
M.Muralitharan	c Masud b Rafique	3
C.R.D.Fernando	not out	1
S.L.Malinga		
Extras	(LB 6, W 1, NB 20)	27
Total	(9 wickets declared)	**370**

SRI LANKA	O	M	R	W	O	M	R	W
Vaas	6	1	25	0	10	4	31	1
Malinga	8	1	44	1	6	1	32	5
Fernando	4	0	29	1				
Muralitharan	14	1	42	3	(3) 10.4	4	18	6
Herath	12	4	38	4	(4) 1	0	1	0

BANGLADESH	O	M	R	W
Syed Rasel	19.2	2	67	2
Shahadat Hossain	20	0	75	2
Mohammad Rafique	37	9	114	5
Enamul Haque II	33	8	106	0
Mohammad Ashraful	1	0	2	0

FALL OF WICKETS			
	B	SL	B
Wkt	1st	1st	2nd
1st	4	41	9
2nd	63	97	35
3rd	155	130	35
4th	156	231	39
5th	156	295	47
6th	158	306	50
7th	158	337	59
8th	170	345	73
9th	176	370	83
10th	188	–	86

Umpires: Asad Rauf (*Pakistan*) (2) and S.A.Bucknor (*West Indies*) (105).
Referee: C.H.Lloyd (*West Indies*) (47). **Test No. 1764/4 (SL386/B39)**

SRI LANKA v BANGLADESH (2nd Test)

At P.Saravanamuttu Stadium, Colombo, on 20, 21, 22 September 2005.
Toss: Sri Lanka. Result: **SRI LANKA** won by an innings and 69 runs.
Debuts: None.

SRI LANKA

S.T.Jayasuriya	lbw b Rasel	13
*M.S.Atapattu	c Masud b Shahadat	11
†K.C.Sangakkara	b Rasel	5
D.P.M.deS.Jayawardena	b Shahadat	2
T.T.Samaraweera	c Shahrir b Rasel	138
T.M.Dilshan	c Masud b Aftab	168
W.P.U.C.J.Vaas	b Rasel	65
M.R.K.B.Herath	lbw b Shahadat	1
M.Muralitharan	b Shahadat	24
C.R.D.Fernando	not out	4
S.L.Malinga		
Extras	(B 4, LB 10, W 1, NB 11)	26
Total	(9 wickets declared)	**457**

BANGLADESH

Javed Omar	b Fernando	18	(2)	c Atapattu b Vaas	9
Shahriar Nafis	c Sangakkara b Malinga	5	(4)	c Samaraweera b Muralitharan	51
*Habibul Bashar	c Vaas b Fernando	18		c Muralitharan b Fernando	10
Nafis Iqbal	c Sangakkara b Fernando	5	(1)	c Sangakkara b Fernando	30
Mohammad Ashraful	c Atapattu b Fernando	42		c Samaraweera b Vaas	26
Aftab Ahmed	c Sangakkara b Fernando	23	(7)	c Samaraweera b Herath	25
†Khaled Masud	st Sangakkara b Muralitharan	26	(8)	lbw b Muralitharan	18
Mohammad Rafique	c Dilshan b Muralitharan	6	(9)	b Herath	9
Syed Rasel	c Vaas b Muralitharan	5	(10)	c Jayasuriya b Herath	1
Shahadat Hossain	c Sangakkara b Malinga	7	(6)	b Vaas	1
Enamul Haque II	not out	2		not out	1
Extras	(B 8, LB 9, W 1, NB 16)	34		(B 7, LB 3, NB 6)	16
Total		**191**			**197**

BANGLADESH	O	M	R	W		O	M	R	W
Syed Rasel	21.3	4	129	4					
Shahadat Hossain	20	3	108	4					
Aftab Ahmed	8	2	33	1					
Mohammad Rafique	23	1	92	0					
Enamul Haque II	18	2	70	0					
Mohammad Ashraful	2	0	11	0					

SRI LANKA	O	M	R	W		O	M	R	W
Vaas	10	0	31	0		13	1	36	3
Malinga	9	1	32	2		7	0	31	0
Fernando	11	2	60	5		10	0	35	2
Muralitharan	14.4	2	47	3	(5)	14	6	28	2
Herath	1	0	4	0	(4)	15.4	3	52	3
Dilshan						1	0	5	0

FALL OF WICKETS

	SL	B	B
Wkt	1st	1st	2nd
1st	28	16	22
2nd	28	46	44
3rd	33	52	56
4th	48	72	131
5th	328	115	136
6th	397	135	139
7th	400	143	172
8th	453	157	194
9th	457	166	196
10th	–	191	197

Umpires: B.F.Bowden (*New Zealand*) (31) and S.A.Bucknor (*West Indies*) (106).
Referee: C.H.Lloyd (*West Indies*) (48).   **Test No. 1765/5 (SL387/B40)**

ZIMBABWE v INDIA (1st Test)

At Queens Sports Club, Bulawayo, on 13, 14, 15, 16 September 2005.
Toss: Zimbabwe. Result: **INDIA** won by an innings and 90 runs.
Debuts: Zimbabwe – C.K.Coventry, T.Duffin.

ZIMBABWE

B.R.M.Taylor	c Gambhir b Khan	13		lbw b Pathan		4
T.Duffin	lbw b Pathan	56		b Khan		2
H.Masakadza	c Karthik b Khan	14		c Kumble b Pathan		2
D.D.Ebrahim	c and b Pathan	24		b Pathan		1
*†T.Taibu	not out	71		c Karthik b Kumble		52
H.H.Streak	c Dravid b Kumble	27		lbw b Pathan		0
C.K.Coventry	lbw b Kumble	2		c Gambhir b Harbhajan		24
A.M.Blignaut	lbw b Khan	4		b Harbhajan		26
K.M.Dabengwa	c Laxman b Pathan	35		lbw b Harbhajan		16
G.M.Ewing	lbw b Pathan	0		lbw b Harbhajan		34
N.B.Mahwire	b Pathan	4		not out		13
Extras	(B 1, LB 7, W 1, NB 20)	29		(B 2, W 2, NB 7)		11
Total		**279**				**185**

INDIA

G.Gambhir	c Taylor b Mahwire	46
V.Sehwag	b Mahwire	44
R.Dravid	c Taylor b Mahwire	77
V.V.S.Laxman	run out	140
*S.C.Ganguly	c Duffin b Ewing	101
Yuvraj Singh	b Dabengwa	12
†K.D.Karthik	c Taibu b Blignaut	1
I.K.Pathan	c and b Dabengwa	52
A.Kumble	c Coventry b Dabengwa	17
Harbhajan Singh	c Coventry b Mahwire	37
Z.Khan	not out	13
Extras	(LB 7, W 3, NB 4)	14
Total		**554**

INDIA	O	M	R	W		O	M	R	W
Pathan	18.5	3	58	5		12	4	53	4
Khan	22	5	74	3		8	1	28	1
Ganguly	1	1	0	0					
Kumble	26	7	71	2		12	2	43	1
Harbhajan Singh	26	5	55	0	(3)	15.5	1	59	4
Sehwag	5	1	13	0					

ZIMBABWE	O	M	R	W
Streak	26	3	91	0
Mahwire	25.3	4	92	4
Blignaut	19	2	96	1
Dabengwa	39	7	127	3
Ewing	42	5	141	1

FALL OF WICKETS

	Z	I	Z
Wkt	1st	1st	2nd
1st	25	88	4
2nd	45	98	9
3rd	119	228	9
4th	124	356	16
5th	193	372	18
6th	197	379	67
7th	210	476	110
8th	269	502	130
9th	269	522	138
10th	279	554	185

Umpires: Alim Dar (*Pakistan*) (23) and D.J.Harper (*Australia*) (52).
Referee: M.J.Procter (*South Africa*) (33).   **Test No. 1766/10 (I388/Z82)**

ZIMBABWE v INDIA (2nd Test)

At Harare Sports Club on 20, 21, 22 September 2005.
Toss: India. Result: **INDIA** won by 10 wickets.
Debuts: Zimbabwe – W.Mwayenga.

ZIMBABWE

B.R.M.Taylor	c Dravid b Pathan	4		lbw b Pathan	4
T.Duffin	c Laxman b Pathan	12		c Dravid b Pathan	10
D.D.Ebrahim	c Karthik b Khan	14		c Yuvraj b Khan	3
*†T.Taibu	c Karthik b Pathan	0	(5)	c Kumble b Khan	1
H.Masakadza	lbw b Pathan	27	(4)	lbw b Pathan	71
H.H.Streak	c Gambhir b Harbhajan	14		c Laxman b Khan	8
C.K.Coventry	c Dravid b Harbhajan	37		c Ganguly b Pathan	25
A.M.Blignaut	c Karthik b Pathan	13		not out	84
K.M.Dabengwa	c Laxman b Pathan	18		c Karthik b Pathan	0
N.B.Mahwire	lbw b Pathan	1		lbw b Kumble	0
W.Mwayenga	not out	14		lbw b Khan	1
Extras	(B 1, LB 3, W 1, NB 2)	7		(B 5, LB 6, W 2, NB 3)	16
Total		**161**			**223**

INDIA

G.Ghambir	c Taibu b Mahwire	97		not out	1
V.Sehwag	c Taibu b Streak	44		not out	14
R.Dravid	b Mahwire	98			
V.V.S.Laxman	lbw b Streak	8			
*S.C.Ganguly	c Taibu b Mwayenga	16			
Yuvraj Singh	b Streak	25			
†K.D.Karthik	b Streak	1			
I.K.Pathan	c Coventry b Streak	32			
A.Kumble	c Ebrahim b Streak	8			
Harbhajan Singh	not out	14			
Z.Khan	c Taibu b Blignaut	2			
Extras	(B 2, LB 11, NB 8)	21		(B 4)	4
Total		**366**		(0 wickets)	**19**

INDIA	O	M	R	W		O	M	R	W		FALL OF WICKETS			
Pathan	15.2	4	59	7		19	4	67	5			Z	I	Z	I
Khan	7	1	24	1		19	4	58	4		*Wkt*	*1st*	*1st*	*2nd*	*2nd*
Ganguly	4	2	10	0	(5)	1	0	8	0		1st	4	75	13	–
Kumble	7	1	19	0		11	3	52	1		2nd	31	198	18	–
Harbhajan Singh	11	3	45	2	(3)	5	0	27	0		3rd	31	219	18	–
											4th	31	245	21	–
ZIMBABWE											5th	75	306	42	–
Streak	32	10	73	6							6th	83	306	85	–
Mahwire	26	5	86	2		1	0	9	0		7th	122	318	201	–
Blignaut	19.3	1	80	1	(1)	1.2	0	6	0		8th	136	342	201	–
Mwayenga	21	6	79	1							9th	138	361	202	–
Dabengwa	9	1	35	0							10th	161	366	223	–

Umpires: Alim Dar (*Pakistan*) (24) and D.J.Harper (*Australia*) (53).
Referee: M.J.Procter (*South Africa*) (34).　　　　　　　　**Test No. 1767/11 (I389/Z83)**

AUSTRALIA v WEST INDIES (1st Test)

At Woolloongabba, Brisbane, on 3, 4, 5, 6 November 2005.
Toss: West Indies. Result: **AUSTRALIA** won by 379 runs.
Debuts: Australia – M.E.K.Hussey.

AUSTRALIA

M.L.Hayden	lbw b Collymore	37	(2) c Sarwan b Gayle	118
M.E.K.Hussey	c Ramdin b Powell	1	(1) c Collymore b Gayle	29
*R.T.Ponting	c Sarwan b Lawson	149	not out	104
M.J.Clarke	c Ramdin b Collymore	5	not out	14
S.M.Katich	c Gayle b Collymore	0		
†A.C.Gilchrist	lbw b Collymore	44		
S.R.Watson	lbw b Edwards	16		
S.K.Warne	c Ramdin b Powell	47		
B.Lee	c Collymore b Powell	47		
N.W.Bracken	c Sarwan b Edwards	37		
G.D.McGrath	not out	6		
Extras	(B 5, LB 13, W 6, NB 22)	46	(B 6, LB 3, W 1, NB 8)	18
Total		**435**	(2 wickets declared)	**283**

WEST INDIES

C.H.Gayle	c Gilchrist b McGrath	10	c Warne b Watson	33
D.S.Smith	b McGrath	88	c Warne b Lee	3
R.R.Sarwan	c Gilchrist b McGrath	21	c Gilchrist b Lee	31
B.C.Lara	lbw b Lee	30	c Hayden b Bracken	14
*S.Chanderpaul	c Bracken b Warne	2	lbw b Bracken	7
M.N.Samuels	c Gilchrist b McGrath	5	not out	17
†D.Ramdin	not out	37	c Gilchrist b Lee	6
D.B.Powell	c Gilchrist b Warne	4	lbw b Bracken	0
F.H.Edwards	b Warne	2	b Bracken	0
C.D.Collymore	c Clarke b Warne	0	lbw b Lee	4
J.J.C.Lawson	lbw b Warne	0	b Lee	1
Extras	(LB 7, W 1, NB 3)	11	(LB 3, NB 10)	13
Total		**210**		**129**

AUSTRALIA	O	M	R	W		O	M	R	W		FALL OF WICKETS			
												A	WI	A	WI
Edwards	21.3	1	94	2		5	0	27	0						
Powell	20	1	100	3		5	1	24	0		Wkt	1st	1st	2nd	2nd
Collymore	26	4	72	4	(4)	11	0	56	0		1st	9	20	71	11
Lawson	14	0	73	1	(3)	6	0	47	0		2nd	101	74	258	53
Samuels	4	0	29	0	(6)	12	1	46	0		3rd	108	134	–	85
Gayle	20	3	49	0	(5)	27	4	74	2		4th	111	149	–	99
											5th	215	161	–	99
AUSTRALIA											6th	273	174	–	105
McGrath	22	3	72	4		11	3	22	0		7th	294	187	–	106
Lee	15	4	59	1		14	4	30	5		8th	369	204	–	106
Bracken	10	4	23	0	(4)	16	3	48	4		9th	417	210	–	114
Warne	28	9	48	5	(5)	2	1	1	0		10th	435	210	–	129
Clarke	2	1	1	0											
Watson					(3)	6	0	25	1						

Umpires: I.L.Howell (*South Africa*) (3) and R.E.Koertzen (*South Africa*) (66).
Referee: M.J.Procter (*South Africa*) (35).

Test No. 1768/100 (A671/WI424)

AUSTRALIA v WEST INDIES (2nd Test)

At Bellerive Oval, Hobart, on 17, 18, 19, 20, 21 November 2005.
Toss: West Indies. Result: **AUSTRALIA** won by nine wickets.
Debuts: Australia – B.J.Hodge.

WEST INDIES

C.H.Gayle	lbw b McGrath	56	b McGrath		4
D.S.Smith	b Lee	4	c Ponting b McGrath		8
R.R.Sarwan	c Gilchrist b McGrath	2	c Gilchrist b Lee		32
B.C.Lara	lbw b Lee	13	c Gilchrist b Warne		45
*S.Chanderpaul	c Hodge b MacGill	39	c Gilchrist b Lee		10
M.N.Samuels	c Gilchrist b McGrath	5	c Hodge b Warne		29
D.J.J.Bravo	c Hodge b MacGill	3	b Warne		113
†D.Ramdin	c Warne b MacGill	2	c Warne b MacGill		71
D.B.Powell	c Gilchrist b Lee	15	lbw b MacGill		0
F.H.Edwards	c Symonds b McGrath	0	not out		2
C.D.Collymore	not out	3	c Gilchrist b Warne		0
Extras	(LB 3, W 1, NB 3)	7	(B 4, LB 12, W 1, NB 3)		20
Total		**149**			**334**

AUSTRALIA

M.L.Hayden	c Bravo b Collymore	110	(2) c Smith b Gayle		46
M.E.K.Hussey	c Sarwan b Bravo	137	(1) not out		31
*R.T.Ponting	b Edwards	17	not out		0
M.J.Clarke	c sub (D.R.Smith) b Edwards	5			
B.J.Hodge	lbw b Collymore	60			
A.Symonds	run out	1			
†A.C.Gilchrist	c sub (D.R.Smith) b Bravo	2			
S.K.Warne	c Sarwan b Powell	1			
B.Lee	c Ramdin b Edwards	18			
S.C.G.MacGill	not out	20			
G.D.McGrath	run out	14			
Extras	(LB 6, W 3, NB 12)	21	(NB 1)		1
Total		**406**	(1 wicket)		**78**

AUSTRALIA	O	M	R	W	O	M	R	W
McGrath	23	9	31	4	25	13	29	2
Lee	13.3	6	32	3	27	4	99	2
Symonds	10	4	17	0	5	1	9	0
Warne	11	2	48	0	39	4	112	4
MacGill	11	3	18	3	24	4	69	2

WEST INDIES	O	M	R	W	O	M	R	W
Edwards	27.4	2	116	3	5	1	16	0
Powell	24	2	117	1	7	1	21	0
Collymore	28	11	54	2				
Bravo	23	2	96	2	(3) 7	1	21	0
Gayle	7	0	17	0	(4) 6	2	16	1
Sarwan					(5) 1.1	0	4	0

FALL OF WICKETS

	WI	A	WI	A
Wkt	1st	1st	2nd	2nd
1st	15	231	4	77
2nd	26	257	27	–
3rd	60	271	62	–
4th	119	306	76	–
5th	119	315	133	–
6th	124	317	140	–
7th	126	324	322	–
8th	130	362	326	–
9th	141	377	332	–
10th	149	406	334	–

Umpires: Alim Dar (*Pakistan*) (25) and R.E.Koertzen (*South Africa*) (67).
Referee: M.J.Procter (*South Africa*) (36).   Test No. 1769/101 (A672/WI425)

AUSTRALIA v WEST INDIES (3rd Test)

At Adelaide Oval on 25, 26, 27, 28, 29 November 2005.
Toss: West Indies. Result: **AUSTRALIA** won by seven wickets.
Debuts: None.

WEST INDIES

W.W.Hinds	c Hayden b Lee	10		st Gilchrist b Warne		15
D.S.Smith	c Hayden b Lee	7		c Ponting b Lee		0
R.R.Sarwan	c Symonds b Lee	16		lbw b Lee		62
B.C.Lara	b McGrath	226	(5)	c Hayden b Warne		17
*S.Chanderpaul	c Gilchrist b Symonds	25	(6)	c Hodge b Warne		4
D.J.J.Bravo	c Ponting b MacGill	34	(7)	b Lee		64
D.R.Smith	c Symonds b MacGill	14	(8)	lbw b Warne		0
†D.Ramdin	lbw b McGrath	27	(9)	c Gilchrist b Warne		28
D.B.Powell	lbw b McGrath	14	(4)	b Warne		2
F.H.Edwards	c Hayden b Warne	10		c Warne b Lee		9
C.D.Collymore	not out	5		not out		1
Extras	(B 2, LB 5, W 1, NB 9)	17		(LB 2)		2
Total		**405**				**204**

AUSTRALIA

J.L.Langer	c Ramdin b Edwards	99		c D.R.Smith b Collymore	20
M.L.Hayden	c Chanderpaul b Bravo	47		not out	87
*R.T.Ponting	lbw b Bravo	56		c Sarwan b Collymore	3
B.J.Hodge	lbw b Edwards	18		c D.R.Smith b Powell	23
M.E.K.Hussey	not out	133		not out	30
A.Symonds	b Bravo	9			
†A.C.Gilchrist	c Chanderpaul b Bravo	6			
S.K.Warne	c and b Bravo	0			
B.Lee	c Ramdin b Bravo	9			
S.C.G.MacGill	b Edwards	22			
G.D.McGrath	b D.R.Smith	5			
Extras	(LB 7, W 2, NB 15)	24		(LB 3, W 1, NB 15)	19
Total		**428**		**(3 wickets)**	**182**

AUSTRALIA	O	M	R	W	O	M	R	W		FALL OF WICKETS			
											WI	A	WI	A
McGrath	30	3	106	3	18	8	25	0			1st	1st	2nd	2nd
Lee	28	3	111	3	17	5	46	4		Wkt				
Symonds	16	5	44	1	2	0	9	0		1st	16	97	2	51
Warne	19.2	2	77	1	33	9	80	6		2nd	19	211	60	55
MacGill	18	3	60	2	11	2	42	0		3rd	53	228	72	110
										4th	121	238	96	
WEST INDIES										5th	237	271	96	
Edwards	23	4	114	3	11	1	52	0		6th	263	277	106	
Powell	24	6	80	0	14	2	40	1		7th	333	277	106	
Collymore	23	1	59	0	20	6	51	2		8th	381	295	160	
Bravo	27	7	84	6						9th	388	388	203	
D.R.Smith	17.3	3	59	1	1	0	1	0		10th	405	428	204	
Hinds	9	1	25	0										
Sarwan					(4)	12	2	35	0					

Umpires: Alim Dar (*Pakistan*) (26) and B.F.Bowden (*New Zealand*) (33).
Referee: M.J.Procter (*South Africa*) (37). **Test No. 1770/102 (A673/WI426)**

AUSTRALIA v WEST INDIES 2005-06

AUSTRALIA – BATTING AND FIELDING

	M	I	NO	HS	Runs	Avge	100	50	Ct/St
M.E.K.Hussey	3	6	3	137	361	120.33	1	–	–
M.L.Hayden	3	6	1	118	445	89.00	2	1	5
R.T.Ponting	3	6	2	149	329	82.25	2	1	3
S.C.G.MacGill	2	2	1	22	42	42.00	–	–	–
B.J.Hodge	2	3	–	60	101	33.66	–	1	4
B.Lee	3	3	–	47	74	24.66	–	–	–
A.C.Gilchrist	3	3	–	44	52	17.33	–	–	15/1
S.K.Warne	3	3	–	47	48	16.00	–	–	5
G.D.McGrath	3	3	1	14	25	12.50	–	–	–
M.J.Clarke	2	3	1	14*	24	12.00	–	–	1
A.Symonds	2	2	–	9	10	5.00	–	–	3

Played in one Test: N.W.Bracken 37 (1 ct); S.M.Katich 0; J.L.Langer 99, 20; S.R.Watson 16.

AUSTRALIA – BOWLING

	O	M	R	W	Avge	Best	5wI	10wM
N.W.Bracken	26	7	71	4	17.75	4-48	–	–
B.Lee	114.3	26	377	18	20.94	5-30	1	–
G.D.McGrath	129	39	285	13	21.92	4-31	–	–
S.K.Warne	132.2	27	366	16	22.87	6-80	2	–
S.C.G.MacGill	66	12	189	7	27.00	3-18	–	–
A.Symonds	33	10	79	1	79.00	1-44	–	–

Also bowled: M.J.Clarke 2-1-1-0; S.R.Watson 6-0-25-1.

WEST INDIES – BATTING AND FIELDING

	M	I	NO	HS	Runs	Avge	100	50	Ct/St
B.C.Lara	3	6	–	226	345	57.50	1	–	–
D.J.J.Bravo	2	4	–	113	214	53.50	1	1	2
D.Ramdin	3	6	1	71	171	34.20	–	1	6
R.R.Sarwan	3	6	–	62	164	27.33	–	1	6
C.H.Gayle	2	4	–	56	103	25.75	–	1	1
M.N.Samuels	2	4	1	29	56	18.66	–	–	–
D.S.Smith	3	6	–	88	110	18.33	–	1	1
S.Chanderpaul	3	6	–	39	87	14.50	–	–	2
D.B.Powell	3	6	–	15	35	5.83	–	–	–
F.H.Edwards	3	6	1	10	23	4.60	–	–	–
C.D.Collymore	3	6	3	5*	13	4.33	–	–	2

Played in one Test: W.W.Hinds 10, 15; J.J.C.Lawson 0, 1; D.R.Smith 14, 0 (2 ct).

WEST INDIES – BOWLING

	O	M	R	W	Avge	Best	5wI	10wM
D.J.J.Bravo	57	10	201	8	25.12	6- 84	1	–
C.D.Collymore	108	22	292	8	36.50	4- 72	–	–
C.H.Gayle	60	9	156	3	52.00	2- 74	–	–
F.H.Edwards	93.1	9	419	8	52.37	3-114	–	–
D.B.Powell	94	13	382	5	76.40	3-100	–	–

Also bowled: W.W.Hinds 9-1-25-0; J.J.C.Lawson 20-0-120-1; M.N.Samuels 16-1-75-0; R.R.Sarwan 13.1-2-39-0; D.R.Smith 18.3-3-60-1.

288

PAKISTAN v ENGLAND (1st Test)

At Multan Cricket Stadium on 12, 13, 14, 15, 16 November 2005.
Toss: Pakistan. Result: **PAKISTAN** won by 22 runs.
Debuts: England – S.D.Udal.

PAKISTAN

Shoaib Malik	lbw b Flintoff	39	c Trescothick b Harmison	18
Salman Butt	c Jones b Udal	74	c Jones b Hoggard	122
Younis Khan	lbw b Harmison	39	c Trescothick b Flintoff	48
M.Yousuf Youhana	b Flintoff	5	(6) c Bell b Flintoff	16
*Inzamam-ul-Haq	c Strauss b Flintoff	53	lbw b Hoggard	72
Hasan Raza	b Harmison	0	(7) c Trescothick b Flintoff	1
†Kamran Akmal	c Trescothick b Hoggard	28	(8) c Pietersen b Harmison	33
Mohammad Sami	c Jones b Hoggard	1	(4) c Jones b Flintoff	3
Shoaib Akhtar	not out	10	c Bell b Giles	11
Shabbir Ahmed	b Flintoff	0	c Jones b Harmison	0
Danish Kaneria	c Giles b Harmison	6	not out	1
Extras	(B 1, LB 7, NB 11)	19	(LB 6, NB 10)	16
Total		**274**		**341**

ENGLAND

*M.E.Trescothick	c Akmal b Shabbir	193	b Shabbir	5
A.J.Strauss	lbw b Sami	9	c Raza b Kaneria	23
I.R.Bell	c Butt b Malik	71	c Akmal b Kaneria	31
P.D.Collingwood	c Akmal b Shabbir	10	lbw b Sami	3
M.J.Hoggard	c Akmal b Akhtar	1	(10) not out	0
K.P.Pietersen	c Butt b Kaneria	5	(5) c Akmal b Sami	0
A.Flintoff	c Malik b Akhtar	45	(6) c Younis b Kaneria	11
†G.O.Jones	b Shabbir	22	(7) b Akhtar	33
A.F.Giles	c Raza b Shabbir	16	(8) b Akhtar	14
S.D.Udal	lbw b Akhtar	0	(9) b Kaneria	18
S.J.Harmison	not out	4	c Younis b Akhtar	9
Extras	(B 8, LB 11, W 1, NB 22)	42	(B 6, LB 1, NB 2)	9
Total		**418**		**175**

ENGLAND	O	M	R	W	O	M	R	W			FALL OF WICKETS			
												P	E	P	E
Hoggard	22	4	55	2	27	2	81	2		Wkt	1st	1st	2nd	2nd
Harmison	16.2	5	37	3	(3) 19.5	3	52	3		1st	80	18	31	7
Flintoff	23	6	68	4	(2) 25	3	88	4		2nd	161	198	124	64
Collingwood	4	1	15	0						3rd	166	251	131	67
Giles	16	3	44	0	22	2	67	1		4th	181	266	266	67
Udal	17	3	47	1	(4) 12	1	47	0		5th	183	271	285	93
										6th	238	364	291	101
PAKISTAN										7th	244	388	295	117
Shoaib Akhtar	27	2	99	3	12.4	1	49	3		8th	260	399	331	166
Mohammad Sami	16	1	76	1	(4) 9	0	31	2		9th	260	400	332	166
Shabbir Ahmed	22.4	7	54	4	(2) 10	0	25	1		10th	274	418	341	175
Danish Kaneria	27	4	106	1	(3) 20	0	62	4						
Shoaib Malik	18	1	64	1	1	0	1	0						

Umpires: B.F.Bowden (*New Zealand*) (32) and S.J.A.Taufel (*Australia*) (27).
Referee: R.S.Mahanama (*Sri Lanka*) (5).   Test No. 1771/61 (P313/E840)

PAKISTAN v ENGLAND (2nd Test)

At Iqbal Stadium, Faisalabad, on 20, 21, 22, 23, 24 November 2005.
Toss: Pakistan. Result: **MATCH DRAWN**.
Debuts: None.

PAKISTAN

Shoaib Malik	c Flintoff b Hoggard	27	c Bell b Flintoff		26
Salman Butt	c Jones b Harmison	26	lbw b Udal		50
Younis Khan	c Pietersen b Flintoff	7	lbw b Hoggard		27
M.Yousuf Youhana	c and b Bell	78	b Flintoff		20
*Inzamam-ul-Haq	run out	109	not out		100
Shahid Afridi	c Trescothick b Hoggard	92	b Flintoff		0
†Kamran Akmal	c Jones b Giles	41	c Jones b Harmison		9
Naved-ul-Hasan	b Harmison	25	c Jones b Harmison		1
Mohammad Sami	c and b Giles	18	(10) lbw b Hoggard		5
Shoaib Akhtar	c Flintoff b Harmison	12	(9) c Jones b Hoggard		14
Danish Kaneria	not out	4	not out		2
Extras	(B 5, LB 3, NB 15)	23	(B 4, LB 5, W 2, NB 3)		14
Total		**462**	(9 wickets declared)		**268**

ENGLAND

M.E.Trescothick	c Akmal b Sami	48	b Akhtar		0
A.J.Strauss	b Naved	12	b Naved		0
*M.P.Vaughan	b Naved	2	lbw b Naved		9
I.R.Bell	c Akmal b Afridi	115	c Akmal b Akhtar		0
K.P.Pietersen	c Yousuf b Akhtar	100	c sub (Asim Kamal) b Naved		42
A.Flintoff	b Akhtar	1	c sub (Hasan Raza) b Akhtar		56
†G.O.Jones	lbw b Afridi	55	not out		30
A.F.Giles	b Afridi	26	not out		13
S.D.Udal	not out	33			
M.J.Hoggard	b Afridi	2			
S.J.Harmison	run out	16			
Extras	(B 1, LB 12, W 1, NB 22)	36	(B 4, LB 8, NB 2)		14
Total		**446**	(6 wickets)		**164**

ENGLAND	O	M	R	W		O	M	R	W		FALL OF WICKETS				
Hoggard	22	0	115	2		16	1	50	3			P	E	P	E
Flintoff	29	2	76	1		27.1	2	66	3		Wkt	1st	1st	2nd	2nd
Giles	20	1	85	2	(4)	17	3	51	0		1st	53	33	54	1
Harmison	24.4	5	85	3	(3)	19	2	61	2		2nd	63	39	104	5
Udal	13	1	60	0		14	2	31	1		3rd	73	107	108	10
Bell	7	1	33	1							4th	201	261	164	20
											5th	346	272	164	100
PAKISTAN											6th	369	327	183	138
Shoaib Akhtar	27	4	93	2		11	2	61	3		7th	403	378	187	—
Naved-ul-Hasan	20	2	63	2		12	3	30	3		8th	431	395	234	—
Mohammad Sami	19	4	51	1		6	1	18	0		9th	446	399	244	—
Shahid Afridi	30.3	3	95	4	(5)	7	2	16	0		10th	462	446	—	—
Danish Kaneria	32	3	102	0	(4)	12	4	27	0						
Shoaib Malik	4	0	29	0											

Umpires: D.B.Hair (*Australia*) (67) and S.J.A.Taufel (*Australia*) (28).
Referee: R.S.Mahanama (*Sri Lanka*) (6).   **Test No. 1772/62 (P314/E841)**

PAKISTAN v ENGLAND (3rd Test)

At Gaddafi Stadium, Lahore, on 29, 30 November, 1, 2, 3 December 2005.
Toss: England. Result: **PAKISTAN** won by an innings and 100 runs.
Debuts: England – L.E.Plunkett.

ENGLAND

M.E.Trescothick	c Akmal b Malik	50	lbw b Akhtar		0
*M.P.Vaughan	c Yousuf b Malik	58	c and b Akhtar		13
I.R.Bell	c Yousuf b Malik	4	lbw b Akhtar		92
P.D.Collingwood	c Kaneria b Akhtar	96	c Raza b Kaneria		80
K.P.Pietersen	c Akmal b Naved	34	c Raza b Kaneria		1
A.Flintoff	c Akhtar b Naved	12	b Kaneria		0
†G.O.Jones	b Kaneria	4	lbw b Akhtar		5
S.D.Udal	c Kamal b Kaneria	10	c Butt b Sami		25
L.E.Plunkett	b Sami	9	lbw b Akhtar		0
M.J.Hoggard	not out	1	b Kaneria		0
S.J.Harmison	c Akmal b Sami	0	not out		0
Extras	(LB 5, NB 5)	10	(B 13, LB 9, W 1, NB 9)		32
Total		**288**			**248**

PAKISTAN

Shoaib Malik	c Plunkett b Hoggard	0
Salman Butt	c Jones b Plunkett	28
Asim Kamal	lbw b Hoggard	5
M.Yousuf Youhana	c Pietersen b Udal	223
*Inzamam-ul-Haq	run out	97
Hasan Raza	c Flintoff b Harmison	21
Shoaib Akhtar	c Udal b Plunkett	38
†Kamran Akmal	c Vaughan b Flintoff	154
Naved-ul-Hasan	not out	42
Mohammad Sami		
Danish Kaneria		
Extras	(B 5, LB 12, W 4, NB 7)	28
Total	(8 wickets declared)	**636**

PAKISTAN	O	M	R	W	O	M	R	W	FALL OF WICKETS			
Shoaib Akhtar	22	6	45	1	19	3	71	5		E	P	E
Naved-ul-Hasan	20	3	76	2	16	3	55	0	Wkt	1st	1st	2nd
Mohammad Sami	18	2	57	2	16	4	39	1	1st	101	0	
Shoaib Malik	14	1	58	3	4	2	9	0	2nd	114	12	30
Danish Kaneria	20	2	47	2	22.1	8	52	4	3rd	115	68	205
									4th	183	180	212
ENGLAND									5th	201	247	212
Hoggard	23	4	106	2					6th	225	516	212
Flintoff	36	8	111	1					7th	249	546	227
Harmison	43	3	154	1					8th	280	636	227
Plunkett	28.2	1	125	2					9th	288	–	248
Udal	18	1	92	1					10th	288	–	248
Collingwood	6	0	22	0								
Bell	2	0	9	0								

Umpires: D.B.Hair (*Australia*) (68) and R.E.Koertzen (*South Africa*) (68).
Referee: R.S.Mahanama (*Sri Lanka*) (7). **Test No. 1773/63 (P315/E842)**

PAKISTAN v ENGLAND 2005-06

PAKISTAN – BATTING AND FIELDING

	M	I	NO	HS	Runs	Avge	100	50	Ct/St
Inzamam-ul-Haq	3	5	1	109	431	107.75	2	3	–
Mohd Yousuf Youhana	3	5	–	223	342	68.40	1	1	3
Salman Butt	3	5	–	122	300	60.00	1	2	3
Kamran Akmal	3	5	–	154	265	53.00	1	–	11
Naved-ul-Hasan	2	3	1	42*	68	34.00	–	–	–
Younis Khan	2	4	–	48	121	30.25	–	–	2
Shoaib Malik	3	5	–	39	110	22.00	–	–	1
Shoaib Akhtar	3	5	1	38	85	21.25	–	–	2
Danish Kaneria	3	4	3	6	13	13.00	–	–	1
Hasan Raza	2	3	–	21	22	7.33	–	–	4
Mohammad Sami	3	4	–	18	27	6.75	–	–	–

Played in one Test: Asim Kamal 5 (1 ct); Shabbir Ahmed 0, 0; Shahid Afridi 92, 0.

PAKISTAN – BOWLING

	O	M	R	W	Avge	Best	5wI	10wM
Shabbir Ahmed	32.4	7	79	5	15.80	4-54	–	–
Shoaib Akhtar	118.4	18	418	17	24.58	5-71	1	–
Shahid Afridi	37.3	5	111	4	27.75	4-95	–	–
Naved-ul-Hasan	68	11	224	7	32.00	3-30	–	–
Danish Kaneria	133.1	21	396	11	36.00	4-52	–	–
Mohammad Sami	84	12	272	7	38.85	2-31	–	–
Shoaib Malik	41	4	161	4	40.25	3-58	–	–

ENGLAND – BATTING AND FIELDING

	M	I	NO	HS	Runs	Avge	100	50	Ct/St
I.R.Bell	3	6	–	115	313	52.16	1	2	4
M.E.Trescothick	3	6	–	193	296	49.33	1	1	5
P.D.Collingwood	2	4	–	96	189	47.25	–	2	–
K.P.Pietersen	3	6	–	100	201	33.50	1	–	3
G.O.Jones	3	6	1	55	149	29.80	–	1	11
A.F.Giles	2	4	1	26	69	23.00	–	–	2
S.D.Udal	3	5	1	33*	86	21.50	–	–	1
A.Flintoff	3	6	–	56	125	20.83	–	1	3
M.P.Vaughan	2	4	–	58	82	20.50	–	1	1
A.J.Strauss	2	4	–	23	44	11.00	–	–	1
S.J.Harmison	3	5	2	16	29	9.66	–	–	–
M.J.Hoggard	3	5	2	2	4	1.33	–	–	–

Played in one Test: L.E.Plunkett 9, 0 (1 ct).

ENGLAND – BOWLING

	O	M	R	W	Avge	Best	5wI	10wM
A.Flintoff	140.1	21	409	13	31.46	4- 68	–	–
S.J.Harmison	122.5	18	389	12	32.41	3- 37	–	–
M.J.Hoggard	110	11	407	11	37.00	3- 50	–	–
L.E.Plunkett	28.2	1	125	2	62.50	2-125	–	–
A.F.Giles	75	9	247	3	82.33	2- 85	–	–
S.D.Udal	74	8	277	3	92.33	1- 31	–	–

Also bowled: I.R.Bell 9-1-42-1; P.D.Collingwood 10-1-37-0.

INDIA v SRI LANKA (1st Test)

At M.A. Chidambaram Stadium, Chepauk, Madras, on 2, 3, 4, 5, 6 December 2005.
Toss: India. Result: **MATCH DRAWN.**
Debuts: India – M.S.Dhoni.

INDIA

G.Gambhir	b Vaas	0
V.Sehwag	c Atapattu b Vaas	36
*R.Dravid	c Sangakkara b Vaas	32
S.R.Tendulkar	lbw b Muralitharan	22
V.V.S.Laxman	run out	5
S.C.Ganguly	c Dilshan b Fernando	5
†M.S.Dhoni	c Gunawardena b Bandara	30
I.K.Pathan	c and b Muralitharan	0
A.B.Agarkar	run out	4
A.Kumble	c and b Vaas	9
Harbhajan Singh	not out	4
Extras	(B 12, LB 2, NB 6)	20
Total		**167**

SRI LANKA

D.A.Gunawardena	c Dhoni b Pathan	4
†K.C.Sangakkara	lbw b Kumble	30
D.P.M.deS Jayawardena	c Gambhir b Kumble	71
T.T.Samaraweera	not out	35
*M.S.Atapattu	b Kumble	7
T.M.Dilshan	not out	8
W.P.U.C.J.Vaas		
C.M.Bandara		
C.R.D.Fernando		
M.Muralitharan		
J.Mubarak		
Extras	(W 1, NB 7, Pen 5)	13
Total	(4 wickets)	**168**

SRI LANKA	O	M	R	W
Vaas	21	14	20	4
Fernando	16	4	58	1
Muralitharan	25	6	60	2
Bandara	11.2	6	15	1

INDIA	O	M	R	W
Pathan	7	0	43	1
Agarkar	10	3	29	0
Ganguly	2	0	16	0
Harbhajan Singh	9	2	34	0
Kumble	15	3	41	3

FALL OF WICKETS		
	I	SL
Wkt	1st	1st
1st	13	5
2nd	45	62
3rd	97	124
4th	108	158
5th	109	–
6th	117	–
7th	118	–
8th	128	–
9th	159	–
10th	167	–

Umpires: M.R.Benson (*England*) (6) and D.J.Harper (*Australia*) (54).
Referee: C.H.Lloyd (*West Indies*) (49).   **Test No. 1774/24 (I390/SL152)**

INDIA v SRI LANKA (2nd Test)

At Feroz Shah Kotla, Delhi, on 10, 11, 12, 13, 14 December 2005.
Toss: India. Result: **INDIA** won by 188 runs.
Debuts: None.

INDIA

G.Ghambir	lbw b Vaas	2		lbw b Vaas	3
*R Dravid	c Mubarak b Muralitharan	24	(5)	run out	53
V.V.S.Laxman	c Sangakkara b Muralitharan	69		c Sangakkara b Vaas	11
S.R.Tendulkar	lbw b Muralitharan	109		lbw b Bandara	16
S.C.Ganguly	lbw b Muralitharan	40	(6)	b Muralitharan	39
Yuvraj Singh	c Mubarak b Bandara	0	(7)	not out	77
†M.S.Dhoni	b Muralitharan	5	(8)	not out	51
I.K.Pathan	c Mubarak b Muralitharan	0	(2)	c Sangakkara b Fernando	93
A.B.Agarkar	not out	14			
A.Kumble	b Bandara	8			
Harbhajan Singh	b Muralitharan	7			
Extras	(B 4, LB 8)	12		(B 9, LB 16, NB 7)	32
Total		**290**		(6 wickets declared)	**375**

SRI LANKA

D.A.Gunawardena	lbw b Pathan	25		lbw b Pathan	9
*M.S.Atapattu	c Gambhir b Kumble	88		c and b Kumble	67
†K.C.Sangakkara	c Kumble b Pathan	3		c Dhoni b Agarkar	33
D.P.M.deS.Jayawardena	lbw b Kumble	60		c Gambhir b Harbhajan	67
T.T.Samaraweera	b Kumble	1	(6)	c Dravid b Harbhajan	0
T.M.Dilshan	lbw b Kumble	0	(8)	b Kumble	32
J.Mubarak	not out	29		lbw b Agarkar	3
W.P.U.C.J.Vaas	c Harbhajan b Kumble	2	(9)	c Harbhajan b Kumble	17
C.M.Bandara	b Pathan	1	(5)	lbw b Kumble	0
M.Muralitharan	b Kumble	9		c Dhoni b Harbhajan	2
C.R.D.Fernando	c Ganguly b Harbhajan	0		not out	2
Extras	(B 4, LB 2, NB 1, Pen 5)	12		(B 2, LB 7, NB 6)	15
Total		**230**			**247**

SRI LANKA	O	M	R	W		O	M	R	W	FALL OF WICKETS				
Vaas	22	5	77	1		21	4	65	2		I	SL	I	SL
Fernando	18	5	43	0	(3)	22	5	75	1	*Wkt*	*1st*	*1st*	*2nd*	*2nd*
Muralitharan	38.4	8	100	7	(2)	38	5	118	1	1st	2	54	12	30
Bandara	17	1	54	2		20	2	74	1	2nd	56	62	42	109
Dilshan	1	0	4	0		4	0	18	0	3rd	133	175	86	119
										4th	254	179	178	119
INDIA										5th	255	179	190	123
Pathan	22	8	34	3		14	2	38	1	6th	255	198	271	131
Agarkar	16	4	40	0		16	4	45	2	7th	255	200	–	199
Kumble	28	6	72	6		36	7	85	4	8th	260	204	–	243
Harbhajan	15.3	0	67	1		25.2	5	70	3	9th	271	219	–	243
Tendulkar	2	0	6	0						10th	290	230	–	247

Umpires: Nadeem Ghauri (*Pakistan*) (3) and S.J.A.Taufel (*Australia*) (29).
Referee: C.H.Lloyd (*West Indies*) (50). **Test No. 1775/25 (I391/SL153)**

INDIA v SRI LANKA (3rd Test)

At Gujarat Stadium, Motera, Ahmedabad, on 18, 19, 20, 21, 22 December 2005.
Toss: India. Result: **INDIA** won by 259 runs.
Debuts: Sri Lanka – W.U.Tharanga.

INDIA

G.Ghambir	c Tharanga b Malinga	19	(2) c Sangakkara b Muralitharan	30
*V.Sehwag	b Malinga	20	(1) c Maharoof b Malinga	0
V.V.S.Laxman	b Maharoof	104	c Sangakkara b Maharoof	5
S.R.Tendulkar	c Mubarak b Muralitharan	23	lbw b Dilshan	19
Yuvraj Singh	c Samaraweera b Muralitharan	0	c Sangakkara b Bandara	75
M.Kaif	c Atapattu b Bandara	4	lbw b Bandara	9
†M.S.Dhoni	lbw b Muralitharan	49	lbw b Muralitharan	14
I.K.Pathan	lbw b Maharoof	82	b Muralitharan	27
A.B.Agarkar	b Malinga	26	c and b Bandara	48
A.Kumble	c Jayawardena b Bandara	21	not out	29
Harbhajan Singh	not out	8	not out	40
Extras	(B 15, LB 13, W 5, NB 9)	42	(B 7, LB 9, W 1, NB 3)	20
Total		**398**	(9 wickets declared)	**316**

SRI LANKA

W.U.Tharanga	c Dhoni b Pathan	2	c Gambhir b Kumble	47
*M.S.Atapattu	c Sehwag b Harbhajan	40	c Kaif b Harbhajan	16
†K.C.Sangakkara	b Harbhajan	41	lbw b Kumble	17
D.P.M.deS.Jayawardena	c Kaif b Harbhajan	0	c and b Agarkar	57
T.T.Samaraweera	c Kaif b Harbhajan	1	c Kaif b Kumble	5
T.M.Dilshan	c Kaif b Harbhajan	65	c Dhoni b Pathan	65
J.Mubarak	b Kumble	13	c Laxman b Harbhajan	18
M.F.Maharoof	c and b Harbhajan	4	lbw b Kumble	2
C.M.Bandara	not out	28	c Sehwag b Kumble	11
M.Muralitharan	st Dhoni b Kumble	3	b Harbhajan	0
S.L.Malinga	c Sehwag b Harbhajan	0	not out	0
Extras	(B 1, LB 2, NB 6)	9	(B 1, NB 7)	8
Total		**206**		**249**

SRI LANKA	O	M	R	W		O	M	R	W		FALL OF WICKETS				
												I	SL	I	SL
Malinga	32	4	113	3		12	2	63	1		Wkt	1st	1st	2nd	2nd
Maharoof	27	11	52	2		6	0	25	1		1st	31	14	0	39
Muralitharan	36	4	128	3	(4)	21	5	90	3		2nd	52	74	9	84
Bandara	24.4	3	69	2	(5)	19	2	84	3		3rd	88	74	34	89
Dilshan	3	0	8	0	(3)	12	2	36	1		4th	88	82	81	96
Mubarak						1	0	2	0		5th	97	105	100	201
											6th	183	144	134	229
INDIA											7th	308	155	174	235
Pathan	10	1	36	1		9	1	31	1		8th	345	198	198	235
Agarkar	6	2	18	0	(3)	11	3	18	1		9th	384	201	247	245
Kumble	25	3	87	2	(4)	34.3	9	89	5		10th	398	206	–	249
Harbhajan	22.2	3	62	7	(2)	31	7	79	3						
Sehwag						3	0	18	0						
Tendulkar						4	0	13	0						

Umpires: B.F.Bowden (*New Zealand*) (34) and Nadeem Ghauri (*Pakistan*) (4).
Referee: C.H.Lloyd (*West Indies*) (51). **Test No. 1776/26 (I392/SL154)**

INDIA v SRI LANKA 2005-06

INDIA – BATTING AND FIELDING

	M	I	NO	HS	Runs	Avge	100	50	Ct/St
Harbhajan Singh	3	4	3	40*	59	59.00	–	–	3
Yuvraj Singh	2	4	1	77*	152	50.66	–	2	–
I.K.Pathan	3	5	–	93	202	40.40	–	2	–
V.V.S.Laxman	3	5	–	104	194	38.80	1	1	1
S.R.Tendulkar	3	5	–	109	189	37.80	1	–	–
M.S.Dhoni	3	5	1	51*	149	37.25	–	1	5/1
R.Dravid	2	3	–	53	109	36.33	–	1	1
A.B.Agarkar	3	4	1	48	92	30.66	–	–	1
S.C.Ganguly	2	3	–	40	84	28.00	–	–	1
A.Kumble	3	4	1	29*	67	22.33	–	–	2
V.Sehwag	2	3	–	36	56	18.66	–	–	3
G.Gambhir	3	5	–	30	54	10.80	–	–	4

Played in one Test: M.Kaif 4, 9 (5 ct).

INDIA – BOWLING

	O	M	R	W	Avge	Best	5wI	10wM
A.Kumble	138.3	28	374	20	18.70	6-72	2	1
Harbhajan Singh	103.1	17	312	14	22.28	7-62	1	1
I.K.Pathan	62	12	182	7	26.00	3-34	–	–
A.B.Agarkar	59	16	150	3	50.00	2-45	–	–

Also bowled: S.C.Ganguly 2-0-16-0; V.Sehwag 3-0-18-0; S.R.Tendulkar 6-0-19-0.

SRI LANKA – BATTING AND FIELDING

	M	I	NO	HS	Runs	Avge	100	50	Ct/St
D.P.M.deS.Jayawardena	3	5	–	71	255	51.00	–	4	1
M.S.Atapattu	3	5	–	88	218	43.60	–	2	2
T.M.Dilshan	3	5	1	65	170	42.50	–	2	1
K.C.Sangakkara	3	5	–	41	124	24.80	–	–	7
J.Mubarak	3	4	1	29*	63	21.00	–	–	4
C.M.Bandara	3	4	1	28*	40	13.33	–	–	1
D.A.Gunawardena	2	3	–	25	38	12.66	–	–	1
T.T.Samaraweera	3	5	1	35*	42	10.50	–	–	1
W.P.U.C.J.Vaas	2	2	–	17	19	9.50	–	–	1
M.Muralitharan	3	4	–	9	17	4.25	–	–	1
C.R.D.Fernando	2	2	1	2*	2	2.00	–	–	–

Played in one Test: M.F.Maharoof 4, 2 (1 ct); S.L.Malinga 0, 0*; W.U.Tharanga 2, 47 (1 ct).

SRI LANKA – BOWLING

	O	M	R	W	Avge	Best	5wI	10wM
W.P.U.C.J.Vaas	64	23	162	7	23.14	4- 20	–	–
M.F.Maharoof	33	11	77	3	25.66	2- 52	–	–
M.Muralitharan	158.4	28	496	16	31.00	7-100	1	–
C.M.Bandara	92	14	296	9	32.88	3- 84	–	–
S.L.Malinga	44	6	176	4	44.00	3-113	–	–
C.R.D.Fernando	56	14	176	2	88.00	1- 58	–	–

Also bowled: T.M.Dilshan 20-2-66-1; J.Mubarak 1-0-2-0.

AUSTRALIA v SOUTH AFRICA (1st Test)

At W.A.C.A. Ground, Perth, on 16, 17, 18, 19, 20 December 2005.
Toss: Australia. Result: **MATCH DRAWN.**
Debuts: None.

AUSTRALIA

J.L.Langer	c Smith b Ntini	37		b Pollock	47
M.L.Hayden	c Rudolph b Ntini	0		c Boucher b Langeveldt	20
*R.T.Ponting	lbw b Pollock	71	(4)	c Boucher b Ntini	53
B.J.Hodge	c Boucher b Ntini	41	(5)	not out	203
M.E.K.Hussey	c Langeveldt b Ntini	23	(6)	c Boucher b Pollock	58
A.Symonds	b Nel	13	(7)	c Gibbs b Langeveldt	25
†A.C.Gilchrist	c Gibbs b Ntini	6	(8)	c Rudolph b Nel	44
S.K.Warne	lbw b Langeveldt	24	(9)	lbw b Kemp	5
B.Lee	not out	19	(3)	lbw b Langeveldt	32
N.W.Bracken	c Boucher b Nel	10		not out	14
G.D.McGrath	c Boucher b Nel	14			
Extras	(B 4, LB 2, W 2, NB 6)	14		(B 5, LB 4, W 1, NB 17)	27
Total		**258**		**(8 wickets declared)**	**528**

SOUTH AFRICA

A.B.de Villiers	b Warne	68	(2)	c Hodge b Warne	12
*G.C.Smith	c Ponting b Bracken	34	(1)	lbw b Bracken	30
H.H.Gibbs	b Lee	21		c Warne b Lee	33
J.A.Rudolph	c Langer b Lee	8		not out	102
A.G.Prince	lbw b Warne	28		lbw b Warne	8
J.M.Kemp	c Hodge b McGrath	7		c Ponting b Warne	55
†M.V.Boucher	c Hayden b Warne	62		not out	13
S.M.Pollock	b Lee	34			
A.Nel	not out	4			
C.K.Langeveldt	lbw b Lee	0			
M.Ntini	c Hodge b Lee	12			
Extras	(B 4, LB 2, NB 12)	18		(B 18, LB 13, NB 3)	34
Total		**296**		**(5 wickets)**	**287**

SOUTH AFRICA	O	M	R	W		O	M	R	W		FALL OF WICKETS				
												A	SA	A	SA
Pollock	19	6	46	1		36	6	98	2	Wkt	1st	1st	2nd	2nd
Ntini	19	3	64	5		34	8	113	1	1st	0	83	37	35
Langeveldt	17	1	100	1		31	3	117	3	2nd	111	127	86	55
Nel	17.2	3	29	3		28	2	104	1	3rd	117	135	129	109
Kemp	3	0	13	0	(6)	11	0	58	1	4th	180	145	184	138
Rudolph					(5)	6.4	1	29	0	5th	185	167	316	250
										6th	199	187	377	–
AUSTRALIA										7th	210	264	444	–
McGrath	18	3	59	1		24	11	39	0	8th	243	282	451	–
Lee	22.2	1	93	5		31	9	83	1	9th	258	283	–	–
Bracken	12	3	46	1	(4)	19	5	37	1	10th	258	296	–	–
Warne	29	4	92	3	(3)	47	21	83	3					
Symonds						3	0	6	0					
Hodge						2	0	8	0					

Umpires: S.A.Bucknor (*West Indies*) (107) and B.R.Doctrove (*West Indies*) (5).
Referee: B.C.Broad (*England*) (15).   **Test No. 1777/72 (A674/SA304)**

AUSTRALIA v SOUTH AFRICA (2nd Test)

At Melbourne Cricket Ground on 26, 27, 28, 29, 30 December 2005.
Toss: Australia. Result: **AUSTRALIA** won by 184 runs.
Debuts: Australia – P.A.Jaques.

AUSTRALIA

P.A.Jaques	c Rudolph b Pollock	2	(2)	lbw b Nel	28
M.L.Hayden	c Smith b Pollock	65	(1)	c Boucher b Kallis	137
*R.T.Ponting	c Gibbs b Nel	117		lbw b Pollock	11
B.J.Hodge	c Smith b Pollock	7		c Boucher b Nel	24
M.E.K.Hussey	b Ntini	122		c Kallis b Smith	31
A.Symonds	c Boucher b Nel	0		c Nel b Kallis	72
†A.C.Gilchrist	c Gibbs b Nel	2		c Prince b Kallis	0
S.K.Warne	c Boje b Nel	9		not out	0
B.Lee	lbw b Ntini	4			
S.C.G.MacGill	b Ntini	4			
G.D.McGrath	not out	11			
Extras	(B 2, LB 4, W 2, NB 4)	12		(B 6, LB 3, NB 9)	18
Total		**355**		(7 wickets declared)	**321**

SOUTH AFRICA

A.B.de Villiers	lbw b McGrath	61	(2)	st Gilchrist b Warne	8
*G.C.Smith	lbw b Lee	22	(1)	c Gilchrist b McGrath	25
H.H.Gibbs	b Symonds	94		b Warne	9
J.H.Kallis	b Lee	23		c Gilchrist b Symonds	9
A.G.Prince	c Ponting b Warne	6		c Hayden b Warne	26
J.A.Rudolph	b Lee	13		b Symonds	4
†M.V.Boucher	lbw b Symonds	23		c Ponting b Warne	5
S.M.Pollock	lbw b Symonds	9		not out	67
N.Boje	b Warne	12		b McGrath	13
A.Nel	c Hussey b MacGill	14		c Gilchrist b McGrath	2
M.Ntini	not out	10		b MacGill	2
Extras	(B 2, LB 7, NB 15)	24		(LB 6, W 1, NB 4)	11
Total		**311**			**181**

SOUTH AFRICA	O	M	R	W		O	M	R	W
Pollock	26	5	67	3		23	5	60	1
Ntini	22.3	3	70	3		8	2	17	0
Kallis	21.5	4	69	0		11	0	58	3
Nel	31	6	84	4		20	3	71	2
Boje	18.1	3	59	0		14	1	65	0
Smith						7	0	41	1

AUSTRALIA	O	M	R	W		O	M	R	W
McGrath	27	13	57	1		15	3	44	3
Lee	28	5	92	3		11	4	23	0
Symonds	20	6	50	3	(4)	4	2	6	2
Warne	21	7	62	2	(3)	28	7	74	4
MacGill	15	3	41	1		16	7	28	1

FALL OF WICKETS				
	A	SA	A	SA
Wkt	1st	1st	2nd	2nd
1st	2	36	53	39
2nd	154	122	82	45
3rd	176	184	131	58
4th	207	192	193	64
5th	207	214	317	72
6th	213	260	321	82
7th	227	265	321	130
8th	239	281	–	166
9th	248	291	–	178
10th	355	311	–	181

Umpires: S.A.Bucknor (*West Indies*) (108) and Asad Rauf (*Pakistan*) (3).
Referee: B.C.Broad (*England*) (16). **Test No. 1778/73 (A675/SA305)**

AUSTRALIA v SOUTH AFRICA (3rd Test)

At Sydney Cricket Ground on 2, 3, 4, 5, 6 January 2006.
Toss: South Africa. Result: **AUSTRALIA** won by eight wickets.
Debuts: South Africa – J.Botha.

SOUTH AFRICA

A.B.de Villiers	c Gilchrist b Lee	2	(2)	lbw b Lee	1
*G.C.Smith	lbw b Lee	39	(1)	lbw b McGrath	5
H.H.Gibbs	b McGrath	27		run out	67
J.H.Kallis	c McGrath b Symonds	111		not out	50
A.G.Prince	lbw b Warne	119		c Ponting b MacGill	18
J.A.Rudolph	c Gilchrist b McGrath	38		c McGrath b MacGill	4
†M.V.Boucher	c Gilchrist b MacGill	5		st Gilchrist b MacGill	11
S.M.Pollock	c Hodge b Lee	46		not out	26
J.Botha	not out	20			
A.Nel	c Hodge b Warne	12			
C.K.Langeveldt	not out	1			
Extras	(B 9, LB 6, NB 16)	31		(B 3, LB 4, W 3, NB 2)	12
Total	(9 wickets declared)	**451**		(6 wickets declared)	**194**

AUSTRALIA

J.L.Langer	b Langeveldt	25		b Langeveldt	20
M.L.Hayden	b Langeveldt	4		c Smith b Botha	90
*R.T.Ponting	lbw b Kallis	120		not out	143
B.J.Hodge	c Rudolph b Nel	6		not out	27
M.E.K.Hussey	c Boucher b Botha	45			
A.Symonds	lbw b Nel	12			
†A.C.Gilchrist	c Boucher b Nel	86			
S.K.Warne	c Boucher b Nel	0			
B.Lee	c Smith b Kallis	17			
S.C.G.MacGill	c Nel b Pollock	29			
G.D.McGrath	not out	1			
Extras	(LB 10, W 2, NB 2)	14		(LB 1, W 3, NB 4)	8
Total		**359**		(2 wickets)	**288**

AUSTRALIA	O	M	R	W	O	M	R	W
McGrath	34	17	65	2	15	2	61	1
Lee	30.4	7	82	3	10	3	48	1
Symonds	23	4	69	1				
Warne	36	5	106	2	(3) 11	1	45	0
Hussey	2	0	12	0				
MacGill	29	5	102	1	(4) 6	1	33	3

SOUTH AFRICA								
Pollock	25	3	109	1	14	2	55	0
Langeveldt	24	4	108	2	14	1	52	1
Nel	24.1	3	81	4	7	0	46	0
Kallis	15	4	25	2	(5) 2	0	8	0
Botha	7	2	26	1	(4) 12.3	0	77	1
Rudolph					11	0	49	0

	FALL OF WICKETS			
	SA	A	SA	A
Wkt	1st	1st	2nd	2nd
1st	16	22	4	30
2nd	69	35	6	212
3rd	86	54	92	–
4th	305	184	123	–
5th	344	222	129	–
6th	355	226	152	–
7th	394	226	–	–
8th	433	263	–	–
9th	449	322	–	–
10th	–	359	–	–

Umpires: B.F.Bowden (*New Zealand*) (35) and Alim Dar (*Pakistan*) (27).
Referee: B.C.Broad (*England*) (17). **Test No. 1779/74 (A676/SA306)**

AUSTRALIA v SOUTH AFRICA 2005-06

AUSTRALIA – BATTING AND FIELDING

	M	I	NO	HS	Runs	Avge	100	50	Ct/St
R.T.Ponting	3	6	1	143*	515	103.00	3	2	5
B.J.Hodge	3	6	2	203*	308	77.00	1	–	5
M.E.K.Hussey	3	5	–	122	279	55.80	1	1	1
M.L.Hayden	3	6	–	137	316	52.66	1	2	2
J.L.Langer	2	4	–	47	129	32.25	–	–	1
A.C.Gilchrist	3	5	–	86	138	27.60	–	1	6/2
A.Symonds	3	5	–	72	122	24.40	–	1	–
B.Lee	3	4	1	32	72	24.00	–	–	–
S.C.G.MacGill	2	2	–	29	33	16.50	–	–	–
G.D.McGrath	3	3	2	11*	12	12.00	–	–	2
S.K.Warne	3	5	1	24	38	9.50	–	–	1

Played in one Test: N.W.Bracken 10, 14*; P.A.Jaques 2, 28.

AUSTRALIA – BOWLING

	O	M	R	W	Avge	Best	5wI	10wM
A.Symonds	50	12	131	6	21.83	3-50	–	–
B.Lee	133	29	421	13	32.38	5-93	1	–
S.K.Warne	172	45	462	14	33.00	4-74	–	–
S.C.G.MacGill	66	16	204	6	34.00	3-33	–	–
G.D.McGrath	133	49	325	8	40.62	3-44	–	–
N.W.Bracken	31	8	83	2	41.50	1-37	–	–

Also bowled: B.J.Hodge 2-0-8-0; M.E.K.Hussey 2-0-12-0.

SOUTH AFRICA – BATTING AND FIELDING

	M	I	NO	HS	Runs	Avge	100	50	Ct/St
J.H.Kallis	2	4	1	111	193	64.33	1	1	1
S.M.Pollock	3	5	2	67*	182	60.66	–	1	–
H.H.Gibbs	3	6	–	94	251	41.83	–	2	4
A.G.Prince	3	6	–	119	205	34.16	1	–	1
J.A.Rudolph	3	6	1	102*	169	33.80	1	–	4
G.C.Smith	3	6	–	39	155	25.83	–	–	5
A.B.de Villiers	3	6	–	68	152	25.33	–	2	–
M.V.Boucher	3	6	1	62	119	23.80	–	1	12
M.Ntini	2	3	1	12	24	12.00	–	–	–
A.Nel	3	4	1	14	32	10.66	–	–	2
C.K.Langeveldt	2	2	1	1*	1	1.00	–	–	1

Played in one Test: N.Boje 12, 13 (1 ct); J.Botha 20*; J.M.Kemp7, 55.

SOUTH AFRICA – BOWLING

	O	M	R	W	Avge	Best	5wI	10wM
M.Ntini	83.3	16	264	9	29.33	5- 64	1	–
A.Nel	127.3	17	415	14	29.64	4- 81	–	–
J.H.Kallis	49.5	8	160	5	32.00	3- 58	–	–
J.Botha	19.3	2	103	2	51.50	1- 26	–	–
C.K.Langeveldt	86	9	377	7	53.85	3-117	–	–
S.M.Pollock	143	27	435	8	54.37	3- 67	–	–

Also bowled: N.Boje 32.1-3-124-0; J.M.Kemp 14-0-71-1; J.A.Rudolph 17.4-1-78-0; G.C.Smith 7-0-41-1.

PAKISTAN v INDIA (1st Test)

At Gaddafi Stadium, Lahore, on 13, 14, 15, 16, 17 January 2006.
Toss: Pakistan. Result: **MATCH DRAWN**.
Debuts: None.

PAKISTAN

Shoaib Malik	c Harbhajan b Pathan	59
Salman Butt	run out	6
Younis Khan	run out	199
M.Yousuf Youhana	st Dhoni b Kumble	173
*Inzamam-ul-Haq	lbw b Kumble	1
Shahid Afridi	c Harbhajan b Agarkar	103
†Kamran Akmal	not out	102
Naved-ul-Hasan	c Ganguly b Agarkar	9
Mohammad Sami	not out	1
Shoaib Akhtar		
Danish Kaneria		
Extras	(B 4, LB 12, W 2; NB 8)	26
Total	(7 wickets declared)	**679**

INDIA

V.Sehwag	c Akmal b Naved	254
*R.Dravid	not out	128
V.V.S.Laxman	not out	0
S.R.Tendulkar		
S.C.Ganguly		
Yuvraj Singh		
†M.S.Dhoni		
I.K.Pathan		
A.B.Agarkar		
A.Kumble		
Harbhajan Singh		
Extras	(B 2, LB 7, W 2, NB 17)	28
Total	(1 wicket)	**410**

INDIA	O	M	R	W	O	M	R	W
Pathan	32	4	133	1				
Agarkar	24	3	122	2				
Ganguly	6	1	14	0				
Harbhajan Singh	34	5	176	0				
Kumble	39.3	2	178	2				
Sehwag	6	0	24	0				
Tendulkar	2	0	16	0				

PAKISTAN	O	M	R	W
Shoaib Akhtar	16.2	6	46	0
Naved-ul-Hasan	16	1	94	1
Shahid Afridi	11	0	55	0
Mohammad Sami	12	1	67	0
Danish Kaneria	10	0	69	0
Shoaib Malik	12	1	70	0

FALL OF WICKETS		
	P	I
Wkt	1st	1st
1st	12	410
2nd	136	–
3rd	455	–
4th	456	–
5th	477	–
6th	647	–
7th	668	–
8th	–	–
9th	–	–
10th	–	–

Umpires: D.B.Hair (*Australia*) (69) and R.E.Koertzen (*South Africa*) (69).
Referee: R.S.Madugalle (*Sri Lanka*) (80).   **Test No. 1780/54 (P316/I393)**

PAKISTAN v INDIA (2nd Test)

At Iqbal Stadium, Faisalabad, on 21, 22, 23, 24, 25 January 2006.
Toss: Pakistan. Result: **MATCH DRAWN**.
Debuts: India – R.P.Singh.

PAKISTAN

Shoaib Malik	c Dravid b Singh	19				
Salman Butt	c Dhoni b Khan	37	(1)	c Tendulkar b Kumble		24
Younis Khan	c Yuvraj b Singh	83		lbw b Singh		194
M.Yousuf Youhana	c Dhoni b Singh	65		run out		126
*Inzamam-ul-Haq	c Dhoni b Khan	119				
Shahid Afridi	c Yuvraj b Kumble	156		c Dhoni b Khan		1
Abdul Razzaq	c Dhoni b Singh	37	(5)	c Laxman b Khan		32
†Kamran Akmal	c Sehwag b Kumble	0	(2)	c Kumble b Pathan		78
Shoaib Akhtar	c Harbhajan b Khan	47	(8)	not out		0
Mohammad Asif	not out	6	(7)	b Khan		0
Danish Kaneria	b Kumble	0	(9)	b Khan		0
Extras	(B 3, LB 4, W 3; NB 9)	19		(B 9, LB 10, W 3, NB 13)		35
Total		**588**		(8 wickets declared)		**490**

INDIA

V.Sehwag	c sub (Imran Farhat) b Razzaq	31				
*R.Dravid	run out	103		not out		5
V.V.S.Laxman	c Akmal b Kaneria	90	(1)	not out		8
S.R.Tendulkar	c Akmal b Akhtar	14				
Yuvraj Singh	c Kaneria b Asif	4				
†M.S.Dhoni	st Akmal b Kaneria	148				
I.K.Pathan	lbw b Razzaq	90				
A.Kumble	st Akmal b Kaneria	15				
Harbhajan Singh	lbw b Afridi	38				
Z.Khan	not out	20				
R.P.Singh	c and b Afridi	6				
Extras	(B 3, LB 15, W 3, NB 23)	44		(W 6, NB 2)		8
Total		**603**		(0 wickets)		**21**

INDIA	O	M	R	W	O	M	R	W		FALL OF WICKETS				
Pathan	19	4	106	0	22	2	80	1			P	I	P	I
Singh	25	3	89	4	22	3	75	1		Wkt	1st	1st	2nd	2nd
Khan	32	7	135	3	(4) 19.4	4	61	4		1st	49	39	52	–
Harbhajan Singh	25	1	101	0	(5) 22	2	78	0		2nd	65	236	181	–
Kumble	35.2	5	150	3	(3) 21	3	118	1		3rd	207	241	423	–
Yuvraj Singh					(6) 9	0	46	0		4th	216	258	488	–
Dhoni					(7) 1	0	13	0		5th	467	281	490	–
										6th	469	491	490	
PAKISTAN										7th	509	529	490	
Shoaib Akhtar	25	7	100	1						8th	567	553	490	
Mohammad Asif	34	6	103	1						9th	584	587		
Abdul Razzaq	28	1	126	2						10th	588	603	–	–
Danish Kaneria	54	6	165	3										
Shahid Afridi	24.4	0	91	2	(1) 4	0	16	0						
Younis Khan					(2) 4	0	5	0						

Umpires: R.E.Koertzen (*South Africa*) (70) and S.J.A.Taufel (*Australia*) (30).
Referee: R.S.Madugalle (*Sri Lanka*) (81).   Test No. 1781/55 (P317/I394)

PAKISTAN v INDIA (3rd Test)

At National Stadium, Karachi, on 29, 30, 31 January, 1 February 2006.
Toss: India. Result: **PAKISTAN** won by 341 runs.
Debuts: None.

PAKISTAN

Salman Butt	c Dravid b Pathan	0	lbw b Ganguly	53
Imran Farhat	c Dhoni b Singh	22	c Tendulkar b Pathan	57
*Younis Khan	lbw b Pathan	0	lbw b Kumble	77
M.Yousuf Youhana	b Pathan	0	lbw b Kumble	97
Faisal Iqbal	lbw b Khan	5	c Tendulkar b Khan	139
Shahid Afridi	b Khan	10	c Tendulkar b Pathan	60
Abdul Razzaq	lbw b Singh	45	c Yuvraj b Kumble	90
†Kamran Akmal	c Dhoni b Pathan	113	not out	0
Shoaib Akhtar	c Yuvraj b Pathan	45		
Mohammad Asif	c Laxman b Singh	0		
Danish Kaneria	not out	0		
Extras	(LB 2, W 2; NB 1)	5	(B 7, LB 7, W 1, NB 11)	26
Total		**245**	(7 wickets declared)	**599**

INDIA

V.V.S.Laxman	b Asif	19	(3) b Asif	21
*R.Dravid	c Akmal b Asif	3	c Akmal b Akhtar	2
V.Sehwag	c Akmal b Akhtar	5	(1) b Asif	4
S.R.Tendulkar	b Razzaq	23	b Asif	26
S.C.Ganguly	c Asif b Razzaq	34	lbw b Razzaq	37
Yuvraj Singh	lbw b Asif	45	c Akmal b Razzaq	122
†M.S.Dhoni	c Akmal b Razzaq	13	c Farhat b Razzaq	18
I.K.Pathan	c Yousuf b Afridi	40	c Faisal b Razzaq	4
A.Kumble	lbw b Akhtar	7	c Farhat b Kaneria	5
Z.Khan	c Akmal b Asif	21	b Kaneria	10
R.P.Singh	not out	0	not out	0
Extras	(B 8, LB 3, NB 17)	28	(B 7, W 5, NB 4)	16
Total		**238**		**265**

INDIA	O	M	R	W		O	M	R	W	FALL OF WICKETS
Pathan	17.1	4	61	5		25	3	106	1	
Khan	15	2	75	1		28	4	103	1	
Singh	16	1	66	3		24	1	115	1	
Ganguly	2	0	9	0	(5)	16	1	68	1	
Kumble	10	1	32	0	(4)	37.1	3	151	3	
Sehwag						1	0	2	0	
Tendulkar						9	0	40	0	

		P	I	P	I
Wkt	1st	1st	2nd	2nd
1st	0	9	109	8
2nd	0	14	122	8
3rd	0	56	280	63
4th	13	56	318	74
5th	37	137	402	177
6th	39	165	598	208
7th	154	165	599	216
8th	236	181	–	231
9th	245	237	–	251
10th	245	238	–	265

PAKISTAN	O	M	R	W		O	M	R	W
Shoaib Akhtar	16	3	70	2		8	1	37	1
Mohammad Asif	19.1	1	78	4		12	1	48	3
Abdul Razzaq	16	3	67	3		18.4	0	88	4
Shahid Afridi	3	0	12	1	(5)	2	0	10	0
Danish Kaneria					(4)	18	0	75	2

Umpires: D.J.Harper (*Australia*) (55) and S.J.A.Taufel (*Australia*) (31).
Referee: R.S.Madugalle (*Sri Lanka*) (82).   Test No. 1782/56 (P318/1395)

PAKISTAN v INDIA 2005-06

PAKISTAN – BATTING AND FIELDING

	M	I	NO	HS	Runs	Avge	100	50	Ct/St
Younis Khan	3	5	–	199	553	110.60	2	2	–
Kamran Akmal	3	5	2	113	293	97.66	2	1	9/2
Mohd Yousuf Youhana	3	5	–	173	461	92.20	2	2	1
Faisal Iqbal	1	2	–	139	144	72.00	1	–	1
Shahid Afridi	3	5	–	156	330	66.00	2	1	1
Inzamam-ul-Haq	2	2	–	119	120	60.00	1	–	–
Abdul Razzaq	2	4	–	90	204	51.00	–	1	–
Shoaib Akhtar	3	3	1	47	92	46.00	–	–	–
Shoaib Malik	2	2	–	59	78	39.00	–	1	–
Salman Butt	3	5	–	53	120	24.00	–	1	–
Mohammad Asif	2	3	1	6*	6	3.00	–	–	1
Danish Kaneria	3	3	1	0*	0	0.00	–	–	1

Played in one Test: Imran Farhat 22, 57 (2 ct); Mohammad Sami 1*; Naved-ul-Hasan 9.

PAKISTAN – BOWLING

	O	M	R	W	Avge	Best	5wI	10wM
Mohammad Asif	65.1	8	229	8	28.62	4- 78	–	–
Abdul Razzaq	62.4	4	281	9	31.22	4- 88	–	–
Shahid Afridi	44.4	0	184	3	61.33	2- 91	–	–
Danish Kaneria	82	6	309	5	61.80	3-165	–	–
Shoaib Akhtar	65.2	17	253	4	63.25	2- 70	–	–

Also bowled: Mohammad Sami 12-1-67-0; Naved-ul-Hasan 16-1-94-1; Shoaib Malik 12-1-70-0; Younis Khan 4-0-5-0.

INDIA – BATTING AND FIELDING

	M	I	NO	HS	Runs	Avge	100	50	Ct/St
R.Dravid	3	5	2	128*	241	80.33	2	–	2
V.Sehwag	3	4	–	254	294	73.50	1	–	1
M.S.Dhoni	3	3	–	148	179	59.66	1	–	7/1
Yuvraj Singh	3	3	–	122	171	57.00	1	–	4
V.V.S.Laxman	3	5	–	90	138	46.00	–	1	2
I.K.Pathan	3	3	–	90	134	44.66	–	1	–
Harbhajan Singh	2	1	–	38	38	38.00	–	–	3
S.C.Ganguly	2	2	–	37	71	35.50	–	–	1
Z.Khan	2	3	1	21	51	25.50	–	–	–
S.R.Tendulkar	3	3	–	26	63	21.00	–	–	4
A.Kumble	3	3	–	15	27	9.00	–	–	1
R.P.Singh	2	3	2	6	6	6.00	–	–	–

Played in one Test: A.B.Agarkar did not bat.

INDIA – BOWLING

	O	M	R	W	Avge	Best	5wI	10wM
Z.Khan	94.4	17	374	10	37.40	4- 61	–	–
R.P.Singh	87	8	345	9	38.33	4- 89	–	–
I.K.Pathan	115.1	17	486	8	60.75	5- 61	1	–
A.B.Agarkar	24	3	122	2	61.00	2-122	–	–
A.Kumble	143	14	629	9	69.88	3-150	–	–
S.C.Ganguly	24	2	91	1	91.00	1- 68	–	–

Also bowled: M.S.Dhoni 1-0-13-0; Harbhajan Singh 81-8-355-0; V.Sehwag 7-0-26-0; S.R.Tendulkar 11-0-56-0; Yuvraj Singh 9-0-46-0.

AUSTRALIANS v ICC WORLD XI

At Sydney Cricket Ground on 14, 15, 16, 17 October 2005.
Toss: Australia. Result: **AUSTRALIANS** won by 210 runs.

AUSTRALIANS

J.L.Langer	b Harmison	0	c Smith b Kallis	22
M.L.Hayden	c Kallis b Muralitharan	111	b Harmison	77
*R.T.Ponting	c Kallis b Flintoff	46	c Boucher b Flintoff	54
M.J.Clarke	c Sehwag b Vettori	39	b Harmison	5
S.M.Katich	run out	0	c and b Muralitharan	2
†A.C.Gilchrist	lbw b Flintoff	94	c Kallis b Muralitharan	1
S.R.Watson	lbw b Muralitharan	24	c Boucher b Flintoff	10
S.K.Warne	c Kallis b Flintoff	5	c Dravid b Flintoff	7
B.Lee	c Smith b Flintoff	1	c Muralitharan b Harmison	3
G.D.McGrath	run out	0	c Smith b Muralitharan	2
S.C.G.MacGill	not out	0	not out	0
Extras	(B 5, LB 11, W 3, NB 6)	25	(B 7, LB 7, NB 2)	16
Total		**345**		**199**

ICC WORLD XI

*G.C.Smith	c Gilchrist b Lee	12	b McGrath	0
V.Sehwag	c Katich b Warne	76	c Gilchrist b MacGill	7
R.Dravid	c Gilchrist b McGrath	0	c Hayden b Warne	23
B.C.Lara	lbw b McGrath	5	c Gilchrist b Warne	36
J.H.Kallis	c Hayden b Warne	44	not out	39
Inzamam-ul-Haq	st Gilchrist b MacGill	1	lbw b Lee	0
A.Flintoff	c Lee b MacGill	35	c sub (B.J.Hodge) b MacGill	15
†M.V.Boucher	c Gilchrist b Warne	0	c Hayden b Warne	17
D.L.Vettori	not out	8	c Ponting b MacGill	0
S.J.Harmison	c Clarke b MacGill	1	lbw b MacGill	0
M.Muralitharan	c Langer b MacGill	2	st Gilchrist b MacGill	0
Extras	(B 1, LB 1, W 1, NB 3)	6	(B 1, LB 2, NB 4)	7
Total		**190**		**144**

ICC WORLD XI	O	M	R	W	O	M	R	W
Harmison	18	3	60	1	12.3	2	41	3
Flintoff	18	3	59	4	16	2	48	3
Kallis	7	1	35	0	3	1	3	1
Muralitharan	30	3	102	2	24	4	55	3
Vettori	17	3	73	1	10	0	38	0

AUSTRALIANS	O	M	R	W	O	M	R	W
McGrath	12	4	34	2	8	4	19	2
Lee	8	1	54	1	10	2	42	1
Watson	6	0	38	0				
Warne	12	3	23	3	(3) 19	4	48	3
MacGill	9.1	0	39	4	(4) 15	4	43	5

FALL OF WICKETS

	Aus	ICC	Aus	ICC
Wkt	1st	1st	2nd	2nd
1st	0	27	30	0
2nd	73	31	152	18
3rd	154	43	160	56
4th	163	134	167	69
5th	260	135	167	70
6th	323	147	170	122
7th	331	151	177	143
8th	339	183	192	144
9th	344	184	195	144
10th	345	190	199	144

Umpires: S.J.A.Taufel (*Australia*) and R.E.Koertzen (*South Africa*).
Referee: R.S.Madugalle (*Sri Lanka*).

LEADING (INTERNATIONAL) TEST AGGREGATES 2005

1000 RUNS

	M	I	NO	HS	Runs	Avge	100	50
R.T.Ponting (A)	14	26	5	207	1444	68.76	6	5
M.E.Trescothick (E)	13	24	–	194	1323	55.12	4	4
M.L.Hayden (A)	14	27	3	138	1192	49.66	4	3
B.C.Lara (WI)	8	15	–	226	1069	71.26	5	–
A.B.de Villiers (SA)	11	19	–	178	1008	53.05	3	5

RECORD:

	M	I	NO	HS	Runs	Avge	100	50
I.V.A.Richards (WI)(1976)	11	19	–	291	1710	90.00	7	5

50 WICKETS

	M	O	R	W	Avge	Best	5wI	10wM
S.K.Warne (A)	14	691.4	2043	90	22.70	6- 46	6	2
A.Flintoff (E)	13	498.2	1553	61	25.45	5- 78	1	–
G.D.McGrath (A)	12	506	1310	59	22.20	6-115	3	–
M.J.Hoggard (E)	13	408.5	1514	58	26.10	7- 61	3	1

RECORD:

	M	O	R	W	Avge	Best	5wI	10wM
S.K.Warne (A)	14	691.4	2043	90	22.70	6-46	6	2

40 DISMISSALS

	M	Dis	Ct	St
G.O.Jones (E)	13	51	50	1
A.C.Gilchrist (A)	14	48	45	3
M.V.Boucher (SA)	11	42	41	1
Kamran Akmal (P)	9	41	33	8

RECORD:

	M	Dis	Ct	St
I.A.Healy (A)(1993)	16	67	58	9
M.V.Boucher (SA)(1998)	13	67	65	2

20 CATCHES

	M	Ct
G.C.Smith (SA)	11	20

RECORD:

	M	Ct
S.P.Fleming (NZ)(1997)	10	28

TEST MATCH CHAMPIONSHIP SCHEDULE

Months indicate the start of a series

2006	Apr	South Africa host New Zealand
		Bangladesh host Australia
	May	England host Sri Lanka
		West Indies host India
	Jun	England host Pakistan
	Aug	Sri Lanka host South Africa
	Sep	Sri Lanka host India
		Bangladesh host India
	Nov	Australia host England
	Dec	Pakistan host West Indies
		South Africa host India
		New Zealand host Bangladesh
2007	Jan	Australia host New Zealand
		South Africa host Pakistan
	Feb	Sri Lanka host Zimbabwe
	Apr	*World Cup in West Indies*
	May	West Indies host Australia
		England host West Indies
	Jun	England host India
	Jul	Australia host Zimbabwe
	Aug	Sri Lanka host New Zealand
	Sep	Zimbabwe host Pakistan
	Oct	India host Zimbabwe
		Bangladesh host New Zealand
		Pakistan host South Africa
		Sri Lanka host England
	Nov	Australia host Sri Lanka
	Dec	Australia host India
		New Zealand host Sri Lanka
		South Africa host West Indies
		Zimbabwe host Bangladesh
2008	Jan	Australia host Sri Lanka
	Feb	India host West Indies
		New Zealand host England
		Bangladesh host Sri Lanka
		Pakistan host Australia
		South Africa host Zimbabwe
	Mar	Bangladesh host South Africa
	Apr	West Indies host New Zealand
	May	England host Zimbabwe
		West Indies host India
	Jun	England host South Africa
		Australia host Bangladesh
	Jul	Sri Lanka host India
	Sep	Sri Lanka host Australia
		Zimbabwe host West Indies
	Oct	India host South Africa
		Pakistan host New Zealand
	Nov	Australia host Pakistan
		West Indies host Bangladesh
	Dec	Australia host West Indies
		New Zealand host Pakistan
		South Africa host England
		Zimbabwe host Sri Lanka
2009	Jan	South Africa host India
		Bangladesh host Zimbabwe
		Australia host Pakistan
		New Zealand host Pakistan
	Feb	New Zealand host Australia
		West Indies host England

	Mar	India host Pakistan
	Apr	West Indies host Zimbabwe
		South Africa host Bangladesh
	May	England host New Zealand
	Jun	England host Australia
	Jul	Sri Lanka host West Indies
	Sep	Pakistan host Bangladesh
	Oct	India host New Zealand
		South Africa host Sri Lanka
		Zimbabwe host England
		Bangladesh host West Indies
	Nov	Australia host Zimbabwe
		Pakistan host England
	Dec	Australia host South Africa
		India host Sri Lanka
		New Zealand host West Indies
2010	Jan	Australia host Zimbabwe
		Bangladesh host Pakistan
	Feb	New Zealand host Zimbabwe
		Pakistan host Sri Lanka
		South Africa host Australia
	Mar	West Indies host India
	Apr	West Indies host Pakistan
	May	England host Bangladesh
	Jun	England host West Indies
	Aug	Sri Lanka host Pakistan
	Sep	Zimbabwe host New Zealand
		Australia host Bangladesh
	Oct	India host Australia
		South Africa host New Zealand
	Nov	Australia host England
		Pakistan host Zimbabwe
		Bangladesh host West Indies
	Dec	New Zealand host Sri Lanka
		South Africa host Pakistan
		India host Bangladesh
2011	Jan	Pakistan host India
	Feb	New Zealand host South Africa
		West Indies host Australia
		Bangladesh host England
	Mar	Pakistan host Sri Lanka
		Zimbabwe host India
	Apr	West Indies host South Africa

LG ICC TEST MATCH CHAMPIONSHIP TABLE

(As at 7 March 2006)

		Rating
1	Australia	129
2	England	113
3	India	111
4	Pakistan	108
5	New Zealand	100
6	South Africa	99
7	Sri Lanka	96
8	West Indies	73
9	Zimbabwe	27
10	Bangladesh	5

SECOND XI CHAMPIONSHIP FIXTURES 2006

3-DAY MATCHES UNLESS MARKED * (4-DAY)

APRIL

Tue 18	Radlett CC	MCC YC v Middx
Mon 24	Manchester (OT)	Lancs v Notts
Tue 25	Stamford Bridge	Yorks v Durham
Wed 26	Hove	Sussex v MCC YC

MAY

Tue 2	Moseley	Warwks v Lancs
Wed 3	Belper Meadows	Derbys v Notts
Mon 8	Derby	Derbys v Yorks
Tue 9	Southampton (RB)	Hants v Warwks
	Oval	Surrey v Essex
Tue 16	Leicester	Leics v Warwks
	Gowerton (*tbc*)	Glam v Middx
	Chester-le-St	Durham v Lancs
Wed 17	Purley	Surrey v MCC YC
Tue 23	York	Yorks v Surrey
	Caythorpe CC	Notts v Lancs
Wed 24	Hinckley	Leics v Derbys
	Uxbridge (Vine L)	MCC YC v Hants
Tue 30	Kidderminster	Worcs v Warwks
	Uxbridge CC	Middx v Essex
Wed 31	Taunton CC	Somerset v Glam
	Uppingham S	Leics v Surrey
	Southampton (RB)	Hants v Yorks
	Cheltenham C	Glos v MCC YC

JUNE

Mon 5	Hove	*Sussex v Yorks
Tue 6	Longhirst	Durham v MCC YC
	Reigate Priory CC	Surrey v Middx
	Bristol	*Glos v Notts
	Dunstall CC	Derbys v Warwks
	Manchester (OT)	Lancs v Hants
	Northampton	Northants v Leics
Tue 13	Knowle & Dorridge	Warwicks v Surrey
	Swallwell CC	Durham v Worcs
	Leeds	Yorks v Northants
Wed 14	Blackpool	Lancs v Glos
Tue 20	Leeds	*Yorks v Lancs
	Stowe S	Northants v Durham
	Cheam CC	Surrey v Glam
Tue 27	Sunderland	Durham v Leics

JULY

Tue 11	Derby	*Derbys v Lancs
Tue 18	Coggleshall	Essex v Middx
	Whitgift S	Surrey v Worcs
	Hove	Sussex v Warwks
Tue 25	Belper Meadows	Derbys v MCC YC
	Stamford Bridge	*Yorks v Warwks
Wed 26	Bristol	Glos v Northants

	Sutton	Surrey v Notts
	Horsham	Sussex v Middlesex

AUGUST

Tue 1	Guildford	Surrey v Durham
	North Perrott	*Somerset v Glos
	tba	Hants v Essex
	Uxbridge (Vine L)	MCC YC v Kent
Wed 2	Crosby	Lancs v Glam
	Hinckley	Leics v Sussex
	Northampton	Northants v Middx
Tue 8	Barnt Green	Worcs v MCC YC
Wed 9	*tba*	Essex v Leics
	Lady Bay SC	Notts v Kent
	Sth North CC	Durham v Derbys
	Taunton	Somerset v Yorks
	tba	Hants v Surrey
	Stratford-upon-Avon	Warwks v Northants
Tue 15	Chester-le-St	*Durham v Yorks
	Milton Keynes	Northants v Surrey
	Panteg	Glam v Leics
	Uxbridge (Vine L)	Middx v Somerset
Wed 16	Worcester	Worcs v Lancs
	Stirlands CC	Sussex v Derbys
	Bristol WI CC	Glos v Hants
Mon 21	Southgate	Middx v Derbys
Tue 22	*tba*	Essex v Warwks
	Canterbury	Kent v Worcs
	Basingstoke	Hants v Somerset
	Hinckley	Leics v Yorks
	Worksop C	Notts v Durham
	Wimbledon	Surrey v Sussex
Wed 23	Radlett CC	MCC YC v Northants
Tue 29	Southport	Lancs v Surrey
	Southampton (RB)	Hants v Kent
	Uxbridge CC	Middx v Yorks
	Hinckley	Leics v MCC YC
Wed 30	Walmley	Warwks v Durham
	Northampton	Northants v Notts
	Chesterfield	Derbys v Glos

SEPTEMBER

Wed 6	*tba*	Essex v Sussex
	Usk	Glam v Glos
	Kenilworth Wardens	Warwks v Hants
	Beckenham	Kent v Surrey
	Todmorden	Lancs v Yorks
	Radlett CC	MCC YC v Durham
Mon 11	Lady Bay SC	Notts v Somerset
Tue 12	Barnt Green	Worcs v Sussex
	Stamford Bridge	Yorks v Essex

SECOND XI TROPHY FIXTURES 2006

JUNE

Mon 19	Southampton (RB)	Hants v MCC YC
Wed 21	Uxbridge (Vine Lane)	MCC YC v Hants
Mon 26	Horsham	Sussex v Kent
	Banstead CC	Surrey v MCC YC
	Bishop's Stortford	Essex v Northants
Tue 27	Cheltenham CC	Glos v Warwks
	Middleton	Lancs v Derbys
Wed 28	Ombersley	Worcs v Warwks
	Glossop	Derbys v Lancs
	Uxbridge (Vine Lane)	MCC YC v Surrey
	Taunton CC	Somerset v Glos
	Ealing	Middx v Northants
Thu 29	Ealing	Middx v Minor C
	Ebbw Vale	Glam v Worcs
	Trent C	Notts v Essex
	Tonbridge S	Kent v Sussex
Fri 30	Radlett CC	MCC YC v Kent
	Port Talbot Town CC	Glam v Glos
	Notts Unity	Notts v Minor C
	Unsworth	Lancs v Leics
	Southampton (RB)	Hants v Surrey

JULY

Mon 3	Southampton (RB)	Hants v Kent
	Tondu	Glam v Somerset
	Todmorden	Yorks v Derbys
	Coventry/Nth Warwick	Warwks v Glos
	Horsham	Sussex v MCC YC
	Shenley	Middx v Essex
Tue 4	North Perrott	Somerset v Warwks
	Normandy	Surrey v Hants
	Northampton	Northants v Notts
	Hartlepool	Durham v Derbys
	Old Hill	Worcs v Glam
	Todmorden	Yorks v Leics
Wed 5	Milton Keynes	Minor C v Essex
	Darlington	Durham v Lancs
	Richmond	Middx v Notts
	Beckenham	Kent v MCC YC
	Old Hill	Worcs v Glos
Thu 6	Hinckley	Leics v Derbys
	Wickford	Essex v Notts
	Milton Keynes	Minor C v Middx

	Bradford & Bingley	Yorks v Durham
	Reigate Priory CC	Surrey v Sussex
	Dorridge	Warwks v Somerset
	Lydney	Glos v Glam
Fri 7	Hinckley	Leics v Lancs
	Radlett CC	MCC YC v Sussex
	Taunton	Somerset v Worcs
Mon 10	Wellbeck Colliery CC	Notts v Northants
	Harborne	Warwks v Worcs
	Charterhouse S	Surrey v Kent
	Chelmsford	Essex v Middx
Tue 11	Seaton Carew	Durham v Yorks
	Horsham	Sussex v Hants
Wed 12	Northampton	Northants v Middx
	Bristol WI C	Glos v Somerset
	South Shields	Durham v Leics
	Canterbury	Kent v Hants
	Usk	Glam v Warwks
Thu 13	Milton Keynes	Minor C v Northants
	Hatherley & Reddings	Glos v Worcs
	Leicester	Leics v Yorks
	Papplewick & Linby CC	Notts v Middx
	Canterbury	Kent v Surrey
Fri 14	Worcester	Worcs v Somerset
	Leamington CC	Warwks v Glam
	Bournemouth CC	Hants v Sussex
	Milton Keynes	Minor C v Notts
Mon 17	Derby	Derbys v Durham
	Neston CC	Lancs v Yorks
	Milton Keynes	Northants v Essex
Tue 18	Hinckley	Leics v Durham
	Milton Keynes	Northants v Minor C
Wed 19	Taunton CC	Somerset v Glam
	Derby	Derbys v Leics
	Bradford & Bingley	Yorks v Lancs
Thu 20	Liverpool	Lancs v Durham
Fri 21	Derby	Derbys v Yorks
	Hove	Sussex v Surrey
	Coggleshall	Essex v Minor C

AUGUST

Mon 7 (8) tba		Semi-Finals

SEPTEMBER

Mon 4 (5) tba		FINAL

MINOR COUNTIES 2006
CHAMPIONSHIP FIXTURES

All fixtures and venues are subject to confirmation. 12.00 and 11.30 starts apply to 1st day only

MAY

28-30	Bovey Tracey	Devon v Dorset
	Mildenhall	Suffolk v Norfolk
	March	Cambs v Bucks
	Hertford	Herts v Beds

JUNE

11-13	Challow & Childrey	Oxfon v Cornwall
	Trowbridge	Wilts v Herefords
	Shifnal	Salop v Wales
	Chester Broughton Hall	Cheshire v Berks
	Sleaford	Lincs v Northumb
	Sedbergh School	Cumb v Staffs
25-27	Dean Park	Dorset v Salop
	Luctonians	Herefords v Oxon
	Abergavenny	Wales v Wilts
	Falkland	Berks v Devon
	Netherfield	Cumb v Lincs
	Gerrards Cross	Bucks v Herts
	Ransomes	Suffolk v Beds
	Benwell Hill	Northumb v Staffs
	Truro	Cornwall v Cheshire

JULY

	Nantwich	Cheshire v Dorset
9-11	Finchampstead	Berkse v Salop
	Torquay	Devon v Herefords
	Banbury	Oxon v Wales
	Camborne	Cornwall v Wilts
	Cleethorpes	Lincs v Norfolk
	Longton	Staffs v Bucks
	Fenner's	Cambs v Cumb
	Bedford Modern School	Beds v Northumb
	Long Marston	Herts v Suffolk
23-25	Dean Park	Dorset v Berks
	Alderley Edge	Cheshire v Herefords

	Swansea	Wales v Cornwall
	Bridgnorth	Salop v Devon
	South Wilts	Wilts v Oxon
	Manor Park	Norfolk v Staffs
	Luton	Beds v Cumb
	Bishop's Stortford	Herts v Northumb
	March	Cambs v Suffolk
	Burnham	Bucks v Lincs
30-Aug 1	Manor Park	Norfolk v Cambs

AUGUST

6-8	Corsham	Wilts v Berks
	Swansea	Wales v Cheshire
	St Austell	Cornwall v Devon
	Banbury	Oxon v Dorset
	Colwall	Herefords v Salop
	Manor Park	Norfolk v Herts
	Slough	Bucks v Beds
	Jesmond	Northumb v Cumb
	Stone	Staffs v Suffolk
	Grantham	Lincs v Cambs
20-22	Dean Park	Dorset v Wilts
	Exmouth	Devon v Wales
	Brockhampton	Herefords v Cornwall
	Reading	Berks v Oxon
	Whitchurch	Salop v Cheshire
	Jesmond	Northumb v Bucks
	Keswick	Cumber v Herts
	Dunstable	Beds v Norfolk
	Bury St Edmunds	Suffolk v Lincs
	Leek	Staffs v Cambs

SEPTEMBER

10-13	(tba – W Div)	**CHAMPIONSHIP FINAL**

MCCA TROPHY 2006 FIXTURES

Group 1	Group 2	Group 3	Group 4
Cheshire	Bedfordshire	Berkshire	Buckinghamshire
Cumberland	Lincolnshire	Cornwall	Cambridgeshire
Hertfordshire	Norfolk	Devon	Herefordshire
Northumberland	Northumberland	Dorset	Oxfordshire
Shropshire	Staffordshire	Wales	Wiltshire

April 30
Cheshire v Cumber (1)   Grappenhall
Northumber v Salop (1)   South Northumber
Suffolk v Beds (2)   Woodbridge S
Staffs v Lincs (2)   Leek
Cornwall v Devon (3)   Falmouth
Dorset v Wales (3)   Bournemouth (DP)
Wilts v Oxon (4)   Westbury
Cambs v Herts (4)   March

May 7
Salop v Cheshire (1)   Shrewsbury
Herefords v Northumber (1)   Colwall
Lincs v Suffolk (2)   Bourne
Norfolk v Staffs (2)   Norwich (MP)
Wales v Cornwall (3)   Abergavenny
Berkshire v Dorset (3)   Falkland
Herts v Wilts (4)   Radlett
Bucks v Cambs (4)   Marlow

May 14
Cheshire v Herefords (1)   New Brighton
Cumber v Salop (1)   Furness
Suffolk v Norfolk (2)   Copdock
Beds v Lincs (2)   Ampthill
Cornwall v Berks (3)   Truro
Devon v Wales (3)   Exmouth

Wilts v Bucks (4)   Trowbridge
Oxon v Herts (4)   Aston Rowant

May 21
Northumber v Cheshire (1)   Tynemouth
Herefords v Cumber (1)   Eastnor
Staffs v Suffolk (2)   Audley
Norfolk v Beds (2)   Norwich (MP)
Dorset v Cornwall (3)   Bournemouth (DP)
Berks v Devon (3)   Finchampstead
Cambs v Wilts (4)   Wisbech
Bucks v Oxon (4)   Ascott Park

June 4
Salop v Herefords (1)   tba
Cumber v Northumber (1)   Barrow
Lincs v Norfolk (2)   Lincoln Lindum
Beds v Staffs (2)   Flitwick
Wales v Berks (3)   Mumbles
Devon v Dorset (3)   Sidmouth
Herts v Bucks (4)   North Mymms
Oxon v Cambs (4)   Challow & Childrey

July 2 – Semi Finals

August 16 – Final
Final   Lord's

PRINCIPAL FIXTURES 2006

CC1	Liverpool Vic County Championship (1st Div)
CC2	Liverpool Vic County Championship (2nd Div)
CGT	Cheltenham & Gloucester Trophy
FCF	First-Class Friendly
LOI	NatWest Limited-Overs International
NL1	Totesport National League (1st Div)
NL2	Totesport National League (2nd Div)
TM	npower Test Match
T20	Twenty20 Cup
UCCE	Univ Centre of Cricketing Excellence

^F Floodlit

Fri 14 – Mon 17 April
FCF   Lord's   MCC v Nottinghamshire

Sat 15 – Mon 17 April
FCF   Chelmsford   Essex v Loughboro' UCCE
FCF   The Oval   Surrey v Durham UCCE
       Hove   Sussex v Cardiff UCCE
       Leeds   Yorkshire v Brad/Leeds UCCE
FCF   Cambridge   Cambridge UCCE v Warwickshire
FCF   Oxford   Oxford UCCE v Derbyshire

Tue 18 – Fri 21 April
CC2   Bristol   Glos v Somerset
CC1   Manchester   Lancashire v Hampshire

Wed 19 – Sat 22 April
CC2   Derby   Derbyshire v Surrey
CC2   Chelmsford   Essex v Northants
CC1   Canterbury   Kent v Durham
CC1   Nottingham   Notts v Yorkshire
CC1   Hove   Sussex v Warwickshire

Wed 19 – Fri 21 April
       Cardiff   Glamorgan v Cardiff UCCE
FCF   Leicester   Leics v Loughboro' UCCE

Thu 20 – Sat 22 April
FCF   Oxford   Oxford UCCE v Middlesex

Sun 23 April
CGT   Chelmsford   Essex v Glamorgan
CGT   Bristol   Glos v Middlesex
CGT   Dublin   Ireland v Hampshire
CGT   Canterbury   Kent v Somerset
CGT   Manchester   Lancashire v Leics
CGT   Nottingham   Notts v Worcs
CGT   Leeds   Yorkshire v Derbyshire

Mon 24 – Wed 26 April
FCF   Cambridge   British Universities v Sri Lankans

Wed 26 – Sat 29 April
CC1   Chester-le-St   Durham v Lancashire
CC2   Cardiff   Glamorgan v Essex
CC1   Southampton   Hampshire v Sussex
CC2   Leicester   Leicester v Surrey
CC1   Lord's   Middlesex v Kent
CC1   Birmingham   Warwks v Yorkshire
CC2   Worcester   Worcs v Somerset

Thu 27 – Sat 29 April
FCF   Cambridge   Cambridge UCCE v Northants
FCF   Durham   Durham UCCE v Notts
       Bristol   Glos v Brad/Leeds UCCE

Sat 29 April – Mon 1 May
FCF   Derby   Derbyshire v Sri Lankans

Sun 30 April
CGT   Bristol   Glos v Ireland
CGT   The Oval   Surrey v Sussex
CGT   Birmingham   Warwks v Scotland

Mon 1 May
CGT   Chester-le-St   Durham v Northants
CGT   Cardiff   Glamorgan v Ireland
CGT   Southampton   Hampshire v Essex
CGT   Canterbury   Kent v Surrey
CGT   Leicester   Leics v Warwks
CGT   Nottingham   Notts v Scotland
CGT   Taunton   Somerset v Glos
CGT   Hove   Sussex v Middlesex
CGT   Worcester   Worcs v Lancashire

Wed 3 – Sat 6 May
CC2   Chelmsford   Essex v Leics
CC2   Cardiff   Glamorgan v Derbyshire
CC1   Southampton   Hampshire v Middlesex
CC1   Manchester   Lancashire v Kent
CC2   Northampton   Northants v Somerset
CC1   Nottingham   Notts v Warwks
CC2   The Oval   Surrey v Glos
CC1   Leeds   Yorkshire v Sussex

Wed 3 – Fri 5 May
       Harrogate   Brad/Leeds UCCE v Worcs

Thu 4 – Sun 7 May
FCF   Worcester   England A v Sri Lanka

Sun 7 May
CGT   Derby   Derbyshire v Leics
CGT   Chester-le-St   Durham v Warwickshire
CGT   Chelmsford   Essex v Ireland
CGT   Uxbridge   Middlesex v Hampshire
CGT   Northampton   Northants v Lancashire
CGT   Edinburgh   Scotland v Worcs
CGT   The Oval   Surrey v Somerset
CGT   Leeds   Yorkshire v Notts

Tue 9 – Fri 12 May
CC2 Leicester   Leics v Glamorgan
CC1 Hove   Sussex v Notts
CC1 Birmingham   Warwks v Hampshire

Wed 10 – Sat 13 May
CC1 Chester-le-St   Durham v Middlesex
CC2 Bristol   Glos v Northants
CC1 Canterbury   Kent v Yorkshire
CC2 Taunton   Somerset v Essex
CC2 Worcester   Worcs v Derbyshire

Wed 10 – Fri 12 May
FCF Durham   Durham UCCE v Lancashire

Thu 11 – Mon 15 May
TM1 Lord's   ENGLAND v SRI LANKA

Sun 14 May
CGT Cardiff   Glamorgan v Sussex
CGT Southampton   Hampshire v Kent
CGT Belfast   Ireland v Surrey
CGT Manchester   Lancashire v Durham
CGT Leicester   Leics v Worcs
CGT Northampton   Northants v Yorkshire
CGT Taunton   Somerset v Essex
CGT Birmingham   Warwks v Derbyshire

Tue 16 – Fri 19 May
CC1 Leeds   Yorkshire v Lancashire

Wed 17 – Sat 20 May
CC2 Derby   Derbyshire v Leics
CC1 Nottingham   Notts v Durham
CC2 The Oval   Surrey v Worcs

Wed 17 – Fri 19 May
FCF Cambridge   Cambridge UCCE v Kent
FCF Southampton   Hampshire v Loughboro' UCCE
     Taunton   Somerset v Cardiff UCCE

Thu 18 – Sun 21 May
FCF Hove   Sussex v Sri Lankans

Fri 19 May
CGT ^FCardiff Glamorgan v Middlesex

Sun 21 May
CGT Bristol   Glos v Kent
CGT Nottingham   Notts v Leics
CGT Edinburgh   Scotland v Northants
CGT Taunton   Somerset v Hampshire
CGT Worcester   Worcs v Durham
CGT Leeds   Yorkshire v Warwks

Tue 23 – Fri 26 May
CC1 Chester-le-St   Durham v Sussex
CC2 Chelmsford   Essex v Glos
CC2 Worcester   Worcs v Glamorgan

Wed 24 – Sat 27 May
CC1 Southampton   Hampshire v Kent

CC1 Manchester   Lancashire v Notts
CC1 Lord's   Middlesex v Warwks
CC2 Northampton   Northants v Derbyshire
CC2 Taunton   Somerset v Leics

Thu 25 – Mon 29 May
TM2 Birmingham   ENGLAND v SRI LANKA

Sun 28 May
CGT Derby   Derbyshire v Scotland
CGT Chelmsford   Essex v Sussex
CGT Bristol   Glos v Glamorgan
CGT Lord's   Middlesex v Ireland
CGT Worcester   Worcs v Northants
CGT Leeds   Yorkshire v Lancashire

Mon 29 May
CGT Derby   Derbyshire v Worcs
CGT Chester-le-St   Durham v Leics
CGT Southampton   Hampshire v Glos
CGT Tunbridge W   Kent v Ireland
CGT Manchester   Lancashire v Notts
CGT Northampton   Northants v Warwks
CGT The Oval   Surrey v Glamorgan
CGT Horsham   Sussex v Somerset
CGT Leeds   Yorkshire v Scotland

Wed 31 May – Sat 3 June
CC2 Swansea   Glamorgan v Somerset
CC1 Tunbridge W   Kent v Warwks
CC2 Oakham S   Leics v Northants
CC2 Whitgift S   Surrey v Essex
CC1 Horsham   Sussex v Middlesex
CC1 Leeds   Yorkshire v Hampshire

Wed 31 May – Fri 2 June
FCF Oxford   Oxford UCCE v Durham

Fri 2 – Tue 6 June
TM3 Nottingham   ENGLAND v SRI LANKA

Fri 2 – Mon 5 June
CC2 Gloucester   Glos v Worcs

Fri 2 June
CGT ^FDerby Derbyshire v Northants

Sun 4 June
CGT Chester-le-St   Durham v Yorkshire
CGT Swansea   Glamorgan v Somerset
CGT Tunbridge W   Kent v Sussex
CGT Oakham S   Leics v Northants
CGT Lord's   Middlesex v Essex
CGT Edinburgh   Scotland v Lancashire
CGT Whitgift S   Surrey v Hampshire

Tue 6 – Fri 9 June
CC2 Derby   Derbyshire v Glamorgan
CC1 Liverpool   Lancashire v Sussex

Wed 7 – Sat 10 June
CC1	Southampton	Hampshire v Notts
CC1	Southgate	Middlesex v Yorkshire
CC2	Taunton	Somerset v Worcs
CC2	The Oval	Surrey v Leics
CC1	Birmingham	Warwks v Durham

Fri 9 June
| | Chelmsford | Essex v Sri Lankans |

Sun 11 June
CGT	Chelmsford	Essex v Glos
CGT	Cardiff	Glamorgan v Kent
CGT	Dublin	Ireland v Sussex
CGT	Manchester	Lancashire v Derbyshire
CGT	Southgate	Middlesex v Surrey
CGT	Nottingham	Notts v Durham
	Taunton	Somerset v Sri Lankans
CGT	Birmingham	Warwks v Worcs

Tue 13 June
| LOI | Belfast | Ireland v England |

Tue 13 – Fri 16 June
| CC1 | Stockton | Durham v Kent |
| CC1 | Nottingham | Notts v Middlesex |

Wed 14 – Sat 17 June
CC2	Chelmsford	Essex v Worcs
CC2	Bristol	Glos v Derbyshire
CC2	Northampton	Northants v Glamorgan
CC2	Bath	Somerset v Surrey
CC1	Birmingham	Warwks v Lancashire

Thu 15 June
| [T20] | Southampton | England v Sri Lanka |

Fri 16 June
| CGT | Leicester | Leics v Yorkshire |
| CGT | FHove | Sussex v Hampshire |

Sat 17 June
| LOI | Lord's | England v Sri Lanka |

Sun 18 June
CGT	Bristol	Glos v Surrey
CGT	Canterbury	Kent v Essex
CGT	Northampton	Northants v Derbyshire
CGT	Edinburgh	Scotland v Durham
CGT	Bath	Somerset v Middlesex
CGT	Birmingham	Warwks v Notts

Tue 20 June
| LOI | The Oval | England v Sri Lanka |

Tue 20 – Fri 23 June
CC2	Derby	Derbyshire v Essex
CC2	Swansea	Glamorgan v Surrey
CC1	Southampton	Hampshire v Durham
CC1	Canterbury	Kent v Notts
CC2	Leicester	Leics v Glos

Wed 21 – Sat 24 June
CC1	Lord's	Middlesex v Lancashire
CC1	Arundel	Sussex v Yorkshire
CC2	Worcester	Worcs v Northants

Sat 24 June
| LOI | Chester-le-St | England v Sri Lanka |

Sun 25 June
CGT	Derby	Derbyshire v Durham
CGT	Chelmsford	Essex v Surrey
CGT	Southampton	Hampshire v Glamorgan
CGT	Belfast	Ireland v Somerset
CGT	Lord's	Middlesex v Kent
CGT	Nottingham	Notts v Northants
CGT	Edinburgh	Scotland v Leics
CGT	Arundel	Sussex v Glos
CGT	Birmingham	Warwks v Lancashire
CGT	Worcester	Worcs v Yorkshire

Tue 27 June
T20	FDerby	Derbyshire v Lancashire
T20	FCardiff	Glamorgan v Worcs
T20	Beckenham	Kent v Essex
T20	Leicester	Leics v Notts
T20	Lord's	Middlesex v Surrey
T20	Northampton	Northants v Warwks
T20	Taunton	Somerset v Glos
T20	Arundel	Sussex v Hampshire
T20	Leeds	Yorkshire v Durham

Wed 28 June
LOI	Manchester	England v Sri Lanka
T20	FChelmsford	Essex v Sussex
T20	Nottingham	Notts v Durham
T20	The Oval	Surrey v Kent
T20	Birmingham	Warwks v Glamorgan

Thu 29 June
T20	Bristol	Glos v Worcs
T20	Southampton	Hampshire v Middlesex
T20	Leicester	Leics v Lancashire
T20	Northampton	Northants v Somerset

Fri 30 June
T20	FDerby	Derbyshire v Leics
T20	Chester-le-St	Durham v Lancashire
T20	FChelmsford	Essex v Hampshire
T20	FCardiff	Glamorgan v Somerset
T20	Lord's	Middlesex v Kent
T20	Nottingham	Notts v Yorkshire
T20	FHove	Sussex v Surrey
T20	Birmingham	Warwks v Glos
T20	Worcester	Worcs v Northants

Sat 1 – Mon 3 July
| FCF | Leicester | Leics v Pakistanis |

Sat 1 July

LOI	Leeds	England v Sri Lanka
T20	The Oval	Surrey v Essex
	Lord's	Cambridge U v Oxford U

Sun 2 July

T20	Beckenham	Kent v Hampshire
T20	Richmond	Middlesex v Sussex
T20	Taunton	Somerset v Warwks

Mon 3 – Thu 6 July

| FCF | Oxford | Cambridge U v Oxford U |

Mon 3 July

T20	Chester-le-St	Durham v Yorkshire
T20	Southampton	Hampshire v Essex
T20	Manchester	Lancashire v Derbyshire
T20	Northampton	Northants v Worcs

Tue 4 July

T20	Bristol	Glos v Glamorgan
T20	Beckenham	Kent v Middlesex
T20	Nottingham	Notts v Leics
T20	The Oval	Surrey v Sussex

Wed 5 July

T20	FCardiff	Glamorgan v Warwks
T20	Leicester	Leics v Derbyshire
T20	Taunton	Somerset v Northants
T20	Leeds	Yorkshire v Notts

Thu 6 – Sun 9 July

| FCF | Canterbury | England A v Pakistanis |

Thu 6 July

T20	FChelmsford	Essex v Middlesex
T20	Southampton	Hampshire v Surrey
T20	Manchester	Lancashire v Durham
T20	FHove	Sussex v Kent
T20	Worcester	Worcs v Glos

Fri 7 July

T20	FDerby	Derbyshire v Notts
T20	FChelmsford	Essex v Kent
T20	Bristol	Glos v Somerset
T20	Southampton	Hampshire v Sussex
T20	Manchester	Lancashire v Yorkshire
T20	Leicester	Leics v Durham
T20	Northampton	Northants v Glamorgan
T20	The Oval	Surrey v Middlesex
T20	Birmingham	Warwks v Worcs

Sat 8 July

| T20 | Chester-le-St | Durham v Derbyshire |
| T20 | Leeds | Yorkshire v Leics |

Sun 9 July

| T20 | Manchester | Lancashire v Notts |
| T20 | Worcester | Worcs v Somerset |

Mon 10 July

T20	FDerby	Derbyshire v Yorkshire
T20	FCardiff	Glamorgan v Glos
T20	Birmingham	Warwks v Northants

Tue 11 July

T20	Chester-le-St	Durham v Leics
T20	Bristol	Glos v Northants
T20	Canterbury	Kent v Surrey
T20	Southgate	Middlesex v Hampshire
T20	Nottingham	Notts v Derbyshire
T20	Taunton	Somerset v Glamorgan
T20	Hove	Sussex v Essex
T20	Worcester	Worcs v Warwks
T20	Leeds	Yorkshire v Lancashire

Thu 13 – Mon 17 July

| TM1 | Lord's | ENGLAND v PAKISTAN |

Thu 13 – Sun 16 July

| CC2 | Bristol | Glos v Essex |
| CC1 | Hove | Sussex v Kent |

Fri 14 – Mon 17 July

CC1	Chester-le-St	Durham v Yorkshire
CC2	Cardiff	Glamorgan v Leics
CC2	Northampton	Northants v Surrey
CC1	Nottingham	Notts v Hampshire
CC2	Taunton	Somerset v Derbyshire
CC1	Birmingham	Warwks v Middlesex

Tue 18 – Fri 21 July

| CC1 | Canterbury | Kent v Lancashire |

Tue 18 July

| NL1 | FChelmsford | Essex v Northants |

Wed 19 – Sat 22 July

CC2	Chelmsford	Essex v Glamorgan
CC2	Leicester	Leics v Derbyshire
CC1	Southgate	Middlesex v Sussex
CC2	Guildford	Surrey v Somerset
CC1	Scarborough	Yorkshire v Warwks

Wed 19 July

| NL2 | FWorcester | Worcs v Glos |

Thu 20 – Sun 23 July

| CC2 | Worcester | Worcs v Glos |
| FCF | Northampton | Northants v Pakistanis |

Fri 21 – Sun 23 July

| FCF | Chester-le-St | Durham v West Indies A |

Sat 22 July

| NL1 | Nottingham | Notts v Lancashire |

Sun 23 July

NL1	Southgate	Middlesex v Glamorgan
NL2	Guildford	Surrey v Kent
NL2	Scarborough	Yorkshire v Leics

Mon 24 July
T20   Quarter-Finals

Tue 25 July
NL1   ^FHove   Sussex v Warwks

Wed 26 – Sat 29 July
CC2   Chesterfield   Derbyshire v Worcs
CC2   Cheltenham   Glos v Glamorgan
CC1   Southampton   Hampshire v Yorkshire
CC1   Lord's   Middlesex v Durham
CC2   Northampton   Northants v Essex
CC1   Nottingham   Notts v Lancashire

Wed 26 – Fri 28 July
FCF   Leicester   Leics v West Indies A

Wed 26 July
NL2   ^FTaunton   Somerset v Kent

Thu 27 – Mon 31 July
TM2   Manchester   ENGLAND v PAKISTAN

Thu 27 – Sun 30 July
CC1   Birmingham   Warwks v Sussex

Sun 30 July
NL2   Chesterfield   Derbyshire v Surrey
NL2   Cheltenham   Glos v Yorkshire
NL2   Southampton   Hampshire v Somerset
NL1   Lord's   Middlesex v Durham
NL1   Northampton   Northants v Notts
        Worcester   Worcs v West Indies A

Mon 31 July
NL2   ^FCardiff   Glamorgan v Essex

Tue 1 – Fri 4 August
CC1   Chester-le-St   Durham v Notts

Tue 1 August
NL2   Cheltenham   Glos v Leics
NL1   ^FBirmingham   Warwks v Middlesex

Wed 2 – Sat 5 August
CC2   Southend   Essex v Somerset
CC2   Colwyn Bay   Glamorgan v Worcs
CC2   Cheltenham   Glos v Leics
CC1   Canterbury   Kent v Hampshire
CC2   The Oval   Surrey v Northants
CC1   Hove   Sussex v Lancashire

Wed 2 – Fri 4 August
FCF   Birmingham   Warwks v West Indies A

Wed 2 August
NL2   ^FDerby   Derbyshire v Yorkshire

Fri 4 – Mon 8 August
TM3   Leeds   ENGLAND v PAKISTAN

Sun 6 August
        Derby   Derbys v West Indies A
NL1   Southend   Essex v Middlesex

NL1   Colwyn Bay   Glamorgan v Warwks
NL2   Cheltenham   Glos v Somerset
NL2   Canterbury   Kent v Hampshire
NL1   Northampton   Northants v Durham
NL2   The Oval   Surrey v Leics
NL1   Hove   Sussex v Lancashire

Tue 8 – Fri 11 August
CC2   Derby   Derbyshire v Somerset
CC1   Manchester   Lancashire v Yorkshire
CC1   Lord's   Middlesex v Hampshire
CC2   Northampton   Northants v Glos
CC1   Birmingham   Warwks v Notts
CC2   Worcester   Worcs v Surrey

Wed 9 August
        TBC   Glamorgan v West Indies A
NL2   ^FCanterbury   Kent v Leics

Thu 10 August
NL1   ^FCardiff   Glamorgan v Durham

Sat 12 August
T20   Nottingham   Semi-Finals & ^FFinal

Sat 12 – Sun 13 August
        Shenley   Pakistanis v West Indies A

Sun 13 August
NL1   Chester-le-St   Durham v Lancashire
NL2   Southampton   Hampshire v Derbyshire
NL2   Leicester   Leics v Worcs
NL1   Lord's   Middlesex v Notts
NL2   Taunton   Somerset v Yorkshire
NL1   Birmingham   Warwks v Northants

Mon 14 August
NL1   ^FHove   Sussex v Essex

Tue 15 – Fri 18 August
CC2   Taunton   Somerset v Glamorgan

Tue 15 August
NL2   ^FDerby   Derbyshire v Glos

Wed 16 – Sat 19 August
CC2   Colchester   Essex v Surrey
CC1   Southampton   Hampshire v Warwks
CC2   Leicester   Leics v Worcs
CC1   Hove   Sussex v Durham
CC1   Leeds   Yorkshire v Kent

Wed 16 – Fri 18 August
FCF   Nottingham   Notts v West Indies A

Wed 16 August
NL1   ^FManchester   Lancashire v Middlesex

Thu 17 – Mon 21 August
TM4   The Oval   ENGLAND v PAKISTAN

Thu 17 – Sun 20 August
CC2   Derby   Derbyshire v Glos

CC1	Manchester	Lancashire v Middlesex

Sun 20 August

NL1	Colchester	Essex v Notts
NL1	Hove	Sussex v Glamorgan
NL2	Worcester	Worcs v Kent

Tue 22 – Fri 25 August

CC1	Chester-le-St	Durham v Warwks
CC2	Northampton	Northants v Leics
CC1	Nottingham	Notts v Kent
CC2	Taunton	Somerset v Glos

Tue 22 August

| NL2 | FLeeds | Yorkshire v Worcs |

Wed 23 August

| NL2 | FSouthampton | Hampshire v Surrey |

Thu 24 August

| | Uxbridge | Middlesex v Pakistanis |

Sat 26 August

| CGT | Lord's | Final |

Sun 27 August

NL1	Chester-le-St	Durham v Sussex
NL2	Canterbury	Kent v Derbyshire
NL1	Manchester	Lancashire v Northants
NL2	Leicester	Leics v Hampshire
NL2	Taunton	Somerset v Worcs
NL2	The Oval	Surrey v Yorkshire
NL1	Birmingham	Warwks v Essex

Mon 28 August

| [T20] | Bristol | England v Pakistan |
| NL1 | Nottingham | Notts v Glamorgan |

Tue 29 August

| NL1 | FNorthampton | Northants v Sussex |

Wed 30 August

| LOI | FCardiff | England v Pakistan |

Thu 31 August – Sun 3 September

| CC1 | Hove | Sussex v Hampshire |

Thu 31 August

| NL2 | FLeicester | Leics v Somerset |

Fri 1 – Mon 4 September

| CC2 | Leicester | Leics v Somerset |

Fri 1 September

| NL1 | FChester-le-St | Durham v Notts |

Sat 2 September

| LOI | Lord's | England v Pakistan |

Sun 3 September

NL1	Birmingham	Warwks v Durham
NL2	Worcester	Worcs v Derbyshire
NL2	Scarborough	Yorkshire v Kent

Mon 4 September

| NL2 | FBristol | Glos v Hampshire |

Tue 5 September

| LOI | FSouthampton | England v Pakistan |

Tue 5 – Fri 8 September

| CC1 | Canterbury | Kent v Sussex |

Wed 6 – Sat 9 September

CC2	Bristol	Glos v Surrey
CC1	Lord's	Middlesex v Notts
CC2	Worcester	Worcs v Leics

Wed 6 September

| NL2 | FDerby | Derbyshire v Somerset |
| NL1 | FCardiff | Glamorgan v Northants |

Thu 7 – Sun 10 September

| CC1 | Chester-le-St | Durham v Hampshire |
| CC2 | Cardiff | Glamorgan v Northants |

Thu 7 September

| NL1 | FChelmsford | Essex v Lancashire |

Fri 8 September

| LOI | FNottingham | England v Pakistan |

Sat 9 – Tue 12 September

| CC2 | Chelmsford | Essex v Derbyshire |

Sat 9 September

| NL1 | Manchester | Lancashire v Warwks |

Sun 10 September

| LOI | Birmingham | England v Pakistan |
| NL1 | Lord's | Middlesex v Sussex |

Mon 11 September

| NL1 | FNottingham | Notts v Warwks |

Tue 12 – Fri 15 September

| CC2 | Taunton | Somerset v Northants |

Tue 12 September

| NL2 | FThe Oval | Surrey v Glos |

Wed 13 – Sat 16 September

CC1	Manchester	Lancashire v Durham
CC1	Birmingham	Warwks v Kent
CC1	Leeds	Yorkshire v Notts

Wed 13 September

| NL2 | FSouthampton | Hampshire v Worcs |

Sat 16 September

| NL2 | Worcester | Worcs v Surrey |

Sun 17 September

NL1	Chester-le-St	Durham v Essex
NL2	Canterbury	Kent v Glos
NL1	Manchester	Lancashire v Glamorgan
NL2	Leicester	Leics v Derbyshire
NL1	Northampton	Northants v Middlesex
NL1	Nottingham	Notts v Sussex

NL2	Taunton	Somerset v Surrey	CC2	Leicester	Leics v Essex
NL2	Leeds	Yorkshire v Hampshire	CC2	Northampton	Northants v Worcs
			CC1	Nottingham	Notts v Sussex
Wed 20 – Sat 23 September			CC2	The Oval	Surrey v Derbyshire
CC2	Cardiff	Glamorgan v Glos	CC1	Leeds	Yorkshire v Durham
CC1	Southampton	Hampshire v Lancashire	**Sun 24 September**		
CC1	Canterbury	Kent v Middlesex	NL		Play-Off

UNDER-19 CRICKET

LIMITED-OVERS INTERNATIONALS

England v India

LOI	Derby	Tue 18 July
LOI	Cardiff	Thu 20 July
LOI	Cardiff	Fri 21 July

TEST MATCH SERIES

England v India

TM1	Canterbury	Wed 26 – Sat 29 July
TM2	Taunton	Tue 1 – Fri 4 August
TM3	Shenley	Sun 6 – Wed 9 August

WOMEN'S CRICKET

WOMEN'S TEST MATCHES

England v India

| TM1 | Leicester | Tue 8 – Fri 11 August |
| TM2 | Taunton | Tue 29 August – Fri 1 September |

WOMEN'S LIMITED-OVERS INTERNATIONALS

England v India

| [T20] | Derby | Sat 5 August |

LOI	Lord's	Mon 14 August
LOI	Shenley	Thu 17 August
LOI	Arundel	Sat 19 August
LOI	Southampton	Thu 24 August
LOI	Southampton	Fri 25 August

FIELDING CHART

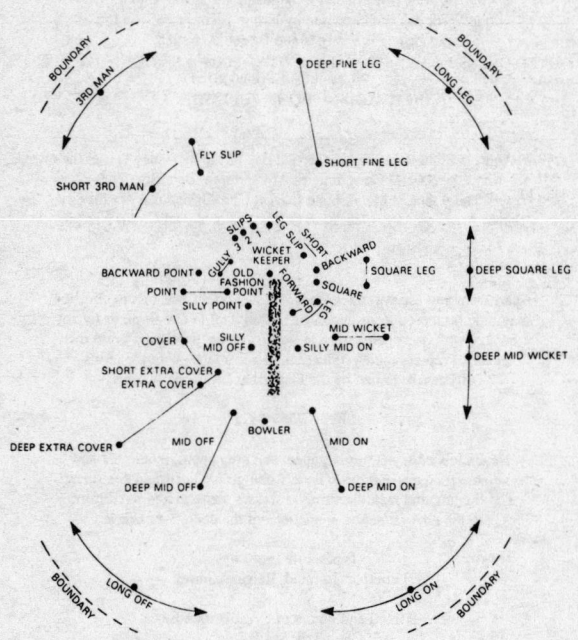

The right of Bill Frindall to be identified as the Author of
the Work has been asserted by him in accordance with the
Copyright, Designs and Patents Act 1988.

First published in 2006
by HEADLINE BOOK PUBLISHING

Cover photographs:
(*Front*) Andrew Flintoff batting on the first day of the 5th Ashes Test at the Oval,
2005 © Getty Images/AFP/Andrew Dennis;
(*spine*) The Ashes © Marylebone Cricket Club/Bridgeman Art Library;
(*back*) Ashes victory celebration © Rex Features/Paul Childs Livepic

1

ISBN 0 7553 1475 1

Headline's policy is to use papers that are natural, renewable and
recyclable products and made from wood grown in sustainable forests.
The logging and manufacturing processes are expected to conform
to the environmental regulations of the country of origin.

Typeset in Times by
Letterpart Limited, Reigate, Surrey

Printed and bound in Great Britain by
Clays Ltd, St Ives plc

HEADLINE BOOK PUBLISHING
A division of Hodder Headline
338 Euston Road
London NW1 3BH
www.headline.co.uk
www.hodderheadline.com